THE AMERICAN CITY
a sourcebook of urban imagery

edited by Anselm L. Strauss

 AldineTransaction
A Division of Transaction Publishers
New Brunswick (U.S.A.) and London (U.K.)

Second printing 2009
First paperback printing 2007 Copyright © 1968 by Anselm L. Strauss

This book is printed on acid-free paper that meets the American National Standard for Permanence of Paper for Printed Library Materials.

Library of Congress Catalog Number: 2006048003
ISBN: 978-0-202-30927-9
Printed in the United States of America

Library of Congress Cataloging-in-Publication Data

The American city : a sourcebook of urban imagery / Anselm L. Strauss, editor.
     p. cm.
  Originally published: Chicago : Aldine Pub. Co., 1968.
  Includes bibliographical references and index.
  ISBN 978-0-202-30927-9
    1. Cities and towns—United States.. I. Strauss, Anselm L.

HT123.A44   2007
307.760973—dc22   2006048003

TO my publisher and my wife who,
like Mr. and Mrs. Shandy and their Tristram,
accidentally gave birth to this offspring.

CONTENTS

6. PERILS OF THE GREAT CITY

7. SUCCESS AND THE PERILOUS CITY

8. POVERTY AND ITS SOLUTIONS

12. THE CITY WITHOUT HUMAN PURPOSE

13. RURAL AMENITIES AND URBAN ATTRIBUTES

14. SUBURBIA

15. VISITORS: FUN AND ESTHETICS

16. CITY PLANNING

17. URBAN IMAGERY AND URBAN THEORY

INTRODUCTION

The readings that comprise this collection barely hint at the immense wealth of commentary produced by Americans about their cities and about urbanization in general. From early days, many Americans have been taken aback at discovering just how urban their nation seemed destined to be. "Cities are here to stay" is a constant refrain both of people who love cities and people who hate them but have to do their best to live with them. Like the course of a fast automobile racing along a dusty road, our urbanization has been accompanied by a great cloud of commentary, composed of dire and hopeful prediction, denunciation, celebration, prescription, advocacy, planning, philosophizing, sociologizing—and from time to time including also what we would now consider genuine social research. All these ingredients of urban commentary present perspectives on the meanings of urbanization.

Some of the perspectives are now archaic, the products of specific times, places, and groups of people. Couched in the language of the day, they cannot but impress us with their provinciality. The more recent commentary may seem more reasonable—or at least more understandable—but only because the authors' experiences with cities are like our own experiences.

Behind these historical differences, however, there persists a remarkable stability of urban images. Indeed, this collection of writings will tend to strike readers as continually transcending time. Olmsted writing about parks in the 1870's, early city planners bemoaning the apathy or greed of citizens, and turn-of-the-century businessmen boasting about their particular cities all seem quite up to date. Just a few words here or a few references there, and their utterances would be applicable to our own cities or our own civic problems.

Most generally, however, the newer perspectives on cities are complex composites of images drawn from older perspectives combined with recently emerged imagery. The emergent derives from recent developments—whether physical, like the latest in urban architcture, or geographic, like the huge sprawl of the "strip city," or political, like the shifting balance of downstate-upstate politics. The emergent imagery also derives from the appearance of new groups, political, religious, and social, on the American scene. In interpreting their experiences with matters seemingly connected to cities, these groups draw upon old stocks of urban imagery, thus creating composite new urban perspectives. Their perspectives are linked with the actions of individuals and groups, and even with institutional planning and functioning.

No single volume can cover all these perspectives, and certainly not all their subtle variants. What I have aimed at in this collection is a sampling of both older and more recent stances toward our cities, the sampling organized mainly around fairly persistent themes. In the first two selections, drawn from my own writings, I have set out what I conceive to be these themes. Readers may add to them as they wish—a game that has delights of its own.

Since this volume is intended to be used both by general readers and by students in courses dealing with urban sociology or urban history or city planning, perhaps I need to say that these readings are offered in a non-judgmental spirit. We should read them as *data*. We can read them with occasional amusement and with respect, but we should beware of reading them as prescriptive. The latter will be a constant temptation, particularly for the more recent writings. My warning applies to the writings of sociologists as well as to those of ministers, city planners, or untitled laymen. There is perhaps one exception to my rule: near the end of this book, various sociologists describe, in research reports, aspects of the lives of groups they have studied. I mean there to underline the perspectives of the groups rather than of the researchers, although even there something of the researchers' stances are discernible. I have no illusion that my own perspectives are not equally reflected by the sampling of materials in this book.

Another way of reading this volume—one which I myself favor—is to regard the many perspectives voiced within it as fair game for a comparative analysis. Properly carried out, such an analysis leads to a *comparative* (sociological) *perspective*: one that takes into account the multitude of other perspectives on the city. The comparative perspective transcends its data—the varied perspectives—but does not thereby become final truth. It does, however, as I hope to show in this book, afford an effective ordering of perspectives, as well as the conditions under which they are held, the behavior of people who hold them, and various important consequences for men and their institutions.

Each set of materials is organized by chapter, and the chapters are introduced by a few paragraphs of commentary. That commentary is meant not only to introduce the materials, but to tie them back to more scholarly or technical literature. Each commentary is followed by a short, annotated bibliography of relevant works, mainly by sociologists or social historians. In some part also, my introductory remarks are intended to underscore where sociologists—the group with whose work I am most familiar—might readily find usable data for pursuing new problems that may be of special interest to them and to their students.

I wish to thank Mrs. Elaine McLarin for managing and solving so very competently the details and problems involved in putting together a volume like this. I also want to thank my colleague, Virginia Oelesen, for listening to and commenting on my initial ideas about this book.

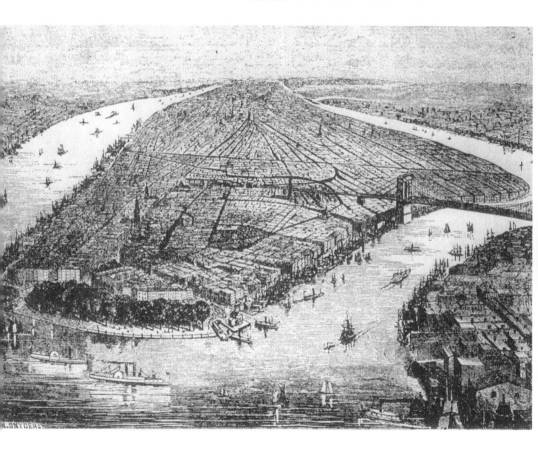

Bird's-eye view of New York, 1880. From J. D. McCabe, *New York by Sunlight and Gaslight*, 1881.

IMAGES AND PERSPECTIVES

THESE two selections set a framework—afford a comparative perspective—for all the readings that follow in this book by focusing on persistent themes in American urban imagery. An occasional reference back to this perspective should enrich the reading of later pages as well as add to the analysis elaborated here.

URBAN PERSPECTIVES: NEW YORK CITY,

Anselm L. Strauss

IN this essay (written in 1955 but hitherto unpublished),
all the protagonists in the novels discussed live in
New York City—a criterion for their selection.
The urban imagery reflected in these novels suggests the
considerable range of perspectives held toward a
large metropolis like New York. These perspectives
include the city as a place of diversity, as a
place of fun and adventure, as a place contrasting
with the countryside, as a dehumanizing
environment, as a place conducive either to continuity
or discontinuity of community and family, and
as a place where complex relationships exist among the
social classes (mobility into and out of classes,
conflict or cooperation among classes).

Looking back from his vantage point as devoted New Yorker—
though by adoption rather than by birth—John Steinbeck has tried to
recapture how he got that way.[1] When, at 23; he first came to New York,
"I saw the city, and it horrified me. There was something monstrous
about it." When he left, not many months later, the city had beaten him.
The city was a place where one could be alone and afraid. Eleven years
later he was back, a minor celebrity. Of himself then, he wrote: "Whereas
on my first try New York was a dark, hulking, frustration, the second
time it became the Temptation and I a whistle-stop St. Anthony. I
reacted without originality: today I see people coming to success doing
the same things I did, so I guess I didn't invent it."

Soon he plunged back to the rural West, convinced that the city was
a trap and a snare. Some years later he finally did settle down in New
York, although even then his country-boy distrust of the city would not
be downed: "I was going to live in New York but I was going to avoid
it. I planted a lawn in the tiny and soot-covered garden, bought huge
pots and planted tomatoes, pollinating the blossoms with a water-color
brush." As he walked the streets for exercise, he gradually got to know
them and the tradesmen on them, and eventually he felt part of the city,

---

1. In the commemorative issue of *The New York Times Magazine,* "New
York, 1653–1953" (February 1, 1953, Section 6, Part 2), "Autobiography: Making
of a New Yorker," p. 26.

albeit his city had a village quality—without its "nosiness." "My neighborhood is my village. I know all of the storekeepers and some of the neighbors. Sometimes I don't go out from my village for weeks at a time."

Each Steinbeck who came to the city was, in some sense, a different man; and each time he perceived, and therefore used, the city quite differently. "Perceived the city" is not quite an accurate term; "conceived" would be better. The urban milieu, or any milieu for that matter, is responded to not merely as physical terrain, a bit of geography, but as symbolic space filled with meaning and peopled with significant persons, artifacts, and institutions.

The newcomer to any city brings with him conceptions of urban life and perhaps of other cities, if not indeed specific notions about this particular city. Whether visiting or migrating to a metropolis of which he knows little beforehand, he must nevertheless learn to cope with it (however brief his stay) by obtaining or developing representations of what kind of a place it is, what can be done there, what the natives are like, and what kind of a visit or life he can have there. The native's experience is not so very different. He has much more leisure to grow into his city, but he does not learn to visualize his city even geographically all at once; neither does he hold unchanging ideas about what kind of a place he lives in. Both he and his urban world change, and both invite re-representation. Steinbeck's story merely speeds up and dramatizes a normally much more drawn out, and thus easily overlooked, process.

In the writings of novelists like Steinbeck, and especially in their works of fiction, the American city rarely appears as mere backdrop, as static stage setting, against which are enacted the sufferings and dreams of men. The city itself is perceived as animate and potent. It makes and breaks men: sometimes promising opportunities and providing for their fulfillment; but sometimes luring or trapping them, and exacting payment. American urban novels, whose characters move in and about a city landscape, provide a composite image of "the city" as conceived over the decades by an enormous number of Americans. This mass of urban folklore can help us construct a mosaic composed of some meanings that cities have had for Americans.

Taken as a group, novelists have portrayed life in the city not only more dramatically—more humanly, if you wish—than their scholarly contemporaries, the sociologists, the geographers, the planners; but they have been less heir perhaps to inherited intellectual views which divert gaze and cramp vision. One may instance here what is perhaps the outstanding single article by a sociologist on the nature of urban life, a paper by Louis Wirth [2] who, in the thirties, systematically set down what amounts to a range of urban perspectives measurably narrower

2. "Urbanism as a Way of Life," in P. Hatt and A. Reiss (Eds.), *Reader in Urban Sociology* (Glencoe, Ill.: Free Press, 1951), pp. 32–48.

than those expressed by the novels in any moderately sizable public library.

Having seen what the novelists have to say about social relations in the city, how their people imagine the city to be and how they cope with and use the city, we shall be in a better position to ask how Americans have come to see their cities in these several ways—and what difference it makes whether cities are conceived from one viewpoint or another.

URBAN HETEROGENEITY

One classic theme of the urban novel pertains to the diversity of every large city's worlds and populations. Drawn from the four quarters of the earth—or at least from neighboring states—the city teems with the people of different races, origins, cultures, and beliefs; not merely peoples of two or even three contrasting classes. This motif is reflected in the local press (boasts of the melting pot and living together, along with reports of ethnic and racial tensions); and in journalistic accounts which attempt to capture the color and spirit of particular cities, whose unique qualities are partly attributed to the characteristics of its diverse populations. Photographers of city life love to show its contrasts: the range of ethnic faces in the crowd, the multiplicity of kinds of city life, as well as the poignancy of Park Avenue and office buildings towering over slum dwellings.

The emphasis on heterogeneity enters into novels in much the same way. The city is a mosaic of worlds: it has many classes, ethnic communities, and neighborhoods. The city is a place, too, where diversity is attendant upon a vast division of labor. Novelists who portray urban occupational life sometimes combine the idea that an occupational world exists within a larger community with another idea that the city can be what it is only because key occupations (the newspaper, the police) function as they do.

Diversity is celebrated for it gives rise to cosmopolitanism. The very multiplicity of populations permits and fosters worldliness—for the city itself and for those of its citizens who "get around." Some critics of suburban growth, ringing an inverse variant on this cosmopolitan theme, have feared that the very homogeneity of suburban populations will lead to conformity and lack of urban dash, color, knowledgability and sophistication. This criticism is beginning to get expression in suburban novels, such as the popular *Tunnel of Love*,[3] where suburban living is pictured as dull and intellectually confining and city itself

3. Peter DeVries (Boston: Little, Brown, 1954).

becomes the symbol of cosmopolitanism and vigor, lost to the suburbanite who finally capitulates to domestic and familial obligations.

THE CITY AS A FEAST

Closely allied to the idea of cosmopolitanism is the complex imagery
of the city as an exciting place. There are several components to this
imagery that ought properly to be distinguished. First of all there is
the city which is physically exciting and satisfying. The skyline, tall
buildings, bridges, stores, city lights, dress and fashion, street scenes
and sounds, urban dialects, the look and the smells of foods: all these
and many more make up the characteristic urban picture. These sights
and sounds are treated not as external to the perceiver, but as necessary
to his very sense of identity, a contributor to and a necessary ingredient
in the stream of personal memories.

Entwined with the physical city is the metropolis as a setting for
exciting events. The stores, bars, brothels, restaurants, and places of
entertainment all profit from the outsider who comes to the great center
for a good time. "A big dirty city is better than a technicolor sunrise out
in the sticks, no matter how many songbirds are tweeting. In the city
you may feel lost, but you also figure you're not missing anything." [4]
E. B. White's popular and poetic volume *Here is New York,* is largely
written from the perspective of the stranger become a New Yorker
(editor of *The New Yorker,* in fact) who has organized his life around
urban excitement and cosmopolitanism: "you always feel that either by
shifting your location ten blocks or by reducing your fortune by five
dollars you can experience rejuvenation." [5]

A third variant of urban excitement is the city as a place of freedom.
Contrast between rural and urban aspects of American life is usually
explicit in this latter imagery. ("Meg came from a small town in south-
western Indiana, a place called Hinsdale, and as far as she was concerned
it could disappear without a trace." [6]) The city is not only a place
where people rise in the social scale, but find release from small town
or rural conformity, and an opportunity to exploit and develop their
native talents. The very anonymity complained about by some natives
and visitors, is viewed as part of the requisite setting for freedom of
action and, fully as important, thought.

In the novels, "excitement" and "opportunity" crisscross other urban
themes. Domestic stability may be seen as inimical to taking full advantage

4. Richard Bissell, *A Stretch on the River* (Boston: Little, Brown, 1950), p. 33.
5. *Op. cit.,* p. 16.
6. Hamilton Basso, *The View from Pompey's Head* (Garden City: Doubleday,
1954), p. 3.

of urban excitement; or class mobility is seen as linked with both opportunity and freedom, as in the discovery of the wider urban scene in the
ethnic second generations; and despite the destructiveness of the city on
family life, the city is seen as having a kind of hard asphalt beauty which
the initiated can appreciate. Even the theme of community in the city,
may be linked with urban excitement, as in the apochryphal joke told
about the tenement woman who refused a vacation in the country with
all its interesting sights, remarking that from her living room window she
too could see some wonderful sights. To many people, city living spells
civilization; even if civilization by no means signifies the same thing to all.

THE RURAL-URBAN CONTRAST

To many others, the city seems a poor place compared with the
small town and the countryside. Whatever the countryside has meant to
rural and small town people themselves, to some city dwellers it has
meant a natural environment and a natural way of living as opposed
to what appears to be the hurly burly, tenseness, impersonality, and
somewhat artificial character of an urban environment. The stereotype
of rural life embodies notions of close kinship and friendship ties, of
intimate and satisfying face to face relationships, of stability, simplicity,
honesty, integrity, concern for associates, and other attributes of tightly
knit groups.

In urban novels, these rural attributes enter in various ways; less rarely
as major themes around which to spin a story than as elements in the
story. Here are a few examples. In *A Cathedral Singer,*[7] the city cathedral
is pictured as the cornerstone of community and stability, and the
symbol by which the present is linked with the past and the future. But
the cathedral is also linked with the rural virtues of peace, safety,
security, serenity, and love of one's fellow man. In Louis Bromfield's
Mrs. Parkington,[8] the virtues of city and countryside are combined in the
person and education of one heroine. She derives from the healthy if
crude soil of a Western community. Together with her ambitious husband,
she invades the Eastern cities. At 84 she looks back, retracing the path
by which they became wealthy and important. Her children are blue-
bloods but without her own rural-based vigor. Yet the city has given to
Mrs. Parkington that sector of her character which is cultivated and
urbane. The important thing about her is that she has managed to
become cosmopolitan while yet retaining a rural identity. "At the one
end of her experience lay Leaping Rock, an utterly barbaric community,
rooted in harsh reality; at the other . . . civilization. Both were good; the

7. James L. Allen (New York: Century, 1916), p. 5.
8. New York: Harper, 1942.

bad-half-civilized ground between them she had never trod, in all her existence.[9] But a variant of rural-urban contrast that is probably more familiar to the sociologist is Ernest Poole's treatment of the breakdown of family ties when a small town family moves to the city, necessitating their reconstruction on a new and urban basis [10] (just as Negro literature today is full of personal breakdown in the great northern cities).

By other commentators on city life, the country is placed in the city, or the city in the country, in order to achieve comical, satirical, or wry effects. Kazin's description of the Jewish slum of Brownsville (Brooklyn) is given punch by his description of the nearby countryside that is not countryside but a garbage dumping ground.[11] In *The Tunnel of Love,* the hero indulges in fantasies of a rural hideout peopled with Hollywood-type girls and activities. A perennial delight to newspaper readers is the unexpected bit of country life found in the city: the fox that wanders down Lake Michigan into Chicago or the duck which hatched its ducklings atop a Milwaukee bridge near the center of town. Rural simplicity is self-consciously turned into sophisticated urbanity: thus Life magazine features an article, "Hick Tricks for City Slicks—Cute, Corny Styles Come in Ahead of Spring": "A spring fashion that has come in early suggests the era when crackers came in barrels. Checked gingham, out-sized bows, stiff white shirt collars and bib-front dresses cut like a farmer's overalls make fresh-faced city girls look something like oldtime country boys." [12] Occasionally the city native laughs at himself, playing upon his reputed ignorance of country things, as when two old friends walking down Broadway perceive a flower, and one bending over to look at it asks what kind is it, and the other replies, "How should I know, I've been out of the millinery business for twenty years!" Some urban humor rests upon placing the sophisticated city person in a rural setting, where he is either helpless or where he ignores the countryside and uses it just as if he were at home (both of these are favorite *New Yorker* themes). Through all of this the rural scene enters into the city's public conception of itself, though we must not suppose either that the rural imagery is accurate or that the same imagery is held by each of the city's many populations.

THE CITY AS A DEHUMANIZING ENVIRONMENT

The harshest view of the large city condemns it *en toto,* or in part, as alien to the gratification of basic human values. The city *per se* is being

9. Ibid., p. 214.
10. *His Family* (New York: Macmillan, 1917).
11. Alfred Kazin, *Walker in the Streets* (New York: Harcourt Brace, 1951).
12. *Life,* February 14, 1955, p. 121.

judged and not some segment of it (as the street which destroys the poor or wealth destroys the rich). The social critic, Lewis Mumford, has incessantly reminded his readers that in the urban environment all classes alike suffer from certain of its brutalizing or destructive features.[13] This severe criticism is couched in a vocabulary built around such terms as: loneliness, strangers, artificiality, front, facade, exploitation, surface, superficial, unnatural, boredom, apathy, routine, dehumanizing machine, meaningless, purposelessness. Explicit or implicit in this lexicon is a rural-urban contrast, with the city coming off the loser.

The indictment—sometimes it is merely a complaint—is an old and popular one. It seems to rest upon three main points. All three are represented in a paragraph drawn from Thomas Wolfe, who is there also suggesting what kinds of people might almost totally denounce the city. Wolfe observed that Southerners who had tried to make a go of it in New York and had failed, then returned home and eventually arrived at the conclusion that city people

> endure their miserable existence because they "don't know any better." City people are an ignorant and conceited lot. They have no manners, no courtesy, no consideration for the rights of others, and no humanity. Everyone in the city is "out for himself," out to do you, out to get everything he can out of you. It is a selfish, treacherous, lonely, and self-seeking life. A man has friends as long as he has money in his pocket. Friends melt away from him like smoke when money goes. Moreover, all social pride and decency, the dignity of race, the authority of class is violated and destroyed in city life. . . .[14]

The first variant of the dehumanizing theme is that the city is an impersonal place, a place that engenders close physical and even social contact without genuine understanding, sympathy, or passion. Even kinship and marital relationships are superficial, without deep meaning. If social relations are occasionally deep and satisfying, they are apt to be transitory. Urban impersonality is played upon in common speech and mass media in dozens of ways, and unquestionably many city persons feel this characterization of the city to be accurate.

A second variant of the theme turns about the notion of mask, show, front, facade, or "game." True feelings are masked, not expressed—as presumably they would be in a more natural environment—hence there is ample room for trickery, fraud, and exploitation. A third variant makes explicit the essential purposelessness of urban existence. Life is routine, boring, or frantic, furious without sound, motion without meaning. People

13. See Lewis Mumford, *The Culture of Cities* (New York: Harcourt Brace, 1938).

14. Thomas Wolfe, *The Web and the Rock* (Garden City: Sun Dial Press, 1940), p. 240.

have become puppets, automatons, and creativity and autonomy are lost.

Usually in the novels, these variants of urban dehumanization are handled in conjunction with other urban themes. For instance, in Wolfe's *The Web and the Rock,* the hero vacillates in tragic tension between his conception of the city as releasing, exciting, freeing and the city as a place which crushes creativeness and purpose, mainly by corrupting taste and sidetracking one's purpose. His protagonist is a native girl, who teaches him both the civilizing inheritance of the city and also the dangers of its wealth and distractions. In Dobson's *The Celebrity,* the hero comes off better after suffering something of the same tension. He wins a book club award for a bestseller, gets drawn into the sophisticated and exhausting round of the famous, and so gets drawn away from his real life's work; but in the end, he returns to his writing (although retaining his earnings) and his market. The author of *Days of My Love* draws a vivid contrast between the specious qualities of commercial life and the depth and naturalness of family relations; and these themes in turn are linked— though the irony is probably unintentional—with the city's blessed anonymity which allows real love to develop between the hero and his mistress, despite a shrewish wife at home.[15] In other novels the loneliness of some urban life is linked with loss of community, with class and ethnic marginality, and with class mobility. Understandably too, the facade or mask theme enters into novelistic criticism of the upper classes. The question raised by all of this, of course, is exactly which urban populations perceive the city as in some sense dehumanizing, and what do they do about it? Assuredly not all city people experience their environment in these terms; and some quite understand how others may so experience it without feeling it impinge upon themselves.

CONTINUITY AND DISCONTINUITY

Another pervasive urban motif deals with stability and change in the city. Some imagery deals with the disintegration, breakup, and even disappearance of groups in the city. Presumably it is the members of such groups, or their close observers, who are struck by this aspect of the city. In softened version, we sometimes hear oldtimers talk nostalgically about the old, now thoroughly changed, neighborhoods; or about a formerly tight-knit kinship circle. The urban novelists portray families breaking up, classes disintegrating, second-generation children leaving their immigrant communities; they do this by describing the deterioration of buildings, the disappearance of landmarks, the invasion of an area by desecrating groups, flight away from the area, the dispersal of kin, the discontinuance of friendships, and the dissolution of ceremonies and in-

15. Leonard Bishop (New York: Dial Press, 1953).

stitutions. If a photographer were to take a picture of a one-time proud church, now broken down and converted into a theater or a Negro church, he would have worked in the spirit of this urban theme. One novel, which turns around the intertwined themes of complete invasion, area disintegration, and mobility, begins and ends with the following: "There was once a block of brownstone houses in midtown residential New York." . . . "The Kelleys and the Abbotts and the Schultzes in the seats of the mighty. They dwell in marble palaces and in towering apartment houses. . . . They have started a new age and a new civilization, and there is no one to say them nay. The brownstone city is no more." [16]

The consequence or the next phase of community dispersal is a number of alienated or marginal persons. Of course the old groups may remain, but persons may stray from them and become marginal men. This is not merely a spatial concept (of in-between worlds) but a temporal one. The marginal have left a group, or it has disappeared under them, and they are in transit to a new world—one which they may or may not find. The sense of personal discontinuity is acute. Hence any novelist who describes this uses an expressive lexicon stressing rootlessness, drift, aimlessness, search without finding, movement without clear direction.

> One got older. One grew soberer. One would like perhaps to see a thread drawn through the years as though they were beads. This year on Charles Street, last year on Tenth; surely these were stations along some route? . . . toward what, and why? . . . And was there something else? [17]

The marginality theme is particularly tied in with class mobility (with its pain of passage and the question of how much to slough off and how much to retain); the theme is often linked also with the city's artificiality and its dehumanization of purpose. On occasion marginality joins with urban excitement, as in Kazin's autobiographical account of his simultaneous discovery of the freedom of the city and the constraint of his ethnic community.[18]

A related cluster of imagery has to do with community in the city. Some of this imagery turns around a movement from marginality to rebirth of community; and some of it pictures the retention of community life despite change. In a novel titled *The Unpossessed,* there is

16. John Wiley, *Queer Street* (New York: Scribners, 1928), p. 1, p. 282.
17. Tess Slesinger, *The Unpossessed* (New York: Simon and Schuster, 1934), p. 6.
18. W. H. White's article on the transient junior executive in the suburbs ("The Transients," *Fortune Magazine,* vol. 47, May 1953, pp. 112 ff.) gains interest from an inverse treatment of mobility: for he attempts to show that these people, though tremendously physically and socially mobile, are not really marginal, since they create community life wherever they move with others just like themselves. Community and marginality are antithetical—just because a community has a more or less integrated past, present, and future. The marginal do not.

portrayed an unrelieved marginality and a human waste without hope: the heroine has an abortion, which symbolizes personal and social sterility, and on the last pages she and her husband leave the hospital and enter their house with no future whatever lying before them—"went in the door and heard it swing to, pause on its rubbery hinge, and finally click behind them." [19]

In other novels, purpose is discovered at the close of the book, and the characters are made to knit their past identities with current ones. In a more than banal sense, they find themselves. In *The View from Pompey's Head,* Hamilton Basso has his hero going home again to his boyhood town and there getting his nostalgia and regret out of his system; once he understands that he really has not left a piece of himself there, in coming to the city, then his past falls into line with his present rather than being disjoined from it. In another book, the heroine marries across class lines, suffers partial disjuncture of identity, but finally reconciles her past with her future, dedicating herself to her immediate conjugal family. In the closing sentences she muses that some day her son "might seem to lose his path, and miss the pattern for a time. And she would understand. . . . It was a great thing to have learned; a gift of comprehension that she could lay at Martin's feet." [20]

The retention of community without such great discontinuity is a less anguished theme, but is of equal importance for understanding urban experience. The emphasis now is upon change without loss of essential continuity. Memory is one link to the past:

> Every city has some locality to which its heroic and civic memories especially cling; and this locality in the city of New York is the historic acre of the Bowling Green. With that spot it has been throughout its existence, in some way or other, unfailingly linked. [21]

Families may move up or down the social ladder, but the generations keep contact and continuity. [22] Marquand's famous story of an old Boston family, *The Late George Apley,* closes with the somewhat errant son, John taking his place within the family firmament: "George Apley died in his own house on Beacon Street on the thirteenth of December, 1933, two weeks after John Apley returned to Boston." [23] Some suggestive essays on Jewish life in *Commentary on the American Scene* [24] deal with this important theme. Jews are pictured as moving upward, uptown, out

19. *Op. cit.,* p. 357.
20. Rose Franken, *Pattern* (New York: Scribners, 1925), p. 348.
21. Amelia Barr, *The Belle of Bowling Green* (New York: A. L. Burt, 1904), p. 3.
22. H. C. Bunner, *The Story of a New York House* (New York: Scribners, 1887).
23. New York: Modern Library, 1940 ed., p. 354.
24. Elliot E. Cohen, Ed. (New York: Knopf, 1953).

of town, and, though developing styles of living which appear externally new, underneath still retain their essentially Jewishness. Key symbols of continuity are Jewish food, family life, gestures, sayings, and a general feeling of ethnic alikeness. Ruth Glazer, in "West Bronx: Food, Shelter, Clothing," [25] satirizes the outsider who coming upon the area thinks: "Ah, those poor people living out their pallid lives in regimented cells, one above the other." But in the West Bronx, the modern wife still cooks chicken and pot roast, and learns to shop in Jewish butcher stores, just as her mother did ("Really, could you buy in the A and P?"). The adolescent boys and girls date, just as they do in the outside world, but this alien pattern leads back, in the end, to the community: to marriage, children, and "the vortex of family existence and the pattern of Bronx living." [26] Community stability of course can turn around rural and class backgrounds as well as ethnicity. The dimensions and subtleties of such modes of keeping community within an urban environment provide tempting plots for the novelist who has himself often been party to such a plot in reality.

SOCIAL CLASS IN THE CITY

Another set of perennial motifs in urban literature consists of the relations of classes to masses and classes to classes. To begin with, the great city is par excellence a place of opportunity, a place where people can and do rise—with all the excitement and turmoil of passage. This theme in literature and in real life is so visible that it hardly calls for much discussion. Its more subtle linkages with rural migration, urban excitement, discontinuity, and marginality have already been suggested.

To some novelists, the city engenders in its wealthiest residents an artificiality of manner and a terrifying decadence of purpose. Upton Sinclair, writing around the turn of the century, takes a rural and upwardly mobile hero into New York society, and through his eyes portrays the deadly round of elite existence.[27] Although initially intrigued and partly captured by the banquets, houses, furnishings, clothes, parties, conversation, and beautiful women that mark the world of wealth, the hero comes eventually to see its essential purposelessness. At best the rich are bored, routinized, addicted to trifles and fads: at worst their life is a corruption, a sham, a facade, a crazyquilt of unreality. Implicit or explicit in this perspective on elite city-ways is a contrast with some other, better, way of life. The latter may be a rural one or the warmer, more real, more purposeful way of a lower class. Hence the elite theme is often inter-

25. *Ibid.,* pp. 301–19.
26. *Ibid.,* pp. 301, 318.
27. *Metropolis* (London: Wener Laurie, 1947, originally published 1908).

woven with the class mobility theme, and occasionally with the downward mobility theme of the disaffected wealthy person abandoning his
class for a lower class in order to find truer identity. In the relatively
optimistic world of the novel, the upwardly mobile hero usually returns
in the closing pages to the place and class where life is more human and
humane. Thus Sinclair in 1908 ends his book with: "I'm going to find
some decent and simple place to live; and I'm going down town to find
out if there isn't some way in New York for a man to earn an honest
living!" Phillips in 1953 has his hero break with his upper-class girl at a
sophisticated cocktail party and retire to Liggetts drug store for "supper"
—"I thought about escape. The word had a glad ring, though not an
exhilarating one. It was too late to be exhilarated. This victory had cost
a lot. . . . I feel as though I'd climbed out of purgatory and I'm waiting
on the edge for my breath to come back . . ." [28] In 1860 Charles Burdett
warned his readers against too much wealth with its destruction of purpose
and family life—the title: *Three Per Cent a Month,* The Perils of Fast
Living, A Warning to Young Men.[29] Now, perhaps, not many Americans
would take his counsel seriously, but enough imagery persists of the
wealthy as corrupt, lawless, individualistic, dissolute, immoral, and frivo-
lous—so that some business leaders feel a need for underscoring elite
sobriety and find it necessary to publicize the contributions to the general
community made by the business community.

A less harsh view of the elite attributes to it certain fine qualities
which nevertheless require balancing with the good qualities of the lower
classes. Those who have been deprived of the advantages of position will,
in turn, be complemented or educated by contact with the high-born.
The masses are pictured as colorful, warm, passionate, vibrant, alive and
natural: the elite as educated, well bred, high minded, and fine but
formal, stiff, and a little colorless, cold, and stifled. Each class gives
something of itself to the other, for the good of both.[30] This theme rather
naturally links with that of class mobility, since it is the mobile who most
frequently make contact: in settlement houses, at parties, and particularly
in the artistic and dramatic world.

A few examples will serve to show some of the dimensions of class

28. *Ibid.,* p. 342; and John Phillips, *The Second Happiest Day* (New York:
Harper, 1953), pp. 406, 409.
29. New York: D. W. Evans.
30. Richard Aldrich once wrote a series of articles about his marriage, "Gertrude Lawrence as Mrs. A" (accompanying blurb: "She grew up in the slums; he
in Boston"), for *Ladies' Home Journal* (1954). One the themes was: "Not all the
changes effected by our marriage were only in Gertrude. Alterations even more
profound went on in me. These were the inevitable results of the exposure of my
cautious, less expansive nature, inhibited by an undiluted Puritan New England
ancestry and by childhood associations and training, to the warm, vital forces that
flowed so richly through her. . . . Scarcely less marked . . . were the changes she
brought about in other members of my family circle."

complementarity. In an unalloyed success story, the poor open vistas to the rich and the rich teach the poor to want the better things of life: "While Eleanor was giving Carminella glimpses of what to the child of the tenements was almost a dream-life, Carminella in turn showed the woman . . . realities which were to her as new and startling phases of life." [31] In another novel,[32] a girl from the slums marries a rich settlement worker, each epitomizing his side of the class equation. Toward the end of the book, their differences are too great, so the woman leaves —to marry a man of her own ethnic community who is as upwardly mobile as she. On the last page, she comforts herself: "Always she would be finer because she had known his fineness." Presumably, despite his anguish, the husband was finer also. In *Toilers and Idlers* [33] the story turns around the romance of a wealthy young man with the poor. Bored with the artificiality and pleasures of his early life, he turns to work under a false name, and becomes revitalized through contact with workingmen. In turn he will contribute something to the education and leadership of the poor through the management of his own factories.

But the fusion of classes can also be combined in one breast, each group adding something essentially fine to the hero's character. Thus two marginal persons, neither truly elite nor any longer really belonging to the masses, are conversing, and one says,

> "I don't pretend that men and women like that are the only ones I want to know, but they make a good foundation for the fancier kind that you add later. I ought to know. I am one. And so are you," he added . . . looking around the great rich kitchen as if to remind Jessie that this was a different milieu indeed from one that would more exactly reflect her origin.[34]

That this is not simply storybook fantasy is testified to by certain aspects of upper and middle class political radicalism, but also by the autobiographies such as those well bred people who worked in the slums around the turn of the century. Emily Barringer,[35] who began her surgeon's career by interning in a Bowery hospital, pictures in vivid terms how she then came into "the bare cold soil of reality," felt the native spontaneity of the population to her own lasting benefit. Mary Simkhovitch, associated with a settlement house in Greenwich Village

31. Edward W. Townsend, *A Daughter of the Tenements* (New York: Lovell, Coryell, 1895), p. 57.
32. Anzia Yezierska, *Salome of the Tenements* (New York: Boni and Liveright, 1923).
33. John R. McMahon (New York: Wilshire Book Co., 1907).
34. Marcia Davenport, *East Side, West Side* (New York: Scribners, 1947), p. 82.
35. *Bowery to Bellevue: The Story of New York's First Woman Ambulance Surgeon* (New York: Norton, 1950), p. 25.

during most of her life, looks back upon her first plunge into that rich, warm, passionate world, and remarks that it "was a question of give-and-take from the start." [36] What gives an urban quality to all this is the assumption, so obvious that it is almost always implicit, that it is in the city that the classes have the great opportunity to make contact and profit from that meeting. This is, then, a great democratic theme of American life, refracted in a particular way.

But democracy can be denied—its fruits withheld with vengeance and forethought, or thoughtlessly, or unconsciously, even unimaginatively. Our novels reflect this in two ways. The first is the classic "invasion" theme; the second is the destructiveness of "the street" and streetlife. In invasion, the lower classes encroach upon the physical, and thus the social terrain, of the better classes; who in turn are then forced, or disposed, to move away. The result is witting or unwitting segregation, and the maintenance of class differences established on different social spaces. The psychology of invasion and flight is very much in public view today, with the core of some of our largest cities suspect, turned over to invading "hordes" of Puerto Ricans, Mexicans, and Negroes, while the more substantial people reside in the suburbs. In the American novel, invasion is entwined, as a theme, with such motifs as class mobility; with the fight to keep culture and family intact; with the struggle to stay in the city and maintain a style of life despite the city's danger, dirt, and ugliness, so that one may still enjoy whatever advantages the city has yet to yield over the suburbs or the small town. The perspective is, of course, that of the invaded. Turned around, it becomes the status mobility of those who invade because they are rising.

For those left behind, there is "The Street," endowed with metaphorical malignancy, symbolizing all the environmental forces massed to degrade its residents, destroy their potentialities, and prevent their rising to better status. Stephan Crane wrote *Maggie, Girl of the Streets* [37] in 1893 around this theme, and forty years later a Negro writer, Ann Petry, portrayed the same tragedy played out on a Harlem street.[38] The frustration and withering impact of the slum is often portrayed by those who have risen out of it, as well as by those who have discovered it and feel that something should be done about it.

From the point of view of the slum dweller, of course, street life may be exciting, familiar, and psychologically supporting rather than an evil; and from the point of view of those who have left it, something like nostalgia, born of ancient loves and sometimes of persistent discomfort in new worlds, for the good old days in the tenements—so that class

36. *Neighborhood: My Story of Greenwich House* (New York: Norton, 1938), p. 96.
37. New York: Johnson Smith.
38. *The Street* (New York: Houghton Mifflin, 1946).

complementarity and class segregation as themes combine in subtle ways within a single person. Something similar, but genealogically reversed, may go on in a person who discovers the richness of the slum's human struggle later in life, and combines horror of street life ambivalently with envy.

PERSPECTIVES: IN SPACE AND TIME

With the spectrum of urban perspectives thus spread out before us, we can begin asking questions about how different populations have imagined and conceived "the city," have sought to cope with it and use it, have shaped its physical layout and created its social relationships—and who, in turn, were shaped and transformed by their residence in urban environs. Certainly no great imagination is needed to begin guessing which groups might be carriers of certain of the perspectives evoked by the urban novels.

We can also grasp how little of urban life can be understood without recognition that urban perspectives arise from historical depths (usually not dreamed of by those holding the perspectives). Urban planners, and sociologists too, have been content with the barest, and not too accurate, outlines of the subjective side of American urbanization. Their conceptions are also part and parcel of the popular folklore and symbolic representations of cities. At worst, the sociological conceptions of urban life are hand-me-downs from older traditions; at best they do no more than scratch the variegated surface of urban social life. The urban historians have given us, for their part, excellent factual accounts of the rise of American urbanization, and a few portrayals of particular cities, sketched in abundant detail but in prosaic framework not so very different than the popular biographies of cities, albeit more judicious and accurate. They picture the city's progress: its rise to fortune or its growing stability, as shown by the development of its civic institutions. Because of academic separatism, historians and social scientists have long shied away from each other, with consequent divorce of urban sociology and urban history—and undoubtedly this has led to a partial impoverishment of both branches of inquiry.

SOME VARIETIES OF AMERICAN URBAN
SYMBOLISM, *Anselm L. Strauss*

THIS second introductory selection is taken from
Images of the American City (New York: Free Press
of Glencoe, 1961, pp. 104–123, reprinted by
permission). It portrays some persistent antitheses
and ambiguities in American life, as they
relate to American cities. As in the preceding
selection, enduring themes of American
urbanization are suggested, notably those touching
on sectionalism versus national centralization,
ruralism versus urbanism, cosmopolitanism versus
specialization, and traditionalism versus modernism.
It will be readily seen that these themes crosscut
those discussed in the preceding pages.

Before we examine how particular populations have expressed themselves about American urbanization, it will be useful to scrutinize some
persistent antitheses in American life. Those controversies—which amount
to basic ambiguities of American values—involve the conflicts of sectionalism versus national centralization, of ruralism versus urbanism, of cosmopolitanism versus specialization, and of traditionalism versus modernism. Instead of discussing those antitheses and ambiguities abstractly, we
shall relate them to the whole subject of American city symbolism in order
to lay another bit of groundwork for the remaining chapters of this volume.
By seeing first some of the larger issues of American valuation as they
pertain to our cities, we shall better be able to understand the predominant urban symbolism of particular regions and populations.

A host of American cities, despite all differences in size, location, or
composition, continually try to validate the claims that they are typical,
authentic American communities. They balance what they are and what
they feel they stand for against a tacitly accepted formula of American
values and national purposes. But the facts and symbols of urban life
become interchangeable in the course of argument, become confused in
meeting the difficulties of expressing a city's hopes and achievements in a
straightforward definitive fashion. They become confused, too, because of
certain ambiguities in what may be assumed to be *the* American way
of life.

This ambiguity of American urbanity and American values is significantly reflected in a lively contention over which city best deserves the title of "most American." The admirers of Chicago, New York, Kansas City, and Detroit, at least, claim honors for the city of their choice. Such claims are not new. As far back at least as 1851, a Baltimorian re-asssured a local audience that Baltimore "may be said to be an epitome of the nation itself"; and upon occasion critics of certain American values may point to one of these cities as a repulsive exemplar of those values. But a uniform, homogeneous American culture spread evenly throughout the nation would allow no city to claim more Americanness than was possessed by other cities; nor could any then base its claim upon a different set of values.

As long ago as 1891, de Rousiers described Chicago as the most American city, remarking that, "It is here, indeed, that the American 'go ahead,' the idea of always going forward . . . attains its maximum intensity." Some fifty-five years later, John Gunther writes that Chicago's "impact is overwhelmingly that of the United States, and it gives above all the sense that America and the Middle West are beating upon it from all sides." In other words, he is stressing less its "striving" than its central position. A thousand miles away, the admirers of New York City stress rather different values. They assert that New York represents the nation at its most civilized and most creative: that it dominates the nation in every way; and that more different kinds of Americans, drawn from more regions, live in New York than in any other metropolis. The proponents of Kansas City dwell upon still different aspects of American culture; George S. Perry, who described that city for the *Saturday Evening Post's* readers, saw it this way:

> Kansas City is a kind of interior American crossroads and melting pot where the Southerner, the Northerner, the Easterner and the Westerner meet and bcome plain John American, with America unfolding . . . "in oceans of glory" in every direction. It got its start on the riches of Boston banks and Western lands and Northern furs. It is not only America's approximate geographical heart, but the center of gravity for her taste and emotion. The soap opera, movie or national magazine that doesn't "take" in Kansas City won't live long in the nation.

Those who would give Detroit the honor of "most American" ignore the virtues of being of pioneer and dead-center America, and claim that Detroit best represents the spirit of modern twentieth-century America, exemplified in the city's superb system of mass production, in its drive, energy, purpose, and fusion of men and machines. Pittsburgh's admirers claim similar industrial virtues for their city. Indeed, a city need not even be among the largest to claim for itself, or to be proclaimed the most typical of America. For instance:

It is a truism to say that Tulsa is the most American of American cities. All the forces that have gone into the making of a Republic have been intensified there. The successive stages through which the country as a whole has passed during three hundred years—Indian occupation, ranching, pioneering, industrial development . . . have been telescoped within the single lifetime of some of the older Tulsans. The result has been the quintessence of Americanism—its violence and strength, its buoyant optimism, its uncalculating generosity, its bumptious independence.

The argument that one city best typifies America is couched in a standardized "logical" form: from a number of desirable attributes, certain ones are selected for emphasis while the remainder are ignored; and it is assumed or asserted that these selected attributes are possessed more abundantly by the admired city. In this way, many facets of American life are overlooked or given secondary status. The argument does not turn upon fact but upon value. Thus, if one values sheer quantity, then New York has most of everything; if one extolls the Midwest as the geographic heart of America and as the possesser of the most widespread and average national values, then he will deny priority to New York. In making such evaluations of their cities, Americans assess the nation's cultural assets and identify themselves with its history and destiny. When they represent a city as most American, they are conceiving it not only as unique and matchless but as the symbolic representative of esteemed national values.

Such great distinction can be claimed for few American cities; hence the citizens of the remaining urban centers must be content with a lesser assertion: namely, that their particular city represents at least one—and probably more—of the important aspects of American life. Thus, Iowa cities are conceived of as good places to live in because they appear to be friendly, peaceful, prosperous agricultural towns; and Fort Worth, Texas, surrounded by cattlemen's country, epitomizes the culture of that region. Such cities are parts of many Americas. The country is vast, its aspects staggeringly varied. Cities need not compete to share the nation's glory, they have only to point to those of their features wherein they typify some aspect, or aspects, of the entire American way of life.

Yet these aspects are not entirely congruent, in fact or in value. One of the most persistent clashes of value on the American scene has long been embodied in the sentimental preference of a rural existence to a thoroughly urban one. When Jefferson spoke of the danger of an American metropolitanism fated perhaps to destroy the sturdy virtues of a predominantly agricultural society, he was but expressing a dichotomy in American thought that persists to this day. Despite the continuous trend toward urbanization, our rural heritage remains potent, entering into American thought and action in increasingly subtle ways.

Eighteenth-century seaboard agriculture was not what farming became on the prairie a century later, nor what it is today in an era of large-scale mechanization. The men who worked the American soil and the life-styles that they evolved have varied greatly in place and time. Yet an American mythology grew up by which it was maintained that agricultural pursuits necessarily bred a certain kind of man. This agrarian mythology is and was a complex set of beliefs consisting of many elements, some of which developed from the several kinds of frontier conditions and others of which evolved after the Civil War in opposition to the dreadful urban conditions. The spirit of this agrarian ideology can be suggested by the following few sentences.

Rural life is slow and unhurried. Men lead natural, rich lives. People are friendly and their relationships are informal, yet orderly. The agricultural population is homogeneous in custom and culture if not in racial stock. The round of existence is stable and the community is religious, moral, honest. Men are, thus, not motivated by purely individualistic impulses. If all farmers do not love one another, at least they understand each other and do not manipulate and exploit each other as do city dwellers. The very physical surroundings are healthy, home-like, restful, not dense with population. Not the least: the rural man is a sturdy democrat, his convictions nourished by his contact with nature itself and with the equalitarian discussion held around the crackerbarrel and in the meeting house.

These conceptions are linked by affect rather than by logic. They evolved under considerably different historical circumstances, some during the development of the New England township, some when the prairie was settled, others while western farmers were castigating the railroad kings, and yet others at a time when rural migrants to cities became demoralized by conditions there. Although the country-city dichotomy has been with us for many generations, the content of the argument on either side has varied from decade to decade—as both cities and countrysides became transformed. Ideas die hard: in the formation of our rural mythology, old ideas accrued to new ones instead of disappearing entirely, despite their incongruence with fact and with each other. Probably no single rural community has ever stressed equally all elements of the entire ideological complex, for its very ambiguity allows its use as an effective resource. The town can use it as well as the village; and the small city can boast of home-like surroundings and friendly atmosphere, in an invidious contrast with the larger urban centers.

Sizeable cities can also be designated as outright embodiments of rural values—as when the citizens of Des Moines aver direct kinship with soil and farm; and in so doing, they may symbolically act in ways more farm-like than the equally business-oriented farmer. The residents of most cities, perhaps, signify their association with sentimental rurality more obliquely, not always recognizing the nature of that feeling of kinship. Cities are referred to by their residents as "The City of Flowers," "The City of Trees," "The City of Homes." They draw upon the rich stock of rural imagery without directly stating their debt. Large cities as they grow to great size abandon such nicknames, which no longer seem to represent what the city has become, but may emphasize in curiously subtle ways that their styles of urban life also partake of America's revered earlier heritage. Chicago—once called "The City of Gardens"—still boasts that it is the city of the prairie, and lays claim to a characteristic friendliness and informality that mark it off from, say, New York or Boston. (As George Perry says, "Chicago is a thousand times more relaxed, less 'mannered' than New York.")

Like the smaller towns, the larger cities may stress one or more of the varied rural themes, thereby cashing in on a much wider ideological complex. The very statement that one's city is a "city of gardens" (albeit gardening is a far cry from farming), arouses connotations smacking of outdoor life, suggestions of qualities bred in close contact with the soil, of urbanites living a life of relaxation rather than of frantic pursuit of excessive monetary gain. The visitor to a city sometimes remarks, also, upon certain paradoxes because, while he notices that the place is marked only by a limited number of rural characteristics, he feels that these are among its important features. What he is really puzzling over is that all rural qualities are supposed to hang together; whereas in this particular city, surprisingly enough, they do not. The perception of such paradoxes is furthered by any obvious juxtaposition of rural and urban character-istics: a city nestled among beautiful mountains but marked by a high rate of crime and by horrendous slums, or a large urban center charac-terized by a noticeably leisured pace of life. Thus about Portland, Oregon, Richard Neuberger remarks: "Torn between her peaceful past and a brawling future as the Pittsburgh of the West, Portland just can't make up her mind. . . . As a result of this strange ambivalence, Port-land is a combination of the rustic and the metropolitan." Similarly, Elsie Morrow writes of Springfield, Illinois, that, "At best, Springfield is a very typical American city, with a special flavor and pleasantness. At worst it is a town which has grown old without ever having grown up. It is something between a backward country settlement and a cosmopolis."

The obverse of such pleasantly toned rural mythology, of course, is an affectively linked set of vices: cities are locales of demoralization, dis-comfort, standardization, artificiality, vulgar materialism, dishonesty, and so on through a richly invidious lexicon. But the rural-urban dichotomy allows black to be called white, and white, black. City dwellers have long characterized their cities as places of progress, opportunity, and excitement, the very image of civilization in contrast to countryside, small town, small city, in contrast, even, to those larger cities which appear provincial. Small cities and even villages have, in turn, affirmed that they participate in an urbane and urbane civilization. Anyone who peruses popular urban histories will notice how very sensitive are their authors about the artistic, musical, and literary "culture" of their towns; they carefully list all "cultural" accomplishments and proclaim the progressiveness of their towns by example and assertion. A town which is not civilized, not progressive, not exciting would seem to have a narrow range of options; its citizens must balance its slight amount of urbanity with presumed rural virtues, or must assert disinterest in (un-American) urban characteristics; or, more subtly, must ignore their place in the backwash of American urbanization and remain content to be where they are.

Whatever else may be true of American cities, they are certainly a most varied lot, being neither cosmopolitan nor all homespun. Nonetheless, particular cities become symbolized as embodiments of different facets of a cheerfully ambiguous rural-urban dichotomy. Thus, emerging styles of urban life receive relatively easy explanation or rationalization. It is as if people were to say: "We are a city like this because we grew up on the prairie, or because we are surrounded by farms, or because our main businesses were founded by farm boys, or because we have no great influx of alien peoples." Likewise, each different population within a single city can rationalize its differential mode of living by appealing to one mythology or another—or to elements of both. Moreover, a city seemingly fated by geographical position and history to be of a certain kind can be envisioned as another kind, and can be directed toward that image by strong interest groups which draw upon different sets of sustaining beliefs. Any city which unquestionably is undergoing change from a commercial to a manufacturing center, or from an agricultural town to a distributing mart, can likewise find ready interpretations to account for otherwise baffling changes in its social characteristics. All such explanations, whether vigorously contested or merely assumed, are answers to that important query: what is the meaning of this city, what kind of a place is it?

The rural-versus-urban conflict that marks American life is crosscut by another ambiguity which turns on a contrast between tradition and modernity. City adherents sometimes stress a lengthy history or a blessedly short one. Votaries of a city with a long history will tend to link its origins with those of the nation itself. Being old—the ideology runs— a long established city is less likely to be crude, vulgar, rough and ready; hence it will be more civilized, more civic-minded, more settled; its citizens will be more stable, have deeper personal and familial roots in the community; its population will be mostly native to it and its immigrants well assimilated; hence, fewer men will have been attracted there merely for opportunistic reasons. The older cities will have more cultivation of leisure, greater delicacy of human relations, and will pay more attention to matters which make for "taste" and "civilization."

But the citizens of other American cities extoll the contrary virtues of youth and scant tradition. They regard their cities as relatively untrammeled by custom and convention. Just because their cities have not had time to settle down, they are supposed not to have developed rigid stances toward handling problems; they are therefore progressive and profoundly democratic, since men have fought their way to success there by their own honest efforts, benefiting neither from hereditary position nor from an elite upbringing. In these younger cities, it is believed that the lines between social classes have not yet grown into impermeable barriers; indeed, they may be denied to exist at all. A young city is conceived of as a place of freedom in still another sense. Its citizens have immigrated there of their own free will because they imagined it to be a place of considerable opportunity. Because the young community permits experimentation and the pursuit of opportunity, it is seen as an exciting place, at least more interesting than the stodgier older cities. Although the latter, by reason of their erlier origins, may perhaps rightfully claim superiority in the arts of civilization—so the argument runs— the more recently founded communities will soon overtake or surpass them; indeed the cosmopolitanism of the older cities may only, in some instances, be a form of decadance.

Ardent speakers for both younger and older cities stress only certain elements in the total available vocabularies; they glory now in a town's experimental attitude, now in its famous traditional styles of cooking; they even combine the attributes of age and youth. Such symbolization occurs without strict regard for fact, since cities, as we have seen, may be represented as rather old when they are actually quite young, and cities of similar age may be conceived of in very different temporal terms.

Tradition and history are often given a peculiar reverse twist, so that certain eastern coastal cities are considered not to have important American qualities, while certain western centers are assigned crucial roles in the making of the nation. It is asserted or implied that there are histories and histories; but the basic history of the country concerns the clearing of the forests and settling of the frontier. The pioneer romance thus crowds out the colonial. Any city whose citizens did not participate in the pushing back of the frontier cannot, therefore, possibly possess the mystical qualities stemming from that glorious enterprise.

But the frontier is a series of conceptions, not merely a set of facts. These conceptions are linked with various rural and urban virtues, with different periods of our history, and with particular American regions as well. In those sections of the country where the frontier as a geographic reality has but recently disappeared, the frontier as a concept refers more to the mining camp and the railroad center than to pioneer agricultural settlements. The frontier was a rough and tough place, where men were men and the hardiest won out. Some of the same associations remain coupled in midwestern remembrances because of the region's boom-town tradition and because of the predominant romance of life on the open prairie. The Midwest is more than the geographic heart of the continent; many believe it to be at the core of what *is* America. Back east, the concept of the frontier has been sufficiently misted over by time so that it is referred to more obliquely ("the founders," "the settlers"), but these terms also carry a considerable charge of regional passion.

The frontier, as an idea, has also broken loose from any regional anchoring; it can be applied to endeavors in industrial, artistic, intellectual, and other non-geographic fields. Consequently, cities building upon the cumulative connotations of the frontier image can be thought of as commercial and industrial pioneers. A great metropolis like New York can strike its admirers as *the* "moving frontier" of the entire American economy and of the nation's civilization. The frontier concept allows some cities to be called currently progressive and others to be linked with the nation's slightly older history, while it may be used with relation to some cities so that it cuts both ways. An example is John Bowman's address to his fellow citizens of the Pittsburgh Chamber of Commerce, in which he reminded them of the city's great pioneer tradition:

> But these qualities in men and women, you say, flared up generally among the pioneers of the time. . . . These qualities, however, did not flare up and stay flared up in any other community for so long a period nor did they reach so intense a glow as they did in Pittsburgh.

He goes on to claim that, "The significant fact now is that Pittsburgh through nearly a hundred years developed a new way of thinking, a new way of acting. These new ways became first nature in the people." And then, by simple transmutation, he views these ways as creative acts, and Pittsburgh's creativeness "was the application of creative ability to industry." This was its great contribution to Pittsburgh. And of course, "the old creativeness, developed here through a long period, is still in Pittsburgh."

But when a city settles down, this turn of events is likely to be greeted by criticism—criticism mixed, however, with expressions of nostalgia and joy over the community's improvements. The citizens may perceive that certain civic characteristics derive from the original pioneer spirit which founded and built the town, however astonished the original settlers might be if they could witness the town's transformation.

When residents identify a city with different rural or urban conceptions and with different kinds of romantic histories, they may also identify it with reference to another persistent American dichotomy: regionalism versus national integration. Since our cities are so widely scattered on such different landscapes, it is difficult not to associate a city with its region. Its domestic architecture, the clothing, speech, and action of some of its residents all proclaim it—and the people themselves sometimes proclaim it with belligerence. As is usual with cultural antinomies, men find ample room for ambiguity and for subtle argument. Two cities of the same region may vie for regional supremacy on symbolic as well as economic grounds. Each will claim to represent the region better; each will stress somewhat different areal attributes. Since no region is entirely homogeneous—if only because of its competing urban centers—there is plenty of room for dispute. In a rapidly changing region, such as the "New South," there may be even less agreement unless the resources of ambiguity are utilized in a way such that one city claims to represent the Old South, while the other is quite content to represent the New South (although a city like Charleston can claim to represent both). A region is usually not exactly coterminous with a state; therefore, a city such as Biloxi, Mississippi, can affirm kinship with New Orleans and with bayou culture rather than with the rest of Mississippi.

Some cities, by virtue of the populations which founded them or immigrated to them later, are considered to be less typical of their regions than are their neighbors; these may compensate by claiming other important American values. Conversely, however, a city may receive great waves of foreign immigrants without serious impairment to its position as a regional standard bearer. A few cities are so new that they and their residents share little in common with the rest of the region, in history or in taste, and so are constrained to build some sort of urban history, however flimsy, or to engage in other ceremonial gestures to reaffirm their association with their region. An interesting case is Kingsport, Tennessee, a small city planned and founded by eastern bankers who were attracted to the site by abundant, cheap white labor. Kingsport's historian, writing when the city was only eleven years old, nevertheless argues that had the village but known it, it "was sleeping only that it might awake into a beautiful prosperous city" for "the moral and mental fibre of the sturdy, resourceful people of the Kingsport community required two centuries in the making." While it "is true that the new city was incorporated and began its municipal life only eleven years ago . . . back of all this, unknown to many of the citizens themselves perhaps, is a setting which would be a pride to any of the oldest cities in the country."

A few urban centers gladly spurn extensive regional affiliation. Their residents prefer to think of them as supra-national, even as "world cities," underline the city's role in the national economy, and flaunt its traits of national leadership, sophistication, cosmopolitanism, size, and other symbols of national and international placement. Some sense of the overwhelming impact of a world city is suggested by the breathless and inadequate ways its admirers attempt to sum it up. Thus, John Gunther, who first compares Chicago (the typical American city) with New York (the world city), writes that Chicago is "the greatest and most typically American of all cities. New York is bigger and more spectacular and can outmatch it in other superlatives, but it is a 'world' city, more European in some respects than American." Some pages later he writes that

> now we come to New York City, the incomparable, the brilliant star city of cities, the forty-ninth state, a law unto itself, the Cyclopean paradox, the inferno with no out-of-bounds, the supreme expression of both the miseries and the splendors of contemporary civilization. . . . New York is at once the climactic synthesis of America, and yet the negation of America in that it has so many characteristics called unAmerican.

Paul Crowell and A. H. Raskin merely say: "New York is not a city. It is a thousand cities, each with its own ninety-nine square miles."

Many citizens of "world cities" make denigrating gestures toward more regionally inclined centers. They refer to those centers as less important, small-townish, hick towns, cow towns, and use other similar epithets. Consequently, these latter places may regard the more worldly centers with a suspicion that gains strength from the historic antagonism between countryside and city as well as from a regional passion against national centralization. However, no single city claims to be a national, or world, city in exactly the same way as any other does; and always regional traits are coupled with non-regional ones (even by residents of New York City).

Sectionalism is closely allied with economic specialization inasmuch as the various continental areas function differently in our national economy. Cities tend to become known for the industries, commercial enterprises, and services that are typical of the surrounding area. National cities, of course, have more varied functions; hence when New York City residents insist that it has "everything," this means more than that it performs all the important economic functions. The full significance of the claim is that all (the best—and possibly the worst) styles of life can be found in New York. But the Florida resort city, the Illinois farm city, or the New England manufacturing town can all be conceived of by their residents as simultaneously truly regional and truly American because what they manufacture or trade or service is necessary to the nation.

Some products or services which are limited to certain cities are of sufficient national importance that those cities come to represent some particular facet of America: Pittsburgh and Detroit come readily to mind. Although not all specialiazions are equally praiseworthy, or even savory, nevertheless observers of such cities as Reno and Calumet City can find ample justification for believing that sex, sin, and gambling are as much a part of American life as are automobiles or opera; and Pittsburgh residents could, until recently, declare that smoke-filled air and labor troubles were the inevitable accompaniment of heavy industrialization. As George S. Perry has phrased it:

> Certainly Reno is an actual and highly special aspect of American life, as much as Monte Carlo is a part of European life. . . . Many Nevadans . . . referring both to the tourist business brought in and the large amount of tax load that gambling pays . . . remark simply: "You don't shoot Santa Claus." . . . For in the American mind, Reno remains to gambling and divorces what Pittsburgh means to steel and Hollywood to movies.

Cities whose range of economic function is exceedingly narrow seem frequently to lack variety of social style and suffer from deficiencies in "culture" and other civic virtues esteemed in most towns. Hence residents from other cities may make them the butts of jibes and the objects of social criticism. In the main, the outsider misses the mark for, like physicians whose identities have grown up around the practice of specific medical skills or about the "ownership" of specific bodily areas, the specialized city tends to glorify its command over special skills and resources. Two spokesmen for a pair of our most specialized cities link special skills with the spirit of America. The first is Malcolm Bingay, writing in *Detroit Is My Home Town:*

> This fluidity of life, this refusal to "jell" or ever to grow old helps to explain why everything that is right or wrong which happens to our nation seems to break here first. It is that very spirit which first conceived the idea of throwing away millions upon millions of dollars of machinery as obsolete to make way for better machinery and greater speed to meet competition. This horror of obsolescence is the "Americanism" which permitted us to triumph in two great wars. . . . Other countries remained static in the sense that while they understood our standardization of parts —to a degree—they never did catch the imponderable elements of mass production in which there is nothing permanent but change.

The second spokesman is Carl Crow, who, in *The City of Flint,* writes:

> The history of the interesting and dynamic city of Flint has been worth recording because it is more than the chronicle of an individual city. It

epitomizes the history of America . . . America is a story of the industrial development which has brought us such a high standard of living.

Citizens who are intensely interested in the furtherance of the arts
congregate in groups and associations that many other citizens believe
are less central to the life of the community than other more vigorous
business, social, and cultural institutions representing the interests of the
town's more typical citizens. Sometimes cultural barrenness is excused
in terms of the city's symbolic age. Given sufficient time, some say, the
city will grow up, develop a rich cultural life, and take its place among
the civilized cities of its size—and, one might add, among some cities
a tithe of its size. The residents of Chicago sometimes use this strategy
to console themselves or to ward off attack, and it is probably commonly
used in other cities. Here is an instance from Birmingham, Alabama:

> Birmingham somehow, for all her pride in the great labors which con-
> verted a cornfield into a great metropolis in little more than the span of
> one man's life, Birmingham is haunted by a sense of promise unfulfilled.
> Her more philosophic citizens are obsessed with this thought. They brood
> and ponder over it, and, searching their souls and the city's history, con-
> stantly seek the reason why. They come up with many answers. One is
> the obvious one of her youth. . . . Another answer is . . . Birmingham is
> a working town. . . . Painting pictures and composing music and writing
> books—even the widespread appreciation of those things—all rather
> come with time.

When a specialized city becomes economically diversified, and creates
or draws to it new populations with new tastes, the imagery associated
with it changes radically. It remains no longer merely a steel city, a
rubber town, or an agricultural community, but is represented widely as
a more cosmopolitan center.

Although every city within the United States is American in a factual
sense, some cities are in some other sense denied that status from time
to time. Many visitors to the Southwest would agree with John Gunther
that there one may feel almost as if he is leaving the United States.
("The first thing I thought was, 'Can this possibly be North America?' ")
But that reaction is not aroused solely by regional geography or by
ethnic culture, for cities may be symbolically driven off the American landscape when they offend deeply felt standards of propriety. One critic of
Pittsburgh some years ago bitterly characterized it as "A city inherited
from the Middle Ages," and only partly admitted that it was one of us.
Reno is frequently a target for obloquy: a *Reader's Digest* article titled
"Reno: Parasite on Human Weakness" is representative; its author,
true to his title, could not admit that Reno is genuinely American.
Even Los Angeles, although it shares national characteristics conspicuously

enough, seems to strike many people as odd or crazy; and, "according to its most severe critics, it is New York in purple shorts with its brains knocked out." The phrase is George S. Perry's; in less fanciful prose he sums up very well the partial denial of status to that large city when he adds that its "civilization has been declared to caricature, in one way or another, that of the entire nation."

The residents of certain other cities sometimes display sensitivity to the ways in which their cities deviate from what they or outside critics conceive to be the normal national or regional urban patterns. Cincinnati has never quite recovered from Mrs. Trollope's visit nor from its reputation as a tradition-bound town located within a progressive, dynamic region. When a city begins its history with a great promise but then suffers relative oblivion, it departs sufficiently from the usual regional expectations to require a set of supporting rationalizations. Thus a loyal resident of Marietta, Ohio, in 1903 mournfully took stock of a century that had passed without much progress for his town. He remarked that

> a city may open the way for progress, and still not progress itself. . . .
> Evidently other cities . . . have excelled her [Marietta] in so many ways.
> . . . But at the beginning of the new century she stands young, strong,
> and vigorous, no longer old, except in name, with an ambition of youth
> and wealth of resource. . . . While it has thus taken a century of ex-
> perience during which time she seems to move forward so slowly, it is
> well to consider that these years were spent in laying a firm and substan-
> tial foundation whereon to build the New Marietta.

In another passage, we can watch a citizen of Vincennes, Indiana, trying to puzzle out why prophesies about cities sometimes fail to materialize. Commenting on Vincennes' bustling future after "a sort of Rip Van Winkle sleep," he wrote:

> This bright prospect although long delayed might have been expected from
> the opinions of the place and its natural advantages expressed by the
> missionary fathers who first visited it. . . . These men were far seeing
> and almost with prophetic vision foretold the future of various places
> they visited. . . . In no instance have their prophetic utterances failed of
> fruition unless it shall be in the solitary instance of Vincennes.

In urging his contemporaries on to greater civic harmony and energy, he added, "They made the same prophetic utterances with reference to Pittsburgh, Cincinnati, Louisville, Detroit, Chicago, St. Paul, St. Louis, San Francisco and many other cities. . . . And why should not their opinions with regard to Vincennes not be realized?"

The residents of most cities can escape feelings of non-typicality simply by stressing other sets of American traits, but when cities develop in astonishingly new ways, their citizens must claim, as I have already suggested, that clearly sanctioned American qualities (rurality, urbanity, sectionality) are actually present or exist in new, somewhat disguised forms.

Most curious of all is the case of New York, a city which has been passionately and repeatedly denied essential American status while its admirers have proclaimed it the greatest city in America. It is one thing to feel that this great metropolis is not the most typical of our cities, that from it foreigners receive a skewed and partial picture of the nation; but it is another matter to believe that New York is partly or wholly not American, or even "un-American." The grounds of attack and defense bring to sharp focus the ambiguity and clash of American values.

In 1894 Theodore Roosevelt published an article titled "What 'Americanism' Means," in which he argued:

> There are two or three sides to the question of Americanism, and two or three senses in which the word "Americanism" can be used to express the antithesis of what is unwholesome and undesirable. In the first place we wish to be broadly American and national, as opposed to being local or sectional.

In the second place, he reports, it is unwholesome for an American to become Europeanized, thus too cosmopolitan; and in the third place, the meaning pertains to those foreign immigrants who do not become quickly Americanized. These antitheses, which run through the arguments for and against New York City, can be found in another article titled "Is New York More Civilized Than Kansas?" which follows almost immediately after Roosevelt's in the same journal. Kansas is defined as the more civilized (that is, as the more American) on a score of grounds, which include its homogeneity of ideal and tradition, its native population, its home life, its lack of class distinction, its religious and moral tone, and its optimal conditions for rearing children. New York is declared not to possess most of these qualities. The author even argues that Kansas is less isolated, in the civilizational as well as the geographic sense, because its greater number of railroads keep it in more intimate contact with all sections of the nation.

Through the years, New York has been accused of being too European, too suspiciously cosmopolitan, too aggressive and materialistic, too hurried and hectic, a city where family life and home life do not flourish but where—it is asserted or suspected—iniquity does. New York seems to sum up all the negative balances in the rural animus against cities, in the sectional argument against centralization and cosmopolitanism, and in the frontier bias against cities which do not share the mystic pioneer experience. No other American city is the target of such great or complete antagonism.

New York's admirers, whether they are native to the city or not, counter these arguments in two ways. They can maintain that the city is not actually deficient in these various regards. For instance, *The New York Times Magazine* makes its business the occasional publication of articles about the city which tacitly or explicitly set out to prove that New York really is a friendly place having unsuspected village-like qualities, a quiet home life, plus bits of rurality and even farming tucked away here and there. They also try to show that the large numbers of immigrants and their children are at least as American as citizens with longer native genealogies. When New Yorkers write about themselves or about their city, their affirmation of urban identity often takes that form. (Al Smith once wrote an article titled "I Have Seven Million Neighbors.")

Side by side with the outright accusation that New York fails to participate in our wholesome, rural, or village heritage runs the assertion that New York is actually our most representative city because it is our greatest. "Greatness" can be attributed on quite different grounds, for each assertion rests upon certain features of American culture judged to be of the highest importance. New York is our last frontier, the place where persons of spirit are drawn as by a magnet. It is the "moving frontier" of American culture, the most important site of progress and innovation. It is the image of America, for here the melting pot is at its most intense and here the New America—racially or culturally—is being forged rather than in the most homogeneous native American centers. Although the same theme of the urban melting pot as the epitome of American civilization is applied to other ethnically diverse cities, New York is a place where all narrow local sectionalism has disappeared: because it is a great world city, as is twentieth-century America—is not this the American century! Even those who hate New York may have to admit New York's typicality on the grounds that if this is the America of today, then New York certainly best represents it. Here, for instance, is Earl Sparling's anguished summation, complete with reference to the pioneer past:

> I find it an appalling place, rich for making money, poor for living. . . . But all of that is one thing. It is a different thing to shrug the whole spectacle away as something completely alien and not American. America cannot be absolved that easily. Not only is New York American, but it is the mirror in which America, after half a century of confusion, suddenly sees herself for what she is. . . . New York is the soul of America. And Americans . . . see it . . . and wonder how all this happened in a free, pioneer land.

Is it any wonder that there is so much ambiguity in the symbolization of this metropolis, this New York which "is at once the climactic synthesis of America, and yet the negation of America in that it has so many characteristics called un-American?" The attitude—and the bewilderment—of many Americans can be summed up in the reactions of a girl from the Midwest who, visiting New York for the first time, exclaimed that it was "just a wonderfully exciting place but so unreal; it doesn't even have trees." It is summed up also in a magnificently paradoxical set of sentences written by the editors of *Fortune* magazine, as they struggled to relate New York City to the national culture:

> New York may be taken as a symbol, or it may be taken as a fact. As a symbol it is a symbol of America; its noisy, exuberant, incalculable towers rise out of the water like a man's aspirations to freedom. As a symbol it is the Gateway, the promise, the materialization of the New World. . . . But taken as a fact, New York is less Dantesque. To most Americans the fact is that "New York is not America." It is un-American in lots of ways. The concentration of power that exists among those spires is itself un-American; so are the tumultuous, vowel-twisting inhabitants who throng the sidewalks.

The confusion continues. Two pages later, when the editors eloquently discuss the city's role as a great melting pot, they wrote, "In that sense New York *is* America," only to blunt the force of that assertion with "more than symbolically."

The strain between ideal and reality, or ideal and presumed fact, runs like a brilliant thread through all our antithetical thinking about America and about our cities. With a fine flair for significant ambiguities, the *Saturday Evening Post* included among more than 145 cities which it surveyed after World War II an article about "a little cow town." Its author asserted that "The *Saturday Evening Post* is running a notable series of articles about American cities. All this is well enough, but . . . if we have any truly national culture, it stems from the small town and near-by farm." George S. Perry, in his book, *Cities of America,* could not avoid including, either, a chapter about a town of two thousand people; and, like the editors of *Fortune,* he uses those interesting terms "fact" and "symbol"—except that he applies them to a small city. "Madison, Wisconsin," he sentimentalizes,

> is both a fact and a symbol that stands for many of the finest traits in the American character. It is a place where independent people get up on their hind legs and have their say. Again, it is a seat of serious learning. Moreover, it is surrounded by that basic harmony that derives from good land that has been treated intelligently and with respect. Finally, Madison's people are almost spectacularly unapathetic. They are concerned,

interested, and willing to do something about almost any public question. In many ways Madison and its environs are a minature model of the ideal America of which many of us dream.

SUGGESTED READING: CHAPTER 1

Scott Greer. *The Emerging City*. New York: The Free Press, 1962.

The author discusses metropolitan developments, explicitly criticizing older images of the city and suggesting what he believes might be a more appropriate one.

Kevin Lynch. *The Image of the City*. Cambridge, Mass.: The Technology Press and Harvard University, 1960.

An architect and planner presents an esthetic and visual perspective on the city, and also explores through preliminary interviews the visual (and sentimental) images of people in Boston, Jersey City, and Los Angeles.

Robert Park. *The City*. Chicago: University of Chicago Press, 1925.

The differential meanings a city can have for different populations, and the relationships between these meanings and life-styles, are explicitly discussed as research topics in this sociological classic.

Morton White and Lucia White. *The Intellectual Versus the City*. Cambridge, Mass.: Harvard University Press and M.I.T. Press, 1962.

The authors aimed to discover the perspectives of American intellectuals toward cities; they concluded that the dominant views were antagonistic. This book is interesting, but the evidence is far from complete.

2

Chicago at Night. Chicago Association of Commerce and
Industry photo.

CONTRASTING
CONCEPTIONS OF
THE SAME CITY

ANY characterization or description of a city is also an interpretation. Even a small city is so many-sided, its people and their activities so varied that different interpretations and characterizations of it are given by its citizens and by its visitors as well. The language of description actually involves a fairly limited range of linguistic conventions. Thus, adjectives are used to modify the city seen as an object: cosmopolitan, smug, serene, bustling. Or the city is personified—endowed with a personality, given a reputation and even a biography. Urban complexity is also handled by thinking of a city as "really" or "essentially" like something else, by use of metaphor or simile ("New York, city with a heart of Nylon"). The imputed qualities of a city, once established by the person describing it, can be elaborated by illustration and pointed anecdote which are aimed at demonstrating how the city's qualities shine through typical events and institutions. And any particular city can strike its citizens or visitors as so unique that they use linguistic conventions asserting merely this uniqueness ("only in San Francisco" or "where else can you find . . . ?").

These linguistic conventions have not been really studied by sociologists or other social scientists. They are, however, excellent indicators of perspectives held not only toward particular cities but toward facets of particular cities. As recent literature in urban sociology has emphasized, anyone who wishes to develop urban theory must work toward a comparative sociology and history of cities. Hence, popular representations of specific cities, though interesting in themselves, can be maximally useful for advancing urban theory only if one thinks comparatively about them.

This means that we must ask not only how do various populations differently conceive of a Chicago, but how do the same types of population regard cities as different as Chicago, New York, Lincoln, Birmingham, Reno, and Atlantic City?

In the three selections that follow—two by visitors to Chicago during the 1890s—these linguistic resources referred to above can be seen plainly. The authors disagree about most details and certainly about the "essence" of Chicago. However, each makes out a good case for his view of that city. We cannot fail to observe that each interpretation of Chicago embodies various of the urban perspectives remarked on earlier, in the preceding chapter.

HOW I STRUCK CHICAGO, AND HOW CHICAGO STRUCK ME, *Rudyard Kipling*

ON his travels through the United States, Kipling's
reactions to American cities were generally
unenthusiastic, but Chicago really aroused
his passion!

I have struck a city—a real city—and they call it Chicago. The
other places do not count. San Francisco was a pleasure-resort as well as
a city, and Salt Lake was a phenomenon. This place is the first American
city I have encountered. It holds rather more than a million people with
bodies, and stands on the same sort of soil as Calcutta. Having seen it, I
urgently desire never to see it again. It is inhabited by savages. Its water
is the water of the Hughli, and its air is dirt. Also it says that it is the
"boss" town of America.

I do not believe that it has anything to do with this country. They told
me to go to the Palmer House which is a gilded and mirrored rabbit-
warren, and there I found a huge hall of tessellated marble, crammed with
people talking about money and spitting about everywhere. Other bar-
barians charged in and out of this inferno with letters and telegrams in
their hands, and yet others shouted at each other. A man who had drunk
quite as much as was good for him told me that this was "the finest hotel
in the finest city on God Almighty's earth." . . .

. . . *Then* I went out into the streets, which are long and flat and without end. And verily it is not a good thing to live in our East for any
length of time. Your ideas grow to clash with those held by every right-
thinking white man. I looked down interminable vistas flanked with nine,
ten, and fifteen storied houses, and crowded with men and women, and
the show impressed me with a great horror. Except in London—and I
have forgotten what London is like—I had never seen so many white
people together, and never such a collection of miserables. There was no
colour in the street and no beauty—only a maze of wire-ropes overhead
and dirty stone flagging underfoot. A cab-driver volunteered to show me
the glory of the town for so much an hour, and with him I wandered far.
He conceived that all this turmoil and squash was a thing to be reverently
admired; that it was good to huddle men together in fifteen layers, one

Excerpted from *From Sea to Sea*, Part II (Garden City, N.Y.: Doubleday, Page
and Co., 1914), pp. 230–248. Copyright 1907 by the author.

atop of the other, and to dig holes in the ground for offices. He said that Chicago was a live town, and that all the creatures hurrying by me were engaged in business. That is to say, they were trying to make some money, that they might not die through lack of food to put into their bellies. He took me to canals, black as ink, and filled with untold abominations, and bade me watch the stream of traffic across the bridges. He then took me into a saloon, and, while I drank, made me note that the floor was covered with coins sunk into cement. A Hottentot would not have been guilty of this sort of barbarism. The coins made an effect pretty enough, but the man who put them there had no thought to beauty, and therefore he was a savage. Then my cab-driver showed me business blocks, gay with signs and studded with fantastic and absurd advertisements of goods, and looking down the long street so adorned it was as though each vender stood at his door howling: "For the sake of money, employ, or buy of, *me* and me only!" Have you ever seen a crowd at our famine-relief distributions? You know then how men leap into the air, stretching out their arms above the crowd in the hope of being seen; while the women dolorously slap the stomachs of their children and whimper. I had sooner watch famine relief than the white man engaged in what he calls legitimate competition. The one I understand. The other makes me ill. And the cab-man said that these things were the proof of progress; and by that I knew he had been reading his newspaper, as every intelligent American should. The papers tell their readers in language fitted to their comprehension that the snarling together of telegraph wires, the heaving up of houses, and the making of money is progress.

I spent ten hours in that huge wilderness, wandering through scores of miles of these terrible streets, and jostling some few hundred thousand of these terrible people who talked money through their noses. The cabman left me: but after a while I picked up another man who was full of figures, and into my ears he poured them as occasion required or the big blank factories suggested. Here they turned out so many hundred thousand dollars' worth of such and such an article; there so many million other things; this house was worth so many million dollars; that one so many million more or less. It was like listening to a child babbling of its hoard of shells. It was like watching a fool playing with buttons. But I was expected to do more than listen or watch. He demanded that I should admire; and the utmost that I could say was: "Are these things so? Then I am very sorry for you." That made him angry, and he said that insular envy made me unresponsive. So you see I could not make him understand.

.   .   .   .

Sunday brought me the queerest experience of all—a revelation of barbarism complete. I found a place that was officially described as a church.

It was a circus really, but that the worshippers did not know. There were flowers all about the building, which was fittted up with plush and stained oak and much luxury, including twisted brass candlesticks of severest Gothic design. To these things, and a congregation of savages, entered suddenly a wonderful man completely in the confidence of their God, whom he treated colloquially and exploited very much as a newspaper reporter would exploit a foreign potentate. But, unlike the newspaper reporter, he never allowed his listeners to forget that he and not He was the centre of attraction. With a voice of silver and with imagery borrowed from the auction-room, he built up for his hearers a heaven on the lines of the Palmer House (but with all the gilding real gold and all the plate-glass diamond) and set in the centre of it a loud-voiced, argumentative, and very shrewd creation that he called God. One sentence at this point caught my delighted ear. It was *apropos* of some question of the Judgment Day and ran: "No! I tell you God don't do business that way." He was giving them a deity whom they could comprehend, in a gold and jewel heaven in which they could take a natural interest. He interlarded his per-formance with the slang of the streets, the counter, and the Exchange, and he said that religion ought to enter into daily life. Consequently I presume he introduced it *as* daily life—his own and the life of his friends.

Then I escaped before the blessing, desiring no benediction at such hands. But the persons who listened seemed to enjoy themselves, and I understand that I had met with a popular preacher. Later on, when I had perused the sermons of a gentleman called Talmage and some others, I perceived that I had been listening to a very mild specimen. . . . All that Sunday I listened to people who said that the mere fact of spiking down strips of iron to wood and getting a steam and iron thing to run along them was progress. That the telephone was progress, and the network of wires overhead was progress. They repeated their statements again and again, One of them took me to their city hall and board of trade works and point it out with pride. It was very ugly, but very big, and the streets in front of it were narrow and unclean. When I saw the faces of the men who did business in that building I felt that there had been a mistake in their billeting. . . .

. . . But I don't think it was the blind hurry of the people, their argot, and their grand ignorance of things beyond their immediate interests that displeased me so much as a study of the daily papers of Chicago. Imprimis, there was some sort of dispute between New York and Chicago as to which town should give an exhibition of products to be hereafter holden, and through the medium of their more dignified journals the two cities were ya-hooing and hi-yi-ing at each other like opposition newsboys. They called it humour, but it sounded like something quite different. That was only the first trouble. The second lay in the tone of the productions. Leading articles which indulge gems such as: "Back of such and such a place," or "We noticed, Tuesday, such an event," or "don't" for "does not" are things to be accepted with thankfulness. All that made me weep was that, in these papers, were faithfully reproduced all the war-cries and "back-talk" of the Palmer House bar, the slang of the barbers' shops, the mental elevation and integrity of the Pullman-car porter, the dignity of the Dime Museum, and the accuracy of the excited fishwife. I am sternly forbidden to believe that the paper educates the public. Then I am compelled to believe that the public educate the paper?

Just when the sense of unreality and oppression was strongest upon me, and when I most wanted help, a man sat at my side and began to talk what he called politics. I had chanced to pay about six shillings for a traveling-cap worth eighteen pence, and he made of the fact a text for a sermon. He said that this was a rich country and that the people liked to pay two hundred per cent on the value of a thing. They could afford it. He said that the Government imposed a protective duty of from ten to seventy per cent on foreign-made articles, and that the American manufacturer consequently could sell his goods for a healthy sum. Thus an imported hat would, with duty, cost two guineas. The American manufacturer would make a hat for seventeen shillings and sell it for one pound fifteen. In these things, he said, lay the greatness of America and the effeteness of England. Competition between factory and factory kept the prices down to decent limits, but I was never to forget that this people were a rich people, not like the pauper Continentals, and that they enjoyed paying duties. To my weak intellect this seemed rather like juggling with counters. Everything that I have yet purchased costs about twice as much as it would in England, and, when native-made is of inferior quality . . . I am an alien, and for the life of me cannot see why six shillings should be paid for eighteen-penny caps, or eight shillings for half-crown cigar-cases. When the country fills up to a decently populated level a few million people who are not aliens will be smitten with the same sort of blindness.

But my friend's assertion somehow thoroughly suited the grotesque ferocity of Chicago. . . . Chicago husks and winnows her wheat by the million bushels, a hundred banks lend hundreds of millions of dollars in the year, and scores of factories turn out plow gear and machinery by steam. Scores of daily papers do work which Hukm Chund and the barber and the midwife perform, with due regard for public opinion, in the village of Isser Jang. So far as manufactures go, the difference between Chicago on the lake and Isser Jang on the Montgomery road [in India] is one of degree only, and not of kind. So far as the understanding of the uses of life goes Isser Jang, for all its seasonal cholera, has the advantage over Chicago. Jowala Singh knows and takes care to avoid the three or four ghoul-haunted fields on the outskirts of the village; but he is not urged by millions of devils to run about all day in the sun and swear that his plowshares are the best in the Punjab; nor does Puran Dass fly forth in a cart more than once or twice a year, and he knows, on a pinch, how to use the railway and the telegraph as well as any son of Israel in Chicago. But this is absurd. The East is not the West, and these men must continue to deal with the machinery of life, and to call it progress. Their very preachers dare not rebuke them. They gloss over the hunting for money and the twice-sharpened bitterness of Adam's curse by saying that such things dower a man with a larger range of thoughts and higher aspirations. They do not say: "Free yourself from your own slavery," but rather, "If you can possibly manage it, do not set quite so much store on the things of this world." And they do not know what the things of this world are.

I went off to see cattle killed by way of clearing my head, which, as you will perceive, was getting muddled. They say every Englishman goes to the Chicago stock-yards. You shall find them about six miles from the city; and once having seen them you will never forget the sight. As far as the eye can reach stretches a township of cattle-pens, cunningly divided into blocks so that the animals of any pen can be speedily driven out close to an inclined timber path which leads to an elevated covered way straddling high above the pens. These viaducts are two-storied. On the upper storey tramp the doomed cattle, stolidly for the most part. On the lower, with a scuffling of sharp hoofs and multitudinous yells, run the pigs. The same end is appointed for each. Thus you will see the gangs of cattle waiting their turn—as they wait sometimes for days; and they need not be distressed by the sight of their fellows running about in the fear of death. All they know is that a man on horseback causes their next-door neighbors to move by means of a whip. Certain bars and fences are unshipped, and, behold, that crowd have gone up the mouth of a sloping tunnel and return no more. It is different with the pigs. They shriek back the news of the exodus to their friends, and a hundred pens skirl responsive. It was to the pigs I first addressed myself. Selecting a viaduct which was full of them, as I could hear though I could not see, I marked a sombre building whereto it ran, and went there, not unalarmed by stray cattle who had managed to escape from their proper quarters. A pleasant smell of brine warned me of what was coming. I entered the factory and found it full of pork in barrels, and on another storey more pork unbarrelled, and in a huge room the halves of swine, for whose use great lumps of ice were being pitched in at the window. That room was the mortuary chamber where the pigs lie for a little while in state ere they begin their progress through such passages as kings may sometimes travel. Turning a corner and not noting an overhead arrangement of greased rail, wheel, and pulley, I ran into the arms of four eviscerated carcasses, all pure white and of a human aspect, being pushed by a man clad in vehement red. When I leaped aside, the floor was slippery under me. There was a flavour of farmyard in my nostrils and the shouting of a multitude in my ears. But there was no joy in that shouting. Twelve men stood in two lines—six a side. Between them and overhead ran the railway of death that had nearly shunted me through the window. Each man carried a knife, the sleeves of his shirt were cut off at the elbows, and from bosom to heel he was blood-red. The atmosphere was stifling as a night in the Rains, by reason of the steam and the crowd. I climbed to the beginning of things and, perched upon a narrow beam, overlooked very nearly all the pigs ever bred in Wisconsin. They had just been shot out of the mouth of the viaduct and huddled together in a large pen. Thence they were flicked persuasively, a few at a time, into a smaller chamber, and there a man fixed tackle on their hinder legs so that they rose in the air suspended from the railway of death. Oh! it was then they shrieked and called on their mothers and made promises of amendment, till the tackle-man punted them in their backs, and they slid head down into a brick-floored passage, very like a big kitchen sink that was blood-red. There awaited them a red man with a knife which he passed jauntily through their throats, and the full-voiced shriek became a sputter, and then a fall as of heavy tropical rain. The red man who was backed against the passage wall stood clear of the wildly kicking hoofs and passed his hand over his eyes, not from any feeling of compassion, but because the spurted blood was in his eyes, and he had barely time to stick the next arrival. Then that first stuck swine dropped, still kicking, into a great vat of boiling water, and spoke no more words, but wallowed in obedience to some unseen machinery, and presently came forth at the lower end of the vat and was heaved on the blades of a blunt paddle-wheel-thing which said, "Hough! Hough! Hough!" and skelped all the hair off him except what little a couple of men with knives could remove. Then he was again hitched by the heels to that said railway and passed down the line of the twelve men—each man with a knife—leaving with each man a certain amount of his individuality which was taken away in a wheelbarrow, and when he reached the last man he was very beautiful to behold, but immensely unstuffed and limp. . . .

The dissecting part impressed me not so much as the slaying. They were so excessively alive, these pigs. And then they were so excessively dead, and the man in the dripping, clammy, hot passage did not seem to care, and ere the blood of such an one had ceased to foam on the floor, such another, and four friends with him, had shrieked and died. But a pig is only the Unclean animal—forbidden by the Prophet.

I was destined to make rather a queer discovery when I went over to the cattle-slaughter. All the buildings were on a much larger scale, and there was no sound of trouble, but I could smell the salt reek of blood before I set foot in the place. The cattle did not come directly through the viaduct as the pigs had done. They debouched into a yard by the hundred, and they were big red brutes carrying much flesh. In the centre of that yard stood a red Texan steer with a head-stall on his wicked head. No man controlled him. He was, so to speak, picking his teeth and whistling in an open byre of his own when the cattle arrived. As soon as the first one had fearfully quitted the viaduct, this red devil put his hands in his pockets and slouched across the yard, no man guiding him. Then he lowed something to the effect that he was the regularly appointed guide of the establishment and would show them round. They were country folk, but they knew how to behave; and so followed Judas some hundred strong, patiently, and with a look of bland wonder in their faces. I saw his broad back jogging in advance of them, up a lime-washed incline where I was forbidden to follow. Then a door-shut, and in a minute back came Judas with the air of a virtuous plough-bullock and took up his place in his byre. Somebody laughed across the yard, but I heard no sound of cattle from the big brick building into which the mob had disappeared. Only Judas chewed the cud with a malignant satisfaction, and so I knew there was trouble, and ran round to the front of the factory and so entered and stood aghast.

Who takes count of the prejudices which we absorb through the skin by way of our surroundings? It was not the spectacle that impressed me. The first thought that almost spoke itself aloud was: "They are killing kine"; and it was a shock. The pigs were nobody's concern, but cattle—the brothers of the Cow, the Sacred Cow—were quite otherwise. The next time an M. P. tells me that India either Sultanises or Brahminises a man, I shall believe about half what he says. It is unpleasant to watch the slaughter of cattle when one has laughed at the notion for a few years. I could not see actually what was done in the first instance, because the row of stalls in which they lay was separated from me by fifty impassable feet of butchers and slung carcasses. All I know is that men swung open the doors of a stall as occasion required, and there lay two steers already stunned, and breathing heavily. These two they pole-axed, and half raising them by tackle they cut their throats. Two men skinned each carcass, somebody cut off the head, and in half a minute more the overhead rail carried two sides of beef to their appointed place. There was clamour enough in the operating-room, but from the waiting cattle, invisible on the other side of the line of pens, never a sound. They went to their death, trusting Judas, without a word. They were slain at the rate of five a minute, and if the pig men were splattered with blood, the cow butchers were bathed in it. The blood ran in muttering gutters. There was no place for hand or foot that was not coated with thicknesses of dried blood, and the stench of it in the nostrils bred fear.

And then the same merciful Providence that has showered good things on my path throughout sent me an embodiment of the City of Chicago, so that I might remember it for ever. Women come sometimes to see the slaughter, as they would come to see the slaughter of men. And there entered that vermilion hall a young woman of large mould, with brilliantly scarlet lips, and heavy eyebrows, and dark hair that came in a "widow's peak" on the forehead. She was well and healthy and alive, and she was dressed in flaming red and black, and her feet (know you that the feet of American women are like unto the feet of fairies?)—her feet, I say, were cased in red leather shoes. She stood in a patch of sunlight, the red blood under her shoes, the vivid carcasses tacked round her, a bullock bleeding its life away not six feet away from her, and the death factory roaring all round her. She looked curiously, with hard, bold eyes, and was not ashamed.

Then said I: "This is a special Sending. I have seen the City of Chicago!" And I went away to get peace and rest.

AN EASTERNER LOOKS AT A WESTERN CITY,
Julian Ralph

JULIAN RALPH was a native New Yorker, known
first as a journalist for such newspapers as the
Daily Graphic and the *Sun,* and later for his magazine
articles and books. *Our Great West,* published in
1893, includes descriptions written for
Harper's Magazine about his travels in the West and
Middle West. It was through such eyes as his
that Easterners got many of their impressions
of western cities.

With few exceptions, the great expositions of the world have been held in Christendom's great capitals, and the cities that have known them have been scarcely subordinate to the expositions themselves in the attractions they have offered to the masses of sight-seers who have gathered in them. Chicago lacks many of the qualities of the older cities that have been chosen for this purpose, but for every one that is missing she offers others fully as attractive. Those who go clear-minded, expecting to see a great city, will find one different from that which any precedent has led them to look for. Those who go to study the world's progress will not find

Excerpted from *Our Great West* (New York: Harper and Brothers, 1893), pp. 1–23, 30–63.

in the Columbian Exposition, among all its marvels, any other result of human force so wonderful, extravagant, or peculiar as Chicago itself.

While investigating the management and prospects of the Columbian Exposition, I was a resident of Chicago for more than a fortnight. A born New Yorker, the energy, roar, and bustle of the place were yet sufficient to first astonish and then to fatigue me. I was led to examine the city, and to cross-examine some of its leading men. I came away compelled to acknowledge its possession of certain forceful qualities which I never saw exhibited in the same degree anywhere else. I got a satisfactory explanation of its growth and achievements, as well as proof that it must continue to expand in population and commercial influence. Moreover, without losing a particle of pride or faith in New York—without perceiving that New York was affected by the consideration—I acquired a respect for Chicago such as it is most likely that any American who makes a similar investigation must share with me.

The city has been thought intolerant of criticism. The amount of truth there is in this is found in its supervoluminous civicism. The bravado and bunkum of the Chicago newspapers reflect this quality, but do it clumsily, because it proceeds from a sense of business policy with the editors, who laugh at it themselves. But underlying the behavior of the most able and enterprising men in the city is this motto, which they constantly quoted to me, all using the same words, "We are for Chicago first, last, and all the time." To define that sentence is, in a great measure, to account for Chicago.

.　　.　　.　　.　　.　　.　　.　　.　　.　　.

I have spoken of the roar and bustle and energy of Chicago. This is most noticeable in the business part of the town, where the greater number of the men are crowded together. It seems there as if the men would run over the horses if the drivers were not careful. Everybody is in such a hurry and going at such a pace that if a stranger asks his way, he is apt to have to trot along with his neighbor to gain the information, for the average Chicagoan cannot stop to talk. The whole business of life is carried on at high pressure, and the pithy part of Chicago is like three hundred acres of New York Stock Exchange when trading is active. . . . It is a rapid and a business-like city. The speed with which cattle are killed and pigs are turned into slabs of salt pork has amazed the world, but it is only the ignorant portion thereof that does not know that the celerity at the stockyards is merely an effort of the butchers to keep up with the rest of the town. . . .

I do not know how many very tall buildings Chicago contains, but they must number nearly two dozen. Some of them are artistically designed, and hide their height in well-balanced proportions. A few are mere boxes punctured with window-holes, and stand above their neighbors like great hitching posts. The best of them are very elegantly and completely appointed, and the communities of men inside them might almost live their lives within their walls, so multifarious are the occupations and services of the tenants. The best New York office buildings are not injured by comparison with these towering structures, except that they are not so tall as the Chicago buildings, but there is not in New York any office structure that can be compared with Chicago's so-called Chamber of Commerce office building, so far as are concerned the advantages of light and air and openness and roominess which its tenants enjoy. In these respects there is only one fine building in America, and that is in Minneapolis. It is a great mistake to think that we in New York possess all the elegant, rich, and ornamental outgrowths of taste, or that we know better than the West what are the luxuries and comforts of the age. With their floors of deftly-laid mosaic-work, their walls of marble and onyx, their balustrades of copper worked into arabesquerie, their artistic lanterns, elegant electric fixtures, their costly and luxurious public rooms, these Chicago office buildings force an exclamation of praise, however unwillingly it comes. . . .

These tall buildings are mainly built on land obtained on 99-year leasehold. Long leases rather than outright purchases of land have long been a favorite preliminary to building in Chicago, where, for one thing, the men who owned the land have not been those with the money for building. Where very great and costly buildings are concerned, the long leases often go to corporations or syndicates, who put up the houses. It seems to many strangers who visit Chicago that it is reasonable to prophesy a speedy end to the feverish impulse to swell the number of these giant piles, either through legislative ordinance or by the fever running its course. Many prophesy that it must soon end. . . . So it seems, but not to a thoroughbred Chicagoan. One of the foremost business men in the city asserts that he can perceive no reason why the entire business heart of the town—that square half-mile of which I have spoken—should not soon be all builded up of cloud-capped towers. There will be a need for them, he says, and the money to defray the cost of them will accompany the demand. The only trouble he foresees will be in the solution of the problem what to do with the people who will then crowd the streets as never streets were clogged before.

This prophecy relates to a little block in the city, but the city itself contains 181½ square miles. It has been said of the many annexations by which her present size was attained that Chicago reached out and took to herself farms, prairie land, and villages, and that of such material the great city now in part consists. This is true. In surburban trips, such as those I took to Fort Sheridan and Fernwood, for instance, I passed the great cabbage farms, groves, houseless but plotted tracts, and long reaches of the former prairie. Even yet Hyde Park is a separated settlement, and a dozen or more villages stand out as distinctly by themselves as ever they did. If it were true, as her rivals insist, that Chicago added all this tract merely to get a high rank in the census reports of population, the folly of the action would be either ludicrous or pitiful, according to the standpoint from which it was viewed. But the true reason for her enormous extension of municipal jurisdiction is quite as peculiar. The enlargement was urged and accomplished in order to anticipate the growth and needs of the city. It was a consequence of extraordinary foresight, which recognized the necessity for a uniform system of boulevards, parks, drainage, and water provision when the city should reach limits that it was even then seen must bound a compact aggregation of stores, offices, factories, and dwellings. To us of the East this is surprising. It might seem incredible were there not many other evidences of the same spirit and sagacity not only in Chicago, but in the other cities of the West, especially of the Northwest. What Minneapolis, St. Paul, and Duluth are doing towards a future park system reveals the same enterprise and habit of looking far ahead. And Chicago, in her park system, makes evident her intentions. In all these cities and in a hundred ways the observant traveller notes the same forehandedness, and prepares himself to understand the temper in which the greatest of the Western capitals leaned forth and absorbed the prairie. Chicago expects to become the largest city in America—a city which, in fifty years, shall be larger than the consolidated cities that may form New York at that time.

.   .   .   .

It seems to have ever been, as it is now, a city of young men. One Chicagoan accounts for its low death rate on the ground that not even its leading men are yet old enough to die. The young men who drifted there from the Eastern States after the close of the war all agree that the thing which most astonished them was the youthfulness of the most active business men. Marshall Field, Potter Palmer, and the rest, heading very large mercantile establishments, were young fellows. Those who came to Chicago from England fancied, as it is said that Englishmen do, that a man may not be trusted with affairs until he has lost half his hair and all his teeth. Our own Eastern men were apt to place wealth and success at the middle of the scale of life. But in Chicago men under thirty were leading in commerce and industry. The sight was a spur to all the young men who came, and they also pitched in to swell the size and successes of the young men's capital. The easy making of money by the loaning of it and by handling city realty—sources which never failed with shrewd men

—not only whetted the general appetite for big and quick money-making, but they provided the means for the establishment and extension of trade in other ways and with the West at large.

It is one of the peculiarities of Chicago that one finds not only the capitalists but the storekeepers discussing the whole country with a familiarity as strange to a man from the Atlantic coast as Nebraska is strange to most Philadelphians or New Yorkers. But the well-informed and "hustling" Chicagoan is familiar with the differing districts of the entire West, North, and South, with their crops, industries, wants, financial status, and means of intercommunication. As in London we find men whose business field is the world, so in Chicago we find the business men talking not of one section or of Europe, as is largely the case in New York, but discussing the affairs of the entire country. The figures which garnish their conversation are bewildering, but if they are analyzed, or even comprehended, they will reveal to the listener how vast and how wealthy a region acknowledges Chicago as its market and its financial and trading centre. . . . Chicago, then, is the centre of a circle of 1000 miles diameter. If you draw a line northward 500 miles, you find everywhere arable land and timber. The same is true with respect to a line drawn 500 miles in a northwesterly course. For 650 miles westward there is no change in the rich and alluring prospect, and so all around the circle, except where Lake Michigan interrupts it, the same conditions are found. Moreover, the lake itself is a valuable element in commerce. The rays or spokes in all these directions become materialized in the form of the tracks of 35 railways which enter the city. Twenty-two of these are great companies, and at a short distance sub-radials made by other railroads raise the number to 50 roads. As said above, in Chicago one-twenty-fifth of the railway mileage of the world terminates, and serves 30 millions of persons, who find Chicago the largest city easily accessible to them. Thus is found a vast population connected easily and directly with a common centre, to which everything they produce can be brought, and from which all that contributes to the material progress and comfort of man may be economically distributed.

A financier who is equally well known and respected in New York and Chicago put the case somewhat differently as to what he called Chicago's territory. He considered it as being 1000 miles square, and spoke of it as "the land west of the Alleghanies and south of Mason and Dixon's line." This region, the richest agricultural territory in the world, does its financiering in Chicago. The rapid increase in wealth to both the city and the tributary region is due to the fact that every year both produce more, and have more to sell and less to buy. . . . Chicago has become the third manufacturing city in the Union, and she is drawing manufacurers away from the East faster than most persons in the East imagine. To-day it is a great Troy stove-making establishment that has moved to Chicago; the week before it was a Massachusetts shoe-factory that went there. Many great establishments have gone there, but more must follow, because Chicago is not only the centre of the midland region in respect of the distribution of made-up wares, but also for the concentration of raw materials. Chicago must lead in the manufacture of all goods of which wood, leather, and iron are the bases. . . .

"Chicago is yet so young and busy," said he who is perhaps the leading banker there, "she has not time for anything beyond each citizen's private affairs. It is hard to get men to serve on a committee. The only thing that saves us from being boors is our civic pride. We are fond, proud, enthusiastic in that respect. But we know that Chicago is not rich, like New York. She has no bulk of capital lying ready for investment and reinvestment; yet she is no longer poor. She has just got over her poverty, and the next stage, bringing accumulated wealth, will quickly follow. Her growth in this respect is more than paralleled by her development into an industrial centre."

So much, then, for Chicago's reasons for existence. The explanation forms not merely the history of an American town, and a town of young men, it points an old moral. It demonstrates anew the active truth that energy is a greater force than money. It commands money. The young founders of Chicago were backed in the East by capitalists who discounted the energy they saw them display. And now Chicago capitalists own the best street railway in St. Louis, the surface railway system of Toledo, a thousand enterprises in hundreds of Western towns.

·   ·   ·   ·   ·   ·   ·   ·   ·   ·

And here one is brought to reflect that Chicago is distinctly American. I know that the Chicagoans boast that theirs is the most mixed population in the country, but the makers and movers of Chicago are Americans. The streets of the city are full of strange faces of a type to which we are not used to in the East—a dish-faced, soft-eyed, light-haired people. They are Scandinavians; but they are malleable as lead, and quickly and easily follow and adopt every Americanism. In return, they ask only to be permitted to attend a host of Luthern churches in flocks, to work hard, live temperately, save thriftily, and to pronounce every *j* as if it were a *y*. But the dominating class is of that pure and broad American type which is not controlled by New England or any other tenets, but is somewhat loosely made up of the overflow of the New England, the Middle, and the Southern States. It is as mixed and comprehensive as the West Point School of cadets. It calls its city "She-caw-ger." It inclines to soft hats, and only once in a great while does a visitor see a Chicagoan who has the leisure or patience to carry a cane.

.   .   .   .

But the visitor's heart warms to the town when he sees its parks and its homes. In them is ample assurance that not every breath is "business," and not every thought commercial. Once out of the thicket of the business and semi-business district, the dwellings of the people reach mile upon mile away along pleasant boulevards and avenues, or facing noble parks and parkways, or in a succession of villages green and gay with foliage and flowers. They are not cliff dwellings like our flats and tenements; there are no brownstone cañons like our up-town streets; there are only occasional hesitating hints there of those Philadelphian and Baltimorean mills that grind out dwellings all alike, as nature makes pease and man makes pins. There are more miles of detached villas in Chicago than a stranger can easily account for. As they are not only found on Prairie Avenue and the boulevards, but in the populous wards and semi-suburbs, where the middle folk are congregated, it is evident that the prosperous moiety of the population enjoys living better (or better living) than the same fraction in the Atlantic cities.

.   .   .   .

It is said, and I have no reason to doubt it, that the clerks and small tradesmen who live in thousands of these pretty little boxes are the owners of their homes; also that the tenements of the rich display evidence of a tasteful and costly garnering of the globe for articles of luxury and *virtu*. A sneering critic, who wounded Chicago deeply, intimated that theirs must be a primitive society where the rich sit on their door-steps of an evening. That really is a habit there, and in the finer districts of all the Western cities. To enjoy themselves the more completely, the people bring out rugs and carpets, always of gay colors, and fling them on the steps—or stoops, as we Dutch legatees should say—that the ladies' dresses may not be soiled. As these step clothing are as bright as the maidens' eyes and as gay as their cheeks, the effect may be imagined. For my part, I think it argues well for any society that indulges in the trick, and proves existence in such a city to be more human and hearty and far less artificial than where there is too much false pride to permit of it. . . .

Chicago's park system is so truly her crown, or its diadem, that its fame may lead to the thought that enough has been said about it. That is not the case, however, for the parks change and improve so constantly that the average Chicagoan finds some of them outgrowing his knowledge, unless he goes to them as he ought to go to his prayers. It is not in extent that the city's parks are extraordinary, for, all told, they comprise less than two thousand acres. It is the energy that has given rise to them, and the taste and enthusiasm which have been expended upon them, that cause our wonder. Sand and swamp were at the bottom of them, and if their surfaces now roll in gentle undulations, it is because the earth that was dug out for the making of ponds has been subsequently applied to the forming of hills and knolls. The people go to some of them upon the boulevards of which I have spoken, beneath trees and beside lawns and gorgeous flower-beds, having their senses sharpened in anticipation of the pleasure-grounds beyond, as the heralds in some old plays prepare us for the action that is to follow. Once the parks are reached, they are found to be literally for the use of the people who own them. I have a fancy that a people who are so largely American would not suffer them to be otherwise. There are no signs warning the public off the grass, or announcing that they "may look, but mustn't touch" whatever there is to see. The people swarm all over the grass, and yet it continues beautiful day after day and year after year. The floral displays seem unharmed; at any rate, we have none to compare with them in any Atlantic coast parks. The people even picnic on the sward, and those who can appreciate such license find, ready at hand, baskets in which to hide the litter which follows. And, O ye who manage other parks we wot of, know that these Chicago playgrounds seem as free from harm and eyesore as any in the land.

The best parks face the great lake, and get wondrous charms of dignity and beauty from it. At the North Side the Lincoln Park commissioners, at great expense, are building out into the lake, making a handsome paved beach, sea-wall, esplanade, and drive to enclose a long, broad body of the lake-water. Although the great blue lake is at the city's edge, there is little or no sailing or pleasure-boating upon it. It is too rude and treacherous. Therefore these commissioners of the Lincoln Park are enclosing, behind their new-made land, a watercourse for sailing and rowing, for racing, and for more indolent aquatic sport.

. . . .

I have an idea that all this is very American; but what is to be said of the Chicago Sunday, with its drinking shops all wide open, and its multitudes swarming out on pleasure bent? And what of the theatres opening to the best night's business of the week at the hour of Sunday evening service in the churches? I suspect that this also is American—that sort of American that develops under Southern and Western influences not dominated by the New England spirit. And yet the Puritan traditions are not without honor and respect in Chicago, witness the fact that the city spent seventeen and a quarter millions of dollars during the past five years upon her public schools.

THE BETTER BUSINESS BUREAU'S
REPRESENTATION OF CHICAGO

A BIT defensive, considering Chicago's reputation at the
time, but the Better Business Bureau of 1930
nonetheless advertises its considered view of Chicago:
city of business and of homes, city at the hub
of the region and yet a world city.

It is high time the business man talked about Chicago and told the truth about the city for Chicago is suffering from the sins of exaggeration. Regardless of who is to blame, Chicago has acquired a bad reputation. The members of the Better Business Bureau realize that the time has come to care about what the world thinks of the city for the city's bad name has ceased to be a joke. It is a detriment to community welfare. Not only does it injure the city's good name; it affects property and business.

The business men who are members of the Better Business Bureau in cooperation with other civic bodies, have determined to rescue the city's good name—not to gloss over crimes and deny facts, but to produce facts and tell the truth. The truth is that Chicago is a prosperous and industrious city where life and property are as safe as anywhere else, where rewards for hard work and decent living are as great as in any other community.

.   .   .   .

Chicago! Growing, glowing, noisy, wind swept Chicago, with her towers and her parks, her squalor and her dust! A prodigy among cities, so acclaimed by friends and foes—a city that so grips the imagination and the curiosity that all who know her talk about her. Everyone who knows anything at all about Chicago has presented his impression to the world. Everyone has talked about the city except the business man. He has been

Excerpted from *Chicago through the Eyes of Business* (Chicago Better Business Bureau, Inc., 1930), pp. 2–3, 13–15, 25–29, by permission of the Chicago Better Business Bureau, Inc.

too busy making the city worth talking about, and yet he alone knows and understands the city for what it really is.

No community has more to offer the average man. In no large city are general living conditions more pleasant than in Chicago. It is a city of homes above the average of the usual crowded metropolis. No city can offer more in the way of business opportunity than those open to the average man and woman in Chicago.

To what end does a city erect buildings, pave streets, dredge harbors and develop industries, but to provide honest work and decent homes for fathers and mothers and children, that they may find life a little easier, may find new fields for achievement and contentment? The end to which any city is built—the mark of its success—is what it provides in work and in homes for its people.

Measured by this standard Chicago is a great city. It is that city which its business men know and which the world should know. The glittering Gold Coast is but a shining rind upon the edge of the city. The slums are but a dull streak across its face. Its gangsters are but a tiny handful of misfit individuals attracting undue notice to themselves by their spectacular noise and clamor. The real Chicago is a city of miles and miles of streets of quiet homes, flanked by peaceful suburbs. Its people are busy men and women, boys and girls, whose hours are crowded with normal interests.

.   .   .   .

Since its founding Chicago has been a shopping center of national importance. The trapper came in once a year for his provisions and clothing. Cattle kings from Texas and Montana came to Chicago to sell their stock and spend their money, taking pianos and silk dresses back to their wives, along with the stories of the elegance of the new three and four story hotels. Chicago todays draws not only commercial traders but personal shoppers for hundreds of miles around. This great influx of money, together with the fortunes spent daily by Chicago people in the loop and neighborhood stores, is great enough to pay off the war debt of a small kingdom. The responsibility which business and the city owes to this great army of spenders who bring their earnings to the Chicago merchants is protected by the Better Business Bureau which for the past three years has waged a ceaseless war against unfair advertising, crooked promoters, swindlers and thieves.

The Chicago shopper is given the best protection in his buying that any city can provide. The bureau records are open to every citizen who wants the assurance that when he buys in Chicago stores, he will get full value for his money. A free bureau of advice concerning the soundness of advertised investments is maintained for the public and business men alike. The commercial importance of this work of the Better Business

Bureau is significant. Not only are the rights of the people who spend their hard earned money protected, but the honest merchant is safeguarded from the unfair competition of white collar bandits, those unscrupulous merchants who destroy business confidence by fraudulent merchandising and advertising.

The old adage that "Men make their money elsewhere but spend it in the east" no longer holds true in the middle west, as Chicago has expanded and become a retail center. A little general store which once stood at Lake and State streets, is now the largest merchandising institution of its kind—the ancestor of the department store. State street shop windows are known the world over and names once sacred to exclusive shops of the Rue de la Paix and Bond street twinkle chastely from suavely elegant doorways of Michigan boulevard.

SUGGESTED READINGS: CHAPTER 2

Paul G. Cressey. *The Taxi-Dance Hall.* Chicago: University of Chicago Press, 1932.

What the city looked like to the taxi-dancer, and to some of her clients, is vividly portrayed.

St. Claire Drake and Horace Cayton. *Black Metropolis.* New York: Harcourt, Brace, 1945.

The images of the city held by Negro Chicagoans were immensely varied, but they were all affected by life in the Chicago ghetto.

Louis Wirth. *The Ghetto.* Chicago: University of Chicago Press, 1929.

Chicago's Jewish ghetto during the 1920's, as portrayed here, deeply colored its inhabitants views of the city— whether they never left the ghetto, left it only to work, or left it behind for a bigger world.

Harvey Zorbaugh. *The Gold Coast and the Slum.* Chicago: University of Chicago Press, 1929.

Contrasting styles of life in, and representations of, Chicago during the1920s. One can see the city as it looked to people in the rooming house area, in the Italian slums, in Chicago's "Towertown," and in the Gold Coast area of the elite.

3

Palace Hotel, San Francisco, 1875. From *Leslie's Magazine.*

THE FRONTIER
AND THE CITY

IN America, cities frequently began as frontier settlements. This was true of the earliest coastal towns, like Boston and New York, and later of large and small cities in every region of the nation. Consequently, one of the pervasive sets of popular imagery about urbanization relates it to the American frontier. Objectively speaking, however, there were numerous frontiers and, of course, numerous types of frontier cities. Some grew up on the rivers; some ran beside railroad tracks; some, like Butte, perched atop mines. And they grew up during different periods of American economic and political development. As a result, the symbolism of frontier and city is even more complex than if we merely had different persons conceiving of a single frontier and a single city. Each selection in this chapter emphasizes a somewhat different aspect of that symbolism.

This kind of data presents both a challenge and an excellent opportunity to urban theorists. Urban historians have not thought comparatively about the range of urban frontiers. At best, they have given us single case studies and have not always recognized the impact of frontier life on later developments in the city and city styles, about which they have written. While urban historians are beginning to recognize that the American frontier was not merely one of forest, plain, and farmland but was also urban,[1] American historians generally still do not understand the considerable part cities have played in national development because they remain, as an occasional urban historian now emphasizes, under the influence either of Frederick Jackson Turner's frontier thesis (free land in the West was vital to national development) or just assume that America was destined to be an agricultural nation. As one historian critic remarks, they therefore continue "to write about the rise of the city in the United States as a deviation from a natural agrarian order." [2] (It is significant that historians did not begin to pay much attention to urbanization until the 1930s.) Guided by such conceptions, most American historians are not likely to examine closely the influence that various urban frontier conditions had on the development of particular cities, on the life-styles created there, or on the general processes of American urbanization. Yet the data for such comparative study abound, both in the increasing numbers of monographs about specific cities and in the rich materials such as are reproduced in this chapter.

Unlike historians, who have at least looked backward into the last century, sociologists have paid little attention either to city origins or to the development of American urbanization. Until recently they have tended to look at cities as they are, rather than as what they now are because of what they have been. Since the last war, however, sociologists have studied urbanization in underdeveloped countries, and so have increasingly been impressed with the varied historical and regional bases of urbanization. Some advocate building a comparative theory about urbanization through studying cities in different countries. Urbanization, in other words, is believed to be affected by the nature of the country in which it evolves, including its resources, stages of economic development, and possibly by the values held by its people. Scholars like Sjoberg have explored some of the difficulties of applying American research methods in these urbanizing but underdeveloped countries,[3] and Reissman has recently suggested a typology of "change" based on a realization that societies as a whole move toward metropolitan expansion.[4]

1. See Richard Wade, *The Urban Frontier, 1790–1830* (Cambridge, Mass.: Harvard University Press, 1961). This monograph argues the importance of Ohio Valley cities in the westward thrust of the nation.

2. Charles Glaab, "The Historian and the American City," In P. Hauser and L. Schnore (Eds.), *The Study of Urbanization* (New York: John Wiley, 1965), pp. 49–80; the quotation is on p. 60.

3. Gideon Sjoberg, "Theory and Research in Urban Sociology, *ibid.*, pp. 157–89, especially pp. 180–82.

4. Leonard Reissman, *The Urban Process* (New York: The Free Press, 1964), especially pp. 212–35.

Examined closely, they are at varying stages of urban development.

Sociologists, then, are increasingly going overseas to make their comparative studies, but have not yet begun to look at American urbanization with the same kind of comparative eye. As we shall note later, sociologists have used American materials to attack certain views previously forwarded by men such as Louis Wirth, noting that he erroneously overgeneralized from Chicago not only to non-American cities but even to other cities in the United States. That is a useful but hardly an extensive use of American data. Comparative data can be found at home as well as abroad. The frontier-regional materials can thus be useful to sociologists as well as to historians.

LAND SPECULATION IN CHICAGO,
John L. Peyton

> THE new cities were looked on as inviting locales for
> investment and speculation. Land booms have
> always attracted speculators to frontier cities. Here is
> how Chicago looked during its early years to one
> visitor from Virginia, who viewed it from
> that perspective.

Chicago was already becoming a place of considerable importance for manufacturers. Steam mills were busy in every part of the city preparing lumber for buildings which were contracted to be erected by the thousand the next season. Large establishments were engaged in manufacturing agricultural implements of every description for the farmers who flocked to the country every spring. A single establishment, that of McCormick, employed several hundred hands, and during each season completed from fifteen hundred to two thousand grain-reapers and grass-mowers. Blacksmith, wagon and coachmaker's shops were busy preparing for a spring demand, which, with all their energy, they could not supply. Brickmakers had discovered on the lake shore, near the city and a short distance in the interior, excellent beds of clay, and were manufacturing, even at this time, millions of bricks by a patent process, which the frost did not hinder, or delay. Hundreds of workmen were also engaged in quarrying stone and marble on the banks of the projected canal; and the Illinois Central Railway employed large bodies of men in driving piles, and constructing a track and depot on the beach. Real estate agents were mapping out the surrounding territory for ten and fifteen miles in the interior, giving fancy names to the future avenues, streets, squares and parks. A brisk traffic existed in the sale of corner lots, and men with nothing but their wits, had been known to succeed in a single season in making a fortune—sometimes, certainly, it was only on paper.

This process was somewhat in this wise—A. sells a lot to B. for 10,000 dollars, B. sells to C. for 20,000 dollars, no money passing, C. writes to his friend D. in New York of the rapid rise in the price. The property had gone in a very short time from 10,000 dollars to 20,000 dollars and would double within ninety days, such was the *rush* of capitalists to the West, and the peculiar situation of this property, adjoining the Depot (on

Excerpted from *Over the Alleghenies and Across the Prairies* (London: Simpkin, Marshall and Co., 1848), pp. 330–36.

paper), of the "North Bend and Southern Turn Great Central Railway and Trans-Continental Transportation Company." D. immediately takes the property at 25,000 dollars, and writes to his friend E. in Boston concerning that wonderful Western place Chicago, relating how property has risen in value and regretting that he is not able to hold on to a very desirable and highly valuable piece of real estate he owns in that city worth 50,000 dollars, but for which he is wililng to take 40,000 dollars, to such extremities is he brought by his necessities. Now E. who is a live Yankee, up alike to business and snuff, sees through the matter, "smells a rat" and of course holds back. The whole affair is about to collapse and result in the bankruptcy of A., B., C., and D.; but D. who is an irrepressible New Yorker, fertile in expedients and full of resources, knows that Southerners "bleed freely," and accordingly before consenting to "go under" determines to try an expedient, and drops a note to his Virginian friend Mr. Old Porte giving him the same story. The old Virginian, Mr. Olde Porte, who has lived in the country on his hereditary acres, like the patriarchs of old, surrounded by his family, bond and free, and his flocks of cattle and sheep, as did Father Abraham, is immediately penetrated with gratitude at the great generosity and kindness of his friend, that absent but ever faithful friend D., who is willing on the score of ancient friendship to make a sacrifice of 10,000 and to accept on his account 40,000 dollars for a property low at 50,000 dollars, and Mr. Old Porte comprehending how advantageous it will be to his children, of whom, as is somewhat common in the Old Dominion, he has a good round baker's dozen, immediately writes to express his gratitude and to accept the property on the proposed terms. Exit Mr. Old Porte on his way rejoicing. He reaches his banker to make arrangements to meet the payments, after having cogitated somewhat as follows:—

"Egad, those New Yorkers are capital fellows, no Yankee about them, descended from the Old Dutch settlers, fine race the Knickerbockers. Why cannot the North and South understand each other better? We might live together like brothers. D——n it I don't think the Yankees quite so bad as people represent. Allowances must be made for the way they are brought up, the devil's not so black as he is painted, we must not forget that they are brothers, must try to eradicate prejudice and get up a national feeling."

Arrived at the Bank he completes the transaction, and encloses to Mr. D. one-fourth of 40,000 dollars which being divided between A., B., C., and D. sets up these enterprising gentlemen, who starting a "wild cat" bank, soon come to the enjoyment of things hoped for.

The probable sequel of such a transaction may be stated in a few words. Mr. Old Porte punctually meets his payments as they fall due, and is constantly kept under the impression that any small extravagance he may indulge among his fellow Virginians, keeping up social life after the style of his ancestors, is a bagatelle to be a hundred-fold made up to his family by the rapid enhancement in the value of his Chicago property. In a few years, Mr. Old Porte is in the course of nature gathered to his fathers, and his estate put in process of settlement. Among other assets to be reduced to cash, are his Chicago 'lots,' which disposed of at auction fetch in round numbers, we will suppose seven thousand dollars, which "outsiders" think a wonderful evidence of the progress of the city, Mr. X. Y. Z. having bought the same five years previously for five hundred dollars and sold it for six hundred dollars. The outside Yankees hearing the estate of the late Mr. Old Porte of Virginia derives the benefit of the rise, will probably say,

"What humbugs those Virginians are, they are always talking about Yankee greed, yet they come all the way to the north-west in search of plunder, hunting for opportunities to make money by gambling speculations. A tree is known by its fruit. Let F.F.V.'s talk as they please of us as a money grubbing race, we know what they are. Let us thank God, we are not as they."

Now this little imaginary transaction is but the truth and substance as to thousands of real transactions which were then, and have been constantly since taking place in Chicago, making the fortunes of some and ruining the estates of others.

CITY OF THE PLAINS, *William H. Dixon*

AN Englishman's reaction's to Denver in 1867
reflected a view of the frontier that was widespread in
the more settled areas of the nation. The
frontier was essentially an uncivilized place, where
morals fell into decay except under exceptional conditions.
The presence of women was one of those conditions.

The men of Denver, even those of the higher classes, though they have many strong qualities—bravery, perseverance, generosity, enterprise, endurance—heroic qualities of the old Norse gods—are also, not unlike the old Norse gods, exceedingly frail in morals; and where you see the tone of society weak, you may always expect to find aversion to marriage, both as a sentiment and as an institution, somewhat strong. Men who have lived alone, away from the influence of mothers and sisters, have generally

Excerpted from *New America* (Philadelphia: J. B. Lippincott, 1867), pp. 95–100.

but a faint belief in the personal virtue and fidelity of women; and apart from the lack of belief in woman, which ought to be a true religion in the heart of every man, the desire for a fixed connection and a settled home will hardly ever spring up. Men may like the society of women, and yet not care to encumber themselves for life. The worst of men expect, when they marry, to obtain the best of wives; but the best of women do not quit New England and Pennsylvania for Colorado. Hence it is a saying in Denver,—a saying confirmed by practice, that in these western cities, though few of the miners have wives, you will not find many among them who can be truly described as marrying men.

On any terms short of marriage these lusty fellows may be caught by a female snare. They take very freely to the charms of negresses and squaws. One of the richest men of this city, whose name I forbear to give, has just gone up into the mountains with a couple of Cheyenne wives. Your young Norse gods are nervously afraid of entering a Christian church.

Denver is a city of four thousand people; with ten or twelve streets laid out; with two hotels, a bank, a theatre, half a dozen chapels, fifty gambling-houses, and a hundred grog-shops. As you wander about these hot and dirty streets, you seem to be walking in a city of demons.

Every fifth house appears to be a bar, a whisky-shop, a lager-beer saloon; every tenth house appears to be either a brothel or a gaming-house; very often both in one. In these horrible dens a man's life is of no more worth than a dog's. Until a couple of years ago, when a change for the better began, it was quite usual for honest folks to be awakened from their sleep by the noise of exploding guns; and when daylight came, to find that a dead body had been tossed from a window into the street. No inquiry was every made into the cause of death. Decent people merely said, "Well, there is one sinner less in Denver, and may his murderer meet his match tomorrow!"

Thanks to William Gilpin, founder of Colorado, and governor elect, aided by a Vigilance Committee; thanks also to the wholesome dread which unruly spirits have conceived of the quick eye and resolute hand of Sheriff Wilson; thanks, more than all, to the presence of a few American and English ladies in the streets of Denver, the manners of this mining pandemonium have begun to change. English women who have been here two or three years, assure me it is greatly altered. Of course Gilpin is opposed—in theory, at least—to all such jurisdiction as that exercised by the Vigilance Committee; but for the moment, the society of this city is unsettled, justice is blind and lame, while violence is alert and strong; and the Vigilance Committee, a secret irresponsible board, acting above all law, especially in the matter of life and death, has to keep things going by means of the revolver and the rope. No one knows by name the members of this stern tribunal; every rich, every active man in the place is thought to be of it; and you may hear, in confidential whispers, the names of persons who are supposed to be its leaders, ministers, and executioners. The association is secret, its agents are many, and nothing, I am told, escapes the knowledge, hardly anything escapes the action, of this dread, irresponsible court. A man disappears from the town:—it is an offence to inquire about him; you see men shrug their shoulders; perhaps you hear the mysterious words—"gone up." Gone up, in the slang of Denver, means gone up a tree—that is to say, a cotton-tree—by which is meant a particular cotton-tree growing on the town creek. In plain English, the man is said to have been *hung*. This secret committee holds its sittings in the night, and the time for its executions is in the silent hours between twelve and two, when honest people should be all asleep in their beds. Sometimes, when the storekeepers open their doors in Main Street, they find a corpse dangling on a branch; but commonly the body is cut down before dawn, removed to a suburb, where it is thrown into a hole like that of a dead dog. In most cases, the place of burial is kept a secret from the people, so that no legal evidence of death can be found.

Swearing, fighting, drinking, like the old Norse gods, a few thousand men, for the most part wifeless and childless, are engaged, in these upper parts of the Prairie, in founding an empire. The expression is William Gilpin's pet phrase; but the congregation of young Norse gods who drink, and swear, and fight along these roads, are comically unaware of the glorious work in which they are engaged.

"Well, sir," said to me, one day, a burly stranger, all boots and beard, with a merry mouth and audacious eye; "well, what do you think of our Western boys?"

Remembering Gilpin, and wishing to be safe and complimentary, I replied, "You are making an empire." "Eh?" he asked, not understanding me, and fancying I was laughing in my sleeve—a liberty which your Western boy dislikes—he brought his hand, instinctively, a little nearer to his bowie-knife. "You are making an empire?" I put in once again, but by way of inquiry this time, so as to guard against giving offence and receiving a stab.

"I don't know about that," said he, relaxing his grim expression, and moving his hand from his belt; "but I am making money."

Gilpin, I dare say, would have laughed, and said it was all the same.

.   .   .   .

Under this man's sway, the city is changed, and is changing fast; yet, if I may believe the witnesses, the advent of a dozen English and American ladies, who came out with their husbands, has done far more for Denver than the genius and eloquence of William Gilpin. A lady is a power in this country. From the day when a silk dress and a lace shawl were seen in Main Street, that thoroughfare became passably clean and quiet; oaths were less frequently heard; knives were less frequently drawn; pistols were less frequently fired. None of these things have ceased; far, very far, is Denver yet from peace; but the young Norse gods have begun to feel rather ashamed of swearing in a lady's presence, and of drawing their knives before a lady's face.

Slowly, but safely, the improvement has been brought about. At first, the ladies had a very bad time, as their idiom runs. They feared to associate with each other; every woman suspected her neighbor of being little better than she should be. Things are safer now; and I can testify, from experience, that Denver has a very charming, though a very limited society of the better sex.

FRONTIER MORALS, *Sarah Royce*

MRS. ROYCE, mother of the philosopher Josiah Royce, wrote a narrative account about the family's migration to California during gold-rush days. The frontier city, as she conceived it, was potentially destructive to family, morals, and churchgoing. Women could either protect their men from demoralization or further it.

Any newcomer into San Francisco in those days had but to seek, in the right way, for good people, and he could find them. But in the immense crowds flocking hither from all parts of the world there were many of the worst classes, bent upon getting gold at all hazards, and if possible without work. These were constantly lying in wait, as tempters of the weak. A still greater number came with gold-getting for their ruling motive, yet intending to get it honestly, by labor or legitimate business. They did not at all intend, at first, to sacrifice their habits of morality, or their religious convictions. But many of them bore those habits, and held those convictions too lightly; and as they came to feel the force of unwonted excitement and the pressure of unexpected temptation, they too often yielded, little by little, till they found themselves standing upon a very low plane, side by side with those whose society they once would have avoided. It was very common to hear people who had started on this downward moral grade, deprecating the very acts they were committing,

From Ralph Henry Gabriel (Ed.), *A Frontier Lady* (New Haven: Yale University Press, 1932), pp. 109–110, 114–118. Reprinted by permission.

or the practices they were countenancing; and concluding their weak lament by saying "But *here* in California we *have* to do such things." Never was there a better opportunity for demonstrating the power and truth of Christian principle, than was, in those days, open to every faithful soul, and, never, perhaps, were there in modern, civilized, society more specious temptations to laxity of conduct. And thus it came to pass, that in this our early California life, while we had the pleasure of associating with those who were true to their convictions, earnest in their religious life, and faithful and lovely in the domestic circle, yet, on the other hand, we often met people, who had let loose the reins of moral government over themselves and families; and consented that others should do so.

.   .   .   .

There were some habits gaining ground among the thoughtless and selfish which gave me uneasiness; and which I could not help feeling presaged evil for the future. One of these was the custom, early begun, of gentlemen manifesting their gallantry by expensive presents to their lady acquaintances. This seemed to be done at first in a sort of off-handed, jocular way; probably without much thought as to its motives or results. There were but few ladies. It was natural there should be a little feeling of rivalry among the gentlemen in competing for the favor of those few. Money, while it was easily lost, was in those days often as easily won. When a gentleman of social disposition "made a strike," as they commonly expressed it, he often liked to tell his lady friends in a laughing way of his good management or unexpected luck. An easy way to introduce the subject was jokingly to toss at her, or in some way offer, a pretty present; and tell her it was a treat on the strength of "so and so."

There were, I am glad to say, ladies of such dignity of character and self-respect as to prevent, without direct effort, any such advances; but there were too many whose cupidity and vanity were stronger than delicacy of feeling, or sense of propriety; and I blushed to discover, by conversations held in my presence, that there were instances of women watching each other, jealously, each afraid the other would get more or richer presents than herself. This evil became painfully prominent, as time went on and more families came to the coast.

.   .   .   .

During those two or three years there first came under my observation some of the unfavorable effects of the great California emigration movement upon American domestic life. . . .

Hints were sometimes heard in conversation, and occasionally appeared in newspaper paragraphs, to the effect that single men were proving a dangerous element in society, by insinuating themselves into the affections of married women, and, in some cases, supplanting husbands. I saw no instance of this kind myself until several years later.

But, in the domestic life of those early days, it was not always the husband that was neglectful and indifferent nor the wife that was faithful. I knew a woman whose every need was richly supplied, her every wish kindly considered by her husband, and, whenever within his means, gratified. He built, as soon as his business allowed, one of the best dwellings to be found in the city where they lived. All was planned according to her directions, and modified to suit her whims. Yet, she was never contented. Pleasant words and smiles rarely greeted him. Imperious demands, and cold criticism embittered his life. He bore it patiently, and meant to keep on enduring; for the sake of those sacred laws to which he ever acknowledged unswerving allegiance. But she contrived in some way, I never knew how, to get possession of a large portion of his property; and then to obtain a divorce. There must have been sad corruption somewhere, or she could never have carried it through.

JOE'S LUCK, *Horatio Alger, Jr.*

ALGER, each of whose tales of success was rapturously awaited by a large audience, felt differently about the frontier than did Mrs. Royce. In writing about Joe's conquest of San Francisco, he portrays a remarkably different city. Joe is in New York when the story begins but, spurred by commendable ambition, he soon takes ship for the golden West.

The afternoon slipped away almost without Joe's knowledge. He walked about here and there, gazing with curious eyes at the streets and warehouses and passing vehicles, and thinking what a lively place New York was, and how different life was in the metropolis from what it had been to him in the quiet country town which had hitherto been his home. Somehow it seemed to wake Joe up and excite his ambition, to give him a sense of power which he had never felt before.

Excerpted from *Joe's Luck* (New York: A. L. Burt, 1887), pp. 36–37, 67–72, 223.

"If I could only get a foot-hold here," thought Joe, "I should be willing to work twice as hard as I did on the farm."

This was what Joe thought. I don't say that he was correct. There are many country boys who make a mistake in coming to the city. They forsake quiet, comfortable homes, where they have all they need, to enter some city counting-room or store at starvation wages, with at best a very remote prospect of advancement and increased risk of falling a prey to temptation in some of the many forms which it assumes in a populous town. A boy needs to be strong and self-reliant and willing to work if he comes to the city to compete for the prizes of life. As the story proceeds we shall learn whether Joe had these necessary qualifications.

.   .   .   .

It was a beautiful morning in early September when they came in sight of the Golden Gate, and entering the more placid waters of San Francisco Bay, moored at a short distance from the town.

All the passengers gazed with eager eyes at the port of which they had heard so much—the portal to the Land of Gold.

"What do you think of it, Joe?" asked Charles Folsom, after a pause.

"I don't know," said Joe slowly. "Is this really San Francisco?"

"It is really San Francisco."

"It doesn't seem to be much built up yet," said Joe.

In fact the appearance of the town would hardly suggest the stately capital of to-day, which looks out like a queen on the bay and the ocean, and on either side opens her arms to the Eastern and Western continents. It was a town of tents and one-story cabins, irregularly and picturesquely scattered over the hill-side, with here and there a saw-mill, where now stands some of the most prominent buildings of the modern city. For years later there was a large mound of sand where now the stately Palace Hotel covers two and a half acres and proudly challenges the world to show its peer. Where now stand substantial business blocks, a quarter of a century since there appeared only sandy beaches or mud flats, with here and there a wooden pier reaching out into the bay. Only five years before the town contained but seventy-nine buildings—thirty-one frame, twenty-six adobe, and the rest shanties. It had grown largely since then, but even now was only a straggling village, with the air of recent settlement.

"You expected something more, Joe, didn't you?" asked Folsom.

"Yes," admitted Joe.

"You must remember how new it is. Ten years, nay, five, will work a great change in this straggling village. We shall probably live to see it a city of a hundred thousand inhabitants."

The prediction seemed extravagant to Joe. Yet it has been more than fulfilled, and now, after a lapse of twenty-five years, the town of shanties has become a stately city of three hundred thousand souls.

The passengers were eager to land. They were tired of the long voyage and anxious to get on shore. They wanted, as soon as possible, to begin making their fortunes.

"What are your plans, Joe?" asked Charles Folsom.

"I shall accept the first job that offers," said Joe. "I can't afford to remain idle long with my small capital."

"Joe," said the young man seriously, "let me increase your capital for you. You can pay me back, you know, when it is convenient. Here, take this gold-piece. You may need it."

It was a twenty-dollar gold-piece which he offered to Joe.

Our young hero shook his head.

"Thank you, Mr. Folsom," he said, "you are very kind, but I think it will be better for me to shift on what I have. Then I shall have to go to work at once, and shall get started in my new career."

"Suppose you can't find work?" suggested Folsom.

"I *will* find it," said Joe resolutely.

"At any rate come with me and see where I put up, so that you can apply to me if you have need."

"I will do that, Mr. Folsom. I don't want to lose sight of you."

"Perhaps we might take lodgings together, Joe."

"I can't afford it," said Joe. "You're a gentleman of property, and I'm a poor boy who has his fortune to make. For the present I must expect to rough it."

"Well, Joe, perhaps you are right. At any rate, I admire your pluck and independent spirit."

There was a motley crowd collected on the pier and on the beach when Joe and his friend landed. Rough, bearded men, in Mexican sombreros and coarse attire—many in shirt-sleeves and with their pantaloons tucked in their boots—watched the new arrivals with interest.

"You needn't feel ashamed of your clothes, Joe," said Folsom, with a smile. "You are better dressed than the majority of those we see."

Joe looked puzzled.

"They don't look as if they had made their fortunes," he said.

"Don't judge by appearances. In a new country people are careless of appearances. Some of these rough fellows, no doubt, have their pockets full of gold."

At this moment a rough-looking fellow stepped forward and said heartily:

"Isn't this Charles Folsom?"

"Yes," answered Folsom, puzzled, "but you have the advantage of me."

"You don't remember me?" said the other, laughing.

"Not I."

"Not remember Harry Carter, your old chum?"

"Good heaven!" exclaimed Folsom, surveying anew the rough figure behind him. "You don't mean to say you are Harry Carter?"

"The same, at your service."

"What a transformation! Why, you used to be rather a swell, and now——"

"Now I look like a barbarian."

"Well, rather," said Folsom, laughing.

"You want me to explain it? You must know, Folsom, that a new country works great changes. Such toggery as I used to wear would be the height of folly at the mines."

"Have you been at the mines?"

"I have only just come from there."

"I hope you have had good luck," said Folsom, once more regarding doubtfully his friend's attire.

"Pretty fair," said Carter, in a tone of satisfaction. "My pile has reached five thousand dollars."

"And how long have you been at work?"

"A year. You know I was a book-keeper in New York on a salary of fifteen hundred dollars a year. I used to spend all my income—the more fool I—till the last six months, when I laid by enough to bring me out here."

"Then you have really bettered yourself?"

"I should say so. I could only save up five hundred dollars a year at the best in New York. Here I have crowded ten years into one."

"In spite of your large outlay for clothes?"

"I see you will have your joke at my expense. Now, what brings you out here? Are you going to the mines?"

"Presently, but not to dig. I came to survey the country."

"Let me do what I can for you."

"I will. First, what hotel shall I go to?"

"There is the Leidesdorff House, on California Street. I'll lead you there."

"Thank you. Will you come, Joe?"

"Yes, I will go to find out where it is."

The three bent their steps to the hotel referred to. It was a shanty compared with the magnificent hotels which now open their portals to strangers, but the charge was ten dollars a day and the fare was of the plainest.

"I guess I won't stop here," said Joe. "My money wouldn't keep me here more than an hour or two."

"At any rate, Joe, you must dine with me," said Folsom. "Then you may start out for yourself in quest of fortune."

"You must dine with *me,* both of you," said Carter. "It is so long since I have seen you that you can't refuse."

Folsom saw that he was in earnest, and accepted.

The dinner was plain but abundant, and all three did justice to it. Joe did not know till afterward that the dinner cost five dollars apiece, or he would have been dismayed.

After dinner the two friends sat down to talk over old times and mutual friends, but Joe felt that there was no time for him to lose. He had his fortune to make. Still more important, he had his living to make, and in a place where dollars were held as cheap as dimes in New York or Boston.

So emerging into the street, with his small bundle under his arm, he bent his steps as chance directed.

"I am all ready for a job," he said to himself. "I wonder how soon I shall find one."

.   .   .   .

When Joe returned to San Francisco, by advice of Mr. Morgan, he sold out his restaurant to Watson and took charge of the latter's real estate business. He rose with the rising city, became a very rich man, and now lives in a handsome residence on one of the hills that overlook the bay. He has an excellent wife—our old friend, Annie Raymond—and a fine family of children. His domestic happiness is by no means the smallest part of Joe's luck.

THE FRONTIER IN AMERICAN HISTORY,
Frederick J. Turner

> TURNER, the great American historian, won his
> reputation for studies of the frontier. Reared in
> the Midwest, he reflected a popular view of the
> relations of frontier-farmland west of the
> Alleghenies to the coastal Eastern region. The
> selection below, written at the turn of the
> century, reflects his rhetoric as well as his
> scholarly approach. It shows a certain ambivalence
> also—and ambiguity—in his handling of the
> dual character of the Midwest, which was increasingly
> becoming industrial as well as agricultural. He
> manages, however, to make the transition to
> industrial magnate from frontiersman without too
> embarrassingly obvious a break of step. His
> ideological ambiguity became increasingly less serviceable
> as the region became increasingly urbanized until,
> later, he suffered considerable personal
> anguish over how to interpret this urban America.

THE MIDDLE WEST

The agricultural preponderance of the country has passed to the prairies, and manufacturing has developed in the areas once devoted to pioneer farming. . . . The settlers of the Old Northwest and their crops have moved together across the Mississippi, and in the regions whence they migrated varied agriculture and manufacture have sprung up.

As these movements in population and products have passed across the Middle West, and as the economic life of the eastern border has been intensified, a huge industrial organism has been created in the province,—an organism of tremendous power, activity, and unity. Fundamentally the Middle West is an agricultural area unequaled for its combination of space, variety, productiveness, and freedom from interruption by deserts or mountains. . . .

. . . .

Excerpted from *The Frontier in American History* (New York: Henry Holt and Co., 1920), pp. 149, 155, 205–206, 220–221, 258–259, 264–265, 267–268. Reprinted by permission.

The ideals of equality, freedom of opportunity, faith in the common man are deep rooted in all the Middle West. The frontier stage, through which each portion passed, left abiding traces on the older, as well as on the newer, areas of the province. Nor were these ideals limited to the native American settlers: Germans and Scandinavians who poured into the Middle West sought the country with like hopes and like faith. These facts must be remembered in estimating the effects of the economic transformation of the province upon its democracy. The peculiar democracy of the frontier has passed away with the conditions that produced it; but the democratic aspirations remain. They are held with passionate determination.

The task of the Middle West is that of adapting democracy to the vast economic organization of the present. This region which has so often needed the reminder that bigness is not greatness, may yet show that its training has produced the power to reconcile popular government and culture with the huge industrial society of the modern world. The democracies of the past have been small communities, under simple and primitive economic conditions. At bottom the problem is how to reconcile real greatness with bigness.

.   .   .   .

THE PROBLEM OF THE WEST

The problem of the West is nothing less than the problem of American development. A glance at the map of the United States reveals the truth. To write of a "Western sectionalism," bounded on the east by the Alleghanies, is, in itself, to proclaim the writer a provincial. What is the West? What has it been in American life? To have the answers to these questions, is to understand the most significant features of the United States of to-day.

The West, at bottom, is a form of society, rather than an area. It is the term applied to the region whose social conditions result from the application of older institutions and ideas to the transforming influences of free land. By this application, a new environment is suddenly entered, freedom of opportunity is opened, the cake of custom is broken, and new activities, new lines of growth, new institutions and new ideals, are brought into existence. The wilderness disappears, the "West" proper passes on to a new frontier; and in the former area, a new society has emerged from its contact with the backwoods. Gradually this society loses its primitive conditions, and assimilates itself to the type of the older social conditions of the East; but it bears within it enduring and distinguishing survivals of its frontier experience. Decade after decade, West after West, this rebirth of American society has gone on, has left its traces behind it, and has reacted on the East. This history of our political institutions, our democracy, is not a history of imitation, of simple borrowing; it is a history of the evolution and adaptation of organs in response to changed environment, a history of the origin of new political species. In this sense, therefore, the West has been a constructive force of the highest significance in our life. To use words of that acute and widely informed observer, Mr. Bryce, "The West is the most American part of America. . . ."

.   .   .   .

This, then, is the real situation: a people composed of heterogeneous materials, with diverse and conflicting ideals and social interests, having passed from the task of filling up the vacant spaces of the continent, is now thrown back upon itself, and is seeking an equilibrium. The diverse elements are being fused into national unity. The forces of reorganization are turbulent and the nation seems like a witches' kettle.

But the West has its own centers of industrial life and culture not unlike those of the East. It has State Universities, rivaling in conservative and scientific economic instruction those of any other part of the Union, and its citizens more often visit the East, than do Eastern men the West. As time goes on, its industrial development will bring it more into harmony with the East.

Moreover, the Old Northwest holds the balance of power, and is the battlefield on which these issues of American development are to be settled. It has more in common with all parts of the nation than has any other region. It understands the East, as the East does not understand the West. The White City which recently rose on the shores of Lake Michigan fitly typified its growing culture as well as its capacity for great achievement. Its complex and representative industrial organization and business ties, its determination to hold fast to what is original and good in its Western experience, and its readiness to learn and receive the results of the experience of other sections and nations, make it an open-minded and safe arbiter of the American destiny.

In the long run the "Center of the Republic" may be trusted to strike a wise balance between the contending ideals. But she does not deceive herself; she knows that the problem of the West means nothing less than the problem of working out original social ideals and social adjustments for the American nation.

.   .   .   .

CONTRIBUTIONS TO AMERICAN DEMOCRACY

Magnitude of social achievement is the watchword of the democracy since the Civil War. From petty towns built in the marshes, cities also arose whose greatness and industrial power are the wonder of our time. The conditions were ideal for the production of captains of industry. The old democratic admiration for the self-made man, its old deference to the rights of competitive individual development, together with the stupendous natural resources that opened to the conquest of the keenest and the strongest, gave such conditions of mobility as enabled the development of the large corporate industries which in our own decade have marked the West.

.   .   .   .

There has been a steady development of the industrial ideal, and a steady increase of the social tendency, in this later movement of Western democracy. While the individualism of the frontier, so prominent in the earliest days of the Western advance, has been preserved as an ideal, more and more these individuals struggling each with the other, dealing with vaster and vaster areas, with larger and larger problems, have found it necessary to combine under the leadership of the strongest. This is the explanation of the rise of those preeminent captains of industry whose genius has concentrated capital to control the fundamental resources of the nation. If now in the way of recapitulation, we try to pick out from the influences that have gone to the making of Western democracy the factors which constitute the net result of this movement, we shall have to mention at least the following:—

Most important of all has been the fact that an area of free land has continually lain on the western border of the settled area of the United States. Whenever social conditions tended to crystallize in the East, whenever capital tended to press upon labor or political restraints to impede the freedom of the mass, there was this gate of escape to the free conditions of the frontier. These free lands promoted individualism, economic equality, freedom to rise, democracy. Men would not accept inferior wages and a permanent position of social subordination when this promised land of freedom and equality was theirs for the taking. . . .

.   .   .   .

Even those masters of industry and capital who have risen to power by the conquest of Western resources came from the midst of this society and still profess its principles. John D. Rockefeller was born on a New York farm, and began his career as a young business man in St. Louis. Marcus Hanna was a Cleveland grocer's clerk at the age of twenty. Claus Spreckles, the sugar king, came from Germany as a steerage passenger to the United States in 1848. Marshall Field was a farmer boy in Conway, Massachusetts, until he left to grow up with the young Chicago. Andrew Carnegie came as a ten-year-old boy from Scotland to Pittsburgh, then a distinctively

Western town. He built up his fortunes through successive grades until he became the dominating factor in the great iron industries, and paved the way for that colossal achievement, the Steel Trust. Whatever may be the tendencies of this corporation, there can be little doubt of the democratic ideals of Mr. Carnegie himself. . . .

.　　.　　.　　.　　.　　.　　.　　.　　.　　.

Whatever shall be the outcome of the rush of this huge industrial modern United States to its place among the nations of the earth, the formation of its Western democracy will always remain one of the wonderful chapters in the history of the human race. Into this vast shaggy continent of ours poured the first feeble tide of European settlement. European men, institutions, and ideas were lodged in the American wilderness, and this great American West took them to her bosom, taught them a new way of looking upon the destiny of the common man, trained them in adaptation to the conditions of the New World, to the creation of new institutions to meet new needs; and ever as society on her eastern border grew to resemble the Old World in its social forms and its industry, ever, as it began to lose faith in the ideals of democracy, she opened new provinces, and dowered new democracies in her most distant domains with her material treasures and with the ennobling influence that the fierce love of freedom, the strength that came from hewing out a home, making a school and a church, and creating a higher future for his family, furnished to the pioneer.

.　　.　　.　　.　　.　　.　　.　　.　　.　　.

She has furnished to this new democracy her stores of mineral wealth, that dwarf of those of the Old World, and her provinces that in themselves are vaster and more productive than most of the nations of Europe. Out of her bounty has come a nation whose industrial competition alarms the Old World, and the masters of whose resources wield wealth and power vaster than the wealth and power of kings. Best of all, the West gave, not only to the American, but to the unhappy and oppressed of all lands, a vision of hope, and assurance that the world held a place where were to be found high faith in man and the will and power to furnish him the opportunity to grow to the full measure of his own capacity. Great and powerful as are the new sons of her loins, the Republic is greater than they. The paths of the pioneer have widened into broad highways. The forest clearing has expanded into affluent commonwealths. Let us see to it that the ideals of the pioneer in his log cabin shall enlarge into the spiritual life of a democracy where civic power shall dominate and utilize individual achievement for the common good.

SUGGESTED READINGS: CHAPTER 3

Carl Bridenbaugh. *Cities in the Wilderness.* New York: Ronald Press, 1938.

An historian's detailed account of the first century of urban life in America, beginning in 1625.

William Haller. *The Puritan Frontier.* New York: Columbia University Press, 1951.

Town planning in a New England Colonial development, 1630–1660.

Richard Wade. *The Urban Frontier, 1790–1830.* Cambridge, Mass.: Harvard University Press, 1961.

An historical study of cities developed on what were then the nation's margins: Pittsburgh, Cincinnati, Louisville, Lexington, and St. Louis.

4

The City of Chicago. From *Harper's Weekly*, September 10, 1859.

CITY DESTINY

MUCH of the popular literature about city destiny has been the work of city boosters, and realtors with land to sell. They persuaded others, and often themselves, that their particular towns were destined to grow and prosper. Their language was, and still is, replete with superlatives. After a city has settled down, its citizens may still use the old images, referring to it as the "Gateway to the West" and perhaps building a monument to symbolize it, as St. Louis has; or referring to it as the "Second City," like Chicago, with an eye on its continued, immense importance.

Pragmatically, Americans have staked their time, fortunes, and sometimes lives on assessments of which cities would grow and which would not. This was a hazardous game, because prospering towns sometimes fell into disastrous declines or became stabilized at low levels of prosperity; because river traffic gave way to railways, or railway companies decided or were persuaded to lay tracks through other towns; or because entire counties or regions declined in economic importance. These aspects of urbanization have been noted and somewhat explored, especially by economic historians. The competition between or among specific cities has been studied increasingly by historians,[1] and to some extent by urban economists.[2]

1. See Glaab, *op. cit.,* for a discussion and bibliography, especially pp. 67–69.
2. See Wilbur Thompson, "Urban Economic Growth and Development in a National System of Cities," in Hauser and Schnore, *op. cit.,* especially pp. 439–42 for a discussion and bibliography.

Sociologists could also with some profit examine these city rivalries for their impact on urban institutions and life-styles.

As for predictions about where our newer cities will be located, what they will look like, and what life there will become, not all Americans were, or are, as percipient as George Tucker, a Virginian economist of considerable foresight, who in 1819 predicted with some accuracy the future course of urbanization in the United States. Even he did not foresee the role of railroads in our urban development for he predicted mainly that inland water routes and lakes were likely places for the development of prosperous cities. While Chapter 17 will illustrate that the game of predicting next steps in urbanization —by social scientists as well as others—continues unabated, the selections in this chapter link prediction to specific questions about city destiny. Forecasting the course of urbanization necessarily involves assumptions about the nature of regions and city growth. Looking backward toward the city's past, after a certain amount of history has unrolled, likewise involves assumptions about where a city is *now* evolving.

THE MIDWEST WILL BE URBAN,
J. W. Scott

A PREVALENT early expectation of the area now
known as the Midwest was that, through the
migration and labor of thousands of enthusiastic
migrants, it would eventually become the world's greatest
agricultural region. The eastern coastal area would
contain the cities; the trans-Allegheny area
would be the nation's breadbasket. Although the
Midwest began its urbanization slowly, it
did begin early. But even as late as 1866, arguments
such as Scott put forth were necessary to
counteract the imagery of the region as essentially
agricultural. (We have already seen Turner, the
historian, later stumbling over this same imagery.)

Almost up to the present time, the whole weight of population in
the United States has lain along the Atlantic shore, on and near its tide
waters, and a great proportion of their wealth was connected with foreign commerce, carried on through their seaports. These being at once
the centers of domestic and foreign trade grew rapidly, and constituted
all the large towns of the country. The inference was thence drawn, that
as our towns of greatest size were connected with foreign commerce, this
constituted the chief, if not the only, source of wealth, and that large
cities could grow up nowhere but on the shores of the salt sea. Such had
been the experience of our people, and the opinion founded on it has
been pertinaciously adhered to, notwithstanding the situation of the
country in regard to trade and commerce has essentially altered. It seems
not, until lately, to have entered the minds even of well-informed statesmen, that the internal trade of this country has become far more extensive,
important, and profitable, than its foreign commerce. In what ratio the
former exceeds the latter, it is impossible to state with exactness. We may,
however, approximate the truth near enough to illustrate our subject.

. . . It may be said, and with truth, that our great seaports have manifest advantages for domestic, as well as for foreign commerce. Since the
peace of Europe left every nation free to use its own navigation, the trade
of our Atlantic coast has probably been five times greater than that carried on with foreign nations; as the coasting tonnage has exceeded the

Excerpted from, "Internal Trade of the United States," *Merchants' Magazine
and Commercial Review*, vol. 8 (1843) pp. 321–22, 325–27, 329.

foreign, and the number of voyages of the former, can scarcely be less than five to one of the latter.

. . . .

It is imagined by some, that the destiny of this valley has fixed it down to the almost exclusive pursuit of agriculture, ignorant that, as a general rule in all ages of the world, and in all countries, the mouths go to the food, and not the food to the mouths. Dr. Chalmers says: "Generally speaking, the *excrescent* (the population over and above that which the country can feed) bears a very minute proportion to the natural population of a country; and almost nowhere does the commerce of a nation overleap, but by a very little way, the basis of its own agriculture." The Atlantic states, and particularly those of New England, claim that they are to become the seats of the manufactures with which the west is to be supplied; that mechanics, and artisans, and manufacturers, are not to select for their place of business, the region in which the means of living are most abundant and their manufactured articles in greatest demand, but the section which is most deficient in those means, and to which their food and fuel must, during their lives, be transported hundreds of miles, and the products of their labor be sent back the same long road for a market. But this claim is neither sanctioned by reason, authority, nor experience.

. . . .

Most countries, distinguished for manufactures, have laid the foundation in a highly improved agriculture. England, the north of France, and Belgium have a more productive husbandry than any other region of the same extent. In these same countries are also to be found the most efficient and extensive manufacturing establishments of the whole world; and it is not to be doubted that abundance of food was one of the chief causes of setting them in motion. How is it that a like cause operating here, will not produce a like effect? Have we not, in addition to our prolific agriculture, as many, and as great natural aids for manufacturing, as any other country? Are we deficient in water-power? Look at Niagara river, where all the accumulated waters of the upper St. Lawrence basin fall *three hundred and thirty five feet* in the distance of a few miles. Ohio, or Kentucky, or western Virginia, or Michigan can alone furnish durable water-power, far more than sufficient to operate every machine in New England. The former state has now for sale on her canals, more water-power than would be needed for the moving of all the factories of New England and New York. Indeed, no idea of our eastern friends is more preposterous than the one so hugged by them, that they, of all the people of the Union, are peculiarly favored with available water-power. We remember reading in the North American Review, many years ago, in an article devoted to the water-power, and its appropriation in the neighborhood of Baltimore, that southwardly from that city, the Atlantic states were destitute of water-power; when every well-informed man should know, that there is not one of those states in which its largest river would not furnish more than power sufficient to manufacture every pound of cotton raised within its boundaries. The streams of New England are short and noisy, not an unfit emblem of her manufacturing pretensions and destiny.

But if our water-power should be unequal to our manufacturing exigencies, our beds of coal will not fail us. One of these coal formations, having its centre not far from Marietta, is estimated by Mr. Mather, geologist, to be of the extent of 50,000 square miles. He says that, in several of the counties of Ohio, the beds of workable coal are from 20 to 30 feet thick. Another coal formation embraces the Wabash valley of Indiana and the Green river country of Kentucky. We know also of its existence in abundance at Ottowa and Alton, in the State of Illinois, and suppose they are in the same coal basin. Another coal basin has been discovered in Michigan, and a fifth on the Arkansas river. In some of these coal regions, and probably in all, beds of iron ore and other valuable minerals for manufacture are abundant.

Will laborers be wanting? Where food is abundant and cheap, there cannot long be a deficiency of laborers. What brought our ancestors (with the exception of the few who fled from persecution) from the other side of the Atlantic, but the greater abundance of the means of subsistence on this side? What other cause has so strongly operated in bringing to our valley the 10,000,000 or 11,000,000 who now inhabit it? The cause continuing, will the effect cease? While land of unsurpassed fertility remains to be purchased, at a low rate, and the increase of agriculture in the west keeps down the relative price of food; and while the population of the old countries of Europe, and the old states of our confederacy is so augmenting as to straiten more and more the means of living at home, and, at the same time, the means of removing from one to the other are every year rendering it cheaper, easier, and more speedy; and while, moreover, the new states, in addition to the inducement of cheaper food, now offer a country with facilities of intercourse among themselves greatly improved, and with institutions civil, political, and religious, already established and flourishing—are farmers, and mechanics, and manufacturers—the young, the active, and the enterprising, no longer to be seen pouring into this exuberant valley and marking it with the impress of their victorious industry, as in times past?

If our readers are satisfied that domestic or internal trade must have the chief agency in building up our great American cities, and that the internal trade of the great western valley will be mainly concentrated in the cities situated within its bosom, it becomes an interesting subject of inquiry how our leading interior city will, at some distant period, say 100 years, compare with New York, the Atlantic emporium. For the purpose of illustration, let us take Cincinnati as the chief interior city. Whether it will actually become such, we design to discuss in a separate paper.

One hundred years from this time, if our ratio of increase for the last 50 years is kept up, our republic will number, in round numbers, 325,000,-000—say 300,000,000. Of this number, if we allow for the Atlantic slope five times its present population, or 40,000,000, and to the Oregon country 10,000,000, there will remain for our great valley 250,000,000. If, to these, we add the 20,000,000 by that time possessed by Canada, we have, for our North American valley, 270,000,000. The point, then, will be reduced to the plain and easily solved question, whether 270,000,000 of inhabitants will build up and sustain greater cities than 40,000,000. As our valley is in shape more compact than the Atlantic slope, it is more favorable to a decided concentration of trade to one point. . . .

.   .   .   .

. . . The introduction of steam in coast and river navigation, and of canals, and railroads, and M'Adam roads, all tending to bring into rapid and cheap communication the distant parts of the most extended continent, is a still more potent cause in favor of internal trade and interior towns. The introduction, as instruments of commerce, of steamboats, canals, rail, and M'Adam roads, being of recent date, they have not had time to produce the great results that must inevitably flow from them. The last 20 years have been devoted mainly to the construction of these labor-saving instruments of commerce; during which time, more has been done to facilitate internal trade, than had been effected for the thousands of years since the creation of man. These machines are but just being brought into use; and he is a bold man who, casting his eye 100 years into the future, shall undertake to tell the present generation what will be their effect on our North American valley, when their energies shall be brought to bear over all its broad surface.

Let it not be forgotten that, while many other countries have territories bordering the ocean, greatly superior to our Atlantic slope, no one government has an interior at all worthy a comparison with ours. . . .

MISSOURI—ST. LOUIS, THE COMMERCIAL CENTER OF NORTH AMERICA, *S. Waterhouse*

TEN years before Scott addressed the readers of
The Merchants' Magazine, a citizen of St. Louis had
predicted, not entirely correctly, the future of *his* city.
The perspective is that of the merchant, who
speaks of St. Louis's destiny as determined by its
favored natural resources, albeit also exhorting
his fellow citizens to act properly so as to
supplement those resources. City rivalry—a frequent
theme in literature about cities—is also an
element in his urging an active effort in order to
make St. Louis fulfill its natural destiny.

St. Louis is ordained by the decrees of phsyical nature to become the great inland metropolis of this continent. It cannot escape the magnificence of its destiny. Greatness is the necessity of its position. New York may be the head, but St. Louis will be the heart of America. The stream of traffic which must flow through this mart will enrich it with alluvial deposits of gold. Its central location and facilities of communication unmistakably indicate the leading part which this city will take in the exchange and distribution of the products of the Mississippi Valley. . . . It is the geographical centre of a valley which embraces 1,200,000 square miles. In its course of 3,200 miles, the Mississippi borders on Missouri 470 miles. Of the 3,000 miles of the Missouri, 500 lie within the limits of our own State. St. Louis is mistress of more than 16,500 miles of river navigation.

This metropolis, though in the infancy of its greatness, is already a large city. Its length is about eight miles, and its width three. Suburban residences, the outposts of the grand advance, are now stationed six or seven miles from the river. The present population of St. Louis is about 200,000. . . .

.   .   .   .

A vast enlargement of our railroad facilities is contemplated. More than 10,000 miles have been projected on the west side of the Mississippi. A quarter of a century may elapse before the completion of these exten-

Excerpted from, *Merchants' Magazine and Commercial Review,* Vol. 55 (1866), pp. 53–55, 56–61.

sions, yet the very conception of them shows that the public mind is alive to the importance of ampler means of communication with the States and Territories of the far West. Most of these roads have received grants of land from the Government, and upon some of the lines the work is already far advanced. . . . The trade of the north-western roads may be partially diverted from St. Louis by the construction of rival lines. But the south-west branch, by its advantages of situation, will compel all connecting lines to be subsidiary to itself; and its commerce, constantly swelled by the traffic of tributary roads, must necessarily flow to St. Louis. The extension of this road would open to settlement vast tracts of valuable land; and, by the impulse of cheap transportation, lead to an extended development of the rich mines of south-western Missouri.

It is to be hoped that our citizens will press forward to an early completion all the roads which will converge at St. Louis. On the east side of the Mississippi an air-line road from Cleveland to this city is now in progress of construction. This road will be a very important accession to our commercial facilities. The great bridge whose arches will, within a few years, span the Mississippi at this point, will put St. Louis in direct connection with the entire railroad system of the Continent. The parallel and meridian lines between oceans and zones will intersect at this city. From this centre roads will radiate to the circumference of our land.

.   .   .   .

The growth of St. Louis, though greatly retarded by social institutions, has been rapid. The population of the city in—

1840	was	16,467
1850	"	77,860
1860	"	160,773

At the lowest rate of decennial increase, St. Louis in 1900 would contain more than 1,000,000 inhabitants. This number certainly seems to exceed the present probability of realization, but the future growth of St. Louis, vitalized by the mightiest forces of a free civilization, and quickened by the exchanges of a continental commerce, ought to surpass the rapidity of its past development.

.   .   .   .

During the rebellion the commercial transactions of Cincinnati and Chicago, doubtless exceeded those of St. Louis. The very events which prostrated our trade, stimulated theirs into an unnatural activity. Their sales were enlarged by the traffic which was wont to seek this market. Our loss was their gain.

The Southern trade of St. Louis was utterly destroyed by the blockade of the Mississippi. The disruption by civil commotions of our commercial intercourse with the interior of Missouri was nearly complete. The trade of the Northern States, bordering upon the Mississippi, was still unobstructed. But the merchants of St. Louis could not afford to buy commodities which they were unable to sell, and country dealers would not purchase their goods where they could not dispose of their produce. Thus St. Louis, with every market wholly closed or greatly restricted, was smitten with a commercial paralysis. The prostration of business was general and disastrous. No comparison of claims can be just, which ignores the circumstances that during the Rebellion retarded the commercial growth of St. Louis, yet fostered that of rival cities.

.   .   .   .

The conquest of treason has restored to this mart the use of its natural facilities. Trade is rapidly regaining its old channels. On its errands of exchange, it visits the islands of the sea, traverses the ocean, and explores foreign lands. It penetrates every State and Territory in the Mississippi Valley, from Alabama and New Mexico to Minnesota and Montana. It navigates every stream that pours its tributary waters into the Mississippi.

But St. Louis can never realize its splendid possibilities without effort. The trade of the vast domain lying east of the Rocky Mountains, and south of the Missouri River, is naturally tributary to this mart. St. Louis, by the exercise of forecast and vigor, can easily control the commerce of 1,000,000 square miles. But there is urgent need of exertion. Chicago is an energetic rival. Its lines of railroad pierce every portion of the Northwest. It draws an immense commerce by its network of railways.

The meshes which so closely interlace all the adjacent country gather rich treasures from the tides of commerce. Chicago is vigorously extending its lines of road across toward the Missouri River. The completion of these roads will inevitably divert a portion of the Montana trade from this city to Chicago. The energy of an unlineal competitor may usurp the legitimate honors of the imperial heir. St. Louis cannot afford to continue the masterly inactivity of the old *regime*. A traditional and passive trust in the efficacy of natural advantages will no longer be a safe policy. St. Louis must make exertions equal to its strength and worthy of its opportunities. It must not only form great plans of commercial empire, but must execute them with an energy defiant of failure. . . .

.   .   .   .

The mercantile interests of the West imperatively demand the improvement of the Mississippi and its main tributaries. This is a work of such prime and transcendent importance to the commerce of the country that it challenges the co-operation of the Government. A commercial marine which annually transfers tens of millions of passengers and hundreds of millions of property ought not to encounter the obstructions which human efforts can remove. The yearly loss of capital, from the interruption of communication and wreck of boats, reaches a startling aggregate.

For the accomplishment of an undertaking so vital to its municipal interests, St. Louis should exert its mightiest energies. The prize for which competition strives is too splendid to be lost by default. The Queen City of the West should not voluntarily abdicate its commercial sovereignty.

If the emigrant merchants of America and Europe, who recognize in the geographical position of St. Louis the guarantee of mercantile supremacy, will become citizens of this metropolis, they will aid in bringing to a speedier fulfillment the prophesies of its greatness. The currents of Western trade must flow through the heart of this valley.

The march of St. Louis will keep equal step with the progress of the West. Located at the intersection of the river which traverses zones and the railway which belts the continent, with divergent roads from this center to the circumference of the country, St. Louis enjoys commercial advantages which must inevitably make it the greatest inland emporium of America. The movement of our vast harvests and the distribution of the domestic and foreign merchandise required by the myriad thousands who will, in the near future, throng this valley, will develop St. Louis to a size proportioned to the vastness of the commerce it will transact. This metropolis will not only be the center of Western exchanges, but also, if ever the seat of Government is transferred from its present locality, the capital of the nation.

HISTORY OF MARIETTA, *Thomas J. Summers*

> AS the urban frontier expanded westward, certain
> cities were left behind in the competition for
> population, resources, and reputation. Some of these
> cities seemed to their founders and first
> residents destined to become the great metropolises
> of their regions. In later years, their local
> historians, no doubt reflecting the sentiments of
> many of their contemporaries, had somehow
> to reconcile present reality with past aspirations.

Not many years past "Old Marietta" was a common term applied to the city wherever it was known. There were, perhaps, two reasons why this familiar term was thus used: the first being the fact of the priority and importance of Marietta in the early history of the West, and thus had reference to the age of the place; the second, the slow progress of the town for so many decades after the beginning of the nineteenth century, when compared with the life and buoyancy of many of her more youthful neighbors.

With reference to these two suggested reasons, it can be said that if the first were the only one, there would be no need of changing the term, for the fact that the settlement of Marietta marks the opening of the Great West and dates more than eleven decades hence, makes all her citizens take pride in calling her "Old Marietta." Who is there that has read or known of the early pioneers as they came and settled at Marietta, but what has a deep regard for them and their work? . . .

.   .   .   .

But while we rejoice in this noble place in history which we as citizens of Marietta occupy, there is another phase of life which belongs to a city. A city may open the way for progress, and still not progress itself. . . . Hence it is that we fear that with the term "Old" when applied to our city that there has been added a meaning that is not as honored as the former, or in keeping with the dignity of the same. There is, perhaps, added a meaning that is intended to reprove the city for being "behind" and "out-of-date." . . . It is then proper to ask if this term embodies not

From *History of Marietta* (Marietta, Ohio: Leader Publishing Company, 1902), pp. 319–20.

alone the "time honored" part of our history, but has in it that element which pictures the city as non-progressive and behind other cities, shall we still cling to it? Shall we not rather be designated by a term which shall embody all that honor belonging to us as the pioneer city, but will at the same time show that we have stepped out of the old non-progressive condition into a state of advancement? With our changed condition let there be a change in the epithet of the city. It is, then, that we pass from the "Old" into the "New" and thus we have "New Marietta."

Does the "New Marietta" imply discontinuity or abandonment of essential identity? Indeed not! The word "New" as thus applied infers that there was once an "Old" and consequently still cherishes the fact that Marietta is old in years that have passed since the pioneers. . . . But at the beginning of the new century she stands young, strong and vigorous, no longer old, except in name, with an ambition of youth and wealth of resource that places her at the head of the progressive cities of the Ohio Valley.

SUGGESTED READINGS: CHAPTER 4

Lois Dean. "Minersville: A Study in Socio-Economic Stagnation," *Human Organization,* Vol. 24 (1965), pp. 254–61.

> The people of Minersville share a feeling of belonging to a vanished golden century and see no future for their community. The relationships of city images, regional economics, and stances taken toward wider issues like the role of the federal government in city planning are nicely brought out in this perceptive article.

Constance Green. *American Cities in the Growth of the Nation.* New York: Harper and Row, 1957.

> A wide-ranging narrative account by an eminent urban historian, touching on the self conceptions of citizens in various cities during the nation's development.

Anselm L. Strauss. *Images of the American City.* New York: The Free Press of Glencoe, 1961. Chapter 3, "The Evolution of Urban Images."

> An analysis of the changing meanings of Chicago and its perceived destiny over many decades, through an analysis of popular histories of that city.

W. Lloyd Warner. *The Living and the Dead.* New Haven: Yale University Press, 1959. Part II, "The Symbols of History."

> Newburyport ("Yankee City") looks back on an old New England past, and celebrates that past and a possible future with a fascinating urban ceremony, analyzed in detail by an anthropologist.

5

American Harvesting Machinery, 1891.

EARLY VERSIONS OF THE RURAL-URBAN DIALOGUE

IN the first decades of the nineteenth century, most
Americans believed that this would continue to be a predominantly
agricultural nation. During those same decades, a dialogue
between urban and rural spokesmen (some of the latter now
living in cities) became increasingly evident. That dialogue has
not ceased, although the specific arguments and claims used, as well
as the spokesmen themselves, have changed over the years,
with the corresponding transformation of cities and countrysides.

The dialogue continues to be fateful for how Americans
regard their cities and for the form of certain urban
institutions. We have already noted that many historians
still adhere to what has been called "the myth" of a
basically rural America. Many sociologists, we shall note
later, have held and probably still hold a similar set of beliefs.
Antagonism still exists in some regions between farmers and the
citizens of nearby towns and cities. State legislators tend greatly to
over-represent the rural vote; the citizens of rural counties tend
to eye at least "the big city" with suspicion. Migrants
from smaller towns are often uneasy in bigger towns, and, as noted
earlier, even large cities may have rural qualities that some
of their citizens point to with pride and satisfaction.
Many of our suburbs are infused with rural or at least
small-town spirit, their streets, churches, and schools echoing

a rural nostalgia. Within large cities we can easily discern the impact of rural conceptions on such institutions as the churches and the free-standing houses, complete with green lawns, and, sometimes, old-fashioned wooden fences. Attempts to maintain or create "neighborhoods" as well as to find a really "friendly" grocer or family doctor are further evidences of an attenuated rurality in urban environments.

In a sense, this entire book reverberates with the continuing and momentous rural-urban dialogue. Urban theorists, we suggest, have not yet begun to think through the implications of this complex imagery. Among the early versions are the selections (except for the last, of more recent vintage) reproduced in this chapter.

THE POLITICAL STATE OF AGRICULTURE and
THE PLEASURES OF AGRICULTURE,
John Taylor

DURING the early nineteenth century, southern
plantation agriculture went into a decline,
mainly because of its impoverished soils. At the
same time, the nation was moving rapidly
toward manufacturing, and an accompanying
industrialism and urbanism. Southern
agrarianism had an articulate spokesman in John
Taylor, farmer and statesman, who blamed agriculture's
decline on the politics of urbanism.

In collecting the causes which have contributed to the miserable agricultural state of the country, as it is a national calamity of the highest magnitude, we should be careful not to be blinded by partiality for our customs or institutions, nor corrupted by a disposition to flatter ourselves or others. I shall begin with those of a political nature. These are a secondary providence, which govern unseen the great interests of society; and if agriculture is bad and languishing in a country and climate, where it may be good and prosperous, no doubt remains with me, that political institutions have chiefly perpetrated the evil; just as they decide the fate of commerce.

The device of subjecting it to the payment of bounties to manufacturing, is an institution of this kind. This device is one item in every system for rendering governments too strong for nations. Such an object never was and never can be effected, except by factions legally created at the public expense. The wealth transferred from the nation to such factions, devotes them to the will of the government, by which it is bestowed. They must render the service for which it was given, or it would be taken away. It is unquestionably given to support a government against a nation, or one faction against another. Armies, loaning, banking, and an intricate treasury system, endowing a government with the absolute power of applying public money, under the cover of nominal checks, are other devices of this kind. Whatever strength or wealth a government and its legal

Excerpted from *Arator, Being a Series of Agricultural Essays, Practical and Political* (Petersburg, Va.: Whitworth and Yancey, 1818), pp. 19–20, 26–29, 35–36, 188–91.

factions acquire by law, is taken from a nation, weakens and impoverishes that interest, which composes the majority. There, political oppression in every form must finally fall, however it may oscillate during the period of transmit from a good to a bad government so as sometimes to scratch factions. Agriculture being the interest covering a great majority of the people of the United States, every device for getting money or power, hatched by fellow-feeling or common interest, between a government and its legal creatures, must of course weaken and impoverish it.—Desertion, for the sake of reaping without labour, a share in the harvest of wealth and power, bestowed, by laws at its expense, thins its ranks; an annual tribute to these legal factions, empties its purse; and poverty debilitates both its soil and understanding.

The device of protecting duties, under the pretext of encouraging manufactures, operates like its kindred, by creating a capitalist interest, which instantly seizes upon the bounty taken by law from agriculture; and instead of doing any good to the actual workers in wood, metals, cotton or other substances, it helps to rear up an aristocratical order, at the expense of the workers in earth, to unite with governments in oppressing every species of useful industry. . . .

The agriculture of the United States, found itself in the happiest situation for prosperity imaginable, at the end of the revolutionary war. It had not yet become such an egregious gudgeon as to believe, that by giving ten millions of dollars every year to the tribe of undertakers, to make it rich, they would return it twenty; and it could avail itself of all the markets in the world, where this ridiculous notion prevailed. There were so many mines of wealth to the agriculture of the United States. The idle clerical, military, banking, loaning, and ennobled classes, as has been stated, do certainly have the effect of raising agricultural prices very considerably; but the agriculturists who pay and maintain these classes, still lose more by them than they gain. . . . European agriculture is gulled or oppressed by others; American, gulls or oppresses itself. The first is no longer weak enough to think, that its battalion of aristocratical items, does it any good; but it is now unable to follow its judgment; the second, though able to follow its own judgment, has adopted the exploded errors heartily repented of by the first, and far outstrips it in the celerity of its progress towards a state of absolute submission to other interests, by shutting out itself from markets enhanced at the expense of other nations; and at the same time by creating the English items of capitalists, or masters for manufacturers, bankers, lenders, armies, and navies. Our true interest was to pay nothing for markets, spurious and swindling to those who buy them, and yet to share in their enhancement of prices. We have pursued a different course, and I do not recollect a single law, state or continental, passed in favour of agriculture, nor a single good house built by it since the revolution; but I know many built before, which have fallen into decay. Our agriculture is complimented by presidents, governors, legislators and individuals; and the Turks reverence a particular order of people as being also favoured by heaven.

.   .   .   .

The arguments to prove the political errors under which our agriculture is groaning, may suggest a suspicion, that I believe that protecting duties, or whatever else shall damp agricultural effort, and impoverish the lands of our country, is the only real and fatal foe to manufacturers; and that a flourishing agriculture will beget and enrich manufacturers, as rich-pastures multiply and fatten animals. He, who killed the goose to come at her golden eggs, was such a politician, as he who burdens our expiring agriculture, to raise bounties for our flourishing manufacturers.—He kills the cause of the end he looks for.

I meet such an insinuation by another argument. Protecting duties impoverish and enslave manufacturers themselves, and are so far from being intended to operate in their favour, or in favour of a nation, that their end and effect simply is to favour monied capital, which will seize upon and appropriate to itself, the whole profit of the bounty extorted from the people by protecting duties; and allow as scanty wages to its workmen, as it can. Monied capital drives industry without money out of the market, and forces it into its service, in every case where the object of contest is an enormous income. The wages it allows to industry are always regulated by the expense of its gain. Monied capitalists constitute an essential item of a government modelled after the English form. To advance this item, for the sake of strengthening the government against the people, and not for the sake of manufacturers, is the object of protecting duties. True, will say many a reader, but that is not the design here. Oh! how reverential is the logician who can prove, that an axe will cut under a monarchy, but not under a republic.

Some king, I believe, requested the merchantile class of his subjects, to ask of him a favour. The greatest, your majesty can grant us, said they, is, to let us alone. Protecting duties are such favours to manufacturers, as the pretended favours of kings are to merchants. They impoverish their customers, the agriculturists, and place over themselves an order of masters called capitalists, which intercepts the profit destined, without legal interposition, for industry. Many other arguments might be urged to prove, that protecting duties beget the poverty of manufacturers; but this is not my subject. To that I return.

.   .   .   .

The farce of legal favour or encouragement, has been so dexterously acted in England, to delude both the agricultural and mechanical interest, the interest of labour, or the majority of the nation, as to have delivered this majority shackled by protecting duties, bounties and prohibitions, into the hands of an inconsiderable monied aristocracy, or combination of capitalists. Into this net, woven of intricate frauds and ideal credit, the majority of the nation, the interest of labour, the agriculturists and mechanics have run, after the baits held out by protecting duties, bounties and prohibitions. From its dreams of wealth it is awakened under the fetters of a monied aristocracy, and unfortunate as Prometheus, it is destined to eternal and bitter toil to feed this political harpy, and to suffer excruciating anguish from its insatiable voraciousness. Sometimes this net has been baited to catch mechanics, at others to catch agriculturists, and perhaps it is but just, that these real brethren interests should fatten the alien tribe of stockjobbers, as a punishment for manifesting a disposition to devour each other.

We farmers and mechanics have been political slaves in all countries, because we are political fools. We know how to convert a wilderness into a paradise, and a forest into palaces and elegant furniture; but we have been taught by those whose object is to monopolize the sweets of life, which we sweat for, that politics are without our province, and in us a ridiculous affectation; for the purpose of converting our ignorance into the screen of regular advances, which artificial interests or legal factions, are forever making in straight or zigzag lines, against the citadel of our rights and liberties. Sometimes after one of these marauding families have pillaged for a thousand years, we detect the cheat, rise in the majesty of our strength, drive away the thief, and sing again into a lethargy of intellect so gross, as to receive him next day in a new coat, as an accomplished and patriotic stranger, come to cover us with benefits.—Thus we got rid of tythes, and now we clasp banks, patronage and protecting duties to our bosoms. Ten per centum upon labour was paid to a priesthood forming a body of men which extended knowledge, and cultivated good morals, as some compensation for forming also a legal faction, guided by the spirit of encroachment upon the rights and property of the majority. Forty per centum is now paid on our labour, to a legal faction guided by the same spirit, and pretending to no religion, to no morality, to no patriotism, except to the religion, morality and patriotism of making itself daily richer, which its says will enrich the nation, just as the self same faction has enriched England. This legal faction of capitalists, created by protecting duties, bankers and contractors, far from being satisfied with the tythe claimed by the old hierarchy, will, in the case of the mechanics, soon appropriate the whole of their labour to its use, beyond a bare subsistence; though in the case of farmers, it has yet only gotten about four times as much of theirs, as was extorted by the odious, oppressive, and fraudulent tythe system. We know death very well, when killing with one scythe, but mistake him for a deity, because he is killing with four.

.   .   .   .

In free countries, are more, and in enslaved, fewer, than the pleasures of most other employments. The reason of it is, that agriculture both from its nature, and also as being generally the employment of a great portion of a nation, cannot be united with power, considered as an exclusive interest. It must of course be enslaved, wherever despotism exists, and its masters will enjoy more pleasures in that case, than it can ever reach. On the contrary, where power is not an exclusive but a general interest, agriculture can employ its own energies for the attainment of its own happiness.

Under a free government it has before it, the unexhaustible sources of human pleasure, of fitting ideas to substances, and substances to ideas; and of a constant rotation of hope and fruitation.

The novelty, frequency and exactness of accommodations between our ideas and operations, constitutes the most exquisite source of mental pleasure. Agriculture feeds it with endless supplies in the natures of soils, plants, climates, manures, instruments of culture and domestic animals. Their combinations are inexhaustible, the novelty of results is endless, discrimination and adaption are never idle, and an unsatiated interest receives gratifications in quick succession.

Benevolence is so closely associated with this interest, that its exertion in numberless instances is necessary to foster it. Liberality in supplying its labourers with the comforts of life, is the best sponsor for the prosperity of agriculture, and the practice of almost every moral virtue is amply remunerated in this world, whilst it is also the best surety for attaining the blessings of the next.

Poetry, in allowing more virtue to agriculture, than to any other profession, has abandoned her privilege of fiction, and yielded to the natural moral effect of the absence of temptation. The same face is commemorated by religion, upon an occasion the most solemn, within the scope of the human imagination. At the awful day of judgment, the discrimination of the good from the wicked, is not made by the criterion of sects or of dogmas, but by one which constitutes the daily employment and the great end of agriculture. The judge upon this occasion has by anticipation pronounced, that to feed the hungry, clothe the naked, and give drink to the thirsty, are the passports to future happiness; and the divine intelligence which selected an agricultural state as a paradise for its first favourites, has here again prescribed the agricultural virtues as the means for the admission of their posterity into heaven.

With the pleasures of religion, agriculture unites those of patriotism, and among the worthy competitors for pre-eminence in the practice of this cardinal virtue, a profound author assigns a high station to him who has made two blades of grass grow instead of one; an idea capable of a signal amplification, by a comparison between a system of agriculture which doubles the fertility of a country, and a successful war which doubles its territory. By the first the territory itself is also substantially doubled, without wasting the lives, the wealth, or the liberty of the nation which has thus subdued sterility, and drawn the prosperity from a willing source. By the second, the blood pretended to be enriched, is spilt; the wealth pretended to be increased, is wasted; the liberty said to be secured, is immolated to the patriotism of a victorious army; and desolation in every form is made to stalk in the glittering garb of false glory, throughout some neighboring country. Moral law decides the preference with undeviating consistency, in assigning to the nation, which elects true patriotism, the recompense of truth, and to the electors of the false, the expiation of error. To the respective agents, the sage law assigns the remorses of a conqueror, and the quiet conscience of the agriculturist.

The capacity of agriculture for affording luxuries to the body, is not less conspicuous than its capacity for affording luxuries to the mind; it being a science singularly possessing the double qualities of feeding with unbounded liberality, both the moral appetites of the one, and the physical wants of the other. It can even feed a morbid love for money, whilst it is habituating us to the practice of virtue; and whilst it provides for the wants of the philosopher, it affords him ample room for the most curious and yet useful researches. In short, by the exercise it gives both to the body, and to the mind, it secures health and vigour to both; and by combining a thorough knowledge of the real affairs of life, with a necessity for investigating the arena of nature, and the strongest invitations to the practice of morality, it becomes the best architect of a complete man.

If this eulogy should succeed in awakening the attention of men of science to a skillful practice of agriculture, they will become models for individuals, and guardians for national happiness. The discoveries of the learned will be practiced by the ignorant; and a system which sheds happiness, plenty and virtue all around, will be gradually substituted for one which fosters vice, breeds want, and begets misery. . . .

The errors of politicians ignorant of agriculture, or their projects designed to oppress it, can only rob it of its pleasures, and consign it to contempt and misery. This revolution of its natural state, is invariably effected by war, armies, heavy taxes, or exclusive privileges. In two cases alone, have nations ever gained any thing by war. Those of repelling invasion and emigrating into a more fruitful territory. In every other case, the industrious of all professions suffer by war, the effects of which in its modern form, are precisely the same to the victorious and the vanquished nation. The least evil to be apprehended from victorious armies, is a permanent system of heavy taxation, than which, nothing can more vitally wound or kill the pleasures of agriculture. Of the same stamp, are exclusive privileges in every form; and to pillage or steal under the sanction of the statute books, is no less fatal to the happiness of agriculture, than the hierarchical tyranny over the soul, under the pretended sanction of God, or the feudal tyranny over the body, under the equally fraudulent pretence of defending the nation. In a climate and soil, where good culture never fails to beget plenty, where bad cannot produce famine, begirt by nature against the risque of invasion, and favoured by accident with the power of self government, agriculture can only lose its happiness by the folly or fraud of statesmen, or by its own ignorance.

THE AMERICAN CITY, *A. D. Mayo*

> THE conception of America as basically a rural nation is vividly expressed in the following characterization of its cities by A. D. Mayo, a minister. He began his book with the assumption that "every wise observer of the affairs of the Republic must confess that our hope of a Christian Democracy is the country life of the nation." His book reflects an attempt to reconcile the all too obviously increasing urbanism with the nation's more "essential" rural foundations.

An American city is essentially a different thing from an European capital. The old cities abroad are the growth of another state of human affairs, and represent quite another phase in the history of human progress than our own. They were the centres of imperial influence; a court, a palace, a royal army, with the peculiar results of such institutions, made them the centres of permanent attraction. Here, too, were the famous seats of the ecclesiastical power that held the monarchy in check, and spite of its corruption, was for centuries the best thing in Europe. And most significant of all, the continental cities were the cradle of freedom, where the mercantile and industrial interest first rallied and beat back the insolent feudalism that ruled over the broad country in the shape of a barbarous nobility; and in the independence of the English and German towns laid the corner stone of the liberty we to-day enjoy. And here were the great

Reprinted from *Symbols of the Capital* (New York: Thatcher and Hutchinson, 1859), pp. 40–44.

foundations of learning and cultivation in the universities, scholars and artists, that are the real sovereigns of modern times. Thus an European city is a nation within a nation, a conglomeration of institutions rooted in the soil of centuries, firmly interlaced into a corporate structure that resists the convulsions of ages. What wonder that Rome, Paris and London, Berlin, Moscow and Vienna should rule the nations they represent as our cities never can control the destinies of America; and that they should exist in all their essential attributes, while dynasties, peoples, civilizations change; the gigantic monuments of the past, that no deluge of modern improvement can move from their foundations.

But an American city is only a convenient hotel, where a free country people come up to tarry and do business, with old recollections of nature haunting them amid its toil and confusion; where the foreigner halts at his landing, and, if able and enterprising, pushes on to the "Far West," where the representative men of various kinds congregate during the few years of their culminating power to organize institutions and policies that represent the property and ideas of the millions that people the fields and villages without. Thus the American municipality can never have more than a representative character. Its money is the accumulation of the country's industry; its commerce is the exchange of the products of the prairie, plantation, lakes and rivers, and thousands of factory villages clustering about innumerable waterfalls among the hills; its scholarship is the growth of far away colleges; its literature culminates in the daily journals; its intelligence is rivalled by country towns; its society does not give the tone to, but is the growth of, the civilization of the district it represents; its politics finally yield to an outside pressure, and its institutions of philanthropy and religion are supported by contributions of men and means from the sects that spread over entire States. It is not the deep, firm root out of which rises the trunk and foliage of a great nationality; rather a boat tossed on the billows of American enterprise and emigration.

Let us rejoice that American cities must be representative, and cannot become our masters until the republic loses all but its name. Thank Heaven, liberty in New York is not compelled to burrow in forts and throw barricades across metropolitan streets, but ranges over her mountain tops, and along her plains, by the shores of her lakes, and down the valleys of her rivers. The open country is our fortress of freedom, and if the people know the worth of this precious boon, they will never permit the temporary classes of their cities to sacrifice it on the altar of municipal ambition. The cities of our State, even our proud "Metropolis," are but houses of industry, entertainment and public utility, built by our people; and while no individual right of the citizen is invaded, let them be so identified in the general body politic, that they cannot be seized by demagogues who would turn them into barbaric castles, fortified by ignorance and vice against the fresh and inspiring growth of new world civilization.

The sophistry of "municipal independence" with which our people are so often befogged, is quite out of place to-day in the United States. It meant something in the middle ages, when a ferocious nobility occupied the country, and held the farmer as a serf, and the gates of the town were the only defence for the merchant and the artisan; but in a State where the land is owned by the people, and an intelligent, virtuous, and prosperous country population build villages and cities for their commerce and convenience, the man who demands that these towns shall cut the vital cord that binds them to their creative and sustaining power, is advocating the cause of the Despotism that is passing away and not the welfare of the Humanity that is to come. Let the free winds of the country blow through every lane and whistle round every corner; let the people of New York always keep their towns in their own hands; then will the city in our republican life be what the garden is to the farm; the inclosure to which every forest and hill, and swamp, and brook and cultivated field has sent its tribute; that amid its bewildering walks and shaded arbors may be seen a representative from every nook and corner of the broad domain, controlled by the genius of a free society and a Christian State.

WHAT CONSTITUTES A MERCHANT,
Charles Edwards

HUNT'S *Merchants' Magazine and Commercial Review,*
beginning in 1839, was read by businessmen
for the latest statistics and news bearing
on trade and manufacturing. From the outset,
agriculture was regarded in its pages as secondary to
trade. (Hunt declared in the first volume that
we are "essentially and practically a
trading people.") This selection and the one that
follows, "The Morals of Trade," are taken from
this magazine. Cities were continually under
attack by farmers' spokesmen; city merchants and
manufacturers returned the fire, but not always from
merely defensive positions.

While the labor of the mechanic moulders or decays after him, the title of merchant is sounded for ages. Cities may be swept to the outline of their foundations; but their merchants are kept in remembrance. Whole nations will war to protect a single merchant: for he carries the honor of his country at the mast of his vessel. . . . His success is the success of that country; and his insolvency causes the firmest institutions of his own land to tremble. The ocean seems to rejoice with the freight of his ships; the winds lend him their breath; the iron appears to have become magnetic for him; his mere cipher is known and respected thousands of miles away; he has been called the steward of the world's stock; while the virtues of the earth are supposed to guide and to sustain him.

With such power in commerce, and such examples before him, the young man, who is looking towards merchandise for his future good, must naturally desire to gain the title of Merchant. What, then, constitutes a Merchant? A word, nevertheless, here, upon the idea which persons at times attach to the mercantile man. They lose sight of the broad space over which he carries his thoughts and property, and fancy his intellect to be as confined as his counting room. . . .

.   .   .   .

Excerpted from *Merchants' Magazine and Commercial Review,* Vol. 1 (1839), pp. 37, 291–92.

There are, also, persons who would sacrifice the merchant for the agriculturist; and consider the latter as all in all. However, gentlemen, the genius of a country who looks to her fields alone, sits like a poor shepherdess upon the mountains, who is content at seeing the waves of the surrounding ocean fashioned into white lambs, and the billows rise like her cattle in anger. The true genius will, with the glance of thought, see how that ocean is panting for the productions of the earth. Such an one proves to be a Minerva, who can and will cast aside her warlike emblems, to place the first vessel upon the sea, and encourage every Jason of her country to steer fearlessly for the golden fleece. The agriculturist bears no comparison to the merchant. Those persons who have lived or visited maritime cities, must, at once, acknowledge this. The merchant can "stand as one upon a rock, surrounded by a wilderness of sea." The farmer must have his rich pasture, a kind climate, and seed to sow. He has to wait for hay time and harvest; the merchant casts his bread upon the waters at all seasons. There is as much difference between them as between an inventor and a mere working man. It is true that Sully looked to the industry of the countryman as the only source of wealth. "Tillage and pasturage," it was a favorite saying of his "are the two breasts by which France is nourished, the real treasures of Peru." It is likewise true that Sully seriously checked national industry by not encouraging manufacturers and commerce.

Trade has this power over agriculture; it increases the wealth of a nation without the labor of producing or fabricating a single article. This is done through fearlessly carrying the dead stock of the agriculturist and planter to places where such stock is not produced. Trade is the foster mother of agriculture. The man of the country may feel himself a priest of nature; but gentleness and a love of the beautiful are also found in a maritime city. Philosophy can move around our wharves as well as repose under a tree. Nature may be studied among us. (although she may be discovered with more difficulty;) and I

> "——rather would entreat thy company
> To view the wonders of the world abroad
> Than, living dully sluggardized at home
> Wear yourself our in shapeless idleness."

The only advantage the farmer possibly can possess, is in a selfish quiet of mind—letting his thoughts merely

> "Hang on each leaf, and cling to every bough."

THE MORALS OF TRADE

Trade is the general name of distribution, and may be united with producing. All farmers, mechanics, artists, teachers, are the producers: while all traders, carriers, agents, are the distributors of wealth, together with the learned professions of law and medicine, who guide and assist in carrying on this great business—the profession of preachers belonging to the producing class, that of teacher. How trade can be dispensed with, or what are the arguments of those who are loud in denouncing it, it is difficult to discover. If the mechanic is improved in his art by giving his attention solely to it, enabling him, by exchange, to command the products of other arts, we see not why the trader is not also improved in his art by his undivided attention to it. The producer wishes to exchange his wheat, his hay, his cotton, for various necessities for his family. Having been occupied in his vocation, he is perhaps ignorant of the texture, soundness, and general value of the various articles needed, and therefore he goes to a person who has made it his study or practice to inform himself upon such points, who makes his purchases for him. In this way he avoids risk: is aided in point of time, convenience, and money; for which aid he pays, by allowing him who acts for him a higher price than he would pay, were he to buy of the original producers of the articles he is in need of. If one may justly pay a lawyer for an opinion respecting the goodness of a title to land; a physician for information respecting diet and exercise, why not also recompense the merchant for his opinion and time? . . .

.　　.　　.　　.　　.　　.　　.　　.　　.　　.

Trade then is as necessary as the professions: it is a profession itself, an art; something that is learned; that requires practice, skill, and judgment. It admits of degrees of success, according to the amount of knowledge, industry, and attention bestowed upon it; and, being founded in the wants of society, may have its laws or morals.

When our hearts are pained by the gross immoralities that prevail in large mercantile and manufacturing towns: when we witness the squalid want and disease that hang upon the skirts of a city; the opportunities that are offered, in the general bustle and hurry, for empiricism and deception in all shapes, we feel disposed to doubt if God ever intended men should

Excerpted from *Merchants' Magazine and Commercial Review*, Vol. 5 (1841), pp. 528–29.

herd together in such large masses, and, without producing, living by the distribution and exchange of the labor of the husbandman and mechanic. On the other hand, too, we picture in imagination the simplicity and security of rural life; the health and purity of country habits. From amid the coal-smoke of a city, its noisy cart-wheels, and the tramping of many feet, we turn our minds to that cottage, where our parents perhaps yet live, with its green, velvet fields, its well-known trees, the very shape of whose branches we recollect, its ancient walks, and unpretending happy appearance. Let not the counting-room or the shop want such dreams and pictures; let them be cherished as sacred; and hugged close to the heart. They will keep alive in us the sympathies of humanity, and purify and freshen those affections which are well-nigh lost or smothered in the jostling of the crowd and the strife of competition.

Nevertheless, such thoughts contain no argument against trade. The evils incident to cities, the suffering, sickness, and vice, that excite our regret, are the result of the misuse of great privileges; not necessary consequences. It is a law of nature that we must pay for all we have; and suffer for all our faults. A man, living alone in a valley, without intercourse with any human being, could not be guilty of dishonesty, of murder —of any vice that belongs to society; but for this exemption from temptation he would pay dearly by the want of that progress, sympathy, and mutual aid which are the great blessings of the social condition. The opportunities for individual improvement are increased, the more numerously men congregate together. A greater number of examples is furnished from which to form an opinion upon a given subject; the objects of science, literature, and art, can be conducted upon a larger scale by the contributions of many individuals. The lawyer has his mind full of information from the variety of questions discussed about him. The physician meets the tendency to disease in cities with a sagacity and experimental knowledge he could never have acquired in a narrower sphere, and the clergyman may be lifted to the occasion and speak with an eloquence proportioned to the danger that surrounds our virtue.

All those arts and inventions for convenience, economy, and health, here find their spur and origin, which taking their rise from the necessities of men congregated together, are spread through the towns and villages of the country, where they never could have originated because never absolutely needful. The facilities of speedy intercourse between cities furnish a highway to the farmer for the transportation of himself and his harvest, whither he would go; who, were it not for the energy of trade, might at this very hour be travelling by the side of his ox-team in the dust or mud of the turnpike. The city—the offspring of trade—is the court where a judgment is put upon the value of every article by actual comparison with others of the same kind. Not only is mind compared with mind, but cloth with cloth, wheat with wheat, and machinery with machinery. Here is made a decision in a day or hour, which a long experience only could arrive at by actual personal trial. These are some of the advantages which accrue to the world from what are called the unnatural herding of men together in cities. These can furnish an offset against those evils which, after all, are so many privileges of humanity. From this crime, vice, and poverty about us, can be traced those institutions which make glad the heart of the philanthropist. Truly are we "made perfect by suffering." What a field for the practice of benevolence and charity! How truly here can it be learned that "it is more blessed to give than receive!"

We shall contend then for the general morality of trade, for these reasons. It is a divine institution. It is the necessary employment of men in a highly social state, which could not exist in any other way.

HUMANITY IN THE CITY, *E. H. Chapin*

IT was not only the merchants who argued the
superiority of the city. The Reverend E. H. Chapin was
raised in Utica, New York, but addressed New
York City congregations in his sermons, published
in such books as *Moral Aspects of City Life*
and *Humanity in the City*. His perspective toward
the big city was basically an approving one.
Indeed, in one sermon he argued passionately that
"a city life is a great school for principle
because it affords a keen trial for principle. The
man who passes through its temptations
and yet holds on, unyielding, to the right will be
proved as if by fire." In the following
selections from *Humanity in the City*, he admonishes
city dwellers to turn to religion for an explanation
of the city's many defects. (Later, in another
selection from the same book, we shall read
his sanction for achieving in the city, provided such
success is imbued with religiosity.)

LESSON OF THE STREETS

I observe that the first lesson of the street is in the illustration which
it affords us of the *diversities of human conditions*. The most superficial
eye recognizes this. A city is, in one respect, like a high mountain; the
latter is an epitome of the physical globe; for its sides are belted by products of every zone, from the tropical luxuriance that clusters around its
base, to its arctic summit far up in the sky. So is the city an epitome of
the social world. All the belts of civilization intersect along its avenues.
It contains the products of every moral zone. It is cosmopolitan, not only
in a national, but in a spiritual, sense. Here you may find not only the finest
Saxon culture, but the grossest barbaric degradation.

.   .   .   .

Idolatry! you cannot find any more gross, any more cruel, on the
broad earth, than within the area of a mile around this pulpit. Dark minds
from which God is obscured; deluded souls, whose fetish is the dice-box

Excerpted from *Humanity in the City* (New York: De Witt and Davenport,
1854), pp. 17–23, 224–25, 227–32, 240–44, 247–52.

or the bottle; apathetic spirits, steeped in sensual abomination, unmoved by a moral ripple, soaking in the slump of animal vitality. False gods, more hideous, more awful, than Moloch or Baal; worshipped with shrieks, worshipped with curses, with the hearth-stone for the bloody altar, and the drunken husband for the immolating priest, and women and children for the victims. . . .

.   .   .   .

In the street, however, not only do we behold these different degrees of civilization, but those problems of diversity, which the highest form of existing civilization develops—the diversities of extreme poverty, and extreme wealth, for instance. Here sits the beggar, sick and pinched with cold; and there goes a man of no better flesh and blood, and no more authentic charter of soul, wrapped in comfort, and actually bloated with luxury.

.   .   .   .

And here, too, through the brilliant street, and the broad light of day, walks Purity, enshrined in the loveliest form of womanhood. And along that same street by night, attended by fitting shadows, strolls womanhood discrowned, clothed with painted shame, yet, even in the springs of that guilty heart not utterly quenched. . . .

.   .   .   .

And, if we would ascertain the practical purport of this lesson of human diversity which is so conspicuous in the street—the meaning of these sharp contrasts of refinement and grossness, intelligence and igno-rance, respectability and guilt—we only ask a question that thousands have asked before us. And yet, it is possible to surmise the purpose of these diversities. We know, for one thing, that out of them come some of the noblest instances of character and of achievement. Ignorance and crime and poverty and vice, stand in fearful contrast to knowledge and integrity and wealth and purity; but they likewise constitute the dark background against which the virtues of human life stand out in radiant relief; virtues developed by the struggle which they create; virtues which seem impossible without their co-existence. For, whence issues any such thing as *virtue,* except out of the temptation and antagonism of vice? How could *Charity* ever have appeared in the world, were there no dark ways to be trodden by its bright feet, and no suffering and sadness to require its aid? I look at these asylums, these hospitals, these ragged schools—a zodiac of beauti-ful charities, girdling all this selfishness and sin—I look at these monuments which humanity will honor when war shall be but a legend, and laurels have withered to dust; and when I think what they have grown out of, and why they stand here, I regard them as so many sublime way-marks by which Providence unfolds its purposes among men, and by which men trace out the plan of God.

.   .   .   .

THE HELP OF RELIGION

.   .   . These very conditions of Humanity in the City, for instance— these conditions of poverty, and responsibility, and relationship, and privilege, and strife, and toil—yea, the lessons which come to us from the crowd as it flows through these streets; constitute a great problem, of which every thinking man will see some solution. . . . . I propose to illustrate the influence of Religion to this effect, first—as a *Conviction;* second, as a *Working Power;* and third, as an *Interpretation.*

I say, then, in the first place, that religion furnishes great help for man in the various issues of life, when he becomes actually convinced that its truths and sanctions are *genuine.* . . . . I do not know that I can better suggest its influence as a help here, in the conditions of the city, than by asking you to imagine what *would* be the state of things in the spheres of toil and traffic—in all the multiform relations of our humanity—if men really apprehended and believed it? *It,* I say—not some special dogma or institution, but the absolute spirit and truth of Christianity. For I do not think that, generally, this *is* actually credited. . . . . For, I ask you, my friends, if it *were* realized, could there be so much abject need among us; so much stony-hearted selfishness; so much shuffling in trade, and corruption in politics, and meanness in intercourse, and foolish superficial living?

.   .   .   .

For I say once more, that a conviction of its reality must be a great help in adjusting the problems of life. And this, because it acts upon the centre of all the sin, and much of the suffering of the world. This personal application of religion stands before all other remedies for the removal of these evils. Others are attempted—others are, in a degree, successful; but none go so deep and produce results so sure.

.   .   .   .

.   .   . The power of *law* has been invoked; and it has its legitimate sphere of operation. It checks the purposed violence. It arrests the overt act. It may consistently be summoned to purify all those channels of social action which it assumes to regulate; and, instead of patronizing the wrong, to set its face and hand against it. Thus it may prevent public harm, though it cannot stop self-injury, and remove occasions of temptation, though it cannot impart moral strength.

.   .   .   .

On the other hand, we have the expedients of the *reformer*. He comes with props and palliatives; soothing some cutaneous irritation, or removing some foul condition. And let us recognize the legitimacy of *his* endeavor. We must approach the human heart through the web of its external circumstances, as well as directly. Nay, often this is the only way by which we can get at it at all. And well may we rejoice over the rescue from specific vices, and commend the zeal and patience which fasten upon some colossal evil to batter and drive it from the world. But notwithstanding such noble achievement, how many have remained among the tombs, or gone back to the wilderness—demoniacs still! It is an old truth, but I say it as though it were in the conviction of a fresh fact forced upon me by these great problems that heave up in the currents of City Life; it is an unavoidable conclusion that there is only one influence that can make safe, and pure, and strong in goodness, those recesses out of which issue so much social evil, and so much personal suffering. And that is the influence not of the law-giver, nor of the reformer; but of the Redeemer. It is that power which flows through the soul in a practical conviction of the reality of religion. It is the help which comes from its inspiration of divine truth and goodness in the breasts of individual men, turning them from evil, rendering them strong against temptation, and sending out from their lives fresh forces of righteousness and love.

.   .   .   .

But religion is not only a help in and for ourselves; it has a ministration for others—for this great mass of destitution and suffering that broods in the midst of the city. Christianity is not merely a theory of existence—it is a *working-power*. Its precepts are practical, and enjoin not merely states of mind and heart, but conditions of activity. . . .

.   .   .   .

But if, turning from the positive achievement, you point to the evils that still exist—if you lift the coverings of respectability and custom from the ghastly facts that are embedded here in our so-called civilization; if you bid me mark the vice, the poverty, the crime, the oppression, the grinding monopoly, the prejudice, the gigantic materialism and practical atheism that are mixed up with it, and seem to be inseparable parts of it; then I ask you—how would it be *without* the Help of Religion? . . .

.   .   .   .

And, if still this problem of human degradation and suffering presses upon us, I say further, that where the constituents of this problem are most prominent, there religion is the most active. The heaviest poverty is belted about by the brightest charities; the hot-beds of crime generate the most radical efforts for its prevention and its cure; and while oppression is at work, setting its dark types upon virgin soil to print off its own shame and condemnation, indignant voices expose it and indignant hearts react against it. And more and more, every day, it is felt and proclaimed that religion is a working-principle —a practical power. . . .

.   .   .   .

We have thus seen that Religion is a Help as to the fact of sin, when men are convinced of it as a great reality; and a help as to the fact of human suffering, because it is a working-power. But, over and above all this, there are problems that perplex us, and demand some answer; problems as to the How, and the Wherefore, and the End. There are times when our thoughts rise above all specific instances, and we take up humanity and existence as a whole, and ask—"What means it all? . . ."
And the only help for us in such a case is the Help of Religion, presenting us, through faith, with an *interpretation* of human life—an interpretation which tells us that what we now experience and behold is only transitional, preliminary, and that we see through a glass darkly, and it doth not yet appear what we shall be.

.   .   .   .

The meaning of these various conditions in the city—the meaning of these sins, and sorrows, and inequalities—the meaning of this tide of life itself that rolls in endless succession through these stony arteries—does it perplex you? Accept, then, the help which religion gives by interpreting it as only preliminary and transitional; only a portion of a wider scheme.

.   .   .   .

See! over your head spreads the great firmament. There are Sirius, and Orion, and the glittering Pleiades. How harmoniously they are related; how calmly they roll! And now, O man! fresh from the reeking dust, and the cry of pained hearts, and the shadows of the grave, do not the scales of unbelief drop from your eyes, when you see the width of God's universe, and feel that His purpose girdles this little planet and steers its freight of souls? You were deceived by your standards of greatness and duration. You thought that this material city, with what it contains, was everything. But *they* have cherished the true view, who in the spirit of the text have interpreted these Conditions of Humanity—the conditions of those who seek and sin and suffer in the busy crowd; of those who rest beneath yonder gleaming tomb-stones. And, as we read what all wise and good men have virtually said, our mortal term contracts, our immortal career opens, our years seem as ticks of a clock, and the entire sum of our life but a minute-mark on the dial of eternity; and this huge metropolis becomes a dim veil, a perishable symbol of real and enduring things.

A LATER VERSION OF THE DIALOGUE,
Walter Burr

A CENTURY after Taylor's protest aganst the growing political power of commerce and manufacturing, a sympathetic critic laid a cooling hand on the still fevered brow of agriculture. Farmers' protest movements will do no good, he argued, but effective political representation will give the farmer what he needs and deserves. In his closing paragraph, Burr explained why the farmer can really depend on that favorable outcome, using an imagery that cheerfully and ingeniously turns the persistent rural emigration to cities into an asset. Burr was a professor of sociology who taught, appropriately enough, at Kansas State Agricultural College.

The professional farm "organizer" marshals statistics to show that farmers have been steadily crowded out of positions of political leadership. They were not crowded out by any other force than the advance of our national civilization. A distinctively agricultural nation is weak, and our sensible farm people, fully as much as any other group, have demanded that we develop industry, finance, and commerce. That meant a period of

Excerpted from "The 'Dirt Farmer' Representing the Farmer," *The Independent,* Vol. 114 (1925), pp. 269–71.

big city expansion. For this rapid development as a manufacturing and commercial people, as well as in order to become world bankers, we demanded the leadership of men who had gone to the top in business.

.   .   .   .

The farmer gets interested in staging a comeback when he feels things are unbearable. That is, the farmer movement is a *protest* movement. It is when times become unbearably bad that he comes raring into the lime-light. He always comes as a fighter. He comes with a protest against the existing order in business, education, or politics—or all together. Often he is more than half right in his contention. But a protest movement can-not live for long, and those who launch it go out with its decline. Two resuits of any such movement assure its speedy death: First, as it meets success, former opposers are wise enough to accept the inevitable and take over enough of the program to rob the reformers of the sane part of their thunder; second, it takes to itself all the disgruntled and disappointed ne'er-do-wells in the country. With the really worth while parts of the program gone to the opposing group, these crazy elements add all of their impossible schemes to the dangerous fragments which remain. Finally, sane and decent people leave the movement entirely. . . .

.   .   .   .

Then how is the American farmer to be given a square deal in public affairs? By giving public affairs a square deal. Important as the actual process of farming is, it is only one of the factors in public affairs. . . .

.   .   .   .

Since farm population turns into city life two million farm-trained children a year, farmers are surer than any other class of a square deal from those who have leadership in public affairs. The old slogan, "Give me a child until he is seven years old, and I care not what you do with him after that," is still true and sound. Statistics show that more than eighty-five per cent of our city and national leaders were born and raised on the farm. The rural neighborhood is the mother and father and school-teacher of nearly all our State and national leaders. "Blood is thicker than water." The blood that flows today in the veins of the big newspaper man in the New York office, Coolidge in the White House, the "Senator from this-or-that State," the railroad president—this is the same blood that flows in the veins of brothers and sisters and fathers and mothers down on the farm.

In other words, the farmers are already in "charge of affairs," through the farm home and the farm school. That's the reason our national life is, after all, so sound. Politics, industry, commerce, education, finance—each one is a business in itself, just as farming is a business in itself. One may go from one calling to another, in this free country of ours, but to very few men is it given to be successful in any two callings at the same time— and the "dirt farmer" is no exception to this rule. He will check his finance up to the financier, his education to the educator, his commerce to the commercial leader, his industry to the industrial manager, his politics to the statesman—while he continues in charge of his farming—and plus that, produces and trains the leaders for all of these activities that make up public affairs.

SUGGESTED READINGS: CHAPTER 5

Albert Blumenthal. *Small-Town Stuff*. Chicago: University of Chicago Press, 1932.

The title itself suggests an evaluative stance on the small town. In this monograph, plenty of ammunition can be found for positive and negative stances toward rurality and urbanity.

Richard Hofstadter. *The Age of Reform*. New York: Alfred A. Knopf, 1955.

Much of the nineteenth-century dialogue, and in particular its political importance, is detailed in this social history.

Henry Nash Smith. *Virgin Land*. Cambridge, Mass.: Harvard University Press, 1950.

This book turns around the fate of the agrarian myth in the development of the Midwest, especially as the area became increasingly commercial, industrial, and urban. The subtitle is, fittingly, "The American West as Symbol and Myth."

P. Sorokin, C. Zimmerman, and C. Galpin. *Systematic Source Book in Rural Sociology*. Minneapolis: University of Minnesota Press, 1930.

In the literature of rural sociology, as well as of "social problems" (as noted by C. Wright Mills), the frequently acrimonious older dialogue between the advocates of rurality and urbanity is sometimes quite explicit.

6

The fate of hundreds of young men: 1. Leaving home for New York. 2. In a fashionable saloon amongst the waiter girls—the road to ruin. 3. Drinking with "the fancy"—in the hands of gamblers. 4. Murdered and robbed by his "fancy" companions. 5. His body found by the harbor police. E. W. Martin, *The Secrets of the Great City*, 1868.

PERILS OF
THE GREAT CITY

DURING the nineteenth century a great many Americans thought
of the city as a perilous place. That perspective had two related
but not entirely identical aspects. The city destroyed people who
were born or migrated there. The city also imperiled the
nation itself. Especially after the Civil War—when cities were
growing rapidly, when country and city grew unmistakably
distinct, when industrialism seemed to overwhelm agriculture
and yet the cities were replete with crime, vice, immorality, and
poverty—the city seemed to threaten its own citizens, those still
living in the countryside, and the very fabric of national life itself.
The complex reform movement that swept the nation toward the
end of the century was profoundly affected by such conceptions
of the city. In later chapters we shall see how they have
carried over into the twentieth century, gradually becoming
muted or incorporated in later conceptions.

American sociology received much of its initial impetus and
direction from such imagery. Virtually all the early sociologists
engaged in reform writing. Most were born in rural areas and
understandably were disposed to help mitigate the city's many
evils. Although today we remember a man like E. A. Ross for
his theoretical writing, he was known far and wide for his
popular books, many of them directly or indirectly concerned
with the perils of the city. At the University of Chicago,

sociologists like Henderson and Zueblin became nationally famous for their writing; today we have forgotten them, although we remember Thomas—who documented how Chicago demoralized immigrants—because he was an outstanding theorist. Since imageries of the city as a place of danger pertained not only to downward mobility but to blocked mobility, it is not surprising to find the town-born W. G. Sumner battling the reformers and arguing for a natural selection in which even children of the poor could rise if they had the necessary ability.

During the 1920s, although Robert Park's program for studying the city was further removed from reformistic tendencies, it received much direction from an attempt to understand for whom the city was perilous—and perhaps what could be done about it. And so Thrasher observed gangs, Shaw studied young delinquents, Cressey did field work in taxi-dance halls, Mowrer interviewed disorganized families, Zorbaugh visited at rooming houses and spoke with slum dwellers who had immigrated from rural areas of foreign countries, while Young wrote about how a sect from rural Russia managed in urban America, Reckless studied Chicago vice, and Frazier published his famous monograph on the rural Negro family in Chicago. Meanwhile, and for years later, as the selection taken from C. Wright Mills' writing makes evident, undergraduates were directed in sociology courses on social problems to all the many problems of urban living.

Although our contemporary debates about delinquency and poverty have somewhat transcended the urban scene, the older imageries of city peril and the evils of urbanization can still be discerned in the arguments and studies of sociologists. As we shall see later, social work and political science, insofar as they pertained to city government, have been quite as much affected by conceptions of the seamy side of American urbanization.

PERILS—THE CITY, *Josiah Strong*

REVEREND JOSIAH STRONG'S catalog of city perils
is fairly comprehensive. It also suggests how
by 1885—the same year that the wave of
"new immigration" hit our shores—large metropolises
seemed to threaten the very existence of the
nation. Strong's sermon is one of many that exemplified
a dichotomous imagery of countryside versus city.

The city is the nerve center of our civilization. It is also the storm center. The fact, therefore, that it is growing much more rapidly than the whole population is full of significance. . . . In 1800 there were only six cities in the United States which had a population of 8,000 or more. In 1880 there were 286.

The city has become a serious menace to our civilization, because in it, excepting Mormonism, each of the dangers we have discussed is enhanced, and all are focalized. It has a peculiar attraction for the immigrant. Our fifty principal cities contain 39.3 per cent of our entire German population, and 45.8 per cent of the Irish. Our ten larger cities contain only nine per cent of the entire population, but 23 per cent of the foreign. While a little less than one-third of the population of the United States is foreign by birth or parentage, sixty-two per cent of the population of Cincinnati are foreign, eighty-three per cent of Cleveland, sixty-three per cent of Boston, eighty-eight per cent of New York, and ninety-one per cent of Chicago.

Because our cities are so largely foreign, Romanism finds in them its chief strength.

For the same reason the saloon, together with the intemperence and the liquor power which it represents, is multiplied in the city. East of the Mississippi there was, in 1880, one saloon to every 438 of the population; in Boston, one to every 329; in Cleveland, one to every 192; in Chicago, one to every 179; in New York, one to every 171; in Cincinnati, one to every 124. Of course the demoralizing and pauperizing power of the saloons and their debauching influence in politics increase with their numerical strength.

It is the city, where wealth is massed; and here are the tangible evi-

Reprinted from *Our Country: Its Possible Future and Its Present Crisis* (New York: The Baker and Taylor Co., 1885), pp. 128–44.

dences of it piled many stories high. Here the sway of Mammon is widest, and his worship the most constant and eager. Here are luxuries gathered— everything that dazzles the eye, or tempts the appetite; here is the most extravagant expenditure. Here, also, is the *congestion* of wealth the severest. Dives and Lazarus are brought face to face; here, in sharp contrast, are the *ennui* of surfeit and the desperation of starvation. The rich are richer, and the poor are poorer in the city than elsewhere; and as a rule, the greater the city, the greater are the riches of the rich and the poverty of the poor. Not only does the proportion of the poor increase with the growth of the city, but their condition becomes more wretched. The poor of a city of 8,000 inhabitants are well off compared with many in New York; and there are no such depths of woe, such utter and heart-wringing wretchedness in New York as in London. Read in "The Bitter Cry of Outcast London," a prophecy of what will some day be seen in American cities, provided existing tendencies continue: "Few who will read these pages have any conception of what these pestilential human rookeries are, where tens of thousands are crowded together amidst horrors which call to mind what we have heard of the middle passage of the slave-ship. To get into them you have to penetrate courts reeking with poisonous and malodorous gases, arising from accumulations of sewage and refuse scattered in all directions, and often flowing beneath your feet; courts, many of them which the sun never penetrates, which are never visited by a breath of fresh air. You have to ascend rotten staircases, grope your way along dark and filthy passages swarming with vermin. Then, if you are not driven back by the intolerable stench, you may gain admittance to the dens in which these thousands of beings herd together. Eight feet square! That is about the average size of many of these rooms. Walls and ceiling are black with the accretions of filth. . . . There are men and women who lie and die, day by day, in their wretched single room, sharing all the family trouble, enduring the hunger and the cold, and waiting, without hope, without a single ray of comfort, until God curtains their staring eyes with the merciful film of death. . . ."

. . . Is it strange that such conditions arouse a blind and bitter hatred of our social system?

Socialism not only centers in the city, but is almost confined to it; and the materials of its growth are multiplied with the growth of the city. Here is heaped the social dynamite; here roughs, gamblers, thieves, robbers, lawless and desperate men of all sorts, congregate; men who are ready on any pretext to raise riots for the purpose of destruction and plunder; here gather foreigners and wage-workers; here skepticism and irreligion abound; here inequality is the greatest and most obvious, and the contrast between opulence and penury the most striking; here is suffering the sorest. As the greatest wickedness in the world is to be found not among the cannibals of some far off coast, but in Christian lands where the light of truth is diffused and rejected, so the utmost depth of wretchedness exists not among savages, who have few wants, but in great cities, where, in the presence of plenty and of every luxury men starve. Let a man become the owner of a home, and he is much less susceptible to socialistic propagandism. But real estate is so high in the city that it is almost impossible for a wage-worker to become a householder. The law in New York requires a juror to be owner of real or personal property valued at not less than two hundred and fifty dollars; and this, the Commissioner says, relieves seventy thousand of the registered voters of New York City from jury duty. Let us remember that those seventy thousand voters represent a population of two hundred and eighty thousand, or fifty-six thousand families, not one of which has property to the value of two hundred and fifty dollars. "During the past three years, 220,976 persons in New York have asked for outside aid in one form or another." Said a New York Supreme Judge, not long since: "There is a large class—I was about to say a majority—of the population of New York and Brooklyn, who just live, and to whom the rearing of two or more children means inevitably a boy for the penitentiary, and a girl for the brothel." Under such conditions smolder the volcanic fires of a deep discontent.

We have seen how the dangerous elements of our civilization are each multiplied and all concentered in the city. Do we find there the conservative forces of society equally numerous and strong? Here are the tainted spots in the body-politic; where is the salt? . . .

. . . The city, where the forces of evil are massed, and where the need of Christian influence is peculiarly great, is from one-third to one-fifth as well supplied with churches as the nation at large. And church accommodations in the city are growing more inadequate every year. Including church organizations of all sorts, Chicago had in 1840 one church to every 747 of the population. In 1851, there was one to every 1,009; in 1862, one to 1,301; in 1870, one to 1,599; in 1880, one to 2,081. I am not aware that the case of Chicago is exceptional. . . . In the large cities generally it is common to find extensive districts nearly or quite destitute of the gospel. South of Fourteenth street, New York, there is a population of 541,000, for whom there is but one Protestant church to every 5,000 souls. That is, here are half a million people only one-tenth as well supplied with moral and Christian influences as the whole country at large. There are wards in New York and other large cities where there is but one Protestant church to every ten or fifteen thousand souls: which means that those wards are from one-twentieth to one-thirtieth as well supplied with churches as the whole land. In Ohio, even including the cities, more than one-fifth of the population is in Evangelical churches; in Cincinnati, by the latest estimate of the population, only one in twenty-three.

If moral and religious influences are peculiarly weak at the point where our social explosives are gathered, what of city government? Are its strength and purity so exceptional as to insure the effective control of these dangerous elements? In the light of notorious facts, the question sounds satirical. It is commonly said in Europe, and sometimes acknowledged here, that the government of large cities in the United States is a failure. "In all the great American cities there is today as clearly defined a ruling class as in the most aristocratic countries in the world. Its members carry wards in their pockets, make up the slates for nominating conventions, distribute offices as they bargain together, and—though they toil not, neither do they spin—wear the best of raiment and spend money lavishly. They are men of power, whose favor the ambitious must court, and whose vengeance he must avoid. Who are these men? The wise, the good, the learned —men who have earned the confidence of their fellow-citizens by the purity of their lives, the splendor of their talents, their probity in public trusts, their deep study of the problems of government? No; they are gamblers, saloon-keepers, pugilists, or worse, who have made a trade of controlling votes and of buying and selling offices and official acts." It has come to this, that holding a municipal office in a large city almost impeaches a man's character. Known integrity and competency hopelessly incapacitate a man for any office in the gift of a city rabble. . . . Popular government in the city is degenerating into government by a "boss." During his visit to this country Herbert Spencer said: "You retain the forms of freedom; but, so far as I can gather, there has been a considerable loss of the substance. . . . Manifestly those who framed your Constitution never dreamed that twenty thousand citizens would go to the polls led by a 'boss.' "

As a rule, our largest cities are the worst governed. It is natural, therefore, to infer that, as our cities grow larger and more dangerous, the government will become more corrupt, and control will pass more completely into the hands of those who themselves most need to be controlled. If we would appreciate the significance of these facts and tendencies, we must bear in mind that the disproportionate growth of the city is undoubtedly to continue, and the number of great cities to be largely increased. The extraordinary growth of urban population during this century has not been all peculiar to the United States. It is a characteristic of nineteenth century civilization. . . . This strong tendency toward the city is the result chiefly of manufacturers and railway communication, and their influence will, of course, continue. If the growth of the city in the United States has been so rapid during this century, while many millions of acres were being settled, what may be expected when the settlement of the West has been completed? The rapid rise in the value of lands will stimulate yet more the growth of the city; for the man of small means will be unable to command a farm, and the town will become his only alternative. When the public lands are all taken, immigration, though it will be considerably restricted thereby, will continue, and will crowd the cities more and more.

This country will undoubtedly have a population of several hundred millions, for the simple reason that it is capable of sustaining that number. And it looks as if the larger proportion of it would be urban. There can be no indefinite increase of our agricultural population. Its growth must needs be slow after the farms are all taken, and it is necessarily limited; but the cities may go on doubling and doubling again. Unless the growth of population is very greatly and unexpectedly retarded, many who are adults today will live to see 200,000,000 inhabitants in the United States, and a number greater than our present population—over 50,000,000— living in cities of 8,000 and upwards. And the city of the future will be more crowded than that of today, because the elevator makes it possible to build, as it were, one city above another. Thus is our civilization multiplying and focalizing the elements of anarchy and destruction. . . .

.   .   .   .

And this peril like the others which have been discussed, peculiarly threatens the West. The time will doubtless come when a majority of the great cities of the country will be west of the Mississippi. This will result naturally from the greater eventual population of the West; but, in addition to this fact, what has been pointed out must not be forgotten, that agriculture will occupy a much smaller place *relatively* in the industries of the West than in those of the East, because a much smaller proportion of the land is arable. The vast region of the Rocky Mountains will be inhabited chiefly by a mining and manufacturing population, and such populations live in cities.

1. In gathering up the results of the foregoing discussion of these several perils, it should be remarked that to preserve republican institutions requires a *higher average* intelligence and virtue among large populations than among small. . . . If the people are to govern, they must grow more intelligent as the population and the complications of government increase. And a higher morality is even more essential. As civilization increases, as society becomes more complex, as labor-saving machinery is multiplied and the division of labor becomes more minute, the individual becomes more fractional and dependent. . . . And, as men become more dependent on each other, they should be able to rely more implicitly on each other. More complicated and multiplied relations require a more delicate conscience and a stronger sense of justice. And any failure in character or conduct under such conditions is farther reaching and more disastrous in its results.

Is our progress in morals and intelligence at all comparable to the growth of population? From 1870 to 1880 illiteracy decreased. While population increased thirty per cent, the illiterate increased only ten per cent. There were in the United States, in 1880, 1,908,801 illiterate voters, "genuine agnostics," who cannot write their own name. At present, *only* one voter in six is illiterate; but judging from a report of the Senate Committee on Education, the proportion will soon increase. That committee estimates the school population of the United States at 18,000,000, of which number "7,500,000 or *five-twelfths of the whole,* are growing up in absolute ignorance of the English alphabet." The nation's illiteracy has not been discussed, because it is not one of the perils which peculiarly threaten the West; but any one who would calculate our political horoscope must allow it great influence in connection with the baleful stars which are in the ascendant. But the danger which arises from the corruption of popular morals is much greater. The republics of Greece and Rome, and, if I mistake not, all the republics that have ever lived and died, were more intelligent at the end than at the beginning; but growing intelligence could not compensate decaying morals. What, then, is our moral progress? Are popular morals as sound as they were twenty, or even ten, years ago? There is, perhaps, no better index of general morality than Sabbath observance; and everybody knows there has been a great increase of Sabbath desecration in ten years. There was three times as much intoxicating liquor used per capita in the United States in 1883 as there was in 1840. Says the Rev. S. W. Dike: "It is safe to say that divorce has been doubled, in proportion to marriages or population, in most of the Northern States within thirty years. Present figures indicate a still greater increase." And President Woolsey, speaking of the United States, says: "On the whole, there can be little, if any question, that the ratio of divorces to marriages or to population exceeds that of any country in the Christian world." While the population increased thirty per cent from 1870 to 1880, the number of criminals in the United States increased 82.33 per cent. It looks very much as if existing tendencies were in the direction of the dead-line of vice. The city, wealth, socialism, intemperance, Mormonism, Romanism, and immigration are all increasing more rapidly than the population. *Are popular morals likely to improve under their increasing influence?*

2. The fundamental idea of popular government is the distribution of power. It has been the struggle of liberty for ages to wrest power from the hands of one or the few, and lodge it in the hands of the many. We have seen, in the foregoing discussion, that centralized power is rapidly growing. The "boss" makes his bargain, and sells his ten thousand or fifty thousand voters as if they were so many cattle. Centralized wealth is centralized power; and the capitalist and corporation find many ways to control votes. The liquor power controls thousands of votes in every considerable city. The president of the Mormon church casts, say, sixty thousand votes. The Jesuits are all under the command of one man in Washington. The Catholic vote is more or less perfectly controlled by the priests. That means that the Pope can dictate some hundreds of thousands of votes in the United States. Is there anything unrepublican in all this?

And we must remember that, if present tendencies continue, these figures will be greatly multiplied in the future. And not only is this immense power lodged in the hand of one man, which itself is perilous but it is wielded without the slightest reference to any policy or principle of government, solely in the interests of a church or a business, or for personal ends.

The result of a national election may depend on a single state; the vote of that state may depend on a single city; the vote of that city may depend on a "boss," or a capitalist, or a corporation; or the election may be decided, and the policy of the government may be reversed, by the socialist, or liquor, or Romish, or immigrant vote.

It matters not by what name we call the man who wields this centralized power—whether king, czar, pope, president, capitalist, or boss. Just so far as it is absolute and irresponsible, it is dangerous.

3. These several dangerous elements are singularly netted together, and serve to strengthen each other. It is not necessary to prove that any *one* of them is likely to destroy our national life, in order to show that it is imperiled. A man may die of wounds no one of which is fatal. No soberminded man can look fairly at the facts, and doubt that *together* these perils constitute an array which seriously threatens our free institutions; especially in view of the fact that their strength is concentrating in the West, where our defense is weakest.

These dangerous elements are now working, and will continue to work, incalculable harm and loss—moral, intellectual, social, pecuniary. But the supreme peril which will certainly come, eventually, and must probably be faced by multitudes now living, will arise, when the conditions having been fully prepared, some great industrial or other crisis precipitates an open struggle between the destructive and the conservative elements of society. As civilization advances, and society becomes more highly organized, commercial transactions will be more complex and immense. As a result, all business relations and industries will be more sensitive. Commercial distress in any great business center will the more surely create widespread disaster. Under such conditions, industrial paralysis is likely to occur from time to time, more general and more prostrating than any heretofore known. When such a commercial crisis has closed factories by the ten thousand, and wage workers have been thrown out of employment by the million; when the public lands, which hitherto at such times have afforded relief, are all exhausted; when our urban population has been multiplied several fold, and our Cincinnatis have become Chicagos, our Chicagos New Yorks, and our New York's Londons; when class antipathies are deepened; when socialistic organizations, armed and drilled, are in every city, and the ignorant and vicious power of crowded populations has fully found itself; when the corruption of city governments is grown apace; when crops fail, or some gigantic "corner" doubles the price of bread; with starvation in the home; with idle workmen gathered, sullen and desperate, in the saloons; with unprotected wealth at hand; with the tremendous forces of chemistry within easy reach; then, with *the opportunity, the means, the fit agents, the motives, the temptation to destroy, all brought into evil conjunction,* THEN will come the real test of our institutions, then will appear whether we are capable of self-government.

OUR CITIES, *John Habberton*

THE accusation that cities are "impersonal" had its roots in a contrast with the countryside, where human relationships were neighborly and sociable. Habberton makes this contrast explicit and also points to the dire consequences of urban impersonality. But considerable ambivalence about city living mars his vigorous denunciation.

A great city is a great sore—a sore which never can be cured.

The greater the city, the greater the sore.

It necessarily follows that New York, being the greatest city in the Union, is the vilest sore on our body politic.

If any one doubts it, let him live in New York awhile and keep his eyes and ears open.

The trouble about great cities is not that they have any impetus or influence especially their own, but that every one, from the vilest all the way up to the best, is compelled by circumstances of city life to often conduct his own daily walk and conversation on lines which are not entirely natural, and which never can be made so.

.   .   .   .

The first deadening influence of the city is that no one knows any one else. Of course every one has some acquaintances, and some people are said to be in the best society and to know everybody, but "everybody" is a relative term, and it never means as much in the largest city as it does in a village of a thousand people. The postman knows everybody by name, and so does the tax-collector and the man who brings you your gas

Excerpted from *Our Country's Future* (Chicago and Philadelphia: International Publishing Co., 1889), pp. 418–32, 442–43.

bill, but individual acquaintance—the touch of elbow—the touch of nature that makes the world akin, must not be looked for in any large city in the Union, least of all in New York, which in spite of two hundred and fifty years of existence, is still so new comparatively that almost all of its prominent citizens were born somewhere else. The names of prominent Americans who reside in New York will naturally occur to any one, yet it is quite safe to say that not one of these gentlemen know by sight and name, let alone by personal acquaintance, more than one person in five who reside within a two-minute walk of his house.

An ex-cabinet officer, a gentleman whose varied abilities have made him known throughout the civilized world, was once asked who was his neighbor on the right. The houses of the two men touched each other, as two houses must, in the city of New York, but the wise and largely acquainted gentleman was obliged to say that he did not know. When the questioner informed him that the person occupying the adjoining house was a notorious thief for whom the police had been long in search, he was astonished and shocked. Nevertheless, when he a few months afterward had his house robbed and drove about violently in a cab in search of the police captain of his precinct, it took him an hour to discover that the said police official resided next door to him on the left. Afterward he was teased about his lack of knowledge of his neighbors, and he admitted frankly that, although he was a man without "airs," and had always made it a custom to fraternize freely with his fellow-men, he knew but two individuals who resided on the same block with himself, and one of these was his own grocer, who occupied a store on the corner.

"If this is so with the green tree, what must it be with the dry?" Men whose sole business is to earn their daily living are glad to find a decent roof over their heads anywhere in a large city and drop into the best place they can find, regardless of who may be their neighbors, and utterly unable to devote any time to their neighbors, even should they be fortunate enough to become acquainted with them. Neighborhood feeling and sentiment, which is of incalculable benefit in all communities not thickly settled, has no influence whatever in a large city. A man may not only live in a house between two people of whom he knows nothing, but the great value of ground in the city of New York and the limited area has compelled the erection of a number of buildings known as "flat" and "apartment" and "tenement" houses, and very few men know the people who live under the same roof with themselves.

.   .   .   .

Of course, if such ignorance may come in the ordinary course of events regarding entirely respectable people, cities must form an admirable hiding-place for disreputable and dangerous characters of all sorts. The time was when a man detected in crime thought it advisable to run away from a large city. But nowadays he knows better. He stays as near home as possible, knowing that there are numberless opportunities for keeping himself entirely out of sight and out of mind of every one who ever knew him. Defaulters who have a great deal of money in their pockets, and also those who have none at all, occasionally find it desirable to go to Canada or Europe, but the rogue who has two or three thousand dollars to spare knows perfectly well that by keeping in-doors in New York he can absolutely escape detection. The police may know him by sight, but the keepers of boarding-houses do not, neither do their servants; and so long as he will remain in his room, have his meals sent to him, and take his exercise and outings only after dark in such disguise as any one can improvise at very short notice, he is entirely safe from detection. . . .

·   ·   ·   ·   ·   ·   ·   ·   ·   ·

Criminals when not actually plying their vocation generally go to large cities, for two reasons: first, to spend their ill-gotten gains in pleasure, and secondly, that as a rule cities are the best hiding-places.

For the same reason that causes desperate criminals to hide in the larger cities, all persons who have in their lives any features which they wish to conceal, find the cities preferable places of residence. One man of large property and some national prominence died a few years ago in the city in which he had been doing business for thirty years, and after he died it was discovered that he had nine wives living, from no one of whom had he ever separated through the formality of a divorce. Each of these nine women imagined herself his own and only wife. Any man, who has formed an undesirable alliance in business or in love or otherwise, knows that with very little trouble he can hide all traces of his mischief by going to a large city to live.

An inevitable consequence is that the number of able but undesirable characters who exist in the cities, having left other places for the good of those who are left behind, have a depressing influence upon the moral atmosphere of other classes of residents. Men meet men whom they never saw before, and whom they are obliged to judge entirely by appearance and professions. It is the same in business as it is in society. Not a year passes in which some adventurer does not impose himself for a time upon the best society of New York and of other cities. And although it would seem that his antecedents might easily be discovered upon the basis of such information as he may feel obliged to give about himself, the fact remains that society is "taken in" quite as often as banks and business men and private individuals. . . .

·   ·   ·   ·   ·   ·   ·   ·   ·   ·

These smart scamps, who are a hundred times as numerous as the newspaper disclosures would lead the public to imagine, have a terribly demoralizing influence upon the young men who flock to the city from all parts of the rural districts as well as upon those who are brought up in the city. To see a rascal succeed has a bad effect upon any one. Even the most righteous man will mournfully quote from Scripture that "the wicked shall flourish as the green bay tree"; that "their eyes stand out with fatness; they have more than heart can wish," where the respectable man has to lie awake nights to devise ways and means of paying his coal-bill and avoiding trouble with his landlord. Business enterprises containing any amount of promise are organized, forced upon the public by smart schemers of whom no one knows anything, and all of them succeed in obtaining a great deal of money. When discovery comes, as of course it must come sooner or later, the villain never makes restitution to any extent and is never adequately punished for his crime. So, the citizen who pretends to be respectable, but always has an eye out for the main chance, is moved by such examples to see whether he cannot do something sharp himself, and get away before the crash comes.

Society in large cities is said to be exclusive. It must be, for its own protection. It cannot possibly be too exclusive. People with and without letters of introduction succeed in forming acquaintances, becoming part of one or another social set, even get into the churches, open bank accounts, go into business, and a year or two afterward are discovered to have antecedents which would make a person of ordinary respectability hold up his hands in horror. Such occurrences have been so common, and the individuals concerned have so often been not only men but women, that the exclusiveness of city society extends even to the churches and school-rooms. The half-grown child attending a public or private school is warned against making any acquaintances whatever except with the children of families whom its parents already know. The member of a church may have a stranger shown into his pew again and again on Sundays, and extend to him the courtesy of an open prayerbook or hymnal, but in self-defence he is compelled to stop at that. The cordiality, freedom of speech, and general recognition, which is the custom in small towns and in rural districts throughout the world, is denied the prudent inhabitant of a city, no matter how hearty his inclination may be to extend a welcoming hand to every one whom he may meet. . . .

.   .   .   .

Nowhere in the world are there more charitable hearts with plenty of money behind them than in large cities, yet nowhere else is there more suffering. Your next-door neighbor may be starving to death and you not know anything about it. You know nothing of his comings and nothing of his goings; he knows nothing of you, and if he has any spirit whatever, and any respect for himself, he would rather apply to the police or to the authorities in charge of the poor than to the people living nearest to him. . . .

.　　.　　.　　.　　.　　.　　.　　.　　.　　.

As nobody knows anybody in the large cities, what is called the floating population have everything their own way, each one for himself. Business wrongs that would not be tolerated for an instant in a smaller community are perpetrated with entire impunity in the large cities. The poorer classes have no strong friend or acquaintance to complain to. Were they in a smaller place they would know some one; probably they would know everybody of any consequence, and also be known, and could quickly bring public sentiment to their aid, but in a large city there is no such opportunity. The only hope of the oppressed is in the courts, which always are overcrowded with business, and can give very little time to any one, and in the press, which is also overcrowded with work, and should not be charged with this sort of responsibility.

Temptation will exist wherever humanity is found, but for a concentration of all temptations, graded to suit all capacities of human weakness, the great city stands pre-eminent. There is no vice that cannot be committed in it—committed with reasonable assurance that it will not be discovered. A man whose habits are apparently correct, who has no known vices, whose daily manner with his fellow-men seems all that it should be, may with entire safety change his manner at night, and re-enact the drama of Dr. Jekyll and Mr. Hyde. It is worse than that. He not only may, but in a great many instances he does. . . .

.　　.　　.　　.　　.　　.　　.　　.　　.　　.

The amount of suffering that exists in all large cities merely through enforced conditions of life passes power of expression. No one has ever yet been able to do the subject justice. Many who have worked among the poor have lost life and hope, and mind itself, in contemplation of the suffering and sorrow which they have witnessed and been unable to relieve. To attempt to care for the poor of a large city affects one very much like an effort to pour water into a sieve; the demand is continual, yet nothing seems to be effected.

Almost everywhere outside of the cities it is assumed at the beginning that those who suffer through their poverty in large cities are either indolent or vicious. A more cruel mistake could not possibly be made. There are many idlers in any large city, as a matter of course, but the great majority of the people work hard to keep soul and body together. . . .

.   .   .   .

A full half of the population of the largest city in the Union reside in tenement houses. The tenement house at best is unfit for human residence if the people who inhabit it expect to enjoy good health, and if the children who are part of almost every family are expected to grow and develop properly in body and soul. Yet the bald fact is that more than half a million of the inhabitants of this country live on several square miles of land in one single city. Land is costly, builders' work is expensive; the cheapest-built houses cost a great deal of money, and consequently the space in them must be divided and subdivided with great skill and detail if the poorer classes are to find habitation at all.

Almost all of this half million people are honest, hard workers. The heads of families are among the first to go to work in the morning and among the last to go to their homes at night. They are those who work for the smallest wages and do the hardest work. They and their families need just as much food to support life as any of the well-to-do portion of the population. But in any large city the necessities of life are costly, and they are particularly so in our largest city. . . .

.   .   .   .

. . . There are Americans of good name and good family now serving in the commoner mechanical capacities in the city of New York, and only a little while ago it was discovered that the wife of a gallant Major-General, who served the United States faithfully during the late unpleasantness, was "living out" as a domestic servant. It is not a result of poverty, misfortune, sickness or anything of the kind. All those horrors are the results, first of all, of city life, of living where no one knows his own neighbors and where the person who falls into embarrassments or is overwhelmed by misfortune has no one to whom to turn, and takes to anything at short notice and in utter desperation, to keep the wolf from the door.

Cities should be suppressed, but that is impossible. They should be properly policed by persons competent to discover and report those most in need of assistance; but that also seems impossible. The only chance left seems to be that the larger the city the greater shall be the missionary work done in it by all denominations. . . . Religious people, regardless of differences of creed, can find no better work in large cities than to search out the needy and endeavor to lift their feet out of the mire and put them in a dry place, to quote from the inspired psalmist in one of his most eloquent passages.

THE LANGUAGE OF THE FENCE, *H. W. Gibson*

> ONE accusation against the city is that it is the source
> of the mass media—a potentially corrupting
> influence on the young. TV, comics, radio, advertising,
> and pornographic magazines have been the chief
> villains in this modern drama. The town
> fence as a communication medium apparently was
> an earlier object of opprobrium.

. . . Parental willingness to shift responsibility upon other shoulders for the instruction of their boys in matters of sex [reveals] an attitude of indifference that is staggering, as well as appalling.

In talking with parents upon this subject they exhibit an attitude of fear lest their boy be not old enough to understand. It is better for parents to tell the facts to their boy two years too early than ten minutes too late, for if the wrong boy comes into the boy's life ten minutes before father or mother becomes his confidential adviser it is too late. Already the author of the "language of the fence" has poisoned his mind. The fact that one hundred and forty-four boys received their first information in sex matters from other boys instead of their parents is a serious indictment against parenthood. "Oh, why didn't my parents tell me!" is the pitiful wail of the habit-bound boy. "Ah, how fortunate for me!" is the satanic reply of the quack who harvests a rich crop of unfortunate students of this fence language. Who is the real sinner, the boy or his parent?

"The City Beautiful" agitation has aroused civic conscience to such an extent that even if the bill board has not been done away with, it is at least better censored. In many cities ordinances forbid the posting of vulgar show bills or scenes depicting murder, but the "language of the fence," in the terms of advertising, is not yet as clean or as honest as it should be. False statements concerning food products and liquids are attractively presented on bill boards which the boy reads on his way to school or work. In many cities the bill board is still the corrupter of morals. Thrilling lithographs in front of moving-picture shows excite scores of boys to criminal acts. These are but other forms of "the lan-

Reprinted from *Boyology* (New York: Association Press, 1919), pp. 192–93.

guage of the fence," greatly influencing the morals of every boy who stands and reads. Many sermons and heart-to-heart talks will be required before the boy will forget the language lesson of the fence.

How can we abolish this school of "fence language"? The destruction of chalk or the voting of bill-board ordinances "won't do the trick." It can only be done through the boy himself. A movement for clean speech, clean sport, and clean living has been quietly influencing thousands of boys in our public schools. Just as boys are responsible for the existence of the language of the fence, so must they be made responsible for its abolishment. . . .

POVERTY AND THE IMMIGRANT,
Robert Hunter

> AS he walked around the streets teeming with
> immigrants, Hunter tells us that he felt
> "an utter stranger in my own city." Although his
> book appeared in 1912, during the flood
> tide of "new" immigration, Americans had been
> having this experience with their cities
> at least since the explosion of Irish into Boston in
> the early 1850's. Hunter, however, is more
> understanding of the newcomers than most natives—
> some of whom moved to the suburban outskirts
> of towns to keep their distance.

In the poorest quarters of many great American cities and industrial communities one is struck by a most peculiar fact—the poor are almost entirely foreign born. Great colonies, foreign in language, customs, habits, and institutions, are separated from each other and from the distinctly American groups on national or racial lines. By crossing the Bowery one leaves behind him the great Jewish colony made up of Russians, Poles, and Roumanians and passes into Italy; to the northeast lies a little Germany; to the southwest a colony of Syrians; to the west lies an Irish community, a settlement of negroes, and a remnant of the old native American stock; to the south lie a Chinese and a Greek colony. On Manhattan alone, either on the extreme west side or the extreme east side, there are other colonies of the Irish, the Jews, and the Italians, and,

Excerpted from *Poverty* (New York: Macmillan, 1912), pp. 261–67, 290–98, reprinted by permission.

in addition, there is a large colony of Bohemians. In Chicago there are the same foreign poor. To my own knowledge there are four Italian colonies, two Polish, a Bohemian, an Irish, a Jewish, a German, a negro, a Chinese, a Greek, a Scandinavian, and other colonies. So it is also in Boston and many other cities. In New York alone there are more persons of German descent than persons of native descent, and the German element is larger than in any city of Germany except Berlin. There are nearly twice as many Irish as in Dublin, about as many Jews as in Warsaw, and more Italians than in Naples or Venice. No other great nation has a widespread poverty which is foreign to its own native people except in so far as it exists in distant colonies in foreign lands. Our foreign colonies are to an important extent in the cities of our own country. On a small scale we have Russia's poverty, Poland's poverty, Italy's poverty, Hungary's poverty, Bohemia's poverty—and what other nation's have we not? England, France, Germany, or Italy may speak almost solely of her native poor, her only poor, the poor of her own blood. In those countries the rich and the poor may meet together, talk together, worship together. In addition to all the elemental bonds of union there are many others growing out of national life. In certain large cities of this country almost everything separates "the classes and the masses" except the feeling which inheres in the word "humanity." The rich and well-to-do are mostly Americans; the poor are mostly foreign, drawn from among the miserable of every nation. The citizens and the slaves of Greece were scarcely more effectually separated.

To live in one of these foreign communities is actually to live on foreign soil. The thoughts, feelings, and traditions which belong to the mental life of the colony are often entirely alien to an American. The newspapers, the literature, the ideals, the passions, the things which agitate the community, are unknown to us except in fragments. During the meat riots on the east side of New York City two years ago, I could understand nothing, as I stood among the mobs of rioters, except that heads were being broken, windows smashed, and that the people were in a frenzy. A few years ago, when living in Chicago in a colony of Bohemians and Hungarians who had been thrown out of employment by the closing of a great industry, I went about among the groups clustered in the streets or gathered in the halls. I felt the unrest, the denunciation, the growing brutality, but I was unable to discuss with them their grievances, to sympathize with them, or to oppose them. I was an utter stranger in my own city. A fire was started by some one; a few buildings were burned. I watched the embittered and angered faces light up with pleasure, but only by such expressions of feeling could I understand what agitated the people of this foreign land. In London, there is an English people; in Paris, a French people; in Moscow, a Russian people. In all these countries there are the masters and the workmen; the rich and the poor, separated by wealth, by position, and by place of dwelling. But in the large cities of America, there are many other things which separate the rich and the poor. Language, institutions, customs, and even religion separate the native and the foreigner. It is this separation which makes the problem of poverty in America more difficult of solution than that of any other nation.

The movement of the poor from one nation to another is one of the astonishing phenomena of modern society. The poor of any country find it possible to move from one extreme of the world to another extreme of the world in quest of better economic or social conditions. The French Canadians move backward and forward between this country and Canada. The poor Italian peasantry of Sicily and southern Italy are even able to come in great numbers from their country to work here during the summer, returning home again for the winter season. In 1898 sixty-six thousand Italian emigrants returned to the port of Genoa. The poorest of the Jews of Russia, the most oppressed peasantry of Asiatic countries, are able to come to the United States to be freed from oppression, or in the hope that by so doing their material condition will be bettered. Rapid and cheap transportation has made possible these remarkable migrations. Nothing shows more clearly than this the change which has taken place in the status of the worker; he is no longer slave or serf, fixed to master or soil; he is free to go where he will, but he has far less security of livelihood than formerly; he is propertyless and proletarian. As a result of these migrations of working men and women national barriers have been beaten down, prejudices overcome, and an intermingling of races and nationalities has ensued in the same country, city, or village, which would have been inconceivable fifty years ago.

While there is a great movement of population from all parts of the old world to all parts of the new, the migration to the United States is the largest and the most conspicuous. Literally speaking, millions of foreigners have established colonies in the very hearts of our urban and industrial communities. For reasons of poverty their colonies are usually established in the poorest, the most criminal, the most politically debauched, and the vicious portions of our cities. These colonies often make up the main portion of our so-called "slums." In Baltimore 77 per cent of the total population of the slums was in the year 1894 of foreign birth or parentage. In Chicago the foreign element was 90 per cent; in New York 95 per cent, and in Philadelphia, 91 per cent. In recent years the flow of immigrants to the cities, where they are not needed, instead of to those parts of the country where they are needed, has been steadily increasing. Sixty-nine per cent of the present immigration avows itself as determined to settle either in the great cities or in certain communities of the four great industrial states, Massachusetts, New York, Pennsylvania, and Illinois. According to their own statements, nearly 60 per cent of the Russian and Polish Jews intend to settle in the largest cities. As a matter of fact, those who actually do settle in cities are even more numerous than this percentage indicates. As the class of immigrants, drawn from eastern and southern Europe, Russia, and Asia, come in increasing numbers to the United States, the tendency to settle in cities likewise increases. For many reasons the centripetal force of the foreign colonies seems irresistible. Already these great foreign cities in our slums have become wildernesses of neglect, almost unexplored and almost unknown to us. Even the settlements touch but few of their vast number. The padrone, enslaving industrially the Italians, the politician, seeking selfish ends, the Jew sweater, and the owner, or agent, of insanitary tenements are the ones who teach the immigrant what America is and what it stands for. Each new shipload increases the profits of these classes, adds to the population of the great cities and colonies, and incidentally adds to its misery.

It is amazing to consider the extent of the foreign element in this country. . . . In many towns nearly one-half of the population is foreign. About 37 per cent of the people of New York City are foreign born or of foreign parentage. In the latter sense, about 80 per cent of the population of Chicago is foreign, in Milwaukee nearly 85 per cent, in Fall River about the same per cent. In no less than thirty-three of our largest cities the foreign population is larger than the native. . . .

. . . Despite the fact that it has been our national custom to spare no expense to educate our citizens, about half the foreigners in the slums are illiterate. And we are presented yearly with an enormous number of adults—this year there will be approximately one million immigrants—a large proportion of whom are illiterate. When they arrive after their fourteenth year, it is very unlikely that they will ever become literate. In a political democracy, where it is of the utmost importance that every citizen should understand the institutions of his country, and should be prepared to by reading for intelligent voting, the illiteracy, which extends to over six millions of our population, should be a matter of concern. The relation of illiteracy to crime is not fully known, but some figures gathered in Massachusetts show that, with the increase of illiteracy, there is an increase in the number of commitments to penal institutions for every crime except that of drunkenness. . . . It is true of every country—it is true of purely American communities—that the poor supply an excess of criminals and deepndents. It is one of the natural results of poverty. . . .

The heaviest burden of the immense immigration is, however, not borne by the state, which, after all, can, when necessary, afford to bear even larger burdens of this character. The real weight is borne by the poorest classes of our community (except those in the almshouses); namely, the unskilled workers. Unskilled labor is already too plentiful; nothing shows it more than the conditions which exist in many parts of the country; in those places where unskilled laborers might profitably themselves, the recent immigrants refuse to go, and instead herd in factory and mining towns and in large cities, pulling like a heavy weight upon that class of laborers which is already too plentiful there. In times of industrial depression, such as we are facing now, the amount of unskilled labor vastly over-supplies the demand for it, and the distress, by reason of enemployment at such periods, becomes a calamity of national importance. We have seen elsewhere how serious the problem of unemployment is at all times. It is nowhere so great as among the classes which are increased by recent immigration. A surplus of laborers enables the meanest employer to oppress his workmen to the very limit of endurance. . . . Carroll D. Wright and Professor Richmond Mayo-Smith have shown how important a factor this over-supply of labor is in creating industrial depressions. The relation of immigration to the oversupply of labor, which, in part, causes industrial depressions, can be clearly seen. Even in times of increasing prosperity and of unusual industrial activity, the unskilled workers are not permitted to profit by the better times. Immigration instantly increases, the labor market is progressively overcrowded, and the wages in unskilled trades are thereby reduced to the lowest limit.

. . . When women come, they also commonly work at such employments as they find open to them. I have seen hundreds of women employed in the stock yards, working in great tubs of blood and entrails, employed in this manner week in and week out, leaving their children at home uncared for in order to assist men in their fight for livelihood. . . . The fear of poverty intensifies the competition between the different nationalities, between the native and the foreigner, between the women and the men, between adults and the children, so that it is absolutely impossible for the unskilled classes to successfully resist oppression. They will work any hours, at any speed, and for almost any wages; they will suffer the direst poverty; they will underfeed their children and themselves; they will sleep in the most insanitary hovels of factory towns or in the darkest rooms of the worst tenements in the cities. The Italians are perhaps as successful as any, and succeed because they are willing to accept the lowest standard of living, the greatest poverty, and the highest morality. It can almost be said that many who win in this competitive struggle win at death.

It is a competition of standards, and the lowest standard prevails. Among the common laborers in coal mining and in the clothing and textile trades, this competition is always too intense. It amounts, at times, almost to a race war, so that the bitterest hatred often exists between the different nationalities. The recent pitched battle between fifty Italian laborers and seventy Irish rock-drillers in one of the Subway pits is an example of what often occurs between the conflicting races. . . .

The tragedy which results from this surplus of labor was strikingly shown in the work of a sculptor, exhibited at the World's Fair in Chicago. It is the custom in some places, in England, for instance, for the foremen of the great factories to go out in the morning to the gate where the workmen, seeking employment, are gathered, and to throw out tickets to the number of employees needed. The group represents an intense struggle to obtain one of these tickets. The man fortunate enough to get it is the central figure. He holds it high above his head, resistant, but looks with compassion upon the struggling ones about him. A withered old man clings to him, begging for the ticket; a youth behind is plotting to seize it; a woman with babe in arms, trampled under the feet of the others, strives to protect the child; a tiny lad, with a wolfish hunger in his face, endeavors to clamber up on others in the hope of seizing the ticket. Let him, who will, go about the factory districts of the country and see this thing enacted in real life, not so obviously dramatical but with agony that is actual. It will then be easy for him to question a national policy of unrestricted immigration.

The political consequences are perhaps out of our province, although they are becoming more and more serious as the foreign colonies become an increasing source of power to corrupt politicians. The greater the poverty, the greater is the dependence of the foreigner upon either padrone or politicians. It has been recently shown that naturalization papers can be had for $5; and a vote means a job. The present methods of naturalization outrage the principles and ideals which formerly under-lay this legal process of initiating the foreigner into the full rights of American citizenship. At present it involves no qualifications on the part of the immigrant and becomes simply another method of encouraging venal voting. It is not easy to say to what extent the foreign elements are responsible for the political corruption in those sections in which they predominate. Our own history is an unclean one. The native element is guilty of the most dangerous political corruption. The Americans are the ones principally who buy up the state legislatures and city councils, who bribe the representatives of the people, and steal every privilege which yields a profit. The Irish-Americans are mainly responsible for bribe-taking because they are the successful politicians. The recently ar-rived immigrants are an unknown quality, but they are learning the game. Their ignorance and poverty make them easy tools. It is undoubtedly true that they play, though perhaps innocently, into the hands of the politicians, and temporarily, at any rate, enhance their power. The conditions in certain sections of New York City and Chicago, and especially in certain sections of Pennsylvania prove this beyond question. Whether or not the dangers to democratic government, which reside in the present political corruption, can be as clearly demonstrated to these foreign elements as to the native element, and whether or not they will respond to the higher appeal, are momentous questions. The personal power of ward politicians and saloon keepers and its appeal to the immediate selfishness of poor immigrants is a mighty political force, perhaps too mighty for the higher appeal to overcome until the mass of immigrants have been sufficiently educated and informed to be reached by the minority from which reform and revolt always emanate. The minority cannot build up a machine; they cannot gain their ends through personal power; they are necessarily dependent to a large extent upon public appeals and literature to make evils known and to demonstrate clearly their proposed reforms. The love and devotion which many of the immigrants manifest for democracy is beautiful and pathetic; but their ignorance prevents them from knowing that their votes commonly support the very men who are selling themselves and their country to the most sinister *Enemies of the Republic.*

THE SEXUAL IMMORALITY OF GIRLS,
W. I. Thomas and F. Znaniecki

> IN their famous monograph, *The Polish Peasant in
> Europe and America,* Thomas and Znaniecki
> made extensive use of documents as
> data. Their interpretation of the court records
> reproduced in the following section is
> representative of how sociologists during the flood tide
> of immigration viewed the deleterious impact of
> the city on immigrants from European countrysides.
> The court records, of course, also reflect perspectives.

101. *Nettie Wieczorek.* "November 16, 1914. Mother died when she was 5 years old. Father married again a few months later. She says her stepmother beats and abuses her, makes her work too hard. The girl ran away from home 3 times, the last time Oct. 14, 1914 [had been sleeping in a toilet]. She does not want to go back." She was given 4 positions as domestic servant within 5 months.

"April 16, 1915, Mrs. Brennan telephoned that Nettie had gone out the previous night and had not returned. April 22, 1915, called at home of Mrs. Brennan where Nettie formerly worked. She refused to take Nettie back as girl was too great a trial and did not have clean personal

Excerpted from *The Polish Peasant in Europe and America* (New York: Alfred A. Knopf, 1927; first edition published in 1918), pp. 1804–1808, 1817–1821. Reprinted by permission.

habits. Said that Nettie had run away on prearranged plan. . . . [A new place was found but Nettie left after 4 months.] August 9, 1915, Nettie found by probation officer in South Chicago in home of Della Fox, delinquent ward of the court, and taken to the Detention Home. August 10, 1915, took Nettie to see doctor . . . who returned unfavorable report [hymen recently broken]. August 25, 1915, talked with Nettie at Detention Home; also talked with Miss Culver, who said that Nettie had a very violent temper and had had a tantrum at the Home, where it took 3 persons to control her. Later I called at Nettie's home and talked with her stepmother who said that Nettie is very hard to control."

The matter was referred to the court. Nettie had run away with a girl and was out all Sunday night. She admitted having met 2 men and had immoral relations with one of them. As it seemed that the other girl might have been to blame, Nettie was given a choice between housework and an institution. She preferred housework and returned to the place where she had been working. "Oct. 26, 1915, I talked to Mrs. Brennan. She stated Nettie has been staying out very late, till 11 and 11:30 P. M., that boys call for her and her thoughts and talk are of men." She was spending all of her wages. One Sunday night a week after the above conversation Nettie failed to return. The stepmother knows nothing of her whereabouts.

"Jan. 3, 1916, Nettie's father called at office, felt very badly over Nettie's disappearance [blamed the court]. He feels she is dead. . . . The police were unable to get any trace of her. Jan. 26, 1916, case in court. Nettie returned home to her father about 10 days ago and he refused to take her. But the next night he did take her in and insisted that she come to court and explain her conduct. She has a very comfortable home with her father, if she behaved. Has a stepmother who seems a very good woman. But Nettie tells me she has been soliciting for 3 months on the streets downtown. It seems almost incredible to me, yet she seems to know all the routine and the ways, mentions several 'rich hotels' where they had 2 beds in a room with bath connected. Said she would go in without any baggage at all and clerks would register them as man and wife. She had no permanent room in the three months, would just use the room the man had engaged for her for the rest of the night. When she did not have a room she would use the money she had for a less expensive room.

"Court: Did you want to do this sort of thing?

"Nettie: Why no, I did not.

"Q. Who first induced you to do that?

"A. Della Fox.

[Probation officer.] "She had gone down to the Beach with Della one time and she said the other day she did not want to do housework because it was so much easier to make money that way.

"Q. How much money have you been given that way?

"A. Three dollars and five dollars was the most.

[Probation officer] "She told her story so complacently, I really believe she needs training."

Nettie was unable to give the name of any man with whom she had associated or of any hotel in which she had stayed. She said they were all down-town and high class hotels. She was sent to the House of the Good Shepherd, with her father's consent.

102. *Marien Stepanek*. Marien was arrested for acting "obstreperous" with another girl in a railway waiting room. She had no underclothing on when arrested [in June]. She was 16 years old, had left home before Easter and had been going much to shows and moving picture theaters. She told a police woman that she had been drugged on the North side and carried to a room by two men on different nights. She had been in the habit of receiving mail at the General Delivery and frequented the Boston Store with a man about 45 years of age whom she claimed was her husband.

Marien said she had "no fault to find" with her home, her father and mother were kind to her but she met a lady by the name of Le Mar and told her she lived in Milwaukee. "And she asked me to live with her, said she was getting a divorce from her husband, and I stayed with her for awhile . . . assisted her with the work." When asked where she met her girl friend she said: "Met her at the Boston Store and did not want to talk to her. And she came up to me and she wanted me to fix it up for her. Said she wanted to get away from home and said I should call up her mother and tell her that she was doing housework and told me to talk as if I was an elderly lady, and I went and did that."

The following letter was received from her while she was away: "Dear Mother, I am feeling fine. Everything is all right, don't worry about me. I am leading high life because I am an actress. I got swell clothes and everything, you wouldn't know me. I had Clara down town one day I was out with the manager. She had a nice time. . . . I never had just nice times in all my life. Everybody says that I am pretty. I paid 65 dollars for my suit and 5 dollars had [hat], 6 dollars shoe 3 gloves 2 dollar underwar 5 dollar corest. Know I have hundred dollars in the bank but I want you to write a letter and say youll forgive me for not telling the truht but I will explain better when I see you and will return home for the sake of the little ones. I will bring a hundred dollars home to you and will come home very time I can its to expensive to liv at a hotel now sent the letter to me this way Genarel Devilery Miss Marion Stephan."

Her father testified: "After Easter got a letter from her something like that one only more in it. She was rich and everything else, which is not so. So she says answer me quick as you can because I go to Milwaukee tomorrow. And I answer it right away to come home as soon as possible. Thought maybe the letter would reach her and heard nothing more until 3 weeks ago and then this letter come and I begging her to come home and be a good girl. She come home and asked if wanted to stay home now and she feel very happy that she is home and thought maybe she would behave. . . . Next day she said she was going for her clothes . . . and I says I go with you. And I could not go and left my boy and girl to go with her Sunday. And she left them in the park and did not come home. Then she was back again Tuesday and in the evening when I come home from work she was not there. . . ."

Marien said she kept company with men for quite a while, giving three names, but she denied immoral relations with any of them. She said she had been going out with another fellow "but he is a gentleman in every way."

"Court: With whom have you had immoral relations?

"A. Cannot remember.

"Q. Have you been to a hotel at any time since you have been away?

"A. Been to a hotel one time with Helen . . . and a girl, Freda Jones. She lives under a different name, Freda Jarvis. . . .

"Q. Did you hear anybody offer $2 at this hotel?

"A. I heard that what Freda said. She was kind of sore. . . . She said about it: 'What they think I am anyhow, stingy fools. Think I am doing anything for $2. . . . Helen and I laughed at her. . . .

"Q. What did you understand by that?

"A. I understood what she meant by it. . . .

"Q. What did you mean by the statement that you are leading a 'high life'?

"A. Meant had been to cabarets and dance halls. Been going to Morrison Ball room . . . and I went to the 'Booster's Club,' that's the old Morrison place."

Marien was sent to the reform school in Geneva but released in September, as her home conditions were good.

.   .   .   .

The sexual immorality of most of the girls here described is thus in most cases clearly a part of a generally unorganized life, and would be as "natural" as any commonplace action if it did not imply, at least in its beginnings, some revolt against existing inhibitions. We have even very little proof that these inhibitions are ever internal and not merely external. . . . The element of revolt against the drudgery and coercion of home life is very strong. Even if the home is not actually bad there is little in it to attract the girl, for the difference between her own education and the traditions of her parents produces an estrangement which prevents an adequate satisfaction of the desire for response, and in view of the traditional supremacy claimed by the older generation, there is no chance of obtaining the recognition which her vanity craves, developed as it is by the continual contact with outsiders. . . .

.   .   .   .

The conclusion as to the significance of sexual immorality in girls of the second generation is perfectly obvious. Illicit sexual tendencies are simply a component—sometimes predominant, oftener subordinate—of a powerful desire for new experience and for general excitement which under the given conditions cannot be satisfied in socially permitted ways. It depends in some measure on individual temperament whether in a given case this desire for new experience will be successfully counteracted by a desire for security which tends to make the girl stay in the beaten path and follow the rules laid down by society. But this depends also, perhaps in a still larger measure, on the question what attractions are offered by society to those who stay in the beaten path. And these attractions are certainly neither many nor strong for the daughter of a Polish immigrant. . . .

.   .   .   .

Perhaps the girl would settle down unrevoltingly to this steady life, however dull, if the apparent possibilities of an entirely different life, full of excitement, pleasure, luxury and showing-off were not continually displayed before her eyes in an American city. Shop windows, theaters, the press, street life with its display of wealth, beauty and fashion, all this forms too striking a contrast to the monotony of the prospect which awaits her if she remains a "good girl." If she felt definitely and irremediably shut off from this "high life" by practically impassable class barriers, as a peasant girl in Europe feels, she might look at all this show of luxury as upon an interesting spectacle with no dream of playing a role in it herself. But even aside from the idea of democracy—which though it does not mean much to her politically, teaches her to think that the only social differences between people are differences of wealth—she feels that some small part at last of this gorgeousness actually is within her reach, and her imagination pictures to her indefinite possibilities of further advance in the future. . . .

THE PROFESSIONAL IDEOLOGY OF SOCIAL
PATHOLOGIES, *C. Wright Mills*

> AS late as the 1940s, some sociologists were also
> condemning "the city," although in somewhat
> more measured prose than that used by
> non-sociologists whose rural biases they shared.
> C. Wright Mills's analysis of "social problems" textbooks
> did not destroy this perspective in future textbooks,
> but he helped to further the view among
> his own readers that industrialization—
> at least in the American "free enterprise"
> variety—has unfortunate consequences for
> people regardless of where they live. As
> an undergraduate, Mills was influenced by such
> institutional economists as Thorstein Veblen,
> and as a graduate student at the University of
> Wisconsin he reacted against agrarian
> liberalism as exemplified by such men as E. A. Ross
> and John Gillin. His own version and critique
> of urban life will become clearer in the selection
> from *White Collar*, which appears later in this reader.

An analysis of textbooks in the field of social disorganization reveals a common style of thought which is open to social imputation. By
grasping the social orientation of this general perspective we can understand why thinkers in this field should select and handle problems in the
manner in which they have.

By virtue of the mechanism of sales and distribution, textbooks tend
to embody a content agreed upon by the academic group using them. In
some cases texts have been written only after an informal poll was
taken of professional opinion as to what should be included and other
texts are consulted in the writing of a new one. Since one test of their
success is wide adoption, the very spread of the public for which they
are written tends to insure a textbook tolerance of the commonplace. Although the conceptual framework of a pathologist's textbook is not usually
significantly different from that of such monographs as he may write, this
essay is not concerned with the "complete thought" or with the "intentions" of individual authors; it is a study of a professional ideology vari-

Excerpted from *American Journal of Sociology*, Vol. 49 (1943), pp. 165–80,
by courtesy of the University of Chicago Press.

ously exhibited in a set of textbooks. Yet, because of its persistent importance in the development of American sociology and its supposed proximity to the social scene, "social pathology" seems an appropriate point of entry for the examination of the style of reflection and the social-historical basis of American sociology.

The level of abstraction which characterizes these texts is so low that often they seem to be empirically confused for lack of abstraction to knit them together. They display bodies of meagerly connected facts, ranging from rape in rural districts to public housing, and intellectually sanction this low level of abstraction. The "informational" character of social pathology is linked with a failure to consider total social structures. Collecting and dealing in a fragmentary way with scattered problems and facts of milieux, these books are not focused on larger stratifications or upon structured wholes. Such an omission may not be accounted for merely in terms of a general "theoretical weakness." Such structural analyses have been available; yet they have not been attended to or received into the tradition of this literature. American sociologists have often asserted an interest in the "correlation of the social sciences"; nevertheless academic departmentalization may well have been instrumental in atomizing the problems which they have addressed. Sociologists have always felt that "not many representatives of the older forms of social science are ready to admit that there is a function for sociology." However, neither lack of theoretical ability nor restrictive channeling through departmentalization constitutes a full explanation of the low level of abstraction and the accompanying failure to consider larger problems of social structure.

If the members of an academic profession are recruited from similar social contexts and if their backgrounds and careers are relatively similar, there is a tendency for them to be uniformly set for some common perspective. The common conditions of their profession often seem more important in this connection than similarity of extraction. Within such a generally homogeneous group there tend to be fewer divergent points of view which would clash over the meaning of facts and thus give rise to interpretations on a more theoretical level.

The relatively homogeneous extraction and similar careers of American pathologists is a possible factor in the low level of abstraction characterizing their work. All the authors considered (except one, who was foreign born) were born in small towns, or on farms near small towns, three-fourths of which were in states not industrialized during the youth of the authors. The social circles and strata in which they have severally moved are quite homogeneous; all but five have participated in similar "reform" groups and "societies" of the professional and business classes. By virtue of their being college professors (all but three are known to have the Ph.D.), of the similar type of temporary positions (other than academic) which they have held, of the sameness of the "societies" to which they have belonged and of the social positions of the persons whom they have married, the assertion as regards general similarity of social extraction, career, and circles of contact seems justified.

.   .   .   .

The "organic" orientation of liberalism has stressed all those social factors which tend to a harmonious balance of elements. There is a minimization of chances for action in a social milieu where "there is always continuity with the past, and not only with any one element only of the past, but with the whole interacting organism of man." In seeing everything social as continuous process, changes in pace and revolutionary dislocations are missed or are taken as signs of the "pathological." The formality and the assumed unity implied by "the mores" also lower the chances to see social chasms and structural dislocations.

Typically, pathologists have not attempted to construct a structural whole. When, however, they do consider totalities, it is in terms of such concepts as "society," "the social order," or "the social organization," "the mores and institutions," and "American culture." Four things should be noted about their use of such terms: (*a*) The terms represent undifferentiated entities. Whatever they may indicate, it is systematically homogeneous. Uncritical use of such a term as "the" permits a writer the hidden assumption in politically crucial contexts of a homogenous and harmonious whole. The large texture of "the society" will take care of itself, it is somehow and in the long run harmonious, it has a "strain toward consistency" running through it; or, if not this, then only the co-operation of all is needed, or perhaps even a right moral feeling is taken as a solution. (*b*) In their formal emptiness these terms are commensurate with the low level of abstraction. Their formality facilitates the empirical concern with "everyday" problems of (community) milieu. (*c*) In addition to their "descriptive" use, such terms are used normatively. The "social" becomes a good term when it is used in ethical polemics against "individualism" or against such abstract moral qualities as "selfishness," lack of "altruism," or of "antisocial" sentiments. "Social" is conceived as a "co-operative" "sharing" of something or as "conducive to the general welfare." The late eighteenth-century use of "society" as against "state" by the rising bourgeoisie had already endowed "society" with a "democratic" tinge which this literature transmits. (*d*) There is a strong tendency for the term "society" to be practically assimilated to, or conceived largely in terms of, primary groups and small homogeneous communities. Such a conception typically characterizes the literature within our purview. In explaining it, we come upon an element that is highly important in understanding the total perspective.

The basis of "stability," "order," or "solidarity" is not typically analyzed in these books, but a conception of such a basis is implicitly used and sanctioned, for some normative conception of a socially "healthy" and stable organization is involved in the determination of "pathological" conditions. "Pathological" behavior is not discerned in a *structural* sense (i.e., as incommensurate with an existent structural type) or in a *statistical* sense (i.e., as deviations from central tendencies). This is evidenced by the regular assertion that pathological conditions *abound* in the city. If they *"abound"* therein, they cannot be "abnormal" in the statistical sense and are not likely to prevail in the structural sense. It may be proposed that the norms in terms of which "pathological" conditions are detected are "humanitarian ideals." But we must then ask for the social orientation of such ideals. In this literature the operating criteria of the pathological are typically rural in orientation and extraction.

Most of the "problems" considered arise because of the urban deterioration of certain values which can live genuinely only in a relatively homogeneous and primary rural milieu. The "problems" discussed typically concern urban behavior. When "rural problems" are discussed, they are conceived as due to encroaching urbanization. The notion of disorganization is quite often merely the absence of that *type* of organization associated with the stuff of primary-group communities having Christian and Jeffersonian legitimations.

Cooley, the local colorist of American sociology, was the chief publicist of this conception of normal organization. He held "the great historical task of mankind" to be the more effective and wider organization of that moral order and pattern of virtues developed in primary groups and communities. Cooley took the idealists' absolute and gave it the characteristics of an organic village; all the world should be an enlarged, Christian-democratic version of a rural village. He practically assimilated "society" to this primary-group community, and he blessed it emotionally and conceptually. "There is reflected here," says T. V. Smith of Cooley —and what he says will hold for the typical social pathologist—"what is highly common in our culture, an ideal of intimacy short of which we do not rest satisfied where other people are concerned. Social distance is a dire fate, achieved with difficulty and lamented as highly unideal, not to say as immoral, in our Christian traditions. It is not enough to have saints; we must have "communion" of the saints. In order to have social relations, we must nuzzle one another."

The aim to preserve rurally oriented values and stabilities is indicated by the implicit model which operates to detect urban disorganization; it is also shown by the stress upon *community* welfare. The community is taken as a major unit, and often its sets the scope of concern and problematization. It is also within the framework of ideally democratic communities that proposed solutions are to be worked out. It should be noted that sometimes, although not typically or exclusively, solutions are conceived as dependent upon abstract moral traits or democratic surrogates of them, such as a "unanimous public will."

"Cultural lag" is considered by many pathologists to be the concept with which many scattered problems may be detected and systematized. Whereas the approach by deviation from norms is oriented "ideologically" toward a rural type of order and stability, the cultural-lag model is tacitly oriented in a "utopian" and progressive manner toward changing some areas of the culture or certain institutions so as to "integrate" them with the state of progressive technology. We must analyze the use made by pathologists of "lag" rather than abstract formulations of it.

Even though all the situations called "lags" *exist* in the present, their functional realities are referred back, away from the present. Evaluations are thus translated into a time sequence; cultural lag is an assertion of unequal "progress." It tells us what changes are "called for," what changes "ought" to have come about and didn't. In terms of various spheres of society it says what progress is, tells us how much we have had, ought to have had, didn't have, and when and where we didn't have it. The imputation of "lag" is complicated by the historical judgment in whose guise it is advanced and by the programmatic content being shoved into pseudo-objective phrases, as, for example, "called for."

It is not enough to recognize that the stating of problems in terms of cultural lag involves evaluations, however disguised. One must find the general loci of this kind of evaluation and then explain why just this form of evaluation has been so readily accepted and widely used by pathologists. The model in which institutions lag behind technology and science involves a positive evaluation of natural science and of orderly progressive change. Loosely, it derives from a liberal continuation of the enlightenment with its full rationalism, its messianic and now politically naïve admiration of physical science as a kind of thinking and activity, and with its concept of time as progress. . . .

.   .   .   .

Another model in terms of which disorganizations are instituted is that of "social change" itself. This model is not handled in any one typical way, but usually it carries the implicit assumption that human beings are "adjusted" satisfactorily to any social condition that has existed for a long time and that, when some aspect of social life changes, it may lead to a social problem. The notion is oriented ideologically and yet participates in assumptions similar to those of cultural lag, which, indeed, might be considered a variant of it. Such a scheme for problematization buttresses and is buttressed by the idea of continuous process, commented on above; but here the slow, "evolutionary" pace of change is taken explicitly as normal and organized, whereas "discontinuity" is taken as problematic. The orientation to "rural" types of organization should be recalled. In line with the stress on continuous process, the point where sanctioned order meets advisable change is not typically or structurally drawn. A conception of "balance" is usual and sometimes is explicitly sanctioned. The question, "Changes in what spheres induce disorganization?" is left open; the position taken is usually somewhere between extremes, both of which are held to be bad. This comes out in the obvious fact that what a conservative calls disorganization, a radical might well call reorganization. Without a construction of total social structures that are actually emerging, one remains caught between simple evaluations.

Besides deviation from norms, orientation to rural principles of stability, cultural lag, and social change, another conception in terms of which "problems" are typically discussed is that of adaptation or "adjustment" and their opposites. The pathological or disorganized is the maladjusted. This concept, as well as that of the "normal," is usually left empty of concrete, social content; or its content is, in effect, a propaganda for conformity to those norms and traits ideally associated with small-town, middle-class milieux. When it is an individual who is thought to be maladjusted, the "social type" within which he is maladjusted is not stated. Social and moral elements are masked by a quasi-biological meaning of the term "adaptation" with an entourage of apparently socially bare terms like "existence" and "survival," which seem still to draw prestige from the vogue of evolutionism. Both the quasi-biological and the structureless character of the concept "adjustment" tend, by formalization, to universalize the term, thus again obscuring specific social content. Use of "adjustment" accepts the goals and the means of smaller community milieux. At the most, writers using these terms suggest techniques or means believed to be less disruptive than others to attain the goals that are given. They do not typically consider whether or not certain groups or individuals caught in economically underprivileged situations can possibly obtain the current goals without drastic shifts in the basic institutions which channel and promote them. The idea of adjustment seems to be most directly applicable to a social scene in which, on the one hand, there is a society and, on the other, an individual immigrant. The immigrant then "adjusts" to the new environment. The "immigrant problem" was early in the pathologist's center of focus, and the concepts used in stating it may have been carried over as the bases for a model of experience and formulations of other "problems.". . .

In approaching the notion of adjustment, one may analyze the specific illustrations of maladjustment that are given and from these instances infer a type of social person who in this literature is evaluated as "adjusted." The ideally adjusted man of the social pathologists is "socialized." This term seems to operate ethically as the opposite of "selfish;" it implies that the adjusted man conforms to middle-class morality and motives and "participates" in the gradual progress of respectable institutions. If he is not a "joiner," he certainly gets around and into many community organizations. If he is socialized, the individual thinks of others and is kindly toward them. He does not brood or mope about but is somewhat extravert, eagerly participating in his community's institutions. His mother and father were not divorced, nor was his home ever broken. He is "successful"—at least in a modest way—since he is ambitious; but he does not speculate about matters too far above his means, lest he become "a fantasy thinker," and the little men don't scramble after the big money. The less abstract the traits and fulfilled "needs" of "the adjusted man" are, the more they gravitate toward the norms of independent middle-class persons verbally living out Protestant ideals in the small towns of America.

SUGGESTED READINGS: CHAPTER 6

Richard Cloward, and Lloyd Ohlin. *Delinquency and Opportunity*. New York: The Free Press of Glencoe, 1960.

A later version of delinquency, and a more recent theory to account for it, than Thrasher's (see below). The emphasis is less on the simple perils of city streets than on the more complex dangers attending urbanization.

E. Franklin Frazier. *The Negro Family in the United States.* Chicago: University of Chicago Press, 1939, pp. 291–334.

The last chapter of this fine monograph gives a graphic description of the disintegration of rural families as they migrate to northern cities. The account was all too prophetic of what has become an obvious feature of the 1960s.

Frederic M. Thrasher. *The Gang.* Chicago: University of Chicago Press, 1927.

An early but still worthwhile sociological monograph on juvenile delinquency in the city.

W. I. Thomas, and F. Znaniecki. *The Polish Peasant in Europe and America* (2nd edition), Vol. II. New York: Alfred A. Knopf, 1927.

The classic account of what happened to Polish peasants when they encountered a big American city, including disorganization of community and family as well as demoralization of men, women, boys, and girls.

7

Return to San Francisco. From *Harper's Magazine*, 1861.

SUCCESS AND THE PERILOUS CITY

ONE of the great themes of American urbanization as indicated earlier is "success" in the city. The city affords marvelous opportunities for social mobility but the countryside and the small town do not. An important variant of this main theme is that success in the city is only won by some people and under certain conditions—for the city is sufficiently perilous that it may destroy those who do not conquer it. This is as true of those who are born in the city as those who migrate to it. The "success against peril" theme is most visibly associated with the larger cities, but closer examination of popular literature about the smaller cities would undoubtedly show the same imagery. To their hinterlands, Memphis and New Orleans simultaneously represented challenge and danger.

This imagery is related in fairly obvious ways to sociological writing, both about cities and about social mobility. Even when the earlier sociologists were inclined to decry the evils of city living, they were inclined to admit that cities were places of opportunity provided aspirants had fortitude and ability. Later sociologists like Louis Wirth betrayed some of the same ambivalence, while Robert Park and his students— like the general populace—were fascinated by the dramatic contrast between the city's poor and the city's rich. The slums were located under the very shadows of the tall Gold Coast buildings!

Success against perilous conditions also appears in the sociological literature about social mobility. In the earlier literature, this is reflected in writings about the sons and daughters of immigrants: some of this second generation might not only be demoralized but some might also adjust to and "do well" on the American scene. Indeed, so might the immigrants themselves. The later sociological concern with vice and crime also led to the conclusion that in these areas, too, there were patterned paths to success as well as to downfall.

In order to relate more recent sociological writing to transmuted versions of the same imagery, one has only to recollect the recent and contemporary concern with such matters as conformity seen as the price of social mobility; family disintegration in the suburbs, because the husband can spend so little time with his wife and children; the illusory promises of the city, which in fact offers little to the white-collar girl; and the tragic migration of southern Negroes and whites to northern cities, which in reality may afford little mobility and result in much demoralization. Indeed, sociologists have been so much focused on polar images of success and failure that it is quite possible, as Berenice Fisher of the University of Wisconsin has pointed out (in an unpublished manuscript), that their conceptions of downward mobility are only meagre representations of the many varieties of downward mobility in America.

The selections in this chapter exemplify different versions of success under perilous conditions, drawn from earlier popular literature. More recent versions will appear later in this book, although they are classified under varying chapter headings to bring out other imageries associated with mobility.

THE STRIFE FOR PRECEDENCE, *E. H. Chapin*

THE Reverend Mr. Chapin warns against financial and
social success for its own sake, but sanctions
success on the urban terrain by linking Christianity
and democracy in an embracing formula.

The city,—in this instance, as in many others, representing the
world at large,—is essentially a race-course, or battle-field, in which,
through forms of ambitious effort, and cunning method, and plodding
labor, and ostentation, the aspirations of thousands appear and carry on
a *Strife for Precedence.*

And, in selecting this phase of human life as the theme of the present
discourse, I observe in the first place—that the desire for precedence is
one of the *deepest* and most *subtle* motives in the soul of man. . . .

  .   .   .   .

But I observe, further, that, while this desire for Precedence is common among men of all conditions, there are some modes of its expression
which are peculiarly excited in a democratic form of society. . . . Here,
where everybody says that all men are equal, and everybody is afraid
they *will* be; where there are no adamantine barriers of birth and caste;
people are anxiously exclusive. And though the forms of aristocracy
flourish more gorgeously in their native soil, the genuine *virus* can be
found in New York almost as readily as in London, or Vienna. And the
virus breaks out in the most absurd shapes of liveries and titles. And
these forms of aspiration are not only absurd because they are inconsistent,
but because they illustrate no real ground of precedence. They are superficial and uncertain. They do not pertain to the man but to his accidents.
He gains by them no intrinsic glory, no permanent good.

  .   .   .   .

Let us, then, consider some of the forms which this struggle assumes
in the streets and the dwellings around us. I remark, in the first place, that
it inspires much of the effort for *wealth.* . . .

Excerpted from *Humanity in the City* (New York: De Witt and Davenport,
1854), pp. 66, 70–75, 77, 86–90.

The destinies of the time are enacted not in Congress or Parliament, but in the Bank of England and in Wall street. It is a mighty power that sits on 'Change, and inspires the great movements of the world; sending its messengers panting through the deep and feeling around the globe with telegraphic nerves. And one may well be more ambitious to wield a portion of this power than to speak in senates, or to sit upon a throne. Here is something that will raise him above the common level; will pay him for long years of sacrifice and contumely; will hide meanness of birth, and scantiness of education, and paint over the stains of damaged character. Here is the most feasible way of distinction in a democracy. The doors of respectability and honor turn on silver hinges. Gravity relaxes, fashion gives way, beauty smiles, and talent defers, before the man of money. He may be an ignoramus, but he possesses the golden alphabet. He may be a boor, but Plutus lends a charm which eclipses the grace of Apollo. He may have accumulated his wealth in a way which would make an intelligent hyena ashamed of himself, but he *has* accumulated it, and the past is forgotten. . . .

Again, consider the illustrations of this strife in the *Style of Living*. It is really a battle of chairs and mirrors, of plate and equipage, and is the spring of the monstrous extravagance that characterizes our city life. For I suppose there is no place on the earth where people have run into such gorgeous nonsense as here—turning home into a Parisian toy-shop, absorbing the price of a good farm in the ornaments of a parlor, and hanging up a judge's salary in a single chandelier. . . .

. . . It is one way of getting a head taller than another upon this democratic level. It is a carpet contest for the mastery in what is called "society.". . .

But enough has been said to illustrate the false element in the great struggle for human precedence. This vicious principle is most comprehensively stated in the proposition, that there is no substantial ground of supremacy in anything that is merely accidental or external to a man. These things may sometimes stand as symbols of true merit and greatness, but they are not themselves proofs of precedence. . . .

And, my friends, the tendency of things is to bring out more and more these real claims to human precedence, and to throw all spurious titles into the shade. This is the radical purport of true democracy, which I take to be the social synonym of *Christianity*. I have shown what inconsistencies and false distinctions swarm here in our midst, under the profession of republican equality. This, however, is because names are *not* things. I don't call that "democracy" which is simply the domineering spirit of self-exaltation in a new shape. . . .

. . . .

Therefore, I regard these spurious claims to precedence—these endeavors after social distinction by virtue of riches, and equipage, and wardrobes—as only evidences of a transition-state. Men, letting go the feudal forms, and still assuming that there is some ground of human precedence, as there really is, have adopted these false expressions of it. They will in turn pass away, and give place to more genuine methods.

But let it be remembered, that these false forms of precedence are not only inconsistent with our social professions and institutions, but they are futile because they are contrary to the Divine Law. Our endeavors in life have a twofold operation, and we must count not only their effect upon others but their reaction upon the fabric of our own inner being. For, whatever honor *men* may attribute to us, we know that there is no real, substantial ground of supremacy except in the excellence and power of our own spiritual nature. And this is acquired not in ostentatious and selfish striving, but when self is least thought of; in the calm work of duty, and when all conception of human merit fades into the Glory of God. And this is the great end to be desired—this strength and exaltation of the soul. This imparts the profoundest significance to that great life-struggle which goes on in these crowded streets The city! what is it but a vast amphitheatre, filled with racers, with charioteers, with eager competitors; surrounded by an unseen and awful array of witnesses. And here, daily, the lists are opened, and men contend for success, for station, for power. But these are meretricious and perishable awards. The real prize is a spiritual gain, a crown that "fadeth not away." And, if we comprehend the great purpose of existence at all—if we look with any eagerness to its intrinsic issues and its final result; we shall heed that decree of Divine Wisdom and Justice that comes down to us through all the vicissitude of life—through all the hurry and turmoil and contention. "If a man strive for masteries, yet is he not crowned, except he strive lawfully."

COMING TO THE CITY, *Horace Greeley*

HORACE GREELEY warns rural youth not to attempt
to scale the city's heights unless properly
endowed by nature and training. But his
primary emphasis is: Stay at home!

Cities are the result of certain social necessities of civilized or semi-civilized Man,—necessities of Trade, of Manufacture, Interchange of Ideas, and of Government: they rest upon and are supported by the Country. Their support is of course mainly voluntary; its amount is controlled by the ability and desires of the rural population. Thus, while almost any farming County might give employment and ample subsistence to five or even ten times its present population, there is scarcely a city in the world whose population is not already quite as large as it has business to employ and income to sustain, while the greater number are constantly crowded with surplus laborers, vainly seeking employment and under-bidding each other in the eager strife for it, until thousands can hardly sustain life on the scanty reward of their exertions, and other thousands are forced to live on public or private charity. Many perish every year, not perhaps of absolute starvation, but of diseases induced by hunger, want and exposure, while a larger number are driven by destitution into evil courses, and close their brief careers of guilty mockery of enjoyment by deaths of shame and horror. Such are some of the dire consequences of the continual over-population of our cities, caused by the insane desire very generally felt to escape the ruder toils and tamer routine of country life. Until some marked change shall have been wrought in the general condition of our rural Industry, so as to render it less repulsive than it now is, our cities must continue over-crowded and full of misery. The naked truth that, as a general rule, no one lives by *bona fide* physical labor who can obtain a living without, and very few live by farming or the like who can live by what are esteemed the lighter and more genteel avocations mainly pursued in cities and villages, explains much of the misery so prevalent all around us. Doubtless, the Monopoly of Land is one of the ultimate causes of this deplorable state of things; thousands annually quitting the country for cities who would cling to the homes of their infancy if they were not the property of others, and would cultivate

Reprinted from *Hints toward Reforms, in Lectures, Addresses, and Other Writings* (New York: Harper and Brothers, 1850), pp. 359–64.

soil like their fathers if they had any soil to cultivate. Having none, they are tempted to seek in some city the employment and independence which seem denied them where they were born.

This choice is almost always an unwise one. In the Country, the young man heartily willing to do anything honest and useful for a livelihood, need seldom wait long for employment that will at least insure him a subsistence. In the Cities, the case is sadly different. A capable, willing, trustworthy man may earnestly seek employment here for months without finding any. And the reason is very clear: There are more seeking work in the cities than work can be found for; and, though the business of most cities annually increases, through the growth of the Country trading with them, yet the pressure for employment in cities constantly outruns the demand for labor, and if New-York were to increase its trade and consequently its population by ten or twenty per cent. a year for the next century, there would at all times be thousands waiting here for chances to do something, and many starved out or impelled to evil courses for want of honest business. The gigantic sea of Foreign Immigration incessantly rolling in upon us, bringing thousands each month to our City (some of them most ingenious, expert and capable) who must have work promptly or go to the Poor-House, and who are inured to lower wages and poorer living than Americans will submit to, will keep the general Labor market glutted and the average recompense of hired labor low for a term of which I can not foresee the end.

—'But do you contend that no American youth should *ever* migrate from the country to one of our Cities?' No, Sir, I do not. What I *do* maintain is this—Whoever leaves the country to come hither should feel sure that he has faculties, capacities, powers, for which the Country affords him no scope, and that the City is his proper sphere of usefulness. He should next be sure that he has ability to procure a livelihood while he shall be laboring to attain that sphere which he regards as his ultimate destination. No youth should migrate to a City without a thorough mastery of some good mechanical trade or handicraft such as is prosecuted in cities, although he may not intend to follow it except in case of dire necessity. Teaching, Clerking, Law, &c. are so very precarious, except to men of established reputation and business, that it is next to madness for a youth to come here relying upon them. With a good trade, a hearty willingness to work, strict temperance and habits of economy, it will be hard to starve out a man who has once found employment; not so with one who is trained only for a Teacher or Clerk, or who 'is willing to do anything' —which means that he knows how to do nothing. With these, our City always has been, always will be crowded—it pays for burying the greater part of them.

The young man fit to come to a City does not begin by importuning some relative or friend to find or make a place for him. Having first qualified himself, so far as he may, for usefulness here, he comes understanding that he must begin at the foot of the class and work his way up. Having found a place to stop, he makes himself acquainted with those places where work in his line may be found, sees the advertisements of 'Wants' in the leading journals at an early hour each morning, notes those which hold out some prospect for him, and accepts the first place offered him which he can take honorably and fill acceptably. He who commences in this way is quite likely to get on.

But for him whose chief object is to live comfortably, or even to acquire wealth by honest industry, the City is not the place. The mass of men and women work far steadier and harder here for a bare subsistence than they do away from the Cities. To say nothing of the ruder manual toil by which no man can support a family in comfort, the average earnings of good mechanics here will not exceed eight dollars per week the year round, or four hundred dollars per annum. This will seem considerable to mechanics who can hire a good house and garden for thirty to sixty dollars, with often a strip of pasture or meadow attached; but let such consider that here almost any kind of a house costs from three to five hundred dollars per annum, and the meanest dog-hole into which a family can be crowded—perhaps up two flights of stairs—will cost one hundred dollars, with like charges for Fuel, Milk, Vegetables, &c. and they will understand the whole subject much better. A good mechanic can support his family better by five days' labor per week in the country than by six in this or almost any great city.

'But men do get rich in the city,'—Yes, they do. One in a thousand of those who come here in quest of fortune achieve it, and they are generally men who would do the same anywhere. Scrutinize closely the lives of those who have made fortunes in cities, and you will find that they were early risers, hard workers, sharp dealers, and close calculators—a sort very difficult to starve. Having thus obtained a good start early in life, the rest was easy; for he must be a natural-born fool or worse who can not with money and credit accumulate property anywhere. The problem we are considering is, How men are to do who have *not* money, or at best have very little.

I am not forgetting that there are some rare but showy instances of men who have made fortunes by some dashing speculation or run of luck in trade—but these are too few to disturb the general calculation. Whoever wishes to try his luck at gambling is not obliged to come to the City for that purpose, or at least need not remove hither. Three days will usually suffice for his purpose.—And, for every large fortune rapidly acquired in Trade or Stocks, fully forty small fortunes (and some large ones) have been lost in the same way. The mushroom millionaire dazzles all eyes by his horses and equipage, his palace, and his plate—he is thought of, talked of—while those who have lost everything by the same turn of the wheel crawl away to die in some out-of-the-way corner, silent and forgotten.

—A single class remains to be spoken of—that of men past their youth, who, often with families dependent on them, seek employment in cities because they have not been successful elsewhere, and, without any special faculty, plunge into some emporium of Commerce to earn in some novel vocation the livelihood among strangers which they can not amid their friends at the pursuits to which they are accustomed. Such men are downright suicides—if they have families, they are worse than that; and whoever aids them in their mad folly is an accessory to their crime. No man should ever change his vocation after thirty unless he has hitherto been a pirate, gambler, pickpocket, or something of the sort, and even then he has but a sorry prospect before him; but for a poor unlucky man to bring a family of children to a City and hope there to support them in some novel pursuit, is the wildest, most desperate infatuation. There is no chance of success—no rational hope that he can struggle on except in the most abject dependence and beggary.

Such are some of the reasons which impel me uniformly to reply unfavorably or not at all to those seeking encouragement in their plans of removing to the City. To bring more here is to increase the prevalence of want and misery among our present redundant population. I might say much more on this theme, but can it be needed?

SOCIETY IN TOWN, *A. D. Mayo*

THE Reverend Mr. Mayo embroiders Greeley's theme
that rural youths should not exchange their
rural homes for unlikely gambles at making city
fortunes. He is, however, confronting more
directly the evident migration into the rapidly
developing cities and the fact that some
men do accumulate fortunes. He also has
some specific warnings for the women in his audience.

The rage of the people of New York for city life is an evil that may
well arrest the attention of the patriot and Christian. The Empire State
contains 46,000 square miles of territory, of which only half, 13,000,000
acres, is cultivated at all, while 13,000,000 acres of unoccupied land,
and untold mineral wealth invite to a century of industrial enterprise. Yet
full one-third of our entire population of three and a half millions, is
huddled into towns and exposed to the influences of American city life.
Our young countrymen are born with a fever in their blood which drives
them from the farm, or the factory, or the mine, where actual production
is the result of their efforts, and economy of health, property, and soul is
promoted, to the town where ninety per cent of the merchants fail, and
the mechanic toils with a pit of starvation ever yawning beneath his feet,
and an ever increasing series of middle men enhances the cost of living,
and pitiless competition of labor and perpetual temptation imperil integrity
of mind and purity of life. Our country girls push for the city as by a
natural instinct, seeming to relish better the intoxicating charm of being
one colored wave of the torrent that rolls along a Broadway than the
centre of a neighborhood among the fields. We have the right to ask
these heedless throngs what purpose drives them to the city; and compel
them to contemplate its nicely balanced advantages and disadvantages before they step over the threshold of nature, and adventure in the labyrinth
of artificial life.

Doubtless, a city is a large labor-saving machine, where the greatest
amount of spiritual energy can be directed to a given point with the least
waste of material resources. It is an undeniable advantage to an able man
to occupy such a tower of observation, whence the forces of civilization

Excerpted from *Symbols of the Capital* (New York: Thatcher and Hutchinson,
1859), pp. 45–55, 276–80.

can be seen in their accumulated vigor and mutual relation. Knowing what is the capacity of society in each department, and how much energy is enlisted for the development of each, he can adjust his own efforts, save himself useless expenditure of his powers, and direct his genius to the exact point of demand. Then it is a privilege to a strong man to enjoy companionship of his equals, to learn to make a straight path through the tangled feet of others as indefatigable as himself; to be drilled and criticised, and finally educated by his peers. This is the great charm of the city to the leaders of every realm of life. Here, too, the tendencies of classes, the need of crowds, and the secrets of public and wide-reaching influence over men, are best to be learned. And the town is a great workshop filled with the best tools in the shape of organized forces and institutions. Labor and business are systematized, society can be taken by the handle, literature is classified, and education and art in every branch assigned to its peculiar department. The caucus, the convention, the city church, the philanthropic institution, are the finest implements to do the kinds of work they represent. Doubtless, these are formidable tools for weak men to handle; and the incompetent man or woman who aspires to their use is like a child in an armory, reaching on tip-toe to lift the sword and bayonet from their rack above its imperilled head; but when a strong man of war appears, he can arm in the least time, with the best weapons. If one is up to the work, and can keep wide-awake without destruction to body and mind, there is a great opportunity in sitting at the end of the wire when the earliest message comes; in catching the last news of fluctuation in trade or society, before it falls into the hands of the reporters; in discerning the premonitory symptoms of all changes that modify the activity of man. The enterprising citizen thus always knows a little ahead of his rural brother, and so has a foot in advance in the race for success.

Able men will, therefore, always face towards the great centres of human activity, and since few young people count themselves fools, the American cities will be the battle-ground of annihilating competition in every department of republican society. From the newsboy whose voice best threads the labyrinth of street noises, to the preacher who knows the magic word that, spoken in the darkest chapel, will fill the street with a crowd of the best mind and heart of the town, every post of profit and influence will be contested inch by inch, and the victor stand at last surrounded by a score of fallen adventurers. The young who rush to the city thinking its brilliant positions are easily secured, do not understand that no man succeeds there otherwise than as a representative of a class; that every citizen who permanently occupies an important position, holds it by virtue of some peculiar power in a certain direction persistently exercised. Many bad people rule in town, but no fool, no mediocre person long occupies a desirable eminence (unless in certain instances where the fools and platitudes need a representative, and choose the genius in stupidity to be their king or queen). That the vast majority of adventurers on the pavement do not succeed; that they work harder, live closer, suffer tenfold the frets and sorrows of life, and peril the best prospects of character beyond comparison with the risks of a country career, is open to every one who will see; and only an insane man will assert that a majority of the one million two hundred thousand people who are waging this pitiless war of competition on the pavements of the Empire State, would not be vastly more useful to themselves and to society, if employed in developing the teeming resources of physical and spiritual wealth that prophecy the future of our noble State.

For out of this very representative character of citizen society spring the formidable disadvantages that to the mass of men quite overbalance the opportunities of the town. The quiet, affectionate youth comes from the genial atmosphere of the rural neighborhood, and finds himself struggling in a rushing crowd of adventurers, each bent on success. For here success is the only alternative of ruin. There is no long-suffering, pitiful community behind the combatant to receive him, wounded and weary in defeat; he must leave the pavement for the country if he fails, and too often there is no home among the fields; and the deep vault of sin and sorrow which runs under every drawing-room and counting-room claims him at the end. But even if this fate is escaped, through what prolonged and withering toils, amid what dangers of health and life, and sanity of soul, does the prosperous citizen approach his reward. The majority of successful dwellers in town are scarred in body and twisted in mind by their prolonged stimulation of all the powers of life, and in grasping the prize of ambition have lost their own best resources of enjoyment. *Happiness does not depend so much on what we have as on a certain freshness of nature that illuminates every corner of our life with a light from within;* and how few preserve that freshness amid the monotonous toils and discouraging collisions of the city.

But the greatest peril besets the soul. He who has impaired his reverence for man, duty, God, and the high religious self-respect which scorns any stooping to success, has made a failure of existence. And it is not easy to elbow the way through crowds of unknown faces—to lose almost the recognition of individual character in the contact with masses—to be forced to treat our best friends as rivals, and the multitude as instruments, without a disastrous decline in that love to man from which grows the reverence for duty and the supreme love of God. It is harder yet to own one's self in a field where society in every direction claims you as one spoke in the wheel of some powerful organization, and to be "left out" is to live in a solitude more fearful than the primitive woods. When the outside of life is so large a point of immediate success, what a temptation to a soul-destroying career of fashion and luxury; and those who know best the seductions of sensuality that lurk beneath the gilding and propriety of the city, most distrust their own power of resistance.

All dangers of the town may be summed up in this: that here, withdrawn from the blessed influences of Nature, and set face to face against humanity, man loses his own nature and becomes a new and artificial creature—an unhuman cog in a social machinery that works like a fate, and cheats him of his true culture as a soul. The most unnatural fashions and habits, the strangest eccentricities of intellect, the wildest and most pernicious theories in social morals, and the most appalling and incurable barbarism, are the legitimate growth of city life. If one has strength of constitution, physical, mental and moral, to push through all these hinderances, and stand upon the summit of the town, doubtless his experience of man is more profound and curious, and his power to dexterously administer affairs greater than in a more secluded position; but who will risk the chances of a strife, where the mass are beaten and the one who outlives his companions succeeds, without deep reflection and for unanswerable reasons? Who but a lunatic will rush into this melee, trusting to luck, where luck is always on the side of the wise and strong?

Therefore, let our young people in the country take much counsel and be very well assured in their own sober judgment, before they cast their lot in the city. Remember that any point of New York is now in vital communication with the centres of civilization, and that every year is bringing all men nearer together. All the essential advantages of our republican life can be secured, by proper effort, in every village and cluster of farms in the Empire State; and the extraordinary successes of towns are but for the few. Let not these few be too eager to vault to their post of ultimate power; if the magnet is in them, the filings will concentrate anywhere; and only by long and patient experiment can any genuine man gain the magic platform whence electric wires course all over the land, and cause a thousand bosoms to thrill at every throb of his heart. For those adventurers who have concluded to sacrifice their manhood to a paltry success, we have nothing to advise; "where the carcass is, there will the eagles be gathered together." But we implore every honest youth in our land to ask this question of his innermost soul: "Am I sure I shall gain enough in happiness, worthy prosperity and manliness, to risk the perils and disadvantages of the town?" For this is the only test, a gain of manhood and womanhood. Oh, how far beneath any noble soul should be the weak hankering for such a success as comes to thousands of families in the city; a gain in money purchased by the sacrifice of honesty and reverence for man, a gain in comforts and luxuries which are a slow poison in the blood; of social position, which changes a sincere wife to a managing mother and a pure child to a reckless young man or a bedizened victim of female vanity; a success that is a dismal failure in all that is fit to be acquired. Better the most obscure lot in the bleakest northern wilderness with virtue, than a palace in town with such a wreck of souls within. Better far the opportunities and joys of our favored country life, for thousands who only leave it to tempt a certain damage to the highest interests of the individual and the demoralization of the republic.

It would be a great triumph of philanthropy if the large class of the poor could be removed from the cities of New York and planted all over her wide territory; and one dollar given to help a pauper family out of town is better charity than a year's support in the garret where they now fight with starvation. And with them all should go thousands who are just living above the precipice of hopeless poverty, whom a few months' suspension of labor will hurl into the abyss of want and crime. And still more imperatively does public economy demand the exit of other thousands of middlemen, who are too able and respectable to fulfill their destiny by gaining a living from the mere handing the necessaries of existence, when they might be producing much that is useful elsewhere. Were our cities swept clean of these classes, there would be still enough to fulfill all the uses of the own; merchants whose talents and character are adequate to manage the machinery and resist the seductions of commerce; workmen of various kinds, whose superior skill and confirmed habits make them at home amid the intricacies of metropolitan industry; professional men, whose laudable ambition, fortified by ample experience, leads them to a municipal platform as their best position; and enough of the rich and cultivated in manners to reform the vices of social life and organize amusements on a generous and Christian scale. But we cannot build cities "to order"; they are and will be the huge receptacles for all varieties of humanity, and represent the worst as surely as the best in our American character. All the teacher of Christianity can do is to take men and women in towns as he finds them, and, spite of disheartening influences, keep on forever warning, instructing and inspiring to virtue.

．　　　．　　　．　　　．　　　．　　　．　　　．　　　．　　　．　　　．

American women are, just now, bewildered by their own position. The great mixture of people in cities and large towns, where customs and fashions originate, divides the mass into a thousand contradictory elements. Society is an uncertain fluctuating ocean, on whose shore every girl stands watching her opportunity to spring aboard the finest craft that is whirled within her reach.

During this formative period of social life, the material advantages of our condition have a fatal fascination to our young country women. There was never a race of men acquiring wealth and position so fast as the young men of America; so every farmer's, mechanic's or merchant's daughter, every girl at her needle, her studies, her schoolteacher's desk, has a mighty temptation to keep the brightest corner of her best eye open for the coming man, who shall appear in his coach at her mother's door, carry her to a beautiful home, and bear her on from triumph to triumph in her social career. Honor to those who fix their eyes on the higher spiritual prizes of American freedom, and live out the resolve to found their success on something better than money and ease; but they are the chosen few. The crowd of American girls do what women would do everywhere; neglect the higher culture of the soul in the scheming or waiting for the sensual advantages of life, and spend the golden years of their first quarter of a century, rather in superficial occupations and inquiring after desirable husbands, than in toiling to become good wives and Republican mothers.

This fearful push for the material prizes of our national life, explains the imperfect education of American young women. Mothers and daughters vie in the cultivation of those temporary graces and accomplishments which are supposed to bring young men to a crisis in the affections, while the solid qualities which can alone retain the love of a rational man, or fit a woman for genuine success, are postponed till life is upon them. It also accounts for the ridiculous imitation of foreign fashions, which makes Boston a sham London, and New York a sham Paris, and arrays the girls of every western town in obedience to the fashion plates of Godey and Harper. It is the chief cause of the restlessness of women, and the want of peace in family and social life; for young women who are crazed with this ambition, cannot be quiet enough to develop that sweetness and strength, which is the rock at the centre of earthly life, and next to God's love, the best support of man. And this is the secret cause of the fearful collapse of female health in America; for standing on tiptoe, watching the chance to leap aboard a fairly, floating palace that wavers over a stormy sea, is not a healthy, though an exciting occupation. It forces children through the grades of girlhood with steam power rapidity to young ladyhood, while they should be romping in pantalets, learning science or household duties under their teachers and mothers. This rush of energy to the surface of life, the excitements, hopes and fears of the young lady's career, leave the deep places of the heart dry, and create a morbid restlessness of the affections, that preys upon the very springs of physical existence; so the majority of American girls, when they have obtained their lover, are not physically fit to become his wife and the mother of his children, and the bright path of girlhood dips down into the valley of shadows, that married life is to woman in thousands of American homes.

This material ambition of the girls drives their companions of the other sex into overheated exertions in business and exhausts their health and freshness, by awakening at one-and-twenty the sense of obligation belonging to forty; while their ill health and practical effeminacy prevent thousands of young men from marrying, and thus fearfully increase the sensuality of the community. It drives the young couple to live beyond their means and sacrifice constant comfort and true family life to occasional splendor and periodical excitement. American men wear out in business keeping up the household, and women wear out in straining after social position. Children are born with the mark of this career upon them, and brought up in a more exaggerated style. The mother at last "breaks down" under social cares, and distractions, and the father has no spot of rest on earth. The American woman has not yet created the American home. As a nation we are jaded, sad, nervous. Our men do not come out of their fine houses with the glory of the Lord shining in their faces, as Moses came down from the mount, but as tired and restless as they went in. The Republican home that shall cheer, console, and elevate the American people, and the Republican Society that is but its extension and idealization, are yet a vision.

THE GIRL WHO EARNS HER OWN LIVING,
Anna S. Richardson

IN 1909, women were still generally warned away from
seeking success in the city, but Richardson
encourages working women to come to the big city
providing they have the proper training and
attitudes. Notice, also, the blurred imagery of the
girl from "smaller city or even a village"
and the "country" girl.

"What experience have you had in this city?" is the question hurled at the newcomer, until she begins to dread it, knowing that the preference will be given to applicants having local references.

It is not to be denied that often the girl from a smaller city or even a village develops into the better clerk or office worker for a Chicago or New York employer than does the city-born girl; but until she has proven her worth, the newcomer must work at the salary of a local apprentice, no matter what her experience in her home town.

The inexperienced city girl must also start at the smallest wages which the superintendent of the establishment dares to offer, simply because the

Excerpted from *The Girl Who Earns Her Own Living* (New York: B. W. Dodge and Co., 1909), pp. 263–66, 281–83.

employer feels that her mistakes will be many and costly, and she will not earn the sum he pays her, no matter how small that may be.

Both the city and the country girl are forced to accept three, four or five dollars per week, quieting their fears by repeating the superintendent's consoling words: "But we will increase your salary as fast as you prove your worth."

But even when a girl tries her level best to prove her worth, and when she gives her undivided attention and efforts to the firm's business, it takes weeks and months to master details and to avoid mistakes. And all that time she must live somehow on what the firm pays her. If out-of-town mothers realized just what this period of probation represented in privation, loneliness, perhaps actual physical discomfort, suffering and hunger, they would do all in their power to keep ambitious but untrained daughters at home. But, unfortunately, mothers who have never worked for their living have false ideas of business life. They see only the well-clad, smiling girls behind counters or in offices, and they do not stop to inquire what price these girls paid for their business training, their present economic independence.

And so, every week of the year, and every day of the week, even including Sunday, the railway trains bring to every large city hundreds of girls utterly unprepared to offer skilled labor in return for living wages, girls who must somehow live while being trained to become real wage-earners.

Only women engaged in social work, representatives of the Travelers' Aid Society and matrons of homes or temporary shelters for working-girls, have any conception of the number of unskilled, untrained girls who plunge into cities without sufficient funds to tide them over a fortnight. These girls honestly believe that within a week they will be working somewhere, somehow, on a salary which will not only permit them to live in city comfort, but to send something home to "the folks." The pathos of their ignorance is not a matter for consideration here. Their relief, their social salvation, is a matter of moment.

No mother should permit her daughter to go to a strange city unless she can provide the girl with funds to pay board and room for a month, which will amount to not less than twenty dollars, and the price of her return ticket in case she fails to find work in that time. The mother who recklessly allows her unskilled daughter to enter a strange city armed only with a week's board and high hopes, is guilty of criminal neglect as the guardian of her child's future.

I wish I could drive this lesson into the heart of every mother who feels that her daughter must go to some large city in order to succeed. If the two are convinced that the home town offers no future for the daughter, then let them prove the sincerity of their conviction by earning enough money at home, even if it means taking in washing and ironing, to insure all or part of the daughter's living expenses for at least three months after she goes to the city.

.   .   .   .

The figures presented in this chapter should prove to the girl who has had a comfortable home in a small city or town that she cannot duplicate home comforts in the larger city on a salary of five dollars a week. Either she must bring with her funds to deposit in bank and draw upon for almost daily needs, or resign herself to a period of stern deprivation. For if she is fortunate enough to secure board and lodging in a working-girl's home for three dollars and fifty cents a week, the remaining dollar and a half must cover a multitude of small expenses.

Unless she is working very near the "home," she must buy her lunch, which represents at the least ten cents per day. In many cities, the "homes" are located at some distance from business centers. This means carfare, at least one way each day, often both trips. Some laundry work she must have done, even if she is permitted to wash gauze underwear, stockings, handkerchiefs, neckwear and other small pieces at her boarding-place. Her shoes will wear out with painful celerity, and her entire wardrobe may have to be renewed, piece by piece, before the promised raise in salary is forthcoming. If she comes to the city unprovided with a black dress, and works in a store, her first expenditure will be for a black skirt and waist. In nearly all city stores the wearing of black and white is obligatory.

Figure this out, item by item, and you will see that the life of the inexperienced and untrained girl in a great city is drab-colored indeed. It will be months before her income will permit her to purchase the pretty clothes of which she dreamed before leaving home, or to indulge in the small pleasures which she pictured as part of every city girl's life.

On the other hand, if a girl has the right sort of business ability behind her ambition, if she can deny herself many little luxuries and for a time devote herself exclusively to mastering the line of work she has chosen, the city holds wonderful possibilities for her. There is always room for the girl with an idea, for the girl who does one thing well, for the girl who is willing, nay, anxious, to learn and to work. But a girl of this sort must hold herself above the cheaper, tinseled life of the big city. She must learn to decline invitations which represent late hours, broken rest, associations that are anything but uplifting. She must find her recreation in the free lectures, the free concerts and the free art exhibits to be found in all progressive cities, and seek her companions at classes for self-advancement, gymnasiums and clubs conducted by institutional churches or organizations like the Young Women's Christian Association.

CITY BOY VERSUS COUNTRY BOY,
J. M. Welding

> ONE influential variant of the city success theme was
> that while the aspiring country boy had to leave
> home to amount to anything, he did owe his future
> eminence to his rural upbringing—he had been
> raised in a physically invigorating and
> morally sustaining environment. Despite J. M.
> Welding's cogent rejoinder in 1892, the rural-background
> imagery has continued in somewhat muted form to
> affect perspectives on success in the city—
> for instance, in the popular accounts about presidents,
> congressmen, and such other of our national
> figures who grew up in homes far away
> from large cities.

"Most of our great men come from the country." Who has not heard this proverb from infancy? In both city and country it passes without question as to truthfulness. *Why* does the country boy outstrip his city rival in the race of life? In reply to this question a number of reasons have been advanced, among the most ingenious of which are the following:

1st. The country boy being inured to a life of labor, becomes hardened, both physically and mentally, and so is enabled to put forth a more vigorous and sustained effort than can the pampered and weakly city youth. [Of course, this goes upon the assumption that the greater proportion of city people are in easy circumstances and so can afford to indulge their youth in a life of ease and sloth. (?)]

2d. The country boy is exempt from the many temptations that beset his urban cousins. [We are hereby prepared to find the average rustic a paragon of innocence, honesty and virtue in general. (?)]

3d. That the short school terms of the country at once afford the youth opportunity to develop his physical powers by labor, and this, in its turn, gives him a zest for study. When, on the contrary, the town boy, while wearied with a long school term, is subjected to the machine system and treadmill routine of graded schools. [This, of course, puts well paid instructors, skilled pedagogy, the kindergarten and the gymnasium at a

Excerpted from "City Boy Versus Country Boy," in George Gunton (Ed.), *Social Economist* (New York: School of Social Economics, 1892), Vol. III, pp. 11–12, 15–18.

sad discount.] All attempts at improvement of the country schools, and the betterment of their teachers, professionally and financially, are met and defeated by this everlasting outcry against introducing the "machine methods of the city."

The proverb cited at the beginning of this article, and the accompanying brood of alleged reasons given in its support; have been, in a manner, incorporated within the general stock of popular beliefs; and so prone is the public to cling to an opinion once rooted in its mind, that the task of proving said opinion to be wrong is a difficult one indeed. The cause of the town boy is nearly hopeless: so much so that it requires considerable boldness to venture upon his defense. Labored efforts have been made by various and sundry writers to establish evidence against the worth of the town boy; but who has ever undertaken his defense? His inferiority is not only insisted upon, but it acquires an added heinousness in the light of the common view of his case, in that he fails *because* of his superior advantages, whereas his rustic competitor is supposed to succeed in spite of disadvantages.

Speaking upon this point it might be as well to remark that the sovereign obstacle against which the town boy has to contend at the very outset of the race, is the discouragement of having always dinned into him the utter hopelessness of his efforts in competing with his country cousin. It is related of Louis XIV that he once propounded to some of the wisest of his courtiers the following question: "Why does a vessel containing ten pounds of water acquire no added weight when a fish weighing one pound is added thereto?" After wrestling for three days and nights with the question, one of them, moved by a bright idea, suggested that the question be changed to—"*Does* a vessel containing ten pounds of water acquire no added weight when a fish weighing one pound is added thereto?" A pair of scales being brought in and a simple experiment made, a royal joke was spoiled and a popular delusion corrected. In a spirit of fair investigation then, let us change the terms of the question to: 1st. *Do* most of our great men come from the country? 2d. *Is* the country boy superior to the town boy physically, intellectually or morally? 3d. *Do* the country schools perform better work in fitting youth for the race of life than is done in the schools of cities? . . .

.   .   .   .

Let us see what there is in the claim that nearly all of the greatest minds are the products of country life. To begin with, we will concede the fact that most of our presidents were farmers' boys, or, at least, may have been between the plow-handles at some time during youth. But in view of the fact that the very latest of our presidents were born at a time when fully ninety-five per cent of the entire population of the New World resided outside of cities and the larger towns, let it be asked the advocates of rural pre-eminence,—supposing the cities to have been capable of producing their proportionate share of the genius fit to discharge presidential duties, what would be the due number of city or town-bred presidents? Again, let it be asked, have our presidents as a class been chosen from among the brightest intellects of our country? Every moderately well-informed person knows that, with a few bright exceptions, our presidents are, to use a colloquialism, made of second-rate timber. The great statesmen, whose names and achievements are before the people, never survive the ordeal of nominating conventions. Some "dark horse" is brought out as a compromise between contending giants. The press of both parties then hunts him from "among the stuff," his virtues and his failings are magnified until in the eyes of the people he is "higher than any from his shoulders and upwards."

Some years ago, an article published—if I remember rightly, in the *Youth's Companion*—was extensively copied and circulated by the press of the country. The writer had sent one hundred postal cards to as many men prominent in politics, education, literature, commerce, arts and sciences. Upon these cards were printed inquiries as to the place of birth and circumstances of boyhood. The answers showed that but ten per cent of these leading men had been born and reared in large cities, while the other ninety per cent had come either from the country, or from *towns of less than five thousand inhabitants*. The writer also mentions the fact that nearly all of these eminent men were beyond sixty in years. The article, being published in 1882, makes it appear that most of these men were born at a period of our history when the purely urban proportion of our population was very insignificant. In 1830, only one person out of thirty-two was an inhabitant of a city of *five thousand* or more inhabitants. Even as late as 1880, the urban population was only eighteen per cent of that of the entire country. Now, what else do these figures show but a complete victory of the much traduced city-bred boys, who, starting in the race numbering less than three per cent of the contestants, come out in the end with ten per cent of the prizes! And then, may we inquire, why should the boys belonging to towns of *less than five thousand inhabitants,* be ranked with the country boys? Having been for ten years a pupil in the public schools of Cincinnati, and having had an experience of eighteen years as teacher in country schools and in graded schools of small towns, I am prepared to affirm that the people of small towns have, by long odds, more points of character in common with city people than with the surrounding rustics. Country people generally affect a degree of superciliousness when comparing their own condition as landed proprietors, with the lot in life of the "town trash"—the laborers and mechanics who form the body of the town's people. But a moderately close observer will soon note the fact that the farmer-folk do not *feel* the contempt to which they give expression.

On the contrary they pay the town-folks the very highest compliment in that they sedulously try to imitate their ways. The degree of culture, intelligence and refinement of a country neighborhood rises in proportion to the nearness of town. Sons and daughters of wealthy farmers are glad to be admitted into the social circles of the small town, whose standard of society is set by the families of professional men, merchants and mechanics. The educational advantages, and the intellectual light engendered by the friction of various elements of society, in even a small town, raises the general average of culture much higher than that which obtains in a rural community. In our larger cities, merchants and others, when referring to city boys, as compared with country boys, are unduly careless in the use of these terms; the latter generally implies, simply, all those who are *not from the larger cities.* By this classification, a boy born and bred in a small town of fifteen hundred, or of four thousand inhabitants, passes for a country boy, although near his home he is alluded to as a "town dude." One proprietor of a large mercantile establishment, whose fad it was to favor young men "from the country" in his choice of employes, was induced by a request of the writer to inquire more particularly as to the antecedents of the nine "country boys" behind his counters. The inquiry opened his eyes to the fact that not one of them had ever been between plow-handles, or had ever combed hay-seed out of his hair.

In looking up the biographies of the many great men who started in life as farmer-boys, we observe this one significant fact, that invariably they availed themselves of the very first opportunity of quitting rural surroundings and employments. They formed the very cream, so to speak, of the country population, which seeking its natural position of affinity with kindred minds of the city, created the impression there that the country is a very magazine of force and mental strength, whereas the simple truth is, that it is but a mass of refuse that remains after the best element has been extracted. On the other hand, no account is kept of the great number of city youths who have chosen farming as their calling, and achieved success therein. The mines and homestead claims of the West tell the tale of pluck and enterprise of town-bred boys. Some of the great wheat farms of Dakota and cattle ranches of Montana are owned and operated by men born in cities and educated in their public schools.

The general tendency is, that whenever a country boy rises to eminence as a man, to add the fact of his country training to his fame. If one of equal eminence is known to have been city-bred, no comments are made as his success is considered as a matter of course. In cases where the early life of a distinguished man has been of a mixed town and country training, it is usual to attribute the entire credit to his rural experience. . . .

WOMEN OF NEW YORK, *Marie L. Hankins*

WOMEN were warned away from seeking success on
the dangerous urban terrain, not only by
ministers and other prominent persons but also by
less eminent people writing in more popular vein. In
her *Women of New York*, Marie Hankins
colorfully describes a number of feminine life-styles,
including some that involve actual or potential
disaster. But note that her women are all city-born.

A New York woman will seldom own that she is poor or unfashionable, until she absolutely suffers destitution. But the destitute are many. It is frightful to think how numerous they are. Our asylums and our public institutions, are filled to overflowing. Yet, alas! the damp hovel, the tottering tenement house, even the corners of empty cellars, the niches of new buildings, and piles of boards or barrels, shelter myriads of starving, shivering, hopeless mortals, every night.

Among the women who thus suffer for their own or others' thriftlessness or crime, none can be found who began life as they will end it. In the homes of wealth, there are very few who were born to the enjoyment of luxury.

The wheel of fortune turns no where so swiftly as in the great metropolis. New Yorkers *must* go up or down, must sink or swim. They make fortunes in a year, or lose them in a day. A friendly push sends some to the top of the see-saw, an unlucky jounce precipitates others head long to the bottom. You cannot crawl up two feet and back one, in Gotham's slippery road. It is either the top or the bottom, towards which we are always progressing. All the better for the lucky ones, and all the worse for those who fall. It is impossible to tell the future life of the child, by the circumstances in which fate appears to have placed it. Make the attempt, and you will soon see your mistake.

Perhaps the principal cause of the rapid approach of want and misery to women reared in ease and plenty, and then thrown upon their own resources, is the idleness in which they are almost universally educated. A fashionable lady is as helpless with her hands, as a Chinese woman is with her feet. Her delicate fingers are shapely and white, it is true, but they are

Reprinted from *Women of New York* (New York: Marie Louise Hankins and Co., 1861), pp. 17–20.

not capable of providing the common necessaries of life, for even one human being. To sew, to make bread, to sweep or wash, would be to degrade herself. To learn a trade or profession, with which, if necessary, she might support existence, would be a drudgery she could not contemplate for a moment. Then her education is superficial, and her accomplishments, even should she be talented, are merely dabbled in, not learned. She can sing, play, paint flowers, and perhaps write poetry—but *only* "a little." She is seldom mistress of any one art, sufficiently to enable her to adopt it as a profession. Her beauty alone, has been well nourished and cared for; and from girlhood, her constant object has been marriage. Once the wife of an eligible suitor, she expects to be supported in a sumptuous style, until her dying day. Should death deprive her of her protector, leaving her unexpectedly penniless, she has no power to struggle with her destiny, but sinks inertly, unless some kind friend or relation proffers his charity. The unfledged bird, the babe of a brief week's existence, is as strong a thing as many a full grown fashionable lady, left to her own resources.

Now and then, sensible people among the wealthy classes give their daughters the power to be independent, by encouraging their talent, or instructing them in some art, by which they might, if necessitated, gain a livelihood. But such common sense is rare. And thus it is that we continually see the poor mount, and the rich fall.

The servant has the use of her fingers, and never need to starve. The milliner, ready to seize at bargains, and turn a penny by some change in the prevailing mode, can make a fortune. The shop keeper's wife is his best aid behind the counter, and by slow degrees each attains a position above that in which she began life. Starting in a shanty, may end in a palace. Yet having once attained an eminence, these very people deny their children the advantages which made them what they are. Believing idleness a mark of superiority, they educated their offspring to an inaction, which degrades both mind and body, renders the girls mere walking fashion plates, and causes the boys to become the dissipated idlers, who will inevitably run through any fortune, and bring themselves and their sisters to beggary.

Women, think of this! Read the various experiences herein presented, and profit therefrom. . . .

SUCCESS AND THE MAN OF CULTURE,
George S. Hillard

IN contrast to the Reverend Mr. Chapin, Mr. Hillard,
a merchant, offers to young and aspiring colleagues
salvation from purely materialistic success, through
profound immersion in reading and the other arts of
a genuinely urbanized civilization. This same message
was repeatedly directed at the *nouveau riche* through
the succeeding decades. Duveen's technique for
selling the paintings of the Old Masters to American
capitalists like Mellon and Frick played on this same
theme of sophisticated, cultured urbanity. But
Hillard also points to urbane pursuits as a
solace for those who fail to become very successful.

To the gentle-hearted youth who is thrown upon the rocks of a pitiless city, and stands 'homeless amid a thousand homes,' the approach of evening brings with it an aching sense of loneliness and desolation, which comes down upon the spirit like darkness upon the earth. In this mood, his best impulses become a snare to him, and he is led astray because he is social, affectionate, sympathetic, and warm-hearted. If there be a young man thus circumstanced within the sound of my voice, let me say to him that books are the friends of the friendless and that a library is the home of the homeless. A taste for reading will always carry you into the best possible company, and enable you to converse with men who will instruct you by their wisdom and charm you by their wit, who will soothe you when fretted, refresh you when weary, counsel you when perplexed, and sympathize with you at all times. . . .

. . . .

In the use of books there is room for such discrimination. Books themselves are of various classes; some are good, some are bad, and many are neither good nor bad. Some are to be studied, some to be read, and some to be thrown into the fire. The profusion of books at the present time, and the ease with which they may be procured, I look upon as by

Excerpted from an address delivered before the Mercantile Library Association at its Thirtieth Anniversary, November 13, 1850 (Boston: Ticknor and Fields), pp. 22–31, 35–38.

no means an unmixed good. There is a great deal of trash current in the form of cheap literature, which, like cheap confectionary, is at once tempting and pernicious. Cheap as these books are in appearance, most of them would be dear at nothing at all. Especially is this true of the swarms of novels, of English and French manufacture, which come warping upon every eastern wind, most of them worthless, and many of them worse than worthless. If you have any purpose of self-culture, one of your first duties is resolutely to abstain from such books, as you would from opium or brandy. . . .

Men engaged in business with a taste for reading are apt to underrate their own intellectual advantages, and to overrate those of men with whom literature or science is a profession. Especially do they magnify the benefits of what is commonly called a liberal education, which means a residence of a certain number of years within the walls of a college. . . . So far as the acquisition of knowledge is concerned, the young men at college have the advantage of you; but not, of necessity, so far as the training of the faculties is concerned. Two youths, for instance, of the same age leave school at the same time, and one enters college and the other goes into a counting-room in Boston. And let us suppose them equally conscientious and equally disposed to make the best use of their opportunities. The collegian works hard, learns much, and acquires honorable distinction, but in the mean time he has perhaps lost his health; for, so far as my observation goes, I should say that one quarter, at least, of the young men who are educated at our colleges leave them with impaired health. From the recluse life which he has led, he is likely to have awkward manners and an unprepossessing address. From not having been trained to habits of self-control, he is perhaps impatient of contradiction, and needlessly sensitive. He is probably conceited, possibly pedantic, and pretty sure to want that sixth sense which is called tact. He knows much of books, but little of men or of life, and from mere confusion of mind incurs the reproach of weakness of character. On the other hand, the lad who enters a counting-room finds himself perhaps the youngest member of a large establishment, and whatever of conceit he may have brought from the village academy is soon rubbed out of him. He learns to obey, to submit, and to be patient; to endure reproof without anger, and to bear contradiction with good-humor. He is obliged to keep his wits about him, to decide quickly, to have accurate eyes and truthful ears, to learn that there are just sixty minutes in an hour, and just one hundred cents in a dollar. He is compelled to bear and forbear, to resist temptation, to struggle down rebellious impulses, and to put on the armor of a brave silence. The hours of his day come freighted with lessons of self-reliance and self-command, and the grain of his character grows firm under the discipline of life.

We are all inclined to pursue too keenly, and to value too highly, what is called success in life, which means a good estate, a distinguished social position, power, influence, and consideration. All the elements that mould the growing mind tend to strengthen this passion. Open the common biographies which are written for our children, and what do you find set down in them? This man, when he was a boy, was docile, diligent, and frugal; he studied hard; he was never idle, and never naughty; he made friends; he acquired knowledge; he laid up all the money that he earned. And what was the result? He became prosperous and powerful and rich; he held high offices and enjoyed great honors, and was esteemed and exalted. If you do likewise, you will be what he was, and gain what he gained. This is but another form of appealing to the love of excelling, rather than the love of excellence,—that inferior motive, which, though it may quicken the faculties, dims the beauty of the soul. . . .

.   .   .   .

In the mercantile profession, the acquisition of property is the obvious index of success. A successful merchant is a rich merchant. The two ideas can hardly be disjoined. Thus the universal passion for the prizes of life is apt, in your case, to take its lowest form, that of the love of money. I would hold up no fanatical or ascetic views of life for your admiration and applause. Wealth brings noble opportunities, and competence is a proper object of pursuit; but wealth and even competence may be bought at too high a price. Wealth itself has no moral attribute. It is not money, but the love of money, which is the root of all evil. It is the relation between wealth and the mind and the character of its possessor, which is the essential thing. It is the passionate, absorbing, and concentrated pursuit of wealth,— the surrendering of the whole being to one despotic thought,—the starving of all the nobler powers in order to glut one fierce and clamorous appetite, —against which I would warn you. This form of idolatry will not only check intellectual growth, but it is adverse to all the delicacies and refinements of virtue. . . .

.   .   .   .

As we are all too much given to make an idol of success, so we shape our lives with reference to this worship. In our calculations, we lay aside the adverse chances. Hence, if we do not achieve success, we are apt to fall into gloomy despair, or bitter repining, or heart-corroding envy. The self-exaggeration of adversity is quite as dangerous to the health of the soul as the self-exaggeration of prosperity. But though fortune and power are desirable things, yet more desirable is that mood of mind which can see them denied without a murmur. My young friends, these considerations come close home to you. You are aware of the inexorable statistics of trade and commerce. You know how few there are that have not, at some period in the course of their business life, encountered disaster and embarrassment. You know how many there are, that, after long struggling with adverse fortune, have at last thrown up their hands, and declined into a recluse condition, and given themselves over to dumb despair. You are all looking forward with hope to the future, and already, in anticipation, grasping the prizes of life. But as the past has been, the future will be. Success and failure will be distributed among you in the same proportion as among your predecessors. Are you prepared to meet the drawing of a blank in the lottery of life? Can you stand and wait, and yet feel that you are still serving? Have you thought of furnishing yourselves with the moral and mental resources which will enable you to rise superior to disappointment and disaster, and to sit down contentedly, if need be, with poverty? We shrink from poverty with unmanly weakness. We exaggerate its terrors, as we exaggerate the attractions of wealth. To our morbid apprehensions, it includes the sting of shame, the burden of self-reproach, the gloom of solitude, and the anguish of a broken spirit. There is, indeed, a pitiless and soul-crushing poverty, which binds and seals the heart with an arctic frost, and shuts out the light of hope, and tries the temper of love, and steals from childhood its blessed prerogative of careless content, and plants by the side of the cradle the lacerating thorns of life; but into this, no man in our country, of average capacity, need fall, except from his vices. There is also a milder and serener form of poverty, the nurse of manly energy and heaven-climbing thoughts, attended by love and faith and hope, around whose steps the mountain breezes blow, and from whose countenance all the virtues gather strength. Look around you upon the distinguished men that in every department of life guide and control the times, and inquire what was their origin and what were their early fortunes. Were they, as a general rule, rocked and dandled on the lap of wealth? No; such men emerge from the homes of decent competence or struggling poverty. Necessity sharpens their faculties and privation and sacrifice brace their moral nature. They learn the great art of renunciation, and enjoy the happiness of having few wants. They know nothing of indifference or satiety. There is not an idle fibre in their frames. They put the vigor of a resolute purpose into every act. The edge of their minds is always kept sharp. In the shocks of life, men like these meet the softly-nurtured darlings of prosperity as the vessel of iron meets the vessel of porcelain. Lift your hearts above the region of wild hopes and cowardly fears. Put on that even temper of mind which shall be a shadow in success and a light in adversity. If wealth and distinction come, receive them in a thankful and moderate spirit. If they do not come, fill their places with better guests. Remember that all which truly exalts and ennobles a man is bound to him by ties as indissoluble as those which link the planets to the sun. Plant yourselves upon God's immutable laws, and fortune and failure will be no more than vapors that curl and play far beneath your feet.

SUGGESTED READINGS: CHAPTER 7

E. Digby Baltzell. *Philadelphia Gentlemen*. Glencoe, Ill.: The Free Press, 1958.

A sociological monograph about the Philadelphia elite; that is, about those who either achieved or have inherited their wealth and social position.

Reinhard Bendix and Seymour M. Lipset (Eds.) *Class, Status and Power* (2nd edition). New York: The Free Press, 1966.

See especially E. Digby Baltzell, " 'Who's Who in America' and 'The Social Register': Elite and Upper Class Index in Metropolitan America," pp. 266–75; R. Richard Wohl, "The 'Rags to Riches Story': An Episode of Secular Idealism," pp. 501–506; Stephan Tharnstrom, "Class and Mobility in a Nineteenth-Century City: A Study of Unskilled Laborers," pp. 602–615.

These three papers are especially interesting when read one after the other. Baltzell is critical of previous discussions of American stratification which were based on study of single communities, and looks for indexes of a national metropolitan elite. Wohl discusses the Alger myth, a vital legend even today. Tharnstrom gives an account of how Newburyport's unskilled laborers lived from 1850 to 1880 and attempts to give historical data on the myth of America as the land of opportunity for all.

Berenice Fisher. *Industrial Education: American Ideals and Institutions*. Madison: University of Wisconsin Press, 1967.

A sophisticated analysis of the kinds of institutions that have evolved in conjunction with ideologies of "opportunities in the city," "education for the urban masses," and the "city as a rational marketplace."

C. Wright Mills. *White Collar*. New York: Oxford University Press, 1951.

This book can be read as a perspective on what happens to white-collar workers in the big city, including those who have migrated there to achieve success there. Mills's perspective is highly critical of the kind of industrial-urbanization which America has developed.

8

Maxwell Street, Chicago, 1947. Chicago Historical Society,
M. Mead, photographer.

POVERTY AND
ITS SOLUTIONS

OUR continual debate over poverty and its relation to cities
is nothing new. Americans have long believed that one awful
consequence of urbanization was a residue of urban poor. What
vary considerably over the decades, however, are the classes
of people called povertystricken, the assigned causes of
their poverty, and the prescriptions for changing city life so that the
numbers of the poor may be reduced or their unenviable
condition mitigated. The selections below illustrate
variants of this enduring urban perspective. Still other variants—
seen in combination with other urban imageries—are illustrated
by the previous selections on the "perils of the city" and by later
selections on city planning.

As noted earlier, sociological literature has always
been affected by urban reform tendencies and by a concern for the
lot of the poor. So that we will not repeat names and influences,
let us note that the study of criminology, in the works of
men like Edwin Sutherland and John Gillin, were much focused,
especially in earlier years, on the connection between crime and
poverty. Even the theoretical writings of as abstract a
thinker as George Herbert Mead, the philosopher who deeply
influenced sociologists, had some roots in his friendship with
Jane Addams and other Chicago reformers. Both he and other
pragmatists, like John Dewey, were struck by the need for

concerted action and consensus in an urban environment where rich and poor had to live together. The writings of Lester Ward, of lower class origins, were also immensely influential in early sociological thought. And now, after some years of post-war affluence, sociologists and other social scientists are engaged again in studies of the urban poor. Just before the recent Johnsonian legislation, A. B. Hollingshead "discovered" the plight of the American lower-lower class when it came to mental disorder in an even more explicit fashion than the earlier Faris-Dunham study, and he urged necessary reforms to help these people. Recent research on geriatrics by sociologists carries on with this general theme.

Without question, sociologists today are deeply involved, in various ways, in the ongoing, persistent dialogue about how to interpret poverty on the American scene. The ecologists among the urban sociologists contribute in more indirect fashion to this same dialogue, as they study spatial forms of the city and the surrounding metropolitan terrain. Those who study cities in Africa and South America are, of course, centrally concerned with urban poverty there in its relation to underdeveloped societies.

RURAL HOMES FOR URBAN CHILDREN,
Charles Loring Brace

> BRACE was a highly respected social reformer; among
> his activities was the institutionalization of
> arrangements whereby urban waifs were adopted into
> farm homes. The resulting combination
> of rural domesticity, farm work, and a country
> environment was bound to counteract the
> evils of the child's previous "street" life. Here Brace
> describes the methods used by the Children's
> Aid Society, and quotes testimonial letters received
> from grateful emigres.

The Founders of the Children's Aid Society early saw that the best
of all Asylums for the outcast child, is the *farmer's home.*

The United States have the enormous advantage over all other
countries, in the treatment of difficult questions of pauperism and reform,
that they possess a practically unlimited area of arable land. The demand
for labor on this land is beyond any present supply. Moreover, the culti-
vators of the soil are in America our most solid and intelligent class. From
the nature of their circumstances, their laborers, or "help," must be members of their families, and share in their social tone. It is, accordingly, of
the utmost importance to train up children who shall aid in their work,
and be associates of their own children. A servant who is nothing but a
servant, would be, with them, disagreeable and inconvenient. They like
to educate their own "help." With their overflowing supply of food also,
each new mouth in the household brings no drain on their means. Children
are a blessing, and the mere feeding of a young boy or girl is not considered at all. With this fortunate state of things, it was but a natural
inference that the important movement now inaugurating for the benefit
of the unfortunate children of New York should at once strike upon a
plan of

EMIGRATION . . .

Simple and most effective as this ingenious scheme now seems—which
has accomplished more in relieving New York of youthful crime and

Excerpted from *The Dangerous Classes of New York* (New York: Wynkoop and
Hallenbeck, 1872), pp. 225–28, 231–33, 261–64.

misery than all other charities together—at the outset it seemed . . . difficult and perplexing. . . .

Among other objections, it was feared that the farmers would not want the children for help; that, if they took them, the latter would be liable to ill-treatment, or, if well treated, would corrupt the virtuous children around them, and thus New York would be scattering seeds of vice and corruption all over the land. Accidents might occur to the unhappy little ones thus sent, bringing odium on the benevolent persons who were dispatching them to the country. How were places to be found? How were the demand and supply for children's labor to be connected? How were the right employers to be selected? And, when the children were placed, how were their interests to be watched over, and acts of oppression or hard dealing prevented or punished? Were they to be indentured, or not? If this was the right scheme, why had it not been tried long ago in our cities or in England?

These and innumerable similar difficulties and objections were offered to this projected plan of relieving the city of its youthful pauperism and suffering. They all fell to the ground before the confident efforts to carry out a well-laid scheme; and practical experience has justified none of them.

To awaken the demand for these children, circulars were sent out through the city weeklies and the rural papers to the country districts. Hundreds of applications poured in at once from the farmers and mechanics all through the Union. At first, we made the effort to meet individual applications by sending just the kind of children wanted; but this soon became impracticable.

Each applicant or employer always called for "a perfect child," without any of the taints of earthly depravity. The girls must be pretty, good-tempered, not given to purloining sweetmeats, and fond of making fires at daylight, and with a constitutional love for Sunday Schools and Bible-lessons. The boys must be well made, of good stock, never disposed to steal apples or pelt cattle, using language of perfect propriety, and delighting in family-worship and prayer-meetings more than in fishing or skating parties. These demands, of course, were not always successfully complied with. Moreover, to those who desired the children of "blue eyes, fair hair, and blond complexion," we were sure to send the dark-eyed and brunette; and the particular virtues wished for were very often precisely those that the child was deficient in. It was evidently altogether too much of a lottery for bereaved parents or benevolent employers to receive children in that way.

.   .   .   .

Having found the defects of our first plan of emigration, we soon inaugurated another, which has since been followed out successfully during nearly twenty years of constant action.

We formed little companies of emigrants, and, after thoroughly cleaning and clothing them, put them under a competent agent, and, first selecting a village where there was a call or opening for such a party, we dispatched them to the place.

The farming community having been duly notified, there was usually a dense crowd of people at the station, awaiting the arrival of the youthful travelers. The sight of the little company of the children of misfortune always touched the hearts of a population naturally generous. They were soon billeted around among the citizens, and the following day a public meeting was called in the church or town-hall, and a committee appointed of leading citizens. The agent then addressed the assembly, stating the benevolent objects of the Society, and something of the history of the children. The sight of their worn faces was a most pathetic enforcement of his arguments. People who were childless came forward to adopt children; others, who had not intended to take any into their families, were induced to apply for them; and many who really wanted the children's labor pressed forward to obtain it. . . . Those who are able, pay the fares of the children, or otherwise make some gift to the Society, until at length the business of charity is finished, and a little band of young wayfarers and homeless rovers in the world find themselves in comfortable and kind homes, with all the boundless advantages and opportunities of the Western farmer's life about them.

.　　.　　.　　.　　.　　.　　.　　.　　.　　.

"YALE COLLEGE, NEW HAVEN, Oct. 11, 1871.
"Rev. C. L. BRACE, Secretary Children's Aid Society:
"*Dear Sir*—I shall endeavor in this letter to give you a brief sketch of my life, as it is your request that I should.

"I cannot speak of my parents with any certainty at all. I recollect having an aunt by the name of Julia B. . . . She had me in charge for some time, and made known some things to me of which I have a faint rememberance. She married a gentleman in Boston, and left me to shift for myself in the streets of your city. I could not have been more than seven or eight years of age at this time. She is greatly to be excused for this act, since I was a very bad boy, having an abundance of self-will.

"At this period I became a vagrant, roaming over all parts of the city. I would often pick up a meal at the markets or at the docks, where they were unloading fruit. At a late hour in the night I would find a resting-place in some box or hogshead, or in some dark hole under a staircase.

"The boys that I fell in company with would steal and swear, and of course I contracted those habits too. I have a distinct recollection of stealing up upon houses to tear the lead from around the chimneys, and then take it privily away to some junk-shop, as they call it; with the proceeds I would buy a ticket for the pit in the Chatham-street Theatre, and something to eat with the remainder. This is the manner in which I was drifting out in the stream of life, when some kind person from your Society persuaded me to go to Randall's Island. I remained at this place two years. Sometime in July, 1859, one of your agents came there and asked how many boys who had no parents would love to have nice homes in the West, where they could drive horses and oxen, and have as many apples and melons as they should wish. I happened to be one of the many who responded in the affirmative.

"On the 4th of August twenty-one of us had homes procured for us at N——, Ind. A lawyer from T——, who chanced to be engaged in court matters, was at N—— at the time. He desired to take a boy home with him, and I was the one assigned him. He owns a farm of two hundred acres lying close to town. Care was taken that I should be occupied there and not in town. I was always treated as one of the family. In sickness I was ever cared for by prompt attention. In winter I was sent to the Public School. The family room was a good school to me, for there I found the daily papers and a fair library.

"After a period of several years I taught a Public School in a little log cabin about nine miles from T——. There I felt that every man ought to be a good man, especially if he is to instruct little children.

"Though I had my pupils read the Bible, yet I could not openly ask God's blessing on the efforts of the day. Shortly after I united myself with the Church. I always had attended Sabbath School at T——. Mr. G—— placed me in one the first Sabbath. I never doubted the teachings of the Scriptures. Soon my pastor presented the claims of the ministry. I thought about it for some time, for my ambition was tending strongly toward the legal profession. The more I reflected the more I felt how good God had been to me all my life, and that if I had any ability for laboring in His harvest, He was surely entitled to it.

"I had accumulated some property on the farm in the shape of a horse, a yoke of oxen, etc., amounting in all to some $300. These I turned into cash, and left for a preparatory school. This course that I had entered upon did not meet with Mr. G——'s hearty approbation. At the academy I found kind instructors and sympathizing friends. I remained there three years, relying greatly on my own efforts for support. After entering the class of '74' last year, I was enabled to go through with it by the kindness of a few citizens here.

"I have now resumed my duties as a Sophomore, in faith in Him who has ever been my best friend. If I can prepare myself for acting well my part in life by going through the college curriculum, I shall be satisfied.

"I shall ever acknowledge with gratitude that the Children's Aid Society had been the instrument of my elevation.

"To be taken from the gutters of New York city and placed in a college is almost a miracle.

"I am not an exception either. Wm. F——, who was taken West during the war, in a letter received from W—— College, dated Oct. 7, writes thus: 'I have heard that you were studying for the ministry, so am I. I have a long time yet before I enter the field, but I am young and at the right age to begin.' My prayer is that the Society may be amplified to greater usefulness.

Yours very truly,

"JOHN G. B."

ONCE A NEW YORK PAUPER, NOW A WESTERN FARMER

"C——, MICH., Oct. 26, 1871.

"Mr. J. MACY:

"*Dear Sir*—I received your very kind and welcome letter a few days since, and I assure you that I felt very much rejoiced to know that you felt the same interest in hearing and knowing how your Western boys and girls get along, as you have expressed in former times.

"In your letter you spoke of the time you accompanied our company of boys to the West as not seeming so long to you as it really was. For my own part, if I could not look to the very many pleasant scenes that it has been my privilege to enjoy while I have been in the West, I do not think it would seem so long to me since we all marched two and two for the boat up the Hudson River on our route for Michigan. There were some among us who shed a few tears as we were leaving the city, as we all expected, for the last time. But as we sped on and saw new sights, we very willingly forgot the city with all its dusty atmosphere and temptations and wickedness, for the country all around us was clothed in its richest foliage; the birds were singing their sweetest songs, and all nature seemed praising our Heavenly Father in high notes of joy.

"In the midst of this enchantment we were introduced to the farmers in the vicinity of A——, and then and there we many of us separated to go home with those kind friends, and mould the character of our future life.

"For my own part, I was more than fortunate, for I secured a home with a *good* man and every comfort of life I enjoyed. I had the benefit of good schools until I was nearly of age, and when I became of age a substantial present of eighty acres of good farming land, worth fifty dollars per acre, was given me, and thus I commenced life. Once a New York pauper, now a Western farmer. If these lines should chance to meet the eyes of any boy or girl in your Society, I would say to them, don't delay, but go to the West and there seek your home and fortune. You may have some trials and temptations to overcome, but our lives seem happier when we know that we have done our duties and have done the will of our Heavenly Father, who has kindly cared for us all through our lives.

"Last winter it was my privilege to be with you all through the Christmas festivities, and it did my soul good to return and enjoy Christmas with you after an absence of nearly fifteen years. I met you there as I also did the Newsboys' Lodginghouse. Those were times of rejoicing to me to see the wickedness we escaped by not staying in your city. When I returned home I brought with me a girl of eleven years of age, and intend to do as well by her as my circumstances will allow. I have been married nearly three years, and by God's grace assisting us we intend to meet you all on the other shore. I have written you a very long letter, but I will now close. I shall be pleased to hear from you again at any time when you feel at liberty to write. Hoping to hear from you soon again, I remain truly your friend,   C. H. J——.''

NINETEENTH-STREET GANG,
Charles Loring Brace

> BRACE tells us of another of his experiments—but this
> one failed. The story will seem all too
> familiar to the modern reader.

Seventeen years ago, my attention had been called to the extraordinarily degraded condition of the children in a district lying on the west side of the city, between Seventeenth and Nineteenth Streets, and Seventh and Tenth Avenues. A certain block, called "Misery Row" in Tenth Avenue, was the main seed-bed of crime and poverty in the quarter and was also invariably a "fever-nest." Here the poor obtained wretched rooms at a comparatively low rent; these they sub-let; and thus in little, crowded, close tenements, were herded men, women, and children of all ages. The parents were invariably given to hard drinking, and the children were sent out to beg or to steal. Besides them, other children, who were orphans, or who had run away from drunkards' homes, or had been working on the canal-boats that discharged on the docks near by, drifted into the quarter, as if attracted by the atmosphere of crime and laziness that prevailed in the neighborhood. These slept around the breweries of the ward, or on the hay-barges, or in the old sheds of Eighteenth and Nineteenth Streets. They were mere children, and kept life together by all sorts of street-jobs—helping the brewery laborers, blackening boots, sweeping sidewalks, "smashing baggages" (as they called it), and the like. Herding together, they soon began to form an unconscious society for vagrancy and idleness. Finding that work brought but poor pay, they tried shorter roads to getting money by petty thefts, in which they were very adroit. Even if they earned a considerable sum by a lucky day's job, they quickly spent it in gambling, or for some folly.

The police soon knew them as "street-rats"; but, like the rats, they

---

Excerpted from *Dangerous Classes of New York* (New York: Wynkoop and Hallenbeck, 1872), pp. 317–19, 321–23.

were too quick and cunning to be often caught in their petty plunderings, so they gnawed away at the foundations of society undisturbed. As to the "popular education" of which we boast, and the elevating and inspiring faith of Christianity which had reared its temples all around them, they might almost as well have been the children of the Makololos in Central Africa. They had never been in school or church, and knew of God and Christ only in street oaths, or as something of which people far above them spoke sometimes.

I determined to inaugurate here a regular series of the "moral disinfectants," if I may so call them, for this "crime-nest," which act almost as surely, though not as rapidly, as do the physical disinfectants—the sulphate of iron, the chloride of lime, and the various deodorizers of the Board of Health—in breaking up the "fever-nests" of the city.

These measures, though imitated in some respects from England, were novel in their combination.

The first step in the treatment is to appoint a kind-hearted agent or "Visitor," who shall go around the infected quarter, and win the confidence of, and otherwise befriend the homeless and needy children of the neighborhood. Then we open an informal, simple, religious meeting—the Boys' Meeting which I have described; next we add to it a free Reading-room, then an Industrial School, afterwards, a Lodging-house; and, after months or years of the patient application of these remedies, our final and most successful treatment is, as I have often said, the forwarding of the more hopeful cases to farms in the West.

While seeking to apply these long-tried remedies to the wretched young population in the Sixteenth Ward, I chanced on a most earnest Christian man, a resident of the quarter, whose name I take the liberty of mentioning, Mr. D. Slater, a manufacturer.

He went around himself through the rookeries of the district, and gathered the poor lads even in his own parlor; he fed and clothed them; he advised and prayed with them. We opened a religious meeting for them. Nothing could exceed their wild and rowdy conduct in the first gatherings. On one or two occasions some of the little ruffians absolutely drew knives on our assistants, and had to be handed over to the police. But our usual experience was repeated even there. Week by week patient kindness and the truths of Christianity began to have their effect on these wild little heathen of the street. . . .

.   .   .   .

Several other lads were helped to an honest livelihood. A Visitor was then appointed, who lived and worked in the quarter. But our moral treatment for this nest of crime had only commenced.

We appealed to the public for aid to establish the reforming agencies which alone can cure these evils, and whose foundation depends mainly on the liberality, in money, of our citizens. We warned them that these children, if not instructed, would inevitably grow up as ruffians. We said often that they would not be like the stupid foreign criminal class, but that their crimes, when they came to maturity, would show the recklessness, daring, and intensity of the American character. . . .

.   .   .   .

But the words fell on inattentive ears.

We found ourselves unable to continue our reforming agencies in the Sixteenth Ward; no means were supplied; our Visitor was dismissed, the meeting closed; Mr. Slater moved away, heavily out of pocket with his humane efforts, and much discouraged with the indifference of the Christian community to these tremendous evils; and the "Nineteenth-street Gang" grew up undisturbed in its evil courses, taking new lessons in villainy and crime, and graduating in the manner the community has felt the past few years. Both the police and the public have noted the extraordinary recklessness and ferocity of their crimes. Once, a mere lad, named Rogers, committed a murder, a few years ago, on a respectable gentleman, Mr. Swanton, accompanied by his wife, in the open street, on the west side of the city. He was subsequently executed. Some have been notorious thieves and burglars.

OUTINGS, *Joseph Lee*

A MORE temporary expedient than having city
children adopted by farm families was to
provide for visits to the country. Those visits took—
and still take—the form of picnics, outings, and
even extended stays at summer camps.

The life of a boy ought not, however, to be all strenuous, particularly in summer. *Non semper tendit arcum Apollo:* even Mr. Roosevelt cannot "play ball" all the time. Baseball is not a boy's play, but his work. In summer we have all of us a desire to go off somewhere and see something new, and it is especially advantageous to the city boy to see some-

Reprinted from *Constructive and Preventive Philanthropy* (New York: Macmillan, 1902), pp. 185–89.

thing of the life of trees and plants and something of the care of crops and animals. The vacation school may establish a visiting acquaintance with nature, but you must stay with a person if you want to really know him. There was some beginning of the sending of children to the country by charitable people as early as 1849, but the first organized work was started in the early seventies. At the present time the amount of this that is done is making it a very considerable factor in the summer life of the city child.

Mr. W. S. Ufford, in his valuable study of the statistics, gives a list of charities which in 1895 sent a total of 356,531 persons out of town, of whom 334,630 were sent for one day, the average stay of the other 21,901 being 9.27 days. The total cost was $122,438. Most of these were still sent to "homes" (in the sense which does not mean home), a good many to private families. Many churches and other organizations, and some factories, now have summer camps and cottages to which children and others are sent.

.   .   .   .

. . . The Boston municipal camp, carried on by Mayor Quincy, in 1898 and 1899, is, I think, the only instance of a municipality undertaking this work.

"The chairman of the local committee of the New York fresh-air fund in one village community weighed every child in the party on arrival, and again after fourteen days in the country. The average age was ten years. The least gain was shown in a four-year-old boy, who added only one pound to his weight, the greatest by an eleven-year-old girl, who gained nine pounds. The average gain for the entire party was four and nine-tenths pounds."

These children come to the country with a more complete ignorance than is easy to imagine. One boy, after watching a large herd of Alderneys, asked, "Say, mister, do you have to buy gum for all them cows to chew?" But familiarity breeds mutual affection between the country families and the children; sometimes, though not in a large percentage of cases, resulting in the settling of the child's family in the country.

A great problem of summer charities is that of Sunday-school picnics. Of the above-mentioned 533 girls, 363 went on from one to ten picnics each. Those who did not go were mostly the younger ones. These picnics are the great interrupters of vacation school work; some of them justify the interruption, but when a boy belongs to half a dozen or more Sunday-schools of different denominations, for picnic purposes only, the question arises whether the churches, in extending their religious influence, ought not to have more regard for the morals of the children.

IMMIGRANTS AND THE CHURCH,
William P. Shriver

> THE reform movement—which addressed itself to
> problems of the urban poor—had a significant
> religious component. Both the migrants from
> rural America and the immigrants from rural Europe
> confronted the churches with opportunities
> to save souls and salve conscience, while
> simultaneously allowing the churches to serve the
> cause of democracy. The religious reformers
> were prolific in inventing serviceable institutions,
> such as the settlement house, the neighborhood house,
> the mission, and the YMCA.

A VOICE CRYING IN THE WILDERNESS [1]

In "the bottoms" of a Western city under the shadow of a great packing works, there is a polyglot community of several thousand souls, including at least fifteen nationalities. In and out among the tawdry homes of this area of human desolation there goes a kindly, great-souled woman, walking where she feels the Christ would gladly have gone. In her heart there is a great desolation also, of infinite longing for the touch of little hands on her face, and the lisping of the tender affection of a little child which she hears now only in memory. But the travail of her soul is being satisfied in an outgoing love to the dirty, neglected little children of "the bottoms." As we set out to discover the ministry of the Church to our recent immigrants, I can conceive of no better thing than to set down here the cry of this woman's heart from this wilderness of human need.

Excerpted from *Immigrant Forces* (New York, 1913), pp. 189–93, 204–205.

1. I believe that from the national point of view the most important work which our American churches have to do to-day is to preach a simple and efficient gospel to the multitudes of immigrants who are coming to our shores. America owes her liberty and her prosperity to the spirit of Christianity which ruled and animated her founders. If our country is to remain true to her original aims, and advances along the line of her first development, she must see to it that the leaven of the gospel of Christ leavens the whole lump of her vastly increasing population— *Henry van Dyke.*

STOP AND SEE

"If the followers of Christ and the people of the Church in their hurryings to and fro would stop long enough to really see the poor tumble-down, unpainted little houses in 'the bottoms,' as bare and comfortless on the inside as they are black and repelling on the outside; if they could only glance into their tiny back yards, where they are fortunate enough to have back yards, near the muddy Kaw where the fogs come up, and near the railroad yards where noisy engines continually belch forth their black smoke and cinders; if they would only pause for a while where the great packing plants and other factories rise, not protectingly, but menacingly, above the humble homes, and in which are swallowed up men, women, and children by thousands, by the labor of whose hands are wrought great wealth for their employers and a mere subsistence for themselves; if they might see, and feel, and know these things for themselves, they would be mastered by a determination which they could not rid themselves of even if they would."

IF

"If women you knew and children you loved actually secured canned goods from the refuse dump, and decayed vegetables thrown away in the market-place, which they ate in preference to accepting charity; if you knew this occurred every day of the year. If you had seen the undersized boy of ten, with circles under his pretty dark eyes, and the hungry look on his sweet, pale face, smile confidently up at his teacher as he asked, 'if she, too, gathered food from the city dump,' and you had noted his look of surprise and regret when told that she did not, because he loved her and thought her very unfortunate indeed. If you could see the lifeless form of a child you knew taken from the old abandoned cistern concealed beneath the rubbish in the back yard, because they did not know the cistern was there, and there was no place for the children to play. If you could see the young foreign men with their handsome faces, and with gifts of mind to enable them to rise, if the means were only placed within their reach, their only center of recreation being some Bulgarian pool-room, Greek coffee-house, or nearby saloon. If you could see these crowded little homes filled with boarders, with no room for a parlor, which is the dream dearest to the hearts of these girls, surpassing even the dream of willow-plumes for their hats, which they attain. If you could see and know the dear old grandmothers, no longer able to go to work, trying to keep house with nothing, or if you could see them sitting in the home of some son or daughter bending over long strips of buttonholes that are never done. If you could see these things, and feel them, and ponder over them, —a great, new compelling purpose would lay hold of your life."

VISUALIZING A MINISTRY FOR THE CHURCH

And then this simple, intelligent, big-hearted American woman, who does not debate with nice and refined discrimination "The Problem of the Immigrant," but puts her own life at their service as fellow human-beings, conjures that larger expression of the Church's ministry which she claims for this community, a community not unlike hundreds of others. "O, for a big, beautiful playground, with a kind-hearted conductor, for boys and girls of ten; and a cheery, well-equipped day nursery for the tots of four, with a mother soul for a matron; and a well-furnished kindergarten with a consecrated kindergartner for the tots between," is the first cry of a heart which understands the meaning and significance of play in a little child's life. Out of her experience of this life of "the bottoms," she asks also for a club for boys, well equipped with a gymnasium, and a club for girls, with cooking and sewing classes, besides instruction in the laws of health and sanitation. In the desolation of this same "bottoms," she covets the warmth and welcome of a neighborhood center, with club and class rooms for the men; with that parlor which these girls are denied for a normal social life; with a gathering place for the mothers, and even the old grandmothers. And this house of the fellowship of Christ she would have radiant with his spirit, and vibrant with his teaching of the forgiveness and love of the common Father, God.

POINTING THE MORAL

I have said that two purposes will have been served in setting down here the heart cry of this woman. She has conceived with fine intelligence the sort of human ministry this desolate immigrant community needs. And she has outlined her program from first-hand, intimate study and contact with the homes, the economic, social, and religious life of this immigrant people. She has made clear the starting place for a ministry of the Christian Church,—an exact and intimate knowledge of the needs. She has felt what so many feel who press into the life of our immigrant industrial communities, the vast ignorance, the almost seeming neglect of those who represent the compassion of Christ in his Church. And, with a patience like unto his own, she asks only that men might stop, and pause, and lift up their eyes and see.

A PROGRAM

The task of the Christian Church with regard to the recent immigrants may be summed up in the following questions: First: How may we put the sympathy and resources of the Christian Church at the service of our recent immigrant and industrial populations? Second: How may we arouse and enrich the religious life of the immigrant and aid its expression in reverent worship and the helpful service of the community? Third: How may we inspire these diverse and polyglot peoples, together with our own and native Americans, with that common sympathy, understanding and ideal purpose which make for American Christian democracy? This program, broadly inclusive, takes account . . . of the sympathy and resources of the American Christian community, which a Christian purpose is bound to place at the service of these people who are on the margin of our social life, who are in greatest human need. . . .

.   .   .   .

A SUBURBAN SETTLEMENT

Many small towns and suburban communities are awakening to the fact that their problems, while of smaller dimensions, are equally acute in their significance to the common life. In Summit, New Jersey, a Neighborhood House, largely maintained by a local church, has been built, at a cost of $5,000, for a relatively small colony of Syrians and Armenians, and more recently of Italians and Poles, employed in a silk mill. This work also is in charge of a young American woman. Many features of city settlement work are employed, for the same human needs prevail, but above all else is the friendly sharing of the neighborhood life. A Sunday-school is maintained in the afternoons with an attendance of 150. On Sunday evenings occasional religious services are held. The outreaching purpose of this work is indicated in needs it placed before the Christian community; "First, a scavenger system under the care of the city; second, a gymnasium that the young men of this section may have a place to visit other than the pool-room or our own somewhat limited quarters; and, third, a gradual increase in knowledge of things as they are, that uptown and downtown, rich and poor, wise and ignorant, may more and more grow together in mutual understanding and purpose for the upbuilding of character and a more perfect realization of the brotherhood of man."

THE SUBJECTIVE NECESSITY FOR SOCIAL SETTLEMENTS, *Jane Addams*

ELOQUENT testimony to a conception that "the
dependence of classes on each other is reciprocal" was
its institutionalization in settlement houses
such as Hull House. There the middle class could
both give something and receive something
precious. In doing so, both classes
would help build a nation that went beyond political
democracy to a truly social democracy.
Unlike Frederick Turner, Jane Addams never doubted
that the city was the battleground of democracy.

Hull House, which was Chicago's first Settlement, was established in September, 1889. It represented no association, but was opened by two women, backed by many friends, in the belief that the mere foothold of a house, easily accessible, ample in space, hospitable and tolerant in spirit, situated in the midst of the large foreign colonies which so easily isolate themselves in American cities, would be in itself a serviceable thing for Chicago. Hull House endeavors to make social intercourse express the growing sense of the economic unity of society. It is an effort to add the social function to democracy. It was opened on the theory that the dependence of classes on each other is reciprocal; and that as "the social relation is essentially a reciprocal relation, it gave a form of expression that has peculiar value."

This paper is an attempt to treat of the subjective necessity for Social Settlements, to analyze the motives which underlie a movement based not only upon conviction, but genuine emotion. Hull House of Chicago is used as an illustration, but so far as the analysis is faithful, it obtains wherever educated young people are seeking an outlet for that sentiment of universal brotherhood which the best spirit of our times is forcing from an emotion into a motive.

I have divided the motives which constitute the subjective pressure toward Social Settlements into three great lines: the first contains the desire to make the entire social organism democratic, to extend democracy beyond its political expression; the second is the impulse to share the race life, and to bring as much as possible of social energy and the accumula-

Excerpted from Jane Addams, Robert Woods, *et al., Philanthropy and Social Progress* (Boston: Thomas Y. Crowell, 1893), pp. 1–10, 15–17, 21–26.

tion of civilization to those portions of the race which have little; the third springs from a certain *renaissance* of Christianity, a movement toward its early humanitarian aspects.

It is not difficult to see that although America is pledged to the democratic ideal, the view of democracy has been partial, and that its best achievement thus far has been pushed along the line of the franchise. Democracy has made little attempt to assert itself in social affairs. We have refused to move beyond the position of its eighteenth-century leaders, who believed that political equality alone would secure all gocd to all men. We conscientiously followed the gift of the ballot hard upon the gift of freedom to the negro, but we are quite unmoved by the fact that he lives among us in a practical social ostracism. We hasten to give the franchise to the immigrant from a sense of justice, from a tradition that he ought to have it, while we dub him with epithets deriding his past life or present occupation, and feel no duty to invite him to our houses. We are forced to acknowledge that it is only in our local and national politics that we try very hard for the ideal so dear to those who were enthusiasts when the century was young. We have almost given it up as our ideal in social intercourse. There are city wards in which many of the votes are sold for drinks and dollars; still there is a remote pretense, at least a fiction current, that a man's vote is his own. The judgment of the voter is consulted and an opportunity for remedy given. There is not even a theory in the social order, not a shadow answering to the polls in politics. . . .

In politics "bossism" arouses a scandal. It goes on in society constantly and is only beginning to be challenged. Our consciences are becoming tender in regard to the lack of democracy in social affairs. We are perhaps entering upon the second phase of democracy, as the French philosophers entered upon the first, somewhat bewildered by its logical conclusions. The social organism has broken down through large districts of our great cities. Many of the people living there are very poor, the majority of them without leisure or energy for anything but the gain of subsistence. They move often from one wretched lodging to another. They live for the moment side by side, many of them without knowledge of each other, without fellowship, without local tradition or public spirit, without social organization of any kind. Fractically nothing is done to remedy this. The people who might do it, who have the social tact and training, the large houses, and the traditions and custom of hospitality, live in other parts of the city. The club-houses, libraries, galleries, and semi-public conveniences for social life are also blocks away. We find working-men organized into armies of producers because men of executive ability and business sagacity have found it to their interests thus to organize them. But these working-men are not organized socially; although living in crowded tenement-houses, they are living without a corresponding social contact. The chaos is as great as it would be were they working in huge factories without foreman or superintendent. Their ideas and resources are cramped. The desire for higher social pleasure is extinct. They have no share in the traditions and social energy which make for progress. Too often their only place of meeting is a saloon, their only host a bartender; a local demagogue forms their public opinion. Men of ability and refinement, of social power and university cultivation, stay away from them. Personally, I believe the men who lose most are those who thus stay away. But the paradox is here: when cultivated people do stay away from a certain portion of the population, when all social advantages are persistently withheld, it may be for years, the result itself is pointed at as a reason, is used as an argument, for the continued withholding.

It is constantly said that because the masses have never had social advantages they do not want them, that they are heavy and dull, and that it will take political or philanthropic machinery to change them. This divides a city into rich and poor; into the favored, who express their sense of the social obligation by gifts of money, and into the unfavored, who express it by clamoring for a "share"—both of them actuated by a vague sense of justice. This division of the city would be more justifiable, however, if the people who thus isolate themselves on certain streets and use their social ability for each other gained enough thereby and added sufficient to the sum total of social progress to justify the withholding of the pleasures and results of that progress from so many people who ought to have them. But they cannot accomplish this. "The social spirit discharges itself in many forms, and no one form is adequate to its total expression." We are all uncomfortable in regard to the sincerity of our best phrases, because we hesitate to translate our philosophy into the deed.

It is inevitable that those who feel most keenly this insincerity and partial living should be our young people, our so-called educated young people who accomplish little toward the solution of this social problem, and who bear the brunt of being cultivated into unnourished, over-sensitive lives. They have been shut off from the common labor by which they live and which is a great source of moral and physical health. They feel a fatal want of harmony between their theory and their lives, a lack of co-ordination between thought and action. I think it is hard for us to realize how seriously many of them are taking to the notion of human brotherhood, how eagerly they long to give tangible expression to the democratic ideal. These young men and women, longing to socialize their democracy, are animated by certain hopes.

These hopes may be loosely formulated thus: that if in a democratic country nothing can be permanently achieved save through the masses of the people, it will be impossible to establish a higher political life than the people themselves crave; that it is difficult to see how the notion of a higher civic life can be fostered save through common intercourse; that the blessings which we associate with a life of refinement and cultivation can be made universal and must be made universal if they are to be permanent; that the good we secure for ourselves is precarious and uncertain, is floating in mid-air, until it is secured for all of us and incorporated into our common life.

These hopes are responsible for results in various directions, preeminently in the extension of educational advantages. We find that all educational matters are more democratic in their political than in their social aspects. The public schools in the poorest and most crowded wards of the city are inadequate to the number of children, and many of the teachers are ill-prepared and overworked; but in each ward there is an effort to secure public education. The schoolhouse itself stands as a pledge that the city recognizes and endeavors to fulfill the duty of educating its children. But what becomes of these children when they are no longer in public schools? Many of them never come under the influence of a professional teacher nor a cultivated friend after they are twelve. Society at large does little for their intellectual development. . . .

.   .   .   .

The University Extension movement—certainly when it is closely identified with Settlements—would not confine learning to those who already want it, or to those who, by making an effort, can gain it, or to those among whom professional educators are already at work, but would take it to the tailors of East London and the dock-laborers of the Thames. It requires tact and training, love of learning, and the conviction of the justice of its diffusion to give it to people whose intellectual faculties are untrained and disused. But men in England are found who do it successfully, and it is believed there are men and women in America who can do it. I also believe that the best work in University Extension can be done in Settlements, where the teaching will be further socialized, where the teacher will grapple his students, not only by formal lectures, but by every hook possible to the fuller intellectual life which he represents. This teaching requires distinct methods, for it is true of people who have been allowed to remain undeveloped and whose faculties are inert and sterile, that they cannot take their learning heavily. It has to be diffused in a social atmosphere. Information held in solution, a medium of fellowship and goodwill can be assimilated by the dullest.

If education is as Froebel defined it, "deliverance," deliverance of the forces of the body and mind, then the untrained must first be delivered from all constraint and rigidity before their faculties can be used. Possibly one of the most pitiful periods in the drama of the much-praised young American who attempts to rise in life is the time when his educational requirements seem to have locked him up and made him rigid. He fancies himself shut off from his uneducated family and misunderstood by his friends. He is bowed down by his mental accumulations and often gets no farther than to carry them through life as a great burden. Not once has he had a glimpse of the delights of knowledge. Intellectual life requires for its expansion and manifestation the influence and assimilation of the interests and affections of others. Mazzini, that greatest of all democrats, who broke his heart over the condition of the South European peasantry, said: "Education is not merely a necessity of true life by which the individual renews his vital force in the vital force of humanity; it is a Holy Communion with generations dead and living, by which he fecundates all his faculties. When he is withheld from this Communion for generations, as the Italian peasant has been, we point our finger at him and say, 'He is like a beast of the field; he must be controlled by force.'" Even to this it is sometimes added that it is absurd to educate him, immoral to disturb his content. We stupidly use again the effect as an argument for a continuance of the cause. It is needless to say that a Settlement is a protest against a restricted view of education, and makes it possible for every educated man or woman with a teaching faculty to find out those who are ready to be taught. The social and educational activities of a Settlement are but differing manifestations of the attempt to socialize democracy, as is the existence of the settlement itself.

I find it somewhat difficult to formulate the second line of motives which I believe to constitute the trend of the subjective pressure toward the Settlement. There is something primordial about these motives, but I am perhaps over-bold in designating them as a great desire to share the race life. . . .

.   .   .   .

We have in America a fast-growing number of cultivated young people who have no recognized outlet for their active faculties. They hear constantly of the great social and mal-adjustment, but no way is provided for them to change it, and their uselessness hangs about them heavily. Huxley declares that the sense of uselessness is the severest shock which the human system can sustain, and that, if persistently sustained, it results in atrophy of function. These young people have had advantages of college, of European travel and economic study, but they are sustaining this shock of inaction. They have pet phrases, and they tell you that the things that make us all alike are stronger than the things that make us different. They say that all men are united by needs and sympathies far more permanent and radical than anything that temporarily divides them and sets them in opposition to each other. If they affect art, they say that the decay in artistic expression is due to the decay in ethics, that art when shut away from the human interests and from the great mass of humanity is self-destructive. They tell their elders with all the bitterness of youth that if they expect success from them in business, or politics, or in whatever lines their ambition for them has run, they must let them consult all of humanity; that they must let them find out what the people want and how they want it. It is only the stronger young people, however, who formulate this. Many of them dissipate their energies in so-called enjoyment. Others, not content with that, go on studying and go back to college for their second degrees, not that they are especially fond of study, but because they want something definite to do, and their powers have been trained in the direction of mental accumulation. Many are buried beneath mere mental accumulation with lowered vitality and discontent. Walter Besant says they have had the vision that Peter had when he saw the great sheet let down from heaven, wherein was neither clean nor unclean. He calls it the sense of humanity. It is not philanthropy nor benevolence. It is a thing fuller and wider than either of these. This young life, so sincere in its emotion and good phrases and yet so undirected, seems to me as pitiful as the other great mass of destitute lives. One is supplementary to the other, and some method of communication can surely be devised. Mr. Barnett, who urged the first Settlement,—Toynbee Hall, in East London,—recognized this need of outlet for the young men of Oxford and Cambridge, and hoped that the Settlement would supply the communication. It is easy to see why the Settlement movement originated in England, where the years of education are more constrained and definite than they are here, where class distinctions are more rigid. The necessity of it was greater there, but we are fast feeling the pressure of the need and meeting the necessity for Settlements in America. Our young people feel nervously the need of putting theory into action, and respond quickly to the Settlement form of activity.

The third division of motives which I believe make toward the Settlement is the result of a certain *renaissance* going forward in Christianity. The impulse to share the lives of the poor, the desire to make social service, irrespective of propaganda, express the spirit of Christ, is as old as Christianity itself. . . .

. . . It may be true, as Frederic Harrison insists, that the very religious fervor of man can be turned into love for his race and his desire for a future life into content to live in the echo of his deeds. How far the Positivists' formula of the high ardor for humanity can carry the Settlement movement, Mrs. Humphry Ward's house in London may in course of time illustrate. Paul's formula of seeking for Christ which lieth in each man and founding our likenesses on him seems a simpler formula to many of us.

If you have heard a thousand voices singing in the Hallelujah Chorus in Handel's "Messiah," you have found that the leading voices could still be distinguished, but that the differences of training and cultivation between them and the voices of the chorus were lost in the unity of purpose and the fact that they were all human voices lifted by a high motive. This is a weak illustration of what a Settlement attempts to do. It aims, in a measure, to lead whatever of social life its neighborhood may afford, to focus and give form to that life, to bring to bear upon it the results of cultivation and training; but it receives in exchange for the music of isolated voices the volume and strength of the chorus. It is quite impossible for me to say in what proportion or degree the subjective necessity which led to the opening of Hull House combined the three trends: first the desire to interpret democracy in social terms; secondly, the impulse beating at the very source of our lives urging us to aid in the race progress; and, thirdly, the Christian movement toward Humanitarianism. It is difficult to analyze a living thing; the analysis is at best imperfect. Many more motives may blend with the three trends; possibly the desire for a new form of social success due to the nicety of imagination, which refuses worldly pleasures unmixed with the joys of self-sacrifice; possibly a love of approbation, so vast that is it not content with the treble clapping of delicate hands, but wishes also to hear the bass notes from toughened palms, may mingle with these.

The Settlement, then, is an experimental effort to aid in the solution of the social and industrial problems which are engendered by the modern conditions of life in a great city. It insists that these problems are not confined to any one portion of a city. It is an attempt to relieve, at the same time, the over-accumulation at one end of society and the destitution at the other; but it assumes that this over-accumulation and destitution is most sorely felt in the things that pertain to social and educational advantage. From its very nature it can stand for no political or social *propaganda*. It must, in a sense, give the warm welcome of an inn to all such *propaganda,* if perchance one of them be found an angel. The one thing to be dreaded in the Settlement is that it lose its flexibility, its power of quick adaptation, its readiness to change its methods as its environment may demand. It must be open to conviction and must have a deep and abiding sense of tolerance. It must be hospitable and ready for experiment. It should demand from its residents a scientific patience in the accumulation of facts and the steady holding of their sympathies as one of the best instruments for that accumulation. It must be grounded in a philosophy whose foundation is on the solidarity of the human race, a philosophy which will not waver when the race happens to be represented by a drunken woman or an idiot boy. Its residents must be emptied of all conceit of opinion and all self-assertion, and ready to arouse and interpret the public opinion of their neighborhood. They must be content to live quietly side by side with their neighbors until they grow into a sense of relationship and mutual interests. Their neighbors are held apart by differences of race and language which the residents can more easily overcome. They are bound to see the needs of their neighborhood as a whole, to furnish data for legislation, and use their influence to secure it. In short, residents are pledged to devote themselves to the duties of good citizenship and to the arousing of the social energies which too largely lie dormant in every neighborhood given over to industrialism. They are bound to regard the entire life of their city as organic, to make an effort to unify it, and to protest against its over differentiation.

Our philanthropies of all sorts are growing so expensive and institutional that it is to be hoped the Settlement movement will keep itself facile and unencumbered. From its very nature it needs no endowment, no roll of salaried officials. Many residents must always come in the attitude of students, assuming that the best teacher of life is life itself, and regarding the Settlement as a classroom. Hull House from the outside may appear to be a cumbrous plant of manifold industries, with its round of clubs and classes, its day nursery, diet kitchen, library, art exhibits, lectures, statistical work and polyglot demands for information, a thousand people coming and going in an average week. But viewed as a business enterprise it is not costly, for from this industry are eliminated two great items of expense —the cost of superintendence and the cost of distribution. All the management and teaching are voluntary and unpaid, and the consumers—to continue the commercial phraseology—are at the door and deliver the goods themselves. In the instance of Hull House, rent is also largely eliminated through the courtesy of the owner.

Life is manifold and Hull House attempts to respond to as many sides as possible. It does this fearlessly, feeling sure that among the able people of Chicago are those who will come to do the work when once the outline is indicated. It pursues much the same policy in regard to money. It seems to me an advantage—this obligation to appeal to business men for their judgment and their money, to the educated for their effort and enthusiasm, to the neighborhood for their response and co-operation. It tests the sanity of an idea, and we enter upon a new line of activity with a feeling of support and confidence. We have always been perfectly frank with our neighbors. I have never tried so earnestly to set forth the gist of the Settlement movement, to make clear its reciprocity, as I have to them. At first we were often asked why we came to live there when we could afford to live somewhere else. I remember one man who used to shake his head and say it was "the strangest thing he had met in his experience," but who was finally convinced that it was not strange but natural. I trust that now it seems natural to all of us that the Settlement should be there. . . .

.   .   .   .

I remember when the statement seemed to me very radical that the salvation of East London was the destruction of West London; but I believe now that there will be no wretched quarters in our cities at all when the conscience of each man is so touched that he prefers to live with the poorest of his brethren, and not with the richest of them that his income will allow. It is to be hoped that this moving and living will at length be universal and need no name. The Settlement movement is from its nature a provisional one. It is easy in writing a paper to make all philosophy point one particular moral and all history adorn one particular tale; but I hope you forgive me for reminding you that the best speculative philosophy sets forth the solidarity of the human race; that the highest moralists have taught that without the advance and improvement of the whole no man can hope for any lasting improvement in his own moral or material individual condition. The subjective necessity for Social Settlements is identical with that necessity which urges us on toward social and individual salvation.

CLERIC URGES NEW MINISTRY TO MEET URBAN NEEDS, *Bernard Weinraub*

THE urban poor are still a responsibility of the church: here is a contemporary version, with suggested activities and institutional arrangements.

The chief executive officer of the Presbytery of New York declared yesterday that "urban man is far more estranged from the Church than we ever dreamed," and proposed a three part program to deal with the problem.

In a blunt report, the Rev. Graydon E. McClellan, the General Presbyter, urged the establishment of a "task force ministry," that might include a social worker in race relations, a housing expert, a guidance counselor and others to "carry out a direct ministry" in parts of the city.

He also proposed the setting up of "a corps of residential chaplains," to work out of store fronts or apartments, and the start of a group of worker-ministers and worker-laymen who would be given housing by the Presbytery, but work in secular jobs.

These "agents of reconciliation," as Mr. McClellan referred to them, would be "scattered out over our city, seeking out the estranged, working in neighborhood organizations, seeking to identify with the oppressed, the transit worker, the dock worker, the dope addict, the person whom the Church now understands so poorly. . . ."

Mr. McClellan issued his annual report—his final one in New York—before representatives of the 117-parish Presbytery here at the Brick Presbyterian Church, Park Avenue and 91st Street. The clergyman, who was named to his present post in 1961, is to leave March 15 to accept a similar position with the Presbytery of Washington, which includes the District of Columbia and parts of Maryland and Virginia.

In his report, Mr. McClellan said "the church has not done well in the city" because, among other reasons, it has focused on "winning converts" and "building up itself."

"The city is full of institutions which concentrate on themselves," Mr. McClellan said, "which seek prestige and preferment and which jostle one another for a place of high visibility."

"Urban man therefore finds it easy to dismiss the church as any one of the rest of such organizations," he added. "Urban man . . . finds it simple to ignore the church for in his eyes it makes so little difference."

In the suburbs, Mr. McClellan said, "the church is a part of the very fabric of social existence."

"In the city, however," he added, "the church is a gaitered anachronism to be regarded benevolently."

The clergyman urged the church to "organize its resources efficiently for mission," declaring that there are "too many small and inefficient congregations to support in the city."

"Churches of less than 500 can't make the grade in the city," he insisted. "Yet it is like proposing a mercy killing for one's grandmother to suggest that a specific old church be closed down or merged, but it's got to come all over New York City."

"The next step great in urban church planning," he added, "is an interdenominational programming of congregational mergers so that we can have larger and more effectively staffed churches."

THE ETHICS OF PROGRESS, *Franklin Giddings*

> LIKE most sociologists in his day, Giddings was
> involved with social reform, although
> contemporary sociologists know him mainly for the
> impetus he gave to empirical social
> research. Giddings's analysis of urban problems,
> reproduced in part below, turns mainly on his views of
> immigration and poverty; it appeared in
> *Philanthropy and Social Progress,* along with papers
> by such reformers as Jane Addams and
> Robert Woods. Giddings's prescriptions for progress
> include some familiar themes: the benefits
> of country life, the dangers of competition, the
> balancing of wealth by a cultured style, and the
> uses of education for the common good.

Unless economic evolution, creating new wants and varying demands, and reorganizing industry to supply them, is going no more rapidly
than the growth of social unrest, or of those political policies that so often
force vast hordes of destitute people into migrations that have no definite
destination, . . . there may be a cruel and ruinous substitution of the lower
for the higher grade of workmen, prematurely and far beyond normal
limits. It would not be unfortunate that the Irishman should displace the
native American, that the French Canadian should in turn displace the
Irishman, and that finally the Hungarian or the Pole should displace the
French Canadian, if the men of the higher standard of life could immediately step into industries of a higher grade. But when this is not possible,
when they can live only by sinking to the level of their more brutal competitors, it is an evil of great magnitude.

Under such circumstances the intense competition of the struggle for
success, due partly to ambition, but primarily to the quickening rate of
industrial and social transformation, piles up in the community a frightful
wreckage of physical and moral degeneration. Every sociologist, every
statistician, has been struck with the seemingly anomalous fact that suicide,
insanity, crime, vagabondage, increase with wealth, education, and refinement; that they are, in a word, as Morselli says, phenomena of civilization.
But the fact is not altogether anomalous, after all. These things are a part

Excerpted from Jane Addams, Robert Woods, *et al., Philanthropy and Social
Progress* (Boston: Thomas Y. Crowell, 1893), pp. 237–38, 242, 245–46.

of the cost of progress, forms that the cost of progress takes when the rate of social activity exceeds the rate of constructive reorganization. Quicken the pace of a moving army, and the number of the unfortunates who will fall exhausted by the way will be disproportionately increased. Besides quickening the pace, let discipline lapse and organization break up, and the number of stragglers will be more than doubled. Increase the strain of any kind of competitive work and derange the conditions under which it is done, and the percentage of failures will rise. That this is the far-reaching explanation of the physical, intellectual, and moral degeneration that we behold on every side, notwithstanding a marvellous multiplication of all the influences that make for good, is not to be doubted by one who will patiently study the facts recorded in moral and vital statistics. Thus, the number of suicides in Italy was 29 per 1,000,000 inhabitants in 1864, when her people were just entering on a new and larger life under national unity. In 1877 it had risen to 40 per 1,000,000. . . .

.   .   .   .

Of the rapid increase of vagabondage, with social unrest and industrial evolution, but a word need be said. Professor McCook, of Trinity College, Hartford, who has made an exhaustive study of this question, finds that we are supporting in this country an army of 48,848 tramps. At the lowest estimate it costs to feed these absolutely worthless wretches $7,938,520 a year. Adding their hospital, jail, and prison expenses, the total becomes $9,000,000.

The end of these things would be social disintegration and paralysis but for a reaction that they start in the public mind. The ethical consciousness of society is aroused and unified by such evidences that civilization and progress are not an unmixed good. The demand becomes daily more imperative for a public and private philanthropy that shall be governed by the results of scientific inquiry; which shall work no longer at cross purposes, but merge their plans and efforts in a unified policy to ameliorate, so far as possible, conditions that man can never wholly remove, but which he can easily make worse. . . .

.   .   .   .

What, then, in concrete detail, are some of the ethical obligations placed upon individuals and upon society by the conditions of social progress?

The law that the progressive, self-governing members of society should lay on themselves must include at least three groups of duties. First, they must resist, personally and in their influence, the tendency to subordinate every higher consideration to that mere quickening of competitive activity which so easily goes beyond its normal function of means to end, to become an irrational, unjustifiable end in itself. Especially in the education of children who are seen to be ambitious, should everything that savors of competition be absolutely put away. The competitive examination of such children is nothing less than essential crime, essential insanity, essential idiocy, for all these things will be among its results. Second, they must resort more freely, as fortunately they are beginning to do, to country-life, and especially must they provide the conditions of country-life to the greatest possible extent for children, not only their own but those of the city poor. Third, they must cultivate that true individuality in the consumption of wealth, which is not only the mark of genuine manliness or womanliness, but which surely acts on economic demand in ways that give a competitive advantage to the higher industrial qualities of men whose own standard of life is high.

The duties that society must discharge in its relation to the general conditions of progressive activity, and to its members who are undeveloped or degenerate, fall also into three groups. First, society must assume the regulation of international migration. Each nation must be made to bear the burden of pauperism, ignorance, and degeneracy caused by its own progress or wrong-doing. Society must also assume the regulation, by industrial and labor legislation, of those industries in which free competition displaces the better man by the inferior. Perhaps in time some of these industries may advantageously come directly under public management, as socialism proposes. Second, society must act on the fact that a proportion of its population must be always practically unfree, by extending compulsory education to the children of all parents who are unable or unwilling to provide in their own way a training that the commonwealth can approve. This education should be as perfectly adapted as knowledge, money, and sincerity of purpose can make it, to the work of fitting the children of the poor for life in a changing, progressive world. Third, society should enslave, not figuratively but literally, all those men and women who voluntarily betake themselves to a life of vagabondage. . . .

A PROGRAM OF SOCIAL WORK,
Simon N. Patten

PATTEN, an eminent economist, is here addressing a
relatively new profession that had emerged
from the long decades of urban reform. Like
most reformers, social workers were
incorrigibly middle-class in origins and attitudes, and
Patten is attacking their naive adherence
to certain middle-class values: "virtue," "income,"
"goodness," "culture," "self-denial." His stance
toward urbanization and poverty reflects his profound
social scientific environmentalism, combined
with an equally profound belief in the contributions of
city people to a democratic America.

There still continues, I fear, a feeling of impatience on the part of
social workers with the philosophy that lies at the basis of their activities.
The books they read or the lectures they hear start out well and often
kindle a real enthusiasm, but in the end they leave the confused worker in
a quagmire of contradictions far from the points of real interest. The
hearer may have had a pleasant evening, but the morning dawns with no
new light on the work of the day. Can the pleasure of the evening be transformed into enthusiasm for work? Is there any relation between thought
and practice? A social philosophy should furnish a hand-book that might
be on the desk of every worker, however humble, and from which might
be drawn the principles and examples that fit the work of the day. Is this
true or can it be made true of the newer social philosophy that is just beginning to gain expounders? The impulses of the thinker are the same as
those that inspire the worker, and the environment he studies coincides
with that within which the worker toils. The gulf between them need not
exist. It will cease when the thought of to-day is so stated that the worker
may comprehend it. This however is no light task, but it is worth a trial
even if it fails.

It therefore becomes the social worker's first task to discover how
faculties may be made active, how industry may be stimulated, and how
men may be surrounded—rich and poor alike—with conditions that shall
renew energy and after every expenditure of it bring it back greater than

Excerpted from *The New Basis of Civilization* (New York: Macmillan, 1912),
pp. 203–204, 211–15, 218–20. Reprinted by permission.

it went out. The measure of increase is the freshness of imagination and the keenness of motive. There is, moreover, another task of equal magnitude. The social worker must examine himself to learn whether or no his own motives and emotions are powerful enough to break the traditions that bind him. Does not he also neglect the distant good, and treat superficial symptoms of disorder? And, most futile attempt of all, does he not struggle to create new traits and to construct new social conventions when he should be striving to make men free by removing the pressure that stifles feeling and disintegrates motive? Let us have more confidence in what nature has implanted in heredity and less in what we as individuals can add to it. Our own forms of culture, our own religion, and our own system of morality seem to be the embodiment of fixed ideals which alone can lift men above the commonplace level of their fellows. Therefore we are urgent in transferring this body of practice to the poor in the hope that it will affect their lives as it has ours. But have we first aroused the imagination and trained it so that these ideals will attract and hold them? Have they the energy, functioning in a proper environment, which will start them toward remote rewards that are not at the moment very desirable? The means of progress are material; its ends are ideal. We will reach the ends only when we lose sight of them in the struggle for material improvements.

The truth of this is partially seen by social workers, but they do not yet see as clearly as they should the distinction between the regeneration of the poverty class and the progress of normal men. The aim of social work is democracy rather than culture; energy rather than virtue; health rather than income; efficiency rather than goodness; and social standards for all rather than genius and opportunity for the few. It may be shocking to put these contrasts so forcefully; I do it, not to depreciate the old ideals closely associated with progress, but to make emphatic the means by which they are reached. In whatever direction progress may seem to lie, an ideal has been erected as the prize to be striven for which shines forth in our thoughts; but the means of reaching it are not also made vivid. And therefore we honor the herculean toilers who strive to cut direct roads toward the goal of the ideal. We encourage self-denial when we should encourage self-expression. We try to suppress vices when we should release virtues. We laud country life when we should strive for the improvement of cities. We judge the poor by their family history when we should judge them by their latent powers. We impose penalties when we should offer rewards. We ask for the gratitude of the poor when we ought to point out their rights to them. We dwell too long upon the weaknesses of the man who drinks and too little upon why the saloon remains at the corner. Too heavy stress is laid on the duties of parents to children and too little upon the obligations of teachers, authors, editors, and doctors, who do, in fact, exercise a stronger influence on the health and character of a city child than its parents can. We also overestimate the power of the home to mould its members, and in consequence neglect to utilize the institutions of city life. We rely on restraint to shape the characters of boys when we should be thinking of their recreations. As the city home becomes smaller its unity is interfered with. The functions it loses are taken over by the growing town, and in their exercise is to be found the process of character making which was carried on in the older form of the isolated home. The farmer knew his farm on which his sons grew up; the wife knew the house, yard, and garden in which her daughters carried on their varied industries. Father and mother were then the natural guides. But now they may never see the parts of the city in which their children work or know of their amusements and temptations. Social workers should idealize and purify the city for this new occupation by the young as the moralists have long sought to preserve the safety of the home. In this transitional period we cannot expect as much aid from the church and Sunday-school as from the newspaper and the political party. They are the agencies by which men transform local abuses into justice and through which men secure the reforms for which they ask.

Character is acquired by example, not by blood; by the activities and amusements in the shop and street, not by the restraints of church and home. The new morality does not consist in saving, but in expanding consumption; not in draining men of their energy, but in storing up a surplus in the weak and young; not in the process of hardening, but in extending the period of recreation and leisure; not in the thought of the future, but in the utilization and expansion of the present. We lack efficiency, not capital; pleasures, not goods; keen present interests, not solemn warnings of future woes; courage to live joyous lives, not remorse, sacrifice, and renunciation. The morality of restraint comes later than the morality of activity; for men need restraint only after poverty disappears. And hence we must return with renewed emphasis to the thought that social work has to do with the means of progress and not with its ends. But the ideals of progress have become so incorporated into our thought that we instinctively place them in the foreground and neglect the activity which must open the way to them.

.   .   .   .

.   .   . Do you desire the evolution of character? Would you help to create new and higher virtues? Are you more zealous for new forms of art than for the spread of what we have? Do you believe that progress comes through genius and heroes or through many slight improvements in the lot of the multitudes? Then progress and culture is your goal, and you should strive for them by direct means. But if you acknowledge kinship with the masses, have faith in humanity and would strive for its elevation, regeneration should be your watchword, and you should promote the interests of the weak rather than to give nurture to the strong. When a social worker accepts this creed and no longer searches for superman, he soon finds that regeneration is prevented not by defects in personality, but by defects in the environment, and that the subjective tests of character to which he has been accustomed must be replaced by objective standards which test the environment. We need not work for regeneration; it will of itself flow from sources we neither create nor control. But we do need to work for the removal of external conditions, which by suppressing and distorting human nature give to vice the power that virtue should possess.

I have laid stress on the self-examination that the social worker should impose on himself. I want to make it equally emphatic that no such test should be applied to poverty men. Their motives, their vices, and their family history should not be made prominent in the tests applied to them. They are what they are because of their situation, which gives them no opportunity to express their inherent but suppressed qualities. We must establish objective standards of efficiency of energy and of living drawn from those who have been released from poverty. It is not necessary to measure the differences in character and virtue between normal men and those on the verge of poverty; it is enough to determine the differences in environment and in the social standards surrounding these two classes. The virtues, the powers, and the energies of the poor will approximate those of the prosperous when the conditions and social standards of the two classes are the same. We must go beyond the tests of personality and family so often employed and set up the standard of each locality as the norm by which the defects and shortcomings of the poor are to be measured. Without such standards social workers cannot determine how much of the poverty about them is due to the ignorance and inefficiency of the poor, and how much to exploitation by their employers; nor can they fix the responsibility of the state in caring for the health and welfare of its citizens. What wages must a workman have in order to be a happy, useful member of his community, and what must the state contribute to this end? These are not vague questions to be answered by some preconceived theory; they demand an actual investigation in each locality and city—which should take precedence over all inquiries into problems of relief, sympathy, or betterment, for no relief or betterment is effective that leaves the person aided below the standard of his fellows. Each social movement should be measured by the number of independent self-supporting families it makes. A failure to reach this objective end means a failure everywhere, for the work must be done again and again until the advantages of independence and efficiency are reached. Nor is it so difficult as it seems to measure the standard of living in a locality; it requires merely a transference of interest from the history and lives of the poor to their environment, their food, and their work. A case is not completely recorded by the account of the failures and woes. Back of them is the crushing force of those external conditions which should be on our schedules even more fully than the items of personal history and misfortune. Measure the conditions of the poor objectively and relieve them fully. Only thus will poverty disappear and democracy be created in which every one is independent and free.

THE CULTURE OF POVERTY APPROACH TO SOCIAL PROBLEMS, *Hylan Lewis*

THE re-emergence during the 1960's of the problem of "poverty" as a great national issue has been accompanied by intense debate about the extent and consequences of poverty and how to improve the position and opportunities of the poor. The debate has led to the proliferation of new terms, such as "culturally deprived," "the disadvantaged," and "the under-privileged." Those terms represent ideological positions, even when a researcher uses them to guide his work. In the paper reproduced below, Hylan Lewis, a sociologist, reminds his colleagues of the ideological coloration of their work, particularly when they use the "culture of poverty" approach. One way of reading his remarks is to regard them as having ancestral roots in the continual (albeit not continuous) debate about urban poverty.

The late Louis Wirth, in the Preface to Karl Mannheim's influential treatise on the sociology of knowledge, *Ideology and Utopia,* declared: "Every assertion of a 'fact' about the social world touches the interests of some individual or group."

An almost incidental allusion to the sociology of knowledge becomes cogent and haunting when I reflect on the theme of this meeting. And Louis Wirth's words written a generation ago make a strong bid to be sharply appropriate to our discussion today of approaches to contemporary social problems—and especially to the culture of poverty approach.

The allusion to the sociology of knowledge is haunting because of considerations related to the semantics of the phrase "culture of poverty."

Excerpted from a paper delivered at the Plenary Session of the Annual Meeting of the Society for the Study of Social Problems, August 29, 1964, Montreal, Canada. Reprinted by permission of the author.

The allusion is compelling in light of the recent convergence of spotlights from different directions and of feverish activities from varied quarters—lay and professional, nonpolitical and political, quasi-scientific and scientific—on the phenomenon which I prefer to call the poverty syndrome.

. . . The social and cultural imperatives that help to make for the popularity and vogue of the term culture of poverty, as well as the consequences that flow from these are crucially important.

The chief dangers lie in the indiscriminate use of certain phrases and in a particular approach achieving near-monopoly status. These contribute to the slowing down or to the stopping of the "democratic dialogue" by which truth and shadings of "facts" about human beings—those who are poor and those who are not poor and those who make social problems and those who do not—are sharpened and updated.

We who are involved with contemporary social problems are at once victims of and contributors to the verbal technology of the times. This has its consequences without regard to how a social problem is perceived, labelled, and defined, and without regard to what people are involved in the problem. The verbal technology of social problems affects students, teachers, researchers, policy makers, practitioners, or "John Q." and "Jane Q. Public. . . ."

Part of the problem comes from the fact that the language of social science and social welfare as applied to social problems is a mixture of the legitimately scientific and of the diluted and the distorted scientific. Social science and social welfare vocabularies have been infiltrated by, and research and action goaded by, faddish and transient and popular shorthand, and by the fetching, the fighting, the soothing, and the seductive catch phrase. The seductive catch phrase reflects the initiative of the mass media mainly, and a tendency for limited trade terms to be adopted and adapted to meet the communication criteria and the circulation needs of the press, television, and radio rather than those of the social science and social welfare professions.

If the focus is on "getting something done" about a particular social problem like poverty there may be positive values in some fledgling concept becoming a spread-eagle catch phrase. This is true particularly for those for whom getting action—any action—on any facet or symptom of living poor is the most important thing at a particular time. But here we are referring to instrumental and tactical uses and effects of phrases like culture of poverty as seen specifically in educational and political uses and gains—and not necessarily knowledge gains. . . .

. . . .

Many students of social problems act as if they are unaware of, or unconcerned about, this kind of unplanned or planned tactical research or tactical uses of it and they appear concerned, sometimes not so much about the consequences of what is happening to society and to the discipline, as they are about the fact that they are not or were not heeded or consulted. Many persons who are involved in working on social problems act ostrich-like about the use that is being made or not being made of their technical skills and concepts; and too many who know what is happening or not happening are wont to pout and piddle.

.   .   .   .

. . . I am pointing to the danger of having too many professionals concerned about social problems who act as if they do not know or do not want to know the score in—the *Realpolitiks* of—the social change game. And there is equal danger in the many who act as if they are afraid of, or incapable of, tangling with some others who are also concerned with doing something about the same social problems but who are able to ignore the researchers of social problems. The researcher and his products are frequently used for tactical rather than substantive scientific or strategic policy-making purposes.

As suggested earlier, we are all in some degree captives of some of the new terms that are being applied to old problems, as well as of some old terms applied in new ways to both old and new problems. . . . And as Wirth noted, some individuals and some groups are potential casualties of these terms and related assertions.

The culture of poverty approach is one of the most popular and best documented of the approaches to the network of social problems involving the contemporary poor in the United States. Related to culture of poverty, but not necessarily neatly, logically, or empirically—and in some instances "spinning off" it—are such terms as lower class culture, culturally deprived, target areas and populations, indigenous leaders and people. These are rapidly getting to be stale, invidious, and sloppy terms. And for better or worse the terms tend to come as easily from the lips of politicians and news commentators, as from social scientists and welfare practitioners.

.   .   .   .

I have little or no quarrel with the culture of poverty approach as a means of understanding and explaining the behavior of some poor people, not yet too clearly defined, so long as it remains just that—an approach that is open and subject to checking and rechecking—and not a bowdlerized slogan. One problem stems from the fact that too frequently the original or scholarly statement of the approach becomes distorted and extrapolated into assertions that both damage or distort the picture of the behavior of many urban poor in the United States. And because of this the picture of social scientists and practitioners as responsible persons may be damaged. The approach also tends to divert and to prevent scientists and laymen alike from looking at the real and primary causes and consequences of being poor. It encourages the application of a specious cultural relativism to contemporary populations in the United States; and it overstresses the differences, and the significance of the differences between the poor and the nonpoor in the United States. It can easily result in a kind of sloganeering and name-calling approach that covers up the real issues. In talking about the poor we are not talking about a group isolated by religion, language, and custom from the United States mainstream—but a category isolated by money, education, lack of jobs, color.

Our evidence supports the assertion that "it is a complex fate and experience to be poor." The disparity between standards expressed and the actual behavior and condition of many of the poor might itself be taken as evidence that there is not a stable, integrated culture of poverty. (For example, in the influential theory of opportunity structure, the main rationalizing idea for current major delinquency programs, posits differential responses to the same value base.)

. . . Could it be that it might be more fruitful to speak of people as being in poor situations, rather than as being poor individuals and products of and carriers of a culture of poverty? The data of the Child Rearing Study in Washington, D.C., point up the similarity of wants and values, if not behavior and conditions, between the poor and the nonpoor. The field materials also show the pragmatic, nonclass, noncultural cast of much of the behavior of many of the low income; and the anticlass, anticultural behavior of others. The data further suggest the checkerboard or straddling quality of the behavior and expectations of many poor. Some of the poor we have known have gone from slum to middle class residential area to slum (or to public housing) in two generations.

Camille Jeffers, a member of the Child Rearing Study Staff, described low income "straddlers of poverty and affluence" she observed during fifteen months of participant-observation in a public housing project. And she said in some of her afterthoughts about child rearing priorities of the mothers she got to know and observe:

> Gradually, I learned that my preconceptions about, and my initial reactions to, the child rearing performances of some of the mothers were quite different from the mothers' opinions of the jobs they were doing. In terms of where they saw themselves, their self-ranking was relatively high, even though . . . they could not always meet the standards they set for themselves. . . . They tended to think they had made, or intended to make, an advance over the child rearing behavior of their parents.

. . . The childhood experiences of some of these mothers . . . reared in poverty, had left a strong, often indelible sense of shame and indignation over . . . having had to live without many of the needed material and non-material things of life. Their efforts to provide something different for their children, whether it was more food, more clothes, or more affection, had a much greater significance than I had first surmised. It stemmed from an insistent, even though unfocused, thrust to do more and better for their children than had been done for themselves.

. . . I began to see how they ranked various aspects of child rearing and to understand the importance they attached to different child rearing demands and needs. And, if these mothers sometimes seemed to see their children's needs more in physical terms than psychological terms, I had only to ponder the [words] of one young mother who, in trying to reconcile herself to her family's circumstances, said 'After all, you have to crawl before you can walk.'

I will conclude these selected comments about the culture of poverty approach to social problems by quoting, with a few minor changes, from the paper, "Culture, Class and the Behavior of Low Income Families," prepared for a Conference on Lower Class Culture sponsored by the National Institute of Mental Health and the New York Youth Commission:

Our intent in this discussion is not to argue that there are no differences —to do so, would be absurd, to say the least; [nor is it to repudiate the culture of poverty approach] it is rather, to stress the need for better understanding of differences, and better planning of change, based upon such understanding. Underscored . . . is the necessity for correct answers about: (1) the significance of the differences between the poor and non-poor, (2) the bases of the differences—and of their persistence, if they persist, and (3) the organization of these differences—and of collective life around them. [Also stressed are the possible injustices to low income individuals and groups—and to the disciplines—that can stem from poorly based assertions and explanations.]

A summing up of some of our concerns about the ways in which culture and class are sometimes used to describe and to explain the behavior of low income people would stress dangers arising from:

(1) Confusions about the meaning and uses of culture and class, and about the kinds and dimensions of behavior to which they might be appropriately and usefully applied;

(2) Questionable extensions of assumptions and of limited data; and what is probably more serious—the partial and garbled versions that filter into other fields and into popular thinking;

(3) Tendencies toward perceptions of culture as fixed and "determinative"—as the inflexible arbiters of life chances as well as behavior;

(4) Preoccupations with culture and class that divert not only from

the consideration of the forces that affect them, but also divert from consideration of the possibilities [of change and stymie sensitivity to] the pace, and the direction of changes. . . .

(5) The urge to order, under one general rubric, varying and frequently disparate behaviors—or aspects of them. In some instances, at least, these behaviors might best be understood, and dealt with, as lacking in the coherence and consistency of cultural systems—and all that this conception connotes;

(6) Tendencies to impute to a total category, such as the lower class, [or the bearers of the culture of poverty] the depreciated—and probably more dramatic and threatening—characteristics of a segment of that category;

(7) Underestimation, or exclusion from attention, of the range in behavior: ". . . for some problems the range rather than the mode may be the crucial datum."

(8) Tendencies to oversimplify complex behavior, frequently obscuring the fact that people today [the poor included, particularly in urban U.S.A.] tend to be "multiple amphibians living in a number of worlds at once"—to use Aldous Huxley's words.

(9) Misplaced emphasis upon differences, to the exclusion and underemphasis of basic similarities and commonalities. Some of these ascribed [or measured] differences are of questionable significance and tenacity, while the similarities might be the keys to understanding behavior—and to programming change. Best results might come from leading to the human [not necessarily special or exotic] strengths of individuals and groups, rather than to their perceived weaknesses.

Our view is that it is probably more fruitful to think of different types of lower class families reacting in various ways to the facts of their position and to relative isolation rather than to the imperatives of a lower class culture. It is important that we not confuse basic life chances and actual behavior with basic cultural values and preferences.

Our experience suggests further that the focus of efforts to change should be on background conditions and on precipitants of the deviant behaviors rather than on presumably different class or cultural values. In other words it is not likely that the way to remove the threat and to reduce the costs of deviant aspects of the behavior of lower class people —or rather segments of the lower class that threaten and cost most at this time—is to be found in direct efforts to change a lower class culture that is perceived as significantly different and alien. Nor is it likely to be found in efforts to indulge (because of a kind of functionalism or cultural relativism), to seal off, or to try to get lower class people themselves to revamp what is presumed to be *their* culture.

The culture of poverty approach has valid, but limited, uses in understanding and in tackling contemporary problems of dependency, delinquency, crime, and mental health. However, the fact that the approach is valid—for certain purposes—and for use on certain levels—does not mean necessarily that in its present form it is either an appropriate guide to action or the most useful single tool to place in the hands of those who have to deal directly with U.S. urban people with problems or with U.S. urban people who are problems.

Because so many of the poor want to be middle class (whatever that is), they are unwitting partners in upholding the system or community that is most invidious with respect to them. The poor themselves—or significant segments of them—are probably themselves the best restraints on, chief victims of, and harshest critics of the minority of poor who may be really anticulture.

It has been said that one of the chief differences between the poor and the nonpoor in the United States is that the poor have fewer options. That they have fewer options is less likely to reflect their own culture of poverty than it is being shut off from the options and rewards of the larger culture—and they are shut off for a wider range of reasons than the culture of poverty can possibly comprehend.

Whether popgun or shotgun or cannon in character—the culture of poverty approach to urban United States poor can hurt. And if it is intended to be a cannon, let's be sure it's pointed in the right direction.

CALIFORNIA FOUNDATION FOR ECONOMIC OPPORTUNITY

THE perspective on urban poverty displayed in this
bulletin stands in self-conscious contrast
to governmental, religious, and other "uplift" programs
for the poor because it emphasizes action
directed by the poor themselves.

FEDERATION OF POOR PLANNED AT OAKLAND CONVENTION

The first statewide convention of delegates from organizations of the poor met in Oakland the last weekend in February and set in motion plans to establish a *California Federation of the Poor*. These plans culminated two days of discussion which sharpened issues confronting these

Excerpted from the California Foundation for Economic Opportunity, Bulletin No. 6, March 1966, pp. 1–3. Reprinted by permission.

groups, produced useful exchange of experience and ideas, and strengthened the determination of the delegates to step-up their local and statewide efforts.

Continuation of the work and plans of the convention is being handled by a provisional steering committee, on which there will be one representative from each participating organization. The committee has tentatively scheduled a meeting in Fresno for later this month. The Federation will include within its structure three statewide councils to serve the interests of welfare rights, tenants and anti-poverty organizations.

The material which follows was taken from drafts being used for the official proceedings and summary of the convention. . . .

.　　.　　.　　.　　.　　.　　.　　.　　.　　.

THEMES AND TONE

The theme of the convention was unity of all low-income groups and the repeated note in all sessions was the necessity for movement by these groups separately and jointly to produce change in the welfare, housing and anti-poverty programs. There was unanimity of feeling that these programs and establishments were now only giving token response and attention to the views and proposals from the poor.

There was anger, indignation and frustration in the voices and comments of delegates, perhaps sharpest against the anti-poverty program which has promised participation to the poor but not delivered on this promise. But criticism was not gentle toward public welfare operations, which appear relatively progressive in state law and regulation but usually punitive and reactionary in local administration. Criticism was also detailed and biting against both public housing authorities and slumlords—the former for failing in practice to realize the early dreams of low-cost public housing, and the latter for perpetuating substandard housing at outrageous rents.

ANTI-POVERTY WORKSHOPS AND RESOLUTIONS

From participants in this workshop came the comment: "The first two hours were spent screaming, explaining, pleading and negating the war on poverty in its present forms." Disenchantment was so marked that feelings ran high in favor of a demand for stoppage of the total program until participation of the poor and upgrading of the program itself was assured. From the workshop and the convention came telegrams to all governmental levels protesting what was reported as a particularly flagrant failure to permit participation and meet poverty problems in Fontana, San Bernardino County.

The resolution from this section emphasized participation of the poor at all stages and levels of the program, an opportunity for them to create and evaluate program proposals, a stepping-up of funding of approved programs, and a new effort to relate these proposals to priority needs of the poor for jobs, for opportunities and for improvement in housing and neighborhood conditions.

WELFARE WORKSHOP AND RESOLUTIONS

This group directed its fire against the repressive, blocking character of administration in most county welfare offices. Resentment was sharp against the "image" of recipients as "chiselers" or "immoral" persons projected by righteous critics of the welfare system through willing news media, and receptive civic groups. Welfare rights organizations cited chapter and verse of their troubles and their achievements in helping their members get the benefits of federal and state laws and regulations despite the negativism of county welfare administration.

The resolutions from this group stressed need for funding from the state welfare system, or other possible resources; urged state administration under a new State Social Welfare Board, including a majority of recipients; abolition of residence laws; meaningful educational and vocational training; and higher housing allowances and maximums in the AFDC program.

HOUSING WORKSHOP AND RESOLUTIONS

The tenants and housing groups reviewed their difficulties with housing authorities and project managers and their low level of protection against abuse by absentee slumlords. On the public housing front discussion pointed up the strange legal fact that local housing authorities were almost a "law-unto-themselves" group—neither supervised nor controlled by federal or state agencies in any clear or comprehensive fashion, and therefore able to treat tenants as if they are serfs. Suggestions came from groups which had been successful in finding out how to deal with this public relic of feudalism. Also spelled out in the workshop were ways to reduce the life and death control of ghetto landlords, although the problems in dealing with code enforcement agencies to obtain action for repairs and decent housing conditions in privately owned slums are becoming more and not less severe.

Resolutions from this group included: Creation of a statewide tenants' council; simpler leases in housing projects, and a change in emphasis from profit to tenant service; rent freezes in all housing, and state rent control; and no urban renewal or removal until slum housing is replaced for those forced to move.

SUGGESTED READINGS: CHAPTER 8

Robert Bremmer. *From the Depths*. New York: New York University Press, 1956.

A useful historical account of the facts of American poverty, views of it by various populations, and institutions set up to eradicate or ameliorate it.

A. B. Hollingshead and F. C. Redlich. *Social Class and Mental Illness*. New York: John Wiley and Sons, 1958.

The discussions in this book, especially of the illness which afflicts "Class V" at the bottom of New Haven's social ladder and the few resources which the people of this class possess for combating their illnesses, preceded the "Great Society's" push toward helping the "disadvantaged"—including offering them community psychiatry.

David Matza. "The Disreputable Poor." In R. Bendix and S. M. Lipset, (Eds.) *Class Status and Power* (New York: The Free Press, 1966), pp. 289–302.

Matza concludes that the disreputable poor "are an immobilized segment of society located at a point in the social structure where poverty intersects with illicit pursuits." In America, this type of "pauperization" persists because of a tradition of poor Irish immigrants and because of the nation's treatment of its Negroes.

Samuel Wallace. *Skid Row as a Way of Life*. New York: The Bedminster Press, 1965.

A study of the "run-down area" characteristic of "almost every American city where the homeless can and do live." The institutions: saloons, pawn shops, cheap restaurants, secondhand shops, all-night movies, missions, flop houses, and dilapidated hotels. The men: the bum, the alcoholic, the drifter, the down-and-outer.

9

On the Eve of the New York Democratic State Convention, September 25, 1934. From left, Former Governor Alfred E. Smith, Governor Herbert H. Lehman, Postmaster General James A. Farley. Wide World Photo.

DEMOCRACY, POLITICS, AND MUNICIPAL REFORM

WHEN urbanization is believed to result in social inequality, then poverty and allied ills are attacked through "uplift," whether social settlements or industrial schools or kindred strategies. However, when the main source of inequality is viewed as political, then the principal corrective consists of political action. Municipal reformers have relied on various means— some on organizational effectiveness, others on arousing an ordinarily indifferent public, and so on. The specific means emphasized depends in considerable degree on who or what is the villain of the drama: a political boss, or powerful business interests, or merely a hitherto uninformed public. What unites all municipal reformers, providing they are interested genuinely in social equality, is the belief that cities are conducive to democracy—at least potentially. Of course, some critics of municipal corruption or inefficiency are interested only in a better city for other people than for those who now run the city.

Such urban images have contributed to the development of American political theory. As two political scientists, Wallace Sayre and Nelson Polsby, have recently written,

> The initial approach of American political science to its subject matter of government and politics shared the strong prescriptive tendencies of the nineteenth-century social sciences. Especially

did the political scientists have a sharp sense of mission when they confronted the political and governmental institutions of urban America. In their view the urban condition was pathological, and they saw it as the proper task . . . to prescribe the required remedies.

This prescriptive mood endured among political scientists for "at least a half century."

Insofar as sociologists have been interested in power, inevitably they too have devoted some portion of their attention to urban politics. A good instance is the Middletown research of Robert and Helen Lynd. When Lloyd Warner, an anthropologist turned sociologist, produced his Yankee Series studies, these provided a very great stimulus to studies of urban elites and political power in the city. The contemporary interest is evidenced in the work of sociologists like Hunter, Dahl, Baltzell, Janowitz, Miller, and Gold. This decade's legislative and organizational effort to alleviate poverty inevitably is producing not only new variants of city-democracy imagery, but a research literature. The sociologists' concern with studies of urban elites during the 1950s has recently been supplemented by political scientists' studies of political decision-making in specific cities. Their work challenges the older interpretations of one or two dominant elites, since the newer research demonstrates more diffuse sources of urban political power than was previously attributed.

THE CITY: THE HOPE OF DEMOCRACY,
Frederic C. Howe

> HOWE was a prominent advocate of municipal reform.
> In the opening sentences of his book, he
> defends the democratic potential of the city
> against the accusations of its critics, who
> were animated by a pronounced rural bias. If our
> cities are not truly democratic, the nation cannot be
> democratic: so, cities are the hope of the future.

Distrust of democracy has inspired much of the literature on the city. Distrust of democracy has dictated most of our city laws. Many persons are convinced that mass government will not work in municipal affairs. Reform organizations have voted democracy a failure. Beginning with a conclusion, they have aimed to temper the failures of an experiment that has never yet been fully tried. They have petitioned State Legislatures to relieve the overburdened city of the duty of self-government. To these men of little faith, we have too much democracy, too wide a suffrage, too many people in our confidence. From their point of view corruption is fivefold. Its origins may be traced to the spoils system, the party machine, the saloon, the foreign voter, and faulty charter provisions. According to them democracy has broken down of its own weight. They conceive our mistake to be an attempt to extend government to the many, and believe that it should be left to the few.

.   .   .   .

We have been living in a false philosophy. We have not what we want, but what we say we want. We want better government. We say we want a business men's government. We already have a business men's government, supplied through the agency of the boss. But he is the broker of unseen principals who own or control the privileged interests which have identified themselves with the government through the aid of the party. Herein lies the explanation of the inertia of the "best" people, the languor of reform, the burdens resting heavy on the shoulders of democracy.

Such evils as these will never be corrected through charter reform, the

Excerpted from *The City: The Hope of Democracy* (New York: Charles Scribner's Sons, 1914), pp. 1, 6–8. Reprinted by permission.

merit system, or the limitation of the suffrage. They are organic, not external. Reform will come and is coming by and through the people. The American city is awakening from below, whence reform has almost always come. New issues are arising of a popular nature seeking a readjustment of the burdens of city life. They seek relief from unjust taxation; the ownership or control of the franchise corporation; the opening up of life to the people through parks and playgrounds. With this has come a demand for great responsiveness in the governmental machinery, so that it will be democratic in substance as well as in form. Distrust of party, the caucus, and the convention is increasing, as well as the intrusion of business interests into the government.

Despite current pessimism, the outlook for the American city is reassuring. The city contains the independent vote. Here are the militant forces of our politics. As time goes on this independence will be extended to the state and the nation as well, with a consequent toning up of the larger issues in American life. To the city, we are to look for a rebirth of democracy, a democracy that will possess the instincts of the past along with a belief in the power of co-operative effort to relieve the costs which city life entails. We already see this manifest in many forms, in our schools, libraries, parks, playgrounds, kindergartens, bath houses, where conservatism has not been so strengthened by vested interests as to be able to resist democracy's coming.

And if democracy has not justified its highest ideals, it has at least given assurances of great vitality in many cities. The city is the hope of the future. Here life is full and eager. Here the industrial issues, that are fast becoming dominant in political life, will first be worked out. In the city, democracy is organizing. It is becoming conscious of its powers. And as time goes on, these powers will be exercised to an increasing extent for the amelioration of those conditions that modern industrial life has created. . . .

THE COMING CITY, *Richard T. Ely*

ELY, a renowned economist and vigorous spokesman for
economic and political reform, gives here his
vision of "the city as a well-ordered
household." Note how carefully he balances between
a business-efficiency perspective on the city and
a moral perspective wherein the social classes
live and work together. He never doubts the key role of
cities for culture and civilization. His illustrative case
materials were designed to give credit for major
reforms where credit was due: to the women!

THE IDEAL OF THE CITY AS A
WELL-ORDERED HOUSEHOLD

Do you not see that when you speak about the city as a well-ordered household you have a rallying cry which may be sufficient to gather about you, in your efforts to secure reform, the best elements from all classes in the community? We use the expression "municipal government is business," and the wage-earner is not deeply moved. In fact, he is skeptical. He says to himself: "Municipal government is business. Then it must be like the factory where I am employed, and where wages were reduced ten cents a day last week. I don't think I like that kind of business." The New York wage-earner may say to himself: "If municipal government is business I am well enough satisfied with Tammany. Tammany furnishes me with work, giving me short hours and high wages. What is the matter with Tammany?" The wage-earner of the 19th ward in Chicago may say: "If I look at municipal government as a business affair, what is the matter with our political boss, Johnny Powers? If we are sick and in need he is always ready to help us. If we or our children become involved in the meshes of the law, and find ourselves in jail, Johnny Powers bails us out. If a member of our family dies he sees that we have flowers and a good funeral, and when great festive occasions like Christmas come around, he does not forget to send us a fat turkey." I am speaking to you about facts and giving you concrete illustrations. If we

Excerpted from *The Coming City* (New York: Thomas Y. Crowell, 1902), pp. 58–61, 71–72, 101–107.

look upon municipal government as business in the narrow sense of the term, after all, what is the matter with Johnny Powers and his like?

But when we utter the words—the *city* must become a *well-ordered household*—we have provided ourselves with a rallying cry which appeals to what is best in all classes. We think about clean streets; we think about a provision of ample school room for all children—something neglected by the low class of politicians in all our cities. We think about improved sanitary conditions, about playgrounds and parks. We think about public baths and other agencies for cleanliness. We have something in our ideal with which to move every father of a family who wants his children to grow up strong and intelligent, and to have a better career in the world than he himself has had. All that is best in our nature is called out by this ideal—the city a well-ordered household. The wage-earner understands it, and is moved by it, and the professional man, however learned he may be, cannot well formulate for himself a higher ideal. It appeals also to the business man, who knowing the difficulties, perplexities, and evil in the business world, would like to escape from it all in public life.

.   .   .   .

THE OUTLOOK FOR THE TWENTIETH-CENTURY CITY

The great field of work has been roughly indicated. We have to prepare for the coming domination of the city, and for an extension of urban conditions even to rural communities. We have to adjust ourselves to some extent to a change of ideals. What shall we say to this? Certainly there is no ground for despair. The spreading out of cities and the extension of urban conditions to country districts may mean, and must be made to mean, a combination of advantages of city and of country. Our ideal in this country has been the domination of the rural community rather than of the city. But if we look back upon past history, and ask ourselves whence the sources of the highest achievements in the way of culture and civilization, we shall find much to give us hope in the prospect of the domination of the city in the twentieth century. As we think about the city during human history we recall Jerusalem, Athens, Rome, Florence, London, Paris, Berlin, sources of religion, learning, and art. Is it without significance that the words "polite" and "urban" are both derived from words meaning city? Is it without significance that Christianity became known in a city, and that the word "pagan" means a dweller in the country? Or is it without significance that the apostle John saw a redeemed society existing as a city?—"And I John saw the holy city, New Jerusalem, coming down from God out of heaven, prepared as a bride adorned for her husband."

I think all of these things are deeply significant, and the significance is perceived in the expression "civic church," which like the expression "the city a well-ordered household," gathers up ideals which are animating those who are giving shape to the twentieth-century city. The city is destined to become a well-ordered household, a work of art, and a religious institution in the truest sense of the word "religious."

. . . .

NOTE.—The following is a reprint of an editorial which appeared in the "Independent" of New York, Nov. 7, 1901. It shows how much the women of that city have been able to accomplish even under very discouraging conditions, and it affords a fine illustration of the work which American women are doing in all parts of our country to improve urban conditions.

THE CREDIT FOR DECENT GOVERNMENT

In the luxurious buffet smoking-car of one of the fast through trains between New York and the West, a dozen gentlemen the other day were discussing the probable outcome of the New York municipal campaign. They were from every part of the United States; they represented every shade of political opinion and various business and professional interests. One, a resident of Salt Lake City, a man of wealth and refinement, who had travelled in every clime, brought the conversation to a focus with this remark: "Well, gentlemen, whether Mr. Low or Mr. Shepherd be elected, New York will continue to be, as it has long been, the best kept and, on the whole, the best governed city on the face of this little planet."

The remark, of course, was received with surprise, and, by one or two residents of Chicago, with almost angry protest; while a New Yorker, reasonably familiar with the situation, but who had taken no part in the discussion, was able in his own mind to anticipate the explanation which was immediately demanded, and was as promptly supplied.

"I mean this," the gentleman from Utah continued; "first, the life and property of a visitor from another city are safer in the streets of New York than in the streets of any other city that I have ever seen; while, as for the city of Chicago, which my friends here represent, it is notoriously the most unsafe town for the stranger, if not indeed for its own citizens, in the United States to-day. I mean, in the second place, that New York has an extensive system of electric railways without overhead wires, and that even telegraph and telephone poles have been removed from all the streets below the Harlem district. I mean, in the third place, that the streets of New York, whatever they may have been in the past, are now well paved and well cleaned. I mean, in the fourth place, that public nuisances of any sort are less frequently met with in the streets and parks of New York than in those of any other city which I visit. And finally, in the fifth place, I mean that, from all that I can gather by observation, from conversation, and from printed material, more earnest and efficient work is done, year after year, by such administrative bodies as the Board of Health, the Department of Charities, and the Park Commissioners to make the conditions of life tolerable for the great mass of human beings living within the municipal district, than is done by similar administrative bodies in any other great city."

To these assertions there was some murmured objection, but no specific reply. Apparently no one was able to prove them untrue. The New Yorker reviewed them one by one in the solitude of his own thoughts as the train sped on, and was obliged to confess to himself that on the whole the Westerner's observations were substantially correct. But the reason for this superiority of New York's administration her citizen found, or thought he found, in causes which had not been mentioned in the conversation, and which reflect little credit upon the politicians of any party; certainly none upon the vile gang whose name is Tammany.

The remark has been repeated until we all are tired of hearing it, that New Yorkers have no civic pride. Possibly this remark is true; we do not know. But whether true or false, one thing at least is true—namely, that New York has an astonishingly large number of citizens in whom the civic conscience is keenly alive; devoted men and women who feel a strong sense of personal responsibility for municipal conditions, as well as for their own private affairs. Among these, perhaps the highest examples of self-sacrificing devotion to the public good are found in the ranks of New York women. To them, as much as to any body of voters, belongs the credit for bringing about such efficiency and decency of municipal administration as we can claim. It is indeed true, as the gentleman from Utah said, that the Department of Charities is on the whole efficient. And why? Chiefly, as all know who are properly informed, because of the untiring lifelong efforts of women like Mrs. Josephine Shaw Lowell, of the Charity Organization Society, Miss Louisa Lee Schuyler, and the late Miss Rosalie Butler, of the State Charities Aid Association, and others who, possibly not so well known, are not less worthy to be named. It is true also that the sanitary administration of New York, the care of the streets, and the protection of the parks, have been, all in all, astonishingly satisfactory when it is considered that the municipal government throughout the greater part of the city's history has been in the hands of thieves as bold as vile, and as vile as human degradation can be. And again asking why? we again find the answer to be as simple and clear as before. In 1896 a little band of women, unable to endure longer the sickening sights and deadly foulness that everywhere defiled our streets and docks, and that rendered the city unsafe to any family, organized the Woman's Health Protective Association of New York. To the labors of this association, more than to any other one agency, we owe the fact that New York is now, outwardly at least, a comparatively decent place. It was this association that made the first systematic investigation of the condition of city stables, of slaughter houses, of bakeries, and of garbage disposition, and which brought a continuing pressure to bear upon the Street Cleaning Department and upon the Board of Health to do their sworn duty to a reasonable degree of thoroughness. The organization keeps out of politics, it cultivates friendly and courteous relations with all officials, of whatever party, and by tact, persistence, and strict attention to its own proper business it has achieved results that no professional reformer in the bottom of his heart would have believed possible.

These achievements by intelligent and earnest women in the fields of public charity and of public sanitation are but two examples among many that might be named of the successful efforts of citizens who are not voters to get such results of decency and efficiency in municipal government as may be possible under the evil political conditions from which we suffer. Not least among these achievements has been the work of the Women's Municipal League, in exposing the partnership between the police department and the most appalling forms of vice.

If, then, New York, in spite of Tammany and Tammany's Republican accomplices, is a comparatively safe and decent town, the credit belongs to those citizens, both men and women, who, looking for no official recognition, or any personal advantage, have given time and strength and means to a quiet but tireless endeavor to make conditions as tolerable as is possible with the existing political machinery. If New York is, in truth, better governed than other cities, it is because New York has more citizens who are sufficiently alive to civic duty to give up their pleasures, and even to sacrifice business interests, in order to work for the public good.

REFORM AND THE SUFFRAGETTE,

Anna J. Cooper

THE meaning of civic and political reform to some
women is made vivid by this "voice from
the South"; to give her words additional significance,
it is worth adding that Anna Cooper was a Negro.

The desire for quick returns and large profits tempts capital oft-times into unsanitary, well nigh inhuman investments,—tenement tinder boxes, stifling, stunting, sickening alleys and pestiferous slums; regular rents, no waiting, large percentages,—rich coffers coined out of the life-blood of human bodies and souls. Men and women herded together like cattle, breathing in malaria and typhus from an atmosphere seething with moral as well as physical impurity, revelling in vice as their native habitat and then, to drown the whisperings of their higher consciousness and effectively to hush the yearnings and accusations within, flying to narcotics and opiates—rum, tobacco, opium, binding hand and foot, body and soul, till the proper image of God is transformed into a fit associate for demons,—a besotted, enervated, idiotic wreck, or else a monster of wickedness terrible and destructive.

These are some of the legitimate products of the unmitigated tendencies of the wealth-producing period. But, thank Heaven, side by side with the cold, mathematical, selfishly calculating, so-called practical and unsentimental instinct of the business man, there comes the sympathetic warmth and sunshine of good women, like the sweet and sweetening breezes of spring, cleansing, purifying, soothing, inspiring, lifting the drunkard from the gutter, the outcast from the pit. Who can estimate the influence of these "daughters of the king," these lend-a-hand forces, in counteracting the selfishness of an acquisitive age?

To-day America counts her millionaires by the thousand; questions of tariff and questions of currency are the most vital ones agitating the public mind. In this period, when material prosperity and well earned ease and luxury are assured facts from a national standpoint, woman's work and woman's influence are needed as never before; needed to bring a heart power into this money getting, dollar-worshipping civilization; needed to bring a moral force into the utilitarian motives and interests of

Excerpted from *A Voice from the South* (Xenia, Ohio: The Aldine Printing House, 1892), pp. 130–31, 133.

the time; needed to stand for God and Home and Native Land *versus gain and greed and grasping selfishness.*

.   .   .   .

In the pioneer days her role was that of a camp-follower, an additional something to fight for and be burdened with, only repaying the anxiety and labor she called forth by her own incomparable gifts of sympathy and appreciative love; unable herself ordinarily to contend with the bear and the Indian, or to take active part in clearing the wilderness and constructing the home.

In the second or wealth producing period her work is abreast of man's, complementing and supplementing, counteracting excessive tendencies, and mollifying over rigorous proclivities.

In the era now about to dawn, her sentiments must strike the keynote and give the dominant tone. And this because of the nature of her contribution to the world.

Her kingdom is not over physical forces. Not by might, nor by power can she prevail. Her position must ever be inferior where strength of muscle creates leadership. If she follows the instincts of her nature, however, she must always stand for the conservation of those deeper moral forces which make for the happiness of homes and the righteousness of the country. In a reign of moral ideas she is easily queen.

A CITY BOSS LOSES AN ELECTION,
A. Julius Friedberg

> ONLY occasionally at annual meetings of the
> National Municipal League for Good Government
> could a dramatic victory over venal politicians be
> reported. One reformer's skepticism about the
> permanence of such victories can be seen around the
> edges of his narrative of "the Cincinnati situation."

A volume has been written of the Cincinnati situation, briefly epitomizing the growth into power of the lately removed boss, and so I trust the members of the League will understand that the limits of a short paper will admit of the barest outline and will necessitate the omission of most of the details of a decidedly interesting story.

The defeated candidate for the mayoralty of Cincinnati at the last November election—your typical respectable boss-tool—unctuously and with unconscious humor gave out on the night of the count that his down-fall was "part of the reform wave that was then sweeping over the country." You will observe that up to that time reform had been scarcely respectable in Cincinnati, and one's personal demerits could be safely hidden under a constitutional immunity from that form of disease. And yet this man spoke the truth. Three months before the election the city, politically speaking, was in a dead calm. It is true, a small coterie of men had been working faithfully, tirelessly, for freedom; discontent there was, here and there; two newspapers, an evening daily and a weekly, had been hammering for several years into the mind of the independent voter the appalling mismanagement and corruption of the public service; but so deep-rooted, so all-embracing was the extensive Republican organization under one George B. Cox—a master-hand, a king among bosses—that the Democratic so-called "Little Boss" stood by, convention time, with a wink of his left eye, and allowed any one who chose, to do the nominating for the minority side. Hope of defeating the machine was for the moment at its lowest ebb; the Democrats, indeed, experienced the greatest difficulty in getting men to run, and the most sanguine reformer felt the need of casting his eye years ahead for the fruition of his labor.

The calm proved to be the proverbial "calm before the storm." So

Excerpted from "The Cincinnati Situation," *Atlantic City Conference for Good City Government* (National Municipal League, 1906), pp. 124–30, 132–34.

many efforts to beat down the powers of corruption, ramified as they were into every circle of the community—business, professional, laboring, social—had failed, that men's spirits were jaded and their despair almost complete. But the ferment had been working, imperceptibly, noiselessly, stirred by the epoch-making events in other cities, and by the bitter truth-telling of the class of men lately dubbed "hysterical creators of the literature of exposure." The investigation of the insurance scandals in New York, the mighty and successful revolution in Philadelphia, the vivid portrayals of the school of Mr. Lincoln Steffens, combined to make the people think once more of their franchise. But their eyes were cast afar. "Things must be pretty bad in other places, but George Cox gives us a pretty good government. We have tried reform before, and besides, we never desert the Republican party, the party of Roosevelt, of the revered McKinley, of Lincoln and Grant and the other dead men." What, then, caused the sudden change—the reversal of a Republican majority of 15,000 out of a total vote of 75,000, into a Democratic majority of 6,000 in the twinkling of an eye? Let us go back a little.

Cincinnati is a community composed largely of Germans and men of German descent, frugal, personally honest, trustful and slow to anger. The city is a solid city, commercially and socially, but, generally speaking, extremely conservative in entering upon new and untried undertakings. Unlike New York, unlike Chicago, it is not a fertile breeding ground for new propaganda, for quick dissemination of new ideas. The *status quo* is hard to overcome. Especially is this true in politics. Cincinnati was a border city, and a great many of its German citizens fought in the Civil War on the Union side under a commander named Siegel. Not long ago one of my acquaintances in his impatience put it thus to his German friend, a rich manufacturer: "Yes, you fought mit Siegel and you vote mit Cox."

Preceding the year 1897 and culminating with that year the Cox organization had become so odious that there was a revolt in the party itself, and the bolters joined with the Democrats in electing as mayor a German by the name of Tafel, a man considered to be honest and decent. But the Tafel fusion administration was so rankly incompetent that it disgusted the electorate. Wrangling among themselves soon destroyed all hope of success, so that before long the renegade bolters, and indeed many of the Democratic components of the crowd in power veered over to Cox; and from that time dates the building up of a machine so powerful that it has been able at the turn of a crank to send out 20,000 men to the Republican primaries. Cox very shrewdly remained unostentatious, and shrewdly associated himself with the business element, flirted with every opponent who was a likely purchase, gave the erstwhile bolters the best offices, and gained the reputation of never breaking his promise. At the slightest sign of a revolt of the people he could turn loose his newspaper organs with the cry of "Tafelism—Fusion—Reform—Horrors," and it always worked. He had the city tightly in his grasp, appointed the judges —never the best men available—cowed the rank and file of the lawyers, frightened saloon-keepers by warning them against the reformer who "would put on the lid," cajoled the young college man and the taxpayer, and punished the doubter.

In 1903 there seemed to be a chance to beat him. The Democrats were weak. . . . The Citizens' Municipal party was organized, partially by submissive Democrats and partially by independent men. M. E. Ingalls, the president of the Big Four Railroad, a prominent citizen, was placed at the head of the ticket to run against Mayor Julius Fleischmann, a young man of large means, pleasure-loving, a popular idol, but of little or no experience, and if not thoroughly subservient to Cox, at least unwilling to take the trouble to cross him. In his wake trailed a number of young men of the type of Nicholas Longworth, jolly fellows all. Ingalls was defeated, but out of the fight a nucleus remained. The Citizens' Municipal party had gathered together a small band of men, devoted to the city and to each other, who resolved that Carthage must eventually be destroyed. At their head was Elliott H. Pendleton, who had been entrusted with the publication of a paper intended to serve only as a temporary campaign sheet—"The Citizens' Bulletin." After the campaign Pendleton was made chairman of the Citizens' party, and for a while he came near to being the whole party. His first resolve was to make the "Citizens' Bulletin" a permanent publication, and from that day to this the "Bulletin" has never missed an issue. It has grown from a four-page hand-bill to a portly sixteen-page weekly paper. Its subscription list grows daily and its readers are the truest of the true. But it must be borne in mind that with all the splendid work of "The Bulletin," and of "The Cincinnati Post" (the Scripps-McRae evening daily), the task was too tremendous to be successful in two years, unless something fortuitous happened. The Associated Press journals, with perhaps one exception, right valiantly bore the banner of Cox, and with sophistry and cant, with appeals to the memory of the revered McKinley, with insidious reminders of the then attractively low tax rate and with solemn warning against Tafelism, fusion and reform, were able to divert the minds of the lovers of the *status quo* from the plunderings of the public treasury, from the abominable condition of the streets, the shameful deterioration of the public schools, the mediocrity of the Bench, the general decay of civic interest and public spirit.

Scenting a slight unrest in the early fall of 1905, the Cox managers, always awake, never over-estimating their strength, deemed it advisable to have on tap a force of registered voters that would render impossible a chance rift in the quiet sky. So they registered them with a vengeance. Men were brought from up river by the boat load, and Kentucky was scoured for negroes to enjoy the city life for a period. They registered them from dives and doggeries, from coal-bins and water-closets—no space was too small to harbor a man. This gave the golden opportunity to a number of brave men headed by J. C. Harper, working with the "Cincinnati Post," a man of indomitable energy and force. Mr. Harper organized the Honest Elections Committee, drew to him a large band of volunteers—young men who had never even dared to join the Citizens' Municipal party—and with the help of the "Post" gave such publicity to the rottenness of the registration lists that the sleeping city turned over once or twice and made a sound that struck the hearts of the gang with terror. Then came the climax.

William H. Taft, Secretary of War, is a son of Alphonso Taft, one of Cincinnati's early notables, and for years has been respected for his independence, his strength, and for his record on the Federal Bench. Moreover, Judge Taft has held six or seven high offices under the Republican party. Coming from the company of Root, then still in the Philadelphia fight, of Bonaparte, prince of reformers, and from Roosevelt, anything Judge Taft might say at that psychological moment was sure to tell. Taft had promised to make one speech in Ohio for the Republican candidate for governor. In that speech, although he praised the Republican governor, himself elected with Cox's help, Taft "went for" the Cincinnati machine. In unmistakable language he cried out that Cox should be defeated, and added that were he to vote he would cast his ballot against the local Republican organization. That was high authority indeed for the disciples of Siegel.

It is a lesson, and a rather confounding lesson, that the word of one man should be powerful enough to change an election. But that is what happened, and the League may well ponder the effect of such influence, which works apart from charters and ballot laws and systems of government, which indeed may as often be exercised for evil as for good.

Cox was beaten and the whole ticket with him—a completely new experience for this generation of Cincinnatians. The new mayor, Judge Dempsey, with his executive board, immediately went to work to try to cope with the army of applicants for jobs. The difficulty of the task may well be imagined. The officers-elect had been chosen by a Democratic convention. Few of the constituents of this convention cared a rap about the separation of city politics from national politics. Demand was immediately made for the appointment of the faithful to the two thousand or more jobs at disposal. On the other hand, everybody knew that the ticket could not have been elected without the help of Republican votes, and there was a great clamor from the Independent Republicans for appointments. And furthermore, the local Civil Service Reform League, the "Citizens' Bulletin," and other civic agencies were insistent for the retention of even Cox men (in the minor positions) who had not been guilty of "pernicious political activity." Notwithstanding the opposition of two of the five of the appointing board, who are Democrats of the old school, some independent Republicans were appointed to office, (notably the street-cleaning superintendent, an educated man of means) and some Cox men whose activity in the old machine had been only what was necessary to keep them alive.

The city departments were found to be in a deplorable condition—the waterworks on the verge of break-down, the streets a mass of ruts and dust-heaps, the election machinery in the hands of incompetent and unscrupulous men, and chaos generally. This was the *impasse* confronting the new officers, themselves untried in public service, with little or no money to go forward with, and with a city council still in the hands of the gang and ready to thwart the executive officers at every step—and so stands the situation to-day. It turns out that many of the men appointed to jobs are unfit, and many of the Republican constituents unworthy of the trust placed in them. The Democrats have succeeded in foisting on the Board machine men of their own stripe—not a whit freer from the collar of their boss than the Republicans of the outgoing administration. On the other hand, hundreds of Democrats who considered themselves entitled to favor for their long years of unrewarded service were halted at the gates of their heaven and now threaten vengeance of one kind or another.

Meantime, what is the attitude of the people? The spasm of revolution against the gang relaxed very considerably soon after the election was over, and many wiseacres, whose wish is perhaps father to the thought, predict a return of Cox next fall. On the other hand, there was, and still is, a disposition to give the new administration an opportunity to "make good," as the phrase is. But consider the tremendous task the new authorities have to cope with. By no means a unit among themselves, with but little new money to make improvements, with the gang press piping merrily away, and the old organization bloody but by no means dead (it still owns the county government), they are treading the steep and thorny path of constructive work, and must show the people something done well before they can begin to hold their advantage.

·   ·   ·   ·   ·   ·   ·   ·   ·   ·

Now, you will ask what advantage is being taken of the opportunity for constructive reform organization? The Citizens' Municipal party, though I believe it and its friends were a most potent factor in molding public sentiment, cannot claim, nor would it choose to claim, any right to dictate the policy of the administration. It is willing to aid in every way it can, but it did not choose the ticket except to endorse as against the Republican machine. The administration numbers in its make-up, it is true, many who are loyal to the City Party idea; but there is no such solidarity of loyalty as to justify a marriage between the two.

The Dana law, which prevented the placing of the names of candidates under more than one designation on the ballot, has been fortunately repealed. So that if events justify, the Citizens' Municipal party may be able, if either of the two national parties will next fall nominate fairly good tickets, to put its strength into the balance. The "Citizens' Bulletin" and the "Post" are keeping up the good fight, though it must be confessed that there has been no such speedy growth of the municipal idea as to justify the conclusion, just yet, that recruits will flock in in such number as to make the Citizens' party the tremendous force it would like to become. Money is very hard to obtain between campaigns—the time organization should go on—and men have not retained their post-election enthusiasm sufficiently to cause them to leave their respective band-wagons. In short, the bed of roses has not even sprouted for the reformers. The trouble is that the gang may mend just enough to get in again, and they may succeed through the sheer inability of the present administration—perhaps through no fault of its own—to "make good."

.   .   .   .

. . . The Citizens' Municipal party . . . stands committed to the principle of complete independence in city affairs from national politics. We have seen that "reform within the party" does not work out as well as some good men seem to think it may, without a workable merit system in force. The fight for that merit system in cities has got to come from without the national political parties, and the quicker we buckle down to the task of missionary work without political emolument, and the quicker we realize that this task must begin by breaking down political machines based on patronage at the disposal of national parties, the better for reform. And in my humble opinion the only hope lies in making it plain to the people that they must vote for men and not for birds.

While it is true that Cincinnati has gone through a cleansing process away from conditions that were more depressing than in any other American city, not excepting Philadelphia, I make no pretence that its problem in the type is different from that which the National Municipal League was organized to cope with. Our lessons from Philadelphia, Minneapolis, New York, Cincinnati, all point to the underlying need for the education of the voter on his personal moral side toward the precept that he must care for his city if he cares for himself, and that he must make sacrifices far beyond the mere brief suspension from the fruits of office incurred by efforts to "reform within the party."

This paper has taken a less optimistic turn than I intended, or than the whole situation, perhaps, warrants. The spirit of better things is abroad; the reformer walks with firmer step and hopes with greater fervor. But he may not yet strut about and crow aloud, for his most difficult work remains still to be planned, let alone accomplished.

BIG KENNEDY AND THE MUGWUMPS,
Alfred H. Lewis

> IN his memoirs, a retired Tammany chief tells a story, no doubt slightly fictionalized but probably relatively accurate, of his predecessor's negotiations with temporary allies, "the forces of reform." The account gives a glimpse of the professional politician's perspective on important aspects of city life—a remarkably different perspective than was (and is) held by municipal reformers.

Before I lift the latch of narration, I would have you pardon me a first defensive word. Conceiving that, in the theory of politics, whatever the practice may discover, there is such a commodity as morals and such a ware as truth, and, remembering how much as the Chief of Tammany Hall I have been condemned by purists and folk voluble for reform as a fashion of City Satan, striving for all that was ebon in local conditions and control, I would remind the reader—hoping his mind to be unbiased and that he will hold fairly the scales for me—that both morals and truth as questions will ever depend for their answer on environment and point of view. The morality of one man is the sin of another, and the truth in this mouth is the serpent lie in that.

.   .   .   .

When the old Chief was gone, Big Kennedy succeeded to his place as the ruling spirit of the organization. For myself, I moved upward to become a figure of power only a whit less imposing; for I stepped forth as a leader of the ward, while in the general councils of Tammany I was recognized as Big Kennedy's adviser and lieutenant.

To the outside eye, unskilled of politics in practice, everything of Tammany sort would have seemed in the plight desperate. The efforts required for the overthrow of the old Chief, and Big Kennedy's bolt in favor

Excerpted from *The Boss* (New York: A. S. Barnes, 1903), pp. ix, 157–68.

of the forces of reform—ever the blood enemy of Tammany—had torn the organization to fragments. A first result of this dismemberment was the formation of a rival organization meant to dominate the local Democracy. This rival coterie was not without its reasons of strength, since it was upheld as much as might be by the State machine. The situation was one which for a time would compel Big Kennedy to tolerate the company of his reform friends, and affect, even though he privately opposed them, some appearance of sympathy with their plans for the purification of the town.

"But," observed Big Kennedy, when we considered the business between ourselves, "I think I can set these guys by the ears. There aint a man in New York who, directly or round th' corner, aint makin' money through a broken law, an' these mugwumps aint any exception. I've invited three members of the main squeeze to see me, an' I'll make a side bet they get tired before I do."

In deference to the invitation of Big Kennedy, there came to call upon him a trio of civic excellence, each a personage of place. Leading the three was our long-time friend, the reputable old gentleman. Of the others, one was a personage whose many millions were invested in real estate, the rentals whereof ran into the hundreds of thousands, while his companion throve as a wholesale grocer, a feature of whose business was a rich trade in strong drink.

Big Kennedy met the triumvirate with brows of sanctimony, and was a moral match for the purest. When mutual congratulations over virtue's late successes at the ballot box, and the consequent dawn of whiter days for the town, were ended, Big Kennedy, whose statecraft was of the blunt, positive kind, brought to the discussional center the purpose of the meeting.

"We're not only goin' to clean up th' town, gents," said Big Kennedy unctuously, "but Tammany Hall as well. There's to be no more corruption; no more blackmail; every man an' every act must show as clean as a dog's tooth. I s'ppose, now, since we've got th' mayor, th' alderman, an' th' police, our first duty is to jump in an' straighten up th' village?" Here Big Kennedy scanned the others with a virtuous eye.

"Precisely," observed the reputable old gentleman. "And since the most glaring evils ought to claim our earliest attention, we should compel the police, without delay, to go about the elimination of the disorderly elements—the gambling dens, and other vice sinks. What do you say, Goldnose?" and the reputable old gentleman turned with a quick air to him of the giant rent-rolls.

"Now on those points," responded the personage of real estate dubiously, "I should say that we ought to proceed slowly. You can't rid the community of vice; history shows it to be impossible." Then, with a look of cunning meaning: "There exist, however, evils not morally bad, perhaps, that after all are violations of law, and get much more in the way of citizens than gambling or any of its sister iniquities." Then, wheeling spitefully on the reputable old gentleman: "There's the sidewalk and street ordinances: You know the European Express Company, Morton? I understand that you are the heaviest stockholder in it. I went by that corner the other day and I couldn't get through for the jam of horses and trucks that choked the street. There they stood, sixty horses, thirty trucks, and the side street fairly impassable. I scratched one side of my brougham to the point of ruin—scratched off my coat-of-arms, in fact, on the pole of one of the trucks. I think that to enforce the laws meant to keep the street free of obstructions is more important, as a civic reform, than driving out gamblers. These latter people, after all, get in nobody's way, and if one would find them one must hunt for them. They are prompt with their rents, too, and ready to pay the highest figure; they may be reckoned among the best tenants to be found."

The real estate personage was red in the face when he had finished this harangue. He wiped his brow and looked resentfully at the reputable old gentleman. That latter purist was now in a state of great personal heat.

"Those sixty horses were being fed, sir," said he with spirit. "The barn is more than a mile distant; there's no time to go there and back during the noon hour. You can't have the barn on Broadway, you know. That would be against the law, even if the value of Broadway property didn't put it out of reach."

"Still, it's against the law to obstruct the streets," declared the real-estate personage savagely, "just as much as it is against the law to gamble. And the trucks and teams are more of a public nuisance, sir!"

"I suppose," responded the reputable old gentleman, with a sneer, "that if my express horses paid somebody a double rent, paid it to you, Goldnose, for instance, they wouldn't be so much in the way." Then, as one exasperated to frankness: "Why don't you come squarely out like a man, and say that to drive the disorderly characters from the town would drive a cipher or two off your rents?"

"If I, or any other real-estate owner," responded the baited one indignantly, "rent certain tenements, not otherwise to be let, to disorderly characters, whose fault is it? I can't control the town for either its morals or its business. The town grows up about my property, and conditions are made to occur that practically condemn it. Good people won't live there, and the property is unfit for stores or warehouses. What is an owner to do? The neighborhood becomes such that best people won't make of it a spot of residence. It's either no rent, or a tenant who lives somewhat in the shade. Real-estate owners, I suppose, are to be left with millions of unrentable property on their hands; but you, on your side, are not to lose half an hour in taking your horses to a place where they might lawfully be fed? What do you say, Casebottle?" and the outraged real-estate prince turned to the wholesale grocer, as though seeking an ally.

"I'm inclined, friend Goldnose," returned the wholesale grocer suavely, "I'm inclined to think with you that it will be difficult to deal with the town as though it were a camp meeting. Puritanism is offensive to the urban taste." Here the wholesale grocer cleared his throat impressively.

"And so," cried the reputable old gentleman, "you call the suppression of gamblers and base women, puritanism? Casebottle, I'm surprised!"

The wholesale grocer looked nettled, but held his peace. There came a moment of silence. Big Kennedy, who had listened without interference, maintaining the while an inflexible morality, took advantage of the pause.

"One thing," said he, "about which I think you will all agree, is that every ginmill open after hours, or on Sunday, should be pinched, and no side-doors or speakeasy racket stood for. We can seal th' town up as tight as sardines."

Big Kennedy glanced shrewdly at Casebottle. Here was a move that would injure wholesale whisky. Casebottle, however, did not immediately respond; it was the reputable old gentleman who spoke.

"That's my notion," said he, pursing his lips. "Every ginmill ought to be closed as tight as a drum. The Sabbath should be kept free of that disorder which rum-drinking is certain to breed."

"Well, then," broke in Casebottle, whose face began to color as his interests began to throb, "I say that a saloon is a poor man's club. If you're going to close the saloons, I shall be in favor of shutting up the clubs. I don't believe in one law for the poor and another for the rich."

This should offer some impression of how the visitors agreed upon a civil policy. Big Kennedy was good enough to offer for the others, each of whom felt himself somewhat caught in a trap, a loophole of escape.

"For," explained Big Kennedy, "while I believe in rigidly enforcin' every law until it is repealed, I have always held that a law can be tacitly repealed by th' people, without waitin' for th' action of some skate legislature, who, comin' for th' most part from th' cornfields, has got it in for us lucky ducks who live in th' town. To put it this way: If there's a Sunday closin' law, or a law ag'inst gamblers, or a law ag'inst obstructin' th' streets, an' th' public don't want it enforced, then I hold it's repealed by th' highest authority in th' land, which is th' people, d'ye see!"

"Now, I think that very well put," replied the real-estate personage, with a sigh of relief, while the wholesale grocer nodded approval. "I think that very well put," he went on, "and as it's getting late, I suggest that we adjourn for the nonce, to meet with our friend, Mr. Kennedy, on some further occasion. For myself, I can see that he and the great organization of which he is now, happily, the head, are heartily with us for reforming the shocking conditions that have heretofore persisted in this community.

We have won the election; as a corollary, peculation and blackmail and extortion will of necessity cease. I think, with the utmost safety to the public interest, we can leave matters to take their natural course, without pushing to extremes. Don't you think so, Mr. Kennedy?"

"Sure!" returned that chieftain. "There's always more danger in too much steam than in too little."

The reputable old gentleman was by no means in accord with the real-estate personage; but since the wholesale grocer cast in his voice for moderation and no extremes, he found himself in a hopeless minority of no one save himself. With an eye of high contempt, therefore, for what he described as "The reform that needs reform," he went away with the others, and the weighty convention for pure days was over.

"An' that's th' last we'll see of 'em," said Big Kennedy, with a laugh. "No cat enjoys havin' his own tail shut in th' door; no man likes th' reform that pulls a gun on his partic'lar interest. This whole reform racket," continued Big Kennedy, who was in a temper to moralize, "is, to my thinkin', a kind of pouter-pigeon play. Most of 'em who go in for it simply want to swell 'round. Besides the pouter-pigeon, who's in th' game because he's stuck on himself, there's only two breeds of reformers. One is a Republican who's got ashamed of himself; an' th' other is some crook who's been kicked out o'Tammany for graftin' without a license."

"Would your last include you and me?" I asked. I thought I might hazard a small jest, since we were now alone.

"It might," returned Big Kennedy, with an iron grin. Then, twisting the subject: "Now let's talk serious for two words. I've been doin' th' bunco act so long with our three friends that my face begins to ache with lookin' pious. Now listen: You an' me have got a long road ahead of us, an' money to be picked up on both sides. But let me break this off to you, an' don't let a word get away. When you do get th' stuff, don't go to buildin' brownstone fronts, an' buyin' trottin' horses, an' givin' yourself away with any Coal-Old Johnny capers. If we were Republicans or mug-wumps it might do. But let a Democrat get a dollar, an' there's a warrant out for him before night. When you get a wad, bury it like a dog does a bone. An' speakin' of money; I've sent for th' Chief of Police. Come to think of it, we'd better talk over to my house. I'll go there now, an' you stay an' lay for him. When he shows up, bring him to me. There won't be so many pipin' us off over to my house."

Big Kennedy left the Tammany headquarters, where he and the good government trio had conferred, and sauntered away in the direction of his habitat. The Chief of Police did not keep me in suspense. Big Kennedy was not four blocks away when that blue functionary appeared.

"I'm to go with you to his house," said I.

The head of the police was a bloated porpoise-body of a man, oily, plausible, masking his cunning with an appearance of frankness. As for scruple; why then the sharks go more freighted of a conscience.

Big Kennedy met the Chief of Police with the freedom that belongs with an acquaintance, boy and man, of forty years. In a moment they had gotten to the marrow of what was between them.

"Of course," said Big Kennedy, "Tammany's crippled just now with not havin' complete swing in th' town; an' I've got to bunk in more or less with the mugwumps. Still, we've th' upper hand in th' Board of Aldermen, an' are stronger everywhere than any other single party. Now you understand;" and here Big Kennedy bent a keen eye on the other. "Th' organization's in need of steady, monthly contributions. We'll want 'em in th' work I'm layin' out. I think you know where to get 'em, an' I leave it to you to organize th' graft. You get your bit, d'ye see? I'm goin' to name a party, however, to act as your wardman an' make th' collections. What sort is that McCue who was made Inspector about a week ago?"

"McCue!" returned the Chief of Police in tones of surprise. "That man would never do! He's as honest as a clock!"

"Honest!" exclaimed Big Kennedy, and his amazement was a picture. "Well, what does he think he's doin' on th' force, then?"

"That's too many for me," replied the other. Then, apologetically: "But you can see yourself, that when you rake together six thousand men, no matter how you pick 'em out, some of 'em's goin' to be honest."

"Yes," assented Big Kennedy thoughtfully, "I s'ppose that's so, too. It would be askin' too much to expect that a force, as you say, of six thousand could be brought together, an' have 'em all crooked. It was Father Considine who mentioned this McCue; he said he was his cousin an' asked me to give him a shove along. It shows what I've claimed a dozen times, that th' Church ought to keep its nose out o' politics. However, I'll look over th' list, an' give you some good name to-morrow."

"But how about th' town?" asked the Chief of Police anxiously. "I want to know what I'm doin'. Tell me plain, just what goes an' what don't."

"This for a pointer, then," responded Big Kennedy. "Whatever goes has got to go on th' quiet. I've got to keep things smooth between me an' th' mugwumps. The gamblers can run; an' I don't find any fault with even th' green-goods people. None of 'em can beat a man who don't pull himself within his reach, an' I don't protect suckers. But knucks, dips, sneaks, second-story people, an' strong-arm men have got to quit. That's straight; let a trick come off on th' street cars, or at th' theater, or in the dark, or let a crib get cracked, an' there'll be trouble between you an' me, d'ye see! An' if anything as big as a bank should get done up, why then, you send in your resignation. An' at that, you'll be dead lucky if you don't do time."

"There's th' stations an' th' ferries," said the other, with an insinuating leer. "You know a mob of them Western fine-workers are likely to blow in on us, an' we not wise to 'em—not havin' their mugs in th' gallery. That sort of knuck might do business at th' depots or ferries, an' we couldn't help ourselves. Anyway," he concluded hopefully, "they seldom touch up our own citizens; it's mostly th' farmers they go through."

"All right," said Big Kennedy cheerfully, "I'm not worryin' about what comes off with th' farmers. But you tell them fine-workers, whose mugs you haven't got, that if anyone who can vote or raise a row in New York City goes shy his watch or leather, th' artist who gets it can't come here ag'in. Now mind: You've got to keep this town so I can hang my watch on any lamp-post in it, an' go back in a week an' find it hasn't been touched. There'll be plenty of ways for me an' you to get rich without standin' for sneaks an' hold-ups."

THE URBAN POLITY,
Milton Kotler

IN 1965, a political scientist confronts a major social
issue—"How can we fulfill urban life as a
political society?" The city is still the hope and the
battleground of democracy, although the
contestants have changed somewhat over the decades.
Kotler's remarks can be read as a
contemporary version of the older good city
government movement, especially that version in which
business interests were eyed with suspicion.

Political thought selects its preferred realities. That makes politics worth thinking about and credible enough for personal action. So I will indulge my taste.

The first reality is that Americans live an urban life, 70 per cent of us more than others. The social issue then is how we can fulfill urban life as a political society. For only polity can shape our association for the greater quality of our lives in public character and private order. Without polity our associations are too often mere entanglements. Our

Remarks introducing a staff discussion on Community Foundations at the Center for the Study of Democratic Institutions, Santa Barbara, California, January 8, 1965. Reprinted by permission of the author.

political task then begins with confronting the city confidently as the place of our lives, and to seek its political foundations.

The second reality is that the major contests of interests are taking place in our cities. It is the ground of new power drawn from old regions, and of shifting power from old urban sources to new ones. The city is the political terrain of the nation and its power is in fast motion.

Its major interest formation is the new middle class. Technology, corporate consolidation, and public economy are transforming that class from a property to wage base. It is a college educated class of salaried administrators, whose primary interest is to secure more objects and persons for service, management, and control. For this purpose the middle class needs a permanently expanding dependent clientele and enough organizational power to protect its function and expanding ranks. Service and expertise are its occupational principles. So the new class seeks to enlarge service programs; refine the qualifications of performance; and control their operation through professional organization. From whom has this new class won its power and what kind of power is it? With what other interest group is it allied? And what, if any, is the character and organization of resistance?

Correspondingly, the lower class has been transformed from production to permanent unemployment. Its value is no longer labor, but dependency. Will it resist its caste subordination into clientelism, by the new middle class? Both groups and allied interests are in daily battle, which is manifested in the recurring disorders that surround housing, education, and welfare administration.

A related urban contest is racial conflict and the move towards integration and equality in the society. This has been taking political shape as it involves new exchanges of power for mutual interest support. These exchanges have established new associations; not only in political party consolidations, but also in social fields of understanding and action.

Fundamentally related to this contest is the violence of the war of generations taking place in the society. There is not only a numerical imbalance of age groups in the society, but a structural imbalance as well. Because of technological unemployment, rapid changes in education, the consolidation of media and consumption etc., today's youth cannot match the prescriptions of their parents about property, income, marriage, religious practice, stability, advancement, etc. This totality of difference between age groups expresses more than typical generational tension. For there are the additional factors of urban concentration, youth organization, and reinforcement of popular culture, which have established the heroic figure and posture of youth. Youth is articulated as the romantic ideal, while failing all traditional values.

Generational exchange has been clearly ruptured. There is an ethical and moral divide. The expression of youth protest has been excluded from the political arena, while middle age has employed the political apparatus for the domestication and pacification of youth. The Job Corps of the Poverty Program is a case in point. To these political control measures, the response of youth can only be violence. This rupture, rather than racial conflict, is the basic foundation of urban violence.

Corporate power has moved its structure and influence to the cities, after a historic collusion with state governments. No longer do public land grabs and privileged tax structures suffice for corporate power. Instead, they require centralization, intellect and skill for the administration of its productive technology. For these and other reasons, the corporation has come full force to the city. Their procession requires favorable opinion to withstand public misgiving. Thus, they have come to control the media, the schools, the press, the university—either by way of ownership, contract, or public service.

How are corporations relating to other forces within the city, like the professions and political machines, and for what exchange of interest? Who do they oppose and seek to weaken? How are they winning the institutional support to develop and establish a durable rhetoric to protect their private power? Which institutions and sectors of the public will object and resist?

Federalism is also moving to the city, through the growth of direct federal-local relations in education, housing, transportation, public welfare, etc. A nation of urban federalism is emerging, while the states gradually become regional administrations of the national government. What new governmental authority will the city get to fulfill this partnership in government, and how will it struggle with the states toward this end? What will happen to national policy when federal-urban relations and reapportionment make the national government more responsive to urban interests, power, and temperament?

The crucial issue of the public control of technology rests in the city. Here the felt effects of technology meet the popular power to question, resist, and even possibly, to democratically guide automation to better purpose. Whether democratic decision can prevail over the private control of technology is questionable. But the issue will have to be met in the city. Only there, within its visible public, can its benefits be tried. Only in the city can its issue gain fire and its judgment be assumed.

These are just some of the contests which make the city the volatile political center of the nation. Yet where is its sufficient public authority to democratically govern these resolutions? Its authority from state government is woefully inadequate to nourish the amity of new exchanges and associations which urban harmony and order require. Even more fearfully, its power is insufficient to control the tempest of power change, and mitigate the inflammations of new class domination. Social judgment is unable to govern these contests of power because there is no municipal authority sufficient to rule and compose the dimensions of these conflicts. In the absence of sufficient authority there can be no pragmatic of social judgment to achieve consensus and govern for the common interest.

From where will the city gain the necessary authority to rule its conflict and establish its peace? Hopefully, from the Federal Government, as the Executive succeeds in furthering federal-urban relations in legislation and administrative practice. The Court will help, no doubt, by identifying constitutional law with urban rights and rule, against state government domination.

Until this trend is achieved the municipal government will remain a mere administrative structure. Its slight authorities today amount to no more than the scope of discretionary power given any administrative bureaucracy. This denigration of the city as a seat of rule has been with us since the federal constitution.

The very forms of corruption typically chronicled about the political machines resemble classical varieties, not of political, but of bureaucratic corruption,—nepotism, graft, police protection, certificates of exception, purchase of privilege and office. Political corruption, on the other hand, turns more on issues of suspension of civil liberties and personal rights, restriction of votes and office, denial of judicial appeal, etc. These corruptions have been more characteristic of state governments than the city. Thus, even its corruption manifests the inadequate authority of the city to rule, rather than its degenerate capacity to do so.

Yet, so long as we fail to credit the political existence of the city, we will correspondingly fail to enhance its authority to rule. Its government will continue to exist in fact and in mind merely as an administration. In consequence, its operations will be considered technical.

The municipal reform and civil service movement in the 20's was an earlier expression of this technical view of city government. That movement failed to achieve the aspirations it sought, because the technical view of municipal government never comprehended the political problems of urban society which require political rule. With the reform movement behind us, the new program of technical administration, favoring area social planning and expertise, stands as the current version of an old misperception. It is against this new technical mission that the task of fulfilling the city as a political society must struggle.

There is both a strong and weak reason for this persistent technical view of municipal government. Taking the weak excuse first, the fervor for technical expertise and area social planning expresses our kind sentiment of mass help for the vast numbers of poor, the unemployed, the helpless aged, delinquents, the Negroes, and others. We argue that speedy help for such larger numbers requires the systematic programming, administration, and expert management of a technical service organization. In failing to recognize that area social planning is more responsive to our own occupational and political interests, we also fail to credit the political nature of the resistance of the poor to the clientelism which we effect.

Turning to the stronger reason for the technical views of the problems of the city, we find that the city is not politically credited in our classic political thought of Founding Fathers, their adopted sons, the Constitution, and Supreme Court judges. The city was never a term of our classical political thought, although it has been dealt with extensively in our traditional literature of social criticism, like Steffens, Veblen, Adams, and Park. The difference that counts is that our classic political thought has a constitutional foundation.

Two features of our political classicism work to exclude the city from its attention. First, the doctrine of limited governmental authority and specific powers relegates the city to state government. Second, the political perspective of our classic thought contemplates the nation as a federal union from which the cities have been excised. Constitutional authority has been the primary issue of our political thought. To that extent, accordingly, the city has neither a place in our classic thought, nor a sufficient standing in our political process.

Liberty of private property was dear to the Constitutional framers. Accordingly, the locus of opposition, namely the cities of the populace, could not be granted legitimate political status or rule. Being certain of the democratic attack of the urban populace on property, the framers propounded what they were less certain of, namely, the inalienability of liberty and the limitation of government. Democracy and the city were left unmentioned in the argument, for the framers had little interest in preparing the historic assault of democracy of property by negative denunciations. And since law must re-enact the constitution, democracy slowly proceeds by a distended and contorted rhetoric of property.

The silence of the city also rests on the nationalism of our classic political thought, for all its federal protestations. Our constitution is national, for it designed the structure of national government. The cities, under state sovereignty, were thus omitted from its attention. Hence, the Idea of the American nation grew without reference to the city and place of the populace. The Idea of our nation grew without a political idea of democracy. The connection of nation and city was lost. The conception of Nation became idealized, abstracted from the "Social Shapes," which Democritus said "men form." Conversely, the city became more sordid by political neglect. Thereafter the two terms moved from simple disassociation to real antithesis: the Nation vs. the City.

So we see how hard it has been in thought and fact to fulfill the existential polity of the city, as a real political society. As to why we should,—the nation is our cities! Our cities are as big as the nation. I recall Scott Greer saying that the important thing about the space-time ratio of modern technology is that because you can get from Los Angeles to San Francisco faster than from downtown L.A. to its airport, then Los Angeles and San Francisco are so close and the Nation is just a short shuttle. For me the significance instead is that it is harder to get to the airport from downtown L.A., than from L.A. to S.F. This means that while the nation may be getting smaller, the city is becoming immense beyond familiar conception. Its enormity far exceeds the distance between cities.

What can we make and must we make of the enormity of urban society? A rich polity of ample authority and democratic rule. For the sake of that taste of democracy, how do we fulfill the city's authority and the people's rule? What kind of government must it have? Should there be one government in the city or many? Can the neighborhoods govern and the city be a common body of ward republics? Johnson of Connecticut at the Constitutional Convention said that what everyone was really arguing about was whether the state is a district of people composing one political society, or as composing many political societies? He was talking about the states. We can ask the same question of the city and rediscover all the meaning that comes with finding new facts about many polities.

I'll stop with that question, which is a good place to start. There is a final note I wish to add. If we agree that the city is our existential polity, albeit today politically uncredited and functionally unformed, then it must become more consciously credited as the real pragmatic forum of our social judgment and political knowledge. So long as what parades as our competent political knowledge about our Nation and the world has no conscious reference to the city as our existential polity, then our opinion will continue to be divorced from practical political foundations in knowledge and experience of our lives. If we do not honor and politically fulfill the terrain of our daily life, we cannot build practical political "judgment" for the common interest from real experience. Our national opinions and intents will then stand as abstractions and attitudes. How badly might we then render a nation. How unwise we could be? How dangerous our misadventure if we continue to govern ourselves and the world by idealizations and abstractions, instead of practical social judgment. How will the misconduct of national idealism spoil our future, as the more exciting possibilities of democratic urban polity, through informed opinion and common judgment instead dim into the background?

SUGGESTED READINGS: CHAPTER 9

Robert Dahl. *Who Governs?* New Haven: Yale University Press, 1961.

A study of the interplay of power groups in a New England City.

Floyd Hunter. *Community Power Structure*. Chapel Hill: University of North Carolina, 1953.

This monograph initiated many later studies of small cities and their political "influentials."

W. Sayre and N. Polsby. "American Political Science and the Study of Urbanization." In P. Hauser and L. Schnore (Eds.), *The Study of Urbanization*, New York: John Wiley, 1965.

An excellent review of urban politics, as studied and theorized about, mainly by political scientists and sociologists.

W. Lloyd Warner. *The Living and the Dead*. New Haven: Yale University Press, 1959, Part I, "Politics and Symbolic Usage."

A fascinating and detailed case study of the career of a political hero (and later villain) in a small New England city.

10

Chicago Police Subduing a Riot. From John Flinn, *History of the Chicago Police*, 1887.

ORDER AND
DISORDER
IN THE CITY

ANY discussion of American urban imagery would be incomplete if it ignored the question of urban disorder—and the associated questions about the ability of police to keep the peace or about the all-too-frequent outbreaks of violence between certain city groups. The selections in Chapter 6 suggested how disorder in American cities looked to some Americans in the past. The selections directly below touch on other variants of this pervasive, persistent imagery.

This imagery links directly to the literature of political science, noted in the introduction to Chapter 9. Also it has profoundly affected the studies and writing of sociologists, as the inclusion below of selections by sociologists indicates. Vice, crime, and the role of the police have long preoccupied the sociologists. Today there is a revival of interest in the functioning not only of police but of the courts. The rising protest against treating addicts as criminals, joined in by sociologists, is part of our contemporary urban literature. So, of course, are the concern with race riots and Negro reactions to police surveillance.

The sociologist's concern with how social order is constructed and maintained naturally leads him to be interested in how social order becomes disrupted or partly breaks down. The discerning reader of such studies often will find there modern variants of both the older rural bias and middle-class reaction to the urban poor.

WHY THE POLICE ARE NOT MORE EFFECTIVE,
William MacAdoo

> MACADOO was chief of police in New York City in
> the early 1900s. He wrote his *Guarding a Great
> City* primarily to explain to a skeptical
> public how difficult was law enforcement in a
> metropolis. He pointed his finger at
> specific groups that restrain or hamper the police in
> their proper duty, and displayed a lively
> skepticism about the efficacy of morals for keeping
> vice and crime within bounds. His description
> of the self-rule of Chinatown speaks volumes for how
> little the police keep order in this section of town.

VICE IN NEW YORK

I was never deluded into the belief that there was any great moral indignation on the part of the community as a whole against betting on horseraces, and I am quite sure that in the so-called respectable quarters the other vices have warm, if concealed, defenders. Large numbers of people are indifferent so long as these vices do not annoy or obtrude themselves offensively on them; others, honestly conscious of moral weakness, are charitably disposed, and quite a number believe it is a necessary condition to a great city; and then, of course, there is a large army of defenders among those who patronize or profit by their existence. I have yet to hear of a police officer being lauded by the general run of people for suppressing gambling or trying to stamp out the sexual vices, with the exception of policy-playing; there public sentiment was practically unanimous. Have you ever heard of any candidate for public office running on that platform? The mother whose children are removed from temptation by his action is pleased with him; a father whose son spent his earnings to batten the spider in the pool room will openly express his friendship. But one only has to go down on any good day to a great race-track in the vicinity of the city to see the well-dressed and orderly people from all conditions of life, the good and the bad, the respectable and the shady, the sport and the banker, and indeed, all classes so well repre-

Excerpted from *Guarding a Great City* (New York: Harper and Brothers, 1906), pp. 76–80, 178–84, 222–24, 226, 347–49.

sented, to understand that in this speculative age and money-crazed country gambling has a strong and almost universal hold on the people. . . .

With the dreams of religious belief and the growth, too, of a complex civilization, there is no doubt a greater toleration of all vices, and the sophistication of youth concerning those social and sexual problems that mark the darker side of life is now openly urged by many parents, with results far from good, I should say. Against advice and knowledge that leads to health and moral well-being no one can wisely say aught, but to familiarize a boy or girl with the chambers of horror and dark sewerways that underlie at points the social structure, will either beget discouragement and disgust, or bitter cynicism and a morbid attraction for the savage and brute freedom of the world of darkness and unbridled license.

With a shifting marriage-tie dissolved by the breath of the divorce court; with a lack of home life in big cities; with the increased number of the unmarried in both sexes, who flit here and there, from this boardinghouse to that hotel, and back; with the close intermingling of the sexes in business and work; with the recognition of common-law marriages and temporary partnerships between the sexes, and with the growth in our big cities of Old-World class distinction, we are far removed from the age of the *Scarlet Letter*. Yet it must be admitted that the vast majority of the citizens of this great metropolis are virtuous men and women, devoted to their families and their homes, and even where the religious and ethical argument for virtue is not held as strongly as in former days, a sophisticated generation cannot fail to recognize that the virtuous family is the true unit upon which all that is good in our present civilization rests, and that, indeed, in more senses than one, virtue is its own reward. These people, therefore, can be relied upon to be either actively or passively friendly to a police administration which seeks rigorously to repress vice, so that at least it shall not intrude upon the notice of decent people or invade respectable and orderly neighborhoods. To allow people to break the law presumes that the police are paid, that high officers grow rich on the blood and tear-stained money of this army of wretched unfortunates, degenerates, and criminals; and, worst of all, these vices in New York are, as it were, syndicated, marshalled, drilled, and employed in the service of men who have grown rich on the weakness and wickedness of their fellows. The owners of property who reap large profits from the base and criminal uses to which it is put; the various business interests which thrive on the very profligacy and prodigality of vice, and who, when it is repressed, complain that with them trade is dull; and, lastly, and more potent than all, those men who have grown rich on crime and vice, to whom it is a legitimate industry, whose millions are stained with the blood and tears of wretched women and outcast men, who own the large Raines law hotels, where the woman is first robbed of the price of her infamy, and, when she is arrested, is compelled to pay them for the bond that releases her—rich and influential, swaggering and blustering, these captains of the industry of vice and crime reach out their influence into most unexpected quarters. They threaten the destruction of honest police captains and demand the transfer of inspectors who do their duty; they hound and persecute an officer who interferes with their schemes or lessens their profits; they drive good and honest policemen into being bad ones; they have a price for every man on the force; they have their agents at the bar, in the courts, and in the newspaper offices; they have friends in every political organization; they have votes to give and money to swell the campaign fund, and open pocket-books for those who can protect them from the law. . . .

.   .   .   .

CHINATOWN

. . . Chinatown has its own government for which two parties at least are generally contending. To this government all Chinamen in the town pay tribute—rent, blackmail, or whatever you may call it. In turn, the top man, if permitted, will deal with the police and the politicians, paying for protection and immunity. Fan-tan, the sale of lottery-tickets, opium-smoking, disorderly houses, and gambling in all its forms, if not strictly repressed are to be found night and day. For this the ordinary Chinaman pays gladly and liberally, and if the police will not harry him, or, as it is called, "police him hard" and often, he has no reasonable fear of the courts. The conviction of a Chinaman is the rarest thing. Few magistrates and juries believe Chinese witnesses, and on cross-examination through interpreters, they sit there moon-eyed and smiling, and contradict themselves a thousand times in half an hour. When the case is closed, if the witnesses on both sides are Chinamen, the best thing to do is to flip a coin in the air and guess head or tail as to which side ought to win. If the police and the magistrates are not eager to convict, all they have to do is to throw up both hands at this medley of testimony and bundle the defendants out of court. When the police themselves have made out a case with their own witnesses, there are so many Chinamen to be sworn for the defense, and so many adjournments and lawyers' arguments, that the case may drag along for months and then be lost in some new excitement.

A crooked policeman runs very little risk in taking graft from Chinatown. Gin Sang keeps a little gambling-place in the basement, hands up his protection rent to another Chinaman, and he in turn to another, until it reaches the top man, who hands it over to the white collector, possibly an outsider, and there it disappears as completely as if it were dropped in mid-ocean. It has been handed up like a bucket of water at a village fire, but no one as yet has succeeded in tracing the chain. In this connection let it be said that in the world of graft there is a slang name for the Commissioner, and in the "olden days" the "collectee" would ask the collector if a certain nicknamed one was interested. A nod and a smile were reassuring.

Chinatown would not exist long if there was any really honest public opinion that wanted it driven out; but it has white friends, influential ones —the real-estate owner, the men in politics, members of rich societies, mistaken philanthropists, a little regiment of lawyers who make money out of it, newspaper men and magazine writers who exploit the sight-seers who think it represents life in China, and some people who distinctly think that it is a decidedly picturesque addition to the town and a good place to take a country friend once in a while to let him see something old and Oriental. If an honest police captain, therefore, attempts to put a heavy hand on the place, there is at once an outbreak of sympathy for these innocent and honest-looking Chinamen, long articles in the newspapers about warring "tongs," and about good Chinamen, bad Chinamen, Christian Chinamen, and police brutality. The big, heavy-handed Celt on the police force is not supposed to understand the finesse of Oriental civilization; he is thought to be too brutal in treating this "yellow peril." Then, too, there is the suspicion, unfortunately founded on too many facts, that in times past corrupt police officials have derived large revenues from this rank and ill-smelling little town. A Chinaman in the shadow of the law would give up everything to a policeman, including his cue and his hopes of heaven, for the law in China means dreadful things if it gets hold of you, and the Chinese are well experienced in the ramifications of graft in their native land.

Not long ago I had, in the office of the Commissioner, Tom Lee, the mayor of Chinatown, so called, and Colonel Mock Duck, as the newspapers nickname him, with their respective counsel. What I am saying here is something in line with the talk I gave Mr. Duck and Mr. Lee, and they were good enough to acknowledge that I was not, even from their point of view, far from the truth. Mock Duck represents what might be called the fighting element; and here again the carrying of deadly weapons plays its part among our polyglot population. If it were not for unceasing police vigilance, every Chinaman in this town would be found carrying a large-sized Colt's revolver. The Chinaman seems to have a great respect for the size of the weapon and wants the very largest caliber. This is easier for a Chinaman than for a white man, because he does not depend on the hip-pocket, but conceals this huge gun in the loose folds of his clothes. I told their representative they ought to practise in the shooting galleries, if they must shoot, as they are wretched marksmen.

On the occasion of their numerous murderous outbreaks they generally kill innocent bystanders. Not long since they killed an Italian woman, and I begged Duck to see that his fellows took to target-practice before beginning again. The Chinese feudist, when he steps out of the alley to fire at his rival, apparently closes both eyes, turns his head, and then works the trigger until the ammunition is exhausted. This accounts for the fact that hundreds of shots are sometimes fired with little or no effect, except possibly to people who are in no wise concerned in the fight. On the other hand, their mode of murder is very cunning. They will start an open row in one street of the town to attract the police, while a section of the clan around the corner are pouring storms of lead into the alleyways, basements, and across the street at their enemies. The best marksmen in Chinatown usually aim for the back. A broad, bloused back is a good target; and as the Chinaman doesn't take any chances, but presses the muzzle against his victim, there is usually some work for the Coroner. . . .

The most noticeable murderous outbreak in Chinatown was recently when they invaded the theatre crowded to its doors, and having fired off several giant fire-crackers among the audience, began pistol practice on a number of selected victims. This was one of the most sanguinary battles in the annals of the town, and, so far as convicting any one, the police and law authorities are helpless. There is moreover, a dangerous tendency on both the part of the police and the other law officers to regard racial outbreaks and murderous affrays, when confined to certain desperate characters, as matters calling for little or no action. If one Chinaman kills another in a feud, public opinion does not seem to command any extraordinary effort to punish the murderer. . . .

If the top Chinamen, their white confederates, and the landlords were not making a great deal of money out of it, Chinatown would not last a week. Detective-Sergeant Costigan gave Chinatown the hardest blows it ever received. He had it on the run, and in another six months or a year there would have been no Chinatown. They were being slowly starved out of it. The white man with a "pull," the rich yellow man at the top, and the other interests that make money out of it, including the tourists' guides, were desperately bitter in their opposition to this new condition of police affairs. It was an opposition that ran deep and strong and carried powerful influences with it. Costigan had under him only seven plain-clothes men, but they were tried, true, and experienced; when it was necessary, outside agents were used.

Whether the operations against the town are directly from Headquarters or the precinct, it has to be made a special post. Of course, if the police policy is to let it run along in its own way, it will go right back to former conditions, and wherever it comes in touch with the police body it will corrupt it, and, moreover, be a trap for foolish women and degenerate men. It will spread and grow like a poisonous ulcer, developing lesser towns in other parts of the city, and then, in addition to all the other social and police problems, we will have a real Chinese question, too, in New York.

.   .   .   .

GAMBLING

The reader must forever get out of his mind the idea that, in New York, pool-selling and gambling are sort of sporadic vices conducted here and there by shady characters, dangerous, disreputable, and criminal men. It is indeed true that the admitted agents who run some of the low order of these places are ex-convicts and men with bad or criminal records, and in a few instances they are desperate and dangerous men. But, taking the thing as a whole, it is simply a vast business run on business principles, backed by men of influence and power, capitalized liberally and on a strictly cash basis; there is no watered stock or over-issuing of bonds on the part of these syndicates; everything is down to actual money.

This great business has its alliance with other business interests. It helps the sale of luxuries, dress, jewels, wines; it asks no questions about rents, it pays the highest; it employs an army of shrewd men with "pulls" in politics, and has friends among the press men; it is a liberal contributor to campaign funds; and, to tell the truth about it, there is no more generous giver to charity. Indeed, some of them are most exemplary church-members, and when the police administration is honest and persistent, some of them are great agitators for reform of other abuses. They hire the best talent at the bar when it is needed. On the big cases, when they go up on appeal, they are represented by the most distinguished and able counsel. They control the pen of able writers. The Louisiana lottery, just before it was exiled, hired a clever and studious writer in Chicago, whom I knew personally, to write a book on gambling from the historical, philosophical, ethical, and moral point of view. It was an intensely interesting history of gambling from the earliest times, with ethical and philosophical deductions favorable to the business. The book was freely distributed to legislators and congressmen and wherever it was thought it would do the most good.

The gambling fraternity in New York have their clearing-houses and exchanges just as well known and just as prominent as those of the business institutions in the lower part of the town. The little fellows in this business, just as in the other big speculative concerns, hang on the words of the top man. . . .

.   .   .   .

When the people become as earnest against pool-selling, gambling, and other prohibited vices, with the almost unavoidable corruption of the police thereby, as they are just now against fraud and peculations in offices of trust, whether in government or insurance companies, and will resent their continuance just as hotly as they would an attempt by the big trusts to raise illegally the price of the necessaries of life, then, and not till then, will this shameless defiance of law cease. If the majority in New York want a wide-open town, as against reasonable restriction or strict enforcement of the law, they will get it even if they have to bribe the police to be allowed to obtain such freedom. The hope for better things lies in arousing them to a true knowledge of the situation and the facts; for their hearts are yet sound, and there are signs in the sky that health-giving winds, which may be a bit rude at first, will soon blow over the face of the land, and convince the managers of the big partisan machines that there are more votes in favor of an impartial and courageous enforcement of the law against prohibited vices than they have hitherto suspected.

.   .   .   .

CIVIC MORALITY

The so-called bipartisan board is a sort of comic-opera idea. It never has worked well and never will. It simply provides for the two leading political organizations to run the police force on avowedly partisan principles in partnership and harmony and under a "gentleman's agreement." This precinct to you, that captain to me; you look after station-houses, I'll take care of the horses; if you won't let me promote Smith, you can't advance Brown; you make a bluff at enforcing the excise, I'll sound the siren to the gamblers. I'll be your wicked partner and you'll be mine, and blessed be the law makers; our responsibilities are beautifully divided, and yet we are so delightfully intertwined, and our interests so closely interwoven, that the party press and the party officers higher up cannot lay an unkindly finger on one of us without every bipartisan nerve of the whole board throbbing with indignation. The whole thing would . . . carry joy to all persons, powers, and interests with which a policeman is supposed to be constantly at war. No longer would we sing, "It was not like that in the olden days," for the olden days—in all their delicious ingenuousness, open-faced contempt for law, simple and childlike amusement at advocates of civic virtue, morality, and common decency and conventional respect for government—would be with us again.

I should think a bipartisan police board of good, old, hard-shelled politicians would be a delightful field for a man with a sense of humor. To listen with assumed gravity to the delegation of leading citizens denouncing some favorite form of law-breaking, while repressing well-springs of mirth at the gullibility and credulity of the people, and then to hear the merry wags burst with laughter after the "leading citizens" had reached the hall, would beat any farce, old or modern, known to the stage.

Until a Mayor can be found who has the courage and conviction to place the fearless enforcement of the law and the impartial administration of justice by the Police Department, of which he is the head, and the courts, of which he is the guardian, above political ambition or advantage, and who will show by his acts that he prefers to go down, even to defeat, fighting like a gallant soldier beside a faithful public officer, rather than insure his safety or conserve his personal comfort by cowardly compromise or shameless desertion, and until a failure to maintain this standard will arouse public opinion, hot, insistent, and irresistible, the era of good government in this and other cities is yet far removed.

KEEPING THE PEACE IN SKID ROW,
Egon Bittner

> THE passages below are excerpts from the field diary of a sociologist who patrolled Denver's Skid Row with its policemen during the summer of 1965. The policemen's conceptions of the locality, its residents and visitors, and of police functions, all come through clearly in these notes. Skid Row and its people look different to outsiders, including some social scientists who have written about these same matters.

DECENT CITIZENRY

As we walked away from this scene, getting back on Larimer, Officer K quite spontaneously proceeded to give me an interpretation of the events, that is, his interpretation of the arrest of the man from Wisconsin and the dealings with the Indian couple. Here is the interpretation. Larimer Street is a place in which a large number of old-timers congregate. A good number of them have small incomes, mainly from pensions and social security. They get their checks at the beginning of the month. The checks are for small amounts. They need to budget to last the month. They like to come down to the bars every evening to have a couple of

Excerpted from *Larimer Tours* (Report No. 32), Police Patrol, Boulder, Colorado (September, 1965), pp. 22–27, 35–36, 41–42, 44–45. Reprinted by permission of the author.

beers. This is what may be called the decent citizenry of the street. These are very vulnerable people. They're unable to protect themselves. Many of them are uneducated. Many of them are not very smart. Most of them tend to be in a state that exposes them to potential exploiters. The exploiters are persons of all ages who come here, have no visible means of support and prey on and live off the older, unprotected pensioners. The exploiters may stay on here. More likely, however, they move from town to town and hit Denver periodically.

Whenever a new man appears on the street, Officer K likes to interview him. He wants to know who the men are that frequent the street. He wants to know the old pensioners and he wants to know the others. He insists on running the street and he wants this to be understood by everybody on this street. As long as he can maintain this state of affairs he can insure some measure of safety for the people who get their fifty or one hundred dollars a month and have to live on it.

THE REIGN OF THE POLICEMAN

The maintenance of this sort of order, through direct scrutiny and continued supervision, is the only guarantee of safety for the poor, old pensioner who has no other place to live. The order is threatened all the time by riff-raff that flock to Larimer. Unless K forcefully impresses his authority on everybody he encounters, a lot of people will be hurt. How unstable the situation is can be best realized by the fact that leaving the street unprotected for two or three nights usually results in disorders and complaints. It is entirely possible that the man from Wisconsin or the Indian couple did not have larceny at heart. But the officer could not let them get away with insolence. It would show others that it is possible to elude his controlling influence.

The moment the reign of the policeman on the beat breaks down, anything might happen and usually most things do. K then told me that he keeps rather detailed notes on all the people he stops to question. He carries a notebook containing such information which encompasses recent encounters. In addition to this, he keeps a file in the back room of one of the bars, to which he resorts whenever he needs additional information. In a certain sense it appears from the officer's comments that he runs the beat quite autonomously, or at least to a great extent, autonomously. Every sign of possible escape from direct control, disobedience to instructions, expressions of hostility, arrogance, insolence, refusal to answer questions properly, all these things are apt to land the newcomer in jail.

HI, NEIGHBOR

From . . . the officer's comments it was quite clear that what he was conducting was not a law enforcement activity in the strict sense but rather a sort of autonomous peace-keeping activity. He worked almost like an independent ruler. He could, of course, invoke the endorsement of the city, the police department, etc. He could call other men to help him out in dire need, but, in general, he seemed to manage his own affairs without advice and without direction. I must add that this autocracy was in the preponderant majority of cases benign, though patronizing. The ruled seemed to accept the domination compliantly and for the most part in good cheer. K's initial approach to persons was invariably lighthearted and easygoing. His favored approach was, "Hi, neighbor!" His decisions, however, were final, and he was apt to decide rather harshly when he was offended. I should have added that as we walked into the Mission about a dozen men were standing outside, and before we walked in the officer shouted loudly for all the men to get inside, and the order was met with full and immediate compliance. As we walked out of the Mission there were again about twelve or fifteen men congregated on the sidewalk, and we went through the same routine. The officer shouted for everyone to go in, and within about ten seconds the place in front of the Mission was clear.

. . . .

One more point about our visit in the Mission: K observed a young man about whom he wasn't sure whether he'd seen him before or not. He consulted with the clerk at the Mission and obtained the man's name and other data, this time, however, not by asking the man but by taking it off the Mission file cards. When I asked him how come he didn't interview the man, he said, because he had a feeling that he already had interviewed, and that he had the information somewhere in his file.

SEVEN DOLLARS A WEEK

After leaving the Mission we went to the William Henry Hotel. We walked upstairs and turned down one of the corridors. At the end there was a man in the doorway. The officer walked up to him and inquired who he was. The man gave his name and said he was just leaving the place to run some errand. The officer walked into the room, poked with his nightstick at clothes and at the bed, turned around and asked the man what he had in his satchel, and the man said he had some papers there. He didn't ask to see them, but turned to the man and said, 'Weren't you sick recently? Didn't I take you to the hospital?' As it turned out this man was once quite ill and the officer was called. This happened some months ago. And he obtained an ambulance for the man and delivered him to the hospital. All this lasted for about five minutes and the conversation was quite friendly, the officer expressing hope that the man would get well and saying he was glad that he felt better now. The man expressed gratitude and every one of his utterances was prefaced by "Sir" and ended with "Sir. . . ." From this room we moved to the other end of the hotel, the officer walking on his tiptoes and listening to what was going on in the rooms.

THE VULNERABLES

As we walked out K pointed out to me that now I had seen in the same hotel and virtually next door to each other the prey and predator. The sick old man being the one he mentions as the person deserving protection and usually not getting enough of protection. The prostitute and the younger man in the room were the ones from whom the older man has to be protected. Only by riding roughshod over the population, only by letting them know every moment of the day who the boss is on the street, is it possible to maintain the sort of order in which some measure of protection could be offered to the vulnerables.

KIDDING

We walked out [of the movie theatre] and on the same path back to Larimer talking about the predicament of the old timer. The officer likes to talk about them. He knows a very, very large number of them by their first names, and they address him by his nickname. All these are men in their sixties, of modest, if not poor appearance. I observed that most are quite comfortable with the officer, kidding, etc.

THE GREAT INJUSTICE

As we walked, K expressed his views on the great injustice: the fact that these men rarely get enough to live on, that after a life of work or service, because a lot of these people are apparently retired servicemen, these men are not provided with adequate means of support by the government. He felt that it was a shame that we are unable to mobilize adequate resources to take care of our own aged. The officer's idea is that we should somehow provide them with a community to live in, in which the conditions would be considerably above what is available to them now.

. . . .

THE SANITARIUM CAFE

The Sanitarium Cafe came up several times as something of a place of refuge for many Larimer pensioners. The proprietor was lauded as a fair man. Not only does he give the old timer his money's worth, but he also keeps the cafe clean of the predators and in this sense provides something of a safe haven for the old timer. As a further item of recommendation for the proprietor of the Sanitarium Cafe, the officer told me that on several occasions the owner has provided some money for the burial of men who die.

. . . .

SWEEPING THE STREET

At this point the time is about eleven-thirty, and I'm enormously impressed by this cold efficiency of keeping the street clean. K is a man who works rather fast. That is, he walks fast. There are continuous glances in all directions, and he's really sweeping the street. Men are being sent home, sent to jail, being ushered into bars or into cafes, out of them, off the street, etc. And it seems like everybody is taken care of. He literally hovers over the neighborhood, and it seems that nothing escapes his attention.

I do not propose that we stopped everyone we met. Persons in bars or cafes are virtually always left alone. Most men in the two blocks of Larimer proper were not addressed, except when they congregated in front of the missions or hotels or when they were obviously drunk. In the sidestreets, however, it was a rare instance that we passed someone. The few men we did pass on sidestreets walked briskly, nodded their heads in greeting and had the appearance of men working in the warehouses located there.

THE DISPLAY OF COMPETENCE

The impression I have is that it is fairly safe to linger in the lights of Larimer after ten o'clock, provided one is not drunk or congregating in groups of more than four or five. But on the sidestreets, one is safe only by displaying obvious evidence of competence and proper justification for passing through the area. To be sure, it is quite easy to distinguish the competent from the incompetent. In fact, however, we did pass a few men I thought we would have stopped, and we stopped one or two I thought we would have passed. I must add that on the sidestreets there is no such thing as simply passing someone. At the very least, there is a greeting exchanged.

THE FAMILIAR AND THE STRANGE

It seems, therefore, that superimposed upon the distinction between the competent and the incompetent is the distinction between the familiar and strange persons. Of those K knows, there are some he addresses by name, some he can tell something about. Others he merely identifies as vaguely known regulars. I would say that these two groups encompass about sixty to eighty per cent of all the people we encountered. I may add that seeing the remaining cohort of strangers against the similar background apparently makes it easy to cope with them.

.   .   .   .

CARTED OFF

Shortly after the rain stopped, K found a man leaning against a wall who was terribly intoxicated. He could hardly speak. He could certainly not stand up under his own power. The officer summoned the scout car and took the identification off the arrested man.

No sooner was he done with doing the write-up of the arrest slip when another man walked by, quite unsteady, and was unable to give an address, who kept pointing to hotels in various directions, and it became quite clear that he had no place to stay. The man was quite intoxicated. But I should think that had K been satisfied that the man lived somewhere in this vicinity he would have let him go. Since he had no place to go, he wrote out an arrest ticket for this man. The arrest ticket was completed by the time the scout car came and both men were carted off to jail.

.   .   .   .

YOU HAD BETTER DO IT

As we walked on we picked up a man whom K had stopped earlier. The man was drunk, not very drunk, but drunk. During the earlier encounter K told this man to make tracks home, and the man promised he would. Now, three-quarters of an hour later, he was found standing in a doorway. It became clear that he did not have a place to stay. And K wrote out an arrest ticket for him, summoned the squad car and sent the man off. Again the whole thing indicated that when you are told to do something by K, you had better do it. And if you don't, you can be sure of landing in jail.

.　　.　　.　　.　　.　　.　　.　　.　　.　　.

SOLID CITIZENS

I want to make one concluding remark. It appears to me, from the two nights of walking on Larimer and from the one night I spent in the radio car patrolling Larimer, that this street has what might be called its solid citizens. These are for the most part older people. All of them drink, and all of them are occasionally arrested. Nevertheless, by and large they are well-liked and are left alone as long as they can monitor on their own. These people are the object of protection by the police officers. In a certain sense the police look out for them. There is between the police, particularly between the officer walking the beat, and the solid citizen a friendly relationship that is continuously maintained by meetings on the street. Most of these people will be on the street in the later afternoon and early evening hours. To some extent these people can count on real help from the police, not merely protection in the event of danger, but advice, guidance, even a handout now and then. I noticed, for example, that K took a cigar from one man, who apparently was also one of these solid citizens, perhaps one who was slightly better off. He took the cigar and gave it to another one who was worse off.

HARD LUCK GROUP

This cohort of the solid citizen has a certain gradation where it slopes off toward the dissolute and unwanted. The continuum shades into younger people who are known to be in trouble, who have lived on the street for some time. These younger people are known to work when they can work, but they are thought to suffer from some form of disability that leads them to drunkenness. The officers are inclined to be generous with these people. They are in some way moved to respect the fact that these people work, as far as they can work, and the officers seem to think that these people are victims of periodic binges. Their own ways of disabling themselves do not earn them contempt but rather pity. . . . There were many instances of these persons, either in a state of intoxication or moving toward a state of intoxication or being sober, who were treated as being down on their luck.

PREDATORS

The hard luck group blends into the third category of persons who are of interest. This last group includes pimps, thieves, prostitutes and other criminals. They are thought to be deliberately vicious. They are more clearly the predators. The distinction between the predators and the hard luck people is difficult, in part, because the predators themselves are quite vulnerable to exploitation.

DISTINCTIONS

Perhaps the most telling distinctions between the three groups are as follows: the old timers are segregated from the rest by their age and the fact that they are residentially stable. The hard luck people are younger and they typically come and go. In the terminology of the street, most of them are on the bum. Both of these groups are easy to spot, in fact they tell you their story at the drop of a hat. They, typically, don't mind being arrested, though they prefer to stay out of jail, even if it means sleeping out. The predators are the hardest to spot, and it appears that in encounters with unknown people the officers first consider this possibility. Perhaps one further reason for the difficulty in distinguishing between the predator and the hard luck person is in fact that the former does not occur on Larimer in good form. There is a streak of bad luck in the predators, and bad luck persons are apt to prey.

Every new person, however, represents a puzzle and causes suspicion. The fact that K hasn't seen you yet is already two strikes against you. When he does see you for the first time, you'd better make a good appearance, and you'd better make yourself known in some way as a respectable citizen, as someone who at least occasionally is sufficiently sober to take care of himself. Once this is demonstrated, then one can count on getting along. Needless to say, the standard of appearance and demeanor I am talking about is relative to the rest of Larimer and quite low indeed.

THE POLICE AS PERCEIVED BY NEGRO BOYS,
Carl Werthman

THESE remarks are eloquent testimony of how "keeping
the peace" looks to teenage Negro and Mexican boys
in one San Francisco slum. They also give
an excellent, if incomplete, idea of what "the city"
looks like to these children. Carl Werthman is a
sociologist and these are fragments from his interviews.

Remember that time we was coming from the show? This cop car
pulls up and these two cops jump out quick. The first stud says, "All right,
God damn you! All you black Africans up against the mother-fucking
wall!" All that shit. So we got up against the wall over there on Market
Street. This long house. You know. So then they started. "Where all you
ignorant sons of bitches coming from?" We say we coming from the
show. "What show?" We say we coming from the Amazon. They say,
"Yeah, we got a call there's a whole bunch of shit going on over there!
I think I'll call all you mother-fuckers in!" So nobody say nothing. So
then he starts again. "What's you name? Let me see you ID!" Finally, this
cop's buddy say, "You want to run them in Joe? They ain't really done
nothing." So then Joe stops. He say, "Now all you black Africans pick up
your spears and go home! I don't want you guys walking up the street!"
We just coming up the street like we always do coming from the show.
That shit happens all the time. There ain't a day that we don't get roused
like that.   (Negro, 16 years old)

Just like over at the Tick Tock and over in Fillmore where they used
to have snacks—and anywhere you go like a public place and a lot of
guys be around. I mean everybody would be buying something and most
of them do be buying something and they be eating it, but the police are
still sitting on you as long as you're there watching every move you make.
And then they converge. And the cops come in with the dogs, about five
or seven carloads and motorcycle cops and they just walk around to everybody to check your car. If your car got one tail light misplaced or anything, they'll give you a ticket. They give you a ticket for anything. For
loitering. Even for not having your car parked right. Now this is supposed

Excerpted from "Gang Members and the Police," unpublished M.A. thesis, University of California, Berkeley, 1964. Reprinted by permission of the author.

to be a public place, but every time you turn around the cops is in there trying to get into something. I heard you couldn't give a person a ticket on private property. But they block off every entrance and come in there and start checking everybody. They bring the whole police station with them.

(Negro, 16 years old)

One time me and a couple of friends, we came down to the corner on Monday night because we was supposed to have our meeting. And we was standing there on the corner bullshitting like we always do, and there was only four of us. Then this cop on a motorcycle pulled over and walked over to us. I seen him before. He rides around the neighborhood a lot. He didn't say nothing. He just zipped down his jacket and there was his big old billy club. And then he started asking questions, identification, what were we doing, and all like that. And he searched us and got our names down on the book and everything. We wasn't doing anything except what we usually do on that corner. [What's that?] Stand there bullshitting. They do anything to get our names on that book. You know. They want us to know they in charge.

(Negro, 16 years old)

I don't know how they know us, but every time you are from a different district they gonna pick you up. Like three Negro boys out on Fillmore. They went out on Fillmore to meet their mother, you know, to get the money so we can go to Oakland that night. The cops say, "You boys from Hunter Point!" And they swore up and down they wasn't from Hunter Point." And they still took them in. They gave them their addresses and everything. They said, "We'll check when we get there." Just cause they was outa their district. Like they say, "If you're out of your district, you going to fight." [Do you guys look any different than the guys who live on Fillmore?] Yeah. They're all short, and their hair's all over their head. You know, you just look different. See, that's their beat over there on Fillmore. They know just about everybody over there.

(Negro, 18 years old)

I got arrested once when we were just riding around in a car. There was a bunch of us in the car. A police car stopped us and it was about ten after ten when they stopped us. They started asking us our names and wanted to see our identification. Then they called in on us. So they got through calling in on us, and they just sit in the car and wait till the call came through. Then they'd bring back your ID and take another one. One at a time. They held me and another boy till last. And when they got to us it was five minutes to eleven. They told everybody they could go home, but they told us it didn't make no sense for us to go home because we was just riding around and we'd never make it home in five minutes. So they busted us both for curfew.

(Mexican, 14 years old)

One Saturday night we were down at the park and these guys were all playing cards. So I just happened to go over there and I was just sitting there watching them. And the cop came and took in seventeen guys. And just cause I was there he threw me in too. They pulled everybody in but they let everybody else go except me and this other guy cause we was eighteen. I got my old lady to get fifty-seven dollars and bail me out, but the other guy didn't have the fifty-seven dollars and he had to stay there for three or four days. I don't think that was right. I wasn't even playing no cards. I got busted for being eighteen. (Negro, 18 years old)

VIOLENCE IN THE CITY,
Robert Blauner

THIS selection is taken from Blauner's "Whitewash over Watts," published a little more than six months after Los Angeles' racial explosion had rocked the country in late summer, 1965; he is attacking the McCone Commission's official report on the riots. Blauner's critique (he is a sociologist) throws into sharp relief two classic—and contrary—conceptions of violence in the city. In this instance, Negroes happen to be involved, but urban violence has been a pervasive theme for many decades. Indeed, one reason American suburbs evolved was that the "better" classes of city people wished to get away from the unprepossessing or violent manners of the lower orders.

On August 24, 1965, just one week after public order had been restored in the south-central area of Los Angeles known as Watts, Governor Pat Brown of California announced the appointment of an eight-man commission of leading citizens. In his charge to the group (which came to be known as the McCone Commission, after its Chairman, John A. McCone, former head of the CIA), Brown asked it to "prepare an accurate chronology and description of the riots"; to "probe deeply the immediate and underlying causes of the riots"; and finally to "develop

Excerpted from "Whitewash over Watts," *Trans-Action,* Vol. 3 (March/April, 1966), pp. 3–4, 7–9, 54. Reprinted from TRANS-ACTION Magazine, Washington University, St. Louis, Missouri, by permission.

recommendations for action designed to prevent a recurrence of these tragic disorders."

For what appears to have been political considerations connected with possible repercussions of the Watts affair on the 1966 gubernatorial campaign, the Commission was given December 1, 1965, as the deadline for the completion of its report. Thus only 100 days were available for a "deep and probing" analysis of the most destructive incidents of racial violence in American history.

.   .   .   .

In view of the conditions under which it was hurried into existence, it should be no surprise that *Violence in the City—An End or a Beginning?* is a slim volume with only eighty-six pages of blown-up type. But the report of the McCone Commission is not only brief, it is sketchy and superficial. Its tone and style are disturbing. There is much glib writing and the approach as well as the format is slick in the manner of our illustrated news weeklies before their recent upgrading. The depth analysis of this fateful outbreak can be read by an average reader in less than an hour—allowing ample time for contemplating the many photographs, both color and black-and-white.

A comparison with the careful and considered report of the Illinois Governor's Commission which analyzed the 1919 Chicago race riots in a 672-page book (*The Negro in Chicago*) that required three years of planning, research, and writing to produce may well be unfair. But with the considerable budget and the academic sophistication available today, more was to be expected than the public relations statement presently in our hands.

It is not only the size and style of the McCone document that are disturbing. Its content is disappointing both in its omissions and in underlying political and philosophical perspectives. There is almost nothing in the report that is new or that gives consideration to the unique conditions of Los Angeles life and politics. As Los Angeles councilman Bill Mills commented, most of the material in the report documents conditions in the Negro ghetto that have been common knowledge to sociologists and the informed public for a generation.

More appalling are the report's deeper failures. With a narrow legalistic perspective that approached the riots in terms of the sanctity of law and order, the commissioners were unable (or unwilling) to read any social or political meaning into the August terror. There was no attempt to view the outbreak from the point of view of the Negro poor. The commissioners also play a dangerous game with the thorny problem of responsibility. The Negro community as a whole is absolved from responsibility for the rioting while local and national leaders (civil-rights moderates and extremists alike) are taken to task for inflaming mass discontent and undermining attachments to law and authority. (In his two-page dissenting comment appended to the main report, the Reverend James E. Jones, a Negro commissioner, criticizes the report for attempting "to put a lid on protest.")

In a crude attempt at "horse-trading" in the responsibility market, the positions of the Los Angeles police department and city administrators are consistently protected. In discounting the relevance of police provocation and city policies to the revolt without presenting any facts or evidence, the Commission not only protects powerful interests; it abdicates its mandate to seek out facts and establish as best as it could the objective reality. My most general and serious criticism of the report is this violation of its responsibility to seek truth and its frequent hiding behind opinion and hearsay.

.   .   .   .

The analytical perspective is overwhelmingly *riot control* rather than collective or crowd behavior. The attempt of responsible Negro leaders to cool off the mobs is discussed, but the major emphasis is on the tactics used by the various law enforcement agencies. After a fairly thorough discussion of the arrest which set off the events, the Negroes who participated in violence are almost excluded from the story. The very language of the Commission suggests that it has prejudged "the meaning of Watts," even though the debate that has been going on in Negro circles as to the apropriate term of reference suggests that determining the character of these events is a real and difficult question.

On page one of the report, the outbreak is called a "spasm" and "an insensate rage of destruction." Later it is called "an explosion—a *formless, quite senseless,* all but hopeless violent protest" (Italics mine). Only in its discussion of the business targets which were looted and burned does the Commission attempt to locate a meaning or pattern in what the rioters did, and here they conclude—unlike most informed observers—that there was no "significant correlation between alleged consumer exploitation and the destruction."

The legalistic perspective of the Commission and its staff seems to have blocked its sensitivity to the sociological meaning of the riots. When viewed simply as an uprising of the criminal element against law and order (aggravated of course by the more social, economic, and political causes of frustration already discussed), the Commissioners need not look seriously at its human meaning nor need they understand what messages may have been communicated by the rocks, gunfire, and Molotov cocktails. Let us not romanticize the Watts violence. I don't claim that everyone involved and everything done had rational motives. But it is a more humble and scientific attitude to leave the question open and to examine the limited evidence that is available. For the assumption of meaninglessness, the emptying out of content and communication from any set of human actions—*even nonrational violence*—reduces the dignity of the actors involved. In the present context it is a subtle insult to Los Angeles' Negroes. The report ostensibly avoids such an insulting stance by minimizing Negro participation and exculpating the bulk of the community from responsibility for the anti-social outbreak—except of course its leaders who aggravated the underlying tension:

> In the ugliest interval which lasted from Thursday through Saturday, perhaps as many as 10,000 Negroes took to the streets in marauding bands. . . . The entire Negro population of Los Angeles County, about two thirds of whom live in this area (that of the riots), numbers more than 650,000. Observers estimate that only about two percent were involved in the disorder. Nevertheless, this violent fraction, however, minor, has given the face of community relations in Los Angeles a sinister cast.

No evidence is presented for the 2 percent estimate, nor for the total of 10,000 participants on which it is based. We are not told how the Commission defines being "involved in the disorder." A number of distortions are apparently obvious, however. Even if 10,000 were the upper limit, this figure would indicate much more than 2 percent participation. For the Negro curfew area of some 500,000 residents contains many neighborhoods of comfortable middle-class people who were far from the riot center; they should be eliminated from a calculation of the extent of participation in an outbreak of the Negro poor and dispossessed. Second, the total population figures include women, children, and the aged. A more appropriate (and still difficult) question would be the extent of participation of young and mature Negro males in the low-income districts that were the centers of the action.

. . . .

My informants reported widespread support within the ghetto for the violent outbreak. Moral approval (as well as active participation) was stronger among youth and among the poor and working-class. Old people and middle-class Negroes were more likely to feel ambivalent and hold back. But there seems to have been at least some participation from all segments of the black community. . . .

. . . .

As the Governor's report correctly notes, the uprising was not organized in advance. Yet it was neither formless nor meaningless. The

Negro crowds were expressing more than the blind rage and the anti-white hate epitomized in the "Burn, baby, burn" slogan. They seem to have been announcing an unwillingness to continue to accept indignity and frustration without fighting back. They were particularly communicating their hatred of policemen, firemen, and other representatives of white society who operate in the Negro community "like an army of occupation." They were asserting a claim to territoriality, an unorganized and rather inchoate attempt to gain control over their community, their "turf." Most of the actions of the rioters appear to have been informed by the desire to clear out an alien presence, white men, rather than to kill them. (People have remarked how few whites were shot considering the degree of sniping and the marksmanship evidenced in accurate hits on automobile lights and other targets.) It was primarily an attack on property, particularly white-owned businesses, and not persons. . . .

.   .   .   .

Any appraisal of the Watts uprising must be tentative. All the facts are not yet known, and it always takes time to assimilate the full significance of historic and traumatic events. I suggest, however, that it was not primarily a rising of the lawless. . . .

.   .   .   .

Instead my interpretation turns on two points. On the *collective* level the revolt seems to represent the crystallization of community identity through a nationalistic outburst against a society felt as dominating and oppressive. The spirit of the Watts rioters appears similar to that of anti-colonial crowds demonstrating against foreign masters, though in America of course the objective situation and potential power relations are very different. On the *individual* level, participation would seem to have had a special appeal for those young Negroes whose aspirations to be men of dignity are systematically negated by the unavailability of work and the humiliations experienced in contacts with whites. For these young men (and reports indicate that males between the ages of 14 and 30 predominated in the streets), violence permitted expressing their manhood in the American way of fighting back and "getting even"—rather than the passive withdrawal which has been a more characteristic response of the Negro poor.

.   .   .   .

The McCone Commission missed the meaning of the Watts revolt due to the limitations inherent in its perspective. The surface radicalism of its language (in calling for "a new and, we believe, revolutionary attitude toward the problems of the city") cannot belie its basic status-quo orientation. The report advocates "costly and extreme recommendations," and while many of their excellent proposals are indeed costly, they are by no means extreme.

Truly effective proposals would hurt those established institutions and interests that gain from the deprivation of Watts and similar communities —the Commission does not fish in troubled waters. Possibly because they do not want Negroes to control their ethnic neighborhoods, they do not see the relation between community powerlessness and the generalized frustration and alienation which alarms them.

In their approach to the integration of the alienated Negro poor into American society, the Commission is guided by values and assumptions of the white middle-class ethos which are of dubious relevance to the majority of lower-class blacks. Their chief hope for the future is the instillation of achievement motivation in the ghetto poor so that they might embark upon the educational and occupational careers that exemplify the American success story. I am not against middle-class values—but in the immediate critical period ahead "middle-classification" will be effective only with a minority of today's poor.

What is needed—in addition to jobs—is an experimental program for finding innovations that might link the values and social patterns of the Negro lower class with the social and productive needs of the greater society, thus reversing the trend toward alienation. Before the meaningful recommendations can be made that are in line with the enormity of the problem, the sociological and cultural character of the Negro low-income community must be understood. The legalistically-oriented Commission— with its primary commitments to control, law and order, a white-dominated *status quo*, and a middle-class ethic—has not been able to do this.

SUGGESTED READINGS: CHAPTER 10

Michael Banton. *The Policeman in the Community*. New York: Basic Books, 1964.

A useful comparative study of several Scotch and American police departments.

Alfred Lee and Norman Humphrey. *Race Riot*. New York: Dryden Press, 1943. Chicago Commission on Race Relations. *The Negro in Chicago*. Chicago: University of Chicago, 1922.

Two of our most disastrous race riots are described in these excellent studies. They are especially interesting when read side by side.

Jerome Skolnik. *Justice Without Trial.* New York: John Wiley, 1966.

Various incompatibilities between enforcing the law and maintaining "order" are demonstrated and analyzed in rich detail; the data were gathered in an urban setting.

Edwin Sutherland. *The Professional Thief.* Chicago: University of Chicago Press, 1937.

Certain of the more subtle problems of keeping urban law and order are made evident by a close reading of this charming book, which is both an autobiographical account by a thief and an annotated commentary by a theoretically minded sociologist.

11

Italian Outdoor Market, Chicago, 1947. Chicago Historical Society, James D. McMahon, photographer.

SOCIOLOGISTS STUDY
SOCIAL WORLDS

HOW are the various urban social worlds related to
specified spaces, areas, and streets of a city? While journalists
and early sociologists both studied these matters, the series of
studies initiated by Robert Park at the University of Chicago was
the first systematic research program into social worlds as
located in symbolic space. The resulting studies, and others carried
out since that era, illuminate—whether explicitly or
implicitly—the urban perspectives dominant in various
social worlds. Sometimes conceptions of social class are
salient, sometimes rurality appears in full force,
sometimes the city's impersonality and anomie, or the city as a
great place for fun, seems to pervade a world. Readers of
these sociological studies can sometimes take for granted that
the researcher has caught the important perspectives of
a particular world; occasionally they must suspect that the
researcher has allowed his own urban imagery to block out
the relevant imageries of the population he has reported.

The selections presented in this chapter, with only two
exceptions, are by sociologists. The selections exemplify
the relative density of sociological knowledge about various
populations in our big cities and suggest why such books as
Whyte's *Street Corner Society,* Wirth's *The Ghetto,* and

Sutherland's *The Professional Thief* are still read. A long
list of researches about urban institutions is part of this same
tradition of sociological research. A continuing
stream of papers and books, such as Sherri Cavan's recent book
on San Francisco bars (*Liquor License,* Chicago: Aldine
Publishing Company, 1966) and the vigorous publications during
the last decade about deviants, who naturally are found or
studied mainly in cities, also are related directly to the
selections reproduced below.

THE GREAT METROPOLIS: SOCIAL WORLDS,
Junius Browne

JOURNALISTIC exploration of the large cities began
to have a considerable vogue in the
mid-nineteenth century, both in the newspapers and
in full-length books. Later this reporting
would be massively supplemented by reformers'
exposés and studies, and much later by
the kind of sociological reporting represented by the
writings of Robert Park and his students at
the University of Chicago. The journalistic
tradition of reporting on colorful local worlds still
exists, of course. Toward these socially distant
worlds, readers sitting comfortably at home
can experience a range of vicarious reactions—
excitement, titillation, horror, indignation, distant
amusement—and even reach an earnest "understanding."

SOCIETY IN THE METROPOLIS

New York is quite as much the fashionable, as it is the commercial
metropolis; for here are the age, the wealth, the caste-feeling and the
social lines of demarcation that so largely aid in forming and sustaining
what is know as Society. In the United States generally the duties we
owe to society sit rather loosely upon "free-born Americans." But in
New York they are such obligations as we feel called upon conscientiously
to discharge, and do discharge upon pain of modish ostracism.

Fashion upon Manhattan Island will admit of no compromise with
Reason, and refuses to listen to the voice of Common-Sense. She demands
her fullest rights, and her devotees yield them with a zeal that savors
of social superstition.

Fully half a million of our population are absorbed in a perpetual
struggle to avoid physical suffering; while a hundred thousand, probably
pass their lives either in being, or trying to be fashionable. That hundred
thousand are very gay, and seem positively happy. Yet their woes and
throes are innumerable; and their struggles with conventionality and

Excerpted from *The Great Metropolis, A Mirror of New York* (Hartford, Conn.:
American Publishing Co., 1869), pp. 31–37, 159–66.

300 : SOCIOLOGISTS STUDY SOCIAL WORLDS

gentility, though less severe, are as numerous as those of the half million with penury and want.

What our best society is will never be determined to the satisfaction of more than one of the cliques, or coteries, or sets that assume to represent it. Each and all of them claim they are it *par excellence;* and each and all go on in their own specific way, saturated with the conviction that they are the conservers and preservers of the finenesses and courtesies, and elegancies of the fashionable elect.

No society in the world has more divisions and subdivisions than ours —more ramifications and inter-ramifications,—more circles within circles —more segments and parts of segments. They begin in assumption and end in absurdity. They are as fanciful as mathematical lines; and yet so strong that they can hardly be broken, and can rarely be crossed.

The grand divisions may be stated, though the sub-divisions may not; for they depend on religious creeds, on community of avocation, on contiguity of residence, and a hundred nameless things. The grand divisions, like all that appertains to society, are purely conventional, wholly without foundation in reason or propriety. They depend upon what is called family, —on profession, wealth and culture,—the last considered least, because it alone is of importance, and deserving of distinction. Family, inasmuch as few persons in this country know who were their great grandfathers, puts forth the strongest claim and makes the loftiest pretension.

The old Knickerbockers, as they style themselves, insist upon it that they should have the first place in society; and, as most of them inherited real estate from their ancestors, that they were too conservative to sell, and too parsimonious to mortgage, they can support their pretensions by assured incomes and large bank accounts, without which gentility is an empty word, and fashion a mockery and a torment.

All the Vans and those bearing names suggestive of Holland, vow they are of the Knickerbocker stock, albeit it is said, some who were Smiths and Joneses two or three generations ago have since become Van Smythes and Van Johannes.

Be this as it may, the actual or would be Knickerbockers are often the narrowest and dullest people on the Island, and have done much to induce the belief that stupidity and gentility are synonymous terms. They have fine houses generally, in town and country; have carriages and furniture with crests, though their forefathers sold rum near Hanover Square, or cast nets in East river; live expensively and pompously; display conspicuously in their private galleries their plebian ancestors in patrician wigs and ruffles, that the thrifty old Dutchmen never dreamed of among their barrels of old Jamaica, or their spacious and awkward seines. They do all those showy things; yet are they degenerate sons of worthier sires, because they have one virtue less than they,—honesty,—and a defect,— pretension,—that puts the bar sinister upon all truly distinguished lineage.

The Knickerbockers incline to entertainments and receptions where dreary platitudes pass for conversation, and well-intending men and women, whom nature would not bless with wit, fall asleep, and dream of a heaven in which they seem clever forevermore.

The livers upon others' means form the second class of our best society, without special regard to their genealogy. They sometimes boast that they do not work themselves, and reveal their vulgarity by the vulgar boast; but fancy that they have inherited gentleness of blood with the fortunes that came unearned into their possession.

Not a few of these have three or four generations of ease and luxury behind them; and consequently the men and women are comely, and have good manners and correct instincts; are quite agreeable as companions, and capable of friendship. To this division of the community, art and literature are largely indebted for encouragement, and Broadway and Fifth-avenue to many of their attractions.

These people patronize the opera, Wallack's, the classical concerts; furnish the most elegant equipage to the Park, and the most welcome guests to Saratoga, Newport and Long Branch. They wear genuine diamonds, and laces and India shawls; speak pure French and elegant English,—many of them at least; and are on the whole, very endurable when they are thrown into contact with persons who value them for what they are, and not for what they are worth.

They are most injured by too much association with each other, and by lack of some earnest and noble purpose in a life they find it difficult to fill with aught beside frivolity.

The cultivatedly comfortable, who are the third and best representatives of our society, give it its best and highest tone from the fact that they are independent, broad and sensible. Successful authors and artists belong to this class, and all the families who have ideas beyond money, and consider culture quite equal to five-twenties. They lend a helping hand to those who are struggling in the sphere of Art, whether the form be marble, colors, sounds, or words; and believe that refinement and generosity are the best evidences of developed character. They give the most agreeable receptions in the city,—quiet gatherings of poets, authors, painters, sculptors, journalists, and actors occasionally,—without vulgar parade, or cumbersome form or wearisome routine. This class exercises a strong and marked influence, and is rapidly increasing; for, though really democratic, it is aristocratic in the true sense.

The new rich are at present stronger and more numerous than ever in New York. They profited by contracts and speculations during the War, and are now a power in the Metropolis,—a power that is satirized and ridiculed, but a power nevertheless. They are exceedingly *prononcé, bizarre,* and generally manage to render themselves very absurd; but inasmuch as they annoy and worry the Knickerbockers, who have less money and are more stupid than they, I presume they have their place and achieve a purpose in the social life of Gotham.

These are the people who flare and flash so at the places of amusements, on the public promenades and in the principal thoroughfares, and whom strangers regard as the exponents of our best society, when they really represent the worst. They outdress and outshine the old families, the cultivatedly comfortable, the inheritors of fortunes, and everybody else, in whatever money can purchase and bad taste can suggest.

They have the most imposing edifices on the Avenue, the most striking liveries, the most expensive jewelry, the most gorgeous furniture, the worst manners, and the most barbarous English. They prejudice plain persons against wealth, inducing them to believe that its accumulation is associated with indelicacy, pretense and tawdriness, and that they who are materially prosperous are so at the price of much of their native judgment and original good sense. After two or three generations, even the new rich will become tolerable; will learn to use their forks instead of their knives in transferring their food to their mouths; will fathom the subtle secret that impudence is not ease, and that assumption and good breeding are diametrically opposed.

The mere adventurers are an itinerant class of New-York society, which flashes and makes a noise for a few months, or years, possibly, and then goes out, and is heard no more. They are of the new rich sort in appearance and manners, but more reckless, more tinseled and more vulgar,—because they are aware their day is brief, and the total eclipse of their glory nigh.

In the Spring we see their mansions resplendent and their carriages glittering oppressively through the drives of the Park and along the Bloomingdale road. In the Autumn, the red flag is displayed from the satin-damasked windows, and placards, on which are inscribed "Sheriff's sale," are posted on the handsome stables, where blooded horses stand ungroomed in rosewood stalls.

The adventurers live upon the top of a bubble which they know will burst soon, but which they design to enjoy while they can. They come here with some means or some credit, and go largely into an operation,— whether in advertising a patent medicine or "bearing" a leading stock, it matters little,—talk largely and coolly of their ability to lose hundreds of thousands without hurting them, but subsequently declare they have made as much; and on this plane of assurance contract enormous debts, and drive four-in-hand to the devil.

How many of these failures do I remember! How like a volcano they blazed, and at last hid their fires in smouldering ashes and unsightly cinders; They had a good time no doubt, in their own estimation, and relished the joke of cajoling the unfortunate tradesmen who played the sycophant for custom. They teach lessons, these adventurers, but give more expensive ones than they take, or are willing to pay for.

The sham and snobbery of our society are in the main indisputable, and far beyond those of any city in the Union; for there is a constant inroad upon the Metropolis of wealthy vulgarity and prosperous coarseness, from every part of the country, giving us more sinners against good breeding than we can conveniently bear, or should be charged with on our own account. Indeed, we have too much of the native article to require importation, and could better afford to part with what grows spontaneously here for the disadvantage of other less pretentious, but more deserving cities.

New York society furnishes such themes for the satirist as no other place can, since its assumption and hollowness are greater, and it pretensions to superiority more insolent.

Wealth is good; but refinement, and culture, and purity and nobleness are better. Everything not dishonest nor dishonorable merits a certain degree of respect and esteem, so long as it does not assume to be other than it is. But, when wealth claims to be virtue, or culture, lineage, or purity elegance, or impudence genius, they all become vulgarized.

When will our American citizens cease to imitate Europe,—copying the vice of the titled, and omitting their virtues? When will they learn that thorough good breeding, as well as entire honesty, consists in daring to seem what they are, and in valuing manhood and womanhood above their accidental surroundings?

THE LAGER-BEER GARDENS

New York, probably, has a German population of one hundred and fifty to two hundred thousand; and it is a part of the social duty of every one of these, if not a point in his worldly religion, to drink beer,—the quantity varying with the intensity of his nationality. Germans and beer are related to each other as cause and effect; and, one given, the other must follow of necessity.

Manhattan, from the battery to Harlem bridge, is covered with beer-saloons and gardens. They are in longitudinal and lateral directions, in the broad thoroughfares of Broadway and Third avenue, and in the out-of-the-way and narrow quarters of Ann and Thames streets. The whole island literally foams and froths with the national beverage of Rhineland; and, from sunrise until midnight, (Sunday excepted, if you have faith in the Excise Law), the amber hued liquid flows constantly from more than ten thousand kegs, and is poured into twenty times as many thirsty throats, and highly-eupeptic and capacious stomachs.

There must be in New York three or four thousand lager-beer establishments, kept and patronized almost exclusively by Germans, who tend to beer-selling in this country as naturally as Italians to image-making and organ-grinding. These establishments are of all sizes and kinds, from the little hole in the corner, with one table and two chairs, to such extensive concerns as the Atlantic garden, in the Bowery, and Hamilton and Lyon parks, in the vicinity of Harlem, not to mention their superabundance in Jersey-City, Hoboken, Brooklyn, Hudson-City, Weehawken and every other point within easy striking distance of the Metropolis by rail and steam.

Of course, Sunday is the day of all the week for patronage of such places, for Teutonic recreation and bibulous enjoyment; and hence the bitter opposition to the Excise Law on the part of the Germans, the greater part of whom are Republicans, but who are not less hostile on that account to the Republican measure. They are determined to have beer on Sundays, and are making every possible effort to render the odious law inoperative by declaring it unconstitutional. They have opened their purses wide, which they rarely do unless terribly in earnest, to regain what they believe to be their rights; and they will never cease agitating the question until permitted to absorb beer when, where, and to what extent they please.

.　　.　　.　　.　　.　　.　　.　　.　　.　　.

The Germans are an eminently gregarious and social people, and all their leisure is combined with and comprehends lager. They never dispense with it. They drink it in the morning, at noon, in the evening and late at night; during their labors and their rest; alone and with their friends; and yet we never hear of their floating away upon the swollen stream of their own imbibitions, or of their ribs cracking and falling off, like the hoops of barrels, from over-expansion. The chief end of man has long been a theme of discussion among theologians and philosophers. The chief end of that portion who emigrate from Fatherland is to drink lager, under all circumstances and on all occasions; and the end is faithfully and perseveringly carried out.

The drinking of the Germans, however, is free from the vices of the Americans. The Germans indulge in their lager rationally, even when they seem to carry indulgence to excess. They do not squander their means; they do not waste their time; they do not quarrel; they do not fight; they do not ruin their own hopes and the happiness of those who love them, as do we of hotter blood, finer fibre, and intenser organism. They take lager as we do oxygen into our lungs,—appearing to live and thrive upon it. Beer is one of the social virtues; Gambrinus a patron saint of every family, —the protecting deity of every well-regulated household.

The Germans combine domesticity with their dissipation,—it is that to them literally,—taking with them to the saloon or garden their wives and sisters and sweethearts, often their children, who are a check to any excess or impropriety, and with whom they depart at a seemly hour overflowing with beer and *bonhommie,* possessed of those two indispensables of peace—an easy mind and a perfect digestion.

Look at them as they once were, and will be again, in Lyon or Hamilton park, on a Sunday afternoon or evening. They are assembled at the popular resort to the number of four or five thousand,—men, women and children, persons of every grade and calling, but all speaking the same language and liking the same drink, which perhaps, more than aught else, makes them a homogeneous and sympathetic people. How entirely contented, and even joyous, are they! The humblest and hardest toilers are radiant with self-satisfaction, as if there were neither labor nor care tomorrow. They drink, and laugh and chat energetically and boisterously, as if they really relished it, and smoke, and sing and dance, and listen appreciatively to music, day after day, and night after night, never tiring of their pleasures, never seeking for a change.

Their life is simple, and included within a little round. Dyspepsia and nervous disorders trouble them not. Every day they labor; every night they rest, lying a solid bar of sleep between the days; each year adding something to their worldly store; always living below their means; thrilled by no rapturous glow; disturbed by no divine ideals; speculative, but calm; thoughtful, but healthy; comfortable, but thrifty; resolved to have and own something if years are given to them, and making their resolution good in real estate, brick houses, and government securities.

How can they enjoy themselves so? think the pale, taciturn, eager-looking Americans at the table opposite. What do they find to talk about so volubly, and laugh at so loudly? How eloquent and witty they must be!

Neither the one nor the other, you will discover, if you listen. They are simple as Arcadians. Little things amuse, trifles interest them. The commonest circumstances, the mere mention of which would weary you, my American friend, are subjects of protracted discussion; and they roar over what would seem to you the merest insipidities. You may be as witty as Voltaire and sparkling as Rochefoucault to your companions. They only smile and look bored again. The most expensive wines stand untasted before you. The great glory of the night, and the beauties of Beethoven and Mozart fall upon you and your friends unmoved; while your German neighbors drink them all in with their lager, and burst into rapturous applause.

Subtle influences those of race and temperament, which nothing can change! Ours is a melancholy brotherhood over whom the Starry Banner waves, and we have purchased our freedom and progress at the price of much of our content. Lager delights you not, nor Limberger either; and the centuries-distant blood of Oedipus is in your veins.

It is a goodly sight to see the Germans, who eat and drink, but eat as they do everything else, with a purpose. No elaborate dainties, no *recherché* viands, no delicate *entremets* for them. Brown-bread and caraway seed, sweitzerkase and Limberger, which no nostril or stomach out of Germany can endure, solid ham, Bologna sausage and blood-puddings appease their vigorous appetites, and preserve their ruddy health; while pipes of strong and by no means choice tobacco yield them all the repose they require.

What a racket they keep up in the pauses of the music, even while it is being played. Food, and drink, and talk, and laughter, hour after hour. They raise their voices; they grow red in the face; they gesticulate; they strike the tables; they seem on the point of mortal conflict; and an American who knew them not would believe murder was about to be committed.

But it is only their way. They are merely discussing the last masquerade, or the claims of Sigel to military reputation. Another round of lager—each person pays for his own glass—will mollify any asperity that may have arisen. Another plate of sweitzer will change the theme, if it be an unpleasant one, and a cabbage-leaf cigar will dissolve into thin air the last traces of ill-temper.

The Atlantic Garden is a favorite resort of the Germans, and one of the noticeable places of New York. It is all under cover, and capable of accommodating twenty-five hundred or three thousand people. It has a large bar-room in front, and smaller ones inside; a shooting gallery, billiard and bowling saloons, a huge orchestrion, which performs during the day, and a fine band that gives selections from celebrated composers during the evening. The entire place is filled with small tables and benches, which are crowded every evening with drinkers and smokers. A confusion of ringing glasses, of loud voices speaking German in high key, of laughter and strains of soft music, float up through tobacco smoke to the arched roof until midnight, when the musicians put away their instruments, the lights are turned out, and the vast place is locked up.

The Atlantic is the most cosmopolitan place of entertainment in the City; for, though the greater part of its patrons are Germans, every other nationality is represented there. French, Irish, Spaniards, English, Italians, Portuguese, even Chinamen and Indians, may be seen through the violet atmosphere of the famous Atlantic; while Americans, who have learned to like lager—even that made in Gotham—and who are fond of music, sit at the little tables, and look like doomed spirits beside their round-faced, square-browed, jolly neighbors. Much may be had there for little, which is less recommendation to the Americans than to the Germans; and they who desire cheap concerts—one may sit there all the evening without a single glass of beer, if he is so minded—can have them every evening in the year.

With all their industry, and economy, and thrift, the Germans find ample leisure to enjoy themselves, and at little cost. Their pleasures are never expensive. They can obtain more for $1 than an American for $10, and can, and do, grow rich upon what our people throw away. They are odd compounds of sentiment and materialism, of poetry and prose, of generous emotion and narrow life, of affection and selfishness, of dullness and shrewdness, of romance and practicality, of opposites of many kinds, but altogether blending into praiseworthy prudence, honesty, industry and enterprise. They are always endeavoring to improve their condition; and, from their constant self-seeking, they soon acquire property, carefully educate their children, ally their descendants to those of Anglo-Saxon blood, and in a few generations become as thoroughly American as the Americans themselves.

A Review of
"THE SOCIAL VALUE OF THE SALOON,"
by E. C. Moore

MUNICIPAL AFFAIRS customarily reviewed
interesting articles on "city conditions"
published in other magazines. The first volume, in
1897, carried a review of Moore's article,
reporting a sociological study of the saloon as a
social center. With remarkably few changes of
wording (as "saloon" to "bar"), but with
hardly any change in basic perspective, this article
might find ready publication today in a
sociological journal. The urban imagery embedded in the
approach is a social world with "friendship and
neighborhood in the midst of the great city."

In the *American Journal of Sociology* for July, Mr. E. C. Moore discusses "The Social Value of the Saloon." The nineteenth ward of Chicago which has a population of 48,280 according to the census of 1896 was chosen as a typical district for investigation. This is a workingman's district, and a large proportion of the inhabitants are unskilled laborers. Besides the saloons, four churches and a few trade unions attempt to meet the social needs of the population. There are no music halls or theatres in the district. Mr. Moore's standpoint is stated as follows: "It was assumed in beginning the investigation that an institution which society has so generally created for itself must meet a definite social demand; and that the

Reprinted from *Municipal Affairs*, Vol. 1 (1897), 576–77.

demand was not synonymous with a desire on the part of society to commit suicide by means of alcoholic poison was granted. The question became that of fixing the demand, of determining the social value. What does the saloon offer that renders it so generally useful, in the economic sense, to the great mass of those who patronize it? For it is use, not abuse, that it stands for."

Mr. Moore enlarges upon the value of the saloon as a social center. "Primarily the saloon is a social center. Few will deny this. It is the workingman's club. Many of his leisure hours are spent here. In it he finds more of the things which approximate to luxury than he finds at home, almost more than he finds in any other public place in the ward. In winter the saloon is warm, in summer it is cool, at night it is brightly lighted, and it is always clean. More than that there are chairs and tables and papers and cards and lunch, and in many cases pool and billiards, while in some few well-equipped gymnasiums can be found which are free to patrons. What more does the workingman want for his club? He already has all that most clubs offer their members—papers and cards and food and drink and service—and being modest in his wants their quality satisfies him. But his demand for even these things is not fundamental, they are but means to his social expression. It is the society of his fellows that he seeks and must have."

While the social value of the saloon under existing conditions is insisted upon, its limitations and imperfections are by no means concealed. "That the saloon functions to certain social wants otherwise not supplied is our thesis. That its wares are poison in their abuse and not in their use is our contention. It is also admitted that social want is very inadequately supplied by the saloon. That a condition in which the idea can express itself in emotional terms only is essentially pathological. But it is believed that the saloon will continue to supply it as long as its opponents continue to wage a war of extermination against all that it represents, instead of wisely aiding social life to reach that plane where its present evil shall no longer be its accidents. The saloon is a thing come out of the organic life of the world, and it will give place only to a better form of social functioning. That a better form is possible to a fully conscious society no one can deny. When and what this form shall be remains for society's component units to declare. The presence of the saloon in an unorganized society is proof conclusive that society can wisely organize the need which it supplies.

"It is hardly necessary to enlarge further upon the evils of the saloon in a protest against the predominance of one-sided statements in the very particular. They are many and grave, and cry out to society for proper consideration. But proper consideration involves a whole and not a half truth, and the whole truth involves its own power of proper action. In the absence of higher forms of social stimulus and larger social life the saloon will continue to function in society, for that great part of humanity which does not possess a more adequate form of social expression the words of Esdras will remain true: It is wine that 'maketh the mind of the king and of the fatherless child to be all one, of the bondman and of the freeman, of the poor and of the rich. It turneth every thought into jollity and mirth, so that a man remembereth neither sorrow nor debt; and it maketh every heart glad.' "

SYMBOLISM, SPACE, AND THE UPPER CLASS,
Walter Firey

> FIREY'S sociological account of Beacon Hill expresses
> the important urban theme of continuity in the
> city. In this instance, the continuity is
> that of the upper class, symbolized by the use of
> urban space as well as legal-political
> battles to protect that space. The world of the upper
> class is located on and rooted in that space.

In common with many of the older American cities Boston has inherited from the past certain spatial patterns and landmarks which have had a remarkable persistence and even recuperative power despite challenges from other more economic land uses. The persistence of these spatial patterns can only be understood in terms of the group values that they have come to symbolize. . . .

.   .   .   .

. . . Beacon Hill is located some five minutes' walking distance from the retail center of Boston. This neighborhood has for fully a century and a half maintained its character as a preferred upper class residential district, despite its contiguity to a low rent tenement area, the West End. During its long history Beacon Hill has become the symbol for a number of sentimental associations which constitute a genuine attractive force to certain old families of Boston. Some idea of the nature of these sentiments may be had from statements in the innumerable pamphlets and articles written by residents of the Hill. References to "this sacred eminence,"

From "Sentiment and Symbolism as Ecological Variables," *American Sociological Review*, Vol. 10 (1945), 141–43. Reprinted by permission of the American Sociological Association and the author.

"stately old-time appearance," and "age-old quaintness and charm," give an insight into the attitudes attaching to the area. One resident reveals rather clearly the spatial referability of these sentiments when she writes of the Hill:

> It has a tradiiton all its own that begins in the hospitality of a book-lover, and has never lost that flavor. Yes, our streets are inconvenient, steep, and slippery. The corners are abrupt, the contours perverse. . . . It may well be that the gibes of our envious neighbors have a foundation and that these dear crooked lanes of ours were indeed traced in ancestral mud by absentminded kine.

Behind such expressions of sentiment are a number of historical associations connected with the area. Literary traditions are among the strongest of these; indeed, the whole literary legend of Boston has its focus at Beacon Hill. Many of America's most distinguished literati have occupied homes on the Hill. Present day occupants of these houses derive a genuine satisfaction from the individual histories of the dwellings. One lady whose home had had a distinguished pedigree remarked:

> I like living here for I like to think that a great deal of historic interest has happened here in this room.

Not a few families are able to trace a continuity of residence on the Hill for several generations, some as far back as 1800 when the Hill was first developed as an upper class neighborhood. It is a point of pride to a Beacon Hill resident if he can say that he was born on the Hill or was at least raised there; a second best boast is to point out that his forebears once lived on the Hill.

Thus a wide range of sentiment—aesthetic, historical, and familial—have acquired a spatial articulation in Beacon Hill. The bearing of these sentiments upon locational processes is a tangible one and assumes three forms: retentive, attractive, and resistive. Let us consider each of these in order. To measure the retentive influence that spatially-referred sentiments may exert upon locational activities we have tabulated by place of residence all the families listed in the Boston *Social Register* for the years 1894, 1905, 1914, 1929, and 1943. This should afford a reasonably accurate picture of the distribution of upper class families by neighborhoods within Boston, and in suburban towns. . . . The most apparent feature of these data is, of course, the consistent increase of upper class families in the suburban towns and the marked decrease (since 1905) in two of the in-town upper class areas, Back Bay and Jamaica Plain. Although both of these neighborhoods remain fashionable residential districts their prestige is waning rapidly. Back Bay in particular, though still surpassing in numbers any other single neighborhood, has undergone a steady invasion of apartment buildings, rooming houses, and business establishments which are destroying its prestige value. The trend of Beacon Hill has been different. Today it has a larger number of upper class families than it had in 1894. Where it ranked second among fashionable neighborhoods in 1894 it ranks third today, being but slightly outranked in numbers by the suburban city of Brookline and by the Back Bay. Beacon Hill is the only intown district that has held to itself a considerable proportion of Boston's old families.

There is, however, another aspect to the spatial dynamics of Beacon Hill, one that pertains to the "attractive" locational role of spatially referred sentiments. From 1894 to 1905 the district underwent a slight drop, subsequently experiencing a steady rise for 24 years, and most recently undergoing another slight decline. These variations are significant, and they bring out rather clearly the dynamic ecological role of spatial symbolism. The initial drop is attributable to the development of the then new Back Bay. Hundreds of acres there had been reclaimed from marshland and had been built up with palatial dwellings. Fashion now pointed to this as the select area of the city and in response to its dictates a number of families abandoned Beacon Hill to take up more pretentious Back Bay quarters. Property values on the Hill began to depreciate, old dwellings became rooming houses, and businesses began to invade some of the streets. But many of the old families remained on the Hill and a few of them made efforts to halt the gradual deterioration of the district. Under the aegis of a realtor, an architect, and a few close friends there was launched a program of purchasing old houses, modernizing the interiors and leaving the colonial exteriors intact, and then selling the dwellings to individual families for occupancy. Frequently adjoining neighbors would collaborate in planning their improvements so as to achieve an architectural consonance. The results of this program may be seen in the draft of upper class families back to the Hill. From 1905 to 1929 the number of *Social Register* families in the district increased by 120. Assessed valuations showed a corresponding increase: from 1919 to 1924 there was a rise of 24 percent; from 1924 to 1929 the rise was 25 percent. The nature of the Hill's appeal, and the kind of persons attracted, may be gathered from the following popular write-up:

> To salvage the quaint charm of Colonial Architecture on Beacon Hill, Boston, is the object of a well-defined movement among writers and professional folks that promises the most delightful opportunities for the home seeker of moderate mean and conservative tastes. Because men of discernment were able to visualize the possibilities presented by these architectural landmarks, and have undertaken the gracious task of restoring them to their former glory, this historic quarter of old Boston, once the centre of literary culture, is coming into its own.

The independent variable in this "attractive" locational process seems to have been the symbolic quality of the Hill, by which it constituted a referent for certain strong sentiments of upper class Bostonians.

While this revival was progressing there remained a constant menace to the character of Beacon Hill, in the form of business encroachments and apartment-hotel developments. Recurrent threats from this source finally prompted residents of the Hill to organize themselves into the Beacon Hill Association. Formed in 1922, the declared object of this organization was "to keep undesirable business and living conditions from affecting the hill district." At the time the city was engaged in preparing a comprehensive zoning program and the occasion was propitious to secure for Beacon Hill suitable protective measures. A systematic set of recommendations was drawn up by the Association regarding a uniform 65-foot height limit for the entire Hill, the exclusion of business from all but two streets, and the restriction of apartment house bulk. It succeeded in gaining only a partial recognition of this program in the 1924 zoning ordinance. But the Association continued its fight against inimical land uses year after year. In 1927 it successfully fought a petition brought before the Board of Zoning Adjustment to alter the height limits in one area so as to permit the construction of a four million dollar apartment-hotel 155 feet high. Residents of the Hill went to the hearing en masse. In spite of the prospect of an additional twenty million dollars worth of exclusive apartment hotels that were promised if the zoning restrictions were withheld the petition was rejected, having been opposed by 214 of the 220 persons present at the hearing. In 1930 the Association gained an actual reduction in height limits on most of Beacon street and certain adjoining streets, though its leader was denounced by opponents as "a rank sentimentalist who desired to keep Boston a village." One year later the Association defeated a petition to rezone Beacon street for business purposes. In other campaigns the Association successfully pressed for the rezoning of a business street back to purely residential purposes, for the lowering of height limits on the remainder of Beacon street, and for several lesser matters of local interest. Since 1929, owing partly to excess assessed valuations of Boston real estate and partly to the effects of the depression upon families living on securities, Bacon Hill has lost some of its older families, though its decline is nowhere near so precipitous as that of the Back Bay.

Thus for a span of one and a half centuries there have existed on Beacon Hill certain locational processes that largely escape economic analysis. It is the symbolic quality of the Hill, not its impeditive or cost-imposing character, that most tangibly correlates with the retentive, attractive, and resistive trends that we have observed. And it is the dynamic force of spatially referred sentiments, rather than considerations of rent, which explains why certain families have chosen to live on Beacon Hill in preference to other in-town districts having equally accessible location and even superior housing conditions. There is thus a non-economic aspect to land use on Beacon Hill, one which is in some respects actually diseconomic in its consequences. Certainly the large apartment-hotels and specialty shops would have represented a fuller capitalization on potential property values than do residences. In all likelihood the attending increase in real estate prices would not only have benefited individual property holders but would have so enhanced the value of adjoining properties as to compensate for whatever depreciation other portions of the Hill might have experienced.

THE WORLD OF FURNISHED ROOMS,
Harvey Zorbaugh

DURING the 1920s, Zorbaugh, a student of Robert Park, studied several of Chicago's social worlds, with an emphasis on the city's diversity and contrasts. Reproduced below are two selections from his *Gold Coast and the Slum*. The first consists of a long document ("the life history of a 'charity girl' "). Her story expresses several classic urban themes: the small-town girl storms the city on her way to success, but fails; the impersonal, heartless city with its consequent lonely, rootless, demoralized denizens; and the search for intimacy, consummated only through immoral adventure.

THE ROOMS

Emporia, Kansas, was my home until I was twenty-two. My father had a small business there. He was an upright, God-fearing man. . . . He taught us to obey the Ten Commandments, to go to church on Sunday, to do all the things the "respectable" do in a small, gossiping place.

We were a large family but father managed to save enough to send me, the oldest, to a small college in the state. And from the time I was a little girl I had music lessons. It is about these music lessons that the story of my life revolves.

Excerpted from *The Gold Coast and the Slum* (Chicago: The University of Chicago Press, 1929), pp. 76–81, by permission of the University of Chicago Press.

I was always looked upon as something of a prodigy about the town. At ten I played at Chopin and Bach. I played my little pieces at church recitals, at firemen's benefits, when mother entertained the Ladies' Aid Society, and at our high school graduating exercises. I was told that I had talent, "wonderful feeling for the soul of the masters," that I ought to go to New York, or abroad, where I could have competent instruction; that some day I would be a concert star.

Through my four years of college this ambition slumbered, but never died. And the day I got my diploma I wrote home that instead of going back to Emporia to marry a "Babbitt" and live on "Main Street," I was going to Chicago to study music. I went home for a stormy week. Father was amazed that I should suggest living alone in Chicago, and sternly forbade my going, saying that if I did he would send me no money—indeed, he had little to send. Mother said little, but when I left she put into my hand fifty dollars which she had been saving for a new dress. All told, when my ticket was bought, I had less than one hundred dollars on which to begin the conquest of a career.

Never shall I forget the time of the night that I arrived at the Northwestern Station, my purse clutched tightly in one hand, and my bag in the other, shaking my head at redcaps, confused and dazzled by the glare of the lights—but my heart singing, my ambition aflame; it was the gate to the promised land. I went to the Travelers' Aid Bureau and inquired how to get to the Y.W.C.A. I walked uptown, carrying my bag, too excited to be tired. I still remember the romantic appeal the sluggish blackness of the river made, gleaming in the lights of the great electric signs. How differently it was to look two short years later!

The first few weeks went by like magic. It was all so strange and maddeningly stimulating to my small-town soul. The "Y" was a pleasant enough place to live—not at all the institutional sort of place I had expected it to be. But even in these first weeks I began to know what loneliness is. Most of my evenings were spent sitting in corners of the sitting-room, watching the old girls playing the piano and victrola, or entertaining their beaux. I got acquainted with a few other newcomers— a girl from Indiana who came to study, like myself, a girl who came from Alabama to get work as stenographer, and four or five others, from small towns in Illinois. All but myself seemed to have acquaintances or connections of some sort in Chicago. And sometimes, when I felt too unbearably lonely, I would go back to the big station in the evening, at the time when the train I came on would be coming in, and watch the faces in the crowd for a face from Emporia.

It was at the "Y" that I had my first acquaintance with that most pitiable figure of the rooming-house world—the old and unmarried woman who works. They were conspicuous in either the cafeteria or the upstairs sitting-room, because of their loneliness—eating lunch at a solitary table, sitting by themselves knitting, with shabby and unbecoming clothes, care-worn faces, and toil-worn hands. I was to learn later some of the tragedies their mute lips harbored.

After six weeks at the "Y" I moved to the Near North Side, to be nearer my music school. And during the next few months I lived at a dozen rooming-houses and homes for girls. The boarding-homes were more comfortable and pleasant, but I was working all day and taking lessons at night. I was out late, and this conflicted with their rules. I soon found a rooming-house was the only place I could live. But it was hard to find a rooming-house where I wanted to live. The rooms I could afford were in gloomy old houses on La Salle Street, bleak and bare, and so large that usually I had to share them with one or two other girls. The beds were hard, and often vermin-infested. The landladies were queer-looking and dowdy, tight-lipped and suspicious of eye, ignorant and coarse. They rarely took any other interest in you than to see that you paid your week in advance. The men and women living in the house were mostly a tough lot. There were goings on that shocked me then—though I would pay scant attention to them now.

My first year is a nightmare as I look back upon it. In order to keep clothes on my back and to pay for my lessons I had to work seven days in the week. My college education had fitted me for nothing. I tried one thing after another—salesgirl at Marshall Field's, milliner's helper, running a simple machine in a garment factory, ushering at a movie, and finally waiting at a "white tile" restaurant. Somehow I never held any of the positions very long.

The days were long and exhausting—up at six, a bath, a cup of coffee on a "sterno" stove, tidy my room a bit, and in the Loop by seven-thirty or eight. Then a long steady grind until five; a mile walk out to my rooming-house; supper in a nearby restaurant—and a plain supper at that; the evening devoted to my lesson or practicing; back to my room at ten-thirty or eleven, often too tired to undress until I had slept an hour or so.

I had come to the city in June. By Christmas my loneliness amounted almost to desperation. I had made no friends—a girl brought up on the Commandments doesn't make friends in rooming-houses or as a waitress very readily. I didn't talk the same language as the girls I worked with. At the theater or the restaurant men often came up to me and said things in a way that made me blush, though often I had no idea what they meant, unsophisticated little fool that I was. Mother was ill, and letters from home came less and less frequently. Shortly after Christmas she died, and the last tie that bound me to Emporia was gone. I was "on my own," and very nearly "on my uppers" as well. But I still had my ambition—I would some day be a great *artiste,* and all this loneliness and hardship would be forgotten. . . .

In February, I think it was, I met a girl from Tennessee at the music school, with whom I became quite friendly. Within a few weeks we decided to get a room together, and we moved over to a house on Dearborn, just north of Division. The house consists of several large old residences thrown together. It has perhaps forty rooms, and there have been as many as seventy roomers in it at one time. It is cleaner than the run of rooming-houses, and quieter, and the man and the woman who run it are decent enough. But you would never mistake it for anything else than a rooming-house. Somehow, one gets to loathe that card in the window—"Rooms"! And the life and people were not much different from those on La Salle Street.

One gets to know few people in a rooming-house, for there are constant comings and goings, and there is little chance to get acquainted if one wished. But one doesn't wish. . . .

.   .   .   .

As the months went by, my lessons cost more and more; I had to work shorter hours to get in my practice; our room was costing more; and I found myself always a week or so behind. It was a humiliating experience to have to cajole the landlady into giving me credit—humiliating to a girl who had been brought up to believe it wrong to have debts. But I got so that I could invent a reason for putting it off as brazenly as the "gold digger" in the next room.

[A year of this had gone by, when one day her music teacher told her there was no hope of her ever realizing her ambitions.] I turned dazedly from the piano. . . . I scarcely heard him. I picked up my music and tossed it into a waste-basket in the corner; and then I walked out of the room.

It was late afternoon, and I walked the streets, neither noticing nor caring where, until late that night I ended up along the embankment in Lincoln Park, and sat down exhausted, on the stone wall by the lake. My head was a bit clearer by now, and I began to take stock of myself. . . .

The ambition for which I had sacrificed, which had kept me alive and going, was dead. There was nothing to hold me to home and family. Mother was dead. No one ever wrote. And my oldest brother, in Chicago a few months before, had told me that father never allowed my name to be mentioned about the house, save to use me as a horrible example of the willful daughter gone wrong—he once referred to me as a street-walker. Those words kept repeating themselves in my mind—"street-walker, street-walker!" And a great bitterness burned in my heart, turning to ashes every love, every tie, every ideal that had held me at home.

Then I began to look at my life in Chicago. What was there in it, after all? My music was gone. I had neither family nor friends. In Emporia there would at least have been neighborhood clubs or the church. But here there was neither. Oh, for someone or something to belong to!

My room-mate had been going to Sunday night services at the Fourth Presbyterian Church, over on the Lake Shore Drive. She told them about me, and one day some pastor's assistant's assistant came to call on me. I went one night after that. I was greeted with ostentatious and half-hearted civility. It was all so impersonal. . . . I never went back; and no other church ever took an interest in me. The only other group I had had anything to do with, outside of my work, had been a social agency from which I had tried to get a little help in the spring. They treated me as impersonally as though I had been a rag doll. There was ringing of buzzers, long documents with endless questionings to be filled out—and not a human touch in it all.

The city is like that. In all my work there had been the same lack of any personal touch. In all this city of three million souls I knew no one, cared for no one, was cared for by no one. In a popular science story in the evening newspaper a few days before I had read how the universe is composed of millions of stars whirling about. I looked up at the sky. I was just like that—an atom whirled about with three million other atoms, day after day, month after month, year after year.

What did I have? I had no clothes, no shows, no leisure—none of the things all girls are supposed to love. My health was breaking under the strain. I was in debt. The answer was, Nothing—absolutely nothing! And there stretched ahead of me long years of nothing, until I married an honest but poor clerk or salesman and tried to make ends meet for a brood of hungry mouths, or until I became one of those broken-down, old working women that I had patronizingly pitied that first week at the Y.W.C.A.

Of course, there were two ways out: I might slip into the lake, there, and end it all. But somehow I didn't think seriously of that. Or I might do as some of the girls in the house, become a "gold digger," play life for what there was in it, pay with what there was in me. The idea half-sickened me, yet I played with it for a while—for so long that I drew up startled at the unknown possibilities that lurked within me, cold at the thought that there was neither person nor thing to hold me back.

.   .   .   .

I never went back to music school. I had been working as a waitress of late, . . . and I kept on with it. But the days and nights were empty now—and at last I knew to the full what loneliness could be. One night a nice boy came into the restaurant—it was one of the larger downtown restaurants—and sat down at my table. He talked to me, as they all did; told me he was from a small town in Oklahoma, that he'd made money, and had come to see the big city. He was friendly, and ended by asking me to a show. I accepted, and we went to a cabaret afterward. In a spirit of reckless bravado, to show the small-town boy I was a city-wise woman, I smoked my first cigarette and took my first drink.

There's no use in making a story of it. He had an engaging smile, and was in search of adventure. I was unutterably lonely—and tired. He said that he loved me, and I was willing not to question too closely. I left the rooming-house, and we took a little flat out near Rogers Park. For a month I played at being respectable, got acquainted with young wives in other apartments, had lovely clothes, lazy hours, ate at the best restaurants, saw the best shows, shopped in smart shops, drove my own car. Then, one day, B. came home and told me he was going back to Oklahoma, and that I wasn't going with him. I said little; I had known it must come, of course, though I had hoped it wouldn't come so soon. There was a generous check. And I moved back into the rooming-house.

TOWERTOWN: CHICAGO'S BOHEMIA,
Harvey Zorbaugh

BOHEMIA is a locale where people drawn from
many worlds reside or visit. Besides this
theme of urban diversity, Zorbaugh's
portrayal of life in Chicago's Towertown during the
1920s caught a number of important urban
themes: the city as a place of freedom
(moral and creative)—including the freeing aspects
of anonymity; the city which is hospitable
to marginal people; the city as a
place for fun and frolic; and urban
cosmopolitanism side by side with urban "front"
or superficiality. As is true of most contemporary
accounts of Bohemias, Zorbaugh's reflected his own
attitudes toward these themes, as well as those of
the people whom he interviewed.

The Towertown of today . . . is largely made up of individuals who
have sought in its unconventionality and anonymity—sometimes under the
guise of art, sometimes not—escape from the conventions and repressions
of the small town or the outlying and more stable communities of the
city. Some of these individuals have a genuine hunger for new experience,
a desire to experiment with life. They run the tearooms and art shops
and book stalls of the "village," or work in the Loop by day and frequent
its studios and restaurants by night. Perhaps, like Collie, they keep a little
red notebook with a list of the things they have always wanted to do, and
strike them off as one experiment in living after another is completed.
Most of these experimenters are young women. For Towertown, like
Greenwich Village, is predominantly a woman's bohemia. . . . It is the
young women who open most of the studios, run most of the tearooms and
restaurants, most of the little art shops and book stalls, manage the exhibits and little theatres, dominate the life of the bohemias of American
cities. And in Towertown the women are, on the whole, noticeably superior to the men.

But these genuine experimenters with life are few. Most of Towertown's present population are egocentric poseurs, neurotics, rebels against

Excerpted from *The Gold Coast and the Slum* (Chicago: University of Chicago
Press, 1929), pp. 91–92, 96–101, by permission of the University of Chicago Press.

the conventions of Main Street or the gossip of the foreign community, seekers of atmosphere, dabblers in the occult, dilettantes in the arts, or parties to drab lapses from a moral code which the city has not yet destroyed. . . . "Self-expression" is the avowed goal of "village" life. And where talent is lacking, self-expression runs to the playing of roles and the wearing of masques, sometimes of the most bizarre sort. . . .

.   .   .   .

The villager is usually content with assuming an eccentricity in dress or manner, an indifference to opinion that is far from real, a contempt for Rodin, Debussy, or Shakespeare, or a pose as the prophet of some new movement in drama, poetry, music, or painting. Once the role is adopted, or perchance thrust upon one, the whole "village" plays up to it, and a personality is crystallized.

> The Neo Arlimusc recently held an exhibit for "Chicago's primitive artist." This primitive artist is P——, a conventional, small business man of sixty-two, who a year ago suddenly began to paint. He had been a clothing peddler in the ghetto, had earned a very mediocre living, but had managed to save a little and had retired. One day the old man dropped some papers from his pocket on which a friend saw some sketches. The old man was much embarrassed, but the friend insisted on taking them to W——, who exclaimed, "This man is a genius, a primitive artist!" P—— had never had a lesson in his life, and paints very crudely. With this encouragement P—— began to paint more crudely than ever. Then it was arranged to give P—— an exhibit. Only his own things were hung. They had an art critic from the University who came and discussed P——'s primitive technique, and a psychiatrist who probed back into P——'s primitive unconscious for the explanation of his turning to painting at so late an age. De K—— got up, and pointing to some Jewish sweatshop scenes painted on old cardboard, exclaimed: "See that? The artist's expression will out! Poverty stricken, he seizes on the only medium available." Then P—— was sent off to New York, where Greenwich Village hailed him as the exponent of a new art form. Under this definition by the group, P—— has ceased to be the timid clothing peddler, sketching and secreting his sketches, having constantly to be reassured he is an artist and has a place in the world, and has accepted the role created for him as the creator of a new and primitive art, and continues to paint more and more crudely.

Behind these masques which the "villagers" present to one another and to the world one usually discovers the egocentric, the poseur, the neurotic, or the "originality" of an unimaginative nature. Occasionally, however, one finds behind these masques young persons who are struggling to live out their own lives, to remake the world a bit more after the fashion of their dreams—young persons who have come from north and west and south, from farm and village and suburb, to this mobile, isolated, anonymous area of a great city where they imagine they may live their dreams. It is these occasional dreams behind the masque, and the enthusiasms, intimacies, disillusionments that are a part of the living out of these dreams, that lend the "village," despite its tawdry tinsel, a certain charm. . . .

.   .   .   .

Transient but intense personal contacts are characteristic of this "bohemian" life of "studio" and "tearoom." Combined with the unconventional tradition of the "village," its philosophy of individualism, and the anonymity which its streets afford, these contacts give rise to unconventional types of sex relationship. Moreover, Towertown's debates on free love and its reputation for promiscuity, coupled with its unconventionality and anonymity, attract to its studios many individuals who are not bohemians, but who seek in Towertown escape from the repressive conventions of the larger community. Many of them become hangers-on of bohemia, but others isolate themselves in its midst.

.   .   .   .

The anonymity and unconventionality of "village" streets attracts to them many who merely want to be "let alone." I was talking one night, near "Bughouse Square," about life in the "village." Afterwards a girl came up to me and said: "Why can't social agencies let us alone? There's at least a year in everybody's life when he wants to do just as he damn pleases. The 'village' is the only place where he can do it without sneaking off in a hole by himself."

Plenty of individuals do use the anonymity of "village" life, however, to sneak off into holes by themselves. Business and professional men use its studio apartments to keep their mistresses. B— and her mother live in a beautiful apartment, with Japanese servants and every luxury. B— is supported by a wealthy business man, married, with a wife and family, who spends occasional week-ends with her. Intervening nights she entertains an army officer, a penniless adventurer, to whom she even gives money. G— is a well-to-do lawyer, and bachelor and keeps his mistress in the village. There are many such cases, especially of young men, "philistines" through and through, who nevertheless like the laissez faire of bohemia. R— is a wealthy dilettante in the arts whose elaborate studio parties are celebrated for the fact that all the women present are his mistresses—past, present, and prospective.

Distorted forms of sex behavior also find a harbor in the "village." Many homosexuals are among the frequenters of "village" tearooms and studios. A friend of mine was asked by an acquaintance to accompany him to the studio of a well-known "villager" to Sunday afternoon tea. There was a large group there. The men were smoking and talking in one end of the room, the women in the other. There was a good deal of taking one another's arms, sitting on the arms of one another's chairs, and of throwing an arm about one another's shoulders. But he thought it was merely that the group were old friends. He was asked to tea again a few weeks later. This time he remained in the evening. Soon the men were fondling one another, as were the women. A man he had met that afternoon threw an arm about him. He got up, went over to the acquaintance who had brought him, and said, "I'm leaving." When they got out on the street he asked, "What sort of a place was that, anyhow?" "Why, I thought you knew," his companion replied, "the best-known fairies and lesbians in Chicago were there."

The intimate and artistic life of the "village" is passed unnoticed by the rest of the city, to which Towertown stands only for these bizarre garret and stable studios, long hair, eccentric dress, and free love. This is due largely to the fact that certain shrewd individuals were not slow to see possibilities in the commercialization of bohemia. Some of these individuals were of bohemia themselves. A group of young women writers in Towertown organized "Seeing Bohemia" trips, at seventy-five cents a head, and conducted curious persons from the outside world through tearooms and studios bizarrely decorated for the occasion.

PATTERNS OF VOLUNTARY ASSOCIATION AMONG URBAN WORKING-CLASS FAMILIES,
Floyd Dotson

ONE feature of working-class life is a restricted associational life. Dotson traces in suggestive outline the alternative kinds of sociability groups used by the urban working class of New Haven.

Sociologists have long recognized a correlation between urbanization and the development of voluntary associations. This observation has commonly been oriented at the theoretical level to the assumption that urbanization as a social process consists of a progressive displacement of "primary" by "secondary" groups in the social structure. The close, intimate, and continuous associations characteristic of the inclusive primary group community give way in the city, it is argued, to intermittent participation in a series of discontinuous groups, most of which are formally and impersonally organized about a single, specific interest.

.   .   .   .

Whatever the adequacy of this theory of existing urban social organization may be as a first approximation, it is now clear that it must be modified in important details. Evidence has accumulated through the researches of Komarovsky and others that formally organized voluntary associations, although numerous in the urban milieu, are unevenly distributed among the various social strata of the population. In general, these investigations indicate that the higher a person's income and class status the greater his social participation.

Significant as these studies are they leave crucial problems unsolved. . . . They do not and cannot tell what forms of social organization are found among those who lack these affiliations.

To investigate these matters a case approach appeared logical at this stage of research in the field. In the project from which the data for this paper were drawn, 50 families were selected from a working-class district in New Haven and interviewed intensively concerning the people

Reprinted from *American Sociological Review*, Vol. 16 (1951), 687–93, by permission of the American Sociological Association and the author.

with whom they maintain face-to-face relationships, in an attempt to discover the nature of their social organization. The results suggest that the "secondary group" nature of leisure time association in the city may be exaggerated in conventional accounts of urban social structure. Although they do not participate to an important extent in formal associations, most of the families studied are neither disorganized nor socially isolated by this lack of participation. The role of informal social participation, particularly within the family and in groups, has, we believe, been consistently underestimated by students of the modern city.

PROCEDURE

Potential candidates for inclusion on the interview panel were chosen at random from the street index of the City Directory. To make the panel as socioeconomically homogeneous as possible, two criteria of selection were imposed once contact with interviewees was established. (1) Since previous studies have shown that unskilled and semiskilled workers tend to lack formal affiliations, it was decided that attention would be concentrated upon them. (2) To guard against the possible retention of associational patterns set in Europe, only those families in which parents were either native stock or American-born were included. . . .

CONFIRMATION OF PREVIOUS STUDIES SHOWING LACK OF PARTICIPATION IN FORMAL VOLUNTARY ASSOCIATIONS

. . . Three-fifths of the men and four-fifths of the women and children in the families studied did not participate at all in formally organized associations. These figures agree closely with Komarovsky's, which pertain to large cities.

The conclusion that formal voluntary associations are relatively unimportant as a source of social contact for most workers becomes all the more inescapable when one considers not only memberships but also actual participation in the activities of the organization. Upon further investigation, 10 of the 29 memberships held by men, and three of the 15 held by women were found to be inactive. None of the 15 memberships held by children was inactive, although by their very nature these are more ephemeral than those of adults.

CHARACTERISTICS OF ASSOCIATIONS WITH ADULT MEMBERSHIPS

A comparison of active and inactive memberships is significant. The formally organized clubs and societies which arouse most interest approximate the informal association in structure and function. . . .

Nominal membership without active participation was found especially in labor unions and the military, fraternal, and ethnic societies. Active memberships tend to be concentrated in athletic and church-affiliated groups.

Labor unions are by their nature largely representative, and rank and file attendance at meetings is notoriously poor. Only one of the six union men on our panel was an active and enthusiastic participant in his local. Veterans' organizations are predominantly middle class in membership; meetings and programs have much in common with business-men's service clubs, and apparently have little appeal for workers. Ethnic societies have apparently progressively lost their appeal as the foreign-born give way to second- and third-generation Americans.[1] Lack of interest in fraternal societies may reflect in part the general decline characteristic of this type of association.

Membership in athletic clubs, on the other hand, tends to be active. While the total number of memberships was small—only five—this figure represents nearly a third of the men between 20–30 years of age, and approximately as many older men had once belonged to such clubs. These tend to be small, local organizations, barely distinguishable from informal types of voluntary associations.[2] Some are organized around the neighborhood bar. Bar keepers are often ex-athletes. They may act as coaches, and perhaps supply money for the jersey sweaters which are normally the only uniform for members. The tavern-keeper leader of a club to which one of our interviewees belonged holds annual dinners at the end of the season for the team and their more faithful fans. Individually, these clubs are ephemeral, but their tradition is thoroughly established in the culture.

Church clubs are second to athletic clubs in the number of active memberships among men. For women, church clubs are by far the most fre-

1. A second generation father of a seventeen-year-old boy remarked concerning the local Pulaski club:

"Yes, we used to belong to that outfit when we was younger, but as me and my wife have got older, we've kinda gotten away from it. We used to like the dances and the parties; they had good crowds down there and we had a lot of fun. But them kind of societies are dyin' out now. Take my kid, he wouldn't be seen dead in a Polish society."

2. This clique-like character is revealed in the remarks of one woman concerning her husband's activities in his club: "Often he don't get home till 11:00 or 12:00 at night. They only practise a couple of hours, but then they sit around three or four more talkin' sports."

quent type of formal association. If the two "mother's clubs" sponsored by the Catholic church to foster interest in the parochial school are included, then nearly half the memberships listed for women . . . are in church-affiliated organizations. The dominance of the church-sponsored club is even more pronounced among children. The scout movement as it appears among the families studied is church-sponsored almost entirely. Likewise, the Gra-Y organization, a grammar-school-age association for boys, is affiliated at the administrative level with the YMCA and is led in New Haven by volunteer workers recruited largely from the Yale Divinity School.

INFORMAL VOLUNTARY ASSOCIATIONS

If the term "clique" connotes a psychologically intimate relationship which involves frequent and regular interaction, then two additional categories are needed to describe adequately the informal voluntary associations of the people whom we studied. These are "friends" and "acquaintances." Close relationships which are best defined as cliques are frequent among kindred,[3] and ubiquitous among unrelated children and adolescents. With marriage, clique associations formed earlier in life tend to be dropped or continued on a less intimate "friendship" basis. "Good friends" are distinguished from "friends" in general. Most of the latter may more accurately be identified as acquaintances.

The acquaintanceship category is large, but vague. It embraces people known in childhood, other than clique-mates, former neighbors, and fellow workers. Such contacts may give a superficial sense of broad participation,[4] but their role in day-to-day activities is a marginal one. Since organized social life must rest upon a firmer basis than acquaintanceship provides, the loosest type of informal voluntary association which can be profitably recognized is the friendship group.

The most striking revelation . . . is the large number of husbands and wives—about two-fifths of the total—*who have no intimate friends outside their own families and relatives.*

In three or four of these cases—as with one elderly couple who had little intimate contact even with the husband's four sons who live in the city—this indicates virtual social isolation. However, this is not the case

3. Whether or not congeniality and recreational units made up entirely of people who are related to each other can be considered voluntary association is a nice question. Suffice it to say that a considerable number of tightly knit clique-like groups of kindred, otherwise undistinguishable in form and function from non-related cliques, were discovered during the course of the study. The important thing, after all, is the sociological reality, not the terminology used.

4. Comments like the following were common during the initial stages of the interview: "Oh, I've got friends all over town. I never stopped to count 'em, but I'll bet you I wouldn't have any trouble namin' 500 of them."

in the majority of these families. Most of them have an active social life within the kin group. Working-class families have been typically large until recently, and, in a long established city such as New Haven, aggregations of kindred may remain relatively unbroken by physical mobility. Groups of this size make it possible to carry on a self-sufficient social life. In at least 15 of the 50 families, leisure-time activities of the husbands and wives were completely dominated by the kin group. In another 28 families, regular visiting patterns with relatives constituted a major, although not exclusive, form of social activity.

NON-KIN CLIQUES AND FRIENDSHIP GROUPS

Cliques founded upon neighborhood propinquity are nearly universal among children and adolescents. Strong adult cliques of non-related persons are less common than those among kindred, but they nevertheless appear in appreciable numbers. Bakke has noted that most adult workers look back to childhood and adolescence for the models of what they think a friendship should be. This observation is corroborated by our material, since nearly all the non-kin clique relationships of adults studied were rooted in the childhood and adolescent period. One of the most tightly knit non-kin adult cliques found consisted of four middle-aged couples. They call this group their "club" and hold regular Friday night meetings in rotation at each other's homes. The activities at these meetings consist largely of visiting and playing cards. In addition to these Friday evening gatherings, they spend many Sundays and holidays together. This clique had its origin some 30 years ago in a Sunday school girl's club to which the wives belonged.

The individual "best friend" relationship (which may be classified as a clique owing to its intensity and duration) is more common than those in which husband and wife both participate. These, too, usually have their origin in childhood and adolescence. A typical example is the wife of one of our families who spoke of the only good woman friend she has outside her own family: "I stood up for her at her wedding. She was married when she was only sixteen, so you can see that's been a long time ago." This woman is now in her late forties.

While most adult clique relationships can be traced back to childhood and adolescence, the fact remains that such cliques usually break down and disappear with the coming of adulthood and marriage. Several factors were identified in our study which help to account for this: (1) courtship and marriage demand a transfer of interest from unisexual to mixed groups, (2) clique relationships need active participation to sustain them, and these activities may be incompatible with marital responsibilities and preoccupations, (3) physical mobility, and (4) social mobility.

The strong clique associations of adolescence are usually supplanted by greater participation in immediate family and kin-group affairs after marriage. Those regular companionable relationships which are retained with outsiders tend to be organized loosely in comparatively unstable visiting and recreational circles made up of ex-clique mates and people met after marriage. These contacts lack the emotional involvement of the clique, and relationships are more casually formed and lost . . . participation in these groups tends to be by couples, while surviving non-kin clique relationships after marriage are likely to be by individuals.

CONCLUSIONS

Additional evidence is presented in this paper that the majority of urban working-class people do not participate in formally organized voluntary associations. The more original contribution lies in the attempt to discover the forms of social organization which structure the leisure-time activities of workers in the absence of formal associations. The central fact which emerges in this connection is the important role which family and kinship continue to play in providing for the companionship and recreational needs of the persons interviewed. Approximately two-fifths of the husbands and wives in the sample had no intimate friends outside the family and kin groups. It was emphasized that in the majority of these cases this does not mean social isolation, but simply that activities are restricted to the members of the kin group.

The theoretical significance of these findings needs to be worked out in greater detail and tested by further empirical studies. Our research was limited within a single city. . . .

.   .   .   .

In brief, the sample studied is representative of a thoroughly urbanized, yet comparatively stable population, rather than the hypothetical average or typical American urban dweller. It seems significant, nevertheless, that within such a population we do not find the wholesale displacement of "primary" by "secondary" groups—with the consequent de-personalization of social relationships—which is implied in the conventional account of urban social life.

RURAL STYLES IN AN URBAN
ENVIRONMENT, *Christen T. Jonassen*

JONASSEN'S paper was written in response to a
debate, then current, over Park's theory of
human ecology. The incidental portrayal of the rural
qualities of Norwegians living in Brooklyn
suggests both how those qualities can
long persist within a population and also the
conditions which further their persistence.

The attempt to discover, describe, and explain regularities in man's
adaptation to space has long been a matter of concern to social scientists
and sociologists. In the United States the ecological school of sociology,
depending primarily on the observation of man in an urban environment,
has concerned itself with this problem. Since Alihan's shattering critique
of the Parkian ecological theory a decade ago, two schools of thought
seem to have emerged. Their discussions have sought to determine whether
or not a science of ecology is possible without a socio-cultural framework
of reference. The crux of the problem seems to center around the relative
influence of "biotic," strictly economic, "natural," and "subsocial" factors
on the one hand, and socio-cultural elements on the other hand. Those
stressing the former as causative factors have been referred to as the
"classical" or "orthodox" ecologists, while those emphasizing the latter
factors might be called the "socio-cultural" ecologists.

Perhaps the best if not the only way to determine where the correct
emphasis should lie is by empirical research. It is hoped that the results
of a research project reported in this paper may contribute toward that
end.

.   .   .   .

The Norwegians in New York have a continuous history as a group
since about 1830 when they formed their first settlement and community
in Lower Manhattan. Since that day the community has moved until it is
now located in the Bay Ridge section of Brooklyn. The first location was
.25 mile from City Hall, the center of the city; the present location is

Excerpted from "Cultural Variables in the Ecology of an Ethnic Group,"
American Sociological Review, Vol. 14 (February, 1949), 32–36, 38–41, by permission of the American Sociological Association and the author.

about ten miles from that point. From 1830 to the present time six fairly distinct areas of settlement may be observed.

I. THE PROBLEM

We shall be primarily interested in the mobility of the Norwegian community. Why did the group first settle where it did, and why did it move from this area to another? We shall want to know why it moved in one direction and not in another, and we shall be interested in the rate and type of movement. . . .

.   .   .   .

II. CULTURAL BACKGROUND OF THE SETTLERS

. . . The Norwegians who created this settlement, unlike those who pioneered in the Western states, came for the most part from the coastal districts of Norway. Norway was in those days underdeveloped industrially and its main means of livelihood were agriculture, lumbering, fishing and seafaring. Many individuals would combine all of these occupations and especially fishing and agriculture which were carried on in the innumerable fjords and inlets of the long indented shoreline of Norway. In these districts a culture based primarily on the sea as a means of transportation and a source of food combined with a little farming has flourished for centuries since the Viking days. The people are trained from their earliest youth in skills necessary to make a living in such an environment. The men and women who founded and continued the Norwegian settlement in New York originated in such environments, and many men joined the colony by the simple expedient of walking off the ships on which they worked as sailors.

Norway, of all the civilized countries in the world, has one of the most scattered populations, the density being only 23.2 persons per square mile as compared to 750.4 for England and 41.5 for the United States. Norway does not have very large cities and its people never live far from the mountains, the fjords, and the open sea. They are for the most part nature lovers and like green things and plenty of space about them.

III. SETTLEMENT AND MOVEMENT OF NORWEGIANS IN NEW YORK

The first Norwegian community which has an unbroken connection with the present one was located about 1830 in the area now bounded by the Brooklyn Bridge, the Manhattan Bridge, and the East River. At that time, along this section of Manhattan were located docks where ships from all parts of the world loaded and unloaded, and here were also located the only large drydocks in New York, capable of repairing large ocean-going vessels. Here also were found the offices of shipping masters, vessel owners, and other seafaring occupations. In this atmosphere of salt water and ships, men familiar with the sea could feel at home. And within walking distance of their homes they found plenty of work as carpenters, shipbuilders, sailmakers, riggers, and dock and harbor workers.

Across the East River lay Brooklyn, a town of some 3,298 inhabitants in 1800. It grew rapidly and became an incorporated city in 1834, and by 1850 it had grown to 96,850 inhabitants. In 1940, the Borough according to Census figures had a population of 2,698,284. Brooklyn gradually superseded New York as a shipbuilding, ship repairing, and docking center. There was the New York Navy Yard in Wallabout Bay. But the center of shipping activity became Red Hook, that section of Brooklyn jutting into the New York harbor, across from the Battery. The Atlantic Docks were completed here in 1848. It also became the terminus of the great canal traffic that tapped the vast resources of the American continent. Here large grain elevators were built to hold grain for ships that came from all parts of the world to load and discharge. . . .

The Norwegians living in New York found the journey by horsecar and ferry tedious and time-consuming. They soon began to settle in Red Hook and the next Norwegian settlement developed in the area immediately adjacent to and north of Red Hook, where a small group of Norwegians settled in 1850. By 1870 the invasion of Brooklyn was gathering speed.

.   .   .   .

The colony developed to the north of Hamilton Avenue. The churches moved over from New York and new churches were established. In the Nineties, this section was one of large beautiful homes and tree-shaded streets. The section became better as one went north and became very exclusive at Brooklyn Heights where the grand old families lived. This section occupied in those days a functional relation to the downtown section of Manhattan that Westchester, Connecticut, and Long Island do today. A contemporary wrote, ". . . the greater part of the male population of Brooklyn daily travels to Manhattan to work in its offices. . . . The very fact that Brooklyn is a dwelling place for New York . . . a professional funny-man long ago called it a 'bed chamber.' " It was actually as the saying went "a city of homes and churches."

Norwegian immigrant girls coming to New York found jobs as domestics in these beautiful homes and Norwegian men, skilled in the building, repair, and handling of ships of all kinds, found plenty of work for their hands in Erie and Atlantic Basins a short distance to the south. The section therefore became a logical location for the development of a Norwegian immigrant community. It offered them everything they needed. The Irish and Germans also moved into this neighborhood, and as it grew more and more crowded the old families moved out. Just as the New Englanders had forced out the Dutch, so now Norwegians, Irish, and Germans were forcing out the New Englanders. The stately old homes were converted to two- and three-family houses, and some to boarding houses. In this neighborhood the Norwegian colony flourished for some decades up to the beginning of the Twentieth Century.

.   .   .   .

The inexorable growth of the city continued. In old South Brooklyn, open places became fewer and fewer and green grass and trees disappeared. Old large one-family houses were torn down to give place to tightly packed tenements. Then it came the turn of the Norwegians, Irish, and Germans to be invaded and succeeded by the southern Europeans, mostly Italians from Sicily.

By 1890, many old downtown families purchased fashionable homes a little further out near Prospect Park, in the Park Slope section, as "a means of getting away from the thickly populated section of Brooklyn," the incentive being the scarcity of houses, plenty of wide open spaces and an abundance of trees and garden spots in the Park Slope area. The residents of the area used to be known as the brownstone people who lived in beautiful mansions, paid their bills monthly, and ordered from the store by telephone. In the beginning of the century, the Norwegians also started to move out of the downtown area and into this section. This became the next center of the Norwegian colony in Brooklyn.

But the city continued to push its rings of growth further and further out and the same process repeated itself all over again. By 1910, the Norwegians were on the move again, this time to the adjoining area of Sunset Park. The docks and shipyards were extended all the way out to Fifty-ninth Street. And in 1915, the Fourth Avenue subway was completed. Electric cars running on Ninth and Fifteenth Streets and Third Avenue and Hamilton Avenue provided transportation to the shipping center at Red Hook.

The center of the Norwegian colony remained in Sunset Park district up to about 1940. The exodus of Norwegians from this section and into Bay Ridge and other outlying sections is now in progress. It is the sections of Sunset Park and Bay Ridge which now constitute the area of the settlement. The present Norwegian settlement is located on the high ground overlooking New York Harbor. For the most part it is a section of one- and two-family houses with small lawns, backyards, and tree-planted streets. The nature of this area was determined by indices which have proved reliable in characterizing urban neighborhoods. . . . No part of this area according to this study displays the characteristics of a slum district. . . .

From the ecological and historical study of the characteristics of the Norwegian community over a period of more than a hundred years, it appears that it has maintained rather consistent characteristics and a functional position in New York since the community was established. Like all other groups, native and foreign, the Norwegians were unable to prevent invasion by other land use and lower status groups; they could maintain the things they valued only by retreating before the inexorable development of the city to new territory where conditions were more in harmony with their conceptions of a proper place to live.

It is apparent from the data of this study that numerous causative factors have operated in determining the location and movement of the Norwegian community in New York: the economic and social conditions of Norway, the economic and social conditions of the United States, the rate and direction of New York City growth, the condition of the neighborhood, available lines of communication between the cultural area and the location of the economic base, and the attitudes and values of the Norwegian heritage. Where they were to settle and the rate and direction of movement was thus largely determined by elements of the immigrants' heritage and the character and needs of the host society of the United States.

Neither one of these factors was *the* determining one. The Norwegians' reaction to this urban environment resulted rather from a judicious balance of all these factors. It is clear from old maps that transportation to Bay Ridge was available as early as 1895, if they had wanted to live there. But this was slow transportation by horsecar in the early days, and the downtown area evidently presented agreeable enough conditions. As the city grew, however, these conditions became less desirable to people who valued plenty of space around them and nearness to nature.

It is apparent that the Norwegian immigrants broke away from the original economic base to a certain extent later. This development depended on the advance of lines of transportation and new technological and economic development and on the fact that the Norwegian culture was becoming ever more industrialized, which gave later emigrants new skills and knowledge that they could apply here. The erection of skyscrapers and use of steel construction in New York gave Norwegian sailors jobs as structural steel and iron workers. They were used to working aloft and their experience as riggers made them particularly valuable for this work. . . .

IV. SOME IMPLICATIONS OF THIS STUDY FOR ECOLOGICAL THEORY

The change of location of the Norwegian community was produced by persons breaking away from the old area and individually choosing a new habitat. Because of its concerted progression in a certain direction to a certain place, the illusion of a directed mass movement is created. But this ecological behavior arises out of the interaction of the realities of the New York environment with the immigrants' attitudes and values. The resulting actions of many individuals are very much alike since they are motivated by very similar attitudes created in conformity with the cultural pattern of Norway. *It is therefore indicated that the movement of these people must be referred to factors that are volitional, purposeful, and personal and that these factors may not be considered as mere accidental and incidental features of biotic processes and impersonal competition.*

It has been stated that immigrant colonies are to be found in the slums or that immigrants make their entry into the city in the area immediately adjacent to the central business district. From the data of this study we are fairly certain that the Norwegian colony has not existed in an area with the characteristics of a slum, and we can be certain that it does not occupy such an area today even though it is the habitat of recently arrived immigrants. It would therefore appear that the statements referred to above can not be taken as generalizations, but apply to certain ethnic or racial groups only.

.   .   .   .

The objective realities of New York thus presented the Norwegians with a multitude of environments to which they might have reacted. It is significant that they reacted primarily to those aspects of the New York milieu that had meaning in their value system. Thus the environmental facts were of little significance *per se* and only as they were incorporated into the value-attitude systems of the Norwegian immigrants.

The movement of the group, when compared with the movements of other ethnic groups in New York and other American cities, assumes some significance. Studies of Italians and Jews reveal different developments. The usual situation in these groups is one in which an area of first settlement is established which stays in one place, and continues to receive new arrivals. As the old immigrants become assimilated and the second generation grows up, they move out to an area of "second settlement," usually far removed from the first in space and time. Thus Italian and Jewish communities in New York are still found in many of the areas, such as the Lower East Side of Manhattan and downtown Brooklyn where they were first established. But there is hardly a trace of any Norwegians in the areas of New York and Brooklyn which they originally inhabited. Furthermore, the development and progression of Norwegian cultural areas in New York show a continuum of space and time and result from the unique character of their heritage in interaction with their new environment. . . .

However, there is no place having the characteristics which Norwegians require adjacent to the present settlement in Bay Ridge. The city is moving in on them from north and west, and there is only water to the east and south. The area is also being invaded by other ethnic groups. Nor is the type of buildings within this area entirely to their liking. It is still predominantly a neighborhood of single- and two-family houses, but a great number of large, high class apartment houses have been built, and the land value has increased so tremendously that wherever zoning permits, this is the type of housing that is erected. It would seem that the Norwegian community in Brooklyn is making its last stand in Bay Ridge with its back to the sea. Its final dissolution is a matter of years. . . .

. . . .

This development has already commenced. Census figures and the changes of addresses for subscribers to *Nordisk Tidende* indicate that many Norwegians are moving to Queens, Staten Island, New Jersey, and Connecticut, where new settlements are forming in environments which are more in harmony with the values of their heritage. Some of these settlements have started as colonies of summer huts, and finally developed into all-year round communities.

The peculiar interplay of a plurality of motives that goes into the determination of ecological distribution of Norwegians is well illustrated by these informants:

> I like it here (Staten Island) because it reminds me of Norway. Of course, not Bergen, because we have neither Floyen nor Ulrik, nor mountains on Staten Island, but it is so nice and green all over in the summer. I have many friends in Bay Ridge in Brooklyn, and I like to take trips there, but to tell the truth when I get on the ferry on the way home and get the smell of Staten Island, I think it's glorious. However, I'm taking a trip to Norway this summer, and Norway is, of course, Norway—and Staten Island is Staten Island.

A man states:

> I arrived in America in 1923, eighteen years old. I went right to Staten Island because my father lived there and he was a ship-builder at Elco Boats in Bayonne, New Jersey, right over the bridge. I started to

work with my father and I am now foreman at the shipyard where we are building small yachts—the best in America. I seldom go to New York because I don't like large cities with stone and concrete. Here are trees and open places.

Another tells what he likes about his place in Connecticut:

I like the private peace up here in the woods. There is suitable space between the cabins so that we do not have to step on each other's toes unless we want to get together with someone once in a while. Since I started to build this house, it is as if I have deeper roots here than in the city. This is my *own* work for myself.

And a woman says:

. . . It is a real joy to get out of the city with all its wretchedness. I go down to the brook where I have a big Norwegian tub. There I sing lilting songs and wash and rinse clothes. Everything goes like play, and before you know it, the summer is over, and all this glorious time is gone and I could almost cry.

.   .   .   .

The assumption that "in general, living organisms tend to follow the line of least resistance in obtaining environmental resources and escaping environmental dangers" has been used as the basis for hypotheses of human distribution in space. Such a statement in the light of this study seems too mechanistic, too simple, and therefore inadequate as an explanation of the distribution of this group in New York. Men need not merely to survive, require not only shelter or just any type of sustenance; they want to live in a particular place, in a particular way. A better description of man's distributive behavior might be: *men tend to distribute themselves within an area so as to achieve the greatest efficiency in realizing the values they hold most dear.* Thus man's ecological behavior in a large American city becomes the function of several variables, both sociocultural and "non-cultural."

INTERDEPENDENT WORLDS: THE SOCIAL INTEGRATION OF QUEERS AND PEERS,
Albert J. Reiss, Jr.

IN this intriguing paper, certain little-known
transactions between "delinquent peers"
(boys) and "adult queers" (men) are described.
Through those transactions, the homosexual and
"straight" worlds repeatedly interact, if
only briefly and in a glancing way. Even this
straightforward research account can be
read as underlining aspects of the urban imagery of
the respective populations, notably anonymity,
impersonality, and human manipulation.

An attempt is made in this paper to describe the sexual relation between "delinquent peers" and "adult queers" and to account for its social organization.[1] This transaction is one form of homosexual prostitution between a young male and an adult male fellator. The adult male client pays a delinquent boy prostitute a sum of money in order to be allowed to act as a fellator. The transaction is limited to fellation and is one in which the boy develops no self-conception as a homosexual person or sexual deviator, although he perceives adult male clients as sexual deviators, "queers" or "gay boys."

.   .   .   .

HOW PEERS AND QUEERS MEET

Meetings between adult male fellators and delinquent boys are easily made, because both know how and where to meet within the community space. Those within the common culture know that contact can be established within a relatively short period of time, if it is wished. The fact that meetings between peers and queers can be made easily is more evi-

Excerpted from "The Social Integration of Queers and Peers," *Social Problems,* Vol. 9 (1961), pages 102, 106–109, 112, 114–15, 116–18. Reprinted by permission of the Society for the study of Social Problems.

1. The word "queer" is of the "straight" and not the "gay" world. In the "gay" world it has all the qualities of a negative stereotype, but these are not intended in this paper. The paper arose out of the perspective of boys in the "straight" world.

dence of the organized understandings which prevail between the two populations.

There are a large number of places where the boys meet their clients, the fellators. Many of these points are known to all boys regardless of where they reside in the metropolitan area. This is particularly true of the central city locations where the largest number of contact points is found within a small territorial area. Each community area of the city, and certain fringe areas, inhabited by substantial numbers of lower-class persons, also have their meeting places, generally known only to the boys residing in the area.

Queers and peers typically establish contact in public or quasi-public places. Major points of contact include street corners, public parks, men's toilets in public or quasi-public places such as those in transportation depots, parks or hotels, and "second" and "third-run" movie houses (open around the clock and permitting sitting through shows). Bars are seldom points of contact, perhaps largely because they are plied by older male hustlers who lie outside the peer culture and groups, and because bar proprietors will not risk the presence of under-age boys.

There are a number of prescribed modes for establishing contact in these situations. They permit the boys and fellators to communicate intent to one another privately despite the public character of the situation. The major form of establishing contact is the "cruise," with the fellator passing "queer-corners" or locations until his effort is recognized by one of the boys. A boy can then signal—usually by nodding his head, a hand gesticulation signifying OK, following, or responding to commonly understood introductions such as "You got the time?"—that he is prepared to undertake the transaction. Entrepreneur and client then move to a place where the sexual activity is consummated, usually a place affording privacy, protection and hasty exit. "Dolly," a three-time loser at the State Training School, describes one of these prescribed forms for making contact:

> "Well, like at the bus station, you go to the bathroom and stand there pretendin' like . . . and they're standin' there pretendin' like . . . and then they motions their head and walks out and you follow them, and you go some place. Either they's got a car, or you go to one of them hotels near the depot or some place like that . . . most any place."

Frequently contact between boys and fellators is established when the boy is hitchhiking. This is particularly true for boys' first contacts of this nature. Since lower-class boys are more likely than middle-class ones to hitch rides within a city, particularly at night when such contacts are most frequently made, they perhaps are most often solicited in this manner.

The experienced boy who knows a "lot of queers," may phone known fellators directly from a public phone, and some fellators try to establish continued contact with boys by giving them their phone numbers. However, the boys seldom use this means of contact for reasons inherent in their orientation toward the transaction, as we shall see below.

We shall now examine how the transaction is facilitated by these types of situations and the prescribed modes of contact and communication. One of the characteristics of all these contact situations is that they provide a *rationale* for the presence of *both* peers and queers in the *same* situation or place. This rationale is necessary for both parties, for were there high visibility to the presence of either and no ready explanation for it, contact and communication would be far more difficult. Public and quasi-public facilities provide situations which account for the presence of most persons since there is relatively little social control over the establishment of contacts. There is, of course, some risk to the boys and the fellators in making contact in these situations since they are generally known to the police. The Morals Squad may have "stake-outs," but this is one of the calculated risks and the communication network carries information about their tactics.

A most important element in furnishing a rationale is that these meeting places must account for the presence of delinquent boys of essentially lower-class dress and appearance who make contact with fellators of almost any class level. This is true despite the fact that the social settings which fellators ordinarily choose to establish contact generally vary according to the class level of the fellators. Fellators of high social class generally make contact by "cruising" past street-corners, in parks, or the men's rooms in "better" hotels, while those from the lower class are likely to select the public bath or transportation depot. There apparently is some general equation of the class position of boys and fellators in the peer-queer transaction. The large majority of fellators in the delinquent peer-queer transaction probably are from the lower class ("apes"). But it is difficult to be certain about the class position of the fellator clients since no study was made of this population.

The absence of data from the fellator population poses difficulties in interpreting the contact relationship. Many fellators involved with delinquent boys do not appear to participate in any overt or covert homosexual groups, such as the organized homosexual community of the "gay world." The "gay world" is the most visible form of organized homosexuality since it is an organized community, but it probably encompasses only a small proportion of all homosexual contact. Even among those in the organized homosexual community, evidence suggests that the homosexual members seek sexual gratification outside their group with persons who are essentially anonymous to them. Excluding homosexual married couples, Leznoff and Westley maintain that there is ". . . a prohibition against sexual relationships within the group. . . ." Ross indicates that young male prostitutes are chosen, among other reasons, for the fact that they protect the identity of the client. Both of these factors tend to coerce many male fellators to choose an anonymous contact situation.

It is clear that these contact situations not only provide a rationale for the presence of the parties to the transaction but a guarantee of anonymity. The guarantee does not necessarily restrict social visibility as both the boys and the fellators may recognize cues (including, but not necessarily, those of gesture and dress) which lead to mutual role identification. But anonymity is guaranteed in at least two senses: anonymity of presence is assured in the situation and their personal identity in the community is protected unless disclosed by choice.

There presumably are a variety of reasons for the requirement of anonymity. For many, a homosexual relationship must remain a secret since their other relationships in the community—families, business relationships, etc.—must be protected. Leznoff and Westley refer to these men as the "secret" as contrasted with the "overt" homosexuals, and in the organized "gay world," they are known as "closet fags." For some, there is also a necessity for protecting identity to avoid blackmail. Although none of the peer hustlers reported resorting to blackmail, the adult male fellator may nonetheless hold such an expectation, particularly if he is older or of high social class. Lower-class ones, by contrast, are more likely to face the threat of violence from adolescent boys since they more often frequent situations where they are likely to contact "rough trade." The kind of situation in which the delinquent peer-queer contact is made and the sexual relationship consummated tends to minimize the possibility of violence.

Not all male fellators protect their anonymity; some will let a boy have their phone number and a few "keep a boy." Still, most fellators want to meet boys where they are least likely to be victimized, although boys sometimes roll queers by selecting a meeting place where by pre-arrangment, their friends can meet them and help roll the queer, steal his car, or commit other acts of violence. Boys generally know that fellators are vulnerable in that they "can't" report their victimization. Parenthetically, it might be mentioned that these boys are not usually aware of their own institutional invulnerability to arrest. An adolescent boy is peculiarly invulnerable to arrest even when found with a fellator since the mores define the boy as exploited.

Situations of personal contact between adolescent boys and adult male fellators also provide important ways to *communicate intent* or to carry out the transaction *without* making the contact particularly visible to others. The wall writings in many of these places are not without their primitive communication value, e.g., "show it hard," and places such as a public restroom provide a modus operandi. The entrepreneur and his customer in fact can meet with little more than an exchange of non-verbal gestures, transact their business with a minimum of verbal communication and part without a knowledge of one another's identity. In most cases, boys report "almost nothing" was said. The sexual transaction may occur with the only formal transaction being payment to the boy.

INDUCTION INTO THE PEER-QUEER TRANSACTION

The peer-queer culture operates through a delinquent peer society. Every boy interviewed in this study who voluntarily established contacts with fellators was also delinquent in many other respects. The evidence shows that contact with fellators is an institutionalized aspect of the organization of lower-class delinquency oriented groups. This is not to say that boys outside these groups never experience relationships with adult male fellators: some do, but they are not participants in groups which sanction the activity according to the prescribed group standards described below. Nor is it to say that all delinquent groups positively sanction the peer-queer transaction since its distribution is unknown.

.   .   .   .

. . . Within the group, boys hear reports of experiences which supply the cultural definitions: how contacts are made, how you get money if the queer resists, how much one should expect to get, what kind of behavior is acceptable from the queer, which is to be rejected and how. Boys know all this *before* they have any contact with a fellator. In the case of street gangs, the fellators often pass the neighborhood corner, hence, even the preadolescent boys learns about the activity as the older boys get picked up. . . . There appear to be several clear-cut norms about the relations between peers and queers, even though there is some deviation from them.

The first major norm is that a *boy must undertake the relationship with a queer solely as a way of making money; sexual gratification cannot be actively sought as a goal in the relationship.* This norm does not preclude a boy from sexual gratification by the act; he simply must not seek this as a goal. . . .

The second major norm operating in the relationship is that *the sexual transaction must be limited to mouth-genital fellation. No other sexual acts are generally tolerated.* The adult male fellator must deport himself in such a way as to re-enforce the instrumental aspects of the role relationship and to insure affective neutrality. . . .

The third major norm operating on the relationship is that *both peers and queers as participants, should remain affectively neutral during the transaction.* Boys within the peer society define the ideal form of the role with the fellator as one in which the boy is the entrepreneur and the queer is viewed as purchasing a service. . . . If the fellator violates the expected affective relationship in the transaction, he may be treated not only with violence but with contempt as well. The seller of the service ultimately reserves the right to set the conditions for his patrons.

.   .   .   .

A fourth major norm operating on the peer-queer relationship serves as a primary factor in stabilizing the system. This norm holds that *violence must not be used so long as the relationship conforms to the shared set of expectations between queers and peers.* So long as the fellator conforms to the norms governing the transaction in the peer-queer society, he runs little risk of violence from the boys. . . . The fellator may violate the affective neutrality requirements to approach the boy and make suggestive advances to him when he is with his age-mates, either with girls or with his peer group when he is not located for "business." In either case, the sexual advances suggest that the boy is not engaged in a business relationship within the normative expectations of the system, but that he has sexual motivation as well. . . . A lower-class boy cannot afford to be cast in less than a highly masculine role before lower-class girls nor risk definition as a queer before peers. His role within his peer group is under threat even if he suffers *no* anxiety about masculinity. Not only the boy himself but his peers perceive such behavior as violating role expectations and join him in violent acts toward the fellator to protect the group's integrity and status.

.   .   .   .

There is another and perhaps more important reason for the use of violence when the peer defined norms of the peer-queer relationship are violated. The formally prescribed roles for peers and queers are basically the roles involved in all institutionalized forms of prostitution, the prostitute and the client. But in most forms of prostitution, whether male or female, the hustlers perceive of themselves in hustler roles, and furthermore the male hustlers also develop a conception of themselves as homosexual whereas *the peer hustler in the peer-queer relationship develops no conception of himself either as prostitute or as homosexual.*

The fellator risks violence, therefore, if he threatens the boy's self-conception by suggesting that the boy may be homosexual and treats him as if he were.

A COSMOPOLITAN WORLD, *Frederick Edge*

SOCIAL worlds may be rooted in urban space, but
many are diffusely organized, difficult to
pin down definitely in space. Some worlds are
"international" (like the jazz world, or
the art world) or at least multinational. Their
members are linked by effective channels of
communication, by common symbolizations
of important events and personages, and by the
existence of certain locales—inevitably in
cities—which function as nodes in a complex
network of communication among members. Social
scientists have yet to develop a language
fully applicable to these symbolic communities. One
such world is the world of chess, with
its various media, famous locales, contests (local,
national, international), and heroes of the
past and present. Among the mythological "greats"
of chess was Paul Morphy who, in 1858 at the
age of 21, traveled to London and Paris,
there defeating the best players of Europe. His
secretary's account of Morphy's greatest feat at one
of Europe's greatest chess locales touches on various
features of the locale and the world, including the
relation of "insiders" to the more general public.

THE CAFÉ DE LA RÉGENCE

Every café has its speciality. At Paul Niquet's, for instance, the
chiffoniers congregate, and at Tortoni's, speculators and politicians. Not
one of these establishments, throughout the city, but has its mark, by
which to distinguish it from its fellows, in the same way as an ugly woman
consoles herself with the belief that she has one quality at least which will
captivate admirers. But the Café de la Régence stands out peculiar from
the rest; it is what they are, and more too. It is an epitome of all.

Now the reader must not suppose I am going to enter on a lengthy
history of this far-famed trysting spot of men of all countries, more
particularly as Mr. George Walker anticipated me many years ago. Everybody knows that the Café de la Régence and the Café Procope are the

Excerpted from *The Exploits and Triumphs in Europe of Paul Morphy* (New
York: Appleton and Co., 1859), pp. 144–45, 159–64.

two oldest in Paris; that the former is so named after the famous Regent Duke of Orleans; that Voltaire, Jean Jacques Rousseau, Duke of Richelieu, Marshall Saxe, Franklin, Robespierre, Napoleon, etc., etc., etc., made it their place of frequent resort for the purpose of playing at chess. I am about to give a daguerreotype of the Régence as Morphy and I found it, and as any one will find it at the present day.

The first thing we caught sight of, on entering, was a dense cloud of tobacco smoke, the product of *tabac de Corporal* and *cigars de la Régie*. The second object was a massive individual, with Titanic shoulders, whom we afterwards learned was Monsieur Morel, or, as they call him there, "Le père Morel," and "The Rhinoceros." Having turned the flank of this gentleman, and our eyes becoming used to the peculiar atmosphere, we observed that tables were placed as close to each other as would admit of one's passing between them, and that chess was being played on some, draughts, cards, and dominoes on others. In a second room, two billiard-tables were in full action, surrounded by still other chess and card parties, whilst the unceasing hubbub arising from the throng seemed to render mental abstraction an impossibility. At a table in the first room, a small crowd was watching the contest between two amateurs of "ye noble game of chesse playe," and Morphy's attention was immediately arrested. I stepped up to the *dame du comptoir* and made inquiries as to who was then in the room, and learned from her that one of the two players Morphy was waching was Monsieur Journoud, "un de nos plus forts," the lady added, as though aware I was a stranger. She informed me that Mr. Harrwitz was then at Valenciennes, but intended to return to Paris at the end of the week, in order to meet Mr. Morphy. On my not expressing any surprise at the mention of the latter's name, she volunteered the information that Mr. Morphy was a celebrated American player, who had beaten everybody he had played with, and that they expected him yesterday. The lady was pleasingly voluble, and I encouraged her; this induced her to add that Monsieur Arnoux de Rivière had just received a letter from a friend in London, apprising him that our hero had left the English capital, and was *en route* for Paris.

Having learned as much as the *dame du comptoir* was able to communicate, I rejoined Morphy, and we took a second look round the room. Sounds of all European languages saluted our ears, and types of different races our eyes. In one corner, a knot of Italians talked, amicably no doubt, in their rapid, quarrelsome manner. At one of the billiard tables, a party of Russians were having it their own way, without fear of listeners; Americans and English, Germans, Danes, Swedes, Greeks, Spaniards, etc., jabbered together regardless of bystanders, making the café a very Babel. Scores of journals were lying here and there—the leading newspapers, in fact, throughout Europe—so that every visitor, no matter what his nationality, could obtain news of home.

The crowd seemed, as it always does, to represent every rank of society. There were military men, from colonels to privates; one or two priests, who seemed somewhat out of their element; well-dressed, aristocratic-looking individuals, who kept together in knots in different corners; and the invariable *pillier de café,* who passes half his existence in such establishments, and the other half in bed. The Cafe de la Régence opens at eight o'clock in the morning, but little or nothing is done until noon, barring the daily visit of some three or four patrons who drink their coffee in silence, and are not seen again until early next day. But at noon men begin to drop in quickly, and, by two o'clock, the room is as full as it can conveniently hold, and so continues until midnight.

.   .   .   .

Awaiting the return of his antagonist, Paul Morphy announced his intention of playing eight blindfold games, simultaneously, in the public café. It is needless to assure my readers that the mere announcement produced the greatest excitement; the newspapers heralded the fact throughout the city, and crowds of strangers came pouring into the Régence, and asking particulars of the *habitués* in relation to the approaching performance. . . .

The blindfold struggle was publicly announced to commence at noon; but, at an early hour, the crowd was already considerable. The billiard-tables in the further room were sacrificed to the exigencies of the occasion; I requested the waiters to put a thick cord round them, so as to rail off a space for Morphy, and a large easy-chair, placed in the *enceinte,* made the whole arrangements as comfortable for him as could be wished. . . .

.   .   .   .

The boards for Morphy's antagonists were arranged in the principal room of the café, numbered as follows:—

No. 1. Baucher,   5. Lequesne,
    2. Bierwirth,   6. Potier,
    3. Bornemann,   7. Préti,
    4. Guibert,   8. Seguin.

Nearly all these gentlemen are well known in contemporaneous chess, and formed such a phalanx that many persons asked whether Morphy knew whom he was going to play against. Monsieur Arnoux de Rivière called the moves for the first four, and Monsieur Journoud for the others; and, all being prepared, Morphy began as usual with "Pawn to King's Fourth on all the boards."

Things went on swimmingly and amusingly. It was as good as a volume of *Punch* or the *Charivari* to hear the remarks made by the excited spectators; more especially when the "openings" were past, and the science of the combatants came out, in the middle of the game. There was the huge "Père Morel," hands in his pockets, blowing clouds from an immense pipe like smoke from Vesuvius, threading his way between the boards and actually getting fierce when anybody asked him what he thought of it. Seeing him seated at the end of the room towards evening, and looking as though dumbfounded at the performance, I said to him, —"Well, Mr. Morel, do you believe now that Morphy can play against eight such antagonists?" He looked at me in an imploring manner and replied,—"Oh, don't talk to me; Mr. Morphy makes my head ache." . . .

.   .   .   .

. . . Monsieur Potier rises from his table to show on another board how Morphy had actually seen seven moves in advance; and Signor Préti gets quite nervous and agitated as our hero puts shot after shot into his bull's-eye; and I had much difficulty in assuring him that no absolute necessity existed for his playing on, until Morphy mated him; but that when he found his game was irretrievably lost, he would be justified in resigning. Monsieur Baucher was the first to give in, although one of the very strongest of the contestants; Morphy's combinations against this gentleman were so astonishing, and the finale so brilliant, that Mr. Walker declared in *Bell's Life*—"This game is worthy of being inscribed in letters of gold, on the walls of the London Club." Bornemann and Préti soon followed, and then Potier and Bierwirth; Messrs. Lequesne and Guibert effecting drawn battles; Monsieur Seguin alone was left. It was but natural that he should be the last, as he was the strongest of the eight combatants, and, truth to tell, he did not believe it possible for any one to beat him without seeing the board; but this Morphy finally effected in some beautiful pawn play, which would have tickled Philidor himself.

Forthwith commenced such a scene as I scarcely hope again to witness. Morphy stepped from the armchair in which he had been almost immovable for ten consecutive hours, without having tasted a morsel of any thing, even water, during the whole of the period; yet as fresh, apparently, as when he sat down. The English and Americans, of whom there were scores present, set up stentorian Anglo-Saxon cheers, and the French joined in as the whole crowd made a simultaneous rush at our hero. The waiters of the Café had formed a conspiracy to carry Morphy in triumph on their shoulders, but the multitude was so compact, they could not get near him, and finally, had to abandon the attempt. Great bearded fellows grasped his hands, and almost shook his arms out of the sockets, and it was nearly half an hour before we could get out of the Café. A well-known citizen of New York, Thomas Bryan, Esq., got on one side of him and M. de Rivière on the other, and "Le Père Morel,"—body and soul for our hero—fought a passage through the crowd by main strength, and we finally got into the street. There the scene was repeated; the multitude was greater out of doors than in the café, and the shouting, if possible, more deafening. Morphy, Messrs. Bryan and De Rivière and myself, made for the Palais Royal, but the crowd still followed us, and when we got to the guardhouse of the Imperial Guard, *sergeants de ville* and soldiers came running out to see whether a new revolution was on the *tapis*. We rushed into the Restaurant Foy, up stairs, and into a private room; whilst, as we subsequently learned, the landlord made anxious inquiries as to the cause of all this excitement. Having done our duty to a capital supper, we got off by a back street, and thus avoided the crowd, who, we were informed, awaited our reappearance in the quadrangle of the Palais Royal.

SUGGESTED READINGS: CHAPTER 11

John Lofland. *Doomsday Cult*. Englewood Cliffs, N.J.: Prentice-Hall, 1966.

An excellent field work study of "conversion, proselytization, and maintenance of faith" in a religious cult. The world of this small urban group is vividly conveyed.

Robert Park. *The City*. Chicago: University of Chicago Press, 1925.

The papers in this classic give the rationale behind the extensive study of Chicago's social worlds during the 1920s, especially one titled "The City: Suggestions for the Investigation of Human Behavior in the Urban Environment."

Caroline Ware. *Greenwich Village*. Boston: Houghton Mifflin, 1935.

New York's Bohemia earlier, as well as now, drew a number of different types of population to live there. Ware, a historian, gives a graphic description of the varied worlds and peoples of the "Village."

William F. Whyte. *Street Corner Society*. Chicago: University of Chicago, 1955. (2nd ed.)

An outstanding participant-observation study of the world of young Italian-American men, in Boston, done in the late 1930s.

12

Glass House. Courtesy of Lee Rainwater.

THE CITY WITHOUT
HUMAN PURPOSE

ONE especially important urban theme has been that cities are
impersonal and inevitably destroy human purposes. The vast
contemporary literature on "alienation," and search for
identity, although not always linked explicitly with urbanization,
is a variant of this criticism of the city. The critics are
sometimes dead set against city life, but, in recent decades
especially, they must accept the enduring existence of cities while
still hoping that cities somehow can be turned to fuller human
purpose. In our time, Lewis Mumford has been the most vocal
and prolific exponent of this perspective. In his writing, and in
that of other such articulate critics as C. Wright Mills, an attempt
is made to explain why urbanization has gone up a blind alley
and what should be done to direct its course. Because the nation
is becoming increasingly urbanized, criticism and prescriptions
are increasingly directed toward the more inclusive metropolitan
area and against "modern life" in general. As one publisher of
social science has discovered, an occasional volume with terms
such as "mass" or "alienation" in the title will help
a publishing house to prosper.

The selections in this chapter should suggest some of the ways
in which sociologists have also been influenced by this perspective
on cities and urbanization. A persistent perspective in urban
sociology has certainly been a recognition and critique of the
city as a place that resulted in anomie, in strikingly impersonal

relations, and in the destruction of human purpose. A counter-perspective, as exemplified in the selections by Janowitz and Davis, shows a much more circumspect treatment of these themes: only some people, and those only to some extent, are affected by those aspects of city living. In somewhat transmuted forms, some of the sociological writing about middle-class suburbs has been critical not merely of small-townish conformity but also of metropolitan-area senselessness and anomie.

The sociologists have also contributed to the great debate over the mass media and popular culture, some deploring the apathetic and anomic features of mass consumption and some emphasizing the redeeming virtues of the general poplace who are creating new life-styles. Though less prevalent than a decade ago, sociological theorizing about "the mass society" also derives from views about the loss of purpose that is actually or supposedly associated with urbanization.

SYMPATHY: COUNTRY VERSUS CITY,

Charles H. Cooley

THESE remarks were written in 1902 by one of
the most enduring of American sociologists,
who taught at the University of Michigan.

The different degrees of urgency in personal impressions are reflected
in the behavior of different classes of people. Every one must have
noticed that he finds more real openness of sympathy in the country
than in the city—though perhaps there is more of a superficial readiness
in the latter—and often more among plain, hard-working people than
among professional and business men. The main reason for this, I take it,
is that the social imagination is not so hard worked in the one case as
in the other. In the mountains of North Carolina the hospitable inhabitants
will take in any stranger and invite him to spend the night; but this is
hardly possible upon Broadway; and the case is very much the same
with the hospitality of the mind. If one sees few people and hears a new
thing only once a week, he accumulates a fund of sociability and curiosity
very favorable to eager intercourse; but if he is assailed all day and every
day by calls upon feeling and thought in excess of his power to respond,
he soon finds that he must put up some sort of a barrier. Sensitive people
who live where life is insistent take on a sort of social shell whose
function is to deal mechanically with ordinary relations and preserve the
interior from destruction. They are likely to acquire a conventional smile
and conventional phrases for polite intercourse, and a cold mask for
curiosity, hostility, or solicitation. In fact, a vigorous power of resistance
to the numerous influences that in no way make for the substantial
development of his character, but rather tend to distract and demoralize
him, is a primary need of one who lives in the more active portions of
present society, and the loss of this power by strain is in countless
instances the beginning of mental and moral decline. There are times of
abounding energy when we exclaim with Schiller,

> "Seid willkommen, Millionen,
> Diesen Kuss der ganzen Welt!"

Reprinted from *Human Nature and the Social Order* (rev. ed.) (New York:
Charles Scribner's Sons, 1922), pp. 146–47, by permission.

but it is hardly possible or desirable to maintain this attitude continuously. Universal sympathy is impracticable; what we need is better control and selection, avoiding both the narrowness of our class and the dissipation of promiscuous impressions. It is well for a man to open out and take in as much of life as he can organize into a consistent whole, but to go beyond that is not desirable. In a time of insistent suggestion, like the present, it is fully as important to many of us to know when and how to restrict the impulses of sympathy as it is to avoid narrowness. And this is in no way inconsistent, I think, with that modern democracy of sentiment—also connected with the enlargement of communication— which deprecates the limitation of sympathy by wealth or position. Sympathy must be selective, but the less it is controlled by conventional and external circumstances, such as wealth, and the more it penetrates to the essentials of character, the better. It is this liberation from convention, locality, and chance, I think, that the spirit of the time calls for.

IMPERSONALITY IN THE CITY,

Robert and Helen Lynd

TWO sociologists, in the second of their two studies
of Muncie, Indiana, make some passing
remarks about the loss of neighborhood (a
preoccupation in the 1920s and 1930s of
many people, including sociologists) and the
consequential increase of urban impersonality.

There may, for instance, be distinct elements of survival value to
the individual, living in a culture characterized by rapid change, in his
learning to "travel light," and to put on and off the physical paraphernalia
of living as readily as he does his coat. But this advantage may be
counterweighted by the marked impairment of those elements in social
organization in a democratic culture which depend heavily upon the
individual's feeling himself to be rooted in the subsoil of neighborhood
and community and therefore personally committed to participating in
terms of *its* problems and *its* future. Here one might conceivably look
for a part of the cause of the "civic indifference" for which Middletown's
prosperous home-owning business and civic leaders so often condemn
the working (and heavily renting) class "across the tracks." [1] On the
personality side, one of man's deepest emotional needs is for a sense of
"belonging." While some adults may lull this need through extreme preoccupation with work or variety of interests, even active adults ordinarily
shun the experience of being socially "lost in the shuffle" while with the
young and the elderly the need to belong to their world is particularly
marked.

Reprinted from *Middletown in Transition* (New York: Harcourt, Brace, and Co.,
1937), p. 188, by permission.

1. One of the major problems of urban living, apparently increasing progressively
as one approaches the metropolitan community, is this weakening of personal identification with neighborhood and community ties. At the extreme, in the metropolitan
community, one tends to witness a society built of individual bricks largely unbound
together by the binding mortar of common community purposes. People are apt to
pride themselves on the fact that they have freed themselves from the localisms
involved in loyalty to Rotary, to church and Ladies' Aid, to civic drives, and to
neighborhood that they regard as characterizing the "small town Babbitt." In so far
as this "freedom" reduces the individual to a social atom related to his fellows
chiefly by their common pursuit of private gain under the impersonal price system,
there is ample basis for questioning whether the freedom may not represent an
acute social pathology rather than a gain. The investigator has suggested elsewhere
the likeness of New York City in the above respects to a Western boom town, full
of the clatter that accompanies physical growth, but socially anarchistic and devoid
of the binding mutual loyalties that derive from settled abode and many shared
common purposes. See "Manhattan Boom Town," *Survey Graphic,* October 1, 1932.

CONSPICUOUS CONSUMPTION: COUNTRY VERSUS CITY, *Thorstein Veblen*

THIS is an old theme, quite prevalent during the
nineteenth century, Veblen does not in these
passages make invidious distinctions
between the countryside and the city; but his
book is in part an attack on the conspicuous
consumption and meaningless idleness of wealthier
Americans, identified with city life. About the same
time, his contemporary, Upton Sinclair, was making a
very similar attack in a scathing novel, *Metropolis.*

It is also noticeable that the serviceability of consumption as a
means of repute, as well as the insistence on it as an element of decency,
is at its best in those portions of the community where the human
contact of the individual is widest and the mobility of the population is
greatest. Conspicuous consumption claims a relatively larger portion of
the income of the urban than of the rural population, and the claim is
also more imperative. The result is that, in order to keep up a decent
appearance, the former habitually live hand to mouth to a greater extent
than the latter. So it comes for instance, that the American farmer and
his wife and daughters are notoriously less modish in their dress, as well
as less urbane in their manners, than the city artisan's family with an equal
income. It is not that the city population is by nature much more eager
for the peculiar complacency that comes of a conspicuous consumption,
nor has the rural population less regard for pecuniary decency. But the
provocation to this line of evidence, as well as its transient effectiveness,
are more decided in the city. This method is therefore more readily
resorted to and in the struggle to outdo one another the city population
push their normal standard of conspicuous consumption to a higher point,
with the result that a relatively greater expenditure in this direction is
required to indicate a given degree of pecuniary decency in the city. The
requirement of conformity to this higher conventional standard becomes
mandatory. The standard of decency is higher, class for class, and this
requirement of decent appearance must be lived up to on pain of losing
caste.

Consumption becomes a larger element in the standard of living in

Reprinted from *The Theory of the Leisure Class* (New York: Modern Library
ed., 1934), pp. 87–89, by permission of the publisher.

the city than in the country. Among the country population its place is to some extent taken by savings and home comforts known through the medium of neighborhood gossip sufficiently to serve the like general purpose of pecuniary repute. These home comforts and the leisure indulged in—where the indulgence is found—are of course also in great part to be classed as items of conspicuous consumption; and much the same is to be said of the savings. The smaller amount of the savings laid by by the artisan class is no doubt due, in some measure, to the fact that in the case of the artisan the savings are a less effective means of advertisement, relative to the environment in which he is placed, than are the savings of the people living on farms and in the small villages. Among the latter, everybody's affairs, especially everybody's pecuniary status, are known to everybody else. Considered by itself simply—taken in the first degree—this added provocation to which the artisan and the urban labouring classes are exposed may not very seriously decrease the amount of savings; but in its cumulative action, through raising the standard of decent expenditure, its deterrent effect on the tendency to save cannot but be very great.

THE MODERN CITY: ANOMIC, IMPERSONAL, MEANINGLESS, *C. Wright Mills*

MILLS'S stance toward the city was complex and
ambivalent. In the following passages, taken
from *White Collar,* he betrays his regional
(Texas) background but also makes fairly explicit
his great disappointment in the directions
taken by the modern city. By 1951, "city" meant
"nation" to men like Mills, so he is
bitterly condemning the very fabric of our
industrial-urban country.

THE BIGGEST BAZAAR IN THE WORLD

It is hard to say who owns the Bazaar. It began when a petty
capitalist left whaling ships for retail trade. Then it became a family
business; some partners appeared, and they took over; now it is a
corporation, and nobody owns more than 10 per cent. From a single
proprietor to what, in the curious lingo of finance, is called the public.
The eldest son of an eldest son has a lot of say-so about its working,
but if he went away, nobody doubts that it would go on: it is self-
creative and self-perpetuating and nobody owns it.

But who runs it? Someone has to run it. . . .

.   .   .   .

. . . It has become so impersonal at the top and bottom that a major
problem is how to make it personal again, and still smooth-running
and continuous.

There are managers of this and managers of that, and there are
managers of managers, but when any one of them dies or disappears,
it doesn't make any difference. The store goes on. It was created by
people who did not know what they were creating; and now it creates
people, who in turn do not know what they are creating. Every hour of

Excerpted from *White Collar* (New York: Oxford University Press, 1951), pp.
166–69, 172–74, 182–84, 187, 189. Reprinted by permission of the publisher.

the day it creates and destroys and re-creates itself, nobody knowing about it all but somebody knowing about every single part of it.

.　　.　　.　　.　　.　　.　　.　　.　　.　　.

In the cathedral, worship is organized; this is the cathedral of commodities, whispering and shouting for its 394,000 assorted gods (not including colors and sizes). In organizing the congregation, the Big Bazaar has been training it for faster and more efficient worship. Its most effective prayers have been formed in the ritual of the Great Repetition, a curious blending of piety and the barking of the circus.

The gods men worship determine how they live. Gods have always changed, but never before has their change been so well or so widely organized; never before has their worship been so universal and so devout. In organizing the fetishism of commodities, the Big Bazaar has made gods out of flux itself. Fashion used to be something for uptown aristocrats, and had mainly to do with deities of dress. But the Big Bazaar has democratized the idea of fashion to all orders of commodities and for all classes of worshipers. Fashion means faster turnover, because if you worship the new, you will be ashamed of the old. In its benevolence, the Big Bazaar has built the rhythmic worship of fashion into the habits and looks and feelings of the urban mass: it has organized the imagination itself. In dressing people up and changing the scenery of their lives, on the street and in the bedroom, it has cultivated a great faith in the Religion of Appearance.

.　　.　　.　　.　　.　　.　　.　　.　　.　　.

THE SALESGIRLS

One of the most crucial changes in the work-life of salesgirls over the last decades is the shift in their relation to customers. What has occurred may be gauged by comparing the outlook of (I) salespeople in small and middle-sized cities, with (II) salesgirls in big metropolitan stores.

I. Sales people, as well as small merchants in the small city, are often proud to say that they know well most of the people they serve. Their work satisfactions spring directly from this experience of the personally known market, from a communalization not with their superiors or bosses, but with the customers.

In the small towns, salespeople feel they are learning human nature at a gossip center. 'I like meeting the public; it broadens your views on life,' one saleslady in her late fifties in a medium-sized jewelry store says.

'I would not take anything for the knowledge I have gained of human nature through my contacts as a saleslady.' This theme of 'learning about human nature' is explicitly connected with the small, personally known character of the market. Again, the comments of a forty-year-old clerk in a small grocery store: 'Meeting the people, I actually make friends in a neighborhood store, because I know their family problems as well as their likes and dislikes,' and, 'I gain from my customers . . . confidences which brings a certain satisfaction in being of help.'

Both salesladies in department stores and women owners of small stores borrow prestige from customers. One saleslady in a medium-sized department store says: 'I like most meeting the public and being associated with the type of customer with whom I come in contact. The majority of my customers are very high type; they are refined and cultured.' A few of the salespeople also borrow prestige from the stores in which they work, some even from handling the merchandise itself. 'I like the displays and the connection with fine china and silverware.'

The power to change people, an attitude that may be considered the opposite of borrowing prestige from the customer, also permits satisfaction. 'I like the satisfaction I secure in my work in improving my customer's appearance,' says a cosmetic-counter woman of about forty. 'I have some very homely customers, as far as physical features are concerned, whom I have transformed into very attractive women.'

Many salespeople try to bring out the human aspect of their work by expressing an ideology of 'service.' This ideology is often anchored (1) in the feeling of being worth while: 'It is a pleasure to serve them. It makes you feel you are necessary and doing something worth while; (2) in the borrowing of prestige from customers; (3) in the feeling of gaining knowledge of human nature; (4) in the tacit though positive identification with the store itself or with its owner. Such elements form the occupational ideology of salespeople in smaller cities; each rests upon and assumes a small and personally known market—the aspect of their work that is primarily responsible for the main features of their ideology. For the emphasis upon the 'handling of people' brings to the fore precisely the experience that wage and factory workers do not have.

II. Salesgirls in large department stores of big cities often attempt to borrow prestige from customers, but in the big store of strangers, the attempt often fails, and, in fact, sometimes boomerangs into a feeling of powerless depression. The hatred of customers, often found in an intense form, is one result; the customer becomes the chief target of hostility; for she is an ostensible source of irritation, and usually a safe target.

Salesgirls in the big city store may be possessive of their own 'regular customers' and jealous of other's, but still when wealthier customers leave the store there is often much 'pulldown' talk about them, and obvious envy. 'The main thing we talk about,' says a salesgirl, 'is the customers.

After the customers go we mimic them.' Salesgirls often attempt identification with customers but often are frustrated. One must say 'attempt' identification because: (1) Most customers are strangers, so that contact is brief. (2) Class differences are frequently accentuated by the sharp and depressing contrast between home and store, customer, or commodity. 'You work among lovely things which you can't buy, you see prosperous, comfortable people who can buy it. When you go home with your [low pay] you do not feel genteel or anything but humiliated. You either half starve on your own or go home to mama, as I do, to be supported.' (3) Being 'at their service,' 'waiting on them,' is not conducive to easy and gratifying identification. Caught at the point of intersection between big store and urban mass, the salesgirl is typically engrossed in seeing the customer as her psychological enemy, rather than the store as her economic enemy.

.   .   .   .

THE PERSONALITY MARKET

In the world of the small entrepreneur, men sold goods to one another; in the new society of employees, they first of all sell their services. The employer of manual services buys the workers' labor, energy, and skill; the employer of many white-collar services, especially salesmanship, also buys the employees' social personalities. Working for wages with another's industrial property involves a sacrifice of time, power, and energy to the employer; working as a salaried employee often involves in addition the sacrifice of one's self to a multitude of 'consumers' or clients or managers. The relevance of personality traits to the often monotonous tasks at hand is a major source of 'occupational disability,' and requires that in any theory of 'increasing misery' attention be paid to the psychological aspects of white-collar work.

In a society of employees, dominated by the marketing mentality, it is inevitable that a personality market should arise. For in the great shift from manual skills to the art of 'handling,' selling, and servicing people, personal or even intimate traits of the employee are drawn into the sphere of exchange and become of commercial relevance, become commodities in the labor market. Whenever there is a transfer of control over one individual's personal traits to another for a price, a sale of those traits which affect one's impressions upon others, a personality market arises.

The shift from skills with things to skills with persons; from small, informal, to large, organized firms; and from the intimate local markets to the large anonymous market of the metropolitan area—these have had profound psychological results in the white-collar ranks.

One knows the salesclerk not as a person but as a commercial mask, a stereotyped greeting and appreciation for patronage; one need not be kind to the modern laundryman, one need only pay him; he, in turn, needs only to be cheerful and efficient. Kindness and friendliness become aspects of personalized service or of public relations of big firms, rationalized to further the sale of something. With anonymous insincerity the Successful Person thus makes an instrument of his own appearance and personality.

There are three conditions for a stabilized personality market: First, an employee must be part of a bureaucratic enterprise, selected, trained, and supervised by a higher authority. Second, from within this bureaucracy, his regular business must be to contact the public so as to present the firm's good name before all comers. Third, a large portion of this public must be anonymous, a mass of urban strangers.

The expansion of distribution, the declining proportion of small independent merchants, and the rise of anonymous urban markets mean that more and more people are in this position. Salespeople in large stores are of course under rules and regulations that stereotype their relations with the customer. The salesperson can only display pre-priced goods and persuade the acceptance of them. In this task she uses her 'personality.' She must remember that she 'represents' the 'management'; and loyalty to that anonymous organization requires that she be friendly, helpful, tactful, and courteous at all times. One of the floorwalker's tasks is to keep the clerks friendly, and most large stores employ 'personnel shoppers' who check up and make reports on clerks' 'personality.'

Many salesgirls are quite aware of the difference between what they really think of the customer and how they must act toward her. The smile behind the counter is a commercialized lure. . . . In the normal course of her work, because her personality becomes the instrument of an alien purpose, the salesgirl becomes self-alienated. . . .

.   .   .   .

Elaborate institutional set-ups thus rationally attempt to prepare people for the personality market and sustain them in their attempt to compete on it successfully. And from the areas of salesmanship proper, the requirements of the personality market have diffused as a style of life. What began as the public and commercial relations of business have become deeply personal: there is a public-relations aspect to private relations of all sorts, including even relations with oneself. The new ways are diffused by charm and success schools and by best-seller literature. The sales personality, built and maintained for operation on the personality market, has become a dominating type, a pervasive model for imitation for masses of people, in and out of selling. The literature of self-improve-

ment has generalized the traits and tactics of salesmanship for the population at large. In this literature all men can be leaders. The poor and
the unsuccessful simply do not exist, except by an untoward act of
their own will.

.   .   .   .

THE ENORMOUS FILE

As skyscrapers replace rows of small shops, so offices replace free
markets. Each office within the skyscraper is a segment of the enormous
file, a part of the symbol factory that produces the billion slips of
paper that gear modern society into its daily shape. From the executive's
suite to the factory yard, the paper webwork is spun; a thousand rules
you never made and don't know about are applied to you by a thousand
people you have not met and never will. The office is the Unseen Hand
become visible as a row of clerks and a set of IBM equipment, a pool of
dictaphone transcribers, and sixty receptionists confronting the elevators,
one above the other, on each floor.

The office is also a place of work. In the morning irregular rows of
people enter the skyscraper monument to the office culture. During the
day they do their little part of the business system, the government system, the war-system, the money-system, co-ordinating the machinery,
commanding each other, persuading the people of other worlds, recording
the activities that make up the nation's day of work. They transmit the
printed culture to the next day's generation. And at night, after the
people leave the skyscrapers, the streets are empty and inert, and the
hand is unseen again.

URBANISM AS A WAY OF LIFE, *Louis Wirth*

IN these passages, taken from this sociologist's famous
paper, Wirth is expressing—although not in
the denunciatory and pessimistic language of
Mills—what he conceives as the essence of
city life. The city as impersonal and anomic does
not constitute his only perspective on urbanism,
but probably it was dominant in his
thought. (Yet in an earlier study of the Jewish
ghetto in Chicago, he portrayed vividly
some of the warm continuity of urban life.) Wirth
drew conspicuously on the writings of
the German sociologist, Georg Simmel, and on a
dichotomy which we have already met in popular
thought—the "urban-rural dichotomy" then current
at the University of Chicago where Wirth taught.

The central problem of the sociologist of the city is to discover
the forms of social action and organization that typically emerge in
relatively permanent, compact settlements of large numbers of heterogeneous individuals. We must also infer that urbanism will assume its most
characteristic and extreme form in the measure in which the conditions
with which it is congruent are present. Thus the larger, the more densely
populated, and the more heterogeneous a community, the more accentuated the characteristics associated with urbanism will be. . . .

.   .   .   .

There are a number of sociological propositions concerning the relationship between (*a*) numbers of population, (*b*) density of settlement,
(*c*) heterogeneity of inhabitants and group life, which can be formulated
on the basis of observation and research.

SIZE OF THE POPULATION AGGREGATE

Ever since Aristotle's *Politics,* it has been recognized that increasing
the number of inhabitants in a settlement beyond a certain limit will affect

Excerpted from *American Journal of Sociology,* Vol. 44 (1938), 9–18, by permission of the University of Chicago Press.

the relationships between them and the character of the city. Large numbers involve, as has been pointed out, a greater range of individuals participating in a process of interaction, the greater is the *potential* differentiation between them. The personal traits, the occupations, the cultural life, and the ideas of the members of an urban community may, therefore, be expected to range between more widely separated poles than those of rural inhabitants.

That such variations should give rise to the spatial segregation of individuals according to color, ethnic heritage, economic and social status, tastes and preferences, may readily be inferred. The bonds of kinship, of neighborliness, and the sentiments arising out of living together for generations under a common folk tradition are likely to be absent or, at best, relatively weak in an aggregate the members of which have such diverse origins and backgrounds. Under such circumstances competition and formal control mechanisms furnish the substitutes for the bonds of solidarity that are relied upon to hold a folk society together.

Increase in the number of inhabitants of a community beyond a few hundred is bound to limit the possibility of each member of the community knowing all the others personally. . . . The multiplication of persons in a state of interaction under conditions which make their contact as full personalities impossible produces that segmentalization of human relationships which has sometimes been seized upon by students of the mental life of the cities as an explanation for the "schizoid" character of urban personality. This is not to say that the urban inhabitants have fewer acquaintances than rural inhabitants, for the reverse may actually be true; it means rather that in relation to the number of people whom they see and with whom they rub elbows in the course of daily life, they know a smaller proportion, and of these they have less intensive knowledge.

Characteristically, urbanites meet one another in highly segmental roles. They are, to be sure, dependent upon more people for the satisfactions of their life-needs than are rural people and thus are associated with a greater number of organized groups, but they are less dependent upon particular persons, and their dependence upon others is confined to a highly fractionalized aspect of the other's round of activity. This is essentially what is meant by saying that the city is characterized by secondary rather than primary contacts. The contacts of the city may indeed be face to face, but they are nevertheless impersonal, superficial, transitory, and segmental. The reserve, the indifference, and the blasé outlook which urbanites manifest in their relationships may thus be regarded as devices for immunizing themselves against the personal claims and expectations of others.

The superficiality, the anonymity, and the transitory character of urban-social relations make intelligible, also, the sophistication and the rationality generally ascribed to city-dwellers. Our acquaintances tend to stand in a relationship of utility to us in the sense that the role which each one plays in our life is overwhelmingly regarded as a means for the achievement of our own ends. Whereas, therefore, the individual gains, on the one hand, a certain degree of emancipation or freedom from the personal and emotional controls of intimate groups, he loses, on the other hand, the spontaneous self-expression, the moral, and the sense of participation that comes with living in an integrated society. This constitutes essentially the state of *anomie* or the social void to which Durkheim alludes in attempting to account for the various forms of social disorganization in technological society.

The segmental character and utilitarian accent of interpersonal relations in the city find their institutional expression in the proliferation of specialized tasks which we see in their most developed form in the professions. The operations of the pecuniary nexus leads to predatory relationships, which tend to obstruct the efficient functioning of the social order unless checked by professional codes and occupational etiquette. The premium put upon utility and efficiency suggests the adaptability of the corporate device for the organization of enterprises in which individuals can engage only in groups. The advantage that the corporation has over the individual entrepreneur and the partnership in the urban-industrial world derives not only from the possibility it affords of centralizing the resources of thousands of individuals or from the legal privilege of limited liability and perpetual succession, but from the fact that the corporation has no soul.

.   .   .   .

DENSITY

As in the case of numbers, so in the case of concentration in limited space, certain consequences of relevance in sociological analysis of the city emerge. Of these only a few can be indicated.

As Darwin pointed out for flora and fauna and as Durkheim noted in the case of human societies, an increase in numbers when area is held constant (i.e., an increase in density) tends to produce differentiation and specialization, since only in that way can the area support increased numbers. Density thus reinforces the effect of numbers in diversifying men and their activities and in increasing the complexity of the social structure.

On the subjective side, as Simmel has suggested, the close physical contact of numerous individuals necessarily produces a shift in the mediums through which we orient ourselves to the urban milieu, especially to our fellow-men. Typically, our physical contacts are close but our social contacts are distant. The urban world puts a premium on visual recognition. We see the uniform which denotes the role of the functionaries and are oblivious to the personal eccentricities that are hidden behind the uniform. We tend to acquire and develop a sensitivity to a world of artifacts and become progressively farther removed from the world of nature.

.   .   .   .

The close living together and working together of individuals who have no sentimental and emotional ties foster a spirit of competition, aggrandizement, and mutual exploitation. To counteract irresponsibility and potential disorder, formal controls tend to be resorted to. Without rigid adherence to predictable routines a large compact society would scarcely be able to maintain itself. The clock and the traffic signal are symbolic of the basis of our social order in the urban world. Frequent close physical contact, coupled with great social distance, accentuates the reserve of unattached individuals toward one another and, unless compensated for by other opportunities for response, gives rise to loneliness. The necessary frequent movement of great numbers of individuals in a congested habitat gives occasion to friction and irritation. Nervous tensions which derive from such personal frustrations are accentuated by the rapid tempo and the complicated technology under which life in dense areas must be lived.

HETEROGENEITY

The social interaction among such a variety of personality types in the urban milieu tends to break down the rigidity of caste lines and to complicate the class structure, and thus induces a more ramified and differentiated framework of social stratification than is found in more integrated societies. The heightened mobility of the individual, which brings him within the range of stimulation by a great number of diverse individuals and subjects him to fluctuating status in the differentiated social groups that compose the social structure of the city, tends toward the acceptance of instability and insecurity in the world at large as a norm. . . .

.   .   .   .

Although the city, through the recruitment of variant types to perform its diverse tasks and the accentuation of their uniqueness through competition and the premium upon eccentricity, novelty, efficient performance, and inventiveness, produces a highly differentiated population, it also exercises a leveling influence. Wherever large numbers of differently constituted individuals congregate, the process of depersonalization also enters. This leveling tendency inheres in part in the economic basis of the city. The development of large cities, at least in the modern age, was largely dependent upon the concentrative force of steam. The rise of the factory made possible mass production for an impersonal market. The fullest exploitation of the possibilities of the division of labor and mass production, however, is possible only with standardization of processes and products. A money economy goes hand in hand with such a system of production. Progressively as cities have developed upon a background of this system of production, the pecuniary nexus which implies the purchasability of services and things has displaced personal relations as the basis of association. Individuality under these circumstances must be replaced by categories.

THE COMMUNITY OF LIMITED LIABILITY,
Morris Janowitz

> NOT long after Wirth's "Urbanism as a Way of Life"
> appeared, Janowitz, also a sociologist at
> the University of Chicago, studied in the 1950s
> the community newspaper of various local
> communities in that city. In suggesting that the local
> community is one of "limited liability," he posed
> an alternative to the perspective that the
> city is a place characterized by extreme impersonality,
> anonymity, and rootlessness.

The analysis of the community press if it reveals nothing else indicates that significant proportions of the residents of the urban metropolis are not "rootless" individuals. Counter-trends to large-scale organization continually develop which modify the impact of technological impersonalization and make possible the gratification of individual needs in the local community. This is a crude statement. Ultimately, the task at hand is to emerge with a theoretical "model" of the local community. Such a "model" will present a meaningful analysis of the complexities

Excerpted from *The Community Press in an Urban Setting* (Glencoe, Ill.: The Free Press, 1952), pp. 207–213, 218, 222–25, by permission.

of the local community and point the way toward constructive support of those mechanisms and institutions which maintain social cohesion.

. . . .

On the one extreme, the present sample reveals that there is a minority of residents (non-readers; 16 per cent) for whom the community press had no meaning and who can be presumed to have practically no commitment or involvement in the community regardless of the amount of their use of local facilities. These individuals are most likely to constitute the "rootless" individuals on whom community social controls have little or no effect. On the other hand, there is another minority (fans; 11 per cent) who find themselves heavily involved with the local community and who are most likely therefore to respond to the pressure of the local community. For the remainder varying levels of involvement emerge.

Interpersonal contacts around the use of local facilities and not mere use of local facilities mold these commitments and involvements. The most direct way in which the social organization of the local community seems to serve these individual needs and motives hinges on its ability to serve the primary group requirements of child-rearing. The local community functions as a community particularly around the needs of its most conspicuous consumers—the children—as the data of this research attest.

Thus, family cohesion becomes central for understanding the inner dynamics of local community involvement since it seems more explanatory than the age, education, income and other such characteristics of the residents. . . .

Community involvement is also linked, but to a lesser degree, to primary group attachments outside of the family, but rooted in the local community. . . . The data at hand indicated that where stable primary groups existed in the local community the community press tended to operate as an extension of real social contacts. Where these contacts were absent the contents of the community press operated merely as a substitute for contact, and thereby negated the impact of the community press in developing local social cohesion. . . .

. . . .

The study of community involvement and orientations by means of the community press seems to highlight a developmental view of the distinction between "community" orientation and "metropolitan" orientation. Local orientations for some broaden out to include wider needs and perspectives, but which do not necessarily eliminate local orientations, although a predominant balance between the two can be discerned. It is as if the individual had the opportunity to make use of community facilities but he augments the satisfaction of his needs by making use of non-community facilities and thereby creating metropolitan orientations. The balance between the two varies from community to community, as can be seen between Atwater, Bethel Park and Carleton Manor. Yet, for the bulk of the sample population, the use of local facilities is impressive and has a significance that wider and broader orientations and identifications do not destroy automatically. It is hardly a case of either one or the other. . . .

The analysis of the community press as a communications system reveals immediately some of the complexities of the process by which the individual and his primary-group affiliations are integrated into the large-scale organization of the urban metropolis. It reveals that despite the growth of mass communications and large-scale organization most individuals are not living in a "mass society" in which they are directly linked to the major agencies of concentrated social and political power. Rather, the growth of large-scale organization has been accompanied by a proliferation of intermediate haphazard-like social arrangements and communication patterns. The local urban community appears to be a complex of social interactions which tends to identify a local elite and local institutionalized patterns for controlling social change. The community press is but one institution that stands intermediate between the individual and the major institutions of the metropolis; and the publisher is but one of the members of this intermediate elite.

.   .   .   .

Moreover, community leadership does seem strikingly associated with residential stability. It is worthwhile noting the degree to which community leaders display residential stability (twenty years or over at the same address), again in contradistinction to the view of the urban community as a "rootless" mass. . . .

The range of collective action which involves the community newspaper—from blood bank campaigns to support for police action—grows out of the leadership position and contacts of the publisher. But, in addition to collective action, social control involves the quest for respectability and morality. The ideology of the community newspaper, and of many other community institutions, seeks to present appropriate symbols of respectability and morality to those who have such motives. Yet for that substantial minority who seek anonymity, avoidance of community involvement and its consequent controls requires little effort.

.   .   .   .

The findings of this study call into question theoretical formulations which see the local community merely in the time perspective of a historical shift from "gemeinschaft" (simple—intimate) social forms to "gesellschaft" (complex—indirect) social forms.

.   .   .   .

It seems appropriate to point out that the generalized description of the urban residential community implied by this research is a community of "limited liability." Our community is clearly not one of completely bureaucratized and impersonalized attachments. In varying degrees, the local community resident has a current psychological and social investment in his local community. In varying degrees, use of local facilities is accompanied by community orientations. The extent and character of these attachments are in good measure linked to the individual resident's predispositions and acts. Raising a family and, to a lesser extent, length of residence and local social contacts predispose him to an acceptance of local community institutions and social controls. In the process, purely "rational" and "instrumental" relations are modified. In this regard, individuals vary in the extreme; some are more capable (or have more need) than others of developing these orientations.

But, in all cases, these attachments are limited in the amount of social and psychological investment they represent. Thus, the notion of a community of "limited liability" emerges. (The term is viewed as similar in many aspects to the individual's commitment of "limited liability" in economic affairs.) The individual, responding to the general cultural norms, is likely to demand more from his community than he will invest. But more significantly, his relation to the community is such—his investment is such—that when the community fails to serve his needs, he will withdraw. Withdrawal implies either departure from the local community or merely lack of involvement. Withdrawal to some extent takes place with individual aging. More often it accompanies changes in the ethnic or social composition of the community. For some the withdrawal is slight since the original investment was slight or non-existent. Finally the point of withdrawal may vary from community to community, from class to class, from ethnic group to ethnic group; but for each individual there is a point at which he cuts off his losses. Seldom is the investment so great that the individual is permanently committed to a community that cannot cater to his needs.

Thus, in summary, the dimensions of the local community point towards emerging social change in the largest metropolitan districts. Motives for community orientation center around the family with its gravitational pull toward the community and to a lesser extent around other primary group contacts. Within a specific local community, significant aspects of social organization operate without respect to socioeconomic status, although deviations (both higher or lower) from the status norms of the community tend to some degree to interfere with community cohesion. Local leadership functions in a social milieu of apparent rationalistic interpersonal contacts but these contacts are surrounded by a network of purely personalistic relations. Local leadership also involves a heavy emphasis on non-partisanship, which is in effect an emphasis on the perpetuation of the status quo. Compromise is the general theme except when fundamental values in the community are impinged by external threats.

The resulting balance of social control at the local community level is one which leaves relatively untouched only a minority of residents, heavily involves another perhaps smaller group in the community, and creates varying degrees of involvement for the bulk of the residents. Many of these elements are indicative of socially adaptive mechanisms seeking and struggling to modify the impact of industrialism and large-scale organization on the local community. This perspective eliminates the necessity of overemphasizing the impersonalized aspects of urban personality and thereby the character of social manipulation in the local community can be seen in its proper limits.

THE CABDRIVER AND HIS FARE: FACETS OF A FLEETING RELATIONSHIP, *Fred Davis*

WHILE a graduate student in sociology,
Fred Davis worked as a cabdriver for one of the
larger taxicab firms in Chicago. His article, based
on his notes and observations over a
six-month period during 1948, places the continuing
sociological concern with urban impersonality
into a fresh context, modifying the
more extreme versions of that theme.

Even in an urban and highly secularized society such as ours, most service relationships, be they between a professional and his client or a menial and his patron, are characterized by certain constraints on too crass a rendering and consuming of the service. That is to say, in the transaction, numerous interests besides that of simply effecting an economic exchange are customarily attended to and dealt with. The moral reputation of the parties, their respective social standing, and the skill and art with which the service is performed are but a few of the non-instrumental values which are usually incorporated into the whole act.

Tenuous though such constraints may become at times, particularly in large cities where anonymous roles only, segmentally related, occur in great profusion, it is at once evident that for them to exist at all something approximating a community must be present. Practitioners and clients must be sufficiently in communication for any untoward behavior to stand a reasonable chance of becoming known, remarked upon, remembered, and, in extreme cases, made public. And, whereas the exercise of sanctions does not necessarily depend on a community network that is closely integrated (or one in which there is a total identity of values and interests), it does depend on their being some continuity and stability in the relationships that make up the network, so that, at minimum, participants may in the natural course of events be able to identify actions and actors to one another.

It is mainly, though not wholly, from this vantage point that big-city cabdriving as an occupation is here discussed, particularly the relationship between cabdriver and fare and its consequences for the occupational culture. Approximating in certain respects a provincial's caricature of the

Excerpted from *American Journal of Sociology*, Vol. 65 (1959), 158–65, by permission of the University of Chicago Press.

broad arc of social relations in the metropolis, this relationship affords an extreme instance of the weakening and attenuation of many of the constraints customary in other client-and-patron-oriented services in our society. As such, its analysis can perhaps point up by implication certain of the rarely considered preconditions for practitioner-client relations found in other, more firmly structured, services and professions.

.   .   .   .

To a much more pronounced degree than is the case in other client-and-patron-oriented services, the occupation of cabdriver provides its practioners with few, if any, regularities by which to come upon, build up, and maintain a steady clientele.

.   .   .   .

The cabdriver's day consists of a long series of brief contacts with unrelated persons of whom he has no foreknowledge, just as they have none of him, and whom he is not likely to encounter again.

.   .   .   .

The cabdriver . . . has no fixed business address, and his contacts with passengers are highly random and singular. To a striking degree he is a practitioner without reputation because those who ride in his cab do not comprise, except perhaps in the most abstract sense, anything approximating a social group. They neither know nor come into contact with one another in other walks of life, and, even if by chance some do, they are unaware of their ever having shared the services of the same anonymous cabdriver. Even were the driver deliberately to set out to build up a small nucleus of steady and favored passengers, the time-space logistics of his job would quickly bring such a scheme to nought. Unable to plot his location in advance or to distribute time according to a schedule, he depends on remaining open to all comers wherever he finds himself. Much more so than other classes of service personnel, cabdrivers are both the fortuitous victims and the beneficiaries of random and highly impersonal market contingencies.

This set of circumstances—fleeting, one-time contact with a heterogeneous aggregate of clients, unknown to one another—exerts an interesting influence on the role of cabdriver.

Unable, either directly through choice or indirectly through location, to select clients, the cabdriver is deprived of even minimal controls. His trade therefore exposes him to a variety of hazards and exigencies which few others, excepting policemen, encounter as frequently; for example:

stick-ups, belligerent drunks, women in labor, psychopaths, counterfeiters, and fare-jumpers. Unlike the policeman's, however, his control over them is more fragile.

.   .   .   .

Goffman speaks of a category of persons who in some social encounters are treated as if they were not present, whereas in fact they may be indispensable for sustaining the performance. He terms these "non-persons" and gives as an example a servant at a social gathering. Although cabdrivers are not consistently approached in this way by fares, it happens often enough for it to become a significant theme of their work. Examples are legion. Maresca tells of the chorus girl who made a complete change from street clothing into stage costume as he drove her to her theater. More prosaic instances include the man and wife who, managing to suppress their anger while on the street, launch into a bitter quarrel the moment they are inside the cab; or the well-groomed young couple who after a few minutes roll over on the back seat to begin petting; or the businessman who loudly discusses details of a questionable business deal. Here the driver is expected to, and usually does, act as if he were merely an extension of the automobile he operates. In actuality, of course, he is acutely aware of what goes on in his cab, and, although his being treated as a non-person implies a degraded status, it also affords him a splendid vantage point from which to witness a rich variety of human schemes and entanglements.

The fleeting nature of the cabdriver's contact with the passenger at the same time also makes for his being approached as someone to whom intimacies can be revealed and opinions forthrightly expressed with little fear of rebuttal, retaliation, or disparagement. And though this status as an accessible person is the product of little more than the turning inside-out of his non-person status—which situation implies neither equality nor respect for his opinion—it nevertheless does afford him glimpses of the private lives of individuals which few in our society, apart from psychiatrists and clergy, are privileged to note as often or in such great variety. . . .

In cabdriving, therefore, propriety, deference, and "face" are, in the nature of the case, weaker than is the case on most other service relationships. This absence contributes to a heightened preoccupation with and focusing on the purely instrumental aspect of the relationship which for the driver is the payment he receives for his services. This perhaps would be less blatantly the case were it not for the gratuity or tip. For the non-cab-owning company driver, the sum collected in tips amounts roughly to 40 per cent of his earnings. . . . For the family man who drives, tips usually represent the difference between a subsistence and a living wage. . . . In occupations where the tip constitutes so large a fraction of the person's earnings, the cash nexus, while admittedly not the only basis upon which patrons are judged, is so important as to relegate other considerations to a secondary place. Will the fare tip or will he "stiff"? How much will he tip? The answers remain in nearly every instance problematic to the end. . . .

.　　.　　.　　.　　.　　.　　.　　.　　.　　.

No regular scheme of work can easily tolerate so high a degree of ambiguity and uncertainty in a key contingency. Invariably, attempts are made to fashion ways and means of greater predictability and control; or, failing that, of devising formulas and imagery to bring order and reason in otherwise inscrutable and capacious events. In the course of a long history a rich body of stereotypes, belief, and practices has grown up whose function is that of reducing uncertainty, increasing calculability, and providing coherent explanations.

A basic dichotomy running through the cabdriver's concept of his client world is of regular cab users and of non-cab users, the latter referred to as "jerks," "slobs," "yokels," "public transportation types," and a host of other derogatory terms. The former class, though viewed as quite heterogeneous within itself, includes all who customarily choose cabs in preference to other forms of local transportation, are conversant with the cab-passenger role, and, most of all, accept, if only begrudgingly, the practice of tipping. By comparison, the class of non-cab users includes that vast aggregate of persons who resort to cabs only in emergencies or on special occasions, and are prone too often to view the hiring of a cab as simply a more expensive mode of transportation.

.　　.　　.　　.　　.　　.　　.　　.　　.　　.

. . . Regular cab users demonstrate in a variety of ways that for them this is a customary and familiar mode of travel. The manner in which they hail a cab, when and how they announce their destination, the ease with which they enter and exit, how they sit—these, and more, though difficult to describe in precise detail, comprise the Gestalt.

There exists among drivers an extensive typology of cab users, the attributes imputed to each type having a certain predictive value, particularly as regards tipping. Some of the more common and sharply delineated types are:

The Sport.—The cabdriver's image of this type combines in one person those attributes of character which he views as ideal. While the Sport's vocation may be any one of many, his status derives more from his extra-vocational activities, e.g., at the race track, prize fights, ball games, popular restaurants, and bars. He is the perennial "young man on the town." Gentlemanly without being aloof, interested without becoming familiar, he also is, of course, never petty. Most of all, his tips are generous.

.   .   .   .

The Blowhard.—The Blowhard is a false Sport. While often wearing the outer mantle of the Sport, he lacks the real Sport's casualness, assured manners, and comfortable style. Given to loquaciousness, he boasts and indiscriminately fabricates tales of track winnings, sexual exploits, and the important people he knows. Often holding out the promise of much by way of tip, he seldom lives up to his words.

The Businessman.—These are the staple of the cab trade, particularly for drivers who work by day. Not only are they the most frequently encountered; their habits and preferences are more uniform than those of any other type: the brisk efficiency with which they engage a cab, their purposefulness and disinclination to partake of small talk. Though not often big tippers, they are thought fair. Thus they serve as something of a standard by which the generosity or stinginess of others is judged.

The Lady Shopper.—Although almost as numerous as businessmen, Lady Shoppers are not nearly as well thought of by cabdrivers. The stereotype is a middle-aged woman, fashionably though unattractively dressed, sitting somewhat stiffly at the edge of her seat and wearing a fixed glare which bespeaks her conviction that she is being "taken for a ride." Her major delinquency, however, is undertipping. . . .

Live Ones.—Live Ones are a special category of fare usually encountered by the cabdriver who works by night. They are, as a rule, out-of-town conventioneers or other revelers who tour about in small groups in search of licentious forms of entertainment: cabarets, burlesques, strip-tease bars, pick-up joints, etc. As often as not, they have already had a good deal to drink when the cabdriver meets them, and, being out-of-towners they frequently turn to him for recommendations on where to go. . . . Often extravagant in their tips because of high spirits and drink, Live Ones are also frequently careless and forget to tip altogether. Knowing that Live Ones are out to "blow their money" anyway, many drivers believe they are justified in seeing to it that they are not deprived of a small portion.

Although the cab culture's typology of fares stems in a large part from the attempt to order experience, reduce uncertainty, and further calculability of the tip, it is questionable of course as to how accurate or efficient it is. For, as has often been remarked, stereotypes and typologies have a way of imparting a symmetry and regularity to behavior which are, at best, only crudely approximated in reality. Too often it happens, for example, that a fare tabbed as a Sport turns out to be a Stiff (non-tipper), that a Blowhard matches his words with a generous tip, or that a Lady Shopper will give fifteen or even twenty cents. The persistence of the typology therefore has perhaps as much to do with the cabdriver's a posteriori reconstructions and rationalizations of fare behavior as it does with the typology's predictive efficiency.

To protect and insure themselves against an unfavorable outcome of tipping, many drivers will, depending upon circumstances, employ diverse tactics and stratagems (some more premeditated than others) to increase the amount of tip or to compensate for its loss should it not be forthcoming. Certain of these are listed below. It should be understood however, that in the ordinary instance the driver makes no attempt to manipulate the fare, believing resignedly that in the long run such means bear too little fruit for the effort and risk.

Making change.—Depending on the tariff and the amount handed him, the driver can fumble about in his pockets for change, or make change in such denominations as often to embarrass a fare into giving a larger tip than he had intended. The efficacy of this tactic depends naturally on the determination and staying power of the fare, qualities which many fares are averse to demonstrate, particularly when it comes to small change.

The hard-luck story.—This is usually reserved for young persons and others who, for whatever reason, evidence an insecure posture vis-à-vis the driver. Typically, the hard-luck story consists of a catalogue of economic woes, e.g., long and hard hours of work, poor pay, insulting and unappreciative passengers, etc. . . . Most drivers, however, view the hard-luck story as an unsavory form of extortion, beneath their dignity. Furthermore, while it may work in some cases, its potential for alienating tips is probably as great as its success at extracting them.

Fictitious charges.—The resort to fictitious and fraudulent charges occurs most commonly in those cases in which the driver feels that he has good reason to believe that the fare will, either through malice or ignorance, not tip and when the fare impresses him as being enough of a non-cab user as not to know when improper charges are being levied. . . .

The "psychological" approach.—Possibly attributing more art to their trade than is the case, some drivers are of the opinion that a cab ride can be tailored to fit a passenger in much the same way as can a suit of clothes. One cabdriver, boasting of his success at getting tips, explained: "In this business you've got to use psychology. You've got to make the ride fit the person. Now, take a businessman. He's in a hurry to get someplace and he doesn't want a lot of bullshit and crapping around. With him you've got to keep moving. Do some fancy cutting in and out, give the cab a bit of a jerk when you take off from a light. Not reckless, mind you, but plenty of zip. He likes that. With old people, it's just the opposite. They're more afraid than anyone of getting hurt or killed in a cab. Take it easy with them. Creep along, open doors for them, help them in and out, be real folksy. Call them 'Sir' and 'Ma'am' and they'll soon be calling you 'young man.' They're suckers for this stuff; and they'll loosen up their pocketbooks a little bit."

In the last analysis, neither the driver's typology of fares nor his stratagems further to any marked degree his control of the tip. Paradoxically, were these routinely successful in achieving predictability and control, they would at the same time divest the act of tipping of its most distinguishing characteristics—of its uncertainty, variability, and of the element of revelation in its consummation. It is these—essentially the problematic in human intercourse—which distinguish the tip from the fixed service charge. . . .

.   .   .   .

Among service relationships in our society, that between the big city cabdriver and his fare is, due to the way in which they come into contact with each other, especially subject to structural weakness. The relationship is random, fleeting, unrenewable, and largely devoid of socially integrative features which in other client and patron oriented services help sustain a wider range of constraints and controls between the parties to the transaction. (Much the same might be said of such service occupations as waitress, bellhop and hotel doorman, the chief difference being, however, that these operate from a spatially fixed establishment, which in itself permits of greater identifiability, renewability, and hence constraint in one's relationship to them.) As a result, the tendency of the relationship is to gravitate sharply and in relatively overt fashion toward those few issues having to do with the basic instrumental terms of the exchange. The very fact of tipping, its economic centrality and the cab culture's preoccupation with mastering its many vagaries reflect in large part the regulative imbalance inherent in the relationship.

By inference, this analysis raises anew questions of how to account for the many more formidable and apparently more binding practitioner-client constraints found in other personal service fields, in particular the professions. To such matters as career socialization, colleague groups, socially legitimated skill monopolies, and professional secrecy there might be added a certain safe modicum of continuity, stability, and homogeneity of clientele. For, given too great and random a circulation of clients among practitioners, as might occur for example under certain bureaucratic schemes for providing universal and comprehensive medical service, the danger is that informal social control networks would not come into being in the community, and, as in big-city cab-driving, relations between servers and served would become reputationless, anonymous, and narrowly calculative.

SUGGESTED READINGS: CHAPTER 12

Richard Dewey. "The Rural-Urban Continuum: Real but Relatively Unimportant," *American Journal of Sociology*, Vol. 66 (1960), 60–66. Herbert Gans. "Urbanism and Suburbanism as Ways of Life: A Re-evaluation of Definitions." In Arnold Rose. (Ed.), *Human Behavior and Social Processes.* Boston: Houghton Mifflin, 1962. Gregory Stone, "City Shoppers and Urban Identification," *American Journal of Sociology*, Vol. 60 (1954), pp. 26–45.

Three considerations of the view that cities are places where relationships are primarily impersonal, segmental, superficial, transitory and predatory.

Scott Greer. "Urbanism Reconsidered: A Comprehensive Study of Local Areas in a Metropolis," *American Sociological Review*, Vol. 21 (1956), 19–25.

Studies like Greer's make evident that there can be considerable "social integration" of residents with their "neighborhoods" and local communities.

Morris Janowitz. *The Community Press in an Urban Setting.* Glencoe, Ill.: The Free Press, 1952.

Janowitz's empirically based conception of the "community of limited liability," suggests the kind of identification urban residents can make with their local communities.

Lewis Mumford. *The Culture of Cities.* New York: Harcourt Brace, 1938.

Mumford is one of the great contemporary critics of modern cities and of the usual styles of city building and planning. In this book, the development of the post-industrial city is linked with impersonality, anomie, routine, and purposelessness.

13

Sweet Summer Time. From *Harper's Magazine*, August 1, 1868.

RURAL AMENITIES
AND
URBAN ATTRIBUTES

THERE are two themes that it is useful to juxtapose because they are inextricably related. The first is the rural image of cities compounded totally of brick, concrete, and stone, an image that is answered with a counterimage that cities too have the rural amenities. The metropolis is defended as not lacking either the physical or moral attributes of the country towns and the farmland. A second theme pertains to the sometimes defensive stances of small town, small city, and farm people. With the growth of large cities, which attracted great numbers of eager migrants from the hinterlands, those who remained behind have frequently the need to defend life in those places. The rural virtues are still stressed, but in combination with genuine urbanity. "We can have the advantages of both" was, and is, the motto.

The "rural" aspects of big-city life are evident in the sociological literature. One need only consider the long history of attempts to study urban "neighborhoods" and "communities" as well as earnest suggestions for their reconstitution when they are threatened by disintegration. The classical writings about immigrant villages and boss politics in the cities are other instances. Less immediately evident is how sociological writing is affected by the theme of the urbanity of small-town life. Of course, both the literature of rural sociology and the more general sociological literature are replete with references to the urbanization of the hinterland. But remarkably few sociological studies,

recent or older, of the small cities and towns of America
exist. Those that we have tend to be focused around special
issues like race relations, as in the books by John Dollard, Hylan
Lewis, Allison Davis and his colleagues, and Ken Morland. There
are also special treatments of certain aspects of small town life,
such as the descriptions of Jewish institutions in small communities. A scattering of monographs on small towns and cities—
including the quite early work of John M. Williams, and the later
studies by Blumenthal, the Lynds, and Warner—are fairly
straightforward studies, with a fair amount of emphasis on the
increasing urbanization of those locales. In seemingly straightforward monographs about small cities, such as *Small Town in
Mass Society* by Vidich and Benson, the small cities are viewed
somewhat critically from some species of metropolitan perspective.
Blumenthal earlier was also impressed by the strictness of social
control and the conformity of small towners. Even the Lynds,
although dismayed by the impersonality of metropolitan life,
made much ado about the conforming spirit of Middletowners
and the homogeneity of their beliefs about the American way.

In general, urban sociology has paid little attention even to
those studies, focusing instead on the great metropolis rather than
on the smaller cities. And although the rural sociologists have
studied many aspects of the smaller communities, they have
been as much advocates of rural reform as serious students of
small town and small city life. It is in that light that we should
perhaps read the last three selections in this part. We need not
take the rhetoric of White and Nicholson at face value to
recognize the need for many comparative studies of small cities,
including their study at varying phases of development and
in relation to their highly variable surrounding hinterlands.

ROOFTOP GARDENERS BRING FORTH BLOSSOMS HIGH ABOVE A CITY OF STONE AND STEEL, *Meyer Berger*

HERE is an implicit answer to the accusation that
the metropolis is only a hectic asphalt jungle,
lacking greenery, flowers, shady trees,
and the quiet life. New York newspapers frequently
print such rejoinders—explicit as well as
implicit—to the curt judgment that New York
is no place to live, but only to visit.

There is a green world high above the pavement that city ground-lings rarely see. Familiar and exotic growths flourish in this sky acreage. The same birds, insects and crawling things that invade open countryside plantings climb to apartment house and skyscraper gardens—as high as thirty-eight floors at Radio City—to rob or destroy crops.

The rural housewife who puts up jams, jellies and preserves from the fruits of farm acreage has a slik-gowned bediamonded sister in town who loves to fill Mason jars and cans with penthouse-grown fruits and berries—when she doesn't have the hired cook do it.

The green-thumbed sisterhood—better than 95 per cent of the tillers of penhouse soil are women—organized the Rooftop Gardeners six years ago. The movement was started by Mrs. Carol Hannig who lives atop 875 Park Avenue and runs the world's largest sand-processing industry.

She got the notion at lectures given by the New York Horticultural Society in 1952. It came to her at one of the sessions that while she could study and enjoy neighborhood penthouse gardens, she knew none of her sky neighbors. She suggested that they meet and exchange ideas, and they snapped at it.

Membership in the Rooftop Gardeners is thirty right now, with the committee considering 101 new applications. These are only a small portion of the 2,500 to 3,000 New Yorkers who use the short-sized rake and hoe on skyline acreage. Many are rich, many are humble.

The busiest and most knowledgeable top-floor husbandman is Hal Lee, a freelance writer on horticulture. He has more than 2,000 plantings on the eleventh floor at 1394 Lexington Avenue, near Ninety-second

The New York Times (April 23, 1958). © 1958 by The New York Times Company. Reprinted by permission.

Street. His crop includes figs, bananas, strawberries, peaches, cherries. He maintains a rich compost heap of leaf mold and kitchen leavings.

Mr. Lee has worked his Lexington Avenue soil the last eleven years. When the Rooftop Gardeners organized they made him president. By and by, though, he turned professional consultant. He wanted to resign then, on the ground that he was a pro, but the resignation was unanimously rejected. He still gets all their business.

Pioneer of the penthouse Maud Mullers is Mrs. Harry Schwartz. She has kept up her penthouse garden atop 944 Fifth Avenue a full thirty-five years. She owns the tallest penthouse trees—a forty-foot honey locust, wide-branched Russian Olive growths, magnolias, fifteen-foot high privet hedge and white birch, peach, apple and cherry trees, among others.

The Schwartzes, like most other crows-nest horticulturists, grow thousands of annuals and perennials. They put their fruits and berries up in jars. They fight off crows, woodpeckers, bats, pigeons, aphids, tent caterpillars and go after all sorts of crawlers with spray guns. They grow magnificent orchids. Their pet dachshund, Penny, cremated, sleeps inside a miniature grave fence under an olive tree.

The Rooftop Gardeners eat under whispering leaves with flower scent drifting across their candle-lit tables. Some sleep in their gardens, under the stars. Some have forsaken the country entirely; just live on their green roofs. One gentleman, a United Nations delegate, has worked a broad putting-green into his garden scheme.

The secret of sky gardening seems to be peat moss. It overcomes the drying effects of lofty winds. Mr. Lee says that dampness from rooftop soil and plantings acts as a humectant—keeps a woman's complexion smooth and soft. He got that from Mrs. Lee, an expert on beauty.

And there's an advantage in having neighbors under you when you're gardening. Last spring Mr. Lee got a telephone call from a tenant three flights down. The man said: "Mr. Lee, get your spray gun handy. Tent caterpillars just passed my window, headed up." It took another hour or so, but Mr. Lee met the invasion at the parapet. The tent caterpillars never established a roof beachhead.

I HAVE 7,000,000 NEIGHBORS,

Alfred E. Smith

ALTHOUGH stressing other values—such as the
complete Americanism of New York
City—Al Smith also retorts to the common
accusation that although that metropolis
is a great place to visit, it is hardly a place to
live. Smith underlines the qualities traditionally
associated with the countryside:
neighborliness, family life, continuity of family and
community, and identification with the city
itself. Like William A. White defending
Emporia (see below), Smith also can claim
that his town is cosmopolitan too!

Any Mr. Smith in any part of the United States will prefer his own
home place to any other part of America, for about him are his family
and friends and the associations of his adult life, if not of his childhood.
These elements are what bind a man's affections to any particular area,
and it will not matter if the place be one of the great centers of population
or a remote and lonely corner of a wilderness, beautiful or bleak, north,
south, east, or west.

I am like all other Mr. Smiths in this regard, perhaps a little more old-
fashioned than most, because I am of the breed that settles down and
doesn't like to move. When you add this quality to justified enthusiasm
for a place you have the sort of deep devotion that I have for New York
City and its environs. I could out-talk any New York Chamber of
Commerce exhorter any minute of the day.

Four generations of my particular branch of the Smith family have
been born on Manhattan Island. My grandson, Alfred E. Smith, IV, was
born in 1931 not many miles from the neighborhood at the extreme lower
end of Manhattan Island where my father and I and my oldest son, Alfred
E. Smith, Jr., first saw the light.

New York is, to me, the ideal part of the United States and although
I take great pleasure in visiting other sections of the country, when I think

Excerpted from *American Magazine*, Vol. 116 (1933), 36–38, 90.

of "My America" I naturally think of New York, particularly New York City.

.   .   .   .

. . . I am no stranger in any part of the metropolitan area. It is to be expected that when every footstep is on known and beloved ground—east side, west side, all around the town—I should have a fundamental peace of mind, which I have.

But, more than this, I am firmly convinced that no spot in the world has greater values for a citizen than my town; and as I stand on top of the Empire State Building and look down on the greatest collection of multitudes and buildings in history, and around and about at dimming landscapes of New Jersey, New York, and Connecticut, I thank God I am a part of this glorious metropolitan life, a part of its art and industry, its culture and its recreations—and I would not trade my lot with a citizen anywhere.

In the last analysis we are all Americans, and New York is just as much America as the plains of Texas, the mountains of Oregon, or the coast of Florida. The lover of the open spaces will never be convinced of the ideal qualities of city life; and the city-bred American forms habits and attachments which would make it difficult for him to accustom himself to live anywhere else. This is fortunate indeed, for were we all to live in cities there would be no one to supply the agricultural needs of the nation.

All of us New Yorkers, of no matter what nationality or creed, find some pride in being a part of the Great City. New York City has always been a magnet. We hear many Americans from other parts of the country get off the old chestnut about "New York is nice for a visit, but I wouldn't live there if you gave me the place."

There is no stronger denial of this sentiment than the fact that thousands of these same Americans move from their home towns into the city of New York every year and millions more cherish a hope of some day living in our country's greatest city.

.   .   .   .

. . . All types of country—from ocean beaches to mountain scenery—lie at Manhattan's door; and it's a pleasant thought to a chronic New Yorker that he doesn't *have* to go anywhere for anything. There is plenty within reach for anyone's lifetime, and all inexpensive. A few cents and a few minutes' time will take you away from the metropolis to the scenic grandeur of northern New Jersey, southern New York, and southern Connecticut, with their Poconos, Catskills, and Berkshires; lakes, rivers, and everything that goes with them. . . .

Like all old-fashioned fathers, I get a great thrill from having my family about me. And I get another thrill (this confession may expose me as a father who has not grown up) in taking my grandchildren on a Saturday or Sunday afternoon to the Zoo, to the Metropolitan Museum of Art to see the great paintings and sculpture, or to the American Museum of Natural History to see how science has re-created the early life on this continent, or to the Aquarium to see the fishes—to any of dozens of such instructive and entertaining institutions. . . .

Of course not all New Yorkers live in apartment or tenement houses. The limits of the city and its suburbs are so wide that many a citizen known as a New Yorker really lives quite a distance from the center of the city and may enjoy a house complete with garden, or even one of the many colonial farmhouses quite isolated and set about with woods and wild life. In fact, I have always believed that one of the most attractive features of New York life is the ability of a resident to select almost any type of dwelling that he may desire and still be within easy commuting distance of the city's many advantages. . . .

.   .   .   .

I like the spirit of New York. It is a happy, neighborly spirit of our enormous population of more than 7,000,000 people. At no time in our history has that neighborhood spirit been better expressed than during the recent troublous times caused by the widespread unemployment. The city itself, as a municipality, has very generously contributed to the relief of suffering and distress. The response of private citizens to private appeal has been marvelous. . . .

I like the seashore, I like the mountains, and I am, after all, an American, but when it comes to selecting my particular part of America, it is unquestionably within the boundaries of New York State and, most of all, within the City of New York.

THE WOMAN ON THE FARM, *Clara Waldo*

WRITTEN at a time when "rural depletion" because
of city-ward migration had become a national
concern, this defense of farm life eloquently, if in
naive terms, states the farmer's case and
points to the rectifying institutions.

While the tendency of the city is to destroy the simplicity of home
life, and to substitute for it the apartment house, the flat, the hotel, the
club, and innumerable cheap amusements away from the home, it is quite
the contrary in the country. Never before was the woman on the farm
striving so hard to make her home attractive as now. She reaches out to
draw from art and science all of the beautiful that she can afford, and such
inventions and conveniences as will shorten and ease her labor, and so
give her more leisure for self-culture.

The woman on the farm is being taught, largely by the Grange, that
she is a valuable citizen, and has a leading part to play on the stage of life.
So she respects herself and her work more than she did, even a decade ago.
She dresses better, practices physical culture, takes a little more rest, reads
more magazines and books, makes herself a better companion to her
children and husband, takes more outings to coast and mountains, camps
with her family at the State Fair and the Chautauqua Assembly, and is
in general a much more cheerful and interesting woman than she has ever
been. With our correspondence schools; with modern languages taught by
phonograph; with art reproductions for 1 cent apiece; with the traveling
library; with current literature at club rates; with lecture courses and
farmers' institutes; with stereopticon views of every famous object on the
earth's surface; with graphophone records of every fine singer, actor,
speaker and orchestra, the woman on the farm is not so far lacking in
general information as one may suppose. Much of culture and society
polish is denied her by reason of her secluded life. But there is a compensation in the universe which gives us on one side what we have missed
on another. So the woman of the farm, while lacking much in "style" and
society small talk, has a comprehensive and practical knowledge of many
things. She is an independent and all-around serviceable person. Indoors
or out she can "lend a hand" where there is need. If her husband falls ill

Excerpted from Mary Douthit (Ed.), *The Souvenir of Western Women* (Port-
land, Ore.: Presses of Anderson and Duniway Co., 1905), pp. 169–71.

or dies, she can manage the business of the farm and bring up the children. Husband and wife on the farm are very close partners in all that concerns their welfare. It is the ideal family life of loving co-operation. To all the members of these ideal rural and surburban homes, the sweet home interests come first. Everything circles around home and mother. There are few distractions, and no unwholesome dissipations to draw the children out at night from their mother's influence. To prove the high character of our country women, and their devotion to love and duty, we have only to point out the many great men and women who have gone forth from these farm homes, to shine in every sort of high position, and to reflect honor upon their bringing up.

The rural free delivery of mail and the rural telephone are great boons to the isolated woman on the farm. She is wishing with all her heart for an enlarged parcels post, so that she may buy more freely from the city merchants.

In the matter of money, the woman on the farm is more independent than her city sister. She earns her pin money by selling poultry, butter and eggs; picking wild berries; making jelly and jam for the city people who go away for the summer; taking summer boarders; picking hops; peeling the chittim bark, and in various other ways. . . .

.   .   .   .

Leadership among women asserts itself in the country as in towns, and the church and Sunday school work goes on much the same. All social gatherings are difficult to keep up because of the scattered homes. For this reason a woman's club does not flourish in the country, nor do literary societies and reading circles. Not many women have a driving horse at their disposal, to go at will, without interfering with the farm work. But wherever a Grange is established no lack is felt in social or educational matters. The Patrons of Husbandry is an ideal order for the country people, including as it does the whole family from the 14-year-old child to the great grand parents. . . .

The Grange upholds woman's suffrage in theory and in practice. Every honor, distinction, and office is open to the woman who, by her character and her ability, can win her way. Thus the women of the Grange learn to debate and discuss all practical and intellectual subjects side by side with the men. Women of the Grange are interested in the same things that call forth the efforts of local woman's clubs. They see that cemeteries, school, and church grounds are kept in neat order, and that trees, vines, and shrubs are set out wherever they can be protected and watered. They inspect the sanitary conditions and the water supply of their district schoolhouses. Matrons of Husbandry are in the advance in urging the addition of nature studies, school gardens, and the work bench to our country school system.

They wish especially to see their children educated towards the farm and not away from it.

The women of the Grange cultivate the true spirit of hospitality. All who come enter into and share their family life. Neighborly kindness to the sick and sorrowing is abundantly expressed in farm communities. While not a trained nurse, the modern woman on the farm informs herself as to the approved methods of caring for the sick and relieving accidental hurts. In the Grange women learn to co-operate in many ways, and the lesson is broadening and beautifying their lives and homes.

All honor to this true woman upon the farm as she sits enthroned among her jewels—the sturdy sons and daughters who will rise up and call her blessed!

> Yes, after the strife and weary tussle
> When life is done, and she lies at rest,
> The nation's brain and heart and muscle,
> Her sons and daughters shall call her blest.
>
> And I think the sweetest joy of heaven,
> The rarest bliss of eternal life,
> And the fairest crown of all, will be given
> Unto the wayworn farmer's wife.

THE PROVINCIAL AMERICAN,
Meridith Nicholson

> IN a symbolic blurring of countryside, village, small
> town, and small city, Meridith Nicholson
> points the moral that people who live outside of big
> cities also live cosmopolitan existences.
> Nicholson lived in Indianapolis, believed then and
> now by many New Yorkers and Chicagoans to
> be the hick town *par excellence.*

What we miss and what we lack who live in the provinces seem to me of little weight in the scale against our compensations,—we are prone to boast,—and we lack in those fine reticences that mark the cultivated citizen of the metropolis. We like to talk, and we talk our problems out to a finish. Our commonwealths rose in the ashes of the

Reprinted from *The Provincial American* (Boston and New York: Houghton Mifflin, 1912), pp. 26–30, by permission.

hunter's camp-fires, and we are all a great neighborhood, united in a common understanding of what democracy is, and animated by ideals of what we want it to be. That saving humor which is a philosophy of life flourishes amid the tall corn. We are old enough now—we of the West—to have built up in ourselves a species of wisdom, founded upon experience, which is a part of the continuing, unwritten law of democracy. We are less likely these days to "wobble right" than we are to stand fast or march forward like an army with banners.

We provincials are immensely curious. Art, music, literature, politics—nothing that is of contemporaneous human interest is alien to us. If these things don't come to us, we go to them. We are more truly representative of the American ideal than our metropolitan cousins, because (here I lay my head upon the block) we know more about, oh, so many things! We know vastly more about the United States, for one thing. We know what New York is thinking before New York herself knows it, because we visit the metropolis to find out. Sleeping-cars have no terrors for us, and a man who has never been west of Philadelphia seems to us a singularly benighted being. Those of our Western school-teachers who don't see Europe for three hundred dollars every summer get at least as far East as Concord, to be photographed "by the rude bridge that arched the flood."

.   .   .   .

In Boston a lady once expressed her surprise that I should be hastening home for Thanksgiving Day. This, she thought, was a New England festival. More recently I was asked by a Bostonian if I had ever heard of Paul Revere. . . .

.   .   .   .

Our greatest gain is in leisure and the opportunity to ponder and brood. In all these thousands of country towns live alert and shrewd students of affairs. Where your New Yorker scans headlines as he "commutes" homeward, the villager reaches his own fireside without being shot through a tube, and sits down and reads his newspaper thoroughly. When he repairs to the drug-store to abuse or praise the powers that be, his wife reads the paper, too. A United States Senator from a Middle Western State, making a campaign for renomination preliminary to the primaries, warned the people in rural communities against the newspaper and periodical press with its scandals and heresies. "Wait quietly by your firesides, undisturbed by these false teachings," he said in effect; "then go to your primaries and vote as you have always voted." His opponent won by thirty thousand—the amiable answer of the little red school-house.

THE COUNTRY NEWSPAPER,
William Allen White

WHITE, a nationally known journalist, was an
articulate defender of small-city
cosmopolitanism. Whatever these towns might
seem like to outsiders, they are not, he
argued, provincial, countrified or deadly dull. The
people who have remained there have
developed, in their own way—and in a very
American way—a distinctly urban mode of life.
Yet these places remain comfortable,
friendly, and easygoing. (This assertion
implicitly challenges the sociologist's long cherished
rural-urban dichotomy.) In his essay on
the country newspaper, White managed also to
touch on many of the urban themes remarked
on earlier, scoring points against the
big cities. His symbolic wedding of town and newspaper
reflected his own editorship of the *Emporia Gazette*.

The country town is one of those things we have worked out for
ourselves here in America. Our cities are not unlike other cities in the
world; the trolley and the omnibus and the subway, the tender hot-house
millionaire and the hardy, perennial crook are found in all cities. Class
lines extend from city to city well around the globe. And American aversion to caste disappears when the American finds himself cooped in a
city with a million of his fellows. But in the country town—the political
unit larger than the village and smaller than the city, the town with a
population between three and one hundred thousand—we have built up
something distinctively American. Physically, it is of its own kind; the
people for the most part live in detached wooden houses on lots with
fifty feet of street frontage, and from one hundred to one hundred and
fifty feet in depth. Grass is the common heritage of all the children—
grass and flowers. A kitchen-garden smiles in the back yard, and the
service of public utilities is so cheap that in most country towns in America
electricity for lighting and household power, water for the kitchen sink

and the bathroom, gas for cooking, and the telephone with unlimited use may be found in every house. In the town where these lines are written there are more telephones than there are houses, and as many water intakes as there are families, and more electric lights than there are men, women, and children. Civilization brings its labor-saving devices to all the people of an American country town. The uncivilized area is negligible, if one measures civilization by the use of the conveniences and luxuries that civilization has brought.

In the home, the difference between the rich and the poor, in these towns, is denoted largely by the multiplication of rooms; there is no very great difference in the kinds of rooms in the houses of those who have much and those who have little. And, indeed, the economic differences are of no consequence. The average American thinks he is saving for his children, and for nothing else. But if the child of the rich man and the child of the poor man meet in a common school, graduate from a common high-school, and meet in the country college or in the state university—and they do associate thus in the days of their youth—there is no reason why parents should strain themselves for the children; and they do not strain themselves. They relax in their automobiles, go to the movies, inhabit the summer boarding-house in the mountains or by the sea, and hoot at the vulgarity and stupidity of those strangers who appear to be rich and to be grunting and sweating and saving and intriguing for more money, but who really are only well-to-do middle-class people.

In the American country town the race for great wealth has slackened down. The traveler who sees our half-dozen great cities, who goes into our industrial centers, loafs about our pleasure resorts, sees much that is significantly American. But he misses much also if he fails to realize that there are in America tens of thousands of miles of asphalted streets arched by elms, bordered by green lawns, fringed with flowers marking the procession of the seasons, and that back from these streets stand millions of houses owned by their tenants—houses of from five to ten rooms, that cost from twenty-five hundred to twenty-five thousand dollars, and that in these houses live a people neither rural nor urban, a people who have rural tradition and urban aspirations, and who are getting a rather large return from civilization for the dollars they spend. Besides the civilization that comes to these people in pipes and on wires, they are buying civilization in the phonograph, the moving picture, the automobile, and the fifty-cent reprint of last year's fiction success. The Woman's City Federation of Clubs is bringing what civic beauty it can lug home from Europe and the Eastern cities; the opportune death of the prominent citizen is opening playgrounds and hospitals and parks; and the country college, which has multiplied as the sands of the sea, supplements the state schools of higher learning in the work of bringing to youth opportunities for more than the common-school education.

Now into this peculiar civilization comes that curious institution, the country newspaper. The country newspaper is the incarnation of the town spirit. The newspaper is more than the voice of the country-town spirit; the newspaper is in a measure the will of the town, and the town's character is displayed with sad realism in the town's newspapers. A newspaper is as honest as its town, is as intelligent as its town, as kind as its town, as brave as its town. And those curious phases of abnormal psychology often found in men and women, wherein a dual or multiple personality speaks, are found often in communities where many newspapers, babble in many voices arising from the dis-organized spirits of the place. For ten years and more the tendency in the American country town has been toward fewer newspapers. That tendency seems to show that the spirit of these communities is unifying. . . .

It is therefore the country newspaper, the one that speaks for the town, that guides and cherishes the town, that embodies the distinctive spirit of the town, wherein one town differeth from another in glory— it is that country newspaper, which takes it color from a town and gives color back, that shall engage our attention at present. . . .

.   .   .   .

But the beauty and the joy of our papers and their little worlds is that we who live in the country towns know our own heroes. Who knows Murphy in New York? Only a few. Yet in Emporia we all know Tom O'Connor—and love him. Who knows Morgan in New York? One man in a hundred thousand. Yet in Emporia who does not know George Newman, our banker and merchant prince? Boston people pick up their morning papers and read with shuddering horror of the crimes of their daily villain, yet read without that fine thrill that we have when we hear that Al Ludorph is in jail again in Emporia. For we all know Al; we've ridden in his hack a score of times. And we take up our paper with the story of his frailties as readers who begin the narrative of an old friend's adventures.

The society columns of our city papers set down the goings and comings, the marriages and the deaths of people who are known only by name; there are gowns realized only in dreams; there are social functions that seem staged upon distant stars. Yet you city people read of these things with avidity. But our social activities, chronicled in our country papers, tell of real people, whose hired girls are sisters to our hired girls, and so we know the secrets of their hearts. We know a gown when it appears three seasons in our society columns, disguised by its trimming and its covering, and it becomes a familiar friend. To read of it recalls other and happier days. And when we read of a funeral in our country newspapers, we do not visualize it as a mere church fight to see the grand persons in their solemn array on dress parade. A funeral notice to us country readers means something human and sad. Between the formal lines that tell of the mournful affair we read many a tragedy; we know the heartache; we realize the destitution that must come when the flowers are taken to the hospital; we know what insurance the dead man carried, and how it must be stretched to meet the needs. We can see the quiet lines on each side of the walk leading from the house of sorrow after the services—the men on one side, the women on the other—waiting to see the mourning families, and to be seen by them; we may smile through our tears at the uncongenial pall-bearers and wonder what common ground of mirth they will find to till on the way back from the cemetery. In lists of wedding-guests in our papers we know just what poor kin was remembered, and what was snubbed. We know when we read of a bankruptcy just which member of the firm or family brought it on by extravagance or sloth. We read that the wife of the hardware merchant is in Kansas City, and we know the feelings of the dry-goods merchant who reads it and sees his own silks ignored. So when we see a new kind of lawn-mower on the dry-goods merchant's lawn, we don't blame him much for sending to the city for it.

Our papers, our little country papers, seem drab and miserably provincial to strangers; yet we who read them read in their lines the sweet, intimate story of life. And all these touches of nature make us wondrous kind. It is the country newspaper, bringing together daily the threads of the town's life, weaving them into something rich and strange, and setting the pattern as it weaves, directing the loom, and giving the cloth its color by mixing the lives of all the people in its color-pot—it is this country newspaper that reveals us to ourselves—that keeps our country hearts quick and our country minds open and our country faith strong.

When the girl at the glove-counter marries the boy in the wholesale house, the news of their wedding is good for a forty-line wedding notice, and the forty lines in the country paper give them self-respect. When in due course we know that their baby is a twelve-pounder, named Grover or Theodore or Woodrow, we have that neighborly feeling that breeds the real democracy. When we read of death in that home we can mourn with them that mourn. When we see them moving upward in the world, into a firm, and out toward the country club neighborhood, we rejoice with them that rejoice. Therefore, men and brethren, when you are riding through this vale of tears upon the California Limited, and by chance pick up the little country newspaper with its meager telegraph service of three or four thousand words—or, at best, fifteen or twenty thousand; when you see its array of countryside items; its interminable local stories; its tiresome editorials on the waterworks, the schools, the street railroad, the crops, and the city printing, don't throw down the contemptible little rag with the verdict that there is nothing in it. But know this, and know it well: if you could take the clay from your eyes and read the little paper as it is written, you would find all of God's beautiful sorrowing, struggling, aspiring world in it, and what you saw would make you touch the little paper with reverent hands.

SUGGESTED READINGS: CHAPTER 13

Herbert Gans. *Urban Villagers.* New York: The Free Press of Glencoe, 1962.

The title of this excellent urban study indicates that there is no dearth of sociological data to counteract the notion that city life has no rural qualities.

Robert Lynd and Helen Lynd. *Middletown.* New York. Harcourt-Brace, 1929. *Middletown in Transition.* New York: Harcourt-Brace, 1937.

The original and follow-up researches of Muncie, Indiana. The residents' perspectives on their city, as well as their imagery of larger cities, are explicitly and implicitly threaded throughout these volumes.

Arthur Vidich and Joseph Bensman. *Small Town in Mass Society.* Princeton, N. J.: Princeton University Press, 1958.

This is a recent sociological study of a small city, interesting both for what is doubtless "true" of the town and its people as well as for the urban bias which permeates the authors' representation of town and residents.

Arthur Wood. *Hamtramck.* New York: Bookman Associates, 1955.

This study of roles in Detroit suggests how rural qualities have lingered on in the descendents of Polish immigrants and colors their urban parish life.

14

Elizabethan Villa, ca. 1850. Duval's Steam Press, Philadelphia.

SUBURBIA

SUBURBS have been a notable feature of American cities since the early nineteenth century; for as the cities expanded in population and size, some residents preferred to live at the outskirts. But they remained essentially urban dwellers, retaining urban comforts and engaging in urban activities. As long ago as 1823, real estate advertisements tempted New Yorkers with "a place of residence with all the advantages of the country with most of the conveniences of the city." The union of rural and urban in suburban imagery is a major urban perspective. But the many variants of that perspective depend on who is talking about suburbs, which kinds of suburbs he is talking about, and when he is talking about them.

Sociologists have been relative latecomers to the dialogue over the forms and meaning of suburbia. An early study of suburban leisure by Lundberg in the 1930s signalized the increasing visibility of suburbs. But the bulk of sociological interest in suburbs has developed since World War II. The ecological wing of sociology is interested in suburban growth; other sociologists are variously interested in suburban institutions, life-styles, and social problems. Unquestionably, some sociological writing on suburbs has assumed that all suburbs have been middle class in population and orientation. Consequently, some of the more recent studies and writing have been intended as correctives; they have emphasized that suburbs are also inhabited by lower socioeconomic classes or, as one Canadian sociologist recently pointed out, that suburbs (around Toronto) are extremely varied in type, population, and style.

Political scientists have also been concerned with political order and power in the suburbs, as their interests have extended into the entire metropolitan area. Sayre and Polsby remark, however, that interest in the central city and the metropolitan area has been greater than concern for the suburbs. As they note, "suburbia in the political process is a related but more neglected phenomenon." Knowledge about suburban politics is for the most part still "abashedly impressionistic." Most generalizations "ignore or blur" variations among the varied types of suburbs. Thus, political scientists have tended to operate with some of the same restrictive images that sociologists have. And neither group has turned back to study suburban life in preceding decades, using the rich material that is available for such studies.

TEN ACRES ENOUGH,
Anonymous

ONE chapter in *Ten Acres Enough* refers to
"Gentleman-farming." Its author, who
considered himself one of that category, tells us
quite explicitly what city living in the country
meant to him. Even this early in the
suburban movement (1864), suburbanites were
defending their migrations from the city in terms of
equal urban amenities and superior rural benefits.

CITY EXPERIENCES—MODERATE EXPECTATIONS

My life, up to the age of forty, had been spent in my native city
of Philadelphia. Like thousands of others before me, I began the world
without a dollar, and with a very few friends in a condition to assist me.
Having saved a few hundred dollars by dint of close application to
business, and avoiding taverns, oyster-houses, theatres, and fashionable
tailors, I married and went into business the same year. . . . The crisis of
1837 nearly ruined me, and I was kept struggling along during the five
succeeding years of hard times, until the revival of 1842 came round. . . .
When in difficulty, we had often debated the propriety of quitting the city
and its terrible business trials, and settling on a few acres in the country,
where we could raise our own food, and spend the remainder of our days
in cultivating ground which would be sure to yield us at least a respectable
subsistence. We had no longing for excessive wealth: a mere competency,
though earned by daily toil, so that it was reasonably sure, and free from
the drag of continued indebtedness to others, was all we coveted.

I had always loved the country, but my wife preferred the city. I could
take no step but such as would be likely to promote her happiness. So
long as times continued fair, we ceased to canvass the propriety of a
removal. We had children to educate, and to her the city seemed the best
and most convenient place for qualifying them for a future usefulness.
Then, most of our relations resided near us. Our habits were eminently
social. We had made numerous friends, and among our neighbors there
had turned up many valuable families. We felt even the thought of break-

Excerpted from *Ten Acres Enough: A Practical Experience* (New York: James
Miller, 1864), pp. 9–10, 12–13, 110–14.

ing away from all these cordial ties to be a trying one. But the refuge of a removal to the country had taken strong hold of my mind. . . . The leading idea in my mind was this—that a man of ordinary industry and intelligence, by choosing a proper location within hourly reach of a great city market, could so cultivate a few acres as to insure a maintenance for his family, free from the ruinous vibrations of trade or commerce in the metropolis. All my reading served to convince me of its soundness. I did not assume that he could get rich on the few acres which I ever expected to own; but I felt assured that he could place himself above want. I knew that his peace of mind would be sure. With me this was dearer than all. My reading had satisfied me that such a man would find Ten Acres Enough, and these I could certainly command.

.   .   .   .

CITY AND COUNTRY LIFE CONTRASTED

The pensive reader must not take it for granted that in going into the the country we escaped all the annoyances of domestic life peculiar to the city, or that we fell heir to no new ones, such as we had never before experienced. He must remember that this is a world of compensations, and that nowhere will he be likely to find either an unmixed good or an unmixed evil. Such was exactly our experience. But on summing up the two, the balance was decidedly in our favor. It is true that though the town close by us had well-paved streets, yet the walk of half a mile to reach them was a mere gravel path, which was sometimes muddy in summer, and sloppy with unshovelled snow in winter. But I walked over it almost daily to the post-office, not even imagining that it was worse than a city pavement. The tramp of the children to school was not longer than they had been used to, and my wife and daughters thought it no hardship to go shopping among the well-supplied stores quite as frequently as when living in the city. Indeed, I sometimes thought they went a little oftener. They were certainly as well posted up as to the new fashions as they had ever been, while the fresh country air, united with constant exercise, kept them in good appetite, even to the rounding of their cheeks, and the maintenance of a better color in them than ever.

As to society, they very soon made acquaintances quite as agreeable as could be desired. Visiting became a very frequent thing; and after a few months I let in a suspicion that the girls found twice as many beaux as in the city, though there the average number is always larger than in the country.

.   .   .   .

Then the walks for miles around us were excellent, and we all became great walkers, for walking we found to be good. Not merely stepping from shop to shop, or from neighbor to neighbor, but stretching away out into the country, to the freshest fields, the shadiest woods, the highest ridges, and the greenest lawns. We found that however sullen the imagination may have been among its griefs at home, here it cheered up and smiled. However listless the limbs may have been by steady toil, here they were braced up, and the lagging gait became buoyant again. However stubborn the memory may be in presenting that only which was agonizing, and insisting on that which cannot be retrieved, on walking among the glowing fields it ceases to regard the former, and forgets the latters. Indeed, we all came to esteem the mere breathing of the fresh wind upon the commonest highway to be rest and comfort, which must be felt to be believed.

But then we had neither gas nor hydrant water, those two prime luxuries of city life. Yet there was a pump in a deep well under a shed at the kitchen door, from which we drew water so cold as not at any time to need that other city luxury, ice. It was gratifying to see how expertly even the small children operated with the pump-handle. In a month we ceased to regret the hydrants. As to gas, we had the modern lamps, which give so clear a light; not so convenient, it must be confessed, but then they did not cost us over half as much, neither did we sit up near so long at night. There were two mails from the city daily, and the newsboy threw the morning paper into the front door while we sat at breakfast. The evening paper came up from the city before we had supped. We had two daily mails from New York, besides a telegraph station. The baker served us twice a day with bread, when we needed it; the oysterman became a bore, he rang the bell so often; and the fish-wagon, with sea-fish packed in ice, directly from the shore, was within call as often as we desired, with fish as cheap and sound as any to be purchased in the city. Groceries and provisions from the stores cost no more than they did there, but they were no cheaper. But in the item of rent the saving was enormous,—really half enough, in my case, to keep a moderate family. Many's the time, when sweating over the weeds, have I thought of this last heavy drain on the purse of the city toiler, and thanked Heaven that I had ceased to work for the landlord.

We had books as abundantly as aforetime, as we retained our share in the city library, and became subscribers to that in the adjoining town. It is true that the road in front of us was never thronged like Chestnut-street, but we neither sighed after the crowd nor missed its presence. We saw no flash of jewelry, nor heard the rustling of expensive silks, except the few which on particular occasions were sported within our own unostentatious domicil. Our entire wardrobes were manifestly on a scale less costly than ever. Our old city friends were apparently a great way off, but as they could reach us in an hour either by steamboat or rail, they quickly found us out. The relish of their society was heightened by distance and separation. In short, while far from being hermits, we were happy in ourselves. I think my wife became a perfectly happy woman. . . .

.   .   .   .

Speaking of visitors from abroad, I noticed that our city friends came to make their visits on the very hottest summer days, when, of all others, we were ourselves sufficiently exhausted by the heat, and were disposed to put up with as little cooking and in-door work as possible. But as such visitations were not exactly comfortable to the visited, so we could not see how they could be any more agreeable to the visitors. Yet they generally remarked, even when the mercury was up to ninety-five, "How much cooler it is in the country!" They did really enjoy either themselves or the heat. But my wife told them it was only the change of scene that made the weather tolerable, and that if they lived in the country they would soon discover it to be quite as hot as in the city. For my part, I bore the heat admirably, though tanned by the sun to the color of an aborigine; but I enjoyed the inexpressible luxury of going constantly in my shirt sleeves. I can hardly find words to describe the feeling of comfort which I enjoyed for full seven months out of the twelve from this little piece of latitudinarianism, the privilege of country life, but an unknown luxury in the city.

TYPES OF SUBURBS,
Everett Chamberlin

> IN terms of social class, Chicago in the 1870s had a
> full complement of suburban styles, as
> indicated by the following descriptions. The
> intervening century has brought many
> changes in suburbs and their styles, but the "status"
> motif certainly persists. The following excerpts
> from Chamberlin's book also suggest
> the varied meanings of suburbs for their
> founders or early settlers.

PARKSIDE

This suburb includes a subdivision consisting of twenty acres, lying between Seventieth and Seventy-first streets, and Stony Island boulevard and Madison avenue. In the neighborhood of the depot of the Illinois Central railroad, it is already well settled, with a fair class of residents.

Property does not range so high in this suburb as in some of its neighbors, but it is scarcely less available. The place has good school and church facilities.

LAKE FOREST

In 1856, the Lake Forest Association was formed by the members of the Presbyterian churches of Chicago. This Company was organized for the purchase of lands at Lake Forest, with a view to erection of a university, and other institutions of learning. About 2,000 acres of land were purchased by the Association, 1,400 of which went into Lake Forest, 39 acres were given to the university for building ground, 10 acres to the female seminary, and 10 acres were set aside for a park. Alternate lots were retained for the benefit of the university, and the others sold; and so rapidly did prices advance, and the suburb take a leading position as the favorite resort of the better class of Chicago's inhabitants, that the scheme proved an undoubted financial success. The Association still holds

Excerpted from *Chicago and Its Suburbs* (Chicago: T. A. Hungerford, 1874), pp. 357, 396–97, 411, 415–16, 451–52.

about 600 acres of land, at prices varying from $300 to $1,000 per acre. . . . The Company have built an elegant hotel overlooking the lake, and carried on different improvements all with admirable results. The hotel has been filled with visitors during the summer, and constitutes a resort which "is becoming [in the language of a Forester] as great a favorite with Chicago people as Newport or Long Branch is to the heated and worn out denizens of New York and other eastern cities."

The university has not yet been built, but excellent educational establishments are found in the village. There is a young ladies' seminary, under the direction of Professor Weston, and an academy for young men under the care of Professor Allen. . . . There are some funds in hand for the erection of the university, but the prosecution of the matter rests with a Board. It is expected that work will not be much longer delayed. There is a fine Presbyterian church in town, of which the Rev. Mr. Taylor is pastor.

Apart from public improvements, Lake Forest boasts of more elegant private residences than almost any other suburb. During the past year three estimable citizens have permanently located themselves in the village. . . . Perhaps the most beautiful place in Lake Forest is that of Mrs. Alexander White, which was purchased by her late husband from H. M. Thompson, Esq. Possessed of a large fortune, as well as refined and luxurious taste, the late proprietor was able to make his estate very beautiful in all respects. The price put upon the place is not less than $100,000. Then the Farwells, dry goods merchants, own lovely palaces in the center of town. Mr. John V. Farwell lives in a turreted baronial castle, built of the concrete made in the town, and presenting a quaint and picturesque appearance. The interior is elegantly finished in black-walnut and cherry. His brother, Hon. C. B. Farwell, has a place on a commanding elevation overlooking the lake. The residence of Mr. Charles Bradley, one of Chicago's leading merchants, is very elaborate and costly. It is a large English cottage, which he has christened "Carlsruhe" and not without reason, for the grounds are as beautiful as that famed German retreat. . . .

RIVERSIDE

No suburb of Chicago possesses greater interest, whether from a historical point of view or from its picturesque surroundings, than the suburb known of late years as Riverside. It is unfortunately the fact that much of the attention of the public which has been directed to it is owing to the continued litigation in which the Improvement Company, having charge of the fortunes of the place, have since the fire been involved. But apart from this, Riverside is worthy of some note. Some five or six years ago, the suburb had no existence on the charts of Cook county. The late city-

MOUNT FOREST

MOUNT FOREST.

Only nine miles from the City, *on the Chicago & Alton Railroad, whose depot is in the heart of the City—has double track and frequent passenger trains. The village is situated upon a* **high ridge,** *which is covered with a growth of* **beautiful forest trees,** *and overlooks a* **clear, deep lake,** *which lies at the foot of the hills. There are* **broad streets, large lots, extensive parks, deep, rocky ravines, flowing mineral springs and enchanting views. No cash payment** *asked of parties making good improvements, and the most liberal terms to all purchasers. Prices during the next six months will be from $3.00 to $10.00 per foot, governed by the location.*

MOUNT FOREST LAND CO.,

143 LA SALLE STREET, CHICAGO.

H. S. DIETRICH, *Real Estate.*
C. B. ATKINS, *Real Estate.*
H. W. FOWLER, *Financial Agent.*

treasurer, Mr. David A. Gage, owned a beautiful farm, lying on the banks of the Desplaines river, well wooded, with many charming points of scenery, and only some four miles from the city limits. Had this city been any other than Chicago, Mr. Gage might to-day be owning his pleasant retreat. But the eye of the far-seeing speculator alighted upon the spot, and the inevitable Company having been organized, the car of progress was speedily set in motion. The locality, in its natural condition, was beautiful; and the opportunity presented for the artist to elaborate upon, and improve the work of nature, was unquestionable. The Company had wealthy and responsible men upon its directorate, whose spirits were speedily aglow with the vision of the bright things before them if they could ever realize their dream of planting on the banks of the Desplaines the model suburb of America. Eastern architects came and surveyed the ground, and shortly afterwards presented a report to the Executive Board of the Association. Their plan was found to be exhaustive and expensive; it brought out with success the leading idea desired, of so laying out the suburb that it should practically be a public park for the benefit of private residents; and, after much debate, it was adopted.

The Company at once raised the funds necessary to proceed with the work. An army of workmen was engaged, and a considerable progress was soon perceptible, in the heavy task before them. The tract of land owned by the Company comprised about 1,600 acres, and of these it was proposed to devote 700 acres for roads, borders, walks, recreative grounds, and parks. The New York landscape artists (Messrs. Olmsted & Vaux) pressed very urgently the necessity of the construction of a carriage road or driveway from the city to the suburb; and, meeting assistance from the town of Cicero and the city of Chicago, the road running from Twelfth street directly to Riverside, 150 feet wide, was constructed. Among the other improvements suggested, and carried into effect, was a complete system of sewerage, the supply of water and gas, the adoption of the curved line for streets, and the planting of innumerable trees. Riverside, before it passed into the hands of the Company, possessed many beautiful groves of trees—elm, maple, and oak; but it was left for the standing wooded land to be utilized to its utmost extent by the skill of the artist. Everything likely to give the place the appearance of a resident park was done. Nor were opportunities offered by the curving course of the Desplaines river neglected. At one place, the river encircles a strip of land, of the shape of a peninsula, and of about one and a quarter square miles in extent, which, together with a neighboring island, has been improved so as to form public parks, access being had to one of them by means of rustic bridges. . . .

Among the other enterprise undertaken and carried to a successful conclusion by the Company, was the erection of a grand hotel. Pleasantly situated, with excellent accommodation, containing a large number of rooms, and all the conveniences of a city establishment, it is a very agreeable place for summer resort. . . .

During the last two years the suburb has made little progress. Litigation, financial embarrassments, and the reports widely circulated, and having some foundation in fact, of the unhealthy character of the location, have continued to retard its growth. The prospects of the place are better than they formerly were, and the persons having charge of Riverside are energetic and persevering, and, their present difficulties removed, will doubtless succeed in restoring the suburb to a more favorable position in public confidence. There is no doubt that both the Desplaines and Fox rivers, lying to the west of Chicago and affording great numbers of very beautiful sites, will soon be bordered with handsome improvements, and be relieved, sooner or later, of the incubus that now rests upon them, viz., a reputation for ague. The most obvious mode of remedying the summer defluxion of these streams is by dredging the channels and docking the shores, when flat, with the product of this operation; also turning into the stream the currents of numerous artesian wells along their banks. We look to see the Desplaines, within fifteen years, an exceptionally choice residence district.

.   .   .   .

PARK RIDGE

This eligible suburb is on the Wisconsin Division of the Chicago & Northwestern railroad, about thirteen miles from the Court-house. It is situated on the dividing ridge between the waters of Lake Michigan and the Mississippi river, and has an altitude of one hundred and thirty feet above the lake. Owing to this altitude, it is especially noted for the salubrity of its atmosphere. It is especially exempt from malarious diseases, and, in the seasons most remarkable in ague history, it wholly escaped the attacks of the shaking demon. In common with most of the suburbs of Chicago, the land was, in the first place, pre-empted and occupied as farms. . . .

Away back in 1855, when the railroad was located, a brick manufactory was started on the present location of Park Ridge, and the unpoetical founders contented themselves with the dull, practical name of Brickton. But the manufacture of bricks proceeded equally well in a hamlet of that name, and, until the occurrence of the great fire, Brickton supplied a large quantity of the red bricks which were sold in the Chicago market. With the fire there came a change—not that the demand for bricks was less, but that the call for good, healthy suburban residence property was more. Brickton shook itself up, and merged into a new name—Park Ridge—one of the best located, as also one of the most promising of the city's suburbs.

The original plat of Brickton comprised only one hundred and sixty acres; but since the name was changed, large additions have been made, chiefly by Leonard Hodges, Esq., J. H. Burns, and J. H. Butler. The village was recently organized, with corporate powers and privileges, and now includes some twelve hundred acres of choice lands. The sentiment of the people being decidedly adverse, there has not, since the settlement of the village, been a single saloon or tippling-house tolerated within its borders. Following this, perhaps almost necessarily, the society of Park Ridge is first class, and its members all reputable, religious and law-loving people. They appreciate so well their pleasant country retreat, that they are decidedly adverse to allowing any objectionable element to obtrude therein. Hitherto they have succeeded, and the future is not likely to see any change in this respect.

.   .   .   .

The town possessses excellent school facilities, a prosperous Methodist church, a Congregational society, and two well attended Sabbath-schools. There are two or three stores; blacksmith's and carpenter's shops; a lumber, wood and coal yard; and a planing mill. A large and extensive manufactory of brick, drain tiles and pottery is in operation; and excellent supplies of building material are to be obtained on the ground.

Among the chief improvements which have been recently completed, must be mentioned the elegant suburban hotel structure, erected, at a cost of $15,000. . . .

The residents of Park Ridge include many business men of Chicago who have generally chosen to erect pleasant, substantial residences, and to adorn the grounds in which the houses stand with all the talent and ingenuity that the landscape artist or lover of esthetics could desire. . . .

THE SUBURBANITE, *H. A. Bridgeman*

THIS perceptive if also rhetorical article appeared
in 1902. Its author anticipated some later
developments, including one that is now at the forefront
of public consciousness: What is the fate of the
central city after the "better classes" move
away, out to the suburbs?

A generation ago debating societies about once in so often threshed over the question of the relative advantages of city and of country life. There were then two distinct human types—the city man and the country man. To them has been added in comparatively recent years a third—the suburbanite. He emerges into view not only at great world centers like London and New York, but in a hundred lesser cities in Europe and America. He differs from both the city man and the country man, for he is the product of new conditions, and upon him a complex set of influences are operating. Ambitious disputants in the lyceums of to-day must extend the scope of their vision and reckon with this latter-day creation. Range him alongside of his urban and rural brethren and let us see what manner of man he is. What causes have produced him? How does he differ from other men, and is he good for anything?

The suburbanite is a recent growth, because cheap and rapid transportation is a modern affair. In other days the choice of residence lay between the purely country and the purely city environment. The Roman noble could have his home either within the city walls or out at Tivoli, but he would hardly think of including the two localities in his daily itinerary. Fancy Maecenas hurrying to catch the eight-six train for the Forum Romanus. The Londoner of twenty-five years ago made his home hard by the Strand or the British Museum. Now he is just as likely to live in Finchley or at Hampstead Heath as within walking distance of St. Paul's. The literary men of the school that has nearly passed off the stage selected either the heart of the city or the country, pure and simple, as their dwelling place. Charles Lamb, for instance, clung with passionate ardor to the brick walls and the narrow streets of the world's metropolis. Tennyson, on the other hand, immured himself in leafy bowers, into which floated bird songs and the murmur of the distant sea. But to-day many of London's foremost literary workers are suburbanites, living close enough

Excerpted from *The Independent,* Vol. 54 (1902), 862–64.

to the center of things to feel often the pulse of human life, and far enough away to escape in some measure its fever and stress.

The cities, it is true, are still the goal of the average American heart, and the question of suburban versus urban residence has, we confess, its pros and cons. As the city man walks brisky to his office in the morning or strolls leisurely uptown in the afternoon; as he saunters over to his club after dinner, or drops into the theater, he may be pardoned for being proudly conscious of the fact that his daily course is not hedged about with threatening time-tables; that he has easy access to the best that the rich, resourceful city offers in the way of music, and theaters, and lectures, and preaching, and libraries; that night and day converging streams, that take their rise all over the world, are depositing their ample cargoes at his very door. He is a dull fellow indeed if his soul is not stirred by the mighty beat of the city heart; by its wonderfully variegated human life; by the tremendous forces for good and ill that in the cities, as nowhere else in the world, maintain perpetual battle.

To be a good city man, to be a Seth Low or a Bishop Potter in New York, a Samuel B. Capen or an Edwin D. Mead in Boston, or a Philip Garrett or a Robert Welsh in Philadelphia, or a Charles J. Bonaparate in Baltimore, to love the city of one's birth or of one's adoption, or to hold in reverence its heroes, to conserve its best traditions, to be ever striving to make it a more beatuiful and a more holy city—that is an ambition which any man, young or old, may well cherish as he would his own honor.

But, on the other hand, Mr. Suburbanite arises and puts in his claim to be heard. "It's all well enough for bachelors and elderly couples and people who like crowds, to reside in town, but if you want to bring up a family, to prolong your days, to cultivate the neighborly feeling, to get acquainted with the stars and the birds and the flowers, leave your city block and become like me. It may be a little more difficult for us to attend the opera, but the robin in my elm tree struck a higher note and a sweeter one yesterday than any *prima donna* ever reached."

Such a burst of enthusiasm, it is true, may signify that the suburbanite is still under the glamour of first impressions, and that his ardor will cool after he has had some experience with late trains and learned how inconvenient it is not to have a drug store just around the corner. But, after all, he is a rare man who once, having migrated to the suburbs, ever takes up permanently his residence in the city again.

For the wholesomeness of suburban life grows upon one. We are sure to get in America, through the rise of numerous little colonies of people who plant themselves five, ten or fifteen miles from town, a renaissance of the old, beautiful neighborhood life that characterized this nation before the rush to the cities began. The piazza of the next house looks inviting, and the temptation is to loiter there a few moments for a friendly chat. The women of the colony get to know each other, not through the conventions of society, but because their children are studying and playing together, and because they utilize the same opportunities for sport or for nature-study. The men, too, become more gregarious, and the club life when once established often becomes something more than a synonym for lounging, smoking and swapping gossip. . . .

·   ·   ·   ·   ·   ·   ·   ·   ·   ·

The opportunity, too, to develop a sound and worthy corporate life is more and more appealing to earnest suburbanites. Not much help can yet be had from those who look upon their suburban homes simply as places to spend their nights and Sundays, but the men whose eyes are being opened to the vision of a better social order—and there is an increasing number of such—turn with hope to the virgin soil of the suburbs. It will take a generation or two of hard fighting to cleanse the big cities of their foulness, but in the suburbs a little patient, wise effort will soon tell upon the common life. The problem of obtaining safe sanitary conditions, good highways and first-class schools is simplified, because the area of treatment is so much reduced. There is no excuse for corporate corruption or for ring rule or for negligent administration of public office in the suburbs. And there are already growing up around the great cities scores of communities, characterized by civic pride and virtue, where the citizens as a body take pleasure in fostering the things that make life for all more rich and worth while. In proportion as this spirit gets more firmly rooted we shall expect not only an approximation to ideal conditions in the suburbs themselves, but a reflex action upon the cities.

For the great danger is that the self-complacent suburbanite will ignore his obligations to the city in which he spends his working hours and earns his daily bread. These obligations continue, even tho he is no longer a citizen of the metropolis. If he evades them he exposes himself to what Rev. Dr. Horton, of London, strikingly calls the "Curse of Suburbanity." Here is the city in whose marts of trade, skyward-reaching office buildings and halls of justice the suburbanite coins his dollar. Shall he and thousands like him, who swell the day population of the city, forget its needs and its just claims when he puts on his overcoat at five o'clock and hurries to the car, or meets his man at the corner, and drives in an elegant trap through beautiful boulevards to his country home? Does he ever stop to think of what he leaves behind him—not merely the grim buildings that keep their silent night watch until their day population comes again, not merely the concert halls and the great hotels and the palatial club houses—but left behind, too, are thousands of men and women and little children living night and day not in the fine houses uptown, but in alleys and rookeries?

Left behind, too, are churches and other agencies for good, weakened by the constant drift to the suburbs. Their field of operation has not been reduced; in fact, it has been increased and rendered also increasingly difficult by the incoming of foreign elements, whose need of education, evangelization and Americanization is great.

What attitude, then, shall the suburbanite take to the city of which he is by necessity still a part? Shall he look upon it simply as a favorable place in which to earn his daily bread—a place that he is well rid of when night comes? Shall he hurry by the slum section and never notice the bundles of rags and misery that now and then disfigure the street? Shall he consider it no concern of his whether or not the city which furnishes him and his children with a living be well governed, whether its streets are clean and its parks large enough for the thousands of people who are crowded into the tenement districts? Because he has become a suburbanite shall he cast off responsibility for the city and center all his interests and all his activities for his fellow men in the suburbs, where the chances are that he will have to go a good ways before he can find a destitute man?

Our ideal suburbanite is yet in the process of evolution. When he emerges he will blend the best traits of the pure city man and the pure country man. He will be like his grandfather, who kept a store in Ruralville in his simplicity, integrity and industry. He will be like his father, the great city merchant, in his firm grasp of large undertakings, in his appreciation of the world movements of the hour. But he will be better than either his father or grandfather. Subjected daily to the influences of both city and country, their constant play upon him will make him broad, symmetrical, responsive to life on all sides and alive to all life's obligations. His suburban home, all that is so bright and heavenly within it, the breath of the rose-bush that is climbing up his veranda, the flickering of the morning sunshine on the path, will strengthen him for the daily grapple with the problems that await him yonder in the noisy town. And every evening as he returns from toil he will bring to his family and his neighborhood much of the city's inspiration, so that they, too, will feel its thrill of life, and its call to strenuous labor while the day lasts.

SUBURBAN NIGHTMARE, *Frederick Allen*

IN 1954, Frederick Allen published an article titled
"Crisis in the Suburbs." Allen was a well-known
journalist and editor of *Harper's*, where
his article appeared. Facing what he called the
"auto age," Allen urged his readers
to accept the facts of modern life: "The days are
passing (if indeed they are not already
past) when one could think of a suburban town
outside one of our cities as a village in the
country. It would be much wiser today,
to think of it as a more or less comfortably spaced
residential area or residential and business
area within the greater metropolis." Thirty years
earlier he had made a previous discovery
about suburbs, which he reported in the next
selection—"Suburban Nightmare." Many
contemporary suburbanites are still
reacting, as Allen did in 1925.

I live in one of the most attractive suburbs of New York. It is built
on rolling hills, with belts of woodland and outcropping ledges; excellent
trains reach it in forty minutes from the city; the houses were mainly designed by architects, rather than contractors, with fortunate results; and
there is not a tenement, a three-decker, or a factory within its limits. The
house which I occupy looks out over several acres of open country, where
on a June evening one may walk beside a little brook and hear wood
thrushes singing in the thickets; and I can reach it from my office in a little
over an hour. It sounds idyllic, now, but my lease will soon come to an
end, and when I think of buying or building I find myself facing the problem which sooner or later confronts every New York commuter. The city
is growing too fast for us.

When the late Dr. Jowett was invited to come to New York to preach,
he asked for only a modest salary and a house "with a bit of green about
it," not realizing that on Manhattan Island only Mr. Frick and Mr. Morgan
and Mr. Schwab and two or three others can afford a bit of green. This is
one of the things for which people go out to the suburbs. They want air
that does not reek of motor exhaust, light instead of the grim shadow of
apartment houses, quiet instead of the clatter of riveters by day and the

Reprinted from *The Independent*, Vol. 114 (1925), 670–72.

squawk of taxicabs by night, neighbors whom they know and to whom their existence is not a matter of utter indifference, and a life whose tempo is less nerve-racking than that of the city. And some of them think it is not unreasonable to hope for still other benefits: for a measure of the informality of country life; for the sight of trees that grow as God intended, and of flowers that have the temerity to bloom outside of florists' shops; for a chance for their children to grow up knowing cows and robins by sight. The New York commuter can get these things now if he is lucky, and can, to some extent, continue to get if he is wealthy, but the odds are against him. The city is growing fast and is swallowing up the surrounding country.

Take our suburb as an example. It is growing like a boom town. Those who have lived in it for ten years are considered old inhabitants. When the trains from the city draw in at night, the crowds that swarm down on to the platform are nearly half as large again as they were a year ago. The price of land has doubled or tripled in five years. New houses are springing up everywhere, and bits of natural greenery, like that on which my windows look out, are doomed shortly for what the real-estate broker, in unconsciously ironic language, is pleased to call "improvement."

A few months ago there were four large tracts of open land, where one could ramble without interruption, within easy walking distance of my house. Last December, one of these tracts was sold to a real-estate corporation for more than a million dollars, and soon they will begin to cut streets through it, break it up into house lots, and make a village of it. They plan to build apartment houses, stores, a moving-picture theatre, and to bring in several thousand people, and they are somewhat surprised that we do not regard them as public benefactors for thus making the suburb bigger and busier.

The second tract was sold in January, also for "improvement." Real-estate men are bickering over the third, and the fourth will follow suit. The groves where we now look for anemones in spring will be sliced through with orderly little streets down which orderly little commuters will hurry to catch the seven-forty-eight train for town, while their wives look into each other's back windows and tell each other that you never would believe, my dear, what goings on there are at Mrs. So-and-So's, right in plain sight of everybody. On Sunday afternoons, the villagers can take their children walking along Woodcrest Avenue or Kenmont Street, but there will be no pastures studded with violets to stroll in, no tumbled stone walls to climb, no lanes to follow between the apple blossoms. An innocuous community with neat oblong gardens before the doors, but a standardized community which has lost the life of the country for that of the town.

Similar things are happening to nearly all the suburbs. Last November, the population of a nearby suburb increased overnight by three thousand. Several new apartment houses were thrown open and immediately filled. That suburb is getting to have a smart metropolitan air; prices, standards of living, and complexions are highly artificial. Recently, in another suburb, I was driving with a prosperous real-estate man. "Do you see that house?" he said to me. "Bought in 1920 for twenty-three thousand dollars and sold this year for thirty-seven. A clear profit of fourteen thousand, and the owner had the use of it all that time." He assured me that the values of houses were going up all over the town, despite frantic building, and referred to them as "homes"—which suggested an interesting problem in definition. A home, to me, is a place where you intend to stay—a century or two, perhaps. To my real-estate friend, a home was an investment (with incidental shelter value) to be turned over, when the market permitted, in order that your next investment might be more pretentious, revealing to all, by the amplitude of its sun porch and the dimensions of its two-car garage, that you were a man of importance and likely to move soon again.

Yet, who can build for permanence when the face of the land is changing so rapidly? You think of buying a house that gives on an open field, and you cannot foresee what will become of that field. You can be sure that it will not stay as it is. In ten years, you may have a view of a row of identical back yards, and a swarm of neighbors not even remotely of your own choosing. All sense of security for the future is lost. With such a gamble before you, is it any wonder that you are driven to think in terms of profitable investment?

Already, we hear our friends talking of "moving farther out." There are two ways of doing this. One is to go out to the outer fringes of our own suburb, where there are still open spaces, before you reach the outskirts of the string of suburbs along the next railroad line. Some people we know are trying these outer fringes. Yet there are disadvantages. Things are comparatively comfortable for those who can afford a chauffeur and two cars. But consider the plight of Mrs. M. who lives three miles from the station and, like most of us, has no chauffeur. She drives her husband to the morning train, meets him at night, drives her children to school, calls for them, drives her maid to the station, and drives miles to see her friends. She told me that in one day she had made twelve trips over those three miles of road. When asked to state her occupation, she wonders whether to say housewife or taxi driver. And even at this price she has little sense of security, for she does not know what sort of community will grow up about her.

To move to another suburb farther from New York means, for the man of the family, spending anywhere from three to four hours a day in travel. I often wonder who the champion commuter of New York is and how far he goes. He must live farther away than Philadelphia or New Haven, for the commuters from these places are numbered by the score.

Probably, he spends over five hours a day *en route;* say, a third of his waking time. If he keeps it up for thirty years, he will have given up ten solid years to reading newspapers in the jiggling light of a train, milling through crowds in subterranean corridors, and being half suffocated in subway cars. Thousands of New York commuters give more than four hours a day to this ordeal, in order that they may have a home not too far from station and store and school, but still in the quiet country.

People speak of improved methods of transportation as though they would solve the problem. They will alter its terms, but how can they solve it? For example, every seat in our commutation trains is now taken and crowds standing in the aisles. No more trains can be run safely on our two tracks at the rush hours, but if the railroad could four-track the line, that would mean faster service, especially for those farther out. But as soon as the service is speeded up, suburbs will become more desirable and the crowds will increase. Never was a circle more vicious. Furthermore, the terminal station cannot handle many more trains, and there is talk of dumping suburban passengers at a new commuters' terminal uptown and wedging them into a proposed subway which will run to Wall Street and the Battery. To anybody who knows what New York subways are like, the prospect is not exhilarating. And when the subway becomes overcrowded, what next?

This is not a New York problem only. It has merely reached New York first. It will soon be as bad in Chicago, though Chicago has more directions to expand in. It will confront other American cities in time, unless the trend of modern life changes. So long as the rush to the cities continues, the movement into the suburbs to escape the turmoil of city life can only defeat its own end.

THE CATHOLIC SUBURBANITE,
Andrew M. Greeley

> THESE passages, written by a Catholic priest who is
> also a sociologist, vividly reflect his perspective
> on suburban life as he tries to transmit his version of it
> to Catholics who live in the suburbs. It bears
> a distinct family resemblance to views
> expressed by suburban religious officials of other
> faiths, especially during the past two decades.

Fifteen years ago, it was fashionable to speak of the days of the
"brick and mortar" priest as something of the dim and distant past. The
period of great construction projects was thought to be over for the Church
in the United States. A plateau had been reached. Today, however, many
a suburban pastor, saddled with a small church, a big debt, a big school,
and a bigger population, must longingly wish that the prophets had been
right. A good part of the Catholic population is moving to the suburbs.
Most Catholics are aware of the immense physical problems involved in
the Church's keeping up with this migration. But few realize to what
extent Suburbia represents a decisive turning point in the history of the
American Church.

We have been, until recently, the Church of the working class. As late
as 1946, 66 per cent of the Catholic population could be classed as members of the lower class (as opposed to less than 45 per cent for most
Protestant groups in the same class). A generation ago, the vast majority
of Catholics were either immigrants who had come in the last tidal wave
of arrivals before World War I or the children of such immigrants. Common labor in the steel mills, stockyards, and construction gangs was the
original occupation of the immigrant. Some of his children inched up the
ladder and became policemen, firemen, workers in public utilities and
transportation. A very few began to achieve success in law, medicine, and
politics.

The situation is changing rapidly. Signs of the change could have
been detected in the 1930's, but the Depression arrested its development.
Since World War II, however, the educational benefits of the G. I. Bill,
the social revolution of the '30's, and the booming Cold War prosperity

From *The Church and the Suburbs* by Andrew M. Greeley. © Sheed and Ward,
Inc., 1959, pp. 51–60. Used by permission.

have caused a profound modification in the fabric of American Catholic life. A great many Catholics are leaving behind their working-class and immigrant roots and becoming successful members of the rapidly expanding middle class. Tens of thousands of young Catholic college graduates have moved into the professions and are becoming an important part of the life of the nation. As a symbol and a summary of this great change, Catholics are moving to the suburbs.

The social and psychological problems arising from the extension of the Church into the suburbs are complex and frightening. There are those who would lament that our boast of being the Church of the poor and laboring is no longer totally accurate. (For that matter, the laboring—if they belong to a militant union—are not likely to be poor in this day and age.) Certainly we must make every attempt to keep a strong working-class base in our Church by trying to convert the new, and largely non-white, lower class. But we must also face the deep and tangled problems that many Catholics are encountering as they become suburbanites.

First of all, there is the problem of the material prosperity of Suburbia. The Church, of course, has never condemned as such the possession of the goods of this world. On the contrary, she has affirmed that a certain moderate comfort is a distinct help to salvation. Nor has the Church opposed the improvements of the age of technology. The Church is not against the machine, atomic energy, or automation. But the problem for the Catholic suburbanite is more subtle. Our national prosperity is based on a constantly expanding economy. Last year may have been a good year, but if this year is not better than last it will be a bad year. The sale of four million automobiles would have been staggeringly good several years ago. This year it would mean a severe depression. If our economy is to remain healthy, it must constantly produce and sell more goods.

If more goods are to be bought, however, more people must feel they need them. So our economy is geared to constantly expanding human needs; and our advertising is fashioned to create these needs. Yesterday's luxuries become today's necessities. What is an interesting novelty today will be a part of the American way of life tomorrow. A car whose design was "years ahead of its time" two years ago is now, from the fashion point of view, obsolete. If the nation is to continue prosperous, its people must want more, more, more.

Such an economic situation may not be in itself an evil. But we have no experience in the ways of harmonizing an expanding-need culture with the traditional teachings of Christian frugality, with the spirit of poverty. It may be possible to want more, more, more and still not lay up treasures in this world where the moth consumes and rust destroys. It may be possible to give no overanxious heed to what we should eat, or what we should drink, or what we should put on when the mass media proclaim in full color that they can array us with greater glory and equip us with greater power than was Solomon's. It may be possible to sit in an air-conditioned ranch-house and watch a color-television set and still not be attached to the things of this world. It may, in short, be possible to harmonize the world of the gadget and the world of the spirit. All these things are possible, but they are not easy.

The Catholic suburbanite is not a crass materialist. He does not pile up possessions for mere love of wealth. He is extremely generous to all sorts of charitable endeavors. He will spare no expense to provide a Catholic education for his large and growing family. He is, in all likelihood, more fervent in his religious duties than were his parents. He is probably an active parishioner and by his own lights an excellent Christian. In fact, he and his fellows have, it would seem, reached a level of *observable religious practice* seldom, if ever, surpassed by a large group of people in the history of the Church.

But the problem of reconciling the gadget and the spirit remains to be solved. In fact, the suburbanite Catholic is hardly aware that the problem exists. So he looks around at his great material wealth (and great it is, by almost any standards that mankind ever knew) and wonders whether his dream house is not getting small, whether he should not get a station wagon with push-button transmission, whether he should not perhaps air-condition the whole house, and whether it's not time to get a power lawn mower or join the local country club. It does not occur to him that such anxieties might interfere with his seeking first the Kingdom of God and His justice.

With prosperity and abundance there comes a second problem for the suburban Catholic. He is a successful, educated, and independent man. True enough, his future may be at the mercy of all sorts of forces out of his control; but he prides himself on the fact that he is a free American and makes his own decisions. His faith is real, but it is by no means the legendary simple faith of the Breton fisherman or the somewhat less simple faith of his immigrant grandmother. He has been taught to question things and to ask why. His priests are no longer the only educated, or even necessarily the best-educated, men in the community. There are a number of people who are capable of assuming the traditional place of the pastor as the single social leader of the neighborhood. The suburbanite feels free to disagree with his clergy on certain procedural matters and to do so forcefully and persistently.

This is not to say that he is anticlerical, but only that the social relationship between the clergy and the laity is changing as an inevitable result of the changing social structure of the world the American Catholic lives in. As one priest sociologist has observed, from the social viewpoint the pastor can no longer afford to be the unquestioned ruler, but now must, if he wishes to be effective, play the role of a quarterback who calls the signals and then co-operates with the rest of the team in the execution of the play.

This subtle change in the accidental structure of the clergy-laity relationship is merely a manifestation of a deeper problem Catholic Suburbia poses. The suburbanite, for all his conformity to the demands of the social groups to which he belongs, is more than a little skeptical of naked authority. "The Church says so" has ceased to be an all-powerful argument. As Father John Thomas has pointed out, the rational foundations of faith and the logical connections between dogmatic beliefs and specific moral imperatives must be made crystal-clear if American Catholics are to be convinced. If an executive of a large corporation cannot be treated in the same fashion as his grandfather, it would follow that something more than the Baltimore Catechism is required for a graduate of a college and professional school.

No one would claim that, absolutely speaking, such changes have to be made; the word of the Church on dogma and discipline is still final. But in the area of sound psychology and effective administration, gradual changes seem inevitable. Authority will not be diminished. It will merely be used in a different way in different times. Progress in this area of the tension between authority and independence is being made, rapidly. Both the clergy and their suburbanite congregations seem patient and eager to learn. But only an incurable optimist would believe that some frictions are not bound to occur as a new relationship between priest and people grows in the suburbs.

A third difficulty facing the Church in the suburbs may be, in the long run, the most perplexing. For in the suburb the Catholic is regarded, at last, as a full-fledged American. The ghetto walls are crumbling. The old national parishes are breaking up. The Catholic suburbanite rides the same commuter train, wears the same brand of suit, reads the same paper, and does the same kind of work as does his non-Catholic neighbor. He may not be completely accepted by Protestants; but he is well on his way. Thirty years ago most non-Catholics were horrified at the thought of Al Smith as President; today many were willing to admit an admiration for Senator John F. Kennedy. Suburbia, with its conglomeration of nationalities and religions, seems the ultimate melting pot. In the externals of life there is little to distinguish the Catholic suburbanite from his Protestant neighbor. Even such old criteria as large families or regular Sunday attendance at church have ceased to be significant.

This Americanization of the immigrant groups is a good thing; but is not an unmixed blessing. Catholics can accept much of the American way of life with little hesitation; but in certain matters—birth control, divorce, and premarital sex experience, for example—we must part company with many Americans. In national parishes and the old neighborhoods, Catholics were somewhat insulated from the infection of pagan influences. In the suburbs they are in the main line of the enemy's fire. This is not to argue that we should retreat into our ghetto. We could not if we wanted to. But the fact must be faced that the suburban Catholic could become *too* American. There is some danger that he will begin to share the common American notion that one religion is practically as good as another. When this happens, he has ceased to be much of a Catholic, no matter how American he may be.

The problems are complex and serious. There are no simple solutions. If the problems are great, however, so also are the opportunities. The Catholic with his doctrine of the Mystical Body may well be able to develop in the suburbs a spirituality which will end the secularism separating the world of the spirit from the world of the gadget. The educated, independent, suburbanite parishioner could become a zealous, dedicated lay apostle bearing witness to the Word of God in areas the priest could never reach.

It is too early to predict the exact shape suburban Catholicism will take. Its techniques and methods are still new and vague. They are being worked out by the system of trial and error, but the final product may well be considerably different from the Catholicism we were used to ten years ago. New things are beginning to stir in the American Church; and we do not know where they will end. The Liturgical Movement, the Catholic Action organizations, Adult Education programs—all hold great promise.

.   .   .   .

There is a considerable amount of controversy as to whether, in the long run, the suburban migration is a good thing for the Church. Such controversy seems pointless. As in all social changes, there are elements of good and bad mixed in a tangled skein. Whether the net result will show the good outbalancing the bad can be determined only by the historians of the future; but what the net result will be depends, under God, on the free will of men. If one tries to survey Catholic Suburbia with some objectivity, one can find many reasons for a cautious hope.

SUGGESTED READINGS: CHAPTER 14

Bennett Berger. *Working-Class Suburb*. Berkeley: University of California, 1960.

> A study made during the period when Americans, including social scientists, were talking rather loosely about suburbs as if they were locales only for middle-class inhabitants.

William Dobriner (Ed.). *The Suburban Community*. New York: G. P. Putnam's, 1958.

A collection of numerous articles about suburbs and suburban life. One can easily discern considerable rhetoric about suburban developments amid presentations of the facts of the suburban movement.

William Dobriner, *Class in Suburbia*. Englewood Cliffs, N. J.: Prentice-Hall, 1963.

A thoughtful study that explores the role of class and ethnicities, the increasing heterogeneity within suburbs, the significant differences among suburbs, and the growing economic interdependence between suburban areas and central cities. Two contrasting examples of suburbs are discussed in detail: Levittown, a mass-produced suburb, and "old Harbour," which has reluctantly changed from a village to a suburb.

John Seely, R. Sim, and E. Loosely. *East Crestwood Heights*. New York: Basic Books, 1956.

An elaborate study of a well-to-do suburb of Toronto, with especially rich materials on styles of life. A Canadian sociologist has recently remarked that Crestwood was not "really" a suburb when it was studied, but it certainly evidenced many of the traits then being attributed to the hectic-paced, middle-class suburb.

15

Tourists at "Work": Fisherman's Wharf, San Francisco.
San Francisco Chamber of Commerce photo.

VISITORS:
FUN AND ESTHETICS

AN enduring perspective on the city, as noted earlier in the
discussion of urban novels, is the city as a feast—
a place that provides great enjoyment to natives and visitors alike.
Cities vary greatly in the kinds of joy-giving images they evoke.
Some cities are noted for their visual beauty, some for
their museums, some for their colorful street scenes, and
some for their night life—these are only a few variants
of this urban perspective. The literature written for
and by tourists and travelers particularly evokes such images.
Quite understandably, these latter ideas may strike the native
resident as unreal, or at least as not genuinely representative of
the true essence of his city.

The social science literature bearing on urban fun and
esthetic enjoyment is not very voluminous. There is, of course,
a considerable and growing interest in the "problems
of leisure" in an affluent urban nation—but how
that leisure bears on what people do and think when they live
in or visit cities has yet to be studied extensively.
Curiously enough, we have more and better information about
what happens in vice areas, whether the visitors are
out-of-towners or citizens of the city, than about almost any
other kind of urban fun. Naturally we have that
information because vice is a traditional urban problem, rather

than because of a genuine interest in the sociology
of those institutions or their visitors. It is also remarkable how
little attention has been given, except by those most directly
concerned, to other urban institutions which are related
to fun and enjoyment: museums and symphony
concerts, for instance. We do have studies of movie and mass
media consumership, but again the research focus is
predominately on consumership as a social problem. As for
urban esthetics, there is precious little, a recent
exception being the exploratory research of an architect and
city planner, Kevin Lynch, who discovered that,
even in much maligned Los Angeles, the citizens as
they drive to work customarily enjoy unsuspectedly
interesting features of the urban landscape.

The specific selections presented below are intended
especially to highlight both the paucity of our
knowledge about fun and esthetic appreciation in the city and
the rich data that could be easily obtained
either through interviews or use of the library. Some earlier
selections are equally relevant to these purposes, for
instance, those on Towertown, Skid Row, and
the Norwegians of New York City.

RENO: SPECIALIZATION AND FUN,
Lucius Beebe

LIKE Las Vegas, Reno is a specialized city whose
trademark is "fun." Visitors flock to such
a locale for one purpose only: to
enjoy themselves in accordance with the types of
fun provided by the city, whose services
are manned either by big-time operators who
know how to provide fun for money or
by natives who have learned how to work at this
kind of trade. Beebe, like other visitors who
have interviewed the natives, has discovered that they
may learn to live with the less than savory image
projected to the nation by their city.

In Reno, Nevada, a community variously celebrated as one of the last outposts of the Old West (which it is) and as the divorce capital of the universe (which it isn't), there is an element known as the see-our-schools-and-churches group. These worthy folk deplore Reno's fame for its glittering night life and social nip-ups and make a practice of button-holing visiting firemen, especially writers, with entreaties to depict Reno as a normal, wholesome American community.

Tell the world about the University of Nevada's ever-growing enrollment, they implore, or the swelling deposits in the swaggering quarter-of-a-billion-dollar First National Bank, but forget Harolds Club and the nocturnal traps that flourish, raw and neon-lit, in town and for miles on U.S. 395 and South Virginia Road.

What the schools-and-churches group fails to understand is that these conventional, conservative qualities are a commonplace elsewhere in the land and that people don't come to Nevada to see more of the same. They visit Reno to get away from precisely these things and to find a relaxed, uninhibited way of life.

Largely, they find it, too, which is just as well, for without the tourist trade Nevada would soon be bankrupt.

The classic example of what visitors want of Reno—and one that causes head shaking among the schools-and-churches contingent—is the

Excerpted from "Reno," *Holiday,* Vol. 24 (November, 1958), 91–92, 166, 169.
Reprinted by permission.

spanking-new Holiday Hotel which glitters decorously beside the Truckee River.

The Holiday was opened two years ago by Norman Blitz, Reno money-bag and real-estate operator who has been called the Duke of Nevada. In what his associates considered a moment of whimsy, Mr. Blitz opened with no gambling on the premises except the ubiquitous slot machines which no one in Nevada considers games of chance anyway. Gambling or no gambling, people noticed, however, that although the Holiday was conspicuously devoid of craps and roulette, it was laid out so that it could open a full-time casino at a moment's notice should the management change its mind.

The hotel was advertised as a place where visitors who disapproved of gambling wouldn't have to encounter it. As a result, patrons stayed away in droves. Even visitors who didn't gamble, it soon appeared, wanted the cheerful twenty-four-hour-a-day tumult of a casino around them. A Nevada hotel without gambling depressed the customers beyond all endurance.

Having proved his point to the satisfaction of everybody save the schools-and-churches element, Mr. Blitz then leased the property with option to buy to Newt Crumley, a hotel man of long experience, retaining a prudent and substantial interest for himself, and the hotel promptly reopened with games past all counting. Overnight the Holiday achieved what the French call a success foolish and now you can't fight your way through the customers happily rolling snake-eyes and pushing chips onto green in the Holiday casino.

The whole episode had a profoundly depressing effect on the schools-and-churches partisans.

Reno's population of 52,000 wouldn't rate passing mention in Ohio or Pennsylvania, and Nevada's estimated one hundred millionaires, most of whom live in and around Reno, would be considered laughable in Texas. Nevertheless, the average Reno resident finds life in the One Sound State, as Nevada likes to call itself because of its absence of any trace of public debt, eminently satisfactory. The average income in Nevada in recent years has been either the highest or second highest in the United States. Life is easy and good in Reno.

Some residents might be hard put to find expression of the fact, but everyone takes satisfaction in being heirs—only slightly removed—to the traditions and spacious way of life of the Old West. Less than half a century ago the last great gold rushes in the continental United States at Goldfield and Tonopah saw Reno swaggering in bonanza. Look from the picture windows of the Sky Room at the Mapes, and on three sides you see the seemingly illimitable reaches of the Great American Desert, a perpetual reminder of the elsewhere-vanished frontier; on the fourth the snow-topped Sierra Nevada rears a last continental barrier between the rest of the United States and California the Golden. There are Stetsons and the broad plainsman's hats known locally as Mormons in the hat racks of the city's hotels. It is difficult to escape a consciousness of the West of only yesterday wherever you go in Reno. Being West as hell is easily the city's greatest asset. It dwarfs all other aspects of the community to insignificance.

Oddly enough, Reno businessmen, save those involved in tourism, display a curious lack of enthusiasm for the state's largest and, indeed, almost only industry of considerable dimensions. And residents of the city never tire of telling the rest of the world that Renoites themselves seldom frequent the town's pleasure palaces. Yet they can hardly wait for a visiting fireman who must be taken on the grand tour. This permits the native to insist at length that he is proof against the blandishments of sin while experiencing them to the fullest.

Visitor and native, on such a tour, will find that the old-fashioned gambling games of the West—faro, rondo coolo, chuck-a-luck and fan-tan—have largely disappeared from the Reno casinos. . . .

Aside from its spurious repute as a divorce center, the most celebrated thing about Reno is Harolds Club, a monstrous perpetual-motion department store of chance that has been made a national institution by some 2300 highway signs in such distant places as U.S. Route 1 in Florida or on the same route outside Bangor, Maine. Harolds is the first thing visitors want to see. It's the largest casino in the state, a philanthropic agency of formidable dimensions and a tourist trap through whose gaudy portals 20,000 visitors pass to pay tribute each summer day.

Occupying a seven-story building in North Virginia Street, Harolds employs more than 1000 specialists, including roulette spinners, dice throwers, barmen, engineers, repairmen, decorators. . . .

Over the years it has given millions of dollars in scholarships at the University of Nevada, one of the provisions being that no Harolds scholar may enter Harolds Club; at improbable times it doubles all pay-offs on winning bets—and almost singlehandedly it finances every important civic project in the Reno community, including the Reno Chamber of Commerce. Sponsors of philanthropies, legitimate or suspect, turn to Harolds with such regularity that a full-time staff of lawyers and investigators is maintained to screen requests.

.   .   .   .

In the normal run of events the overwhelming bulk of revenue at Harrah's and Harolds, as in other popular resorts in downtown Reno, derives from slot machines and relatively small-time players in such unsophisticated games as craps and blackjack. . . .

TOKYO: ENJOYMENT PLUS ADDITIONAL MEANINGS, *Yoshie Egawa*

SOME years ago (1955), a young woman from
Tokyo wrote a paper for a graduate class
in sociology at the University of Chicago. The paper
bore the title: "Images of Tokyo by
Foreign Visitors." Parts of her paper are reprinted
here. Miss Egawa based her analysis on a
reading of magazine articles by Americans about
Tokyo. We need not be concerned with
the accuracy of her analysis: it was quite
sufficient for underlining some kinds of enjoyment
which Tokyo affords American visitors.
In addition, the city seems to arouse certain
other images derived from the experiences
of Americans with their own country and own lives,
including images of modernity versus
traditionalism, continuity versus discontinuity, and
quiet ruralism versus an all too disturbing
urbanism. In her paper, Miss Egawa also comments
on Americans' images of Tokyo: so that we
get the effect of a mirror which mirrors a mirror.
[I have not been able to locate Miss Egawa so that I
might both thank her for the use of her paper and
apologize for the occasional liberties taken with her not
yet quite accurate use of English prose.—ED.]

"To a visitor from the Far West, Tokyo presents two possibilities of interest which are inexhaustible: opportunities of getting thoroughly lost, and an almost unlimited element of novelty." This opening phrase from "In the Streets of Tokyo" (*Outlook,* September 29, 1913) . . . pictures the first shock and the following state of mind of a foreign visitor to Tokyo, especially people of Western origin. . . . The same writer goes on to describe:

In these large features, Tokyo has the interest of a novelty so radical that it is doubtful if it ever quite fades even from the sight of the foreigner who has made the old town his home. Novelty sometimes lies in degree of difference from the things to which one is accustomed; in Tokyo it lies not in degree but in kind. . . . Between the Occidental and the Japanese city there is a fundamental difference of outline and of detail.

What then are the categories Westerners draw on to describe this strange city? How do they perceive our city?

Looking at these articles, it seems apparent that "contrast" is made in a hackneyed vocabulary. Their first shock of novelty is thus the contrast of East and West or ancient and modern. . . . Equally obvious to us is that on the whole the foreign view is inevitably biased in some degree by preconceived stereotyped images of Japan, unmistakably out-of-date at any period. . . . Although the content of these stereotyped images need not be as simple and unsophisticated as this: "In the eyes of some foreigners— especially those who have never been here—it is a sugary land of cherry blossom and Cho-Cho-Sans, heaving long sighs in the shade of twisted pines over the infidelities of imaginary Pinkertons—a country where . . . kimono-clad figures live in paper houses with quaint gardens and mossy steps." *(Ibid.)* None of their views are independent of that sort of influence. To cite an instance, a war correspondent on his way to Korea stopped overnight in Tokyo and made a sketch of a street scene, absurdly and unrealistically drawing the shape of Japanese houses and the style of childrens' hairdos to meet the images and expectations of what a Japanese street would be like for magazine readers in his homeland. Likewise, pho- tographic evidence of Japanese ritualism well labelled as medieval, or some survivals of the pure East, is fondly snapped by foreign observers either out of curiosity or nostalgic sentiment. . . .

In every article, both new and old, a dominant category used to describe Tokyo is the contrast of East and West, and ancient and modern, as if by common consent, though the entanglement of these four elements is not at once intelligible to us from the different culture. "The contrast between old and new, which is frequently another version of the contrast between what is traditional and what is Western, is written into many aspects of Tokyo" ("Berlin and Tokyo," *Japan Quarterly,* 1955). Or "since the opening of travel to Japan, there is perhaps no place in the world where the East and the West mix more than in the capital" ("Tokyo," *Overland Monthly,* January, 1910). There are similar sentences in other articles too numerous to mention. Also, unfailingly the first and most impressive contrast is caused by "the architectural beauty smack in the middle of Tokyo. . . . Here, concrete office buildings form a modern backdrop for the bridges and parks of the ancient Imperial Palace, which stands among beautifully landscaped lawns and fragrant, lotus-filled moats" ("I've Got a Yen for Japan," *American Magazine,* 1955). This contrast is never so striking to the eyes of our Japanese natives, for whom co-existence and mixture of these elements seems to be harmonized through time. This kind of contrast is not of course confined to the physical appearance of the city but most amazingly is found in the intricacy of the city life itself. "In Tokyo, there is no frontier, and the contrasts are everywhere. They are those of ancient and Modern Japan, as closely interwoven in the life of a huge city as they are in that of each individual" ("Berlin and Tokyo," *op. cit.*). . . .

What appears beautiful and what looks ugly are worth noting. Despite personal differences in taste, foreigners unanimously agree on choosing places where the pure East presents itself as a beautiful spot. This Oriental beauty is nothing but the appreciation of natural beauty which is absolutely rid of any tint of artificiality. "Tokyo is not beautiful, though it has localities of great beauty; parks of great age and of a mysterious and impressive charm. Modern Japan is finding in its ancient temple-grounds parks which have a quality distilled by time, which no skill of the landscape artist can overtake and capture by the swift methods of to-day" *(Ibid.)*. In the same way, they admire the grove which is not planted but grows naturally. "In Tokyo itself there is a wonderful grove of trees of most curious contorted shapes, which are much admired and well hung with poems at the proper season" ("Tokyo," *Chatauqua*, 1904). The Japanese garden, likewise, is a chief attraction because of its natural beauty. Even in the midst of the city they have this pleasure: "Sometimes, if a gate or door stands open, one may get a glimpse of one of those charming gardens which enshrine silence and privacy in the crowded capital" *(Outlook, op. cit.)*. Or "Tempting and strange as these sights were, my greatest pleasure was exploring the lonely private gardens that abound in Japan" *(American Magazine, op. cit.)*. So the old shrines and temples scattered around the city are their resting places where they can easily get lost in Oriental charm. . . . "One afternoon I discovered a shadowy temple set back from the busy street, and I entered the quiet, tree-lined refuge to rest on a simple stone bench" *(Ibid.)*. Notice the encounter of the East which happens quite abruptly or utterly unexpectedly. . . .

The difference between the crowded business sections and the tranquil semi-rural districts lying to the north and north-west is paid attention. "Varied styles of architecture, many of them grotesque and entirely out of keeping with the general aspect, are perhaps the main feature of the business section and there is a superficial air of Westernization about the buildings and the people in the streets. All this, however, changes as soon as the quiet of the suburban districts is reached, picturesque Japanese-style wooden dwellings taking the place of the great eight-storied reinforced-concrete office buildings and of the three-storied stucco-fronted atrocities, which are such an eyesore in many parts of the city" ("Tokyo" *Nineteenth Century*, no date). This writer ends up in praise of the semi-rural parts of the city with their traditional Japanese-style houses. . . .

Cultural contrasts in the Tokyo streets, however, much more excite their interest and awaken curiosity, though by no means separable from the physical appearance and layout of the streets. Let me quote what is East to most foreign visitors. The alfresco mode of living which overflows into the street. Various features of it stimulate their interest because of dissimilarities with Western street scenes. "Street life and street crafts have survived in Tokyo while in the West (in particular in the States) they have almost all been swept away" *(Berlin and Tokyo, op. cit.).* Another observer makes a pointed observation: "The Tokyo street is a drawing room, restaurant, playground, workshop, and public thoroughfare combined—as in Italy where the skies also are blue and homes small and overcrowded." . . .

Perhaps a still more characteristic trait of the foreigner's view can be detected in an attitude toward the changing phases of the city. Undoubtedly the riddle of a newborn product of cultural fusion must be the main attraction, a pregnant stimulus because all is blurred in the necessity and chance of a unique cultural situation. Yet we Japanese perceive clearly their mixture of praise and regret to every pace and phase of our changing city culture, either for its great strides toward Western conveniences or for its loss of ancient grace. The Great Westerner thus is our teacher, our parent, and a friend who is a little jealous, superior in his full-fledged civilization but with an incurable inferiority complex to our littleness, pretty shapes and gracious decorum, whose watchful eye is full of ambivalence and easily beguiled by the façade of our cultural complexity.

Yet their expectancies for the emergence of a new Tokyo culture are full of hopeful opinion, with some idealistic views of what the Oriental city must be like. That is, I guess, the main reason why they are rather patient of any shapelessness or naughtiness this city ofttimes gets into, just like actions of a growing child are sometimes seen as inevitable—though at the moment it is unknown to foreigners in what way and into what this cultural confusion will finally settle. A recent article says:

> Tokyo is still in the middle of a glorious post-Treaty binge. Without some appreciation of what release and independence meant to the Japanese, we can scarcely make a fair assessment of what is happening in Tokyo today. In the circumstances, it is rather silly to keep wagging a Western finger at all this Tokyo naughtiness, or to wax pious over the nudist camps that have replaced the traditional Japanese theatre. Some time will have to pass before Tokyo can proclaim its intentions. After the binge will come the hangover, then the period of remorse and reaction, and then, we hope, the social compromise that will blend democracy with moderation. . . . As a sketchy summing up, today's print of Tokyo could not possibly indicate how the colors will finally set. Many of the gaudier hues will be toned down, if not actually shaded out, and the ultimate art form will depend a great deal on the influence of rival schools abroad" ("New Tokyo," *This Is Japan,* 1954).

Among the articles in an earlier issue of another magazine, a similar point: "In Tokyo the West has met the East, and out of civilization, in which the ideals of the two hemispheres are fusing" ("Tokyo Today," *Geography*

Magazine, 1932). These sanguine views of the city's culture make it possible to prevent jumping at a conclusion drawn from superficial cultural cosmetics and to wait for the appearance of a real Tokyo. . . .

> Of course a million things are wrong with Tokyo, and every wrong thing was contributed by the West, none the less so because Young Tokyo appears to have taken to it all with a bewildering gusto. How, with the ancient dignified amenities of the geisha system, the new Japanese can put up with this hybrid culture is one more perplexing aspect of the Mysterious Orient. Of course the place is knee-deep in anomalies; what would they matter if the fundamental norm were not so splendid and desirable. Japan is superb because it is reasonable, and tranquil and austere and civilized; it must be granted its aberrations. Japan has shown her skill at adaptation, how she can absorb a technique or a method and improve on it. If the post-war Tokyo has created itself in the image of an Oriental Milwaukee, it is that much easier to live in, if only because the spirit that inhabits it is Japanese. ("Is this Japan?" *Japan Quarterly,* 1956)

But equally there is that nostalgic sentimentality toward the loss of beautiful sights of the East for the sake of modernizing the city life. "Today Tokyo is a city of broad streets, of many splendid buildings, of spacious parks. For the tourist it has lost much of its charm; but, after all, it belongs to the Japanese" *(Geography Magazine, op. cit.).* In another magazine: "Of such losses the picturesqueness of old Yedo is certainly one. Modern Tokyo grows year by year more western, and less beautiful, and a great deal easier to live in. . . . Assuredly one must rejoice, and yet—one has the feeling that one used to have when one's best kitten grew up into a big clumsy cat. Can beauty and convenience never learn to live together?" *(Chatauqua, op. cit.).* The last question seems to be a problem which inevitably comes to the Western mind. But is this same question posed by Westerners while confronting the prodigious change of Western cities? And do they always feel a nostalgic reminiscence for the vicissitudes of Western cities in their straight-line process of modernization? . . . [But] old Japan and its cultural seat of Tokyo [can be] conceived as closer to the first principles of civilization than the new Japan and the new face of Tokyo.

> If, as I believe, the first aim of a wise civilization should be to increase the average individual's opportunities of rational happiness, then the old Japan was nearer to wisdom than the new. . . . In the streets of Tokyo to-day, as in Glasgow or Chicago or Berlin, the "progress which is measured by statistics" has produced, and is producing, material and spiritual ugliness. There has been, no doubt, a notable advance in the experience and machinery of life, but it is an advance not only unaccom-

panied by any indication of increased happiness and morality, but one which reveals in itself many symptoms of unrest and discontent. ("Tokyo Revisited," *Scribner's, 1921*)

Missing the things gone in the city, an old lane or an obliterated street corner, is by no means a sentiment peculiar to the stranger from the West, but his longing for lost street scenes might differ from ours since he lacks a cultural background—if not wanting in some historical knowledge and perspectives about this city. This means that foreigners may possibly indulge in more flights of fantasy, projecting their yearnings for the tranquility of soul (which seems to be a psychic need for them). This nostalgia quite often may surpass the notion of necessary reform in modern city life, which is an unavoidable problem to native citizens living in the maelstrom of the flowing tide of Western culture. The foreigners, thus, often take a position of conservatism and oppose even the changes necessary in our city for modernization.

OCCUPATIONAL TOURISTRY, *Ruth Pape*

CERTAIN occupations offer splendid possibilities for
visiting cities that are exciting. In the
following paper, a perceptive nurse offers some
conclusions, based on her research,
about the structural conditions that permit
a period of "touristry" for young nurses.

Every year millions of working Americans are on the move. Summer only brings an increase in the year-round tide of vacationers who travel within the confines of their two, three or four weeks off from the job. Only the very wealthy can maintain a permanent vacationer status, although the retired or unemployed may be able to cover as much territory while bumming around. Besides the vacationers, however, there are travelers who are making more or less permanent migrations in search of a better job, a better climate or a better neighborhood. Some also are following migratory jobs, as in agriculture, or intermittently migratory ones, as with lumbering or construction work. There are even some occupations into which travel is built as a requisite feature, as in the transportation indus-

Excerpted from "Touristry: A Type of Occupational Mobility," *Social Problems,* 11 (1964), 336–37, 339, 340–42. Reprinted by permission of the Society for the Study of Social Problems.

try, the Foreign Service and the military. But this is hardly voluntary mobility for, when the Navy invites a young man to see the world, the itinerary is hardly of his own choosing.

But there is a group of people who do work, who travel more or less where and when they please, who seem never to have been described or analyzed in the literature of geographic or occupational mobility. Well-known to despairing employment agencies and employers, these people are practicing what I choose to call "touristry," a form of journeying that depends upon occupation, but only in a secondary sense in that it finances the more primary goal, travel itself. Performing a highly-demanded service which is easily documented, either by a transferable license or by relatively simple tests, they are able to spend a longer time at touring than a simple vacation would allow by merely taking a job in the area they wish to sample and keeping it only as long as features unrelated to the job continue to be attractive.

.   .   .   .

PRESENT EMPLOYMENT CONDITIONS

Nurses who wish to travel now have many alluring choices. Air and shiplines, the Peace Corps, and the armed services all stress exotic foreign service. But for those less willing to submit to the accompanying time restrictions and commitments, there is still the self-planned and self-limited route of touristry. It is true that there are some countries where it is not possible or desirable to work (so that nurses would wish to save for a *bona fide* vacation to go there), but more and more nurses are finding ways to extend their touristry even beyond national boundaries.

That nurses turn their licenses almost directly into travel tickets may be seen in the recruiting advertisements in almost any nursing journal. Beside the usual details of salary, installation description and fringe benefits, may be found frequent references to the local attractions either present or within easy range. Whether these are effective or not, hospitals in metropolitan areas are often largely staffed by nurses who come not only from other locales but other states and countries as well.

For many years it has been common knowledge that there is an almost universal shortage of nurses. Hawaii is presently the only state that does not need, in various stages of desperation, every nurse that can be attracted. California, for example, must recruit roughly 75% of its work-force from nurses trained outside the state. It is no wonder then that the process of establishing licensure has been made as efficient and painless as possible, reportedly making it possible for a nurse with sufficient and adequate documents to begin work after only "a few minutes" at the office of the California Board of Nurse Examiners. Even those whose transcripts must be sent for may work in the interim with an easily obtained temporary license. Within nursing, California, along with New York, is noted for having the most stringent requirements for graduate nurses.

.   .   .   .

INITIATION OF THE TOURISTRY PATTERN

Although nursing students do not often give it as a reason for going into nursing, possibly the easy transferability of practice may be one of those secondary selling points that draw a large number of travel-minded girls into nursing schools. As graduation approaches, among the growing and sharpening fantasies of goals for the students are the shared dreams of where they will go. The potential tourists become aware of mutual interests and thus may band together to prepare for their trip. At graduation, the girls are restrained only by the need to take and pass their licensing examinations, then to earn enough money to get wherever they plan to go and pay a month's rent when they get there. Whenever this is accomplished, the touristry-bent nurse bursts onto the employment market in earnest, not only ready to leave her childhood status but also her childhood neighborhood, at least as far as the years in the schooling area have made this represent it.

The rates and timing may vary but graduation usually sees a number of newly married girls who have gone directly on with the traditional feminine mode, thus skipping over the interim of independence and irresponsibility. At this stage, few girls plan to remain unmarried, unless they are committed to religious goals, are far older than the usual, or are settled into a pattern of deviance that does not include marriage. Many young graduate nurses report, however, that although they fully expect to marry, it is not part of their immediate plans and they can well imagine working the two years that statistically fall between a girl's coming onto and leaving the labor market for the first time.

These are the girls who say they are not yet ready for marriage, who want to see something else before they settle down, but who are also willing to admit that marriage may come along any moment and change those ideas. These are the nurses who may be seen working in many of our metropolitan hospitals with only a few months' working experience behind them, usually at their training hospital. They have come in groups of two or more, located a furnished apartment, sharing costs and chores, and then gone looking for a job, usually intent on all working together too.

TOURISTRY IN OPERATION

What makes them different from workers migrating in search of greener job pastures is that, for them, a job is merely the way to support themselves decently while they see the sights, sample the social life, have a bit of fun and then move on. These nurses do not follow any orientation to work as a central focus of living; their attention is directed to values outside the job environment and they use their work as a means to other, unrelated ends.

Thus the standards they do use in evaluating a job seem unrelated to those used by career oriented nurses or any who would try to apply professional standards. In touristry, pay is naturally the prime consideration since this is the main reason for working at all. Nurses from the East and South are attracted to the higher pay offered in the West without taking into account the comparably higher costs of living there. But pay schedules are fairly standardized within a region and there is no tradition of individual negotiation. Immediately after salary comes a concern with hours. Hospital-scheduling, as for any 24-hour institution, conflicts with the work-day that most of the American public puts in. The lack of predictable days off also interferes with any attempts at long-range planning. Another consideration of high importance, that euphemistically masquerades under the heading of "social opportunities," is the quantity of available young men in the immediate and surrounding areas. One factor that bears most directly on quitting, but also figures in job acceptance, is the strenuousness of the job. There are few nursing jobs nowadays that are routinely exhausting, but these girls insist on enough energy after work to engage in the social activities that are their prime interest. Thus it happens that whenever the turnover of staff becomes exceptionally heavy, a certain portion of those remaining will soon quit because the added work they must do leaves them unable to lead their non-work lives as they would wish.

TERMINATION OF TOURISTRY

Just as surely as it can prevent touristry, so marriage will put a stop to it as a pattern. The irresponsibility interim of the young girl's life can also be closed by a call to return home to attend to family crises, such as illness or death. Of course, returning home may also mean that the girl, without considering settling down, has found touristry to be unsuitable for her personally. Some find that they are greatly disappointed with what they meet in travel, that things are not so much better than they were at home. Others may rapidly find that they are frankly homesick and were never cut out for touristry.

There are a certain number of working nurses who, with the passage of time and the approach of their thirties, begin to suspect that marriage may not be as inevitable as they had expected at twenty-two. Among other reactions may well be the appearance of concern for an occupational future and such attendant factors as advancement and security. These nurses may travel again, but their moves are then more likely to have a direct relation to the more classical forms of work oriented mobility.

THE "PERMANENT" TOURIST

A very few nurses may find travel so entrancing that they will continue it even as a prime pattern. In my sample group, there were two staff nurses who realized that they were fairly well past the age of inevitable marriage, who had considered settling into a career commitment pattern but had given this up. One had already applied to the U.S. Foreign Service and was only awaiting acceptance before quitting. The other had only vague ideas of when and where she would be next but characterized herself as "one of the movers." Both fantasized the ideal husband as one whose job required extensive travel. Although neither were actually settled into an orientation toward future security, there is probably a point where it is simpler and less risky to combine touristry with occupation in one of those fields or agencies where travel is a necessary characteristic.

SUGGESTED READINGS: CHAPTER 15

Harold Finestone. "Cats, Kicks and Color." In Howard S. Becker (Ed.), *The Other Side,* New York: The Free Press of Glencoe, 1964.

This article emphasizes the fun and the esthetic elements in the drug user's way of life. Finestone makes explicit what is reflected, sometimes more implicitly, in many studies of urban vice. Both visitors and natives use cities (of all sizes) as places of illicit, or not quite proper, enjoyment.

Orrin Klapp. *Symbolic Leaders.* Chicago: Aldine Publishing Company, 1964.

This stimulating book can be read profitably for the deeper meanings of popular culture heroes (such as baseball players, movie stars, and singers) in an urbanized nation. It also suggests some of the deeper symbolism of what it means to go to ball games and to the movies, or to engage in other types of urban recreation.

Kevin Lynch. *The Image of the City.* Cambridge, Mass.: The Technology Press and Harvard University Press, 1960.

The kinds of esthetic, especially visual-esthetic, enjoyment had by residents of Los Angeles, Boston, and Jersey City are suggested by many quotations taken from interviews with these people. Even dull cities and routinized actions—like driving to work—provide esthetic excitement and various species of enjoyment.

Anselm L. Strauss. *Images of the American City.* New York: Free Press, 1961, Chapter 5, "The Visitor's View."

Some causes and consequences of visitors' images of certain cities; also the natives' views of "fun" sections of their own cities.

16

How Suburbanites Get In and Out of Town. Los Angeles
Chamber of Commerce photo.

CITY PLANNING

SINCE there are variable perspectives on any given city, its
citizens can scarcely reach total agreement on how
to change or improve their city. As a result, "city planning"
means different things to different segments of the city's
population. What some people regard as planning, other people
may even not recognize or may even refuse to
acknowledge as planning. The evolution of American cities has
been immensely influenced by the planning of
businessmen—whether that planning is, in today's jargon,
integrated or fragmented and whether it obviously
reflects vested interests or only the planners' conceptions of the
total public interests. Often opposing these business
concepts of where the city should be directed are the views
of "professional planners," of concerned good
citizens, and of architects and others interested in fine buildings
or serviceable parks. The great difficulties faced by
those latter groups, considering the massive array of
vested interests which determines the final shape
and substance of the physical city, is suggested by Leonard
Reissman, a sociologist who remarks that the practicing planner
finds "his hands are too often tied . . . because there are few
legal avenues open by which he might reverse
[the current trends]. He is forced to dance to a tune not of

his choosing. He is prevented at almost every step
from action by the jealousy of newly won authority, and
above all by a prevailing urban philosophy of
laissez faire." Consequently the planner, Reissman suggests,
ends by merely juggling street patterns, expanding highway
facilities, purchasing more land for increasing amounts of money,
and providing a few additional services. "The practitioner,"
Reissman concludes, "who understands the total
situation, must endure endless frustration." Probably that is
much too strong a conclusion, since some practicing planners
are civic officials who do not aspire at all to leave their
imprint on the city, while others are satisfied to have only a
little impact on its physical and social structures.

The selections below illustrate various of the views about
city planning, and they embody many of the urban images
touched on earlier.

THE UTOPIAN CITY: ALTRURIA,
Titus K. Smith

> DURING the last decades of the nineteenth century,
> when the realization became more
> widespread that most Americans would henceforth
> live in cities, urbanized utopias as a form
> of idealized planning began to appear in print. The
> utopian city reflects what its author finds most
> dissatisfying about contemporary city life
> and expresses his views of the good
> urban life—even if it has to be lived in the
> heart of the countryside.

Stepping over to the telephone, he called up the hotel of the town, and ordered a dinner to be cooked and sent to his home forthwith. "We have a telephone in every house, for use in all the everyday affairs of life," said he. This seemed an improvement even on New York, and when John told me we should be eating our dinner in thirty minutes, I was still more pleased.

"You see," said John, "our central kitchen or hotel expects such orders, and has the very latest appliances to fill them with dispatch. . . . The town has over 3,000 inhabitants, and the hotel is run for the accommodation of our people quite as much as for strangers. Our orders are filled at about the cost of materials and labor, which makes it cheaper than to consume one's own time in preparing food. We have no servants in Altruria. Nevertheless, we command all the help we need, and on a moment's notice. We do not employ each other. The town affords employment for every citizen. The services of the man who was here to-night will be charged up to my account, and for any services which I render I receive due credit." . . .

.   .   .   .

. . . When I got downstairs he stood ready with a smaller road-wagon, which he called a light roadster.

.   .   .   .

Excerpted from *Altruria* (New York: Altruria Publishing Co., 1895), pp. 29–30, 32–35, 37, 39–40, 46–49.

"All this land that we have traversed is in Altruria township, and is the property of the Altruria Corporation, organized to do a cooperative farming and manufacturing business," John stated. "With these swift road machines we can go to the ends of the farm in a few minutes, so that distance is annihilated; consequently, all our people, though farmers, live in town, and have every city convenience which ensures close association, water, sewer, light, heat, transportation, all furnished at reasonable cost, and cheaper than any individual household could supply itself. All our work is done under a system of voluntary co-operation scientifically adjusted to the seasons of nature, so that time and substance are economized to the highest degree, and the work of all is greatly lightened. None, however, is compelled to work; but, 'no work, no pay,' for we believe with St. Paul, that, 'he who will not work, neither shall he eat.' But the bugbear of work is removed from us. We all work from religious conviction. In fact, no one can be an Altrurian who is not a real Christian." . . .

. . ."This is the secret of our good health and happiness in Altruria; we have no care (worry). Twelve years ago, although still young, I felt myself getting old. Care was ever with me. I entered the mad race for wealth for fear I should not have even enough. I found that those who did achieve extraordinary success and bought themselves immunity from care, reached the goal only by running over their weaker fellows. Agriculture, under the old system, was lonesome and melancholy. I began to think whether success in any sphere was after all worth the seeking. Between the private monopolies and free competition all the nobler instincts of man were stunted. Accidentally I came across Altruria. At first I was skeptical, wondering whether the scheme was not too good to be real. But I tried it; actual experience gave me confidence, and we have been here ever since."

One thing I noticed especially about Altruria; its streets are clean, almost, as the halls of the houses; and the vehicles came and went noiselessly. The whole town was queenly in appearance and service, and yet every arrangement was a natural simplicity at a minimum expense. Flowers there were in profusion everywhere. Each house had a plot of ground of about half an acre, and on this space each householder had his garden and pursued his own fancies in floriculture, etc. There was not an architectural poem in terra-cotta or granite or similar material.

"You Altrurians," said I, as we had returned to the veranda, "are veritably working gentlemen. If our workers in New York had such homes they would consider themselves in the millennium."

"Yes, and reversely, we Altrurians consider them as being in a veritable hell," said John. "And yet your people could be even better conditioned than we are; their natural opportunities are superior."

.   .   .   .

"Perhaps nothing can more fully awake us to this danger than a clear view of the world. And to make the lesson the better applicable to ourselves, let us imagine that we had decided to abandon our Altrurian life, and tomorrow would see us disband and become a part of the world. As man cannot live without land, there would be a wild scramble among us for the better portions of the soil of Altruria township. The stronger would take their larger portions, and the weaker their smaller ones. Some would have an abundance of water for irrigation; others none except a small supply for domestic use. Is there anything under Heaven which could keep these neighbors in substantial equality and fraternity under such conditions? Nothing. Then would enter greed, envy, and all the vile brood of egoism. Selfishness would reign supreme. By and by, some of the smaller holders of sterile portions would abandon their holdings, or if they should remain, the children would show their superior sense in leaving. Where would they go? To the cities, into the stores and factories, to become the economic slaves of the industrial world, which is heartless. 'There is no sentiment in business.'

"Go with me now forward into the time of another generation. Some of the grandchildren of our cultured Altrurian stock are found in the lowest city tenements, their offspring to be reared in the vilest environments, amidst filth; and schooled early in vice and crime. Others have become factory operatives, live in their employer's houses and trade at his store— slaves in everything save name, and the option of seeking another master under similar conditions. Their despoilers will honor themselves by contributions to the charities, the necessity for which they have created by the economic system under which they operate. The robbed are offered their own goods in charity, and powerless to resent the insult. If in that dire extremity the gospel should be preached to them, would it not fall on their ears as a mockery? Would they not feel that instead of receiving the bread of life they were being offered a stone?

"They flee back to the country to regain land and freedom. But economic value now stands between them and possession. They must here also become the servants of those who are in possession of the primary factors of production through the ownership of economic value.

"Such is the search, the vain search, of the 'Gentiles' after the things of this world before they seek the kingdom. At every step they and their children in every generation are harrassed by inequalities, envyings, bickerings, strifes, thefts, murders; all the fruit of their selfishness, their egoism. Now, what I have pictured as your future, should you abandon Altruria, is to-day the actual state of the outside world. The masses are economic serfs. The producers retain of their products only sufficient to barely feed and clothe themselves. They pile up prodigious fortunes, and have no part therein.

"Here, in Altruria, we are joint owners of the factors of production— land and machinery. Consequently we maintain an approximate equality. We have no shamed poor to receive the charity of the fawning rich. Our children are not humiliated while still in their innocence. One child is the peer of every other child. Their opportunities for acquiring the tools of intelligence and skill are the same. None need leave school at the beginning of its teens to help support poor parents, for no parents among us are poor.

"None of us are lonely, as are the agriculturists of the outside world. We are all near neighbors, and enjoy the quickening impulses of an intelligent society, and mutual aid comes quickly in case of sickness or bereavement."

.   .   .   .

"It is enough, my friend, I see it all."

"I am delighted to hear it," said John. "If you will go back to New York and settle up your affairs and come again, we will renew your life, multiply your joys, and when you die it will be with a clear conscience, and you will go 'not like the quarry slave at night, scourged to his dungeon, but sustained and soothed with an unfaltering trust' that God is your father, and with a knowledge that you have been a true brother to every child of His."

PLANNING AND THE CITY'S "GOOD,"
Robert H. Talbert

> IN his book on Fort Worth, a contemporary
> sociologist sums up his conception of what makes a city
> good, making clear his belief that unless there is
> careful city planning not only will the desired end
> not be attained but chaos may actually result from
> the unguided urban growth.

"OUR FAIR CITY"

Possibly since the beginning of urban life men have pointed with pride to their own town. Local pride and patriotism have been a common belief of urban dwellers from time immemorial, and many have agreed with Saint Paul in concluding, "I am a citizen of no mean city." In the United States today one hears from the lips of the residents of almost every city something similar to the following summary statement:

> Our city is noted as a city of fine residences, good schools, and strong churches—a good place to live. From thousands of sources one hears this theme in some form. Local citizens point with pride to their fine school buildings, their beautiful new auditorium, their expensive stadium. Or they take their visitor along tree-lined streets of magnificent residences, through their spacious parks.

Certainly the characteristics mentioned in the above statement are desirable and may be visible evidence of a community's awareness for the welfare of its citizens. But those who are interested in an objective evaluation of community life must go further. They must determine whether the fine buildings are merely a facade behind which lie less desirable conditions. For citizens interested in the nature of their community, there must be the recognition that the welfare of the whole community is affected by the living conditions of each part of it. Conversely, individual human welfare is a function of the general welfare.

The evidence which is available suggests that in reality some citizens do live in mean cities. As one writer has concluded:

Reprinted from *Cowtown—Metropolis* (Fort Worth, Texas: Manney Co., 1956), pp. 260–64, by permission of the author.

But as a matter of fact many of our cities are mean in their provisions for health, comfort, education, recreation and other features of a good life. This is partly because of lack of resources, but it is partly because their citizens do not know what a city can be and should be, and what some American cities have made themselves and do not know their own city in comparison with others.

Other students of American community life have come to the same conclusion, that there are in reality significant differences in the quality of living available in different urban areas.

BASIC QUESTIONS

Such conclusions as to the nature of American cities lead logically to at least three basic questions. First, is it correct to conclude that some areas are in reality better places to live? Second, is it possible for individual citizens or groups of citizens to improve their city, or is improvement or degeneration a function of basic influences beyond the control of the individual community? And finally, is it possible to agree as to what makes a city good? The writer is of the opinion that the answer to each of these three questions must be given in the affirmative. However, it must be recognized that objective measures are essential in working toward an adequate answer to the third question.

THE NEED FOR OBJECTIVE MEASURES

An adequate understanding of a city's functioning, and proper consideration of its potential for growth and development, require objective measures which will reveal present conditions and future possibilities. That is, the study of community life must seek to create an honest balance sheet of accomplishments and failures for the present, and an awareness of future needs. While many surveys of this type have been attempted for individual cities, there are relatively few studies which provide the basis for comparative analysis. Three such attempts can be briefly considered. The oldest of the three comparative studies was done by E. L. Thorndike and published under the title, *Your City*. Thorndike studied 310 cities in the United States, and used some 297 measures to arrive at what he calls the "general goodness of cities." Although Thorndike's approach emphasized material accomplishments, it does reveal significant differences between cities in terms of such basic needs as education, health, library facilities, and similar basic institutional needs. Most recently Robert C.

Angell has attempted to measure the relative "moral integration of cities." For Angell, the major factors differentiating cities revolve around the quality of local leadership and the willingness of citizens of individual cities to work together for their general welfare.

Still another attempt to provide qualitative differences between cities has been made by Austin L. Porterfield in developing what he calls an Index of Urban Integration. Basic to Porterfields's index of community quality is a composite measure labeled ACID. Each of the letters refers to a combination of several series of data. The A portion of the composite index measures the degree of anomie; the C is composed of various sub-series and provides a measure of conflict between rival groups; the I pro-vides a relative measure of interpersonal disaffection; and the D gives a measure of the influence of depressed classes. Porterfield thinks of the composite ACID index as representing a continuum along which individual cities would fall. In each of these attempts to differentiate between cities, although each has utilized different measures, there is the common purpose of seeking to determine the relative goodness of cities.

The differences between the measures briefly outlined above suggest some of the difficulties in arriving at general agreement as to what a city should have. A great majority of citizens would agree as to the necessity of good streets, sanitary sewers, and similar material accomplishments. Less general agreement would be achieved in deciding what other roles the city government should play in community improvement. Thus, there would be serious disagreement as to whether public authority has certain types of responsibilities, such as that of providing low-rent housing units for low-income families. In a less obvious way, there would be some disagree-ment as to the proper asthetic goals for the community, or what should be the goals in the field of morality.

Even so, while such disagreements do exist, they do not make impos-sible the task of urban improvements. In line with this idea, the following list of desired goals is presented. This listing is intended to suggest the basic needs which will make the urban community a fit place in which to live. The basic needs would include the following:

1. A stable economy.
2. An educational system which successfully transmits the necessary skills and understanding for mature living in our society.
3. A program of health and sanitation which successfully utilizes the current knowledge of medicine and science.
4. Stable family life.
5. Effective religious experiences.
6. A program of recreation which is both re-creative and conducive to the development of mature adults.
7. A physical structure which maintains maximum standards for safety, convenience, and the aesthetic needs of the people.

8. A program for housing the population which will recognize the needs of people.

Admittedly, these are only broad generalizations. Yet they are believed to be the basic requirements for effective community life. They are intended to provide goals which will give direction to action somewhat as a map shows us which way we want to go. And like a map, they suggest ways which can be travelled—with effective leadership. Actually, of course, there are available more detailed "maps" or "blueprints" for each of the generalizations listed above. The major problem at the present is in making the general public aware of the needs for the future and familiar with the knowledge which is available.

As this is written the Gruen Plan for the development of Fort Worth has been introduced. This plan calls for major changes in the central business district, and related planning for the entire city and metropolitan area. . . . Whether the Gruen Plan or some other is adopted, it does emphasize the necessity of planning. In the opinion of the writer the alternative (no plan) will lead inevitably to chaos.

THE CITY BEAUTIFUL: TREES, PARKS, AND OTHER OPEN SPACES, *Frederick Olmsted*

FREDERICK OLMSTED built many of our country's finest city parks; he was an effective spokesman for the public park movement as well. This movement did not at all challenge the city, it only challenged the city as a purely commercial venture. Olmsted's statement joins the city conceived as an efficient (and necessary) machine with the city as a beautiful and healthy locale. His statement includes an early version of the current anti-smog argument and discussion.

It is hardly a matter of speculation, I am disposed to think, but almost of demonstration, that the larger a town becomes because simply of its advantages for commercial purposes, the greater will be the convenience available to those who live in and near it for co-operation, as well with reference to the accumulation of wealth in the higher forms,—as in seats

Excerpted from "Public Parks and the Enlargement of Towns," *Journal of Social Science, 3* (1871), 10–25.

of learning, of science, and of art,—as with reference to merely domestic economy and the emancipation of both men and women from petty, confining, and narrowing cares.

It also appears to be nearly certain that the recent rapid enlargement of towns and withdrawal of people from rural conditions of living is the result mainly of circumstances of a permanent character.

We have reason to believe, then, that towns which of late have been increasing rapidly on account of their commercial advantages are likely to be still more attractive to population in the future; that there will in consequence soon be larger towns than any the world has yet known, and that the further progress of civilization is to depend mainly upon the influences by which men's minds and characters will be affected while living in large towns.

Now, knowing that the average length of life of mankind in towns has been much less than in the country, and that the average amount of disease and misery and of vice and crime has been much greater in towns, this would be a very dark prospect for civilization, if it were not that modern Science has beyond all question determined many of the causes of the special evils by which men are afflicted in towns, and placed means in our hands for guarding against them. It has shown, for example, that under ordinary circumstances, in the interior part of large and closely built towns, a given quantity of air contains considerably less of the elements which we require to receive through the lungs than the air of the country or even of the outer and more open parts of a town, and that instead of them it carries into the lungs highly corrupt and irritating matters, the action of which tends strongly to vitiate all our sources of vigor—how strongly may perhaps be indicated in the shortest way by the statement that even metallic plates and statues corrode and wear away under the atmospheric influences which prevail in the midst of large towns, more rapidly than in the country.

.   .   .   .

It has happened several times within the last century, when old artificial obstructions to the spreading out of a city have been removed, and especially when there has been a demolition of and rebuilding on a new ground plan so some part which had previously been noted for the frequency of certain crimes, the prevalence of certain diseases, and the shortness of life among its inhabitants, that a marked improvement in all these respects has followed, and has been maintained not alone in the dark parts, but in the city as a whole. . . . Strange to say, however, here in the New World, where great towns by the hundred are springing into existence, no care at all is taken to avoid bad plans. The most brutal Pagans to whom we have sent our missionaries have never shown greater indifference to the sufferings of others than is exhibited in the plans of some of our most promising cities, for which men now living in them are responsible. . . .

It is evident that if we go on in this way, the progress of civilized mankind in health, virtue, and happiness will be seriously endangered.

.   .   .   .

Let us proceed, then, to the question of means, and with a seriousness in some degree befitting a question, upon our dealing with which we know the misery or happiness of many millions of our fellow-beings will depend.

We will for the present set before our minds the two sources of wear and corruption which we have seen to be remediable and therefore preventible. We may admit that commerce requires that in some parts of a town there shall be an arrangement of buildings, and a character of streets and of traffic in them which will establish conditions of corruption and of irritation, physical and mental. But commerce does not require the same conditions to be maintained in all parts of a town.

Air is disinfected by sunlight and foliage. Foliage also acts mechanically to purify the air by screening it. Opportunity and inducement to escape at frequent intervals from the confined and vitiated air of the commercial quarter, and to supply the lungs with air screened and purified by trees, and recently acted upon by sunlight, together with opportunity and inducement to escape from conditions requiring vigilance, wariness, and activity toward other men,—if these could be supplied economically, our problem would be solved. . . .

Would trees for seclusion and shade and beauty, be out of place, for instance by the side of certain of our streets? It will, perhaps, appear to you that it is hardly necessary to ask such a question, as throughout the United States trees are commonly planted at the sides of streets. Unfortunately they are seldom so planted as to have fairly settled the question of the desirableness of systematically maintaining trees under these circumstances. In the first place, the streets are planned, wherever they are, essentially alike. Trees are planted in the space assigned for sidewalks, where at first, while they are saplings, and the vicinity is rural or suburban, they are not much in the way, but where, as they grow larger, and the vicinity becomes urban, they take up more and more space, while space is more and more required for passage. That is not all. Thousands and tens of thousands are planted every year in a manner and under conditions as nearly certain as possible either to kill them outright, or to so lessen their vitality as to prevent their natural and beautiful development, and to cause premature decrepitude. Often, too, as their lower limbs are found inconvenient, no space having been provided for trees in laying out the street, they are deformed by butcherly amputations. If by rare good fortune they are suffered to become beautiful, they still stand subject to be condemned to death at any time, as obstructions in the highway.

What I would ask is, whether we might not with economy make special provision in some of our streets—in a twentieth or a fiftieth part, if you please, of all—for trees to remain as a permanent furniture of the city? I mean, to make a place for them in which they would have room to grow naturally and gracefully. Even if the distance between the houses should have to be made half as much again as it is required to be in our commercial streets, could not the space be afforded? Out of town space is not costly when measures to secure it are taken early. The assessments for benefits where such streets were provided for, would, in nearly all cases, defray the cost of the land required. The strips of ground reserved for the trees, six, twelve, twenty feet wide, would cost nothing for paving or flagging.

The change both of scene and of air which would be obtained by people engaged for the most part in the necessarily confined interior commercial parts of the town, on passing into a street of this character after the trees had become stately and graceful, would be worth a good deal. If such streets were made still broader in some parts, with spacious malls, the advantage would be increased. If each of them were given the proper capacity, and laid out with laterals and connections in suitable directions to serve as a convenient trunkline of communications between two large districts of the town or the business centre and the suburbs, a very great number of people might thus be placed every day under influences counteracting those with which we desire to contend. . . .

.   .   .   .

There will be room enough in the Brooklyn Park, when it is finished, for several thousand little family and neighborly parties to bivouac at frequent intervals through the summer, without discommoding one another, or interfering with any other purpose, to say nothing of those who can be drawn out to make a day of it, as many thousand were last year. And although the arrangements for the purpose were yet very incomplete, and but little ground was *at all* prepared for such use, besides these small parties, consisting of one or two families, there came also, in companies of from thirty to a hundred and fifty, somewhere near twenty thousand children with their parents, Sunday-school teachers, or other guides and friends, who spent the best part of a day under the trees and on the turf, in recreations of which the predominating element was of this neighborly receptive class. Often they would bring a fiddle, flute, and harp, or other music. Tables, seats, shade, turf, swings, cool spring-water, and a pleasing rural prospect, stretching off half a mile or more each way, unbroken by carriage road or the slightest evidence of the vicinity of the town, were supplied them without charge, and bread and milk and ice-cream at moderate fixed charges. In all my life I have never seen such joyous collections of people. I have, in fact, more than once observed tears of gratitude in the eyes of poor women, as they watched their children thus enjoying themselves.

The whole cost of such neighborly festivals, even when they include excursions by rail from the distant parts of the town, does not exceed for each person, on an average, a quarter of a dollar; and when the arrangements are complete, I see no reason why thousands should not come every day where hundreds come now to use them; and if so, who can measure the value, generation after generation, of such provisions for recreation to the over-wrought, much confined people of the great town that is to be?

For this purpose neither of the forms of ground we have heretofore considered are at all suitable. We want a ground to which people may easily go after their day's work is done, and where they may stroll for an hour, seeing, hearing, and feeling nothing of the bustle and jar of the streets, where they shall, in effect, find the city put far away from them. We want the greatest possible contrast with the streets and the shops and the rooms of the town which will be consistent with convenience and preservation of good order and neatness. We want, especially, the greatest possible contrast with the restraining and confining conditions of the town, those conditions which compel us to walk circumspectly, watchfully, jealously, which compel us to look closely upon others with sympathy. Practically, what we most want is a simple, broad, open space of clean greensward, with sufficient play of surface and a sufficient number of trees about it to supply a variety of light and shade. This we want as a central feature. We want depth of wood enough about it not only for comfort in hot weather, but to completely shut out the city from our landscapes.

The word *park,* in town nomenclature, should, I think, be reserved for grounds of the character and purpose thus described.

Not only as being the most valuable of all possible forms of public places, but regarded simply as a large space which will seriously interrupt cross-town communication wherever it occurs, the question of the site and bounds of the park requires to be determined with much more deliberation and art than is often secured for any problem of distant and extended municipal interests.

A Promenade may, with great advantage, be carried along the outer part of the surrounding groves of a park; and it will do no harm if here and there a broad opening among the trees discloses its open landscapes to those upon the promenade. But recollect that the object of the latter for the time being should be to see *congregated human life* under glorious and necessarily artificial conditions, and the natural landscape is not essential to them; though there is not more beautiful picture, and none can be more pleasing incidentally to the gregarious purpose, than that of beautiful meadows, over which clusters of level-armed sheltering trees cast broad shadows, and upon which are scattered dainty cows and flocks of black-faced sheep, while men, women, and children are seen sitting here and there, forming groups in the shade, or moving in and out among the woody points and bays.

It may be inferred from what I have said, that very rugged ground, abrupt eminences, and what is technically called picturesque in distinction from merely beautiful or simply pleasing scenery, is not the most desirable for a town park. Decidedly not in my opinion. The park should, as far as possible, complement the town. Openness is the one thing you cannot get in buildings. Picturesqueness you can get. Let your buildings be as picturesque as your artists can make them. This is the beauty of a town. Consequently, the beauty of the fields, the meadow, the prairie, of the green pastures, and the still waters. What we want to gain is tranquillity and rest to the mind. Mountains suggest effort. But besides this objection there are others of what I may indicate as the housekeeping class. It is impossible to give the public range over a large extent of ground of a highly picturesque character, unless under very exceptional circumstances, and sufficiently guard against the occurrence of opportunities and temptations to shabbiness, disorder, indecorum, and indecency, that will be subversive of every good purpose the park should be designed to fulfill.

. . . .

A park fairly well managed near a large town, will surely become a new centre of that town. With the determination of location, size, and boundaries should therefore be associated the duty of arranging new trunk routes of communication between it and the distant parts of the town existing and forecasted.

These may be either narrow informal elongations of the park, varying say from two to five hundred feet in width, and radiating irregularly from it, or if, unfortunately, the town is already laid out in the unhappy way that New York and Brooklyn, San Francisco and Chicago, are, and, I am glad to say, Boston is not, on a plan made long years ago by a man who never saw a spring-carriage, and who had a conscientious dread of the Graces, then we must probably adopt formal Park-ways. They should be so planned and constructed as never to be noisy and seldom crowded, and so also that the straightforward movement of pleasure-carriages need never be obstructed, unless at absolutely necessary crossings, by slow-going heavy vehicles used for commercial purposes. If possible, also, they should be branched or reticulated with other ways of a similar class, so that no part of the town should finally be many minutes' walk from some one of them; and they should be made interesting by a process of planting and decoration so that in necessarily passing through them, whether in going to or from the park, or to and from business, some substantial recreative advantage may be incidentally gained. It is a common error to regard a park as something to be produced complete in itself, as a picture to be painted on canvas. It should rather be planned as one to be done in fresco, with constant consideration of exterior objects, some of them quite at a distance and even existing as yet only in the imagination of the painter. . . . I hope you will agree with me that there is little room for question, that reserves of ground for the purposes I have referred to should be fixed upon as soon as possible, before the difficulty of arranging them, which arises from private building, shall be greatly more formidable than now.

To these reserves,—though not a dollar should be spent in construction during the present generation,—the plans of private construction would necessarily, from the moment they were established, be conformed.

I by no means wish to suggest that nothing should be done for the present generation; but only, that whatever happens to the present generation, it should not be allowed to go on heaping up difficulties and expenses for its successors, for want of a little comprehensive and business-like foresight and study. In all probability it will be found that much can be done even for the present generation without greatly if at all increasing taxation, as has been found in New York.

THE CITY BEAUTIFUL: MUNICIPAL ART,
Frederick S. Lamb

A QUARTER of a century after Olmsted's plea for
parks and trees, Frederick Lamb, an artist
born in New York City, made another kind of
plea: that cities should be graced with
beautiful municipal art. Lamb's critique of urban
ugliness and his proposals for relieving
it constitute an argument not much improved on
seven decades later.

It seems strange that the American mind, usually so quick to appreciate the pecuniary value of any movement, has not seen the civic advantage of Municipal Art. There is a completion of cities just as there is a competition of individuals, and this competition has remained unrealized by the citizens of Greater New York. In fact, until recently, everything has been done, or left undone, to make our city as unattractive as possible. Improvements when introduced have been costly and misdirected. Millions have been lavishly expended at a late date to accomplish what could easily have been obtained at a small expenditure had the question been taken in time; millions expended, which, if expended under competent direction, would have accomplished double their present results.

Parks, which in the natural growth of the city should have been reserved, are now acquired at an enormous expenditure, and no sooner is a small section secured for the citizens than it becomes the mark of hostile legislation, and every interested corporation seeks to appropriate it for its own use.

Every new invention, every new innovation presages some new monstrosity. Every company, traction or otherwise, every inventor seems at liberty to assume a portion of the light and air left the poor public for their own benefit. Streets are rendered almost lightless, buildings tower to the skies, and the poor foot-passenger is left sunless and cheerless to wonder why the whole of Manhattan should have too much building on the one hand and too little on the other.

The so-called utilitarian spirit, the so-called progress, the so-called practical citizen have much to answer for. One of the most beautiful loca-

Excerpted from "Municipal Art," *Municipal Affairs.* Vol. 1 (1897), 674–76, 678–
79, 682–86, 688.

tions granted a people for a home has been ruthlessly ravaged. Every natural advantage, every natural beauty has been ignored; every opportunity sacrified to the steady onward march of serried streets; natural drainage, natural levels, so disregarded that not only portions of the city proper, but surrounding sections, have become menaces to health. Old landmarks are obliterated; historical monuments destroyed; buildings of national importance sold for second-hand building material; rivers, fields and commons of the old villages swept away, and in their place the factory or rear tenement appears. The most impressive river front ever granted a city is bereft of all natural beauty. The depredation extends to the opposite shores, and the historic section of Pleasant Valley is a fitting place for oil refineries and stock yards.

Remember Manhattan of the past, and look at it now! Where are the gifts so lavishly bestowed by nature. Central Park, a monument to the genius of its designers, Vaux and Olmstead, and Riverside Drive alone remain. City Hall Park, one of the few of the early reservations, has been encroached upon because the city officials were too parsimonious to pay a moderate sum for a suitable site for the New York Post Office. City economy has been matched by corporate greed, and the beautiful St. John's Park, absorbed by the New York Central, has been forever lost to Greater New York, thus eliminating another of the few remaining breathing places.

The belief that in some unknown way New York was exempt from all rules governing other cities must have indeed been held by those in charge of the city. Not only all aesthetic questions, but even the most common laws of sanitation and everyday living, have been ignored, until New York with its filthy streets, rear tenements and corrupt government, has become the laughing-stock of foreign countries and a shining example of the failure of free institutions.

Reviewing the records of the past fifty years, it would be difficult to imagine a more disastrous management of city affairs—a management producing or permitting conditions, to correct which will take untold energy and untold wealth. Why we should have been willing to sacrifice natural advantages and recklessly, wastefully disregard the material at hand, remains and always will remain a mystery.

Nor is this waste and misapplied extravagance confined to the past. Every day we have new evidence that the same reckless spirit is at work. In the Riverside Extension, recently adopted, we learn that the city has accepted a scheme which involves an expenditure variously estimated at from three to seven millions of dollars, and yet those who have carefully looked into the question tell us that had the proposed driveway been made sixty feet wide, and "the natural grades followed more closely, the Extension could have been built for one million five hundred thousand dollars, and would have been better adapted to the present street plan." The scheme adopted has been characterized as "an outrage" by the comptroller, and a leading paper in speaking of the Viaduct states that "certainly no competent person can have been asked to consider what will be the effect of the proposed construction upon one of the most commanding and attractive points of view upon Manhattan Island, for any competent person would have answered that it would be so injurious as to be almost ruinous." The Harlem with its many advantages might easily have rivalled the Seine. The natural formation of the land lends itself to the picturesque construction for which the foreign river is so justly famous. The future growth of the city will necessitate the construction of many bridges in addition to those already in place, and had the officials in charge in past years been wise enough to have reserved this section, a picturesque river frontage second to none in the world could have been secured. Tardiness in action has defeated this purpose. Corporate interests have already secured river rights, and Harlem is rapidly becoming a commercial centre with all its attendant drawbacks.

A spasmodic effort has been made in the Speedway to redeem the short-sightedness of former generations. An enormous sum of money, some five millions of dollars, has been set aside. The project hastily conceived has been rushed through without the aid of expert advice, and so far as completed looks more like a railway cut than a driveway in the suburbs of a great city. As usual, natural formation, natural beauties have been ignored, and what might have been one of the most interesting features of our city is now commonplace in the extreme.

And during all these years what has the artist said or done? How has he met his responsibilities to the Municipality?

.   .   .   .

But in studying the development of these societies, leagues and federations, we find little if any of the true communal spirit which made the cities of the middle ages the art centres of Europe. We find the desire to "make any sacrifice for art," "art for art's sake," on every hand. Yet for years these very enthusiasts have tolerated commonplace architecture, obstructed streets, telegraph poles, elevated roads, bill boards, every advertising monstrosity conceived by the human mind, and have, from morning until night, wandered among the worst aggregate of public fixtures ever produced by any city in the world, and have wandered speechless. The evening may possibly have been devoted to "art for art's sake," profound discussion of the impressionistic theory, or the necessity of a closer "study of nature." Absolute truthfulness to life may have absorbed the time and attention of the members, but certainly no organized effort was made by any society until a recent date to ameliorate the condition of the city. And what efforts have been put forward have been more in the form of criticism than formative action. We hear of protests from societies, objections from leagues and federations, but what creative, aggressive action is being taken by any art organization? How are our individual artists meeting their personal responsibilities to civic art? Is it by allowing the absorption by city and corporate interests of all natural breathing places? Is it by permitting the destruction of all the beautiful old Dutch and Colonial mansions? Is it by allowing the obliteration of historic memories? Is it by giving up without protest, franchise after franchise, grant after grant, until corporate interests become most powerful and a menace to all advance, to all improvement? Is it by permitting the architecture of every avenue to be but the constructional frame for the support for a series of nondescript signs? Is it by permitting each thoroughfare to be filled with telegraph poles, electric lights, lamp posts, execrable in design, elevated roads and other obstructions? Is it in this way he meets his responsibility?

. . . .

Art must be indigenous to be of value. Art must appeal to the great masses of the public to regain its educational influence. Foreign examples may be studied, and foreign pictures reproduced, but unless art tells the lesson of the human heart, unless the cry of human suffering is echoed there, unless the daily struggle of the individual is felt and recorded, unless all the aspirations, hope and prophecy for the future are expressed, art must of necessity have fallen far, far short of the mark and failed to accomplish its mission. . . .

Let us go back to first principles and again attack the problems of every day life with the experience of past ages to help us. Let us not be led astray by the individualism of the present age. Let us not be deceived by the glamour of easel work, but let us realize that art to be of value must answer the question of utility and not relegate itself to the exclusiveness of aristocratic appreciation. In so far as art fails in this respect, just so far it loses its claim to the title of Municipal Art, and just so far it alienates the sympathy of the great majority of our citizens. Let the architects devise schemes for historic and monumental buildings. Let our engineers endeavor to solve the problems of technical construction, and solve them in such a way as to obtain the necessary result without violating every aesthetic principle. Let our sculptors so work, that when their statues and allegorical groups are complete, their city is benefited. Let the mural painter in his every effort so work that the simplest object in his hands becomes a thing of beauty. Let him refuse no opportunity, no task however simple, and let his every effort, whether remunerative or unremunerative be for the beautification of his city and its homes, and let all "allied arts" and kindred professions unite in their efforts to raise *their* home—The Greater City of

New York—from the common place level of a simple manufacturing centre. . . .

.   .   .   .

Look for one moment at the field for work. The Harlem River, mutilated as it is, is not yet beyond the hope of redemption. Prompt and vigorous action may still wrench victory from defeat. The river front with all its present complications, may through judicious legislation be vastly benefited. The crusade for small parks, so ably carried on, may be broadened into a demand for public recreation buildings. The present street fixtures must in time be replaced, and can then be designed under competent super-vision. Franchises not yet granted may be so qualifiedly conferred as to insure artistic success. Church property, educational concessions may when bestowed be accompanied with the condition that upon removal, the property must revert to the city at a proper valuation, thus insuring as the city grows and these institutions follow its progress, the reservation of these small holdings for the use of the city. The exemption from taxation, the many concessions made might at least insure the city the option of purchase at a fair valuation, when the property no longer fulfills its original purpose. Public signs must be required to be more uniform and less obtrusive. The recent rapid development of the artistic poster is but one of the many instances of the possibilities in this direction. . . .

Markets, so essential to the life and economical existence of the community, could, instead of being as at present a drawback to the section in which they are placed, be so designed as to contain not only food products, but shrubs and flowers, and the stalls for these could be so placed as to appeal to the most fastidious critic. The union would be to the advantage of both, and as in all true reforms, the public would also be benefited.

.   .   .   .

And why should the city restrict its efforts to its own limits? Why should its artists confine their study to local questions, when the surrounding country may at any moment be annexed? In advance of the rapid growth of our city, much can be accomplished at comparatively small cost under competent guidance. Many preliminary steps may be taken, and taken in the right direction, although the final completion of the work may for years be deferred. Forethought is far more valuable than afterthought. One million of dollars judiciously expended now may save millions at a later date. Then why these absurd restrictions to city limits, why these imaginary state lines? Why should not the common sense of the community overstep these artificial barriers and treat the suburbs with as much care as the city itself?

We are told that eventually the Newark Meadows are to be reclaimed, drains placed, canals dug, dykes raised, and from the present barren marsh, a second great city will spring. Is this project to be left unstudied because an artificial state line intervenes? Is this work, one of the greatest of the day, to be left to mediocre ability? Is this question like all others to be unappreciated until from sheer force of necessity, something is done and done ill-advisably? Could any engineer, could any architect, could any artist dream of a problem more fraught with possibilities? The utilitarian treatment of Holland, the aesthetic dream of Venice lie at our very door.

.   .   .   .

And yet we know that down deep in the hearts of the people is a strength, a force, an energy, which when roused will sweep all before it; an energy which, when once started, will not rest until what is now most censured becomes most praised.

Who will arouse this latent force? Who will touch this latent sympathy? Who will guide the great reactionary wave which will inevitably sweep the country? Past experience has shown that unless under expert guidance, the best of effort may fall far short of the mark. In this crisis, the city must turn to its professional members, and from them expect, nay demand, the benefit of their technical training. Let no artist echo the scathing denunciation now being poured upon this city. Let no artist complain of the "lack of art atmosphere," of the lack of an "appreciative audience," of the "want of sympathy," so long as he refuses to answer the call of duty, and aid *his* city with *his* best effort and *his* ability.

This is the field; the battle is waging; the issue is before us. Shall the victory be secured?

THE CITY CLUB AND THE CITY BEAUTIFUL,
Leslie Miller, Dr. MacAlister, and S. S. Fels

FOLLOWING an address (by a Mr. Kelsey) to the
City Club of Philadelphia, Mr. Miller, Dr.
MacAlister, and Mr. Fels made some
comments pertaining to the role of the City Club in
making the city a better and more beautiful
place in which to live and work. The year was 1910.

DR. MACALISTER: ". . . We have another gentleman here to-day
who has been active in the work of beautifying and benefitting the city
whose name is familiar to you all, and I know you will be glad to listen
to Mr. Leslie W. Miller, Principal of the School of Industrial Art."

MR. MILLER: "I am interested in the plan for a better city not only
from the social point of view, but from every other point of view; and I
am delighted that there is now in the city of Philadelphia so good a platform on which to discuss this vital question, and so warm a place in which
schemes for the betterment of the city on topographic and other lines,
beautiful and industrial, may be considered, as right here in the City Club.
I want to congratulate the members of the Club on the magnificent promise
of the work they have undertaken here. I think that the City Club is the
one influence we have been waiting for. Since I came to Philadelphia, I
have met many good people who have had earnest schemes for promoting
and beautifying the city, but I think it is in a place like this particularly
that all these schemes should be brought together. I believe that people
will learn here what it means to plan, and how necessary it is to plan things
before you can ever hope to have them.

"Mr. Kelsey brought home to us in a most forcible manner the necessity of getting together in this work. Our city has never been conscious of
its needs before. We have taken everything for granted, believing that the
city was well able to take care of itself.

"William Penn planned Philadelphia. He planned it admirably, and he
planned it beautifully. He thought out how the city was bound to grow,
and he plotted it on a broad scale, with wide streets, considering the needs
of those days, with little spots of green here and there, and he thought
everybody's house would have its green surroundings. He planned the town

Reprinted from *City Club of Philadelphia Bulletin* (issued by the City Club of
Philadelphia), Vol. 2, No. 2 (1910), 60–61.

as Washington and L'Enfant planned Washington. They provided for its growth as a capital city. He planned it as Peter the Great planned St. Petersburg. But the plan, so admirably formulated years ago, has been entirely outgrown, and the kind of civic consciousness which underlay its creation has somehow gone to sleep. Now that civic consciousness is awakening, and one of the first things thought of is the taking up of the work that the fathers did so well. We must take cognizance of the new problems of a big city which the founders could not possibly foresee.

"I hope that one result of Mr. Kelsey's able address to-day will be to bring home to the mind of every man here a recognition of the dignity, the overwhelming importance of intelligent planning for the future of this city. Whether you take it up from the point of view of playgrounds, from the point of view of school houses, or from the point of view of commercial development, the situation is one to command our thoughtful attention. The city itself, as well as any of its children, has the right to a strong and healthy development. It has the right to its own existence, and to progress along noble lines.

"Let us not sympathize with the disposition in some quarters to belittle the movement for intelligent city planning. We have neglected it absolutely for two hundred years. We have let the plan go on just as Penn founded it, letting streets grow and grow in length indefinitely, cutting down a hill here, or filling up a little stream there, and turning both into eye-sores instead of the restful places of beauty that they should have remained.

"There are plenty of us here who cannot take a proper interest in the whole city planning movement because we are interested in some particular feature or branch of the whole. I can speak heartily of the needs of the schools, because I am associated with them. We may say that the parkway can wait, that the City Beautiful can wait, and we may say, let us have more kindergartens and all that. Now, let us learn to take a look at our needs in a little bigger way than that. The development of the banks of the Schuylkill, something for which we have been planning for twenty years would give a playground of which every child of the city would be glad to take advantage, and would at the same time do away with the conditions along the Schuylkill which have so long been a stench in our nostrils. There is not any thing that we need more than a clean beautiful city. There is nothing which will promote the usefulness of our school houses so much as a pleasant place for the children to play. The community as a whole does not need economic conveniences and facilities for travel and time-saving so much as it needs beautiful open spaces in which every man, woman and child can enjoy the moments of leisure. Our grid-iron system of streets was good enough when the city was small, but now that it is large, and it is necessary to go clear around two sides of every square in order to get from one corner to another, the system proves how miserably inadequate it is to the needs of the present.

"An intelligent city plan for the future will provide not only better means of communication, but it will provide for the spread of that system of breathing-spots laid out by Penn. We must bear in mind that our responsibility for the city is going to increase with every year of our life. Old ideas must be absolutely swept away. We must take within our view a district certainly not less than thirty miles in a radius from the city hall, for only on such a scale can the needs of the future be provided for.

"The city planning idea is not visionary, it is practical. Do not sneer at it and say that the city's growth will take care of itself by-and-bye. But let us unite to make our city what it should be, healthy and noble, worthy of its history and its mission."

DR. MACALISTER: "I think it is worth while to observe that these things can be done. There was probably no more unpromising city in the world from the aesthetic standpoint than the city of Chicago a few years ago. Many of you know what the conditions were. But Chicago took up the situation, formulated a comprehensive plan, which has been executed to a considerable extent, and the consequences is that the city to-day presents a wonderful contrast with respect to health, beauty and attractiveness to what was the case less than a dozen years back. We have begun to think here along the same lines. Our natural situation is far better than that of Chicago, and it is possible to make Philadelphia one of the most beautiful cities of the world. We must not forget that Boston realized its duty in this respect some years ago, with a result that it now has miles and miles of beautiful surroundings, magnificent avenues, bosky woods, and gardens in every direction. Our city can do as much, and perhaps more."

MR. S. S. FELS: "Dr. Kelsey mentioned something about the land restricted areas in this country, and the direction in which the talk has gone leads me to say a word about getting rid of our old ideas, as Dr. Kelsey said, and considering conditions as they are now. I believe that there is a direct connection between our want of playgrounds and of planning for the city in a broader way, and our land system. That question is one which it would be well for the City Club to take up for discussion. People are discussing it more and more. I am connected with the Vacant Lots Association of Philadelphia and I know that a great deal of land lies idle, benefitting the community in no way whatever. When the city wants to buy lots it must pay two or three times the proper amount. It seems to me that some scheme of taxation could be devised so that land could not be held for speculative purposes. This is a very broad and weighty question, one which it would benefit our members to study, and therefore I ask our Secretary, who has charge of these matters, to bring this question up for discussion in a little deeper way. I believe more people are thinking than are saying anything about it."

PLANNING AND COMMERCIAL
ORGANIZATIONS, *Ryerson Ritchie*

THE introduction to this speech, given to the
same City Club of Philadelphia by Mr. Ritchie of
Boston, reads: "The members who attended the
Long Table Luncheon of the Club on Saturday,
February 26, 1910, were deeply interested in
Mr. Ritchie's address on 'Commercial Organization.'
Mr. Ritchie is an expert organizer of commercial
bodies and has had more than twenty-five years of
succcessful experience in this field of work. . . .
President George Burnham, Jr., presided
at the meeting." Mr. Ritchie presented only one
of a variety of American businessmen's
views about city planning.

MR. BURNHAM: ". . . Mr. Ritchie has had a wide experience in the
organization of commercial bodies in other cities also. During the past
two years he has been in Boston and has succeeded in getting the various
organizations of that city, which were pulling apart, to try to do substantially the same work. I have great pleasure in introducing to you Mr.
Ritchie.

MR. RITCHIE: "As communities differ in character, so do commercial
bodies. Cleveland, Chicago, Detroit, Boston, Philadelphia and all American
cities differ in important respects. A commercial association that is suitable
for one city is not likely to fit the needs of any other. Each is a separate
entity and must in its own way solve the problems that are peculiar to it.
If the business men of Philadelphia believe that broader organized work
should be done for the city, they must find out what kind of an organization is most fitting, how that organization is to be supported, and what
specific work is most urgent.

.   .   .   .

". . . The successful business organization must stand for those incisive
methods and broad principles that enterprising men of high character adopt
in their own business or professional lives. Each important question affect-

Excerpted from *City Club of Philadelphia Bulletin* (issued by the City Club of
Philadelphia), Vol. 2, No. 7 (1910), 74–79.

ing the city or its commerce should have the benefit of expert research and study and the critical advice and counsel of the men who are best fitted to pass upon it. Methods of procedure should be followed that insure business like analysis and harmonious action.

"It is too often true that at the very outset of movements for the promotion of trade and manufacture the average commercial body disregards the established standards of business—it usually starts with a blare of brass trumpets. In the East as in the West, we have the Boosters' Club, the Boosters' League, the Chamber of Hustlers and a variety of associations with equally appropriate nick names; and they are all supposed to be conducted by staid intelligent business men.

.   .   .   .

"In the United States municipal advertising is receiving much attention and large sums of money are paid for this purpose. Many so-called commercial bodies think that the advertising and exploiting of their cities are their chief mission as well as a measure of their efficiency. Much of this advertising reminds us of the circus-bombastic, strongly colored by exaggeration. . . .

"Large sums are expended annually upon spectacular displays and pageants—gaudy, flimsy, flamboyant flashes of so-called civic enterprise. They are little more than popular carousals and are actually hurtful to the reputation of the city and its commerce. . . .

"The chief aim of some commercial organizations is to make their city known as 'The Great Convention City'; to secure many conventions and build great convention halls. Within the past few years millions have been invested by cities of the United States in fine structures which are especially fitted for but infrequently used by visiting assemblies. Now, what is the effect of over crowding the community? Why, the whole city is put into an uproar. The thoroughfares and and street cars, public buildings and grounds are over crowded. The merchants, transportation lines, hotels, saloons, etc., may profit for a day or two, but the strain, the wear and tear, the damage to property, the interference with regular and legitimate business—these offset any profit or benefit that may come. Conventions that have a commercial, scientific or educational value, doubtless are an advantage, but the assembling of any crowd of mixed people creates a dangerous and abnormal condition in the city, and such a condition is not to be preferred to the orderly and steady course of things. The addition of one little industry that brings fifty families to the city who live contentedly and prosperously, and move about 365 days in the year is of much more value than the sudden influx and outgo of a visiting crowd.

"It is not a little disconcerting to be told that in this year of 1910 quite a few 'big' civic movements, fathered by new or combined commercial bodies, are the 'greatest' movements on the continent, which means 'in the world.' Each one of this class of organizations aims to get more industries, do bigger advertising, secure greater conventions, and boost more than any other in the whole universe. The members who do nothing but pay their dues are led to expect great things. The newspapers that like booms and boosts expect great things, the insistent demand of the crowd of onlookers is for great things; but great things are not accomplished by such means and the public loses faith.

"This exaggerated self-importance on the part of many commercial bodies and their emotional civic enterprise lead them to scatter their interests and undertake too much. They become strenuous, impetuous, hasty, over-enthusiastic. The scattering of effort over a wide-range of interests inevitably brings dissatisfaction and weakens efficiency. Time and influence are lost, while experience and wisdom are being gained. It is better to begin with the wisdom of the business man, by concentrating upon a few of the important problems and by selecting those that have a commercial bearing or those public issues that should be measured by the straight rule of business. I would rather see a new organization begin its work with three instead of thirty committees: it is more certain to attain concrete results and gain prestige. Just as in business life, sure progress is marked by the accomplishment of one thing at a time and thus talents rapidly multiply. . . .

"The establishment of new industries is of far more importance to a city than fairs or festivals, conventions or advertising, booming or boosting. The increase in the employment of capital and of mechanical and manual labor should be a responsibility of the central organization. The securing of new industries is a business enterprise and should follow the established rules of business. A still hunt is one of these rules. The manufacturer, if he is a good business man, wants it clearly understood that the location he may choose for his business is as good or better than any other place.

"There is strong competition among American cities for new industries and those cities that know themselves, their advantages and drawbacks, and pursue a business like policy, will succeed in exact proportion to the ability and wisdom shown by their promoting agencies. If a city, knowing itself, exercises wisdom and diplomacy as well as enterprise and tenacity, it can accelerate its growth commercially. The first question is—what industries are best fitted for the city? Those that can be advantaged by a location here are the industries to seek. Those industries that are looking for money to establish themselves, for bonuses, for tax exemption or land gifts are undesirable in any community and from the standpoint of business. The meritorious industry can readily be distinguished from the indigent concern.

·　　·　　·　　·　　·　　·　　·　　·　　·　　·

". . . When commerce favors a community there is something wrong with its business men if its does not rise to its opportunities. The centre of all organized activity is the city itself; and the city's character is as clearly marked by the lines of business or class of industries located there as it is by the native character and the acquired culture of its people. If you mentally compare a number of cities you will think of one as modest, unassertive, unpretentious; another as self-laudatory, conceited, bombastic; a few as self-satisfied, self-conscious, self-important. Some citizens impress one as common-place, vulgar; others as refined, respectable. It is easy to know a city,—personally. One need only look about in the streets; note the faces, voices, manners, read the newspapers, the head lines, the advertisements; examine the signs and sign-boards, question the policemen, or the man on the street. As the material progress of the community depends upon commerce, so commerce depends upon the community. The citizen has a moral obligation, makes the community socially and gives it its composite personality. The city reflects the intelligence, worth and energy of its people. It is like a garden: if it is neglected it will run to weeds.

"Changes are coming fast in trade and industry: of late years there has been a veritable transformation. Not long ago competition was the life of trade, but now combination is fast squeezing the life out of competition. The swift drift of commerce calls for an understanding of economic geography. If the trust is objectionable so also is combination among merchants. Whatever our views may be as to monopolies and price regulation, we must all agree that the organization is fast taking the place of the individual. Communities must organize to safeguard and promote their interests. The cities are slow in doing what the great business institutions have done and are doing. Has any of our great cities taken full advantages of its opportunities? What American city has made a thorough and scientific study of its facilities and resources, and of the factors and elements of its development?

.   .   .   .

". . . The centers of action are our cities—and the cities should lead. We know very well that Philadelphia will continue to grow and prosper, but are existing conditions in themselves sufficient to insure its greater future? Individual enterprise will do much, but individual enterprise *massed* can do almost anything within reason. Make the intelligence of Philadelphia single minded in purpose and you can exercise irresistible influence and power. Philadelphia has competitors and rivals. If she intends to pass her rivals and competitors, she should have a united organization—one that serves as the brain of the city—sees ahead, comprehends the whole situation and develops each factor and agency within its grasp.

"The changes that have come to the business world and to the urban communities have reformed the so-called commercial association. Formerly, the board or exchange was held together by some commercial interest. Today these organizations ought to be, and many of them are, held together by a communal interest. The business interests are already organized for their own protection and advantage. The welfare and growth of the community affect business and often touch it intimately. The virile commercial association should be a civic society; and if it is not a civic society it has little or no public influence—and that is right. A commercial body that does not care for the city, as a city, is not even a good commercial body.

. . . .

". . . Many American cities have recently gone through a period of critical self examination. The work of refinement has been begun and is being furthered through the initiative, enterprise and influence of organized bodies of business men. These movements are not conducted by parties nor by partisans, not by the organized politicians nor the unorganized public. It is the business association that is finding the weak and the strong places in the body politic, and by business-like and professional treatment is strengthening them.

"Aside from trade and industrial interests we find the associations of business men concerned about parks, playgrounds and boulevards; civic centers, city planning and better housing; public health, sanitary improvements and street cleanliness; honest government, wise legislation and better citizenship; new charters, economic methods and higher efficiency; more enterprise, better business management of our cities. One has but to think of a dozen or more of our economical centers to recognize the fact that the recent notable development of many American cities stands to the credit of the new spirit back of the modern association of commerce. It seems to me that the influences and motives that stimulate the energy and underlie the ambition of these institutions give great promise for the future.

"There is ample evidence that the common interest has come to be the recognized concern of business men, and as one consequence their associations are receiving into membership and securing the aid of our ablest and most patriotic men. On any public issue it is not difficult now to call into active service the busiest men of the city. And by reason of this voluntary service the cities of America are receiving, and will more and more receive the benefit of keen analysis, judicial criticism and businesslike treatment of commercial problems. Our business bodies will, figuratively speaking, hold a magnifying glass over the public treasury and the public service and aided by their talents and loyalty cure many ills of our so-called democratic government.

"On the one hand it may be said that it is not an ideal condition when a democratic people, with sovereign rights, look to any class of citizens for protection and aid. The business men of the city form a class, and we know very well that in that class business honor has ever had a hard fight against the avarice of business. But, on the other hand, honor is the keystone of the arch of commerce and no class can be more safely trusted with public responsibilities: moreover, none is more respected by the mass of men."

BUSINESS VISION AND CIVIC SPIRIT,
John Ihlder

> JOHN IHLDER was the Secretary of the Board of
> Trade Committee on Municipal Affairs in Grand
> Rapids, Michigan. By 1909, he could
> characterize "the reformer" as old-fashioned, and
> advocate a different kind of program:
> first, "securing betterment by calling attention to
> measures rather than men"; and then,
> "putting before the people a city plan, a scheme
> showing the city's possibilities and
> indicating the way it should develop." While some
> of the rhetoric of this Board of Trade
> Committee is taken from the good government
> reformers, no doubt the Board's vision of
> this small city was colored by the members'
> occupations and respectable social positions.

We do not aim to be reformers, but performers. The underlying principle of our work is that if we can interest the people in the building of the city, efficiency and honesty in government will follow inevitably. This does not mean stimulating the public by a series of spectacular proposals, though, of course, these are necessary occasionally; but interesting them in the daily routine of city work, making them take in it the same steady interest that they feel in their own concerns, explaining to them clearly both the methods and the effects of keeping streets clean; extending sewers and water mains; following an intelligent financial policy—subjects usually considered dry and uninteresting, but an understanding of which is necessary to intelligent and effective citizenship, and an understanding of which makes city building a game of intense interest.

Reprinted from "The Development of Civic Spirit," *Cincinnati Conference for Good City Government* (National Municipal League), 1909, pp. 424–32.

With these, of course, we are constantly holding out the vision of the city of the future. It has seemed to us that the fault of militant citizens in the past has been that they have constantly fought for negatives, to lessen evil, to drive bad men out of office and that they have neglected to make routine city work attractive to the average man. So we are experimenting on the other method. We fight for positives, we assume that city officials represent the people and so we try to influence them for the city's good by making the people take an intelligent, public-spirited interest in what their officials are doing. We take no part in the selection of the candidates, basing our hopes for progress on the increasing foresight and understanding of the people whom those candidates represent. Aside from this general educational campaign which is carried on unceasingly by means of committee meetings whose discussions are published in the newspapers, by addresses delivered before neighborhood associations, by literature circulated broadcast and by civic revivals, we occasionally take definite action for the adoption by the government of some concrete measure, such as home rule, a lodging-house ordinance, Arbor Day distribution of trees and plants.

In Grand Rapids we have not yet such tangible monuments to the success of our efforts as Harrisburg can show. We have not equalled Denver or Cleveland in the creation of great public improvements. But this is due to two causes. First, we have been at work a shorter time. Second, we have adopted a different method, slower but, we believe, destined to be much more permanent in its results. Instead of making the improvements themselves the chief objects of our endeavors, we have made them incidental. Our main object has been to arouse the people to a constructive interest in the city and its problems, to study with them its needs and resources and then to act with them in carrying out plans which commend themselves to others as well as ourselves.

This is a long-time process, but its effects, we believe, will be worth the time, for when results come they will be not merely a group of public buildings or a pure-water supply, but an active and intelligent citizenship which will give us all these things which we desire and what is more, a citizenship which will regard Grand Rapids as a common heritage in the intelligent development of which all are vitally concerned. That will mean not only specific public improvements but also honest and efficient government, wholesome and sanitary living conditions, a city designed to make the most of all its advantages so that its people may live the fullest and happiest lives.

It is difficult to trace the beginnings of any great movement, for beginnings are always obscure and the men who made those obscure beginnings, who first contended against indifference and ridicule are, while the hardest to find, those most deserving of honorable mention. There probably never was in the history of Grand Rapids or any other American city a time when there was not a small group of men striving earnestly and unselfishly for civic betterment. But it was less than two years ago that this group learned how to make the mass of the people sympathize and co-operate. Yet the work done before must not be minimized, for it planted here and there all over the city seeds which now are sprouting, which we who came later are cultivating with the prospect of making them spread into an abundant harvest.

I mention this because there is in all of us a tendency to ignore the painful and apparently fruitless, but absolutely necessary, preliminary work when at last large results begin to appear.

About two years ago we struck the combination which now is giving results. Only this fall, yes only within these past few days, have we seen the effects of our work become so evident that we appear before you to-day confident that our method is right, that the future of our city is safe. There probably will be setbacks, human progress has never been without them, but we have reason for faith that barring some unforeseen and uncalculable disaster we are on the way to making of Grand Rapids a true and an efficient democracy, one in the operation of which nearly every citizen will take a live, constructive, far-seeing interest. We have taken our citizens and our officials as we found them, we began our work at a time when reformers were discredited and disliked as mere faultfinders, however worthy their motives; when our people had indeed freed themselves in large measure from thralldom to national parties in their municipal elections but when they still thought of the city in terms of politics and when, consequently, they were, as it seemed, incurably pessimistic of any good thing being done by the city as a city. This, may I say parenthetically, seems to be an unfortunate effect of the work of the old-fashioned reformer who sought to accomplish good by devoting his energies to exposing evil.

But to begin on the story. Grand Rapids has long been, from the point of view of the party machine politician, a stiff-necked community. It has paid the penalty by being passed over when there were plums in the shape of state institutions to be distributed. But such penalties may be well afforded when in the opposite scale are thrown the rewards of independence. When men are needed the party turns to us. Among our citizens are a United States senator and an ambassador, while the congressman of the district has opened an office within our boundaries in order that he may come within the charmed circle of our fellowship. These are tacit acknowledgments of the leadership which Grand Rapids has now in the state. For years the city led the direct primary fight. The first victory was won when the legislature enacted a law giving only to us the privilege of choosing candidates by direct vote. So successful was this measure that the law has recently been made state-wide. Then we began to demand a non-partisan direct primary. This, of course, was met with bitter opposition at Lansing, and not only was the demand refused but through "a clerical error" our old primary law was so changed as to become inoperative. So for a season we were thrown back on the old caucus method of choosing candidates. This seeming set-back had one great advantage. During the time the direct primary law was in operation its opponents had denounced it as not having brought forward so good a class of candidates as had the old caucus system. That it brought out the voters and made them take a part in selecting office-holders such as they had never done before was too patent for argument. When, therefore, the caucus was unexpectedly restored much interest was shown as to the men who would be nominated for office. The advocates of the caucus were put on their mettle. And as a result they renominated for the principal offices the very men who had been nominated under the direct primary the time before. So that point was settled. Even when trying to make a record the caucus could not improve on the work of the direct primary.

But before all this, in 1904-5, we had secured through a fortunate combination of circumstances, a non-partisan mayor. Nominated by the Democrats after a bitter factional wrangle that cost him the support of a considerable section of his party, he was elected largely by Republican votes. Taking this as a mandate to disregard party lines, he tried to guide himself by only one consideration, the good of the city. To that administration we look back as to the beginning of most of what is encouraging in our government. Then was started the great work of flood protection, two concrete walls four miles long beside the river which divides the city, a new charter which abolished many unnecessary offices, began the work of consolidating power and responsibility, established the principle of choosing administrative officers regardless of politics and retaining them so long as they show ability and industry, and a remodeled school board. Before the school board had been an unwieldy, patronage-bestowing body of twenty-four men elected by wards. Now it is a compact public-spirited body of nine men elected at large.

All these changes were born of much discussion, for the non-partisan mayor was one who talked in public instead of in the seclusion of his private office. The charter as finally adopted was far from perfect; this was the beginning of such public discussion of big matters and some of the suggestions coming in late were incorporated hurriedly. But this charter was a great improvement on the old. And more important still, the discussions which it started have continued until to-day the mass of people in Grand Rapids know fairly well what they want in the way of government.

It was a result of all this discussion that the Municipal Affairs Committee of the Board of Trade found its work. We were at that time still of the belief that a good system of government should work itself without more than sporadic help from the people. But a few men saw the fallacy of this belief. The Board of Trade had taken considerable interest in the framing of the new charter and after that instrument was finally completed its Municipal Affairs Committee took upon itself the task of continuing to work for the city. In this committee was gathered a considerable part of that small group of militant citizens above referred to. Outside of their organization were many associations designed to secure better government by selecting candidates for office, by bringing pressure to bear upon candidates already selected or by uncovering the misdeeds of officials. There is no need of reciting their names for every city contains similar associations. The Municipal Affairs Committee therefore set itself a different task, that of securing betterment by calling attention to measures rather than men. It began along lines familiar to all of you, the abatement of the smoke and bill-board nuisances, an Arbor Day distribution of trees and plants. Then it conceived the audacious project of putting before the people a city plan, a scheme showing the city's possibilities and indicating the way it should develop. The committee's purpose was to put before the people a vision of their city as it may be, trusting that once that vision had penetrated into their consciousness they would select as their representatives men capable of making the vision real. That was about three years ago.

Since then the history of the city plan has been the history of Grand Rapids.

Of course, so sweeping a statement as this needs explanation. During those three years many things not only important in themselves, but significant of the future, have taken place. The new school board has proved itself worthy of the people's confidence by making a transformation in our system of education. The Public Library has grown into an institution which through its branches and depots and its free lectures reaches every neighborhood. The Municipal Affairs Committee has expanded both in membership and in purpose until it covers a field it did not dream of three years ago. And all over the city there have sprung up neighborhood improvement associations, the object of which is to bring people together for the common good.

But remembering all this it still seems to me that the past three years the history of the city plan has been the history of Grand Rapids, for the great purpose of the plan was not to show us how we could best bring about certain material improvements. It was to put before us a vision of the city as we may make it, and by the power of that vision draw us all together in one great fellowship.

When it first broached the subject the committee was greeted with jeers and mockery. That anyone should dream of putting through a great altruistic project in a practical, individualistic community seemed to the man on the street the height of the ridiculous. It was bound to run counter to selfish interests which would block it. Futile attempts to secure little improvements, such as rounding off the corners of a street jog, were recalled. If it was impossible to carry through these small projects because selfish interests stood in the way, one must be crack-brained who seriously proposed to extend the chief business street of the city through a built-up district, or to create a new civic center several blocks away from the existing public buildings.

Many of the leading men of the town took this attitude—judges, manufacturers and merchants. But here and there among them we found, sometimes when we had least expected it, one who had a larger vision, one who realized that the large project may succeed where the small one fails, because the large project seems worth while and because it fires the imagination.

In spite of jeers and ridicule the committee took its work seriously. This, it must be remembered, was before town planning had become what it is to-day, almost a common-place in America. A report showing the waste in money and duplications due to lack of planning in the past was prepared and submitted to the directors of the Board of Trade. They indorsed it and even recommended that the Board raise the money with which to secure a town plan. This recommendation was, however, disregarded on the ground that as the plan must needs be carried out by the city government, that government should be responsible for its preparation.

This entailed more cost in time, but a cost well afforded. The aldermen, needless to say, could not understand what we were driving at. Finally, however, a committee of three was appointed by the council and after months of argument and persuasion they were induced to recommend the appointment of a commission of nine citizens to take up the matter. But no money was given these citizens. They spent a winter at the task and then found it too big for them unless they could get expert advice. But expert advice costs money and that the council was in no mood to give, for to the aldermanic mind the whole scheme was folly without a single practical feature in it. So the Municipal Affairs Committee came to the commission's aid by giving the first civic revival.

Charles Zueblin, then connected with the University of Chicago, was engaged as the revivalist. Requests for formal endorsement were sent to every society and lodge in the city. Literature was distributed broadcast.

Revival week began with discouragement. Rain poured down and the attendance at the meetings was small. But day by day the attendance increased and at last hundreds had to be turned away. On Saturday eighty of the representative business men attended a conference luncheon and voted that money should be provided for a city plan report. That evening and on Sunday petition cards were circulated at the revival meetings. On Monday the council granted the appropriation.

This was the first great triumph. It lay not so much in having secured the money for a report, as in having made the people take a living interest in their city's future.

Almost a year elapsed before the report appeared, but it was a well-spent year. The commission held frequent meetings which were fully reported in the newspapers. When Messrs. Carrere and Brunner, our expert advisers, came to Grand Rapids their doings were fully chronicled. They were taken before the common council, before the Board of Trade, public meetings were held at which they addressed the people. So, when at last the report appeared the people had come to have some understanding of what it meant.

Since its appearance last May the report has been growing steadily in popular favor. Still we did not feel confident enough of its hold upon the people to demand immediate compliance with its recommendations. So this month we held our second civic revival. Again we engaged Mr. Zueblin, but instead of holding all our meetings in one place, we sent him about the city, in the endeavor to reach audiences who would not come down town. The last meetings were on Sunday in our largest theater, which was filled. Again we made the effects of the revival definite by holding a conference luncheon attended by more than one hundred business men and city officials. There we adopted a program endorsing the city plan report and recommending that we take up one great improvement at a time, but meanwhile, as opportunity offers, do what we can to further those whose turn comes later. In consonance with this program we decided to concentrate our efforts this winter upon a campaign for pure water. At the same time, however, we demanded that a new fire-engine house, which it was proposed to place in the way of the extension of our chief business street as recommended by the report should be moved back, additional property being bought for the purpose, so that when the turn of this improvement comes we may find it easier, not more difficult of accomplishment.

But again I wish to point out to you that what we are aiming at is not a series of public improvements. These are only incidental. What we desire is the creation of a new sense of citizenship, a new and vital interest in the city as our common heritage. If we can secure that the improvements will follow inevitably. And in order that we may secure that we are going about our improvements slowly, giving the people time to think and understand. We have our plan which will enable us to do our work wisely, more wisely we believe than if we had carried on a whirlwind campaign for a big bond issue which would have made possible all the work at once. For such a campaign, we fear, would be followed by reaction. The great object having been attained, there would have followed lethargy and indifference. What we hope for is steady improvement as a result of steady interest, improvement not only in the physical appearance of the city, but in its government and in the lives of its people.

SOCIAL POWER AND THE REAL ESTATE
BOARD, *Donald H. Bouma*

THE author is a sociologist, the year is 1962. His
descriptive analysis shows a real estate
board displaying considerable control over the destinies
of a small city. The urban perspective
reflected in the board's activities is distinctly
business-oriented, although expressing also a desire for
a physically attractive (single-family homes) city.

The real estate board was selected as the research focus because of
several indications during the exploratory phase of the study that it was in
a key position of influence in Grand Valley. Those in authority positions
and heads of organizations in the city frequently mentioned the board as
being an effective force in the making of community-wide decisions.

A study of the alignment of community groups on several controversial
issues which went to the voters for decisions revealed that the real estate
group had been victorious in each instance, while other groups also
suggested as having influence, such as the Chamber of Commerce and
the newspapers, had been defeated several times. The city's leading newspaper editorialized as follows: "We know from what has happened in
the past that it is almost essential that any proposal to undertake a civic
and school expansion program have the real estate board's support if it is
to succeed."

The Grand Valley board had also been recognized by both state and
national real estate associations for its effective community participation.
It had been given the highest award granted by the National Association of
Real Estate Boards for "civic activity." Mentioned specifically were the
assistance of the local board in framing a new city zoning ordinance, the
successful fight for rent decontrol, assistance to the city in its land value
survey in preparing for scientific reassessment of the city, and its active
support in helping to pass a two-mill twenty-year tax increase for a school
building program.

.   .   .   .

Excerpted from "Analysis of the Social Power Position of a Real Estate Board,"
Social Problems, Vol. 10 (1962), 123, 125, 130–32. Reprinted by permission of the
Society for the Study of Social Problems.

The factors found to be significantly operative in the social power position of the board in Grand Valley include the social cohesion of the group and its mechanisms of social control, the financial structure of the organization, the cumulative character of social power, the social capital available to the group because of the technical information it possessed, the awareness of the value systems of various publics, direct participation of board members in authority positions, the handling of opposition groups, and the adequacy of the legitimation processes. . . .

.   .   .   .

The cumulative aspect of social power is also indicated by the fact that those who are concerned with getting a decision made tend to consult the group known to have been effective in shaping past decisions. These consulting and conferring processes open up new areas in which the power group can influence community decisions, and the process is carried on in its own back yard. Instead of having to go to the voters or having to assert itself in the arena of authority on given issues, the board finds issues being brought to it and can involve itself in decision-making in its very early stages. Further, the influence is exerted in non-public manner so that the risk of arousing negative community reaction which so often is the response to a position of social power, is minimized. Thus a pattern of success in the decision process provided for the board the basis for maintaining and extending the social power position.

A fourth factor in the analysis of the social power position of the real estate board was its possession of knowledge and technical information in certain strategic areas in the decision-making process. Realtors were uniquely knowledgeable concerning taxation, assessments, city planning, zoning, housing, residential segregation, industrial and commercial relocations, and the like.

Since the property tax was the primary source of income for the support of municipal functions, and since any enrichment or extension of city and school services involved, generally, a shift in the property tax rate, the board's knowledge in the area of taxation placed it in a crucial position for influencing a whole array of allied community decisions. When the city devised a new city-wide zoning code the real estate board was asked to appoint a committee of its members to work with the planning department. The new ordinance was drawn in relation to the overall master plan to direct the outward growth of the city and to redevelop and rehabilitate certain areas in the city. The opportunity and ability to influence the construction of a zoning ordinance with such far-reaching consequences for the future growth, development, and rehabilitation of the community indicated another facet of the social power position of the board.

A fifth factor which explained the competency of the board in influencing community decisions was its awareness of, sensitivity to, and identification with the value systems of the community.

The real estate business is of such a nature as to develop in the realtors a keen awareness of the value systems of the community, primarily because of its intimate contact with people from all classes and segments of the community. . . .

Further, this close contact covers all segments of the community, cutting across racial, ethnic, economic, religious and other groupings. Through the contacts of individual realtors, the board developed an awareness of value systems. For example, few members of the Chamber of Commerce came into close contact with the customer. This was especially true of those chosen to the board of directors, generally the most prominent business men in the city. What contact there was with customers was on a momentary basis or, in the case of many businesses, on a selective basis, so that no general awareness of values resulted.

.   .   .   .

This awareness of and sensitivity to community values enabled the board to determine the kinds of positions the public would support and partially explains the success pattern of the board. However, this also acted as a check on its social power position. Points were reached beyond which the board dared not go because of a fear that public reaction would interfere with the business possibilities of the individual realtor. This was one of the few limits to the social power position.

Not only was the board aware of and sensitive to value systems, but it also identified itself with these value patterns. One of the esteemed values in the community was home ownership, and each year Grand Valley is listed as a leading city in the country in percentage of home owners. Throughout its history the board had strongly identified itself with the interests of property owners, and fought battles in their name. . . .

.   .   .   .

Because of its identification with the interests of home owners the board could successfully legitimize its decisions on community issues in terms of home owner values. One member put it this way: "We were opposed to public housing because we felt that it would hurt our pocketbooks, but we talked tax threat to home ownership to the people." If the board was opposed to a suggested change it told the public that the proposal would involve a tax increase which was a "threat to home ownership."

When the board shifted its stand and favored a tax increase for schools, the legitimation was still in terms of home ownership and property values. In public statements the board told people that the suggested increase was best "for the home owner and taxpayer since antiquated and crowded school buildings hold back a community and affect property values."

The board's repeated stands against higher taxes, of course, easily identifies it with general community values. Everybody is presumably opposed to higher taxes. Although inadequacy of city and school services could conceivably backfire on the group responsible for the low taxes, diversion channels for the negative affect were opened up by charging city and school officials with unwise use of the "adequate" funds available.

Finally, the community took pride in being a conservative city, and it was characterized by a very slow growth pattern which necessitated few changes. The conservative stands of the board, generally urging a negative vote on issues, harmonized with this value.

A sixth factor in the power position of the real estate board was the direct participation of realtors in the arena of authority through the elective and appointive positions held by individual members. In such cases there was a confluence of the two aspects of social power—influence and authority—which were distinguished earlier. The realtor-councilman is as a realtor a member of a group having influence and, as a councilman, a member of a group having authority. In such situations the interaction between the two facets of social power becomes extremely close, and at times it is difficult to discern to what extent the influence structure is acting in the arena of authority, or to what extent the authority structure is used to advance or retard the cause of the influence structure.

The holding of authority positions by realtors opened up additional possibilities and unique channels for the exercise of influence. Realtors had extensive membership in the state legislature. After farmers and lawyers, the third largest group was made up of real estate and insurance men. For years two of the three state representatives from Grand Valley were members of the real estate board. This not only provided the board with direct access to the legislature for the implementation of decisions in that arena of authority, but also provided the board with observation posts so that impending decisions which affected its interests could immediately be brought to its attention.

.   .   .   .

These were some of the important ingredients of the social power position of the real estate board in Grand Valley. It had successfully influenced many community decisions, both in the arena of authority and in the arena of public elections. Although social power is generally evaluated negatively in our society, and the image of the "man of power" or the "power group" is largely a negative one, the board exercised its power with a minimum of negative public reaction. For one thing, the board did not involve itself in every community decision—only those it considered major ones—and never endorsed candidates in elections. Further, it handled well the legitimation function and was able to make its position seem valid and right.

CITY PLANNING AND THE SYMBOLISM
OF SPACE, *Walter Firey*

CERTAIN parts of cities may be deeply invested with civic meaning. In Washington, D.C., the green areas, which contain some of the nation's greatest monuments, constitute sacred locales. In Boston, as Firey's account shows, the Common carries such a freight of symbolism as to maintain the area against the direct invasion of business enterprises. City planning also has taken this symbolism into account.

If we turn to another type of land use pattern in Boston, that comprised by the Boston Common and the old burying grounds, we encounter another instance of spatial symbolism which has exerted a marked influence upon the ecological organization of the rest of the city. The Boston Common is a survival from colonial days when every New England town allotted a portion of its land to common use as a cow pasture and militia field. Over the course of three centuries Boston has grown entirely around the Common so that today we find a 48-acre tract of land wedged directly into the heart of the business district. On three of its five sides are women's apparel shops, department stores, theaters and other high-rent locational activities. On the fourth side is Beacon street, extending alongside Beacon Hill. Only the activities of Hill residents have prevented business from invading this side. The fifth side is occupied by the Public Garden. A land value map portrays a strip of highest values pressing upon two sides of the Common, on Tremont and Boylston streets, taking the form of a long narrow band.

Before considering the ecological consequences of this configuration

From "Sentiment and Symbolism as Ecological Variables," *American Sociological Review*, Vol. 10 (1945), 143–46. Reprinted by permission of the American Sociological Association and the author.

let us see what attitudes have come to be associated with the Common. There is an extensive local literature about the Common and in it we find interesting sentiments expressed. One citizen speaks of:

> . . . the great principle exemplified in the preservation of the Common. Thank Heaven, the tide of money making must break and go around that.

Elsewhere we read:

> Here, in short are all our accumulated memories, intimate, public, private.
> Boston Common was, is, and ever will be a source of tradition and inspiration from which the New Englanders may renew their faith, recover their moral force, and strengthen their ability to grow and achieve.

The Common has thus become a "sacred" object, articulating and symbolizing genuine historical sentiments of a certain portion of the community. Like all such objects its sacredness derives, not from any intrinsic spatial attributes, but rather from its representation in peoples' minds as a symbol for collective sentiments.

Such has been the force of these sentiments that the Common has become buttressed up by a number of legal guarantes. The city charter forbids Boston in perpetuity to dispose of the Common or any portion of it. The city is further prohibited by state legislation from building upon the Common, except within rigid limits, or from laying out roads or tracks across it. By accepting the bequest of one George F. Parkman, in 1908, amounting to over five million dollars, the city is further bound to maintain the Common, and certain other parks, "for the benefit and enjoyment of its citizens."

What all this has meant for the spatial development of Boston's retail center is clear from the present character of that district. Few cities of comparable size have so small a retail district in point of area. Unlike the spacious department stores of most cities, those in Boston are frequently compressed within narrow confines and have had to extend in devious patterns through rear and adjoining buildings. Traffic in downtown Boston has literally reached the saturation point, owing partly to the narrow one-way streets but mainly to the lack of adequate arterials leading into and out of the Hub. The American Road Builders Association has estimated that there is a loss of $81,000 per day in Boston as a result of traffic delay. Trucking in Boston is extremely expensive. These losses ramify out to merchants, manufacturers, commuters, and many other interests. Many proposals have been made to extend a through arterial across the Common, thus relieving the extreme congestion on Tremont and Beacon streets, the two arterials bordering the park. Earlier suggestions, prior to the construction of the subway, called for street car tracks across the Common. But "the controlling sentiment of the citizens of Boston, and of large numbers throughout the State, is distinctly opposed to allowing any such use of the Common." Boston has long suffered from land shortage and unusually high real estate values as a result both of the narrow confines of the peninsula comprising the city center and as a result of the exclusion from income-yielding uses of so large a tract as the Common. A further difficulty has arisen from the rapid southwesterly extension of the business district in the past two decades. With the Common lying directly in the path of this extension the business district has had to stretch around it in an elongated fashion, with obvious inconvenience to shoppers and consequent loss to business.

The Common is not the only obstacle to the city's business expansion. No less than three colonial burying-grounds, two of them adjoined by ancient church buildings, occupy downtown Boston. The contrast that is presented by 9-story office buildings reared up beside quiet cemeteries affords visible evidence of the conflict between "sacred" and "profane" that operates in Boston's ecological pattern. The dis-economic consequences of commercially valuable land being thus devoted to non-utilitarian purposes goes even further than the removal from business uses of a given amount of space. For it is a standard principle of real estate that business property derives added value if adjoining properties are occupied by other businesses. Just as a single vacancy will depreciate the value of a whole block of business frontage, so a break in the continuity of stores by a cemetery damages the commercial value of surrounding properties. But, even more than the Common, the colonial burying-grounds of Boston have become invested with a moral significance which renders them almost inviolable. Not only is there the usual sanctity which attaches to all cemeteries, but in those of Boston there is an added sacredness growing out of the age of the grounds and the fact that the forebears of many of New England's most distinguished families as well as a number of colonial and Revolutionary leaders lie buried in these cemeteries. There is thus a manifold symbolism to these old burying-grounds, pertaining to family lineage, early nationhood, civic origins, and the like, all of which have strong sentimental associations. What has been said of the old burying-grounds applies with equal force to a number of other venerable landmarks in central Boston. Such buildings as the Old South Meeting-House, the Park Street Church, King's Chapel and the Old State House—all foci of historical associations—occupy commercially valuable land and interrupt the continuity of business frontage on their streets. Nearly all of these landmarks have been challenged at various times by real estate and commercial interests which sought to have them replaced by more profitable uses. In every case community sentiments have resisted such threats.

In all these examples we find a symbol-sentiment relationship which has exerted a significant influence upon land use. Nor should it be thought that such phenomona are mere ecological "sports." Many other older American cities present similar locational characteristics. . . .

THE REDEVELOPMENT OF
WEST END, *Herbert J. Gans*

> A SOCIOLOGIST who did an excellent field study of "an
> inner-city Boston neighborhood," gives here,
> first, the reasons why the city officials
> decided to redevelop West End; then he tells how
> the residents responded to the redevelopment
> plans as they slowly evolved and became implemented.
> Gans' account shows vividly several classic
> urban perspectives in sharp contrast and conflict.

REDEVELOPMENT: THE CITY'S REASONS

There were many reasons for the city to redevelop the West End. Boston is a poor city, and the departure of middle-class residents and industry for the suburbs has left it with an over-supply of tax-exempt institutions and low income areas that yield little for the municipal coffers. Through the federal redevelopment program, the city father hoped to replace some of the low-yield areas with high-rent buildings that would bring in additional municipal income. Moreover, they believed that a shiny new redevelopment project would cleanse its aged, tenement-dominated skyline, and increase the morale of private and public investors. This in turn would supposedly lead to a spiral of further private rebuilding in the city.

The West End was thought to be particularly suitable for redevelopment. Because of its central location adjacent to Beacon Hill and near the downtown shopping area, real estate men had long felt that the area was "ripe" for higher—and more profitable—uses. The long block fronting on the Charles River was considered attractive for luxury housing. Some businessmen believed that the decline of the downtown shopping district

Excerpted from *The Urban Villagers* (New York: The Free Press of Glencoe, 1962), pp. 285–98, 304, by permission of the publisher. © The Free Press of Glencoe, a division of the Macmillan Co., 1962.

could be ended by housing "quality shoppers" on its fringes. Moreover, Massachusetts General Hospital was expanding rapidly, and its trustees had long been unhappy about being surrounded by low-income neighbors.

The process of buying and clearing land and relocating residents, however, is expensive. Indeed, no redevelopment project of any scale is likely to be approved unless there are definite assurances that the cleared land will be purchased by a builder. Moreover, Boston had already had an unfortunate experience with its first redevelopment scheme: the "New York streets" project, planned for industrial re-use, which had stood virtually empty for several years after it had been cleared. But because of the West End's favorable location, developers and investors displayed interest from the beginning in making the area a high-rent district.

Political considerations also had to be taken into account, for the project had to be approved by the City Council and the Mayor. Here, too, all the signs were promising. The business community and the city's newspapers were favorably inclined, as were the political leaders of the city outside the West End. And even the West End protest seemed muted. Some years earlier, when it had been proposed to clear the North End, th citizens and the political leaders of that area had raised such an outcry that the project was immediately shelved. But the local politicians in the West End were too few and too powerless for their protests to be heeded. Nor could the West Enders themselves make their voices heard. The Save the West Committee's protest was noted, but as the group's membership was small, and since the Beacon Hill civic leader who supported it was known for his sponsorship of unpopular—and strange—causes, the Committee, in effect, had no political influence. Moreover, the local settlement houses and other caretaking agencies all approved of the redevelopment, partly because their lay leaders were drawn from the Boston business community, and partly because the staffs of these agencies felt that the fortunes of the West Enders would be thereby improved. The Catholic Archdiocese, whose local church was to be saved for architectural reasons, also gave its blessing. Consequently, both the Mayor and the City Council voted for the project, the latter almost unanimously.

Finally, all of Boston was convinced that the West End was a slum which ought to be torn down not only for the sake of the city but also for the good of its own residents. This belief was supported by the general appearance of the area, by studies that had been made in the West End by public and private agencies, and by stories that appeared in the press. . . .

.   .   .   .

Once the relevant agencies had given their blessings, the redevelopment officials went into action, using the procedures they had established in the city's first redevelopment project, and the guides and requirements set up by the federal government. When the site office had been established, the Authority then carried out appraisals to determine the prices to be paid the owners of structures, and a relocation survey to aid in the resettlement of the tenants. After the Authority had taken over the land under eminent domain, it also became responsible for the supervision and maintenance of the buildings, and for the collection of rents. In accordance with the federal law, it made plans to assure that every West Ender would be relocated into a "decent, safe, and sanitary" dwelling unit elsewhere; in public housing, should the family's income make it eligible; or in other apartments that West Enders could find either on their own, or with the help of the Authority were they not eligible for public housing. If tenants paid their rent while in the West End, they received a moving allowance of $25 per room of furniture once they had moved. Should the unit to which they moved fail to meet the triple criterion of standardness, the Authority promised to find them another place in which to live. In these activities and others, the Authority staff believed itself to be acting in the best interests of the city and of the West Enders as well.

THE WEST ENDERS' PERCEPTION OF THE REDEVELOPMENT PROCESS

To the West Enders, the many years between the announcement that the area would be redeveloped and the actual clearing of their neighborhood appeared quite differently than it did to the city and its officials. No one with whom I talked was quite sure when the West Enders had first heard about the plans for redeveloping their neighborhood. The Planning Board's recommendation in 1949 had been made public; of course, and the press had also carried stories of the preliminary planning studies that had begun in 1951. At that time, the residents were opposed to the redevelopment, but did not feel themselves sufficiently threatened to be alarmed. . . .

.   .   .   .

Tenants, and resident owners whose buildings were still occupied, were almost unanimously opposed to redevelopment. Some of the tenants in the most dilapidated structures were hopeful that government action would provide them with better places to live. But the vast majority of West Enders had no desire to leave. As I have tried to show throughout the book, they were content to live in the West End, and were willing to overlook some of its physical defects in comparison with its many social advantages. Those who had been born there cited the traditional belief that "the place you're born is where you want to die." Even criticism of the area would sometimes be stilled by the remark, "never disparage a place in which you've grown up." Many of the people who had left the West End at marriage would come back occasionally—if only to shop—and one man whose family had left the area shortly after his birth twenty years earlier insisted that "you always come back to the place of your childhood."

Most people were not very explicit at that time about their feelings toward the area. Since the West End still existed and since they had never known anything else, they could not estimate how its disappearance might affect them. "What's so good about the West End? We're used to it," was one quite typical comment. Subsequently, however, I heard more anguished remarks that indicated how important the area and its people were to the speaker. In December, 1957, the day after the federal government gave the city the go-ahead, one young Italian man said:

> I wish the world would end tonight. . . . I wish they'd tear the whole damn town down, damn scab town. . . . I'm going to be lost without the West End. Where the hell can I go?

Another West Ender told me: "It isn't right to scatter the community to all four winds. It pulls the heart out of a guy to lose all his friends." Shortly before the taking, a barber in his early sixties ended a discussion of death that was going on in the shop with these comments:

> I'm not afraid to die, but I don't want to. But if they tear the West End down and we are all scattered from all the people I know and that know me, and they wouldn't know where I was, I wouldn't want to die and people not know it.

Perhaps because most people were opposed to the redevelopment, they could not quite believe that it would happen. Over the years, they began to realize that the redevelopment plans were in earnest, but they were—and remained—skeptical that the plans would ever be implemented. Even on the day of the taking, the person just quoted told me: "I don't believe it; I won't believe it till it happens. I'll wait till I get my notice. . . . You'll see, they'll start at the lower end, and they'll never come up here."

There were several reasons for the West Enders' skepticism. First, they had considerable difficulty in understanding the complicated parade of preliminary and final approvals, or the tortuous process by which the plans moved back and forth between the Housing Authority, the City Council, the Mayor, the State Housing Board, and the federal Housing and Home Finance Agency. Instead of realizing that each approval was one step in a tested and finite administrative procedure, the West Enders saw it as merely another decision in a seemingly purposeless, erratic, and infinite series. Thus, when the federal housing agency did give its final approval in the winter of 1957, most West Enders did not understand that this was the last step in the process. They recalled that the same agency had approved it several times before, without any visible result. Thus, they felt certain that there would be more meetings, and more decisions, and that twenty-five years later, the West End would still be there.

Their failure to understand the process can be traced back partly to the poor information that they received from the press and city agencies. The latter, assuming that West Enders understood the nature of the process, did not attempt to describe it in sufficient detail. Moreover, city officials did not see that to West Enders, all government agencies were pretty much the same, and that notions of city-state-federal relationships were strange to them. The West Enders in turn paid little attention to the press releases, and were more receptive to distorted facts and the many rumors that they could hear from friends and neighbors.

Moreover, they noted that official announcements were vague about when things would begin to happen in the West End, and that if estimates were given, they were usually wrong. . . .

Nor could West Enders really conceive of the possibility that the area would be torn down. They had watched the demolition of parts of the North End for the Central Artery—the city's expressway system—and while they disapproved, they realized that a highway was of public benefit and could not be opposed. But the idea that the city could clear the West End, and then turn the land over to a private builder for luxury apartments seemed unbelievable.

Their skepticism turned to incredulity when the city awarded the redevelopment contract to the second highest bidder. The lawyer's ties with the Mayor convinced them that the redevelopment was a politically motivated plot to take the West End for private profit with government help. The idea that a private builder could build apartments then estimated to rent for $40 to $50 a room—more than they were paying for five- and six-room apartments—was hard to believe. And that the government could encourage this venture seemed incomprehensible except as a result of political corruption, the exchange of bribes, and the cutting in of politicians on future profits. . . .

Thereafter, all of the steps in the process were interpreted as attempts to scare the West Enders out of the area, so that the values of the buildings would be reduced and the private developers could buy them more cheaply. But even then, people were skeptical that this scheme would come to fruitation, partially because it was so immoral. Many West Enders argued that only in Russia could the government deprive citizens of their property in such a dictatorial manner.

Also, West Enders found it hard to think far ahead. Even if they could admit to themselves that the area might eventually be "thrown down"—as they put it—it was still difficult to think about what might happen years hence, especially in the absence of incontrovertible evidence. As already noted, Housing Authority announcements were not considered reliable. Nor were announcements and newspaper stories generally accepted as evidence; people had to see more concrete examples of the city's plans before they would believe that the city was in earnest. For example, the registered letters, which the Redevelopment Authority sent to all West Enders indicating that it had taken over the area, were less persuasive than the announcement that as of May, 1958, rents were to be paid not to landlords but to the city's relocation office. Only when people saw their neighbors—and especially their landlords—going to that office to pay their rents did all of them realize that the end had come. . . .

And finally, of course, West Enders simply denied the possibility of redevelopment because they did not want it to happen. They were content to live in the West End, and could not imagine living elsewhere, or going about the city looking for "rooms."

As a result, life in the West End went on as always, with relatively little overt concern about the redevelopment, and with even less public discussion of it. On the days following the announcement of another decision in the process, people would talk about it heatedly, but then it would be forgotten again until the next announcement. There had been so many announcements, and so many meetings, and nothing ever seemed to happen afterwards. Surely it would be safe—and easy—to assume that nothing would ever happen.

As a result of this attitude, the oncoming redevelopment had little impact on the lives of most West Enders until the very end. The daily routine continued as before. . . .

.   .   .   .

The caretaking agencies knew, of course, that the area would be redeveloped, and were not in doubt over the outcome of the long process. This knowledge, the gradual reduction in the number of their clients, and the appearance of some of the lower-class newcomers, sapped their morale. For although most of the agencies and their staffs were in favor of the redevelopment, they were also sorry to see the neighborhood torn down, and its residents dispersed. . . . The caretakers also tried, with little success, to prepare the West Enders for what was about to happen. Some of them urged the redevelopment agency to improve its relocation procedures, but by then it was too late.

The best illustration of the lack of impact of the redevelopment process on the West Enders was the failure of the Save the West End Committee to attract their overt support, and the absence of other forms of protest. As noted earlier, the Committee came into being in 1956, when a handful of West Enders met with a local civic and political leader who had long been interested in the West End. An upper-class Bostonian whose family and forebears had been active in caretaking projects in the area since the turn of the century, he helped to build the park, pool, and boating area along the banks of the Charles River and had participated in other improvement projects since the 1930's. He felt that the West End was not a slum and also argued that the city had no right to take private property—especially that of poor people—for luxury apartment buildings. He promised to support the group politically and financially, and with his help, the Committee rented a vacant store in the area. Over the years, it held a number of meetings, spoke at public hearings, published pamphlets and leaflets, went to Washington to try to overturn the decision, and eventually took its case to the courts. The Committee sought of course to enroll the neighborhood in its work, but attracted only a small—although loyal—group of members, who kept up a steady barrage of protest over the years. Not until the very end, however, did they gain a wider audience.

One of the major obstacles to the Committee's effectiveness in its own neighborhood was its outside leadership. . . Moreover, the other active members—and the people who originally asked for his guidance—were neither typical West Enders, nor the kinds of people who could enroll them. Among the most active were an Italian writer and an artist, a young Jewish professional, a single Polish woman, and a number of elderly ladies who lived in the Charlesbank Homes. . . .

The Committee, however, did not develop a program that would require West Enders as a whole to take action. Its pamphlets and speeches expressed the same indignation and incredulity felt by all, but it did not ask them to act, other than to come to meetings, help the Committee in its mailings, and stay in the West End.

Yet all of these considerations for the Committee's lack of success in gaining active neighborhood support paled before the most important one: the inability of the West Enders to organize in their own behalf. Indeed, other causes were only effects of that basic inability. Had the West Enders flocked to meetings in larger numbers, the leadership would probably have gone to someone whom the residents would have followed. As it was, they watched the activities of the Committee with passive sympathy. Some were suspicious; they argued that the Committee consisted of people who had been left out when the graft was distributed; that the leadership was Communist; and that a Jewish officer of the Committee was related to one of the developers. The majority however, did agree with all that the Committee claimed, and shared in its anger. But even then they could not break out of the peer group society, and organize in common cause. It was impossible to fight city hall; this was a function of the local politician. If he failed, what else was there to do? Action-seeking West Enders would

have relished a march on City Hall to do violence to the officials principally associated with the redevelopment, but the act of joining with neighbors to work together for halting the redevelopment was inconceivable. At
the meetings at which West Enders spoke, they spoke as individuals, about
their own individual cases. The local politicians who appeared at these
meetings spoke *to* the West Enders rather than *for* them; they convinced
the audience of their own opposition to the redevelopment, and tried to
display themselves as loyal representatives of the West End. But they too
were unable—and perhaps unwilling—to organize an effective protest
movement.

.   .   .   .

The truth was, that for a group unaccustomed to organizational activity,
saving the West End was an overwhelming, and perhaps impossible, task.
Indeed, there was relatively little the Committee could do. The decision
to redevelop the West End had been made early in the decade, and it
had received the blessings of the city's decisive business leaders and politicians. The West End's local politicians all opposed the redevelopment, but
were powerless against the unanimity of those who favored it. As noted in
Chapter 8, the election of city councilors at large rather than by wards
since 1951 had reduced the influence of individual districts. Smaller areas,
with few voters, were especially hard hit; and the West End, which was
losing population at this time, was virtually disenfranchised. Nor did the
West End have other attributes of power such as those displayed by the
neighboring North End, which had successfully repulsed efforts toward its
own redevelopment. This area had a larger population and a much larger
business community—some of it politically influential. Most important,
the North End was the center—and symbol—of Italian life in Boston. Its
destruction thus would have been a threat—or at least an insult—to every
Italian voter in Boston, and the city's politicians simply could not afford to
alienate this increasingly influential vote. Conversely, although the Italians
were also the largest group in the West End, they were not in the majority.
And since they had attained a plurality only comparatively recently, the
area had never really been considered an Italian neighborhood. Thus, it
is doubtful whether even a unanimous turnout in opposition by the West
Enders would have been sufficient to set in motion the difficult process of
reversing years of work by local and federal agencies, and giving up the
large federal grant that financed the clearance of the area.

.   .   .   .

I was told that before the West End was totally cleared—and even
afterwards—West Enders would come back on weekends to walk through

the old neighborhood and the rubble-strewn streets. The last time I saw the area, it had been completely leveled except for the buildings that had been marked for preservation. A museum of Yankee artifacts and the library—now closed—remained at one corner, the Hospital at another. The Catholic church—where services were still being held for parishioners living on the Back of Beacon Hill—stood in lonely isolation in the center of the cleared area. The Hospital had graded some of the adjacent property for temporary parking, and at a far corner, fronting on the river, the first of the new buildings were going up. The cleared area looked very tiny, and it was hard to imagine that more than 20,000 people had once lived there.

DILEMMAS IN URBAN RENEWAL,
Harold Goldblatt

IN recent decades, urban renewal programs have
been among the important developments
in urban planning. Harold Goldblatt, a sociologist,
gives an illuminating analysis of the many dilemmas
that confront the interested parties to renewal
programs, like the Adams-Morgan program undertaken
recently in Washington, D.C.

Adams-Morgan confronted the urban renewal administrator with a series of dilemmas or critical choices which could not be avoided. Each choice promised good consequences on either side of the dilemma and bad consequences as well. The dilemmas are probably not unique to Adams-Morgan. More likely they recur wherever community improvement sets itself similar objectives and strategies for realizing them.

One of the major dilemmas of Adams-Morgan grew out of the fact that it is in an area consisting of three socially distinctive sub-areas. Area A and Area C are opposite poles of the social continuum, ranging from upper middle class to lower working class. Area B is in between. By all accounts the total area was in no sense a community to begin with, did not think of itself as a community, and would be difficult to make into one. Yet this is what the demonstration project set itself to attempt. The alternative—to define the three areas as separate communities—would

Excerpted from "Citizen Participation in Urban Renewal in Washington, D.C.," a report to the Washington, D.C., Health and Welfare Council of the National Capital Area, 1966. Reprinted by permission of the author and the Council.

have meant giving up two of the three important goals: the goal of racial integration, the goal of class integration, or the goal of citizen participation. The latter point requires some elucidation.

We noted in Chapter III that the sociological literature on social participation almost consistently reports findings of maximum participation in civic affairs at the middle of the social structure. The very poor do not take part in what are essentially middle-class social groups either for want of social skills, or because of subtle discouragement. The very rich have their own distinctive social groups which not only tend to transcend localities within the city but even to be of a more cosmopolitan nature. In Adams-Morgan, local leadership for the nascent community was sought from Area A and B, the more affluent of the three sub-areas. But this meant inclusion in one demonstration area of a wide gamut of social and racial groupings with correlative diversity of social and economic interests. The technical problem, to find social formulas which would reconcile divergent or conflicting viewpoints becomes increasingly more complicated the less homogeneous the social grouping. But to work with homogeneous groups in an effort to simplify the social engineering means to abandon the goals of racial and class integration.

The first of the dilemmas confronting the demonstration project thus was one of definition. The project sought to create a local "community." By any definition of the term, "community" means a social grouping set off from adjacent groups. Efforts to delimit the geographical boundaries of communities range from the more or less impressionistic methods of the Chicago school of urban sociology (Robert Park and his students) to the precise quantitative methods of Shevky and Bell. But all are more or less arbitrary. The modern metropolitan city is indisputably an organic whole composed of sub-communities or so-called "natural areas." For example, the second precinct is different from other areas; west of Rock Creek Park is different from the east. Georgetown is distinctive; so too are the Southwest, Capitol Hill, Foggy Bottom, etc. But it is rarely plain where the one "natural area" leaves off and the adjacent "natural area" begins. This question of the indeterminacy of the boundaries of so-called "natural areas" ceases to be an academic exercise when efforts must be set in motion to create a local community set off from adjacent areas by sentiments of local patriotism. Community means people who "belong" and others who do not; community means "we" contrasted with "they"; community means interests held in common contrasted with conflicting or at least different interests of other communities; community means identity of interests of group members overriding the special interests of sub-groups or individuals. Community means cohesion overriding divisiveness. Community means also *organization* of component parts, sub-areas, families, individuals. A community, finally, is a social organization of sub-groups.

The second dilemma confronting Adams-Morgan was the issue of whether to organize citizen participation in existing community organization or to create community organizations de novo. The outcome of the experience has led the former staff of the Demonstration Project to conclude that it was a mistake to attempt organization specifically for the sake of renewal. Since they did not undertake the alternative route, the use exclusively of pre-existing organizations in the community for the purpose, they were not really in position to evaluate that latter alternative. Where the problem stands is this: to organize the community for the specialized objective of urban renewal requires full-time professionals and is a lengthy process. It is expensive and time consuming. Moreover it puts the new organizations in competition with the pre-existing ones with all the opportunity this creates for rivalries of leadership within the locality and for the right to represent the locality in its dealings with the outside world, its social environment. On the other hand, not to organize specifically for urban renewal is to put this social interest second to the primary purpose of the existing organizations, if not in competition with it. There is, moreover, a more serious problem, namely that pre-existing organizations have been able to recruit only a fraction of the residents of the area and this fraction is smallest where it is needed the most—in the poorest, most blighted areas.

The way out, seemingly obvious, is to combine both methods, creating an organization which co-opts existing voluntary associations and creates others de novo only where none already exist. But this "solution" may be really only a paper solution. In the first place this approach actually *was* followed, to some extent. Both the Adams-Morgan Planning Committee and Adams-Morgan Planning Council seated representatives from citizen associations and civic associations that antedated the formation of these groups as well as representatives from block groups created *de novo*. This "solution" brought with it a characteristic dilemma commonly resulting from the co-optation of existing organizations. The civic and citizen associations were, of course, members of citywide organizations with formal policy orientations transcending the specific local issues and, at least to some degree, bound by the policy orientations of the citywide organization. Thus the stage was set for cross-pressure upon the Adams-Morgan organization by the dual membership, that is dual allegiance of member organizations created for other purposes than the local renewal or with previous commitments to other organizations. The history of Adams-Morgan very plainly shows the outcome: the schism was along the lines of pre-existing block groups and block groups created *de novo*.

Another dilemma in regard to citizen participation stems from the recruitment patterns. Existing block groups already have, formally or informally, a de facto membership policy or principle of social selection. And even when formally the organization is open to all residents with no eligibility restrictions other than geographic, in subtle ways an organization acquires a preferred social type and a less preferred social type, criteria of loyalty, and criteria of fitness for membership along political, social, and economic lines. The experience of the Kalorama Citizens Association illustrates the rejection of dissenters on grounds of disloyalty to the association and sabotage of its majority position until "such time" as the clear and present danger of renewal might be removed. On the other hand, not to admit such organizations is to create rival organizations in the same area with the danger of jurisdictional disputes and bewilderment to the non-participants who are courted by both organizations.

Another set of dilemmas grow out of the urban renewal decisions proper. The first of these involves the question of time. To freeze the area in its current land-use pattern pending the development of a comprehensive plan is beyond the social power of the renewal administrations. Not to do so endangers the plan, threatening it with obsolescence, both social and technical, before the moment of truth can arrive. Just this did occur in Adams-Morgan and was ultimately the grounds offered for rejection of the plan.

The pressure of time also bears, of course, on citizen participation. To involve the local residents in the planning process is a long time-consuming process; the temptation is to short-circuit the process wherever possible. One method is to exclude or to discourage dissenters who lengthen the discussion process so greatly by their objections to majority opinion. To do this, however, is to run the possibility or even the probability that the minority opinion will seek out and find other ways of making its influence felt on the final outcome. There appears to be some question as to whether this actually did or did not occur in Adams-Morgan. The surface events appear to be that the dissenting opinion when bypassed, ignored, or voted down by the majority in Adams-Morgan went "over the head" of the community organization to the ultimate source of power, that is the House District Committee, and there found in Representative Dowdy's subcommittee a willing and able ally. Others believe, however, that the community organization in Adams-Morgan never had any real power to influence the outcome but was merely a social toy to begin with, tolerated until it was poised at the threshold of achievement and then quickly and decisively disallowed. On balance the evidence seems against this latter view. We should have to view District and Federal agencies as either accomplices or dupes of the process of toleration and rejection and the substantial sums of money expended as merely the expense of citizens allowed to amuse themselves at the game of urban planning. We should also have to believe that their public denunciations in the press of the actions of the National Capital Planning Commission were merely pro forma. A better reading in the writer's opinion is the enactment of a "community conflict" in which one side won and the other lost; lost were the funds expended by Federal and District allies of the losers.

Still another dilemma grows out of the choice of renewal modes. We have already classified modes of renewal according to the extent of the change they involve. The least extensive change is required by code enforcement. Code enforcement, however, creates its own dilemmas. A rigorous enforcement of the code does not affect the total patterning of land use and so does little to alter the "incompatibility of land uses." It also does little to increase the housing inventory available for residential use. On the other hand, a basic change in the pattern of land use cannot be accomplished by citizens through any do-it-yourself program. Hence yet another dilemma of citizen participation in urban renewal grows out of the chain of means to ends.

Urban renewal in the sense of physical improvement of the area is ultimately accomplished by men working as architects, engineers, or construction workers at repair or restoration or rebuilding. Examples of direct activity by residents are, however, few for a significant reason. Among the examples listed for Adams-Morgan are "clean-up," "fix-up," "paint-up," "plant-up," rodent control, and the like. Significantly enough, the newspaper accounts attribute such activities to children, to the volunteers residing in Hollyday House (Church of the Brethren), and to lower-working-class residents. More extensive repairs, restoration, or rebuilding must involve the employment of men trained in the construction trades (laborers, carpenters, bricklayers, plumbers, electricians, etc.). Citizen participation in urban renewal at this point ceases to be do-it-yourself activity and becomes instead a means of inducing property owners to spend money on the employment of others skilled in such work, or in persuading owners to borrow money from the bank if they can, or in organizing an amateur non-interest bank to loan funds to homeowners unable otherwise to obtain credit.

Hence the dilemma: If renewal is to be accomplished without reliance on Federal funds, it must be accomplished by local citizens who for the most part are unskilled at such work and have little credit for employment of those who do. And on the other hand, the employment of craftsmen takes the renewal effort out of the hands of purely local citizens and necessarily involves not only District but Federal officials as well.

A rigorous enforcement of the code induces some owners to change the use of the property from residential to non-residential so diminishing the inventory of housing available to low-income groups where the need is greatest; on the other hand a lax enforcement of the code, which discriminates against home owners while absentee owners escape, permits the blighting process to continue.

SUGGESTED READINGS: CHAPTER 16

Herbert Gans. *The Urban Villagers.* New York: The Free Press of Glencoe, 1962.

When the "West End: An Urban Village" was about to be redeveloped by city planners, Gans, a sociologist, studied the process from the viewpoint of the people who lived in West End. The difference between planners and residents (including many Italian-Americans) was immense.

Peter Rossi and Robert Dentler. *The Politics of Urban Renewal.* New York: The Free Press of Glencoe, 1961. Harold Kaplan, *Urban Renewal Politics: Slum Clearance in Newark.* New York: Columbia University Press, 1963.

Two monographs that vividly describe the struggle of political interests implicated in this kind of urban planning.

Sam Warner (Ed.). *Planning for a Nation of Cities.* Cambridge, Mass.: Harvard University Press, 1966.

Papers by a number of experts on planning, housing, and urban problems.

Louis Wirth, *Community Life and Social Policy: Selected Papers.* Chicago: University of Chicago Press, 1956.

Discussions of localism, regionalism, and centralization and the metropolitan region as a planning unit.

17

San Francisco Zoo. Photo: Linda Klink.

URBAN IMAGERY AND URBAN THEORY

THE two selections that follow provide different kinds of summations for this book. The first describes the recent changes in imagery that reflect and influence the directions of change now occurring in American urban life. The second suggests the areas and strategies of research that will contribute to a more adequate body of urban theory than we now have, and demonstrates how the kinds of data presented here can be used for this purpose.

THE LATEST IN URBAN IMAGERY,
Anselm L. Strauss

THE urbanization of America continues apace, its
emerging forms and consequences as problematic
as ever. Our contemporaries—scholars,
businessmen, journalists, planners, government
officials, and just plain interested citizens—
are trying to make sense of urbanization and
wondering or predicting where it is going next. As
always, the stakes are high and the institutions tend to
follow in the wake of the imagery.

As the United States progressed from an agricultural nation to a
markedly urbanized one, each step of the way was paralleled by Americans' attempts to make sense of what was happening. This ideological
accompaniment to the objective facts of national urbanization was shot
through, during the nineteenth century, with contrasts drawn between urban
and rural styles of life. These contrasts still persist in muted forms.

However, the imagined polarity between country and city or town and
city no longer dominates the American scene. It was succeeded some
decades ago by a presumed polarity of city and suburb—a polarity which
followed in the wake of a vastly increased suburbanization and the flight of
great numbers of city dwellers to the suburbs in search of fresh air, safe
and quiet streets, genuine communal life, better standards of domestic
living, financial profit, and—as sociologists have so often stressed—more
prestigeful locales in which to live. But the imagined polarity of suburb and
city is already breaking down, and new imagery is beginning to take its
place. This imagery suggests some of the kinds of questions that Americans
are raising about the destinies of their metropolitan areas. It also points
to the particular ways in which Americans are attempting to make sense
out of the often puzzling facts of today's urban milieu.

What is going to be the fate of American cities? The envisioned alternatives, in answer to this momentous question range from the continued
dominance of cities to their actual disappearance. The *New York Times,*
perhaps only for purposes of provocation, recently raised the alternatives
in this way:

Reprinted from Anselm L. Strauss, *Images of the American City* (New York:
The Free Press of Glencoe, 1961), pp. 246–54, by permission.

One hundred million Americans are now living in metropolitan areas, including their central cities.

Will the new pattern of settlement result in the eventual dwindling of great cities like New York, Chicago and San Francisco? Will they be just islands of national business headquarters, financial clearing houses and other specialized functions within great flat seas in which the other activities of our national life will mingle?

Or will our historic cities sparkle brighter by contrast with the sprawling urbanized regions which they will serve as centers of culture as well as commerce?

Far from dominating the American scene today, the big cities are on the defensive, at least in some ways. Our magazines are full of stories about cities fighting to make a "comeback" and cities are combating "The threat of strangulation by the suburbs." One emerging concept of the fate and function of the metropolis is that it can serve as "the core" of the entire metropolitan area. By "the core," urban planners and civic propagandists may mean either centers of business or cultural functions, or both. For instance, the mayor of Detroit, like many other civic leaders, advocates strengthening downtown districts so that they can serve as strong magnets to attract people from distant suburbs, either for daily visits or for permanent residence. Hence, he advocated building expressways to bring suburbanite shoppers into the downtown area: "If we don't make it possible for them to come back, they will build large shopping areas in the outlying communities and we will lose that business." To some other metropolitan champions, "the new metropolis" connotes somewhat less hardheaded emphasis upon business and more upon cultural and political leadership of cities.

New concepts are also emerging of who shall—or should—live in the central city. Here, for instance, is the view of William Zeckendorf, probably the most influential of American urban redevelopers:

> There is a swing back to the cities of the highest-grade type of tenant. He is generally aged 45 and upward. He has raised his children; he has reached the peak of his earning power; his house is now superfluous in size; he is tired of commuting.
>
> That man, if you provide him with appropriate living conditions in the central areas of the cities, can be reattracted on a scale never dreamed of before to a way of life that is impossible to obtain in the suburbs.

He adds, and here we may see how new is the concept involved, that: "For each 10 people that the city loses to the suburbs, it can get 10 times their collective buying power in people who return." In the hands of people like Zeckendorf, the concept of "redevelopment" has now come to mean a combination of things: partly the replacement of slums with upper-income housing; partly the renovation of "downtown U.S.A." But other planners and influential citizens urge—on moral as well as on economic grounds— that the city ought not to be given over only to the wealthier residents; and in fact, others keep pointing to the steady abandonment of the large cities to Negroes, who are thus effectively segregated within the greater urban area.

While cities are "fighting back" against suburbs, the transformation of suburban areas is being accompanied by a reinterpretation of life as it is lived there. In place of a relatively undifferentiated "suburb"—a symbolic area contrasting with an equally symbolic city—a differentiated set of popular concepts is appearing. As those suburbs near the city's actual boundaries become increasingly crowded, virtually parts of the city, the "better class" of residents who live further out refer disdainfully to those older suburbs. They make subtle distinctions among the relative qualities of various communities—knowledge essential when unwanted ethnic groups or Negroes may tomorrow set up residence in certain of those locales. Especially since the enormous extension of the suburban rings all the way into the next states, it was inevitable that someone would make a distinction between suburbs and suburbs-beyond-the-suburbs. Spectorsky's "exurbia" and "suburbia" has met this need. The sociologists themselves, spurred on by William H. Whyte's discovery of a certain kind of suburb, chock-full of youthful transients, are beginning to wonder about different kinds of suburban styles.

In past decades, a momentous aspect of the suburban dream was the wish to reinstate, or establish, the emotionally satisfying bonds of community and neighborhood. For more civic-minded souls, a suburban community also represented a reasonably good way to enter into the political process; something that was much more difficult to effect within the crowded city wards. Both aspirations have attracted much acid comment in recent decades. The imagery of a truer political democracy has not always been easy to put into practice, especially as the suburbs have grown larger or have become the locus of clashes between uncompromising social classes. As for the bonds of community and neighborhood, two kinds of criticism have been directed against these. One is uttered by suburbanites who expected the friendliness and democracy of an ideal small town, but who were bitterly disappointed by the realities of suburban living. They accuse the suburb of false friendliness, of mock neighborliness; they claim that it has not a democratic atmosphere at all, that it is ridden with caste and snobbery. Another kind of criticism is leveled by both suburbanites and outsiders against the achievement of too much "community." It is said that there is no real privacy in most suburbs and that so deadening is the round of sociability that little time can remain for genuine leisure. While most critics are willing to admit that friendship and communal ties are to be valued, they deride the standardization of suburban communities and their all too visible styles of life (the barbecue suppers, the PTAs, the suburban clothing, the commuting). Since World War II, criticism has continued to mount about the suburban way of life. The new kinds of suburbs are too homogenous in population, too child-dominated, too domestically oriented, too little concerned with intellectual or cultural pursuits—or so they seem to the critics.

When conceived in such terms, suburbanization represents to inveterate lovers of the city a genuine threat to urban values—a threat even to the nation. In place of the earlier derision of the suburb as an uncomfortable or inconvenient place to live, and added to the fear of the suburb as a threat to true democracy (because it enhances class distinctions), we now observe an increasing concern over the continued exodus to suburbs. If it is true that suburban life is inimical to much that has made the city exciting, freeing, and innovative, then—it is felt—there is cause for alarm. Despite the counter argument that the suburbs now have theaters and concerts, the city as the great central local for the arts, and for civilized institutions generally, still remains convincing as an image to many city residents. Even intellectuals living in the suburbs betray uneasiness about their abandonment of former habitats and pursuits: and the growing literature of the suburban novel portrays the city as a creative foil to the dull, if necessary, domesticity of suburbia.

The intellectuals, too, are joined by urban politicians and by urban businessmen in despairing of the suburban movement. According to Zeckendorf, "Satellite towns, which are the product of decentralization, are parasites, jeopardizing the entire fiscal and political future of our great municipalities." He like others, argues how it is detrimental to the whole metropolitan community, and thus ultimately to the nation, that suburban cities should refuse to be incorporated into the nearby dominant metropolis.

Such incorporation, or annexation, is one of the burning metropolitan issues of the day. "Does Your Community Suffer from Suburbanitis?" queries *Colliers,* as it publishes the comments of two noted therapists who analyze this civic disease. They argue that cities have always gained needed breathing space by annexation of outlying areas, but that since 1900 the suburban residents have successfully prevented annexation through fears that they would have to pay higher taxes, would be affected by corrupt municipal governments, would be lost in the huge cities. Yet, as these pleaders for annexation say, these arguments are losing force, for annexation, although hard fought by many towns, appears to be a growing movement.

Thus, a new imagery about the city and its suburbs is appearing. The city as an invading malignant force which threatens the beauty of the suburban village has been a fearful image held by suburbanites for many years, an image which has been expressed in antagonism against new kinds of neighbors, in complaints about loss of rural atmosphere, and in a continual flight further outward. But a reverse aspect of the city is supplementing another image—namely, that the former idyllic suburban landscape is, or is becoming, a thing of the past. The services which the central city can offer the nearby communities are inestimable, or at least are better than can be locally supplied, for the suburbs are no longer relatively isolated, autonomous, proud towns. If old, they have been swamped with population, and, if new, they have been erected too quickly and lack adequate services or were built with an eye to future growth of population.

Although most suburbanites still undoubtedly imagine the central city to be different from the suburbs, already some prophets are beginning to visualize very little true difference between the two locales. They delight in pointing out, if they are themselves city dwellers, that the suburbs are fully as noisy as the city; that traffic is becoming as onerous in the towns as it is in the metropolis; that city people are wearing the same "suburban" kinds of informal attire. The suburbanite is beginning to notice these things himself.

The lessening of differences between suburb and city—by the increasing suburban densities and the possibility of planning cities for good living —seems destined to bring about further changes in the urban imagery of Americans. Very recently several new images have appeared. Thus one sociologist, Nathan Glazer, who loves cosmopolitan city life and who is afraid that it cannot flourish in suburbia, has argued that suburbia itself is in danger of invading, in its turn, the big city. This is a new twist, is it not? Glazer's argument is that because redevelopers have combined certain features of the garden city (superblocks, curving paths) and Corbusier's skyscraper in the park, they have in a large measure destroyed "the central value of the city—as meeting place, as mixing place, as creator and consumer of culture at all levels." If poorer classes are better off now than they were in our older great cities, the rich and middle classes are worse off; artists, poets, intellectuals and professors also have less propitious circumstances in which to flourish. The city core itself,

> the part that people visit, that eager migrants want to live in, that produces what is unique, both good and bad, in the city, as against the town and the suburb. What has happened to that? Strangely enough, it loses the vitality that gave it its attraction.

Glazer asserts that the very density of nineteenth century cities forced city planners to build towns at the rim of existing cities, rather than to plan for better cities. We have now, he argues, to plan for the metropolis without losing that essential cosmopolitanism which makes it great. A rich and varied urban texture must be created, "and this . . . cannot be accomplished by reducing density." Whatever it is that has gone wrong with our cities, he concludes, "one thing is sure: nothing will be cured by bringing the suburb, even in its best forms, into the city." This is a radically different kind of argument—and imagery—than that of the city boy who merely refuses to take up residence in the suburb because he believes life there is intellectually stultifying.

In either case, though, the critic of suburbia takes the city as his measuring rod: he assumes the city as the locus for a frame of mind, a style of life. The proponent of suburbia reverses the procedure and measures the city against a healthier, saner, more sociable suburban counterpart. There is, of course another, and transcending, position whereby one may avoid taking sides, saying that both city and suburb have their respective advantages; people who own homes in both locales doubtless suscribe to that particular imagery.

Yet another transcending imagery is possible:

> We are going to have to learn a wholly new concept of a city—a great sprawling community covering hundreds of square miles, in which farms and pastures mingle with intense developments, factories and shopping centers, with the entire area run purposefully for the common good. . . . These wonderful new cities, aren't as far in the future as they may sound.

Notice the wording: we have to learn a "wholly new concept of a city," and "these wonderful new cities" that are just around the corner. These terms signify a claim that the dichotomy of city *versus* suburb is no longer defensible in the eyes of some Americans. In its turn, this dichotomy is in some danger of the same dissolution as its predecessor, the country-city polarity. When Americans can maintain no longer that the two locales differ then we can expect new imageries to arise—new interpretations of the latest phases of urbanization.

One can almost see them being born. Only four years ago, *Fortune* magazine published a series of articles on the "exploding metropolis," closing with William H. Whyte's "Urban Sprawl." Whyte begins his report on the state of American metropolitan areas by warning that their fate will be settled during the next three or four years. "Already huge patches of once green countryside have been turned into vast, smog-filled deserts that are neither city, suburb, nor country." That last phrase forebodes the invention in the near future of a less neutral, more descriptive, term than the sociologists' colorless "metropolitan area." Whyte himself coins no new term, but his attitude toward the region eaten into by urban sprawl reflects something new. He reports a conference of planners, architects, and other experts that was convened by *Fortune* magazine and by *Architectural Forum* to tackle the problem of remedying the worst features of urban sprawl. This group made recommendations, based upon the assumption that large amounts of suburban land need to be rescued before they are completely built upon in distressingly unplanned ways. As Whyte says, "it is not too late to reserve open space while there is still some left— land for parks, for landscaped industrial districts, and for just plain scenery and breathing space." The language—and the outlines of these recommendations—are consciously very like that of earlier generations of city planners who were concerned with the problems of urban density; although the current situations, as everyone recognizes, involve a more complex interlocking of city, suburb, county, and state.

Americans are now being told in their mass media that soon they will "be living in fifteen great, sprawling, nameless communities—which are rapidly changing the human geography of the entire country." They are beginning to have spread before them maps of these vast urban conglomerations which are not cities but are nevertheless thoroughly urban: "super-cities" and "strip cities." They are being warned that America's urban regions are already entering upon a new stage of development, "even before most people are aware that urban regions exist at all." And even before the recently coined concept of "exurbia" is more than a few years old they are being confronted with "interurbia," which represents simply all the land not actually within the denser urban strips of land but within the urban regions, an area within which few people live on farms but where almost everybody commutes to work—not necessarily to cities "but to factories and offices located in small towns." As the polar concepts of city and suburb thus dissolve, Americans are being invited to think of urbanization in newer, more up-to-date terms. The new terms, however technically they may be sometimes used, refer no less than did the older vocabulary to symbolic locales and associated sentiments.

STRATEGIES FOR DISCOVERING
URBAN THEORY, *Anselm L. Strauss*

THE selection below was written to stimulate types of research which might lead to the discovery of an integrated and maximally useful urban theory about American cities. There is no such theory today, any more than there was eight years ago when Gideon Sjoberg remarked that the dominant theoretical orientation in urban sociology could "hardly be termed full-fledged theories" and that "a consistent general theory of urbanism, though perhaps unattainable, should be the goal toward which we strive." [1] The selection does not offer a blueprint for launching specific researches or develop a theory by which to approach urban data; it suggests a set of strategies—which together constitute a stance—for studying cities and their populations to discover which problems are most relevant for developing a general but grounded urban theory.

IDEOLOGY AND ITS CONSEQUENCES

As a first step, I suggest that urban sociology (and/or social psychology) could profit greatly from a critical scutiny of itself and its past. The conceptions which inform sociologists' writings are essentially identical to, and not always more sophisticated than, those found in the popular media. Indeed, virtually all the important urban sociologists during any decade, from Henderson or Zueblin at the turn of the century to Greer today, can, without stretching credulity, be viewed as articulate spokesmen, excellent rhetoricians, for less sophisticated versions of the same views about cities. What C. Wright Mills demonstrated for the rural biases of "social problems" literature, could just as easily be demonstrated for the relevant biases in contemporary sociological writing about poverty, urban race relations, delinquency, suburbia and other public issues. The "all-too-American" views of cities held by sociologists have had at least two major

Excerpted from Anselm L. Strauss, "Strategies for Discovering Urban Theory," in Leo F. Schnore and Henry Fagin (Eds.), *Urban Research and Policy Planning* (Beverly Hills, Calif.: Sage Publications, 1967), pp. 81–98, by permission.
    1. "Comparative Urban Sociology," in R. Merton *et al.* (Eds.), *Sociology Today* (New York: Basic Books, 1959), p. 356.

consequences for their urban sociology. I only mention these consequences here, since the remainder of this chapter deals with their implications.

In the first place, a remarkably small range of potentially relevant topics has been studied from sociological perspectives. A corollary is that sociologists have bunched their research around relatively few topics or areas. Thus, we have an abundance of research about major cities (where "social problems" have been so obvious) but comparatively little about life as lived in regional centers, in small cities, or in specialized cities like Reno, Flint or Birmingham. We have writing far out of proportion to its probable import for urban theory about poverty, vice, delinquency and urban crime, while the recent spate of interest in middle-class suburbs flows from the same ideological source: concern with a social problem. The occupations we know best through many researches either have not been much studied with direct focus on their urban aspects (medicine, nursing, for instance) or have been studied because they relate to reformistic concerns (prostitution, political bossism, teaching, real estate brokerage).

The case of the realtor is particularly instructive: he has been studied somewhat in relation to race relations and to city planning, but we know almost nothing about the network of social relationships within which he and his clients operate, say, in suburbs and suburban counties. Except from personal experience, no sociologist could begin to write a systematic account of relationships which exist among realtors, bank employees, contractors, local politicians, investment brokers (professional and amateur) and other relevant parties to realtors' transactions. In short, an unfortunate consequence of sociologists' commitments to ideological positions or of their concern with public issues has been to limit severely the areas which they have studied, and possibly has led them also to overconcentrate on certain other areas.

The character of theory about urban social relations has also been negatively affected for the same reasons. Anyone who has taught a course or read through available textbooks in urban sociology must know that "hodge-podge" is an accurate description of urban theory, at least those portions of it that deal with social relations in the city. When sociologists are relatively consistent in their views of city life, then their theories are deeply colored by one or more ideological positions. When they are eclectic, as in the textbooks, then their ideological positions shift from chapter to chapter and sometimes from paragraph to paragraph. The elements of urban theory tend merely to be refinements of common sense conceptions about urban social relations, however sophisticated the language and however "data-based" are the supporting facts. I shall not attempt to demonstrate these assertions: I make them only as an introduction to the statement of a position.

STRATEGIES FOR URBAN RESEARCH

The cardinal strategies that I shall suggest and discuss—quite aside from specific areas of research also to be discussed later—are as follows.

First, study the unstudied. The reasoning behind this strategy is not merely that already too much is known about too small a range of topics, but that quite literally we do not know the most fertile topics for developing a powerful urban theory. I do not mean to suggest that nothing can be learned through further studies of the police, skid-row residents, or delinquents, or of any other repeatedly studied subject; but these may have less pay-off for understanding our cities and the social relations within them than many another area of research.

Second, study the unusual. The reasoning behind this strategy is that urban sociologists have assumed that they know the important topics for developing theory, but this assumption is questionable, if only because they have been captives of their ideological positions and their concerns with reform. Whether questionable or not, however, the assumption can be checked only through deliberate study of topics which not only have been untouched but may seem so trivial as not to warrant study.

Third, study an area which is enmeshed in public debate only after taking steps to minimize ideological entrapment. The reasoning behind this strategy is: if the sociologist is interested in entering the public debate as such, he need not be concerned with research except for rhetorical purposes; but if he is interested in urban theory—and in contributing to the public issue through the application of theory—then he *must* guard against ideological commitments. Later I shall suggest a specific tactic for doing this.

Fourth, where possible study any topic comparatively. This strategy is not always feasible, but I advocate it. While single case studies are useful, a comparative procedure yields more urban theory, and more quickly. For instance, the study of a number of suburban banks will yield more theory than the study of one or two banks "in depth." If the banks are sampled according to theoretical considerations, then the theoretical yield is likely to be still greater. This "theoretical sampling" should be directed by theory, but it should pertain less to banks as organizations than it does to banks as they relate to urbanization and urbanites. In addition, the strategy of comparative analysis implies that the scattered literature on a great variety of urban groups, communities, institutions and processes be reconceptualized in accordance with a concerted attempt to develop a systematic and integrated theory of urban social relations.

This set of strategies does not lead automatically to a specific number of areas of research; but it does imply a redirection of sociologists' energies and perspectives, and to some extent a broadening of their methods.

A further implication is that the redirection leads to new intersections with the urban studies of colleagues in other fields. It is remarkable how little interchange there is between urban sociologists and urban historians, or with economists whose work sometimes bears directly on social relations in metropolitan areas. The overlapping work of sociologists and political scientists, both of whom are interested in urban politics, is much better developed. The recent writing of Norton Long seems especially to have stimulated sociologists.

The remainder of this chapter will consist of a relatively few suggestions bearing on the kind of research implied by the four strategies. My remarks about research areas should not be regarded as more than suggestions. Each reader will doubtless find other areas that impress him as more interesting and possibly as more fruitful for theory development. What is of more importance than the specific research areas is the general perspective implied by the set of strategies.

UNSTUDIED AREAS

VARIETIES OF CITIES

Since the terrain that is still relatively unstudied or untouched is very great, perhaps its discussion might begin with a rather glaring omission in our urban studies. Sociological generalizations about urban social relations are based principally on studies of large American cities and a few smaller ones. Some inkling of what has been omitted, besides differentials in size, is suggested by a series of articles about American cities which appeared in the *Saturday Evening Post* during the late 1940s: over 100 cities, from all sections of the nation, were covered. Even a casual scrutiny of the articles suggests a range of potentially relevant dimensions which bear on urban social relations.

There are cities which are generally considered by their citizens and neighbors to be regional centers—representative of their geographic area. There also are cities located "in" a region, many of whose citizens are symbolically as well as actually linked closely with non-regional geography. There are specialized cities: for sin, for more regular transient recreation, for resort living, for old folks, for conventions, for manufacture of a small range of products, for turning out legislative business. There are towns which have had glorious histories but have dim futures; there are towns with little history but great futures; towns with minor histories and seemingly little future. There are cities which consider themselves rivals of certain nearby cities, and ones which rival distant cities. There are cities which are run by outsiders, and one which are governed by insiders—by old elites or by new elites. There are cities which seem to be entirely surrounded by middle-class suburbs, and cities with an enormous variety of suburbs. According to Gans, "The primary task for urban (or community) sociology seems to me to be the analysis of the similarities and differences between contemporary settlement types." He confines himself to a thoughtful exploration of suburbs with the city's "inner" and "outer" areas.

Finally, all cities bear the marks of their geography, in style, as well as in predominant business—river cities, agricultural towns, mining towns, mountain cities, seaports. (Since agriculture or mining are very different in different regions, even such terms imply multiplicity.) Sociologists need not have gone overseas to challenge Wirth's generalizations about city life! Indeed, an immense amount of popular writing implicitly or explicitly has challenged the "impersonality" and heterogeneity views of "the city."

In recent years, probably due largely to the more scattered location of sociologists themselves, a number of researches have been done on populations within a greater variety of cities. The implications of this material for urbanism have yet to be worked out for simple empirical purposes, let alone for urban theory, but any good introductory textbook lists a number of such studies.

URBAN ICONS

The dimensions I have touched on should readily suggest some foci around which research might be organized. Two others—implicit in the above—are especially worth emphasis, the more so as they fall somewhat outside the usual attention of sociologists. Cities might well be studied, contemporaneously and historically, in terms of their icons. These are important—at least for various groups within a given city—for helping to set the city's style, for bringing a sense of belonging to citizens, for representing the city to outsiders, even for giving direction to planning and to the evolution of its institutions. The symbolism of Washington for the nation, and the prominence of its icons (the Capitol, the White House, and so on) is an obvious instance. A less obvious example is the complex of meanings represented by Chicago's various prominent icons. Chicago's business spirit and cosmopolitanism formerly were represented by such visual icons as Marshall Field's, the railroad depots, State Street, the "Loop," and skyscrapers like the Wrigley Building and the Tribune Tower. Although these Chicago icons still function for some populations, no doubt, nowadays the bustling commercialism and cosmopolitanism are more likely to be represented by Michigan Avenue, Rush Street, the double-towered apartment building complete with marina at its base, the lake front, and O'Hare Airport—claimed to be the nation's busiest air terminal. Chicago is represented through these icons on countless posters and postcards, in the mass media, and in the speech of natives and visitors alike: "crossroads of the nation," "second city," and bustling "forward-looking" business mart.

Of course, different populations emphasize different icons, including some I have not mentioned. What is needed for the development of urban theory is a series of cumulative studies of different types of icons, for different cities, and for different populations within those cities. And since the meanings of these icons are never static, we need a focus on change also: for instance, it would be interesting to know what happened in Brooklyn just before and after the Dodgers left.

SYMBOLISM OF TIME

Another perspective from which cities might usefully be studied is in terms of their symbolism of time. Actual time and symbolic time are not always closely associated; in any event, they are different items. Thought and speech about cities are replete with temporal imagery. Cities are represented as oriented toward the past, the present, or the future; as being old or young; as settled or conservative; or are referred to by other temporal terms. American cities frequently are characterized according to a future-oriented growth model ("expanding," "increasing," or "progressing") or an inverse growth model ("declining" or "decreasing"). They can also be described in terms of a metaphor of biological development, losing and gaining attributes rather than merely more or less of the same thing. The very terms used to describe city development are borrowed from the language of human development. For decades, Chicago has been described as "adolescent," but Milwaukee, which is about the same age, tends to be described as middle-aged and settled.

A great many questions are raised by this temporal and metaphorical treatment of cities. When does a city stop being represented as being young and become adolescent, why, and by whom? How long can a city exist without being regarded as old, or even middle-aged and settled down? When a city changes, what must be done before a claim legitimately can be made, or safely supported, that a new stage in city development has been reached? What happens to temporal symbolism when a city is invaded by new waves of immigrants: is it conceived to be the same city, a different one, and in what degree, and by whom? There are a whole battery of research questions which bear on how different segments of a city may attempt to make public their temporal conceptions, make them predominate in the mass media, and stamp them into the city's physical structure. (Pittsburgh's recent "rejuvenation" is a nice instance, and one that has implications for the temporal aspect of urban theory.)

Leonard Schatzman has suggested to me that fruitful studies might be made of how different populations regard "what the city used to look like

and what it looks like now." For instance, old-time natives in San Francisco sometimes complain bitterly about the high-rise apartments that are
"spoiling" the old skyline; while newcomers usually do not know what
the older city looked like, and so may (some do) find the skyline enchanting or exciting. Such temporal considerations unquestionably affect the
public battles over a city's physical aspects.

SYMBOLISM OF SPACE

Another area of research is the symbolism of space: it is relatively
unstudied by urban sociologists, despite the many ethnic, "natural area,"
stratification and even suburban studies. These studies have been confined
principally to large cities—a point I shall not emphasize except to suggest
that research on the same ethnic group (say of Jews or the Irish) in
diverse cities (say, Norfolk, Milwaukee, Santa Fe, Stockton, Lincoln, and
Meridian, Mississippi) might show some surprising things about the range
of urban experience and the use and symbolism of space. A wonderfully
suggestive study of space was published some years ago, although it has
been little referred to since, by Christen Jonassen who described the
ecology and successive movements of a Norwegian community in
Brooklyn, with an appropriate focus on the Norwegians' rural symbolism
of space (Jonassen, 1949). His study illustrates both the potential value
of research on symbolic space per se and the value of choosing little-
known urban and suburban groups for study. Most of our community
studies pick up something of how people perceive and use urban space,
but few studies are much focused on the more subtle meanings of space
for the city's residents.

As I write these lines, Chicago Poles bitterly assail the police who
protect Negro demonstrators on their march through Polish areas. Negroes'
desire for housing there runs afoul of a fierce sense of possession of land—
which is not simply a bunch of streets but village parishes. Ten years ago,
another Chicago parish defended itself against invaders by constantly
stationing armed guards at major entry points for some weeks.

Any city—any metropolitan region—might be viewed as a complex
related set of symbolized areas. Any given population will be cognizant
of only a small number of these areas: most will lie outside of effective
perceptions; others will be conceived in such ways that they will hardly
ever be visited and will even be avoided. When properly mapped, any
given area will be symbolized differently by several, if not by numerous,
populations. In consequence, our cumulative research tells us more about
the symbolic meaning of space for simple residential areas than for complex areas used and symbolized by diverse groups. One urgent task of
urban theory is to develop categories and related hypothesis about the
differential symbolism of space, and the differential behavior associated

with that symbolism. This aspect of theory has rather obvious implications for land use, recreation, urban aesthetics, and so on. The exploratory research suggested by Lynch is especially worth perusing in this regard.

WORLDS WHICH TRANSCEND SPACE

One great gap . . . in urban sociology is a failure to take cognizance of the many social worlds which are not closely linked with specific urban spaces. Ethnic groups are spatially locatable, so it makes sense to study them in terms of space. But many urban worlds are diffusely organized and difficult to pin down definitely in space, since their members are scattered through several or many urban (and rural) areas. Although the chief institutions of an urban world (fashion, jazz, drama, chess, art, bridge, stamp collecting, baseball, or lesbianism) are necessarily located somewhere, the important attributes pertain more to the shared interests and activities of "members" of these worlds. I venture to say that the standard sociological concepts are not especially suited to understanding either these worlds or the behavior of their members.

Probably, we shall even have to discover the most useful kinds of research questions to ask about these worlds. Perhaps these questions might include how the local, national, and international versions of a given world (like chess) interlock; and how the margins of certain worlds (homosexual and ballet) overlap. The existence of mass media (magazines for sports fishermen or hi-fi enthusiasts) and special institutions (the Museum of Modern Art or the New York Metropolitan Opera House) to specified worlds is more obvious than their meanings for their various consumers. The relationship of a world's professionals and amateurs is perhaps another good research question. These worlds are far more absorbing to, and so better covered by, popular writers than by sociologists; but one can hardly be content with popular description and explanation.

AMERICAN SYMBOLISM: URBAN AND CULTURAL

In a stimulating article Lois Dean recently analyzed the psychological gestalt of a community which she named "Minersville." The people of this community share a feeling of belonging to a golden vanished century, and an almost complete alienation from a federal government which they believe is antagonistic and non-responsive to their values. Dean concludes that planning which operates on the principle of federal collaboration with local initiative is unlikely to work well, if at all, with such communities. Translated into the language of the preceding discussions of city-types and the sociology of time, space, and social worlds, we can see the more easily that Minersville and other towns and cities require study in terms of where they fit—temporally as well as regionally, symbolically as well as physically—into the American scene. Granted that people who are located differentially in a city's social structure inevitably differ in their views of the city, in their actions toward it, in their styles of living within it, and in what they wish to preserve or forget about its past; nevertheless, those cities can be studied globally in relation to the American scene.

Chicago is a good example. As I have documented in *Images of the American City,* Chicagoans from the very beginning thought of their city as destined to become a world center, not simply a regional city. Fairly quickly it overtook other cities in population and resources, and was not surpassed by any other city until recently; now Los Angeles contests Chicago's right to be called "the second city." Since Chicago overtook St. Louis (after the Civil War) it has had New York as its key rival—but not vice versa. Chicagoans are still sensitive to judgments by New Yorkers that Chicago and the Midwest are only "the provinces." Chicago shares a regional suspicion of the East as epitomizing distinctions of class, as over against more equalitarian and democratic spirit of a region established under conditions of frontier democracy. Chicago also shares in the ambiguous definition of "the midwest"—a region which shifted, in fact and in symbol, from being the nation's breadbasket to being one of our greatest industrial areas.

I do not claim that all Chicagoans are bathed in all of this symbolism, but only that they and their city (and metropolitatn region) can profitably be studied in such terms. Regional and urban historians are more apt to bring such considerations into their research, but only for more strictly historical or chronological purposes. Urban sociologists either are unaware of such considerations or do not thoroughly explore what such considerations might imply. The final book in Lloyd Warner's Yankee City Series goes further in this direction that almost any other study of an American city by a sociologist or anthropologist, although the earlier volumes are not consistently informed by the later insights about symbolism. A steady focus on matters of symbolism, I suggest, would teach us a great deal about social relations in given urban settings. Comparative studies, as will be suggested below, would also build such a focus on a theory of urban relations in America.

STUDY OF THE UNUSUAL

Since there is no end to the suggestions that can be made for studies of the unstudied, I turn now to the related second strategy: studying the unusual. This strategy should lead ingenious researchers to groups and institutions whose study might more quickly develop aspects of urban theory than research on less "regular" areas. Again, convinced readers will wish to devise their own list of researches, after reading the few suggested below. Howard Becker has suggested to me that even the somewhat studied underworld still is largely *terra incognita.*

THE TRIVIAL

First of all, we should take seriously the game of studying phenomena which seem trivial. For instance, I have engaged in some fieldwork at shops where wigs are sold and quickly found categories suggested by the data that bear, for instance, on matters of urban privacy (how salespeople and customers, reciprocally and respectively, handle potentially embarrassing exposure; how breakdown of protective maneuvers fail and with what consequences), and public display (how customers learn to display themselves through wigs; for what audiences; and how the wigmaker or salesman teaches display). Fieldwork at second-hand furniture auctions suggests the fruitfulness of studying the more sociological aspects of little-noted economic behavior. Careful observation of spatial movements on a bus route suggests ways of maintaining distance, reserve, dignity, and privacy under crowded urban conditions. Twenty-four hour vigils, by students, at a downtown street corner suggest a number of hypotheses about the use and symbolism of space, as well as ideas about nighttime careers. Similar observation and interviewing in a variety of parks reveals a number of unsuspected personal careers and urban worlds.

THE ODD

A corollary tactic is to choose the "odd" or "different." For instance, rather than studying the usual occupations, or those that seem important to the city's functioning, why not study those that are little noted, even in popular magazines? They might turn out to be strikingly informative about city life. For instance, we might study bill collectors if only because they visit virtually all sectors of the metropolitan area, and probably experience some not-so-ordinary encounters. Everett Hughes' suggestion of some years ago that sociologists study the "low" occupations (garbage collection) or the "dirty-work" of the professions (abortionist physicians, ambulance-chasing lawyers) is also a guideline to discovery of the unusual urban worker. Barney Glaser has pointed out to me that most of the city's functionaries whose services keep its physical structure "going" have scarcely been studied, if at all, by urban researchers: for instance, garbage collectors, firemen, electricians, and workers in the sewerage and water systems. The subway guard, the bus driver, the garbage mechanic, the nighttime office cleanup lady are among the more lowly, unusual workers; but higher occupations like professional fund-raisers or radio announcers might also prove to be informative subjects for research.

Minor Economic Activity

An associated tactic is to choose some category of economic activity, or some business, which is not likely to be studied for its importance to the city. (One of the most informative urban studies I ever read, a thesis at the University of Chicago, was about Chinese laundries and laundrymen.) Once this tactic is stated, the studies almost suggest themselves: auctions of all types (art, antique, industrial); second-hand sales of various goods (clothes, furniture, yachts); varieties of land purchase and sales (as suggested earlier); and so on. Some of these businesses and markets are much studied by economists, but their sociological aspects are yet to be explored, especially as they might pertain to urban social relations.

Study of the Streets

One more suggestion for studying the unusual: it would certainly be productive to study systematically the social relationships that exist on certain types of streets. What network of social relations exists on the Negro main streets which parallel the white main streets in many a Southern small city? What about the recognizable evolution of certain streets as they change from "far-out-bohemian" to what might be termed "shoppers' bohemian?" In fact, what about the change of any business street in any characteristic direction whether upward in the standard scale of business or downward? Again, I know from study of certain streets that unusual relationships, businesses, and functions can be discovered: for instance, in a Negro neighborhood a "basement store" was by day also a nursery for children of recent migrants and at night a gathering place for teen-age jazz enthusiasts and a kind of social club for adults. Of course, such studies should not be confined to purely business streets. Even fairly conventional streets, if studied in terms of an evolving urban theory, probably would be highly profitable, especially in types of cities that are not yet much studied. Students in urban sociology courses, according to Virginia Olesen, continually raise the question: "How does urban life, e.g., San Francisco, differ from so-called suburban life, for those of similar status and education?" One efficient way to find out is to study a number of streets where similar people, of comparable status and education, live and shop.

MINIMIZING IDEOLOGICAL COMMITMENTS

Some pages ago, I remarked that urban sociologists had allowed their ideological commitments profoundly to affect their research. If a researcher wishes to study some aspect of urban relations that is quite involved in public debate, his best defense against his own (usually unwitting) commitments is to undertake an initial research into the various ideological commitments which others have made about the phenomenon—poverty, let us say, or social mobility—including those made in previous decades by sociologists, as well as laymen. A historical perspective on the rhetoric of public issues is necessary because rhetoric has historical roots; arguments have a way of getting repeated with slight variations of imagery, emphasis and language. Contenders in the current forum can thus be "placed" and their arguments treated as behavior, to be taken into account in studying "the topic"—one that the researcher will inevitably then define differently than when he began his inquiry.

Although space does not permit extended discussion of this strategy, perhaps a brief example will induce others to use it. Louis Wirth's "impersonality of urban relations" is a popular theme not only in the writings of many sociologists but in the speech and writing of others, laymen and specialists alike. Variants of the theme are easy to find in the nineteenth- and twentieth-century literature, whether by journalists or ministers or novelists or farmers. Some urban dwellers have had their styles and behaviors crucially affected by this view of cities; others have rejected it, or never even encountered it. The sociologist's task is to determine the variants of this impersonality theme (and there are many); to discover which kinds of groups, and under what specified conditions, see segments of urban life in those terms, and with what consequences to themselves, their institutions, and other groups. Explicit studies with such a focus are rare.

This means that sociologists who have written and acted on the assumption of urban impersonality are also fair game for study—especially those who, like Wirth, have influenced city planners or, like C. Wright Mills, have affected popular thought. Other influential exponents of urban impersonality, like Lewis Mumford, should be studied by urban sociologists, rather than ignored or treated as remote founts of wisdom.

I cannot resist adding that the controversy over "popular culture," in which many social scientists have become embroiled, can be conceived as embodying views of the city as depersonalized, impersonal, and anomic. That assertion, whether true or not, suggests that urban imageries or themes intertwine in marvelously complex ways. Part of the task of urban sociology—both for its own development and minimizing researchers' ideological commitments—is to trace out the connections among those imageries. Just what difference has it made to Americans and their cities that some cities have been visualized as especially corrupting to rural migrants who failed to conquer it, but also especially conductive to rural migrants' making it up the social ladder? What kinds of institutions have been spawned by the intersection of themes like "opportunities in the city," "education for the urban masses," and "the city as a rational market-place"? What has been the impact on urban planning of versions of the city as "depersonalizing," "aesthetically depressing," "morally corrupting," as antagonistic to physical health, but at the same time as conducive to the very highest civilization? Perhaps these questions seem a light-year away from the discussion of the protective strategy against ideology with which this section started, but just these kinds of questions are necessary, I believe, for transcending the arguments which usually backstage the research we do in "hot" public areas.

Comparative Studies

The fourth strategy that I suggest should guide many urban studies is the deliberate use of comparative method. Most studies of urban social relations have been case studies: one or two suburbs, one or two occupations, a neighborhood, a city institution, or a type of institution. Case studies are certainly useful for various purposes, but they are deficient for *discovering* a systematic, integrated theory about urban social relations. They are deficient because the researcher finds himself extrapolating to more general theory, buttressing his own data with occasional data or interpretations drawn from selected studies, but without developing the *grounds* of that more general theory. He may even attempt little or no wider interpretation of his data, thereby throwing the burden on those of his readers who are interested in wider theory. I believe this case approach to be a chief reason for the disparate character of theory of urban relations.

Where we are weak is not in how to *verify* theory, but in how to *discover* theory. Thus, I draw a distinction between discovery and verification. The line between the two activities is not sharp, and is not hard and fast. Certainly research can embody both activities. But during the last few decades sociologists have tended to develop the verification side much further than the discovery side. In the eyes of methodologists, case studies tend to be thought of as only preliminary, affording hypotheses to be tested by more rigorous methods. I am asserting just the opposite view: case studies give great depth of knowledge, and therefore are probably very good for verifying theoretical formulations. I do not think they take us very far, or very fast, in discovering and formulating integrated theory. They tend to give bits and pieces of relatively unrelated theory. Their accumulation affords inventive readers the opportunity to formulate some generalizations, which they may use in lectures or research, but these hardly add up to integrated or fully public theory. To continue the piling up of informative case studies would seem an unwarranted act of faith, if we are interested (to use Sjoberg's phrase) in a consistent, general theory.

Insofar as theory is the goal (not for its own sake, simply, but also for its pragmatic consequences), the alternative is a self-conscious use of comparative method. . . .

In accordance with initial hunches or hypotheses, the researcher can begin to "theoretically sample" various groups or institutions. For instance, even without sophisticated hypotheses, one might wish to study realtors in various kinds of urban or suburban areas, to see what similarities and differences in their behavior, relationships, and institutions would quickly become apparent. At a more sophisticated level, one might wish to sample urban or suburban locales where he suspected various urban images might predominate among the population: for instance, a rural imagery, an impersonality imagery, a class-conflict imagery, a status-climbing imagery, a city-as-fun imagery; or any combination of such imageries.

In this kind of study—because his aim is the discovery and *not* the verification of theory—the reasearcher need not know everything about realtors or everything about the locale; he only needs to know enough to feel quite certain about the phenomena directly at the center of his interests. This kind of comparative focus "rather quickly draws the observer's attention to many similarities and differences . . . these contribute to the generation of theoretical categories, to their full range of types of continua, their dimensions, the conditions under which they exist . . . and their major consequences. . . . The observed differences and similarities speedily generate generalized relations among the theoretical categories, which in turn become the hypotheses soon integrated into the . . . theory." All the research problems or areas suggested earlier are amenable to this type of theoretical sampling and comparative analysis.

In this kind of comparative research for discovering theory, data that are already published become highly relevant—not for buttressing a researcher's theoretical formulations, but as relevant as his own first-hand data for the discovery of theory. For this purpose, researchers are thoroughly warranted in drawing on published data. Thus anyone who might wish to study the symbolic use of space will find plenty of material in the sociological literature. Most of it would be inadequate for testing theory, but it is quite adequate for stimulating the development of theory. Some of the published data are not in the form of another researcher's conclusions, but will actually be his raw data, including quotations from his informants. A good example of such data is the hobo's conceptions and uses of urban space, as detailed descriptively in Anderson's early monograph of the hobo. Use of all these data for general comparative purposes—a form of secondary analysis—is perfectly legitimate when one's aim is the development of theory.

A NOTE ON METHOD

It should be readily apparent that many of the research areas suggested in this paper probably require extended field observation, and even some measure of participant observation. One should not, however, foreclose on any alternative method which appears appropriate for an area under study. But I call attention to field observation precisely because the monographs of the early "Chicago school" were based mainly on that method. Since their publication, field methods have greatly developed and should be used wherever deemed helpful or necessary.

There is perhaps more point to my urging that historical and humanistic documents be used as data. Although little used by American urban sociologists, these documents can be of considerable value for exploring the forms, functions and meanings of cities. In fact, if readers take seriously any of my suggested strategies or research areas, they will find themselves turning to such documents. Some of our needed urban research simply cannot be accomplished without such materials—abjuring them only leads to the impoverishment of our theory and even of our descriptive knowledge. As I have remarked elsewhere, comparative studies cannot do without documentary research if only because use of documents— found in the library and elsewhere—is sometimes speedier and more efficient than first-hand collection of observational, interview, or questionnaire data. A recent study in urban history that should be of considerable interest to urban sociologists, and which illustrates the kinds of documents available besides those found in libraries, is Warner's study of three Boston suburbs. While historians make excellent use of such documentary materials, they do not address themselves to the same range of problems as those noted above, although there is much overlapping of interest, of course, between them and urban sociologists. Indeed, use of such materials would almost certainly bring historians, sociologists, political scientists, economists, and humanists closer together in their separate explorations of "urban problems," as well as provide correctives for their separate types of blindness. That planners, architects, statesmen, and other political men of affairs might also profit from such collaboration seems very probable.

SUGGESTED READINGS: CHAPTER 17

Barney G. Glaser and Anselm L. Strauss, *The Discovery of Grounded Theory*. Chicago: Aldine Publishing Company, 1967.
Subtitled "Strategies for Qualitative Research," this book discusses the logic and various methods of generating theory.

Jean Gottman. *Megalopolis.* New York: Twentieth Century Fund, 1961.

The conception to which the title of this book refers, is becoming part of the imagery of urban America. Gottman, a European geographer, discusses the striking merging of cities into lengthy urban belts.

M. Grodzins, "Metropolitan Segregation," *Scientific American* Vol. 197 (1957), 33–41.

One of the first articles that signaled the dramatic change of our central cities from predominantly white to predominantly Negro. This image, of course, has become part of today's visual, verbal, and emotional language.

Philip M. Hauser. "A Billion People in the United States?" *United States News and World Report,* November 28, 1958, p. 82.

A well-known demographer and urban sociologist contributes toward the popular image of American cities.

Jane Jacobs. *The Death and Life of Great American Cities.* New York: Random House, 1961.

Jacobs offers a critique of some dominant trends in big-city planning, and a passionate defense of some virtues of the older, more crowded, but more "colorful" city. She contributes incidentally to some of the emerging imagery of our cities.

Lightning Source UK Ltd.
Milton Keynes UK
UKOW041947140513

210666UK00001B/90/P